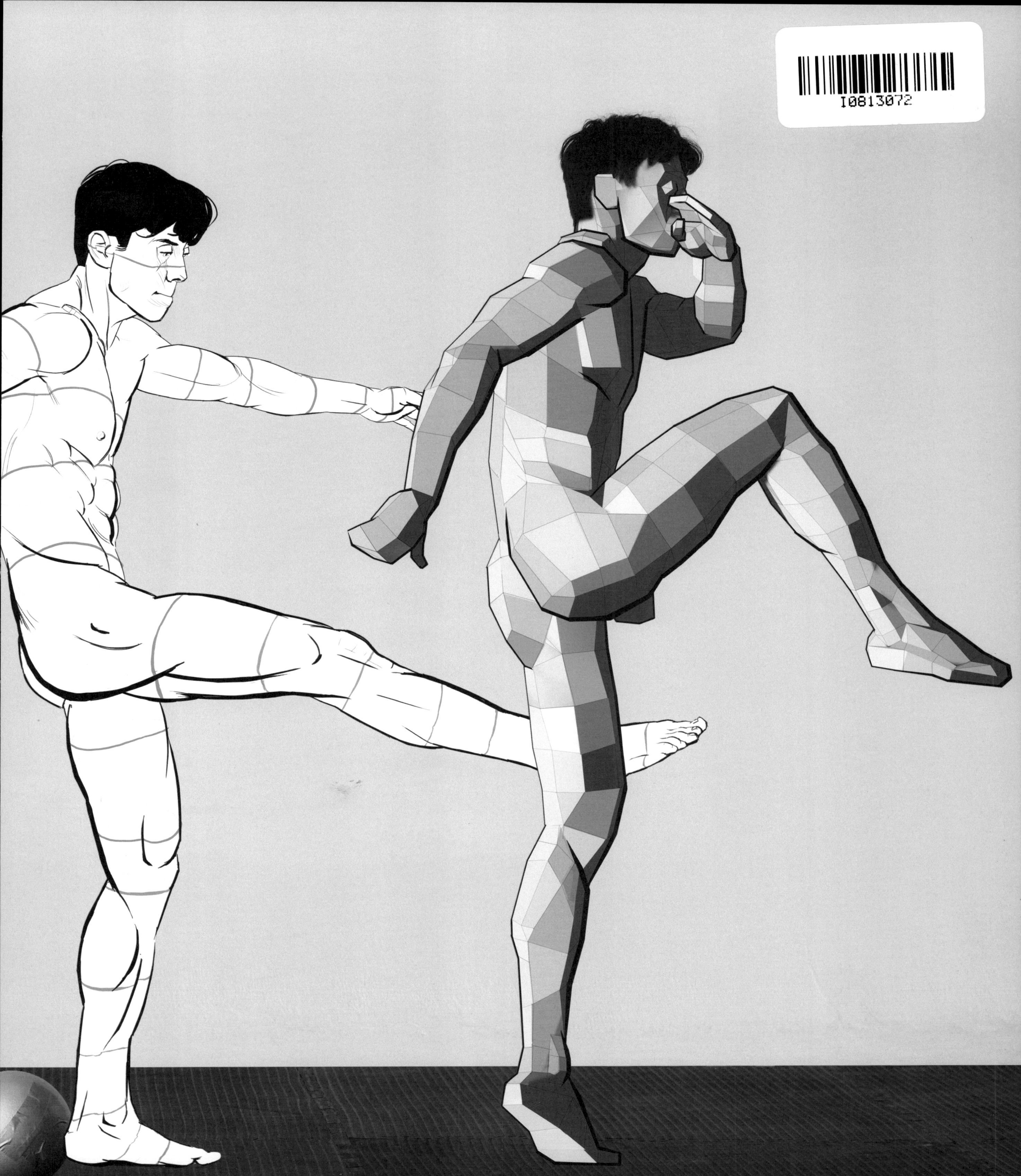

ANATOMY IN MOTION

An artist's guide to capturing dynamic movement

Written and illustrated by **Charlie Pickard** | Photography by **Robin Bharaj**

3dtotalPublishing

3dtotalPublishing

Correspondence: publishing@3dtotal.com
Website: store.3dtotal.com

First published in the United Kingdom, 2024, by 3dtotal Publishing.

Address: 3dtotal.com Ltd,
29 Foregate Street, Worcester
WR1 1DS, United Kingdom.

Hard cover ISBN:
978-1-915992-02-4

Printed and bound in China
by C&C Offset Printing Co., Ltd

Visit store.3dtotal.com for a complete list of available book titles.

Editor: Marisa Lewis
Designer: Fiona Tarbet
Lead Editor: Samantha Rigby
Lead Designer: Joseph Cartwright
Studio Manager: Simon Morse
Managing Director: Tom Greenway

FSC
MIX
Paper | Supporting responsible forestry
FSC® C008047

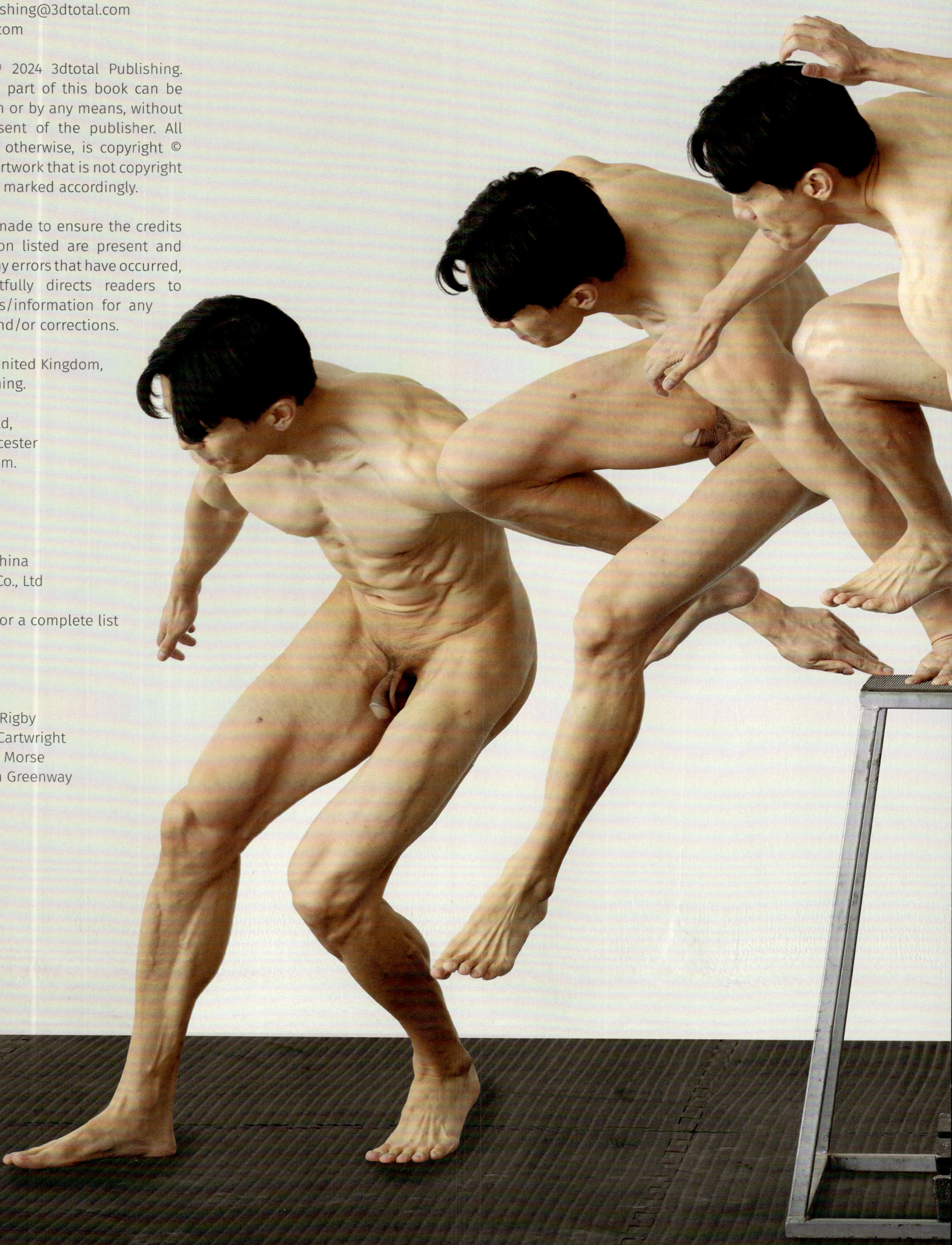

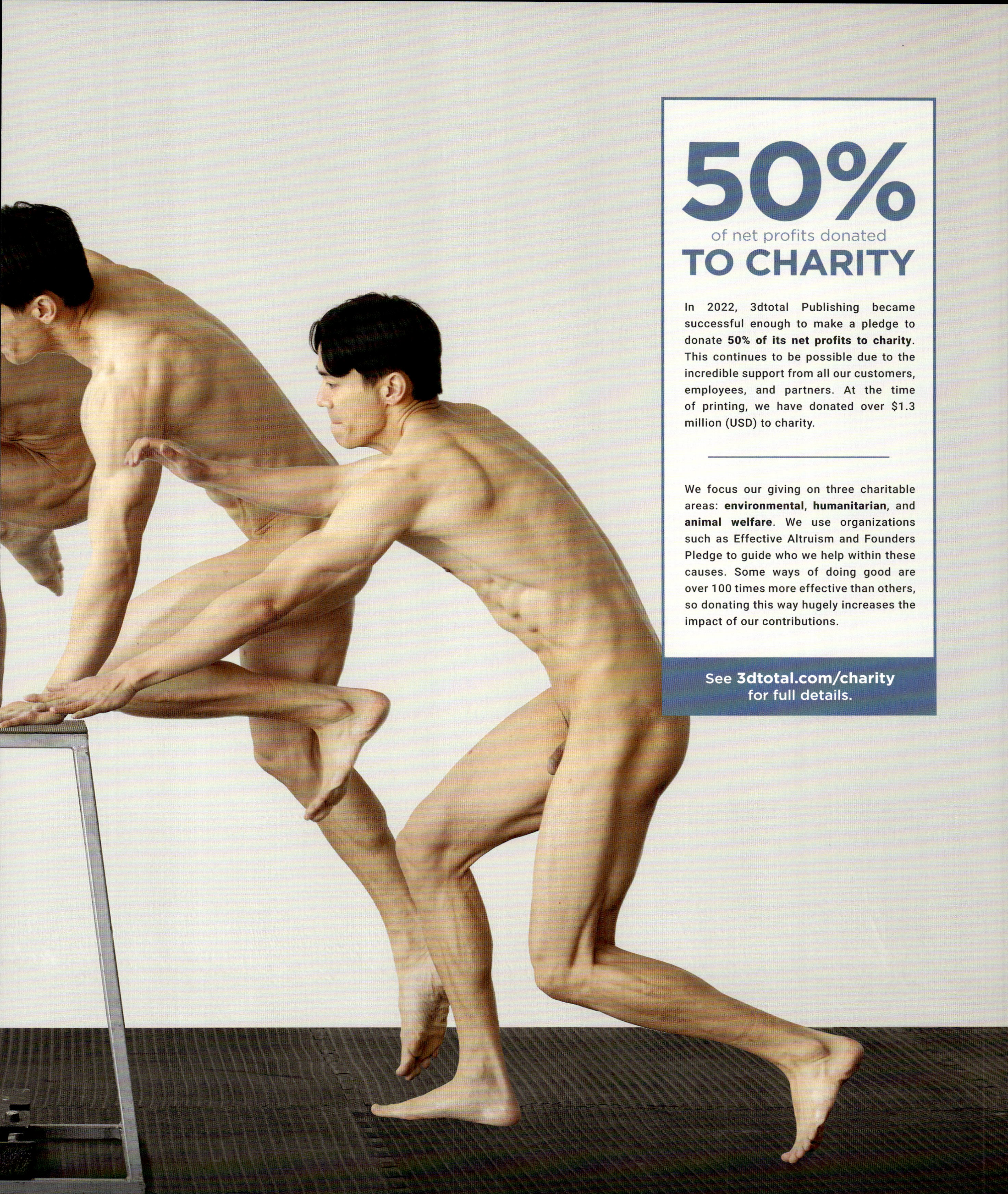

50%

of net profits donated

TO CHARITY

In 2022, 3dtotal Publishing became successful enough to make a pledge to donate **50% of its net profits to charity**. This continues to be possible due to the incredible support from all our customers, employees, and partners. At the time of printing, we have donated over $1.3 million (USD) to charity.

We focus our giving on three charitable areas: **environmental**, **humanitarian**, and **animal welfare**. We use organizations such as Effective Altruism and Founders Pledge to guide who we help within these causes. Some ways of doing good are over 100 times more effective than others, so donating this way hugely increases the impact of our contributions.

See **3dtotal.com/charity** for full details.

Contents

The basics of motion

Basic body movements

Full-body actions

Introduction

For as long as humans have been making art, we have been depicting the human figure. Some of the earliest figurative artwork we can access is some 40,000 years old and this obsession has never left us. It has been, and likely always will be, a boundless source of inspiration for as many generations as there are artists. The reason for this is simple: *this subject is us*. If we want to make art that speaks to others on a human level, there can be no more powerful symbol. The influence of this ever-powerful subject can be felt in all of the artwork around the world and throughout history.

Many cultures have taken this influence in many wonderful directions, but perhaps nowhere has been as dedicated to its representation in as high fidelity as the West. The history of Western art can be characterized by this eager desire to recreate the human figure faithfully. We only need to look at the gorgeous works this has wrought throughout history as evidence.

This chasing after realism in representation has taken us towards many realms of study and led to many fascinating discoveries. The subject of this book is one of these areas of study: anatomy, the study of the pieces and forms that make up the human figure. Some say the roots of this particular study go as far back as ancient Egypt, though it did not reach its modern form until the Renaissance. It is a fascinating subject and I am excited to explore it with you.

The particular focus of this book will be the anatomy of motion and this is, in my opinion, the proper perspective from which to study anatomy as artists today. The human body is fundamentally a machine of locomotion. Its form evolved as a response to stresses in its environment. One of the most important demands on all of us is the ability to move through our world, and so, the core of the design of the human body is set up to enable us to move.

For us as artists, studying how the body functions can be the greatest tool to remember the complicated structure the body presents. It is truly an awe-inspiring, overwhelming structure in its complexity: ingeniously subtle, graceful, and powerful in equal measure. Through the lens of motion we are offered a great way to imprint this structure on our minds, distilling all of the raw information into a usable state. This perspective is often referred to as 'function over form' and has placed movement at the centre of many studies that teach figurative art.

However, anatomy has not always been approached this way. The ancient Egyptians, though glorious at their craft, seemed to show little interest in depicting this aspect of the human form. Their artworks, though exquisite, are generally quite stiff in posing (**image a**). It is not until the ancient Greeks that we start to see a real interest in portraying realistic anatomy. It is said that Greek sculptors worked directly from nude athletes in the ancient gymnasiums to achieve their wonderfully naturalistic results. Their works have been a marvel ever since (**image b**).

This study directly from the nude is not dissimilar to what we will see in these pages. This book gathers many reference photos of nude models moving, as the ancient athletes would have, through various actions. Snapshots of actions help us see exactly what is going on. The Greeks could have only captured glimpses of this as they worked. We're lucky to live in this age!

a.

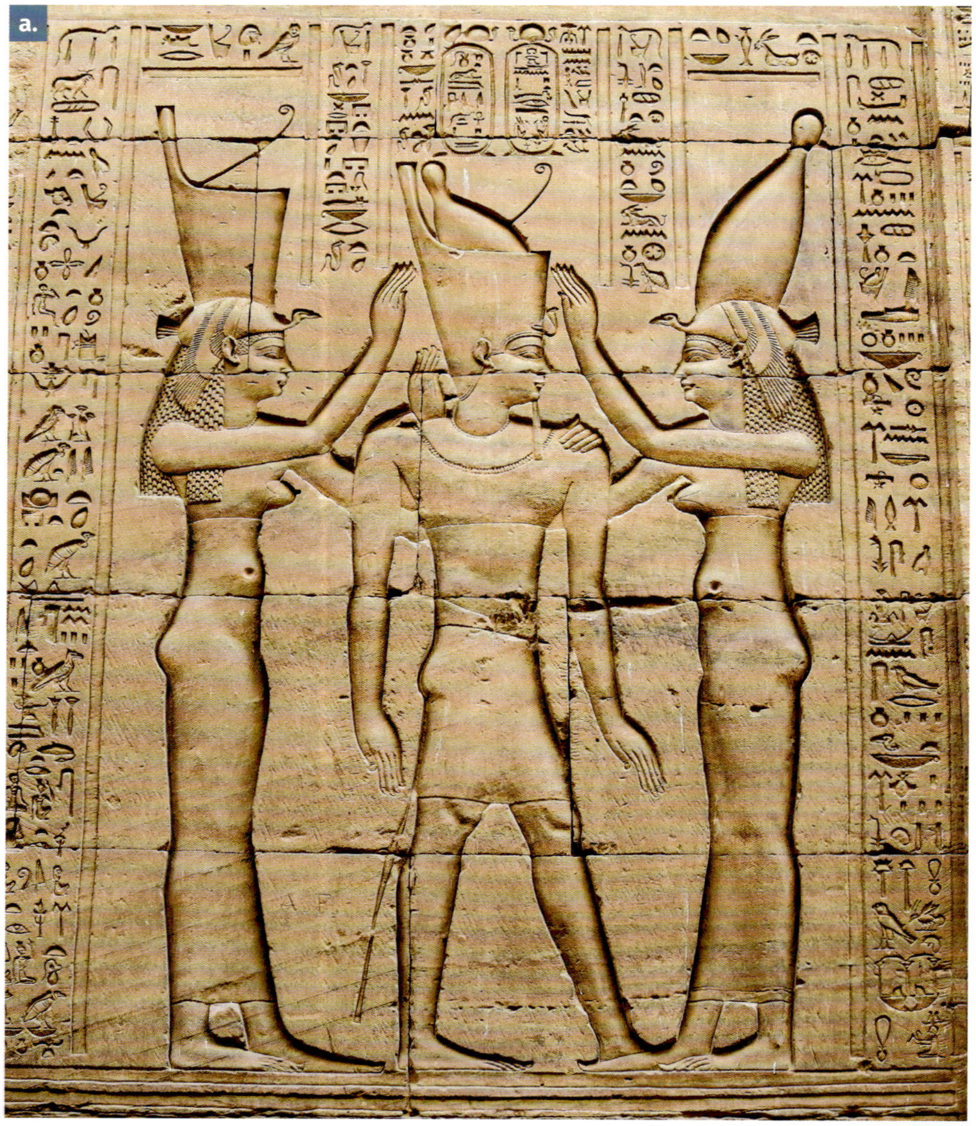

Carvings at the Temple of Edfu, Egypt (c. 237–57 BC). *Photo by AXP Photography on Unsplash*

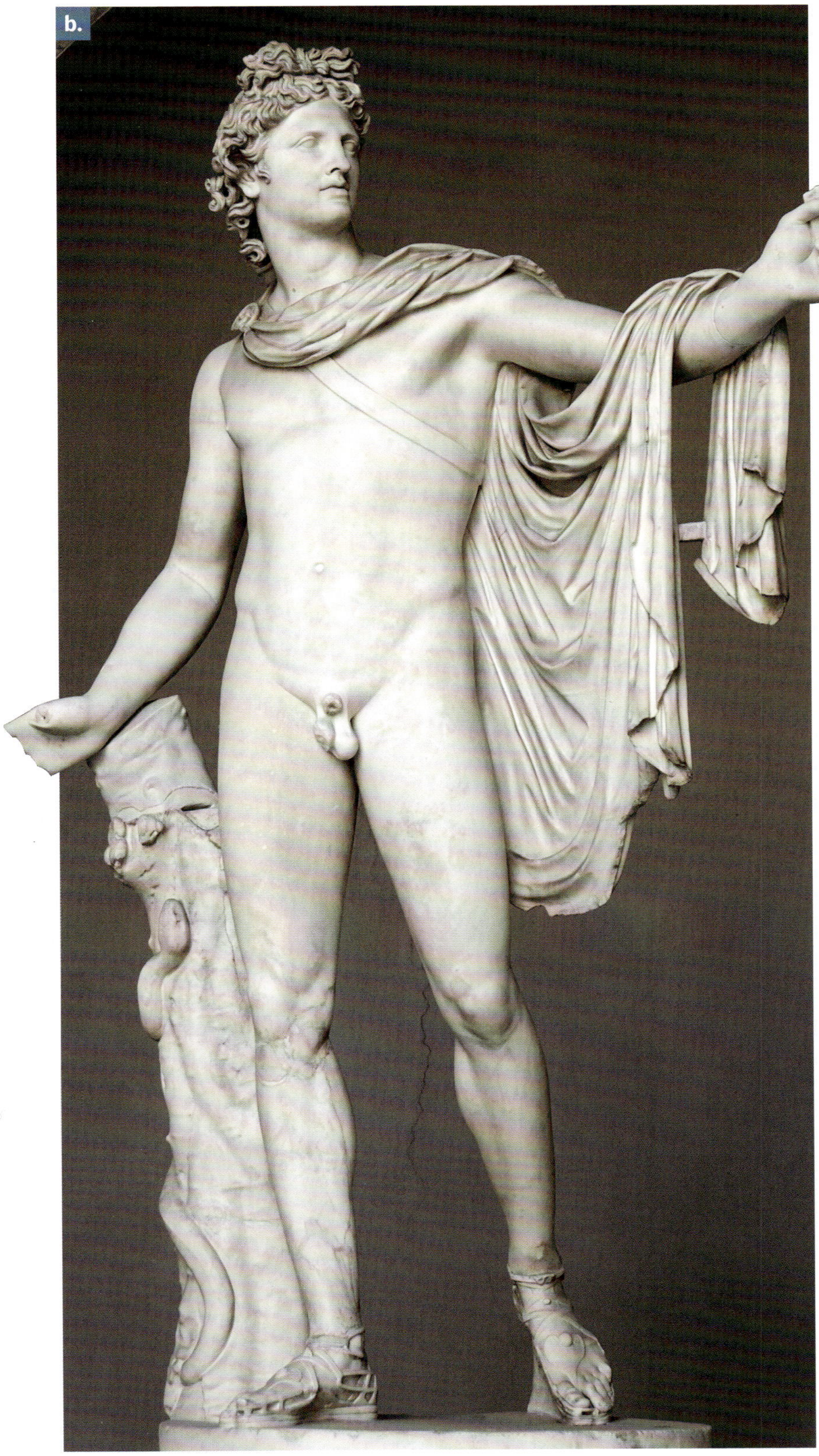

b.

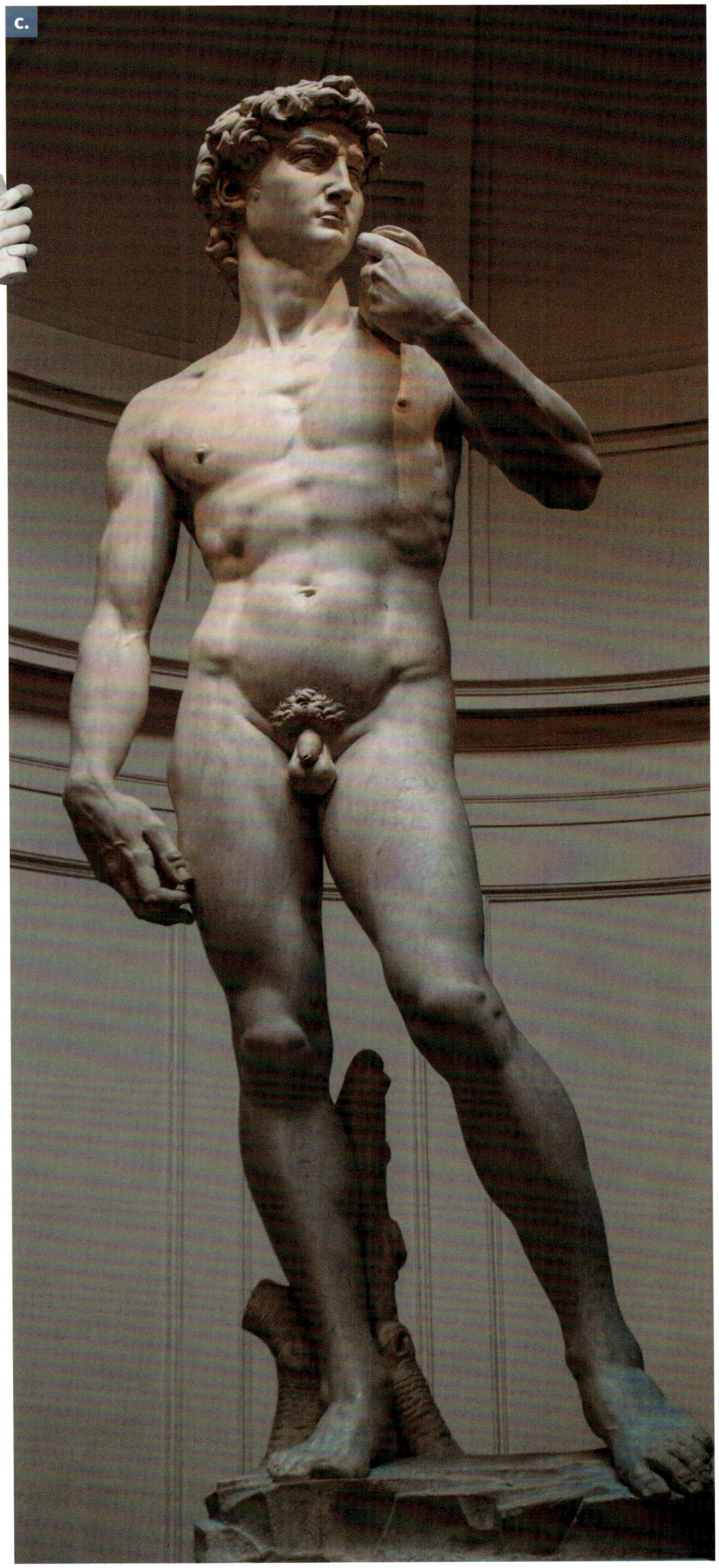

c.

Roman copy of Leochares' *Apollo Belvedere* (original c. 330–320 BC).
Photo by Marie-Lan Nguyen via Wikimedia Commons

Michelangelo's *David* (c. 1501–1504).
Photo by Èric Teixidó on Unsplash

Bernini's ***Apollo and Daphne*** **(c. 1622–1625).**
Photo by Daderot, CC0, via Wikimedia Commons

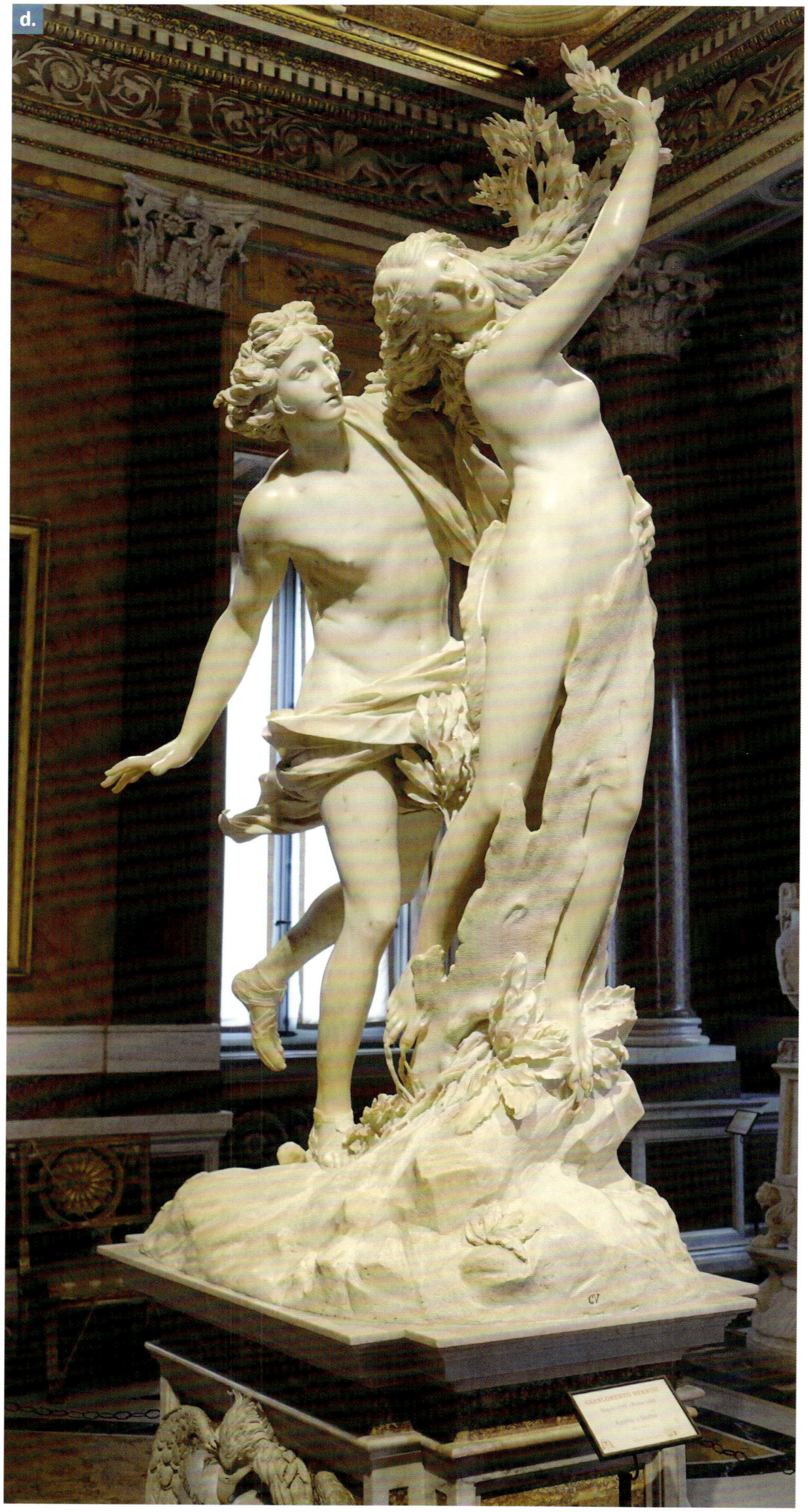

After the ancient Greeks, there was a long gap in interest in this sort of work. It wasn't until the Renaissance from the fourteenth to the sixteenth centuries – an era of creativity and discovery that took Europe from the Middle Ages into the modern world – that it was picked up again by artists such as Michelangelo (see **image c** on the previous page). Alongside this interest in depicting natural posing came the Age of Enlightenment (seventeenth and eighteenth centuries) and a new scientific attitude. This was when the science of anatomy in the true sense was developed. Artists were so hungry for this knowledge that they dug up and dissected corpses! Luckily, we now have books and other ways to access and study that knowledge. We owe a great deal to those artists, and their artwork speaks for itself.

During the Baroque period (around 1600 to 1750), capturing dynamic motion became the explicit goal of an entire movement in art. It was characterized by chasing truly powerful depictions of explosive action. In my opinion, nowhere was this captured more powerfully than in the works of the sculptor Gian Lorenzo Bernini. Bernini shows us a moment in time, captured in all its essence (**image d**).

In the more recent past, moving pictures and animation have given rise to new forms of creation that stretch the art of movement to new and ever greater heights. Whether it be the fantastic paintings of George Bellows' boxers, or the brilliant animations of Richard Williams or Glen Keane, we have seen artists who are not content to just reproduce movements exactly, but who exaggerate and heighten them. They have taught us that we can aim for and achieve a *feeling* of movement. This is a wonderful lesson – one we should not ignore.

As artists in the modern age, we are heir to all of this hard-won knowledge, aimed at this singular goal of understanding ourselves through the depiction of the human figure. I have made the study of this subject my life's work and it is a well that has not run dry (**image e**).

e.

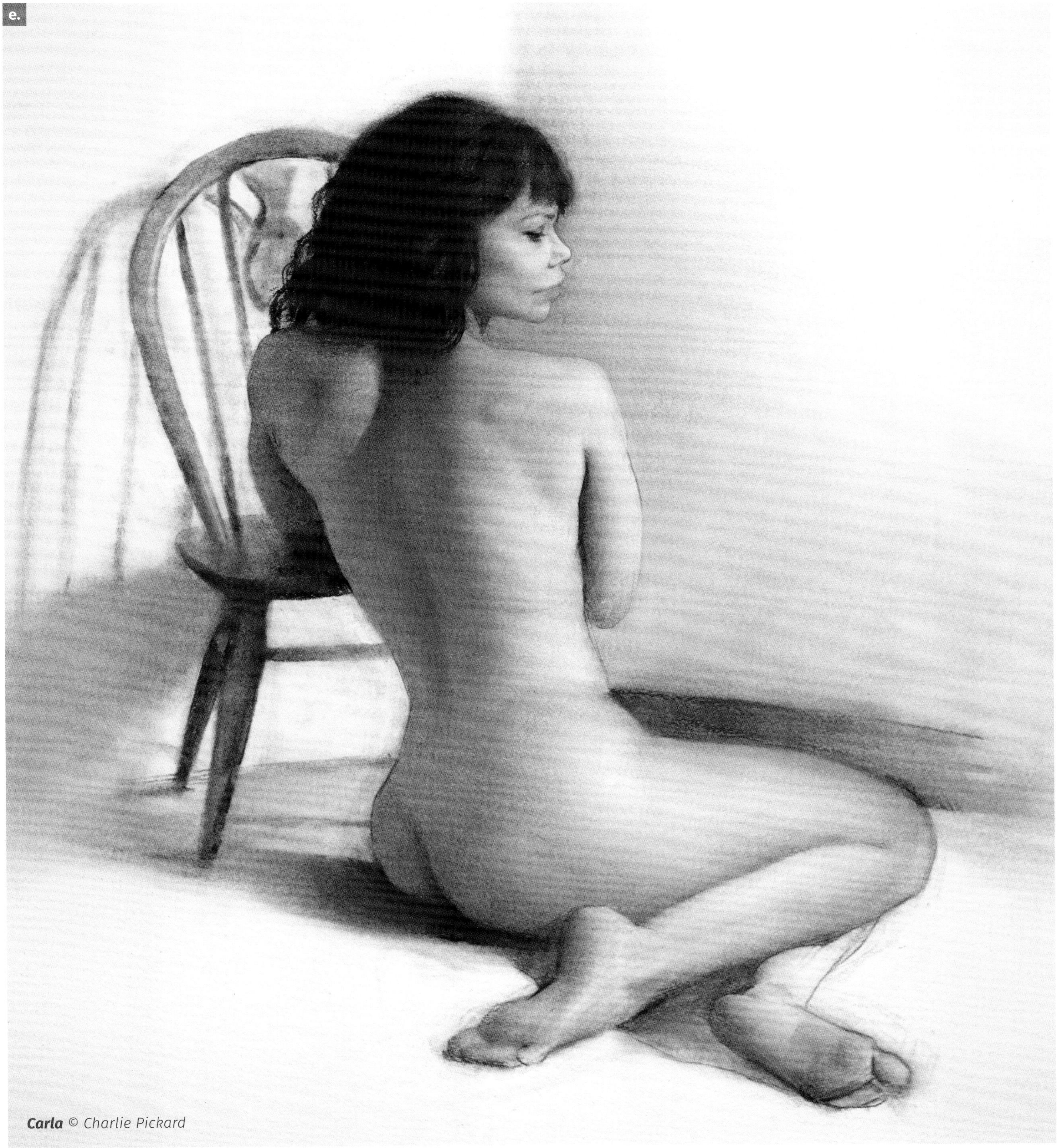

Carla © Charlie Pickard

Locomotion principles

As we begin our study of the human body in motion, it is important that we first speak about some of the fundamental principles that our bodies use to move. The human body can be thought of as having three main layers: bone, muscle, and fat. The bones are the most fundamental of these three structures, but alone they are inert and cannot move. The fatty tissue is more responsible for the body type we observe and will follow the shapes set up by the two lower structures (bone and muscle). Of these three, the layer most responsible for movement is the muscular layer. This is where we will primarily focus our study.

What makes up a muscle? How does it create the forces necessary for movement? Every muscle is made up of two types of tissue:

- **The tendons.** These form the connection from muscle to bone, and as such need to be stiff and strong so as not to get damaged easily. This causes them to be fairly immoveable.
- **The 'muscular body'.** This part is formed of many fibres running between the two tendons. This is where most of the force of the muscle is generated. As such, it can vary quite a lot in size, and will be where we observe the most changes through movement.

How does the muscular body generate force? The mechanism behind this is simple. The muscle starts in a 'relaxed' state, with its fibres flexible and long. When a movement is desired, the brain sends an electrical signal ('action potential') to the muscle through the nerves, which causes the muscle to 'activate'. When the muscle is activated, the fibres that make up its body enlarge. This increases the size of the muscular body and makes it inflexible. The result of the enlargement is a shortening of the entire length of the muscle, causing a force towards the centre of the muscular body. This simple process is responsible for all of the varied movements we observe in the body.

The basic parts of a muscle

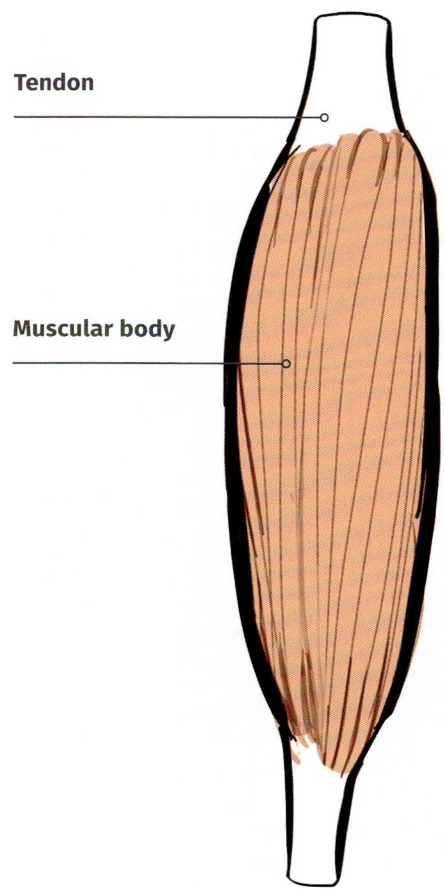

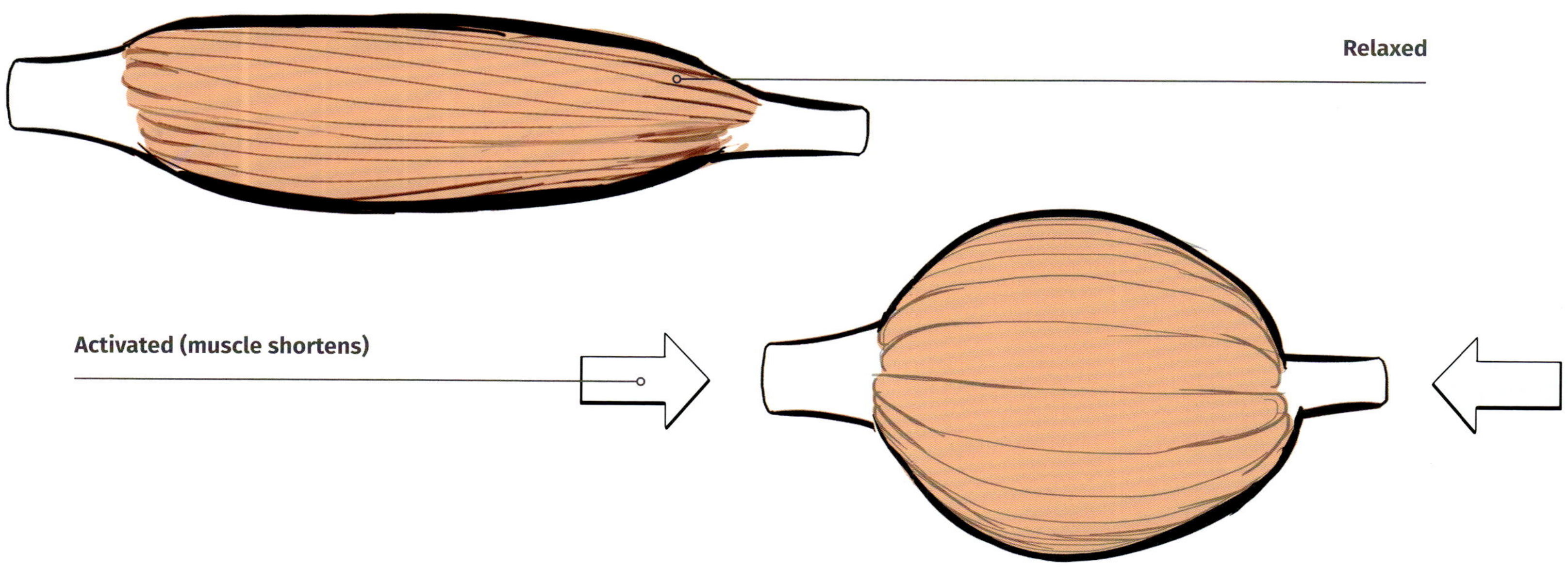

You can visualize the muscular body like a hydraulic pump – the pump (or muscle) compresses towards the centre

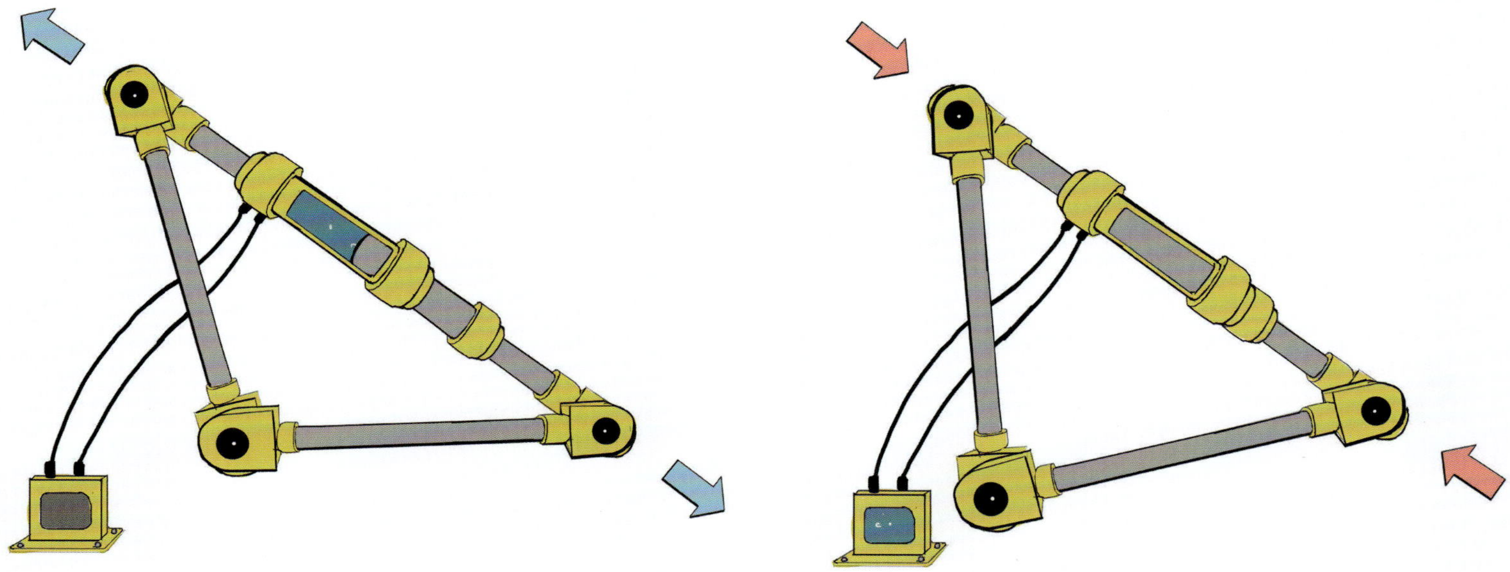

We can understand how this basic effect causes movement between the bones if we take a look at the simple machine of the hydraulic joint. As you can see in the hydraulic joint shown above, like in the muscular body, there is a central moving part that contracts. Since the parts on either side cannot change shape, a movement is created in the central joint.

The exact same mechanism happens in the arm. The tendons, attached to the hard bones on either side, are forced to drag the bone along with them when the muscle activates and contracts. This causes a movement in the joint (the elbow, in this case). This leads us to an important mechanical truth for movement in the body: *every muscular body must move over a joint in order for movement to occur*. This idea holds true for all the movements of the bones and is important to remember as we continue our studies.

One way that the muscles are different from a hydraulic press is that, while the mechanical joint exerts a force in both the direction of its expansion and contraction, muscles do not work this way. The only force exerted by the muscle is when it contracts, which means the available force can only ever be exerted one way.

The muscle changes shape as it expands and contracts

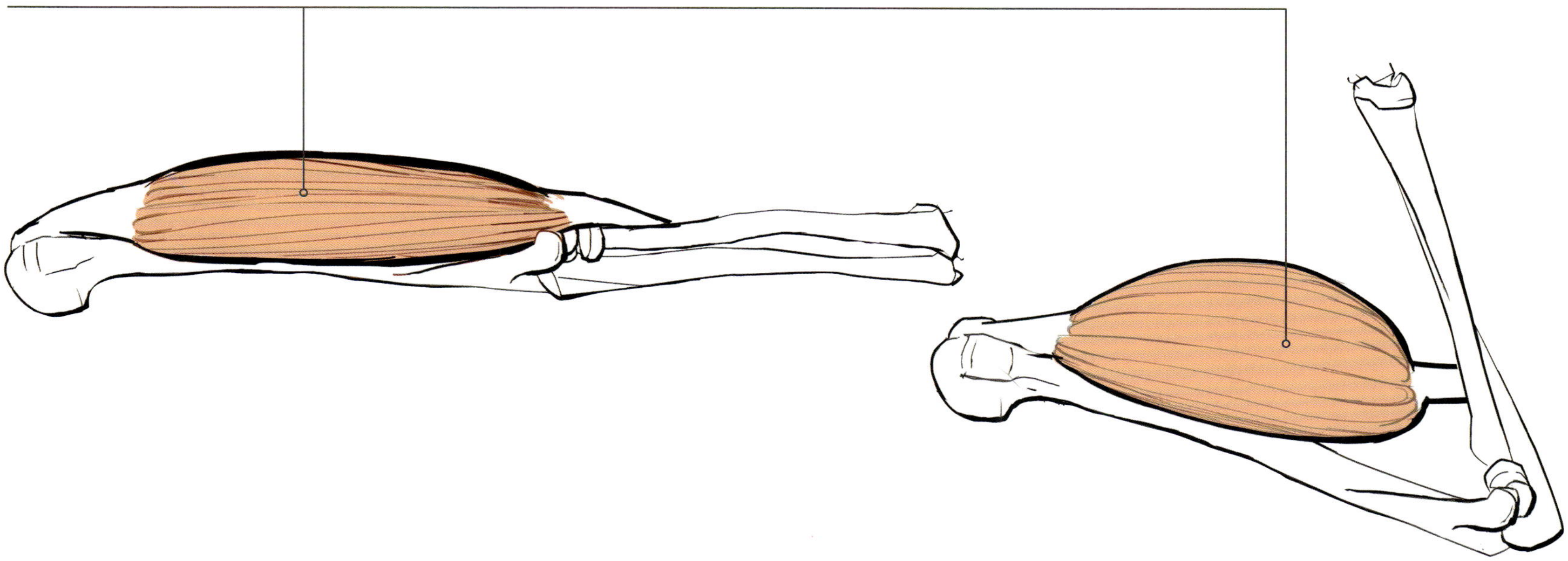

A muscle can also be visualized as a pulley system – the pulley (or muscle) can only exert force in one direction

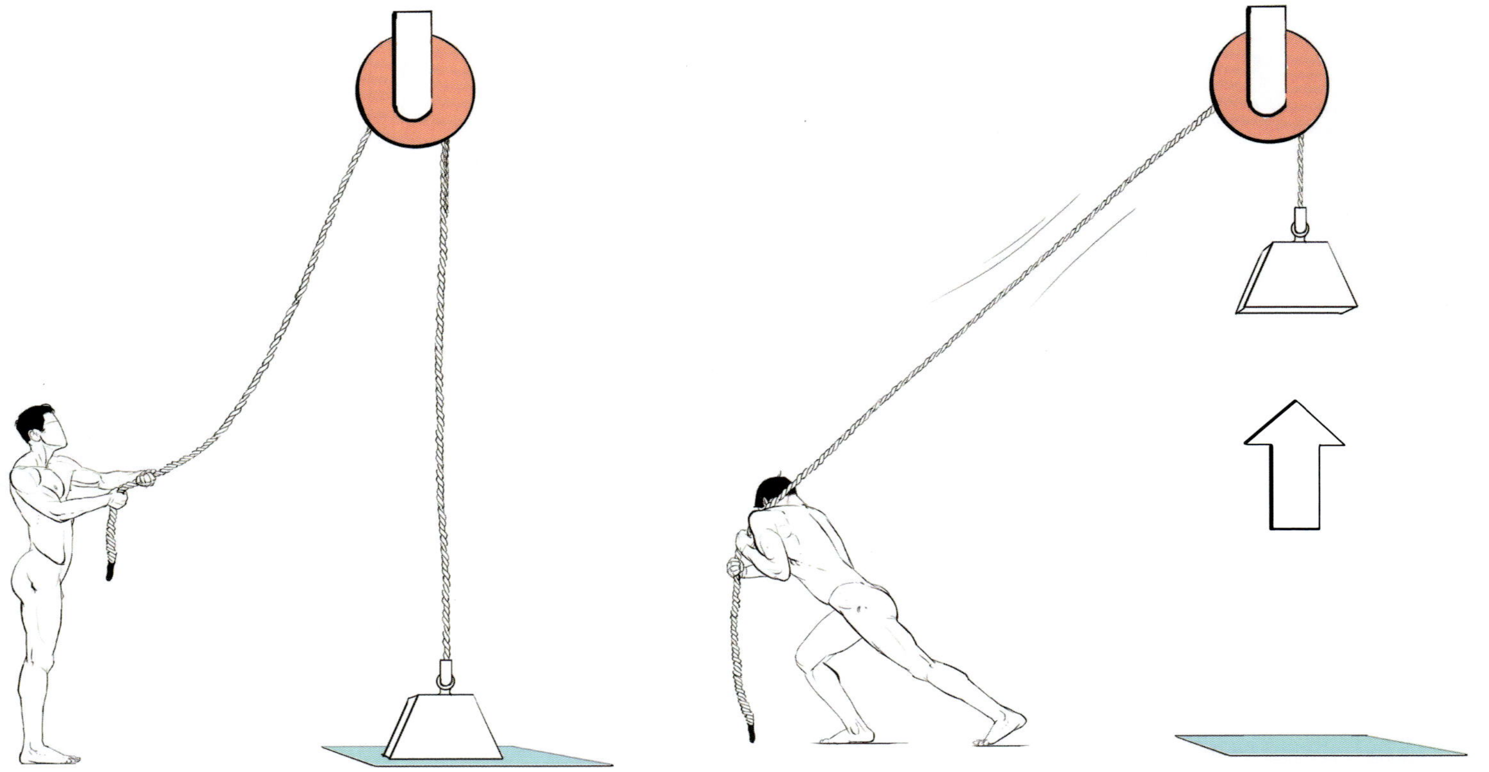

Another useful mechanical analogy that will help us understand this is the idea of a simple pulley raising a weight. The figure shown above can only pull down on the rope to pull the package up. He cannot push the rope back up and has to rely on gravity to return it to the ground.

This problem of one-way action makes movement slightly more complex to understand. Our body needs another force in order to provide the complex movement we need to move through the world. Luckily the body has an elegant solution to this problem that we will discuss on page 16.

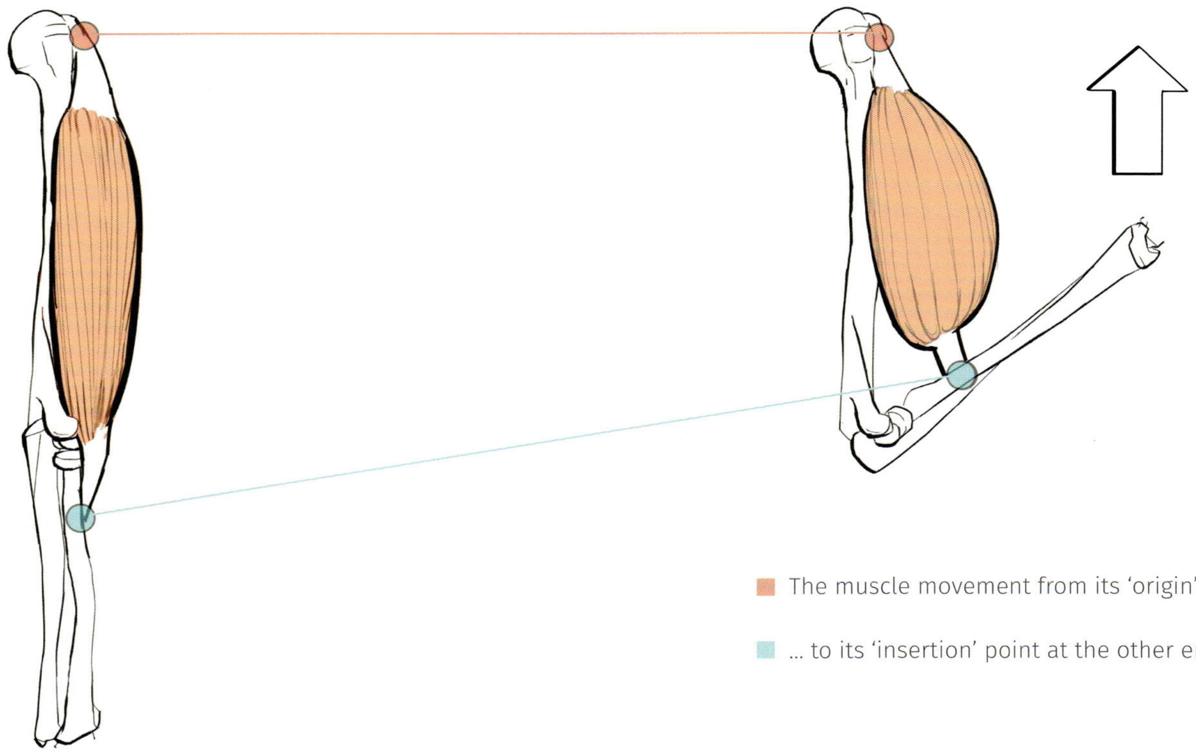

■ The muscle movement from its 'origin' point ...

■ ... to its 'insertion' point at the other end.

The muscle is relaxed and elongated in shape

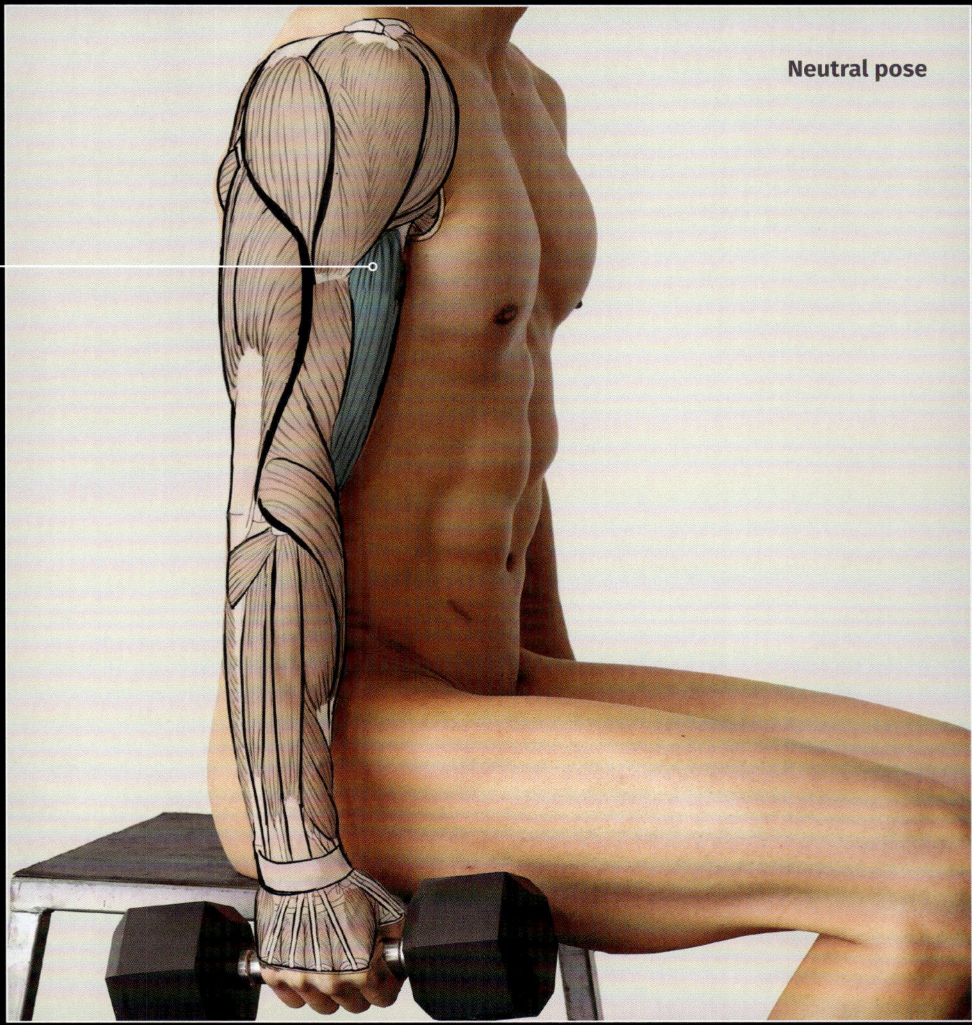

Neutral pose

Let's have a look at how these principles work in action on a live model. If we take the simple movement of the arm flexing, we can see all of these elements at play. The muscle in its relaxed position is long and slender, and once flexed becomes rounded and engorged. The tendons on either side do not change in shape or size.

These basic ideas are what govern all of the movements in the body, so study them well. As you move through the book, try to consider how they affect the changes in shape in all of the following poses and references. It's simple once you know it.

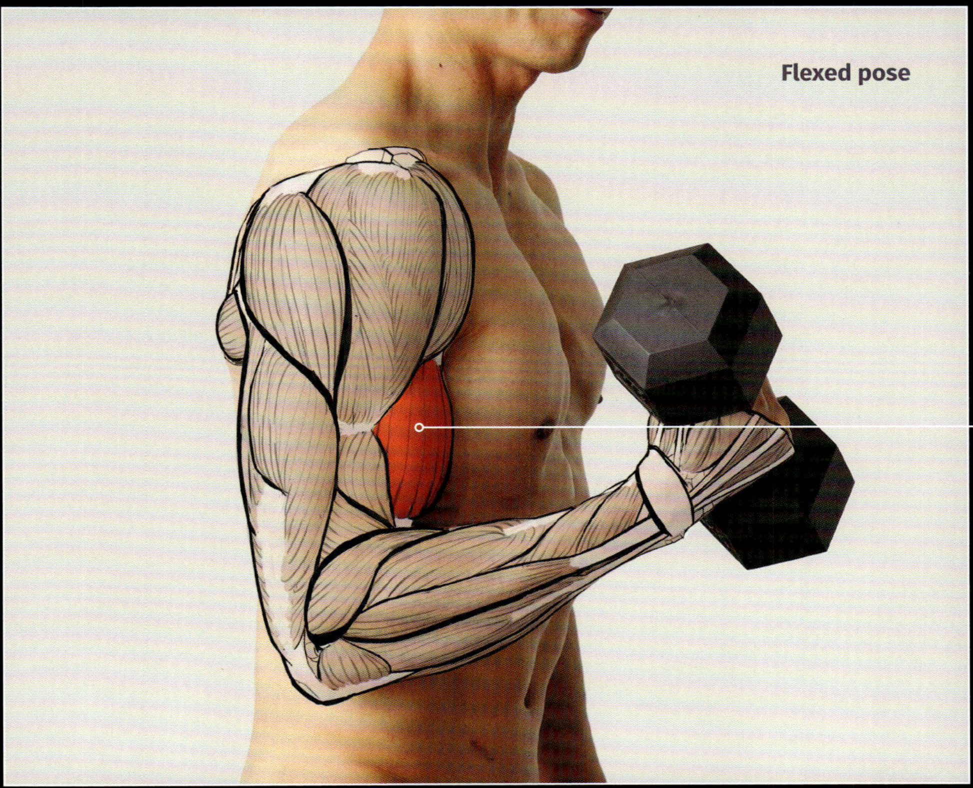

Flexed pose

The muscle is activated and its shape contracts

Types of muscle

While the basic principle we covered on the previous page is true, it is hugely simplified. The human body is incredibly complex. In order for us to have the full story of how the body is composed, we need to learn about the different ways that muscles are formed, the ways in which they can change, and the effects that change can have on their movement.

The first variable is the number of muscular 'heads'. In fact, if we change our simplified muscle to have two heads instead of one, we land on a familiar muscle: the biceps (**image a**). 'Biceps' actually means 'two-headed' in Latin. The reason the muscle splits up, in this case, is to give two slightly different directions to the force it can output, making our control over movements much more specific. As you can see in the case of the biceps, one 'head' goes over the joint of the humerus (upper-arm bone) and the other more directly to the coracoid process of the scapula (a bony protrusion on the front of the shoulder).

a.

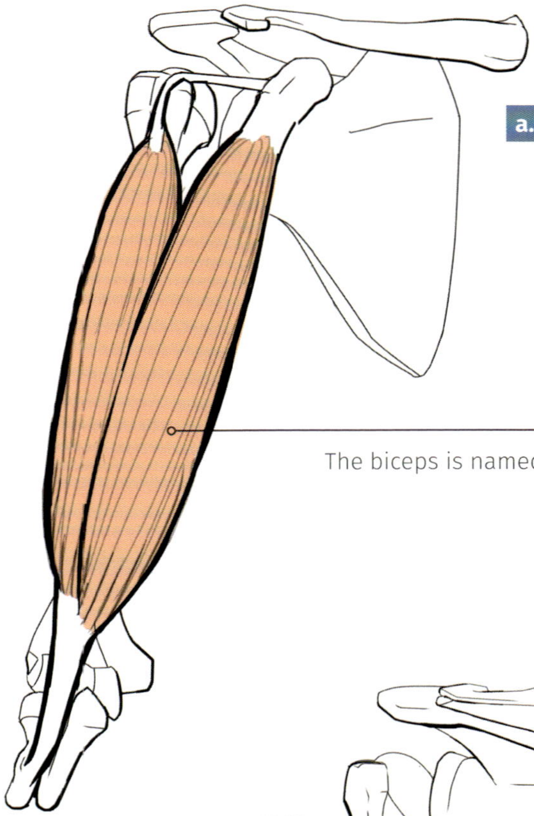

The biceps is named after its two 'heads'

c.

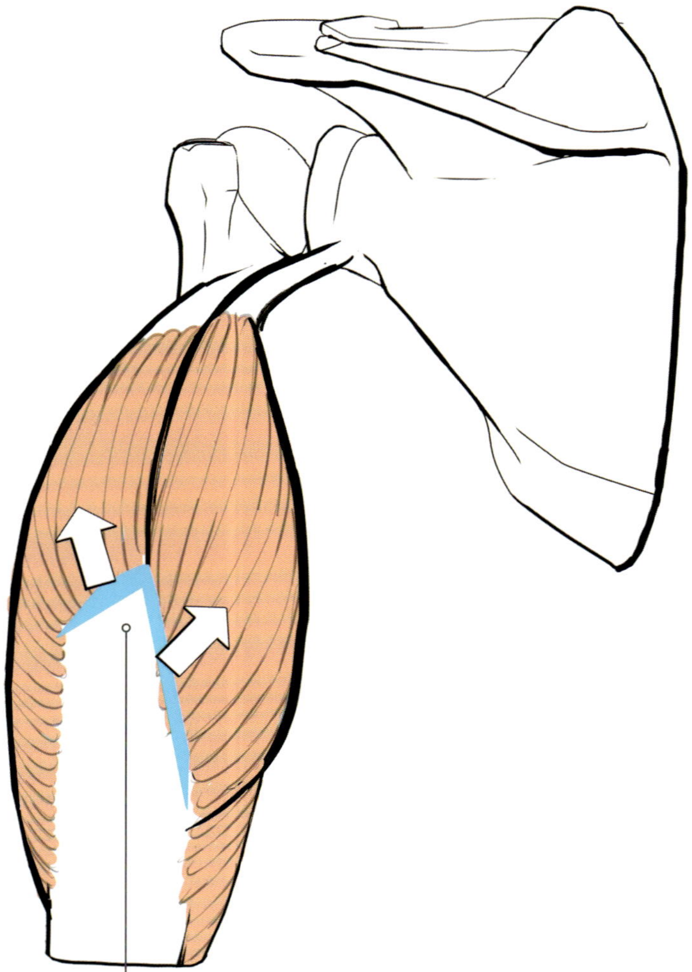

The triceps' attachment points allow it to exert force in multiple directions

b.

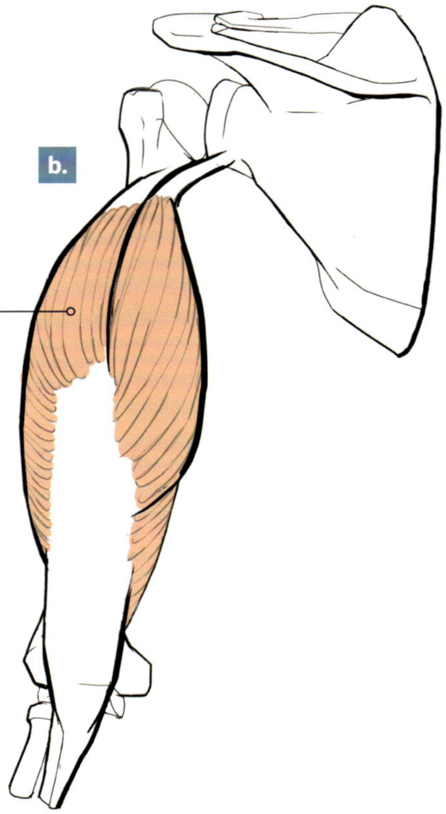

Another factor in a muscle's form is the shape of the tendon to which it attaches. In the case of the biceps, the tendon shape is merely an extension of the muscle heads, but this is not always the case. We can see this in full effect on the triceps (meaning 'three-headed') (**image b**). This muscle inserts into a larger common tendon that takes on a characteristic shape that is important to its function. Like the biceps, the main reason for this change is to allow different directions of force (**image c**).

The force put out by a muscle will always run along the direction of its fibres, and these fibres will commonly move perpendicular to the shape of the tendon. If you recognize the shape of the tendon, you can surmise the function of the muscle.

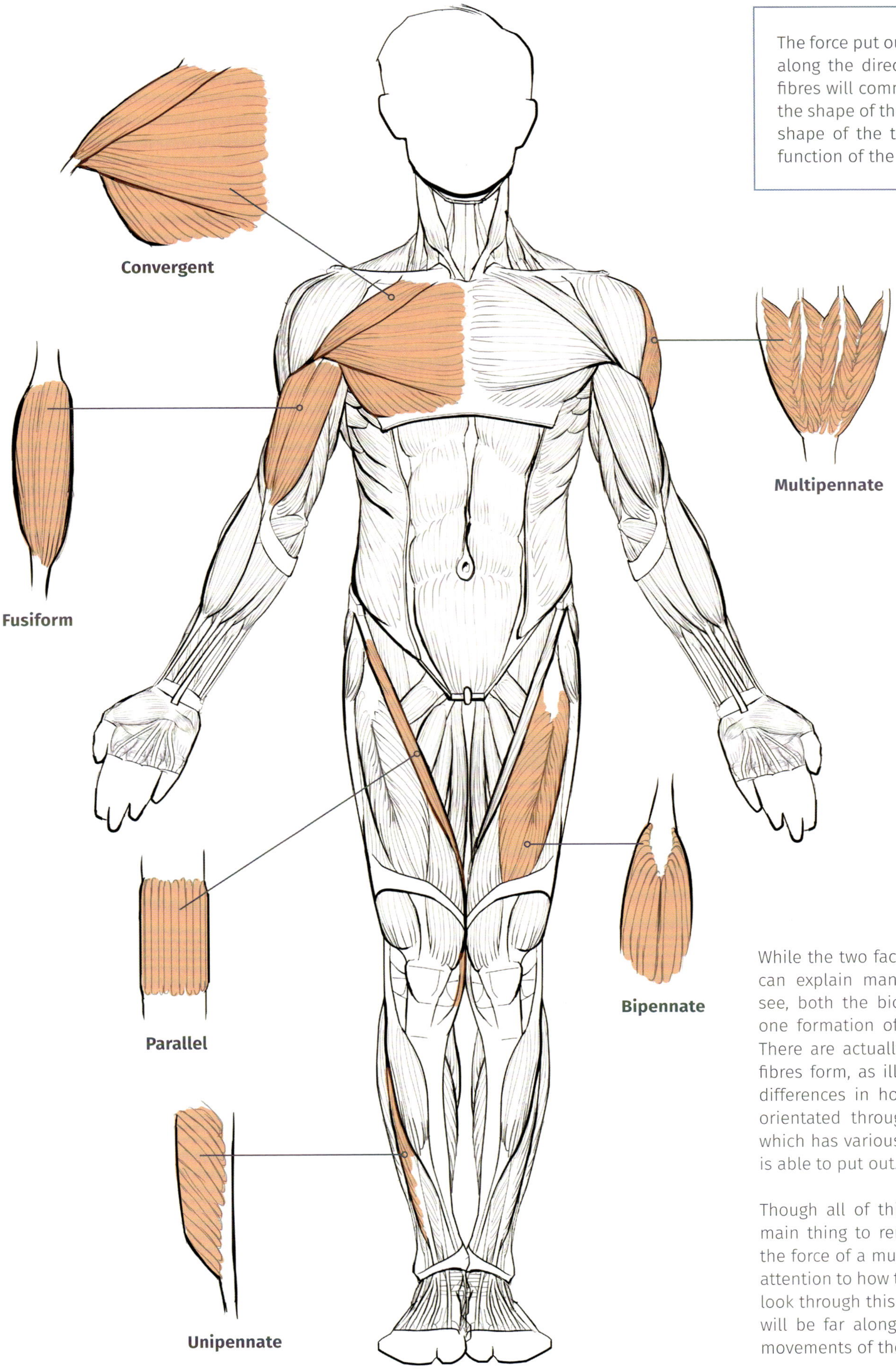

While the two factors of heads and tendon shape can explain many of the changing muscles we see, both the biceps and triceps only represent one formation of a muscle, known as 'fusiform'. There are actually a few other ways that muscle fibres form, as illustrated here. These are largely differences in how the fibres of the muscle are orientated throughout the body of the muscle, which has various effects on the force the muscle is able to put out.

Though all of this may seem overwhelming, the main thing to remember is that the direction of the force of a muscle always follows its fibres. Pay attention to how these fibres are orientated as you look through this book. Understand them and you will be far along the path of understanding the movements of the muscles.

Antagonistic pairs

As we discussed previously, each muscle is limited to only one direction of movement. This creates a problem for us. How can a body part return to its original position once moved? Again, the answer is simple: *there's another muscle going the other way*. This other muscle, attached to the other side of the joint, can answer the original force in the opposite direction. This basic setup of muscles is called an 'antagonistic pair'. The acting muscle is called the 'agonist' and the other is the 'antagonist' (from 'anti-agonist'). As one muscle contracts, the other relaxes.

The biceps and triceps of the arm are one example of an antagonistic pair. The biceps acts as the main agonist for the movement of flexion (see page 60) and the triceps acts for the movement of extension (see page 58). Therefore, these muscles are the 'flexors' and 'extensors' of the upper arm, respectively. This pair is only one simple example but this relationship occurs throughout the body. This leads us to a general rule for the make-up of the body: *wherever there is a muscle creating a plane of movement, there will be an antagonistic muscle creating the opposite movement.*

This setup of **antagonistic pairs** also rather elegantly solves another important problem of moving the bones: the problem of having precise control. The solution is easiest to see with another simple analogy. Look at the figure at the top of the opposite page, pulling down on a heavy pole. He has to work hard to get the pole moving. Once it has started its descent, however, he has no way of stopping it, as he can't push on the rope. The result of all this can only be a nasty accident. If only he had more control!

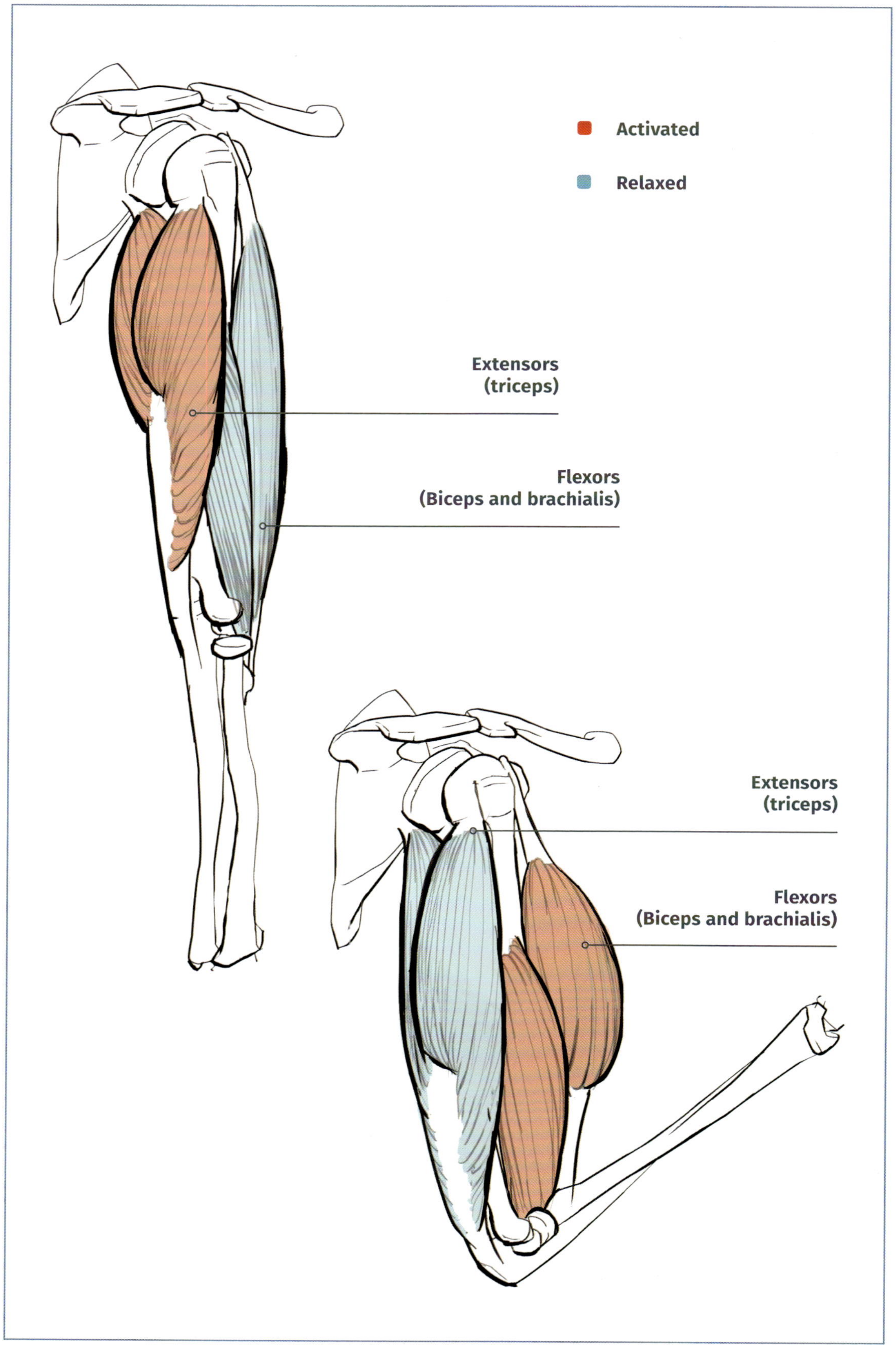

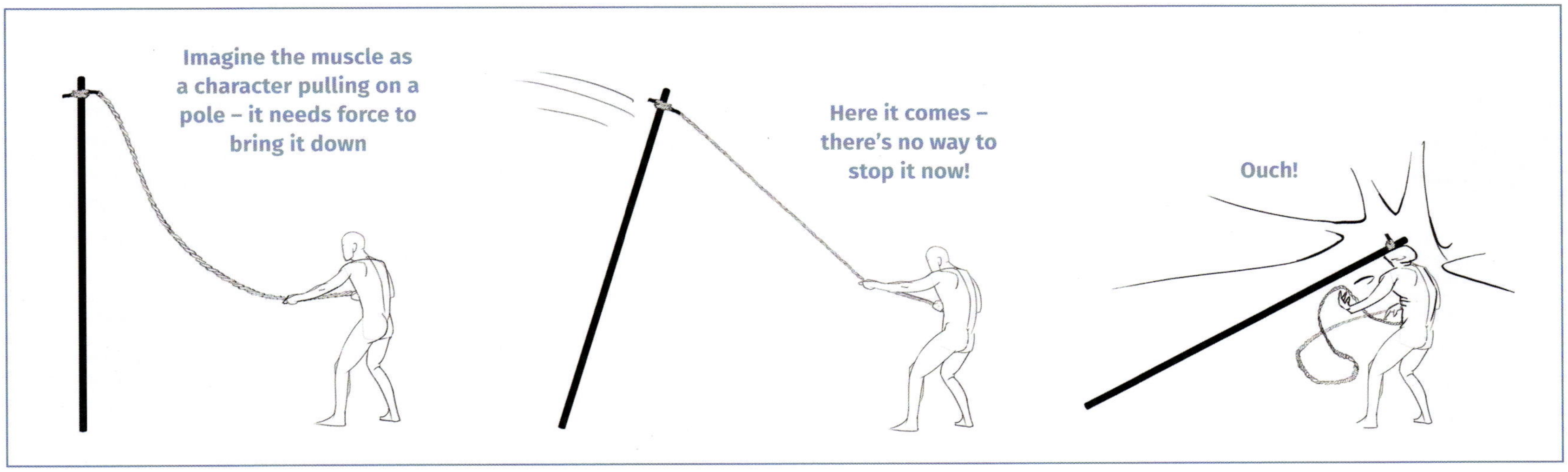

This lack of control would be a major problem in the body. Without proper control, movement of limbs might happen too suddenly, causing injuries and perhaps even breaking joints. However, if we give our figure a friend on the other side of the pole, the pair can work together to move the pole safely and with control. The same amount of force is needed to get the movement going, but once the pole starts to fall, the figure on the other side can begin to pull, creating an antagonistic force and slowing its descent (**images a–d**). In this way, any position of the pole can be held for as long as our figures can endure. The more relaxed one figure is, the harder the other has to work. This is how antagonistic pairs of muscles are able to give us such precise control over the position of each limb. As one side becomes more and more active, the other side becomes more and more relaxed. It's a wonderful system.

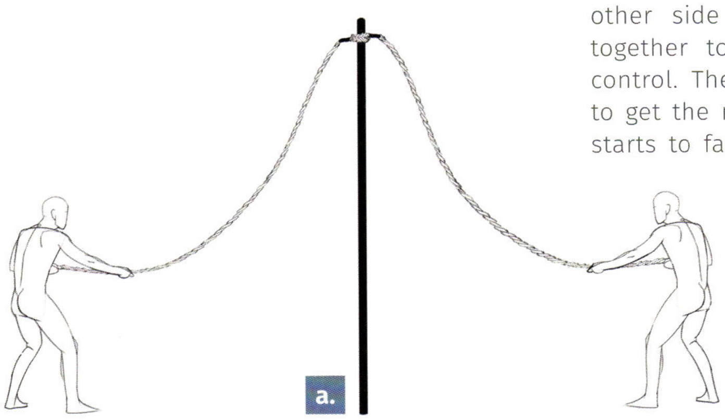

a.

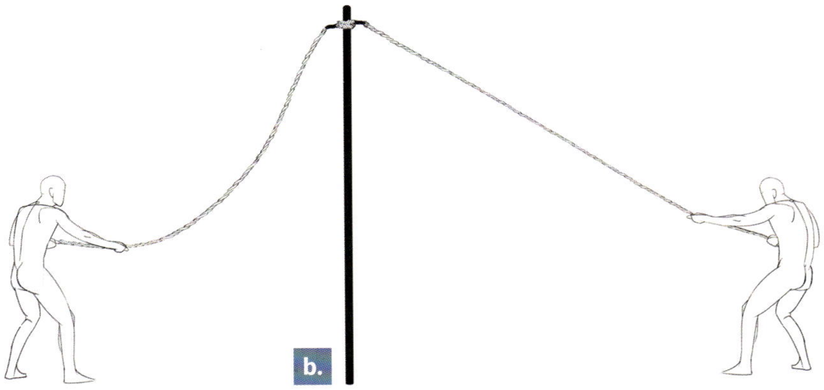

b.

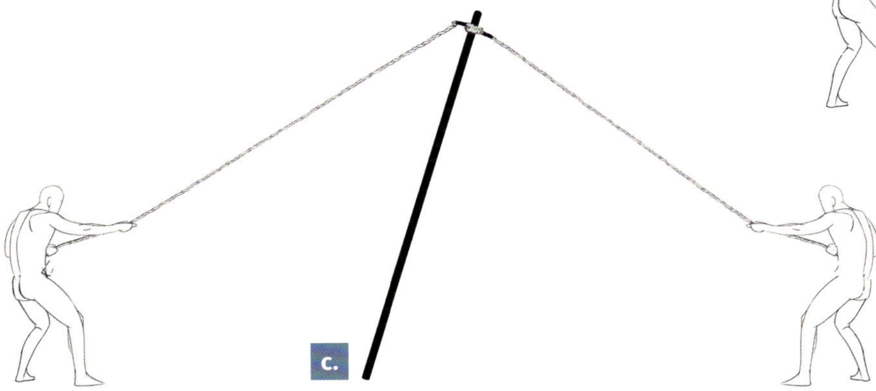

c.

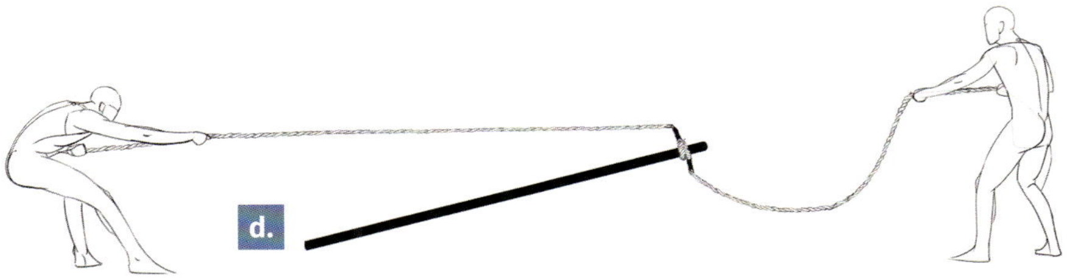

d.

If we give our figure (or muscle) a companion pulling in the opposite direction, together they have greater control over the action

Let's see just how this antagonistic relationship presents with a live model. In the fully extended position (below), the triceps is activated and enlarged while the biceps has reached its full relaxed length. In the fully flexed position (far right), the opposite is true: the biceps is activated and bulging out, while the triceps is fully relaxed and stretched.

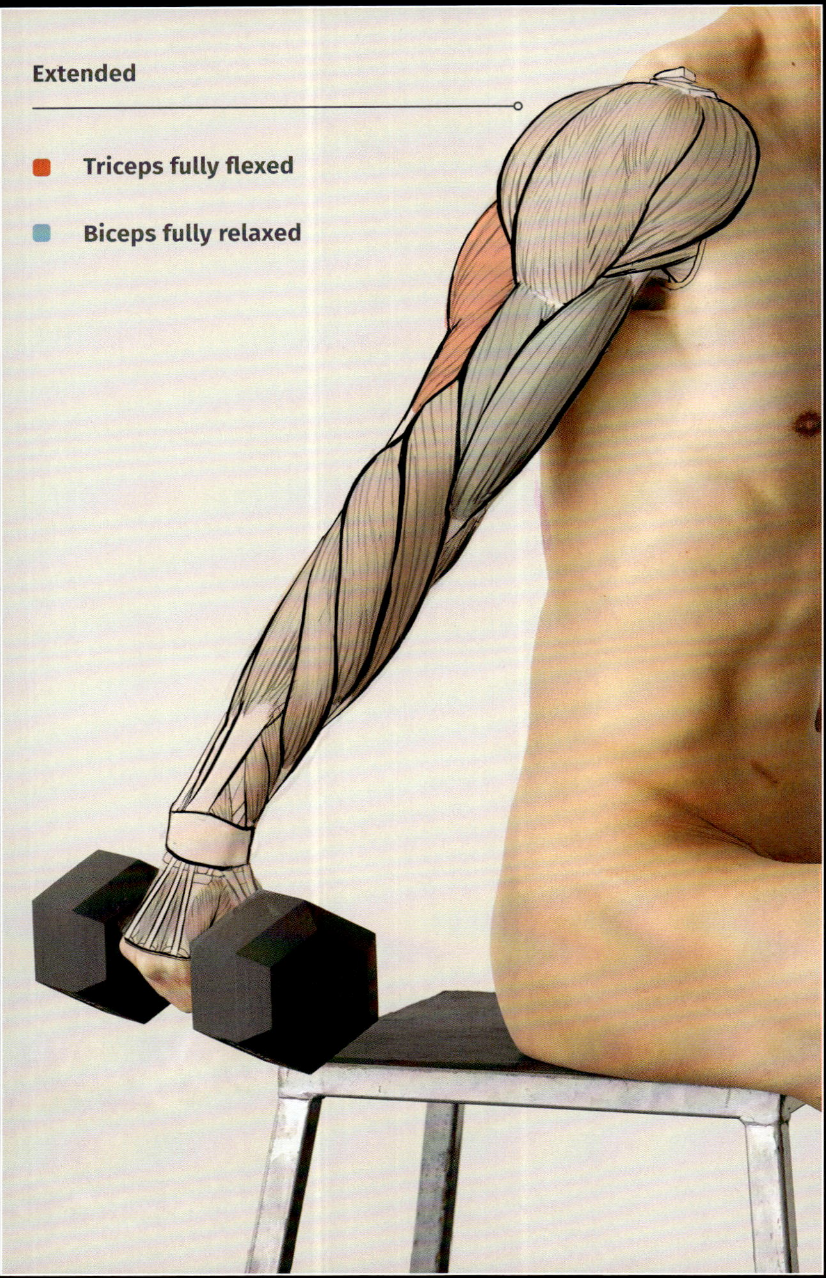

In the neutral position (below), the arm is more evenly activated, with neither side being fully activated or stretched. As you study the poses and movements in this book, always take note of which main antagonistic pair is at work in the movement. Which muscle relaxes while the other contracts? Figuring this out is the key to making your figures appear naturally posed.

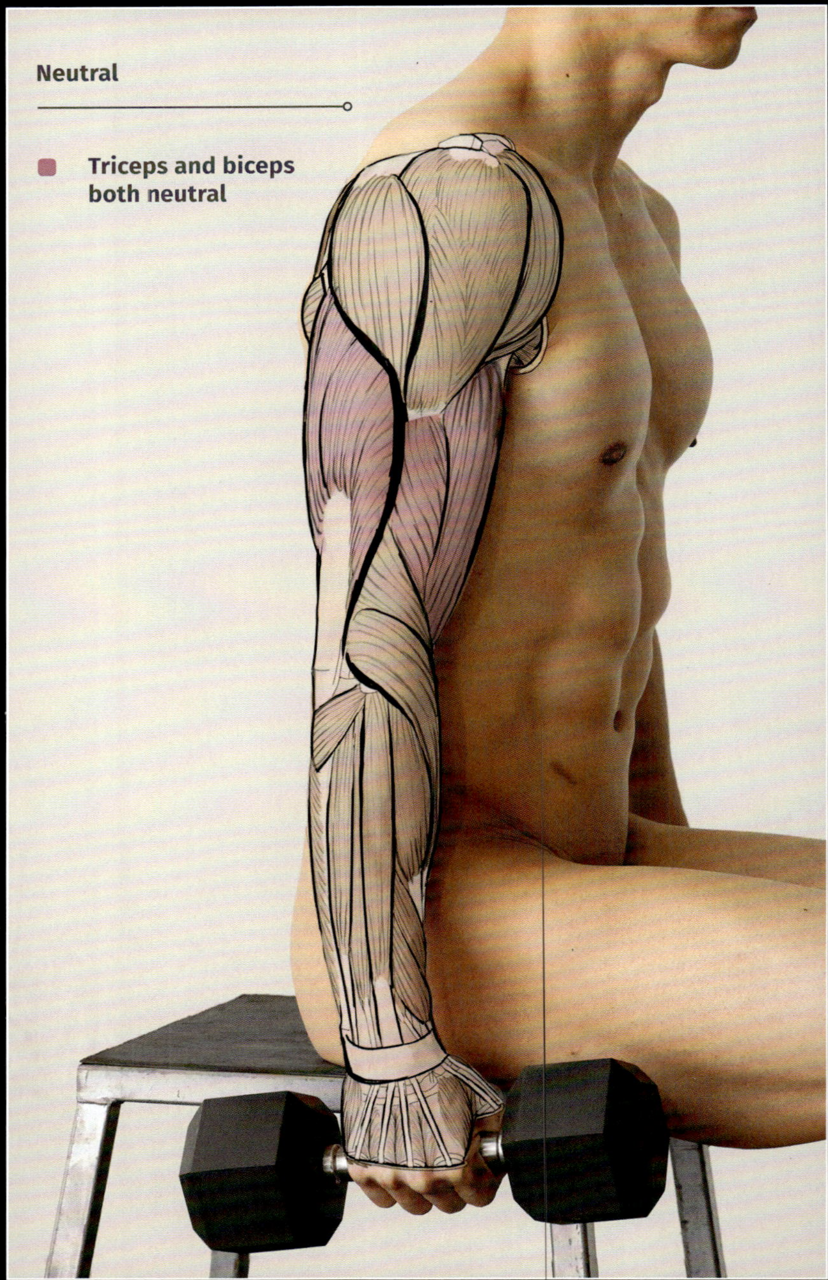

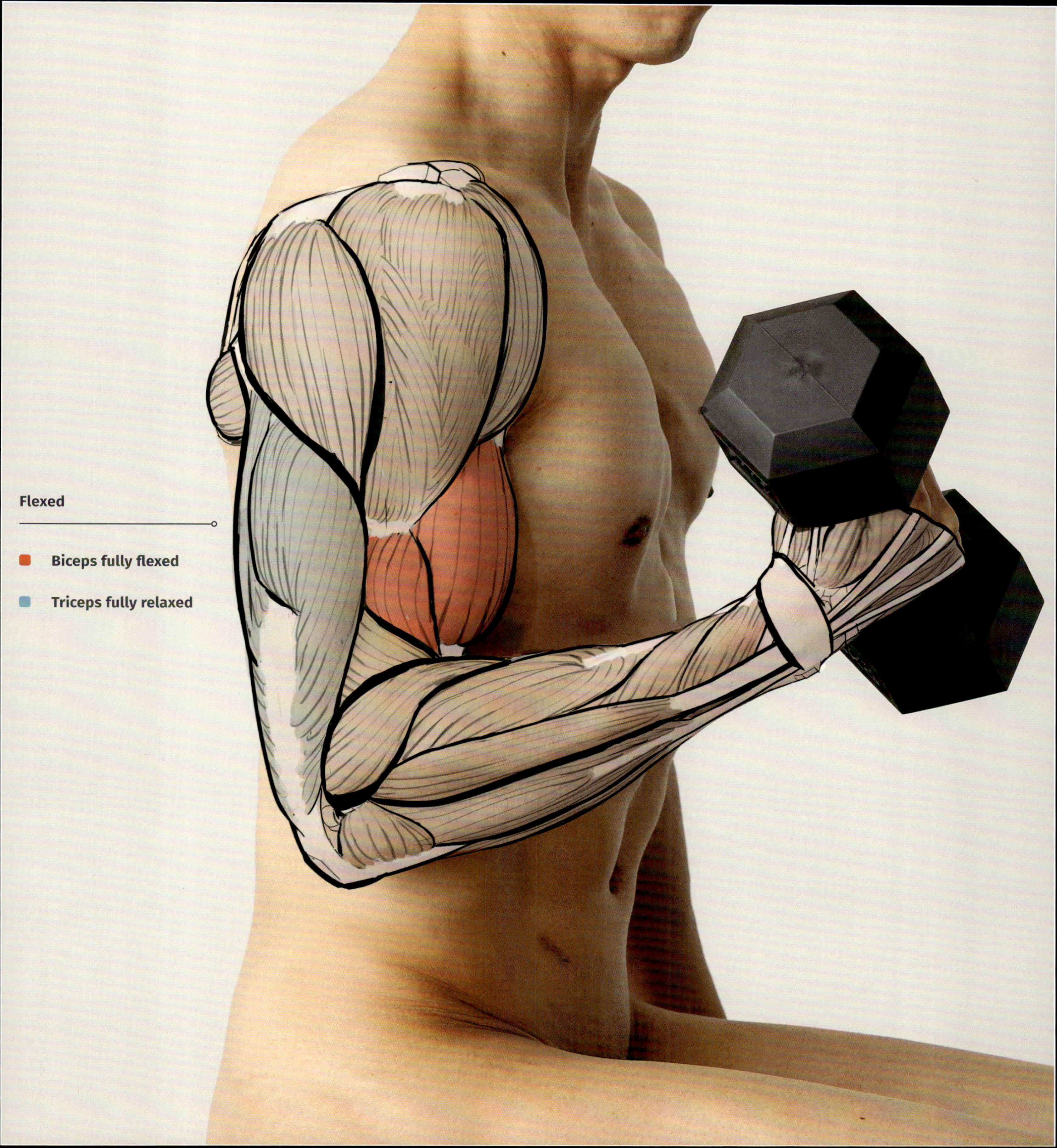

Flexed
Biceps fully flexed
Triceps fully relaxed

Active and passive design

The knowledge that much of the body consists of antagonistic pairs will be massively useful to us when we attempt to simplify or exaggerate the complexities of the human form. This leads us to the concept of active and passive shape design. Active shapes comprise a lot of sudden changes in direction, while passive shapes present as more simple and flowing.

In general, when depicting a body part, we want to keep one side of the form active and the other passive. We can see the effect of this in the classic 'pillowcase' example. When both sides of the pillowcase are equal and straight, the pillow has no weight – it appears as if it is floating. If we add a more active squashed side to one half, we are immediately able to see much more weight acting on the pillowcase. This is the strength of contrast in active and passive design.

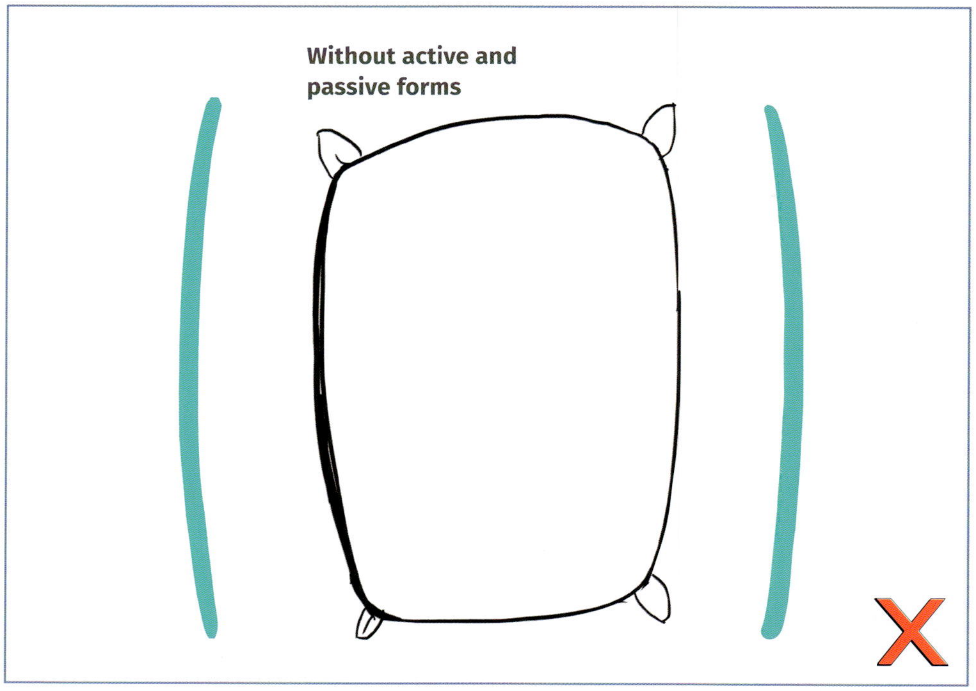

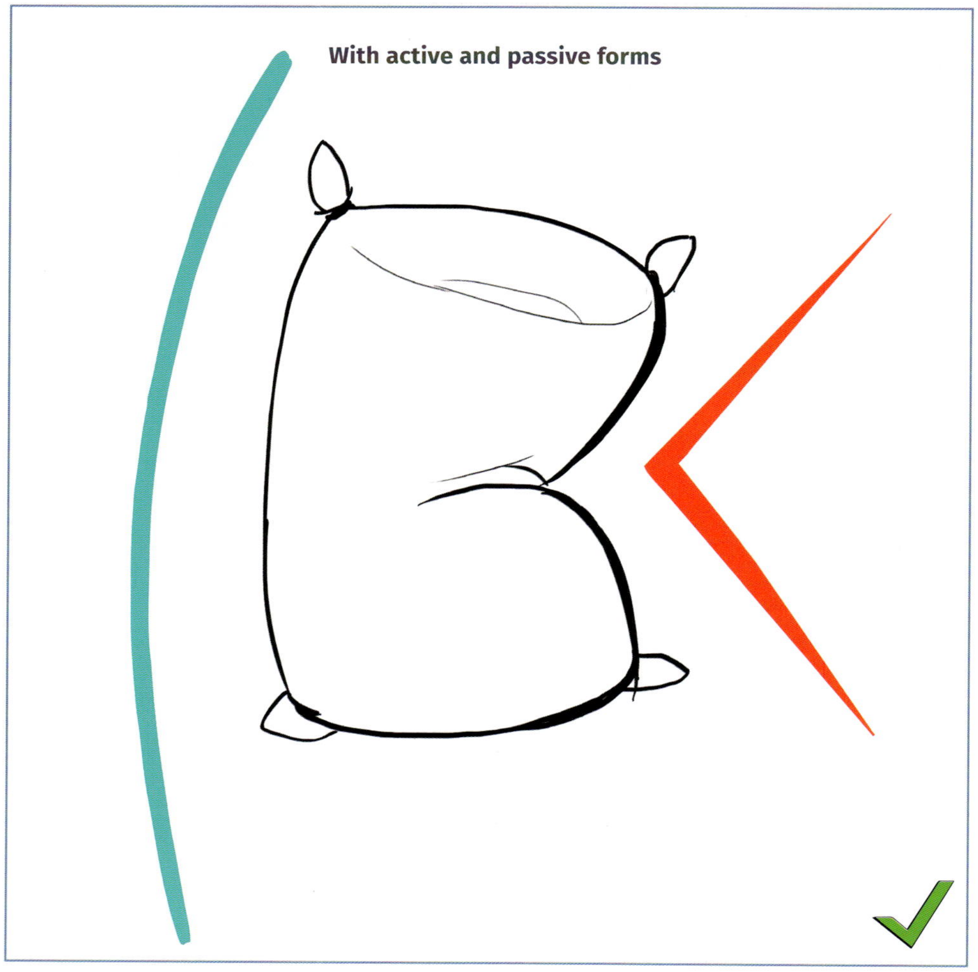

While the pillowcase is a fairly simple example, this idea holds true for every area of the body in action. This is because of the previously discussed antagonistic pair relationship. We can see how these two ideas interlock if we take a look at the same example of the arm moving from flexion to extension. In both examples, the active side of the arm is also filled with active shapes and lots of anatomical details; in contrast, the inactive side is stretched out, displaying a more passive design and far less anatomical detail.

When we first start learning anatomy, it is often tempting to try to use our hard-won knowledge everywhere in a drawing and place muscular details throughout. This is a common mistake resulting in a figure that looks tense all over. If we want to achieve a naturally posed look, it is as important to leave anatomical details out of the stretched side as it is to emphasize them in the active side.

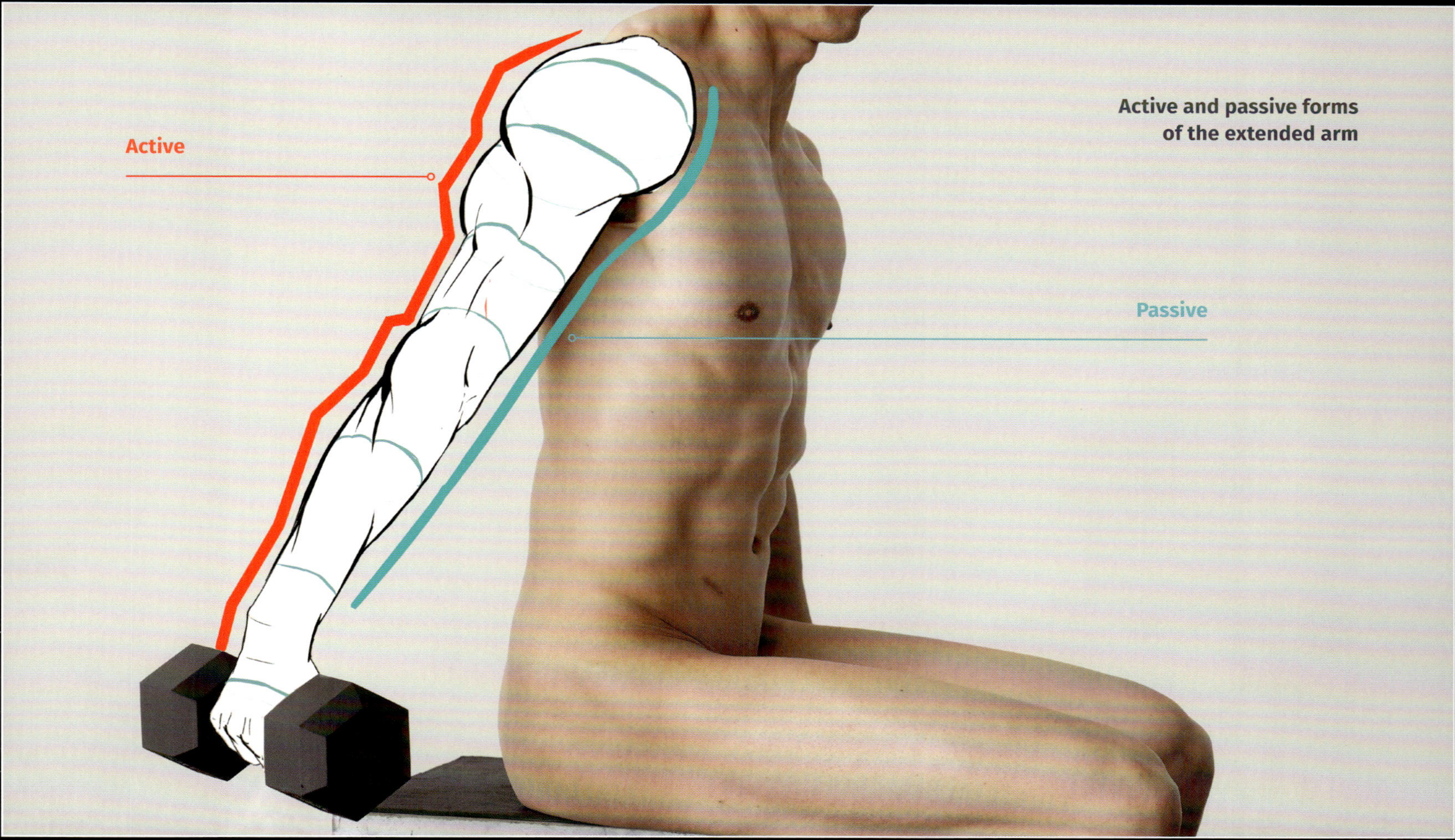

Active and passive forms
of the extended arm

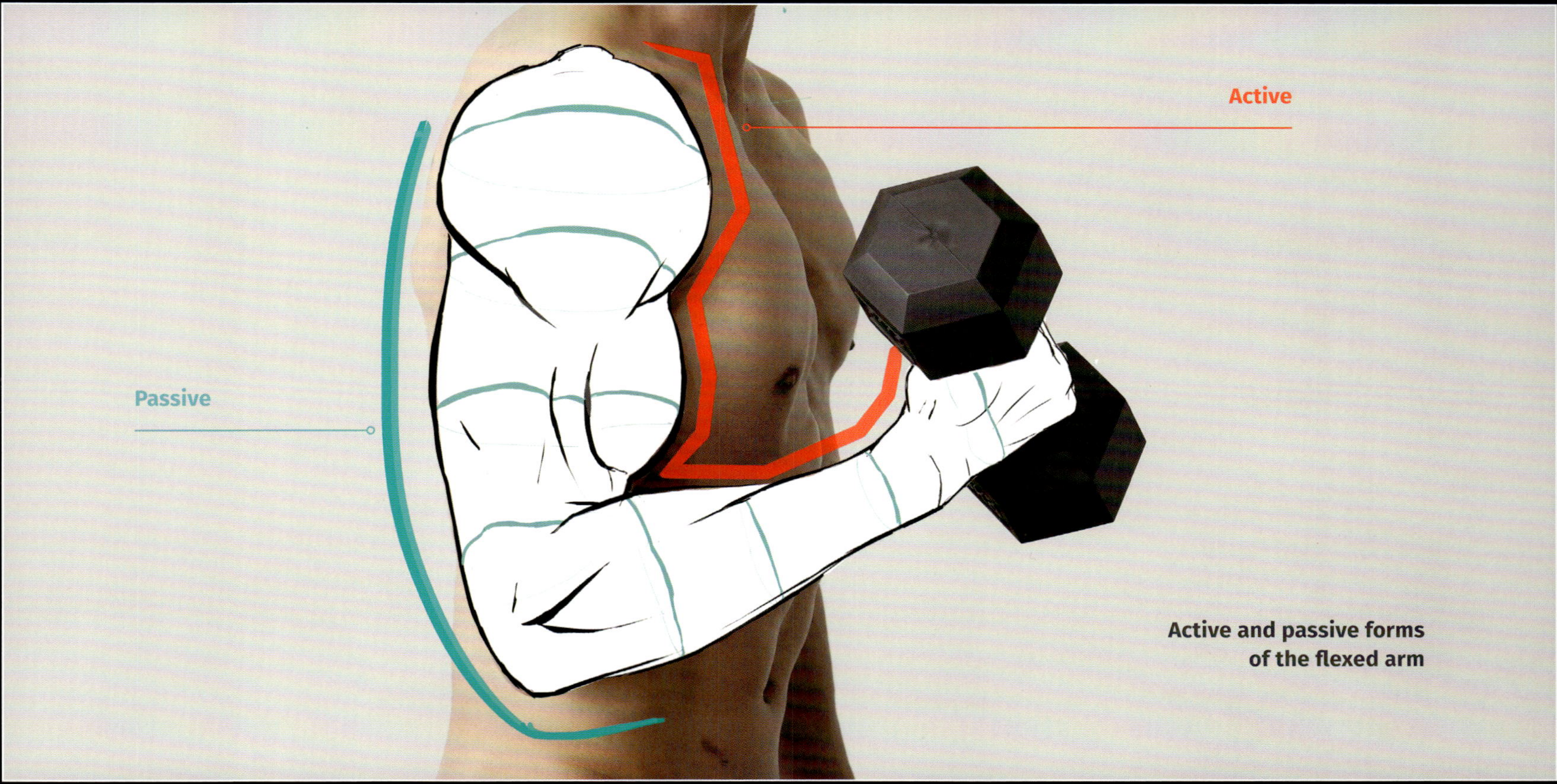

Active and passive forms
of the flexed arm

This special relationship between active and passive holds true for full-body poses as much as it does for individual body parts. We can see a strong example in this beautiful gymnastic movement. What is wonderful to see is that these poses create an active and passive relationship on either side of the pose, and the passive side flips as the model progresses through the movement. It won't always be as obvious as the extreme bends and curves shown on the top and bottom left, but this relationship is one of the signs of a good pose.

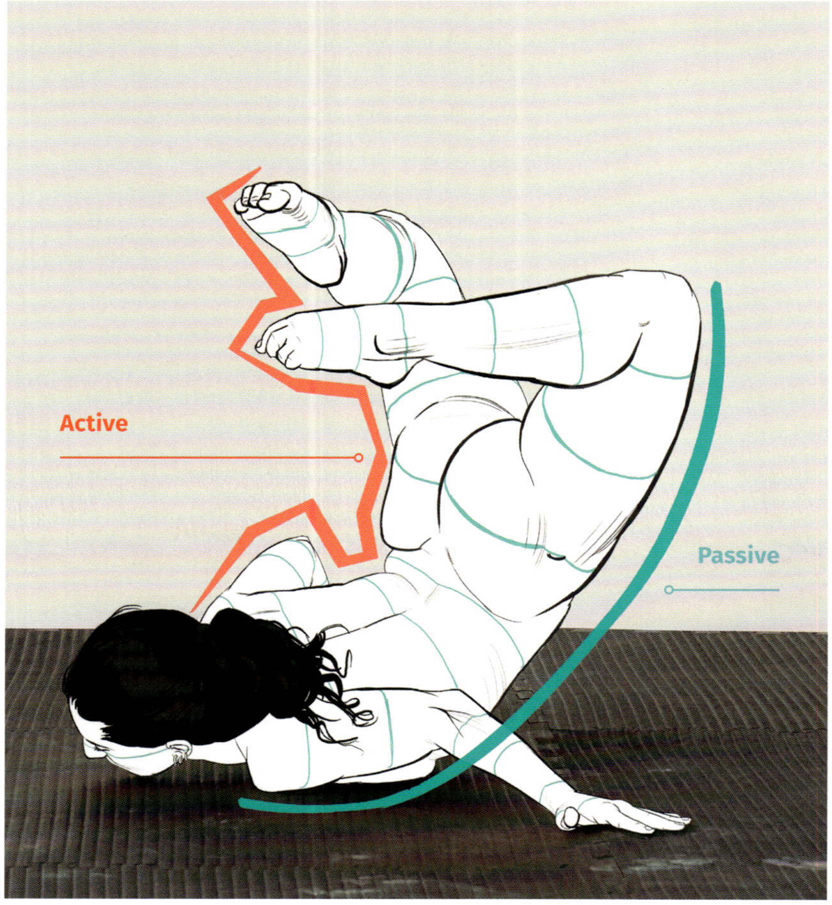

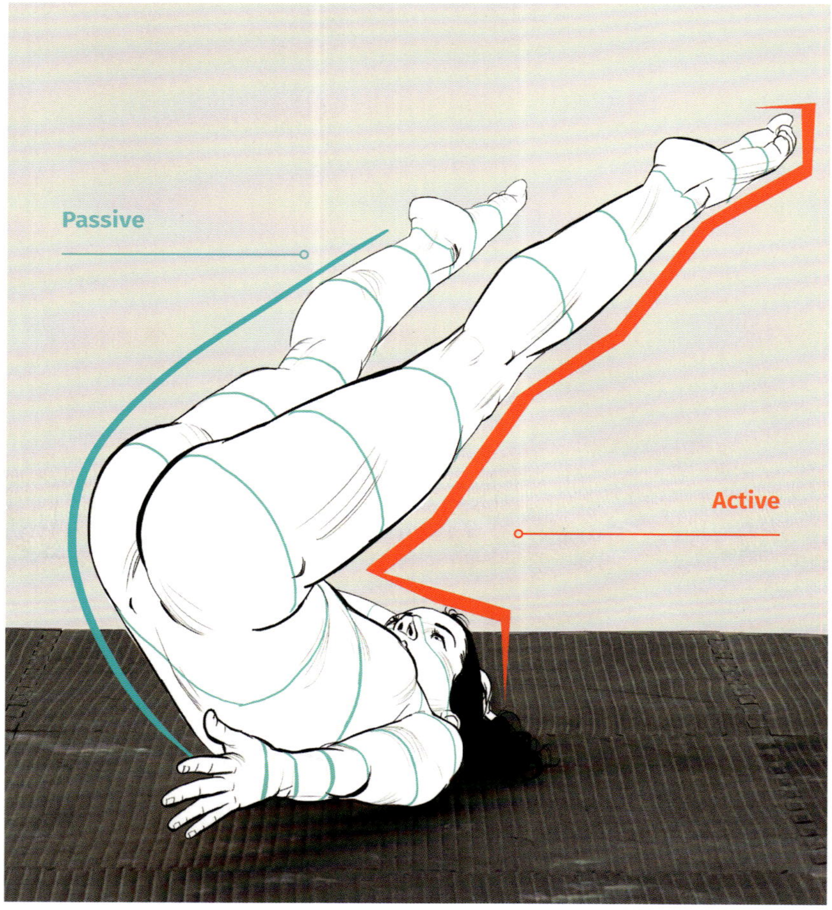

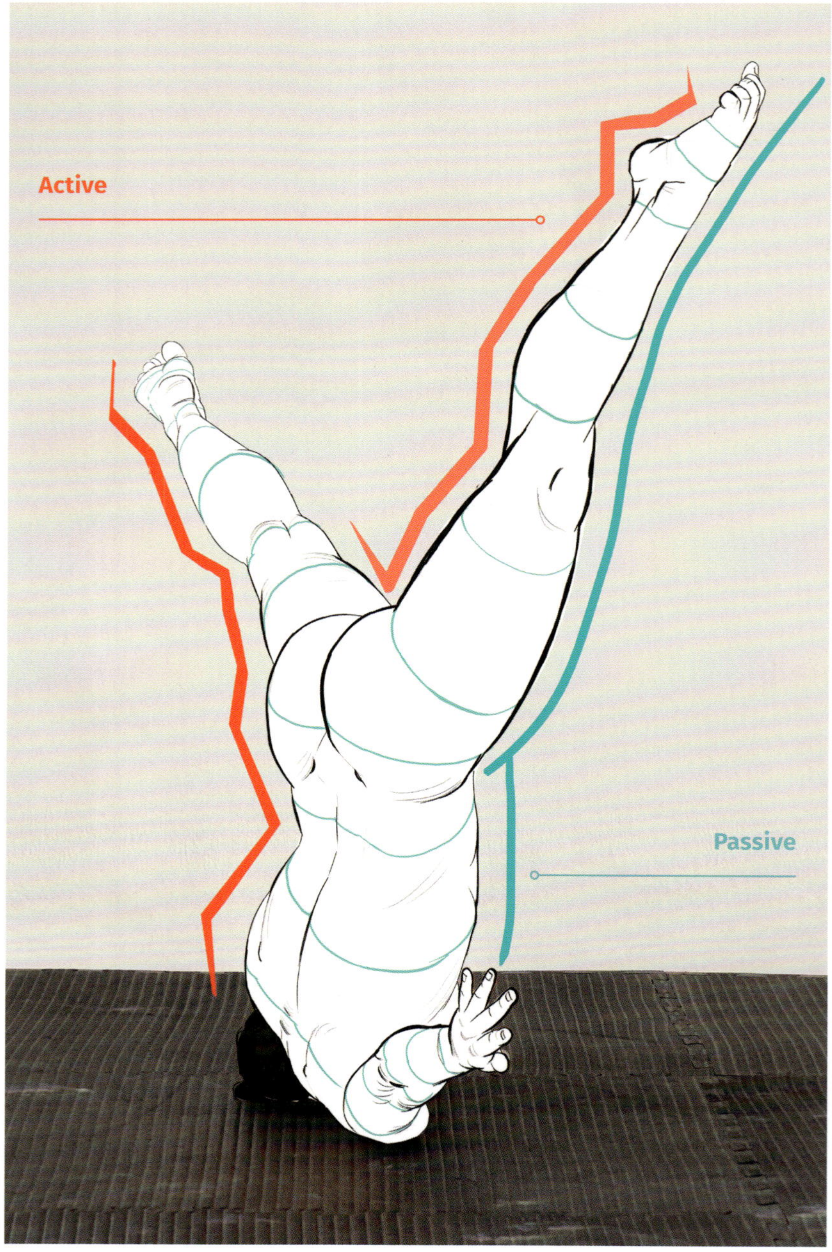

Active and passive forms in dramatic full-body gymnastic poses

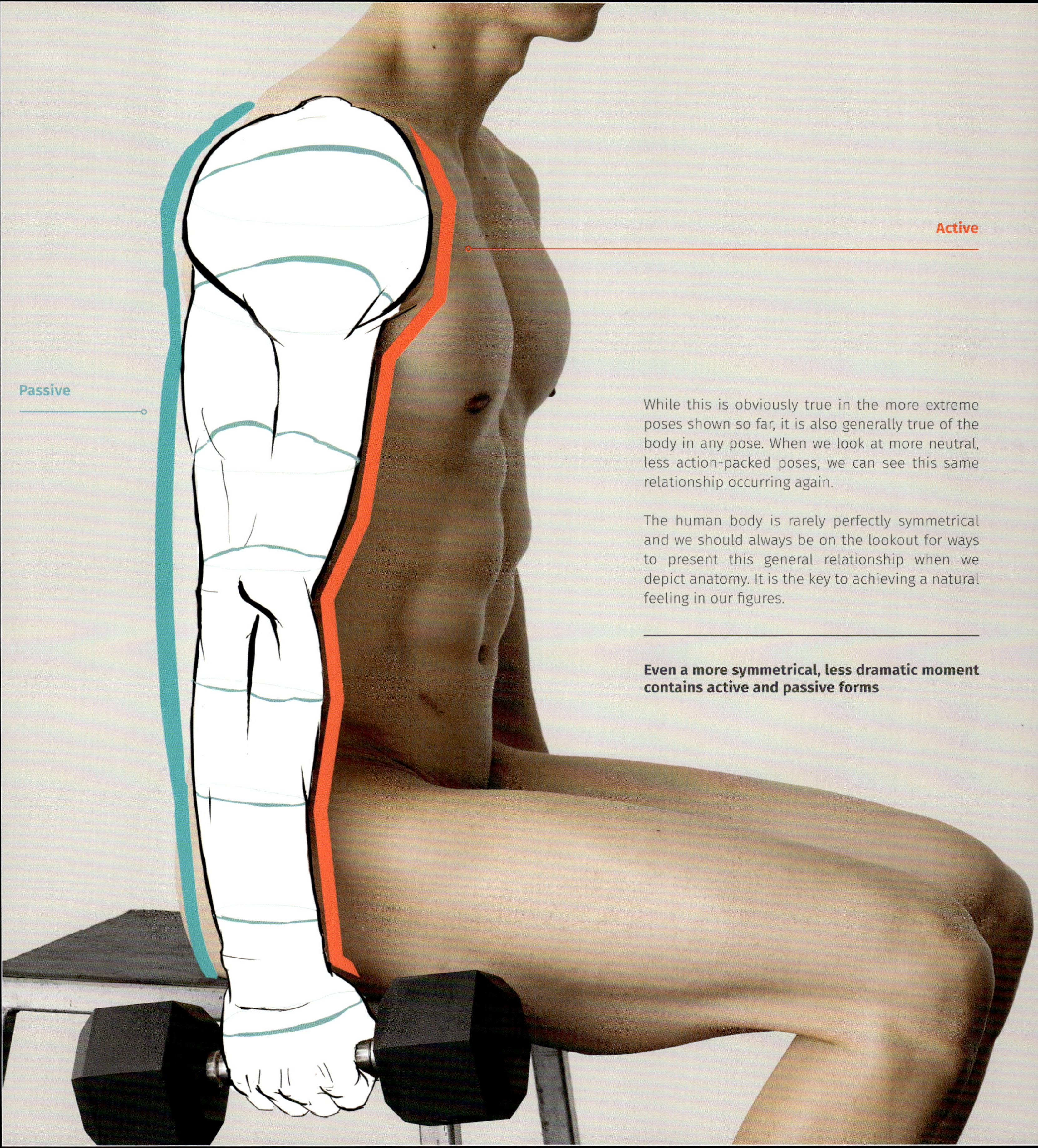

While this is obviously true in the more extreme poses shown so far, it is also generally true of the body in any pose. When we look at more neutral, less action-packed poses, we can see this same relationship occurring again.

The human body is rarely perfectly symmetrical and we should always be on the lookout for ways to present this general relationship when we depict anatomy. It is the key to achieving a natural feeling in our figures.

Even a more symmetrical, less dramatic moment contains active and passive forms

Types of motion

Before we look at the specific anatomy of the figure in movement, it is important that we first make clear the different types of motion available to the body through its various joints. As we do this, we will also take note of another important consideration: the general range of motion of all the various parts of the body as isolated movements.

The reason it is important to study these in isolation is that many of the movements compensate for each other to fill out the body's available range of motion when it is in full motion. This can give us an inaccurate sense of what is possible with the figure. It is important we know the limits of each part of the figure, so that we do not exit the range of possible motion. This mistake is easy to make as working from imagination can completely break the pose, so study the diagrams shown here well.

Arm movements

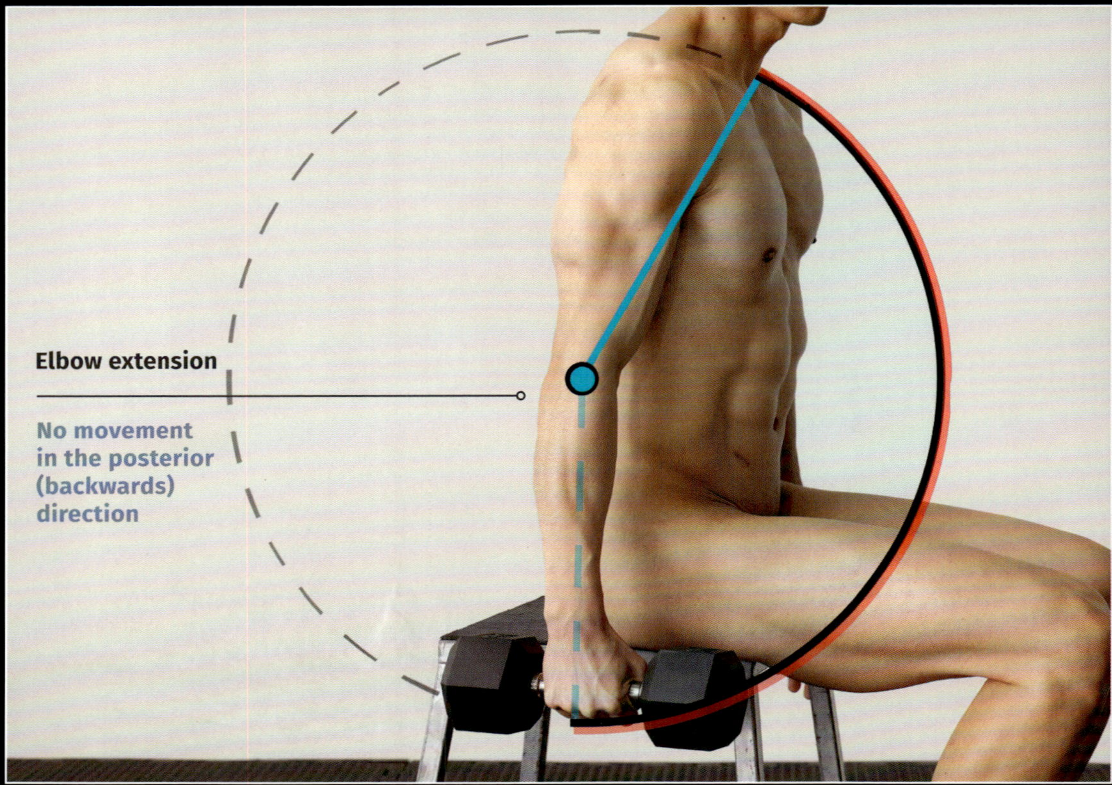

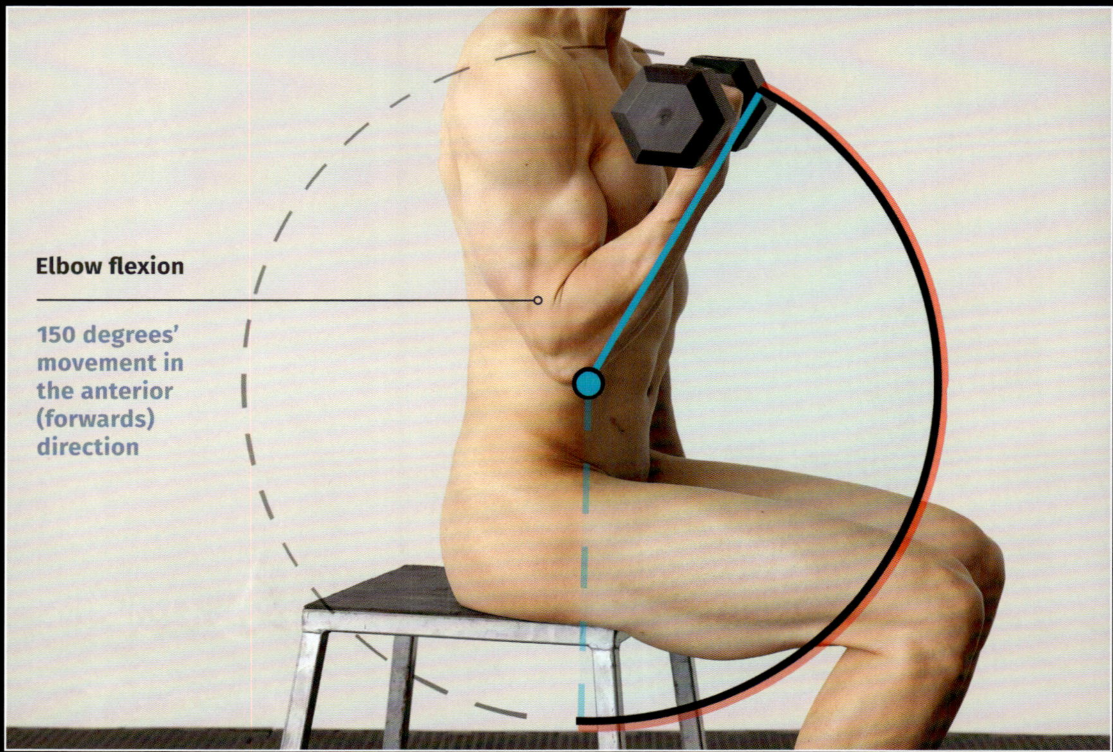

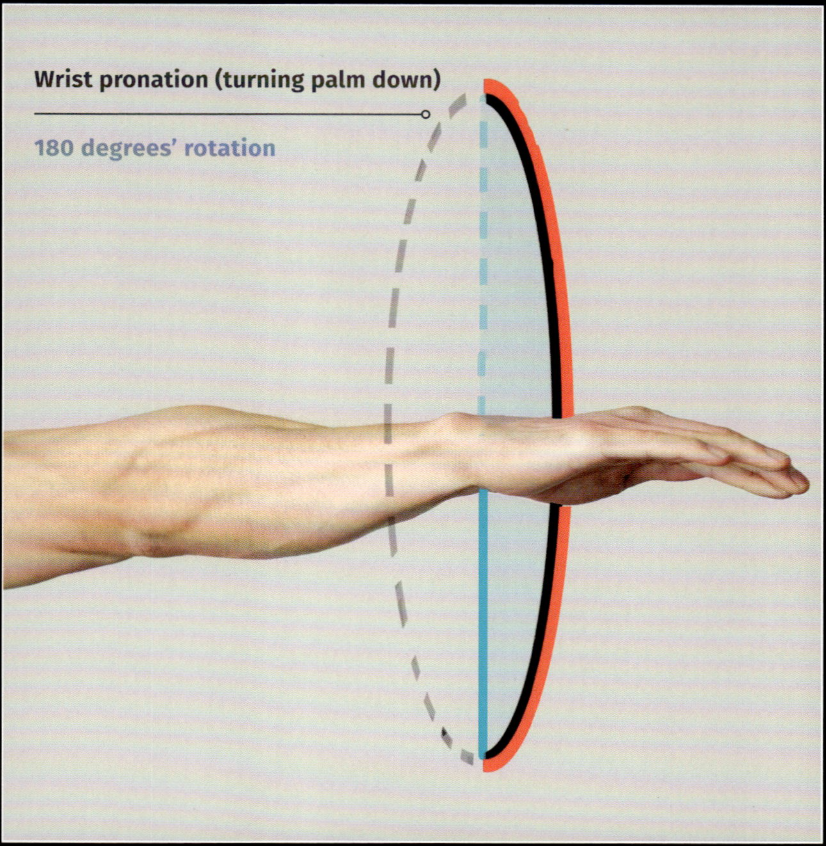

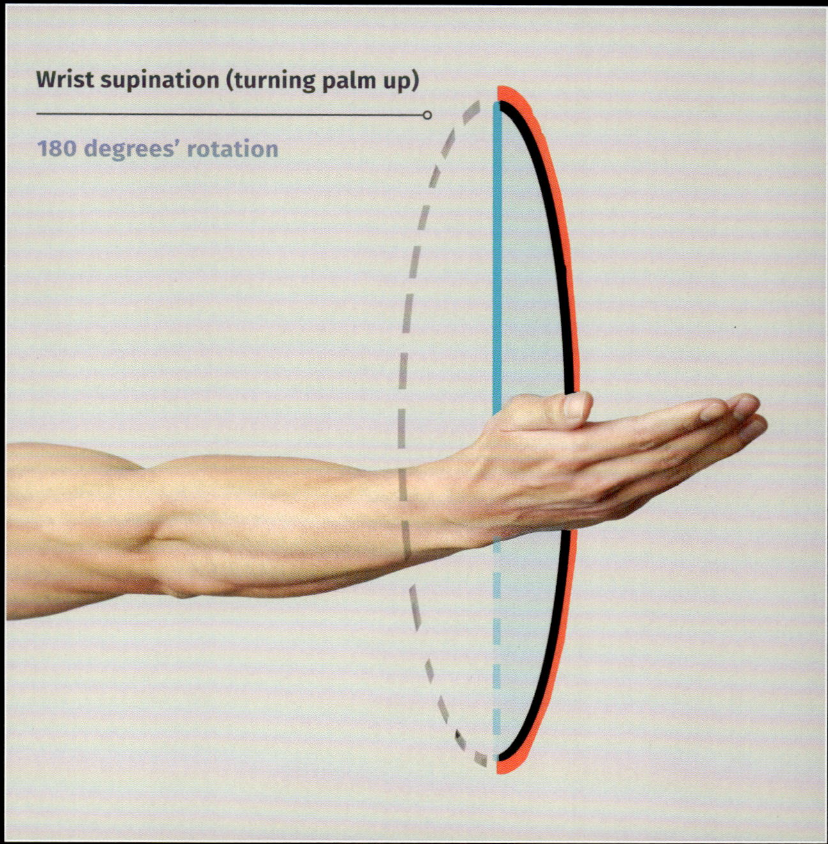

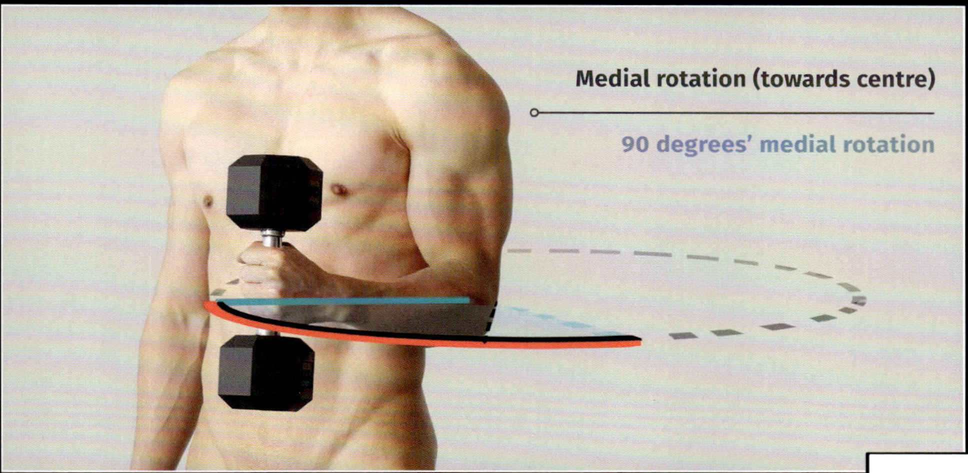

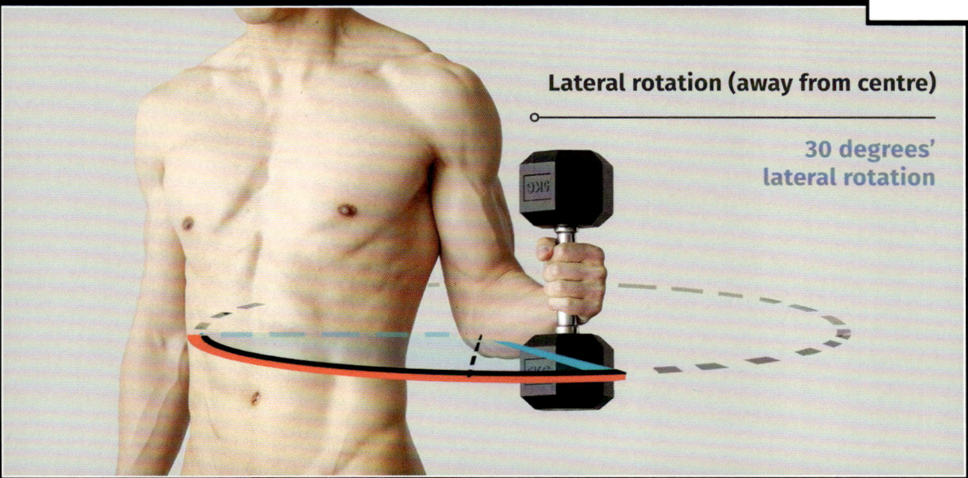

Rotation scope (top view)

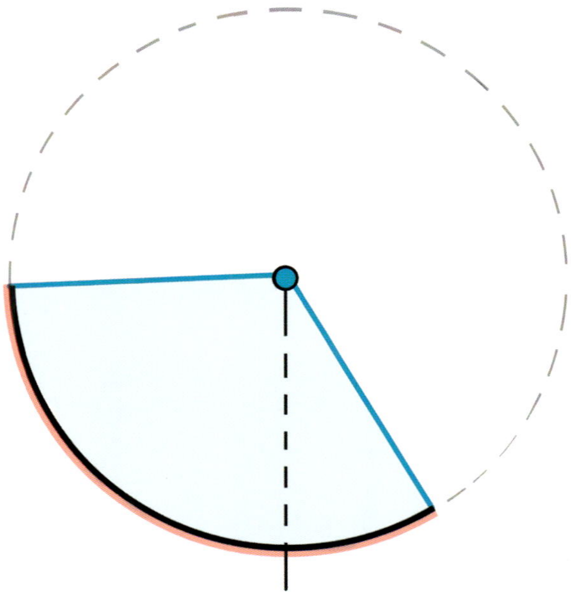

The degrees of movement available when rotating the arm from a neutral centre line

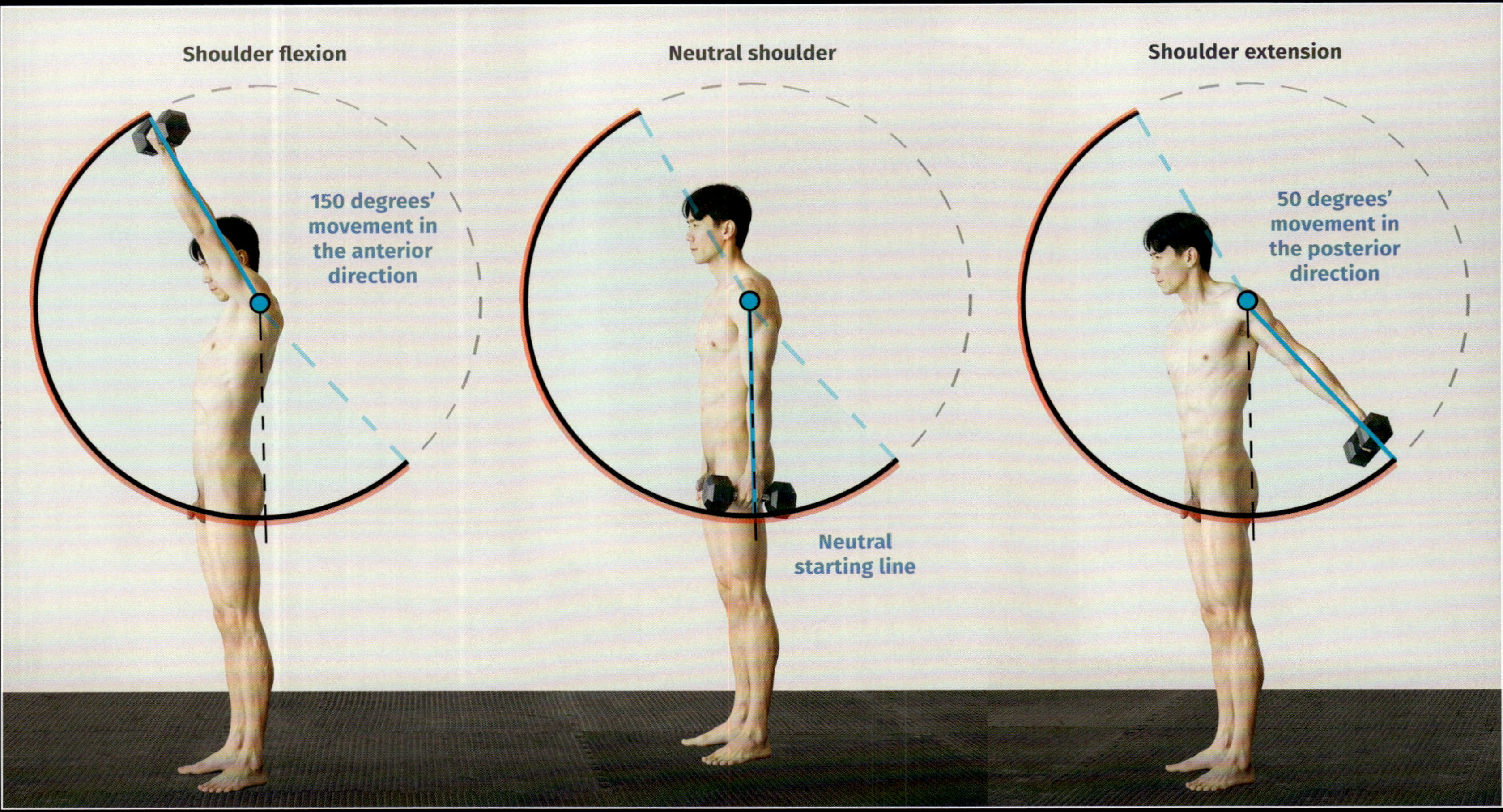
Shoulder flexion
Neutral shoulder
Shoulder extension
150 degrees' movement in the anterior direction
50 degrees' movement in the posterior direction
Neutral starting line

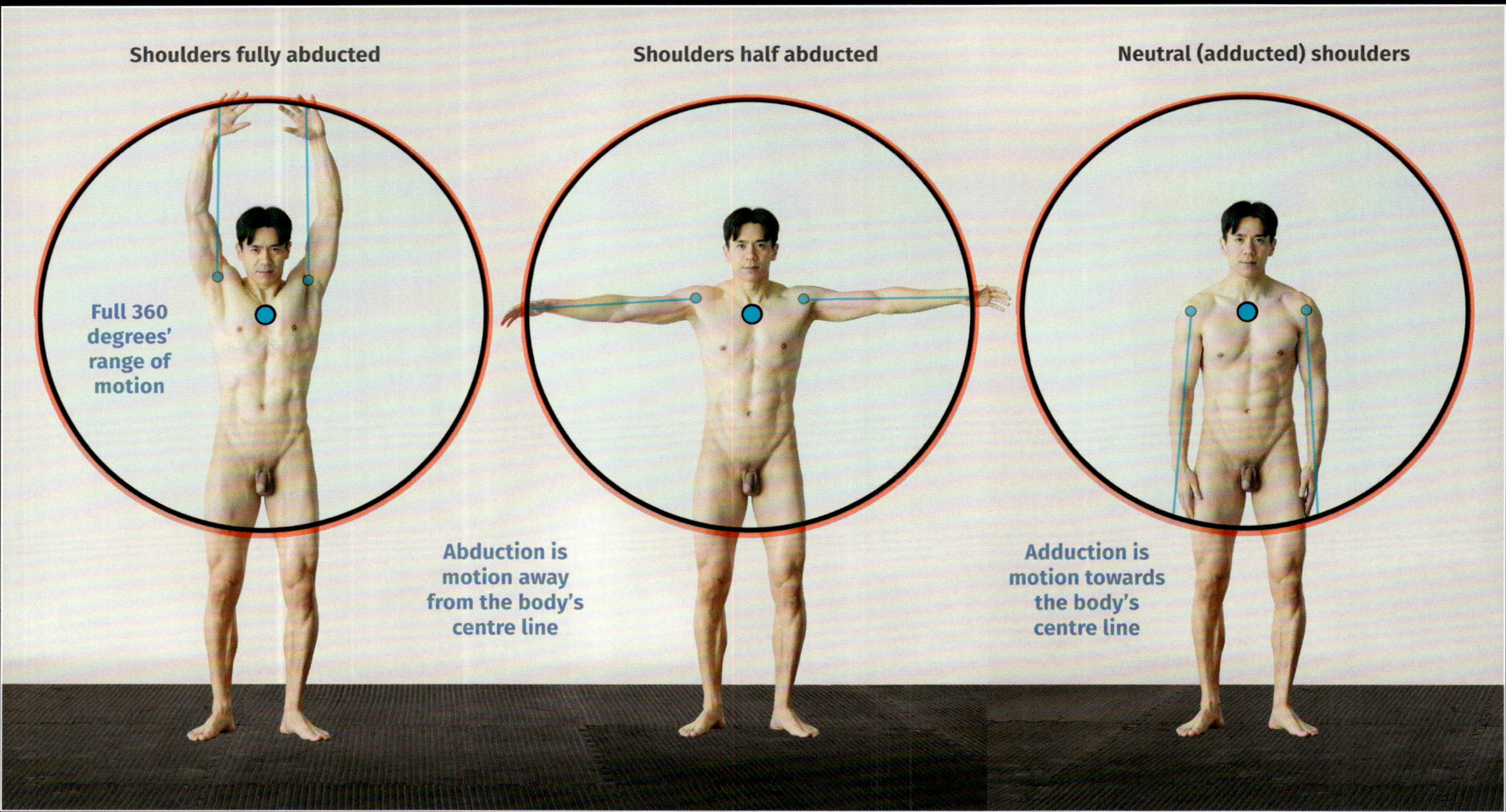
Shoulders fully abducted
Shoulders half abducted
Neutral (adducted) shoulders
Full 360 degrees' range of motion
Abduction is motion away from the body's centre line
Adduction is motion towards the body's centre line

Scapulohumeral rhythm

An important element to understand about the shoulder joint is how much of an impact the movement of the scapulae (shoulder blades) has on the movement of the shoulder joint. The arm does not simply move on its own. In fact, without our scapulae, we would have a considerably reduced range. This is most clearly seen from the back view.

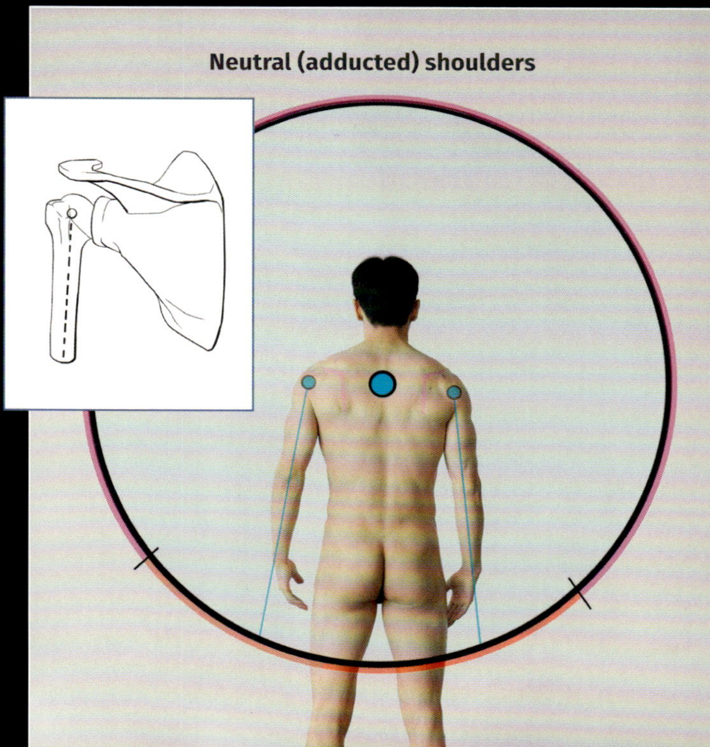

Neutral (adducted) shoulders

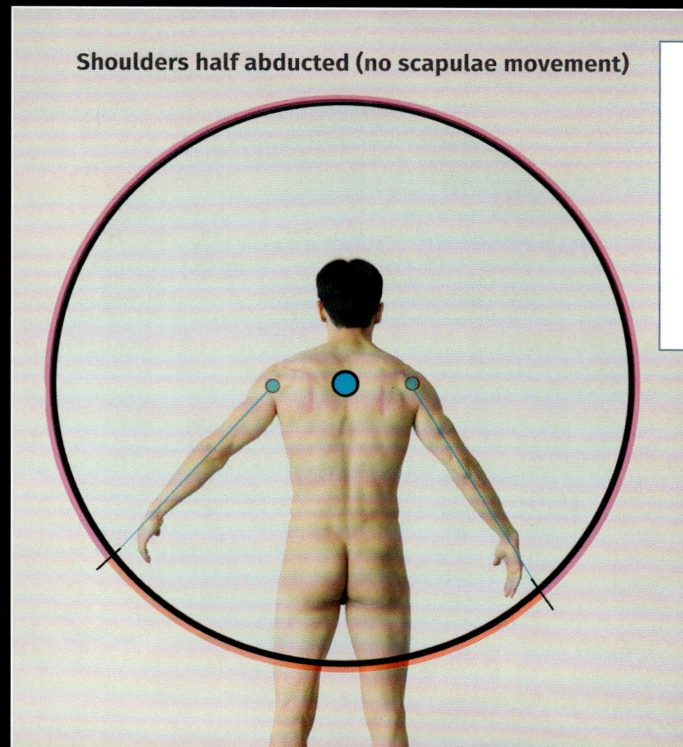

Shoulders half abducted (no scapulae movement)

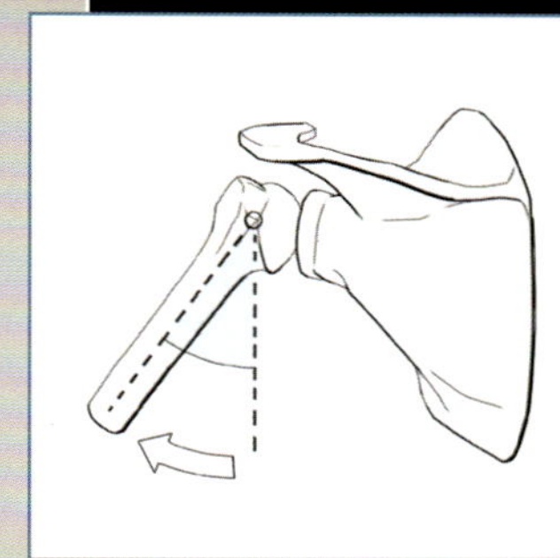

Without movement of the scapulae (shoulder blades), the shoulders have a limited range of only 50 degrees of abduction, out of the possible 180 degrees

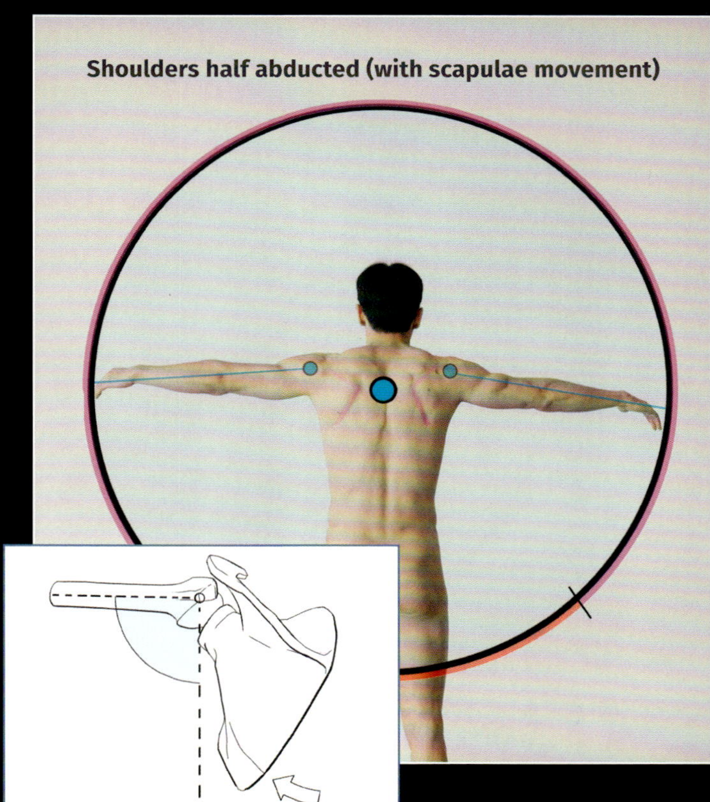

Shoulders half abducted (with scapulae movement)

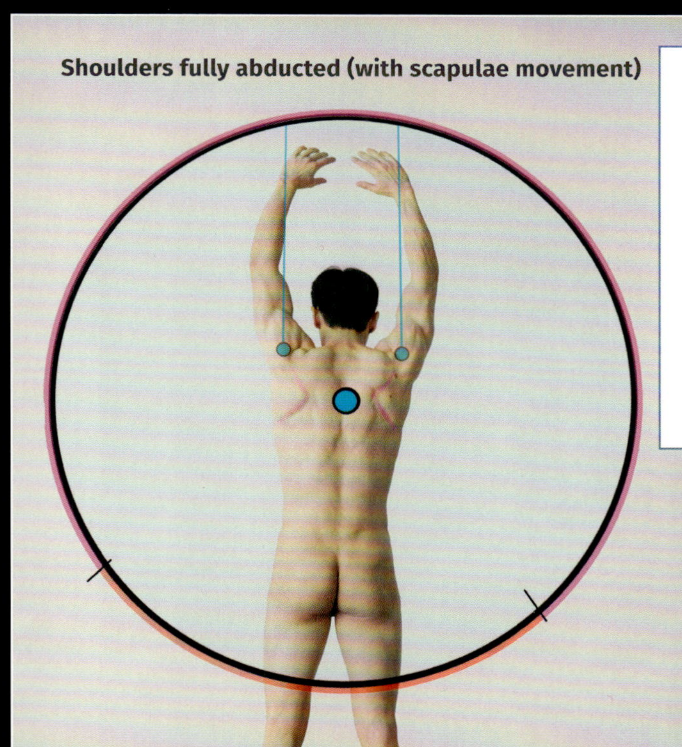

Shoulders fully abducted (with scapulae movement)

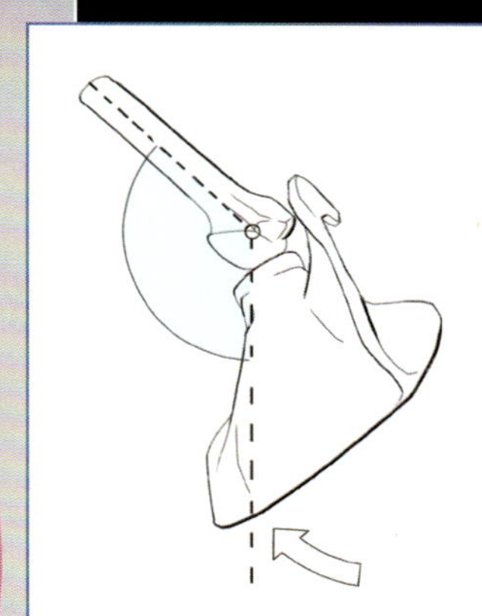

Above 50 degrees, the model can move through the entire rest of the range, entirely down to the movement of the scapulae. Don't forget this when drawing the arms!

Leg movements

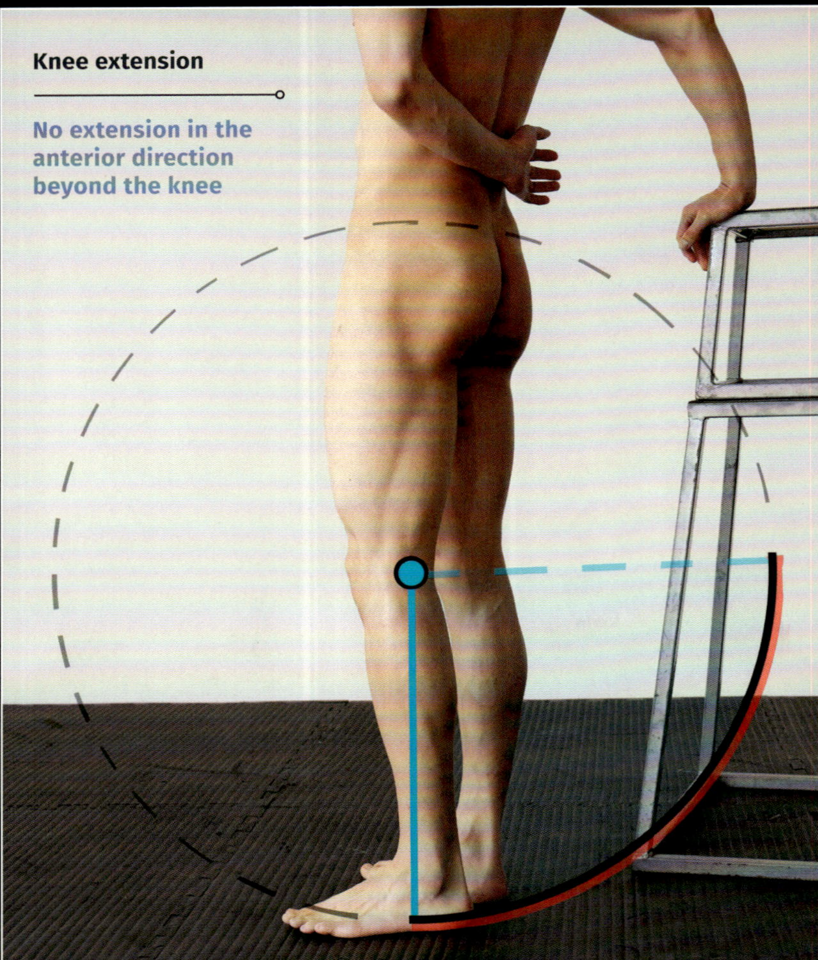

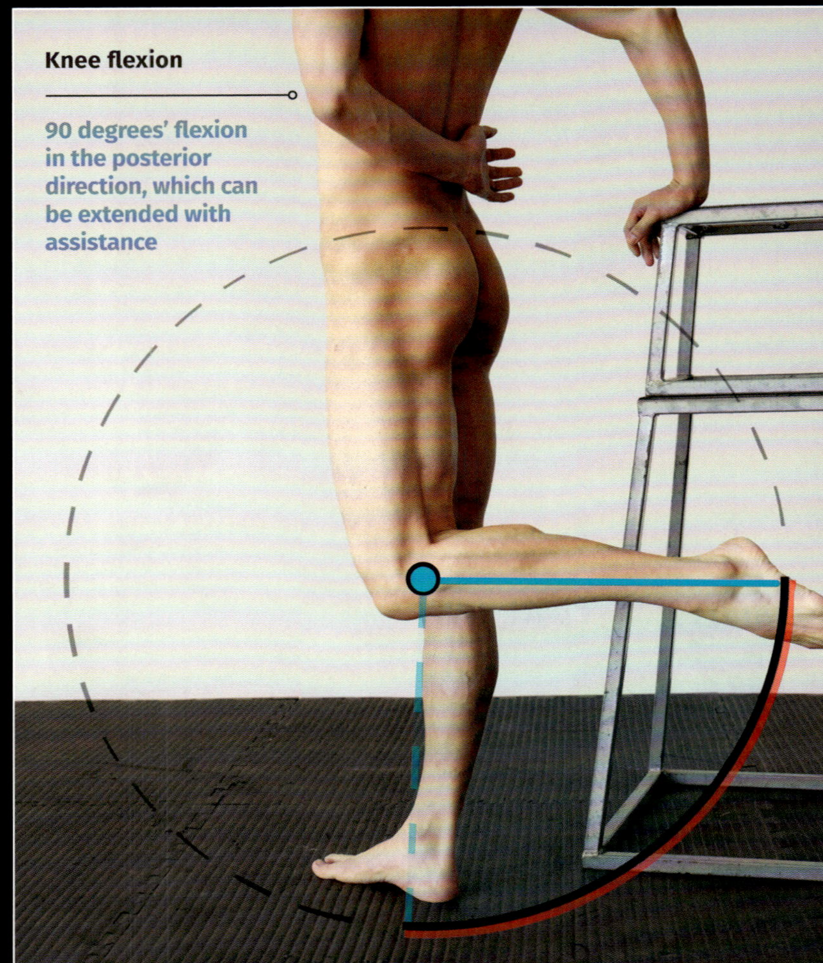

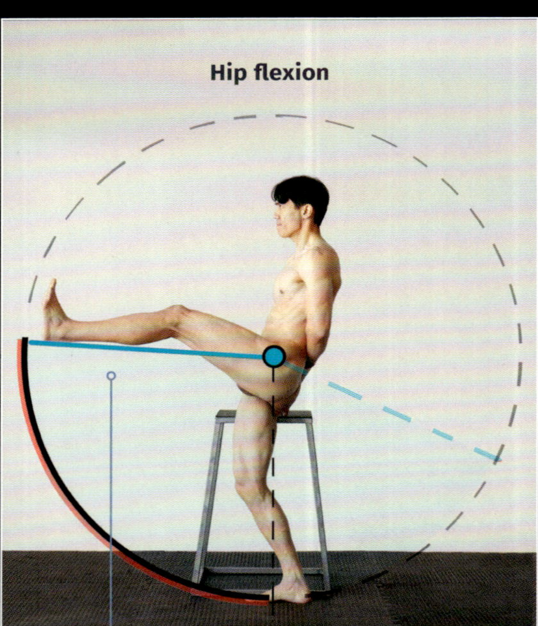

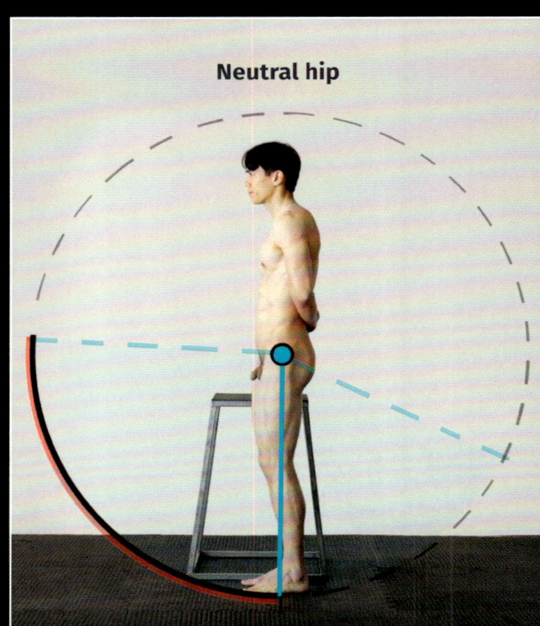

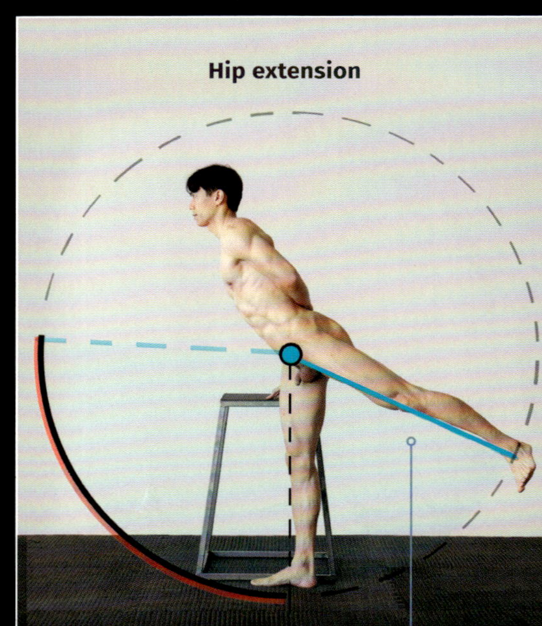

90 degrees' flexion in the anterior direction, which can be extended with assistance

50 degrees' flexion in the posterior direction

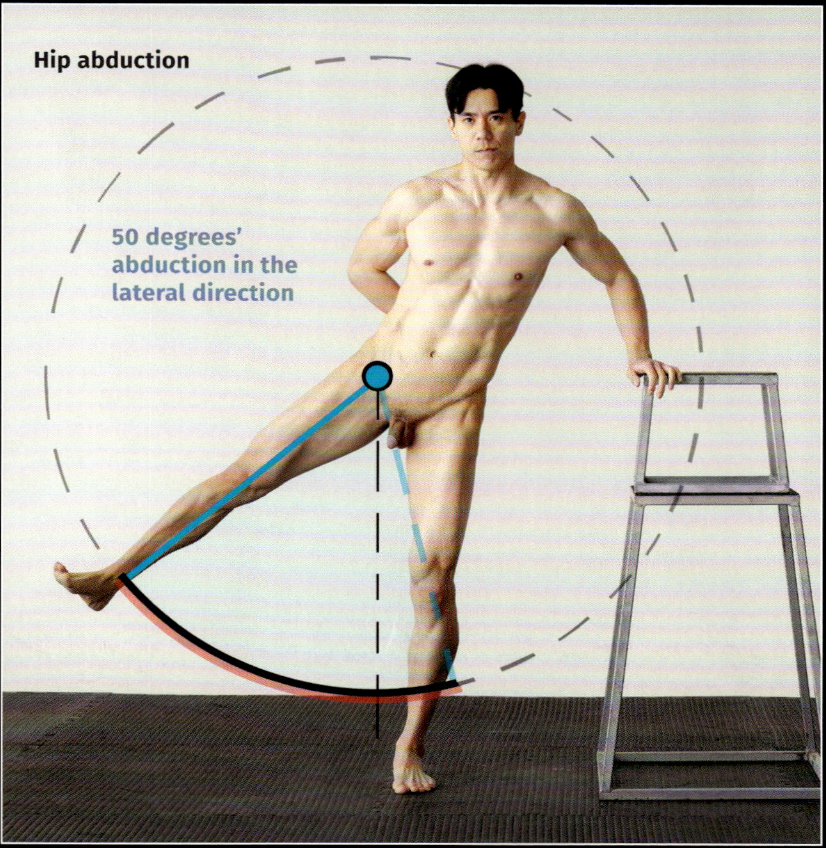
Hip abduction
50 degrees' abduction in the lateral direction

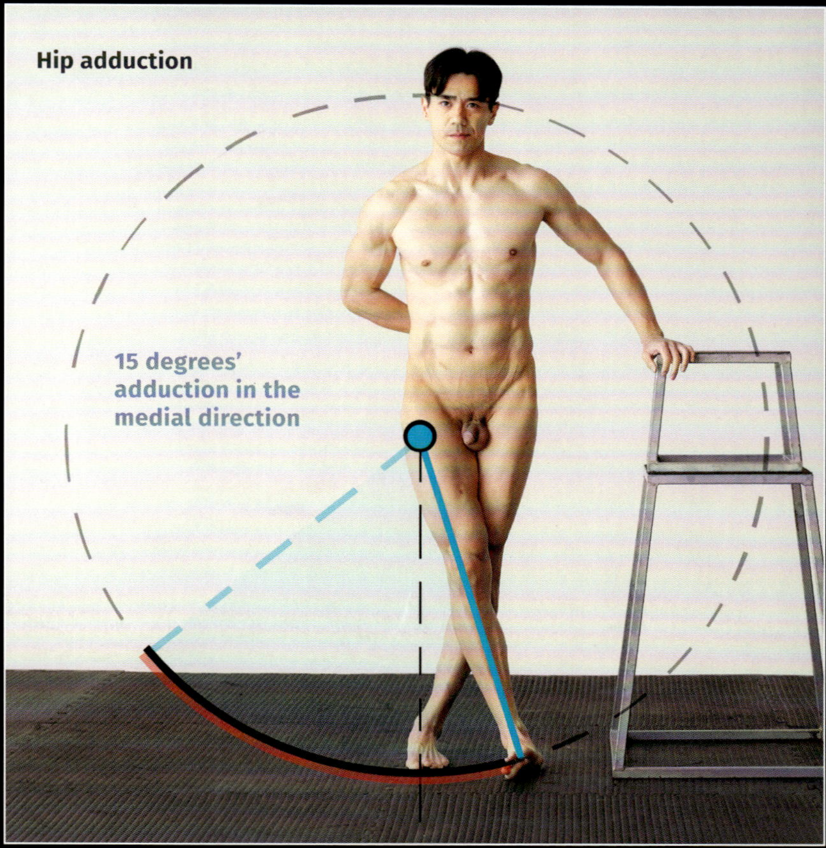
Hip adduction
15 degrees' adduction in the medial direction

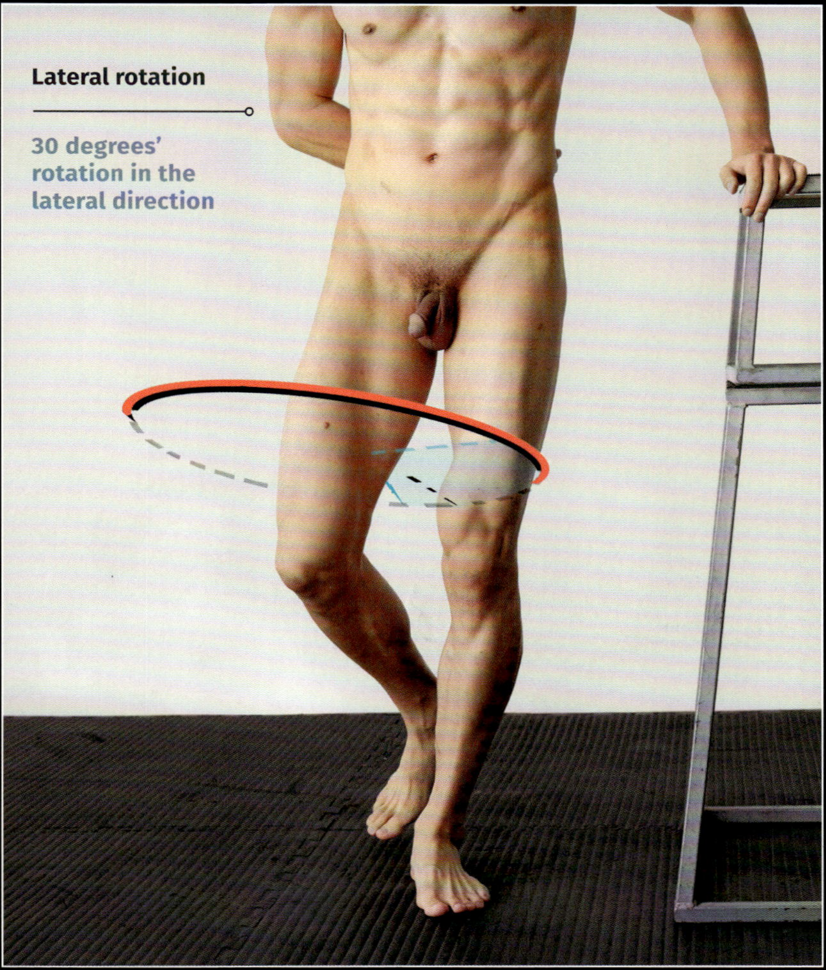
Lateral rotation
30 degrees' rotation in the lateral direction

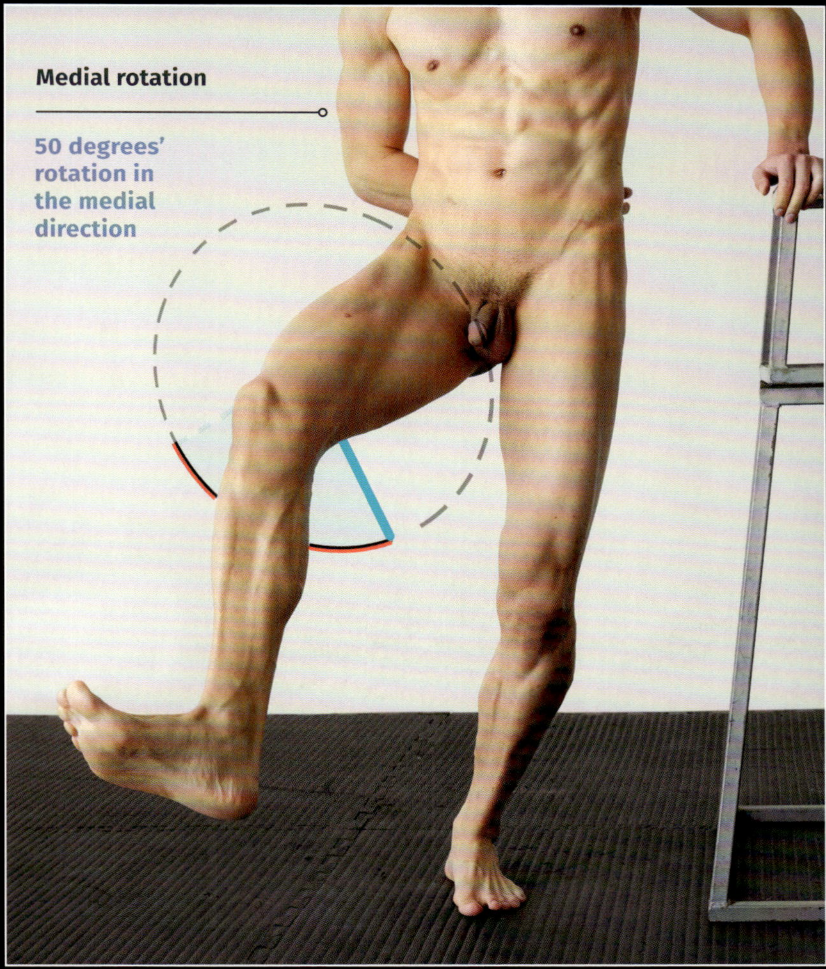
Medial rotation
50 degrees' rotation in the medial direction

Upper-body movements

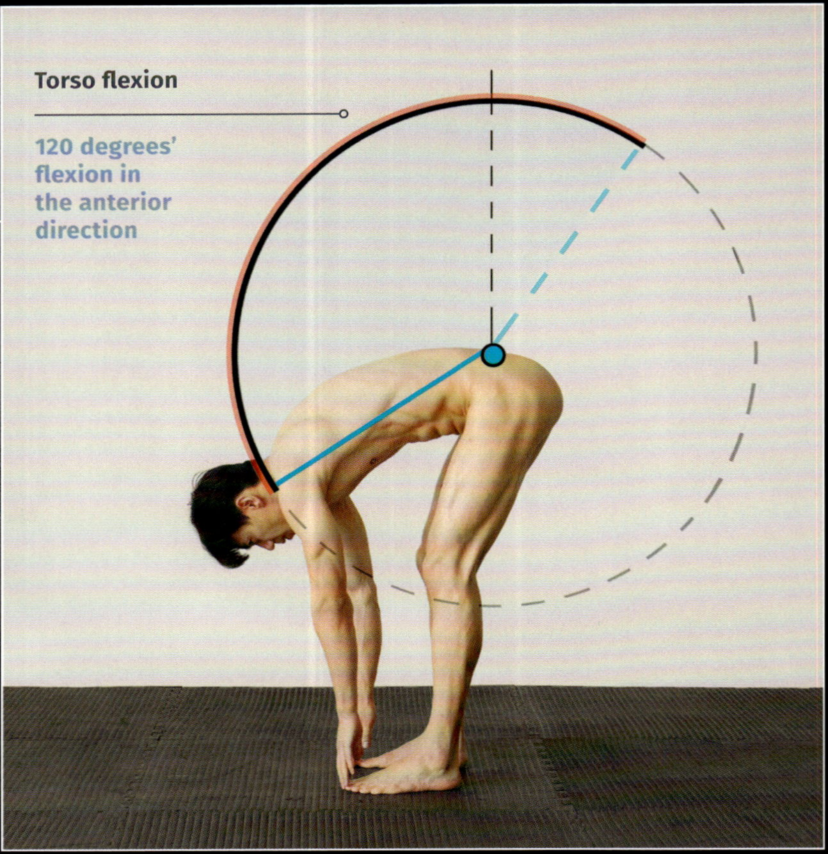

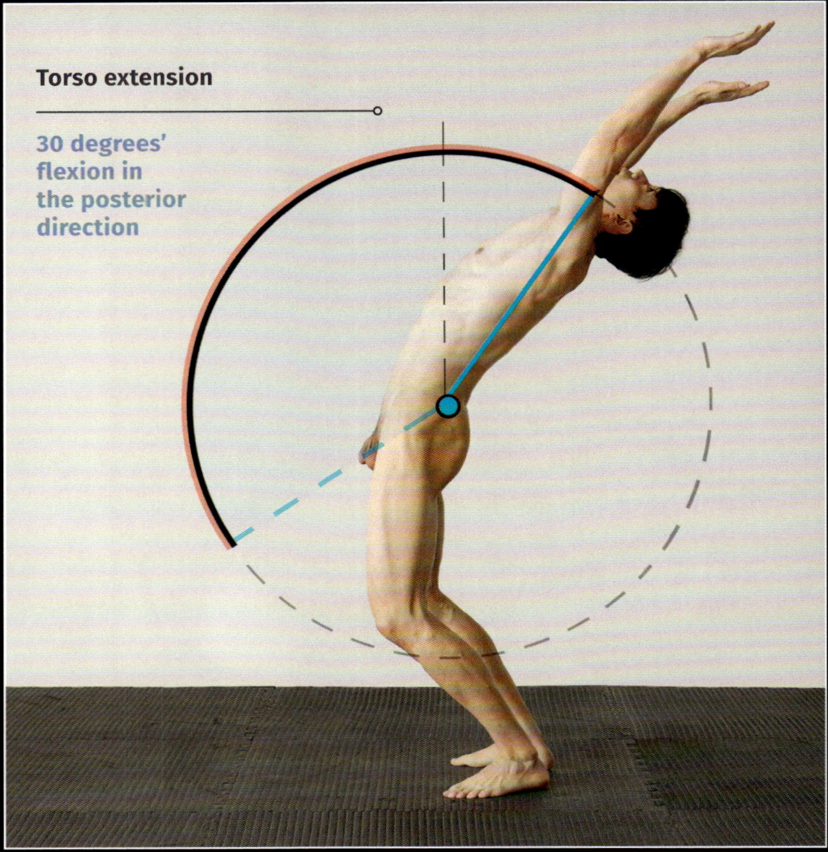

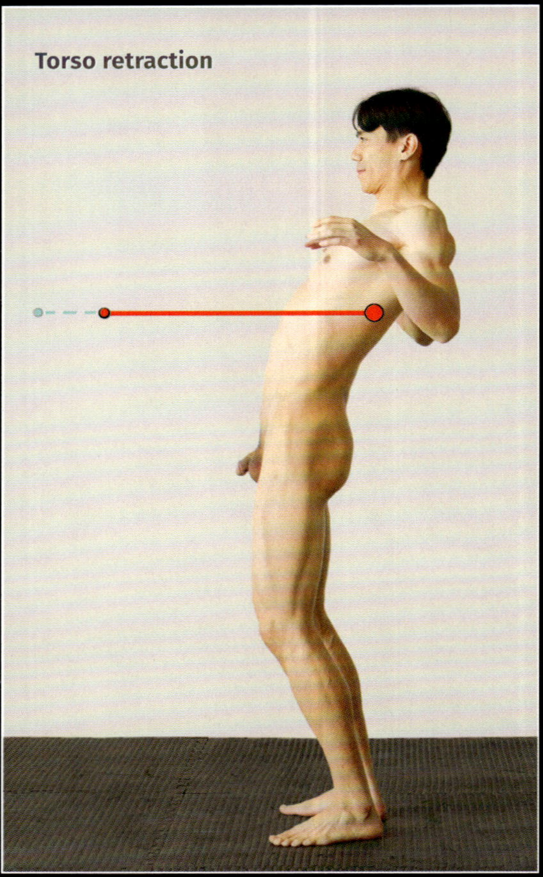

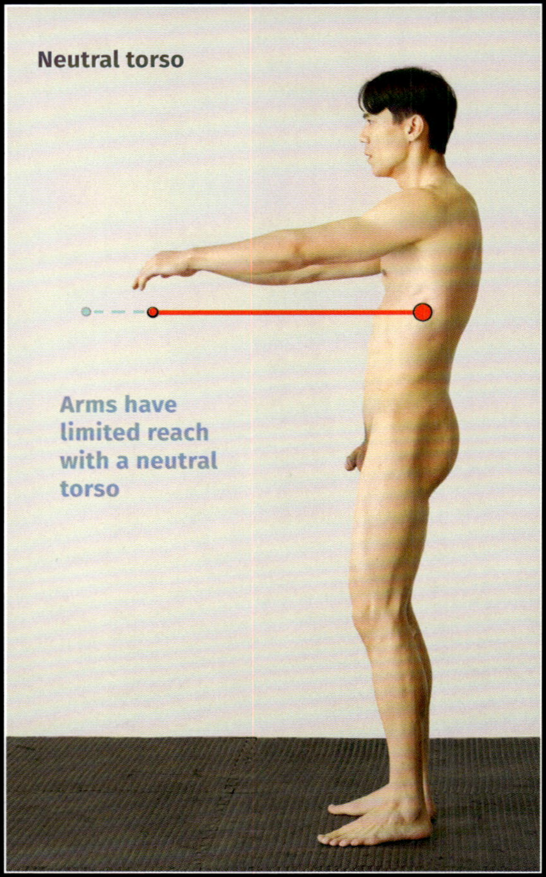

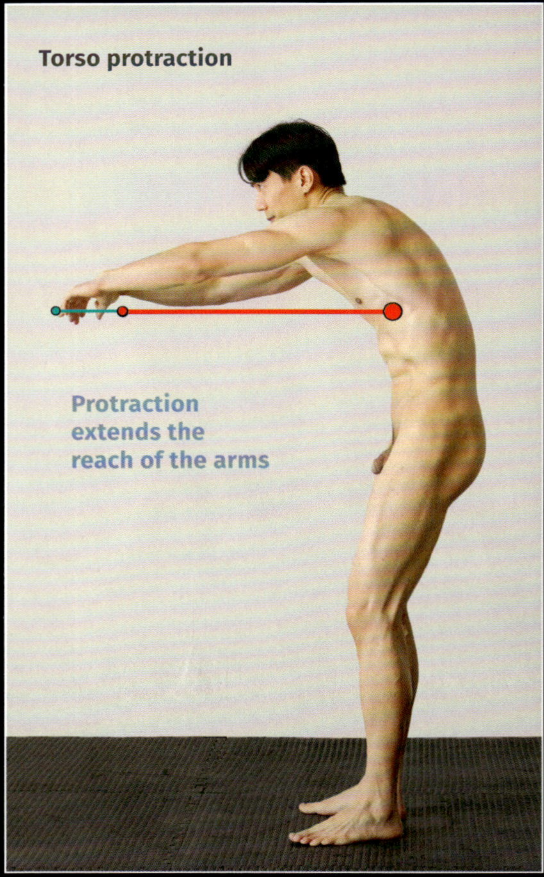

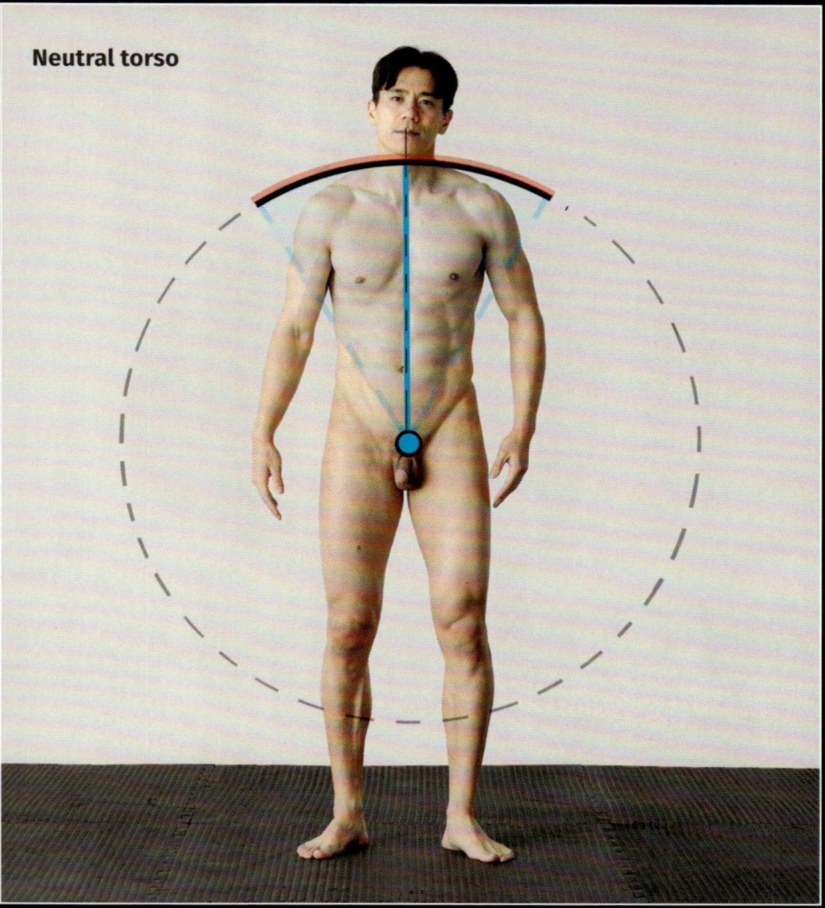
Neutral torso

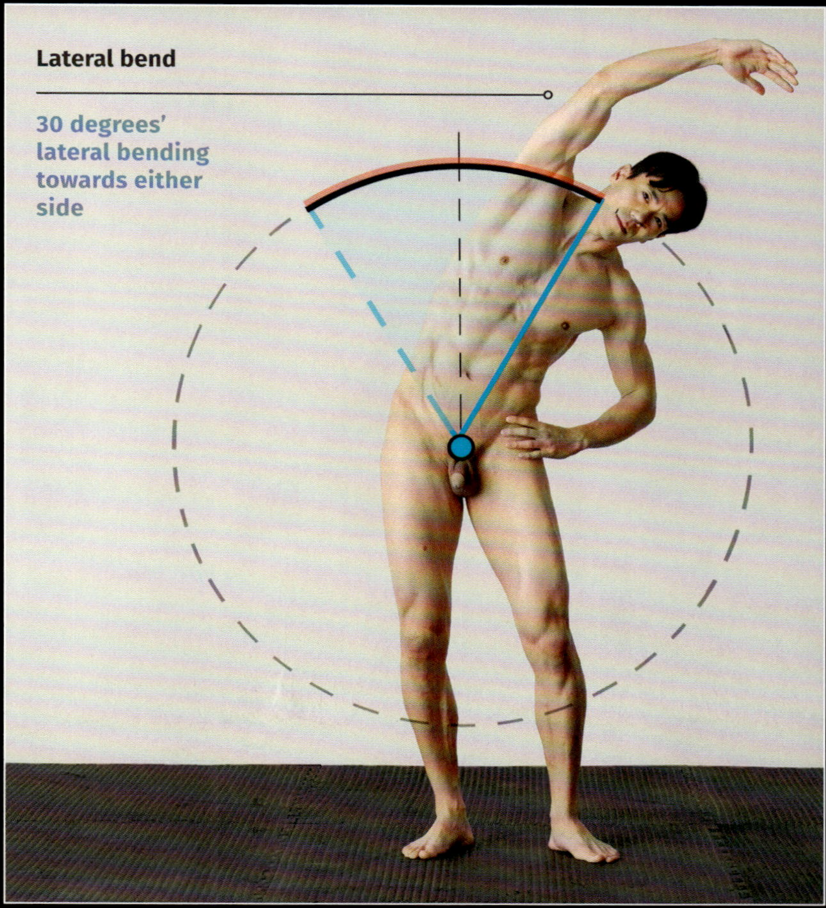
Lateral bend
30 degrees' lateral bending towards either side

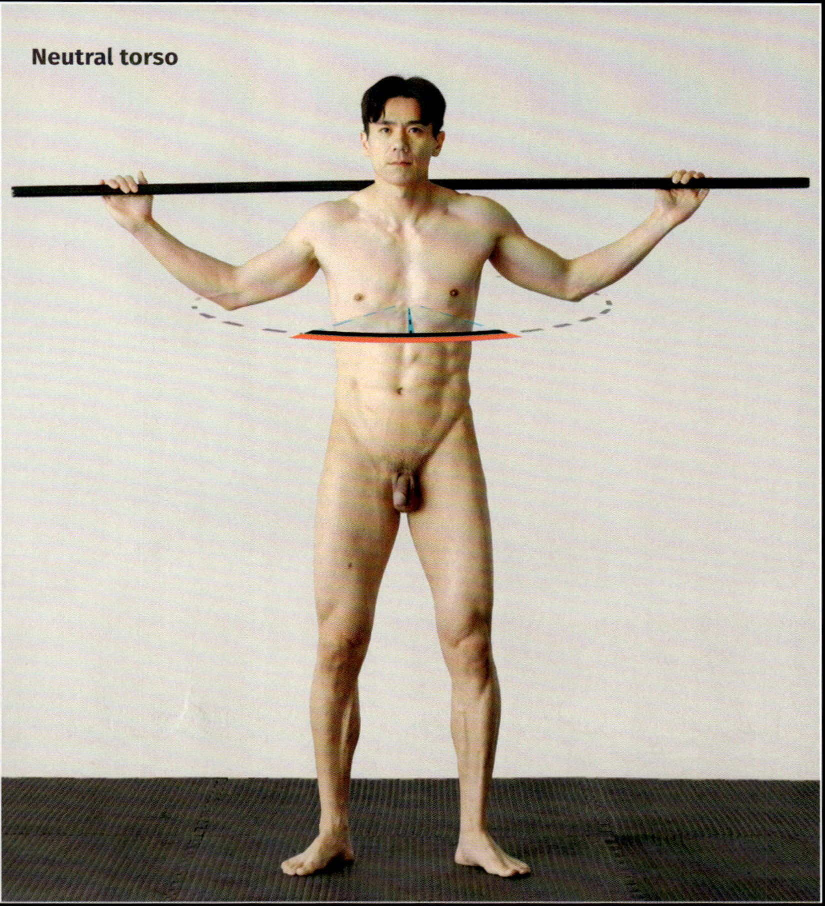
Neutral torso

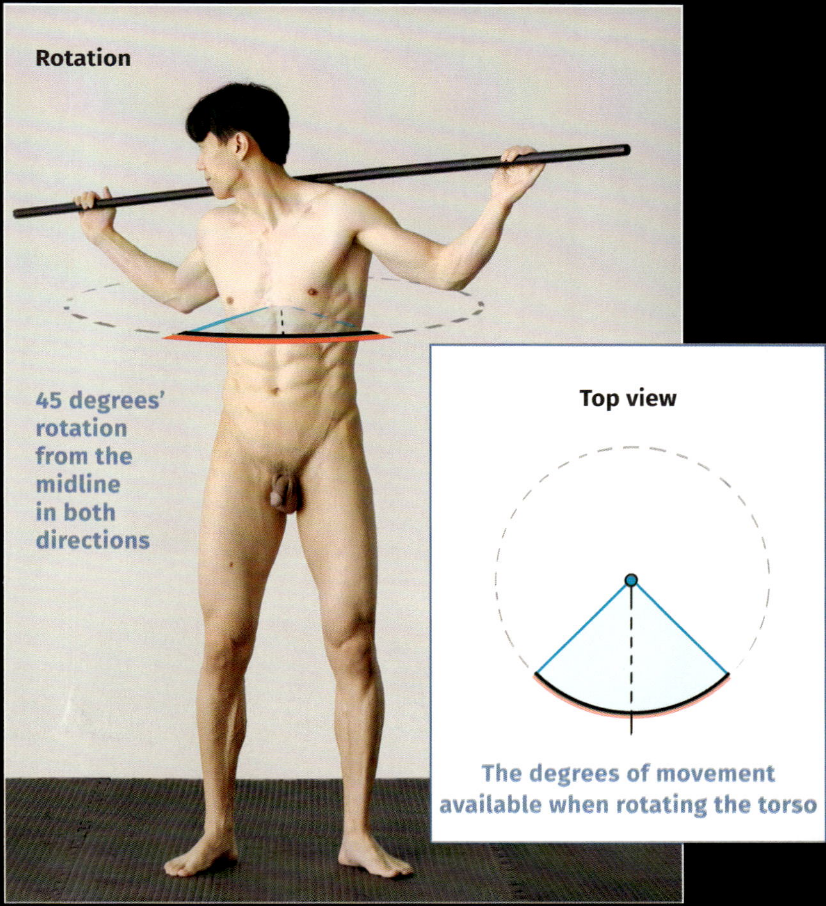
Rotation
45 degrees' rotation from the midline in both directions
Top view
The degrees of movement available when rotating the torso

Head and neck movements

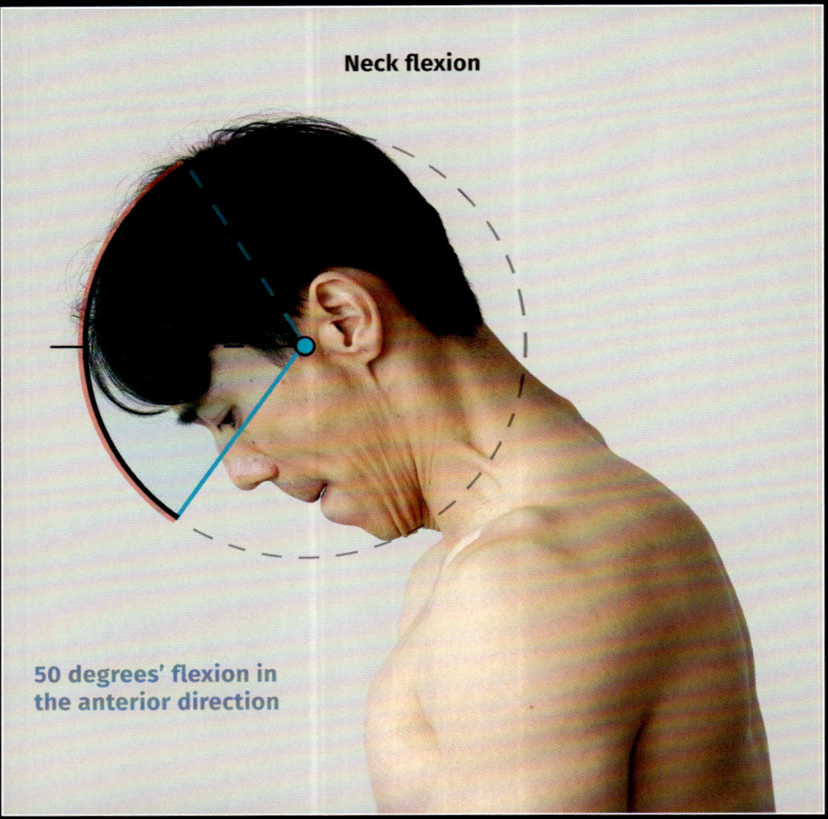

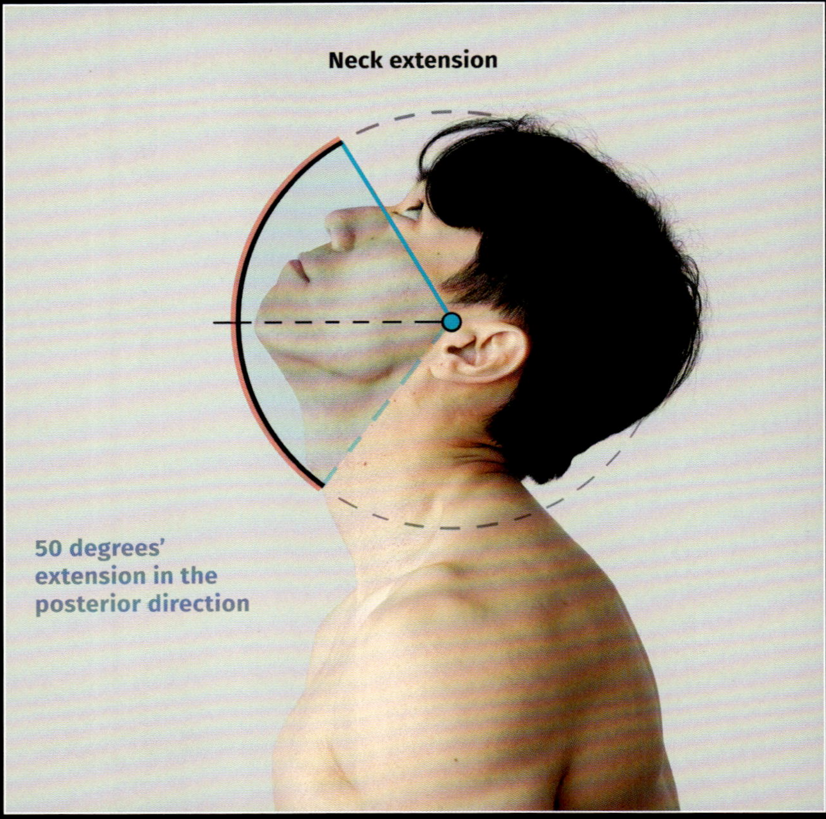

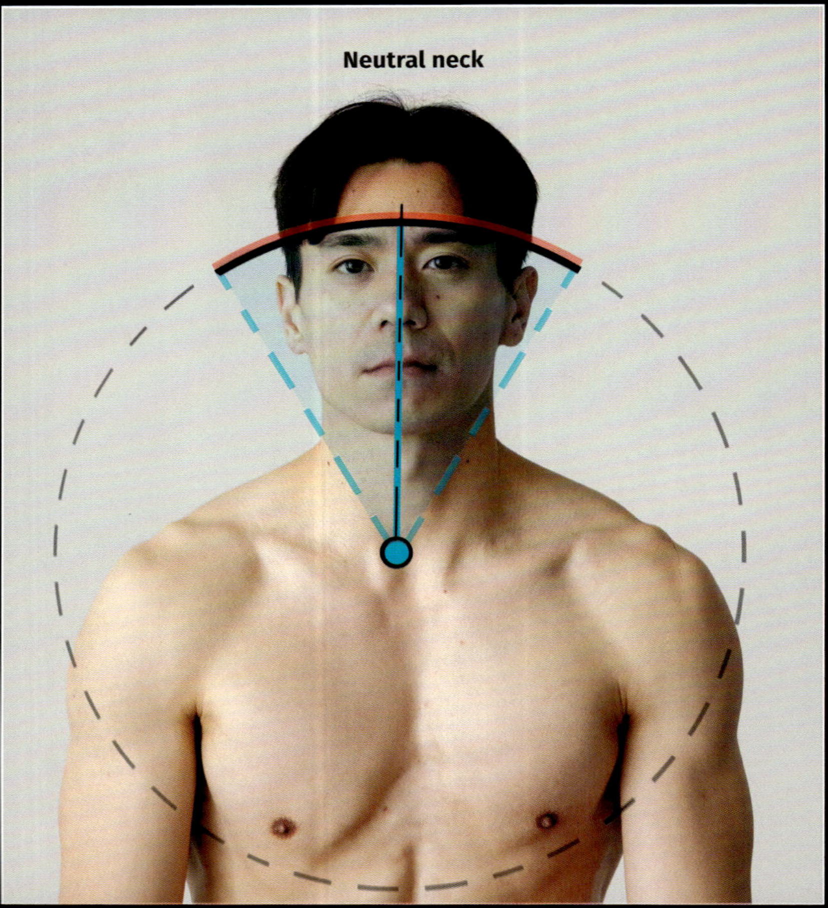

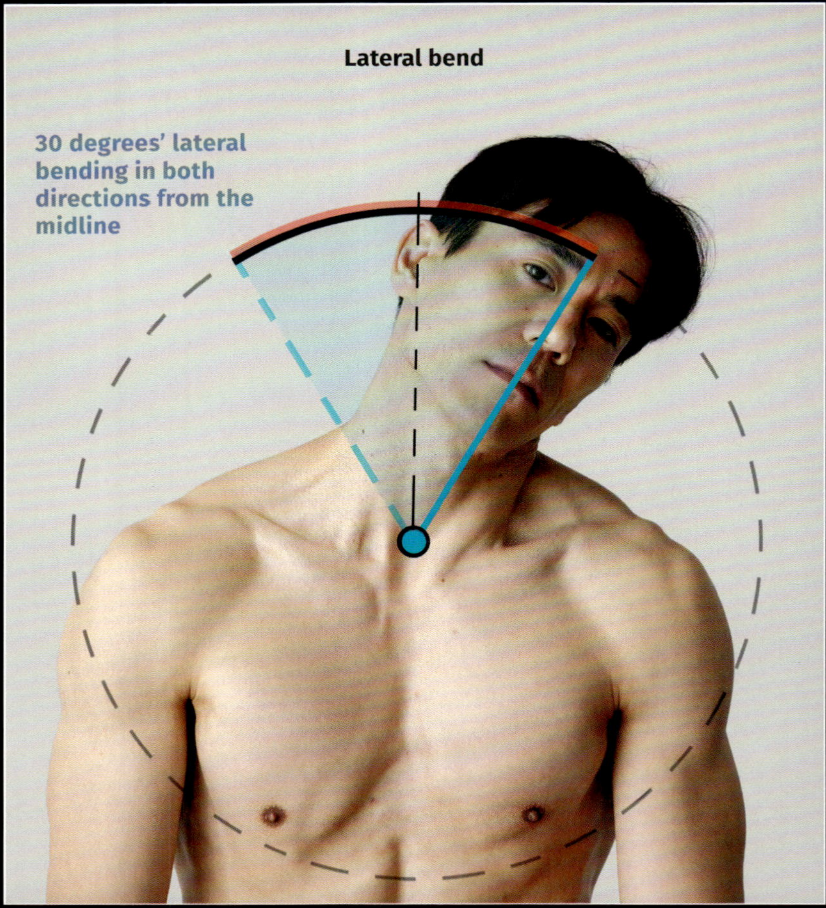

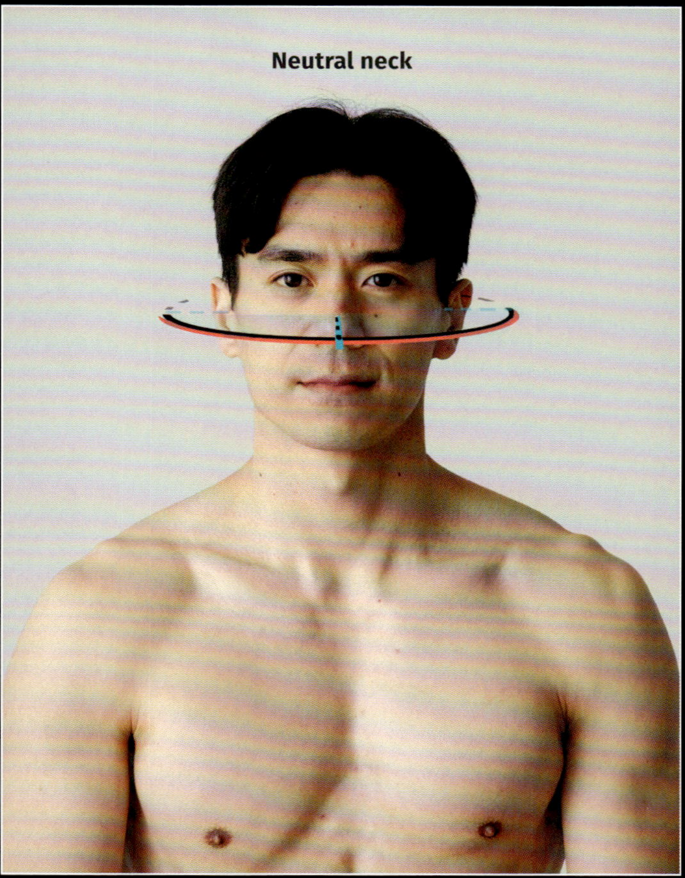
Neutral neck

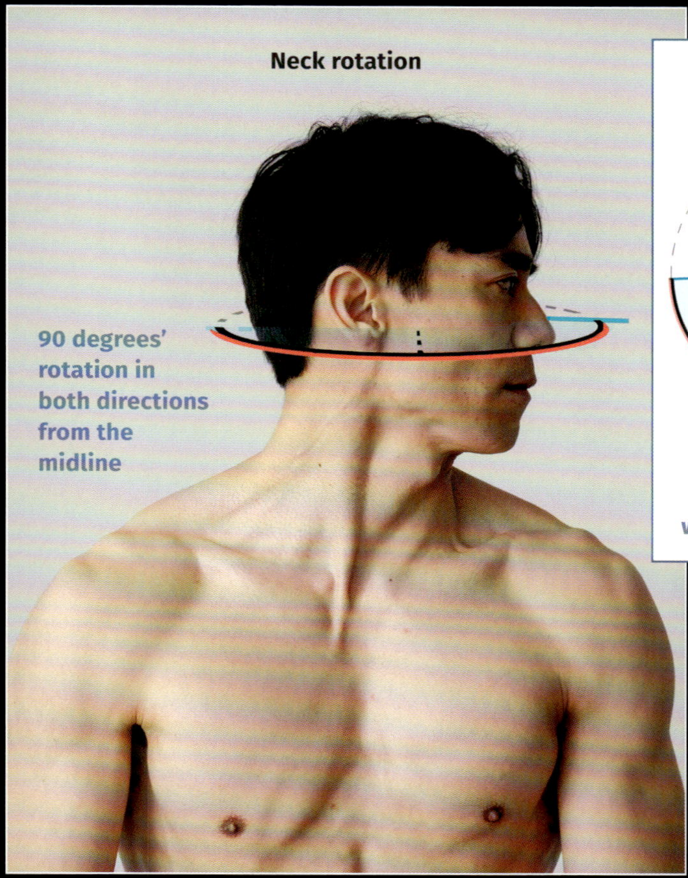
Neck rotation
90 degrees' rotation in both directions from the midline

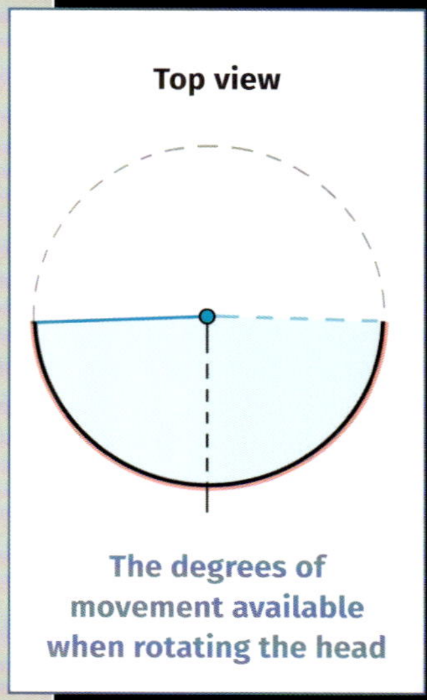
Top view
The degrees of movement available when rotating the head

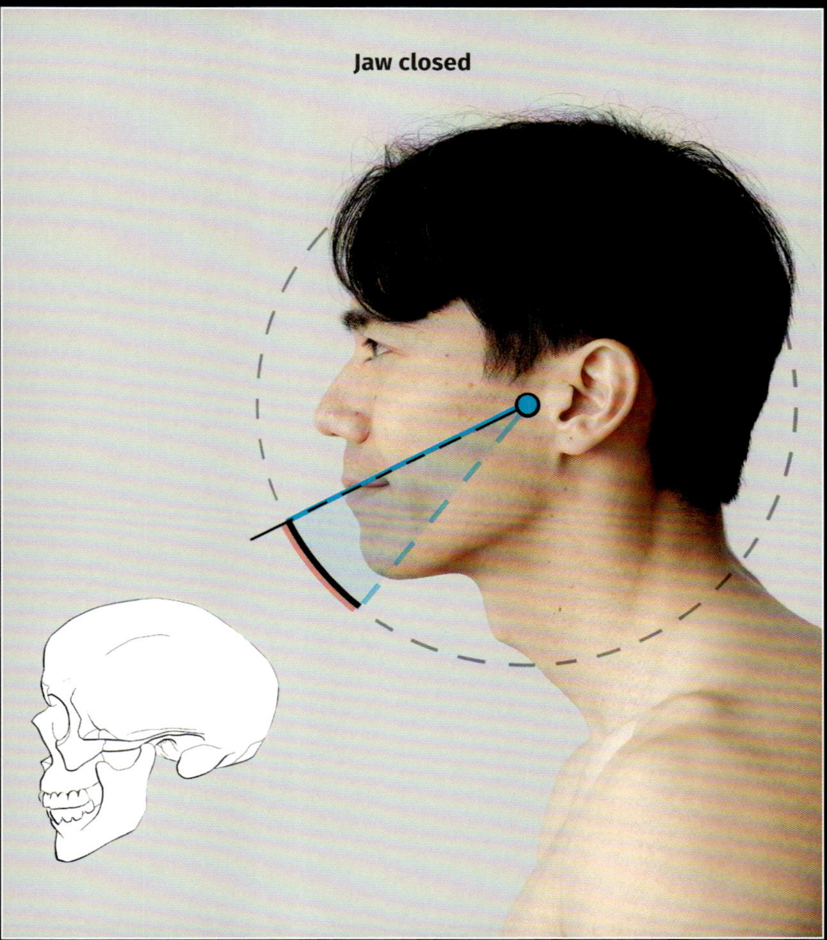
Jaw closed

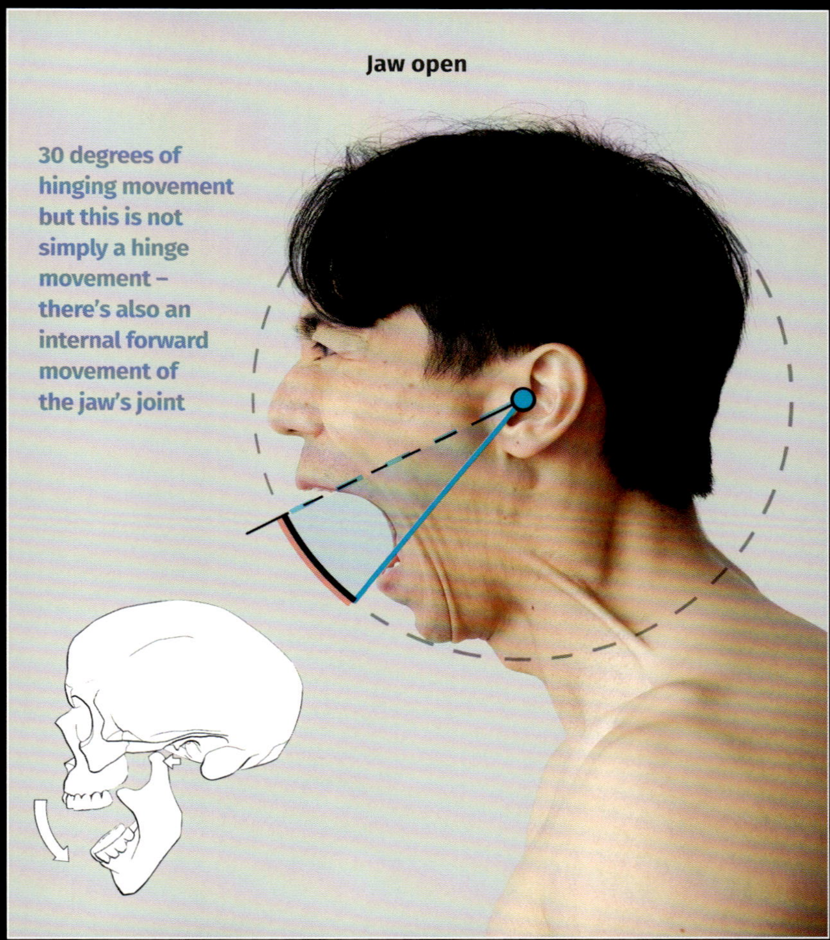
Jaw open
30 degrees of hinging movement but this is not simply a hinge movement – there's also an internal forward movement of the jaw's joint

Gesture drawing

It may seem daunting to move from individual, simple movements to full-figure complex ones. The simple movements of individual forms alone can feel difficult enough, and multiplying these difficulties through an entire figure may seem near impossible. In the face of this daunting complexity, it is important that we first discuss some ways to simplify and approach the main idea of a pose before we get too caught up in the details. Gesture drawing is our most important tool for grasping these larger qualities of a pose.

This is a style of drawing where we try to limit how many lines we use to represent the figure, with the aim of distilling it down, without details, to its main idea. We can then push and exaggerate this idea as much as we like in our drawing. On this page, I have included simple schema of the basic lines this type of drawing might include on a male and female figure. We can bend these lines to fit many poses. Of course, it should always be remembered that these lines are not strict for every pose. They must be flexible, so feel free to change them to fit the idea of the pose you are going for.

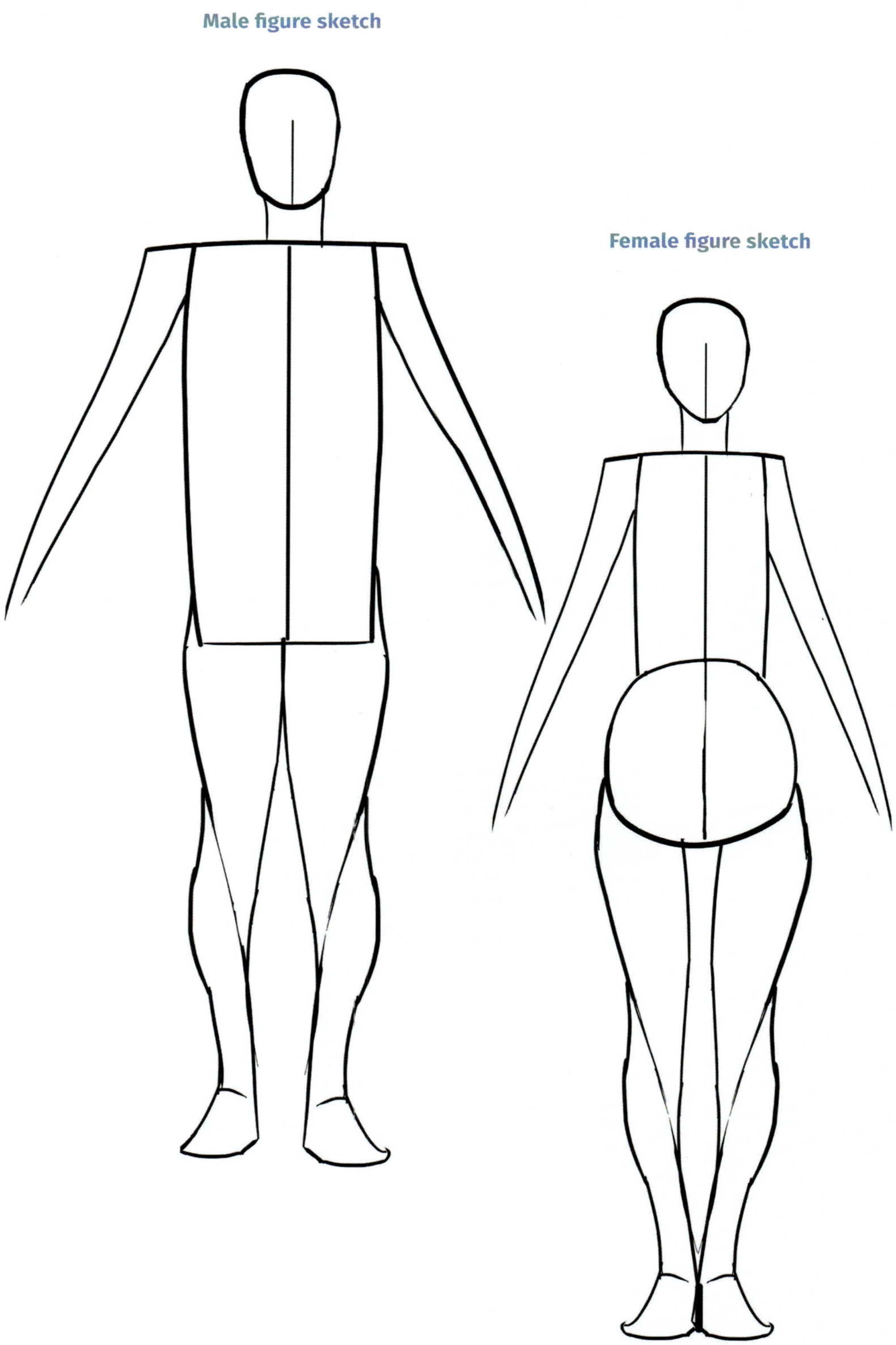

Here are some lines that a gesture drawing might typically include

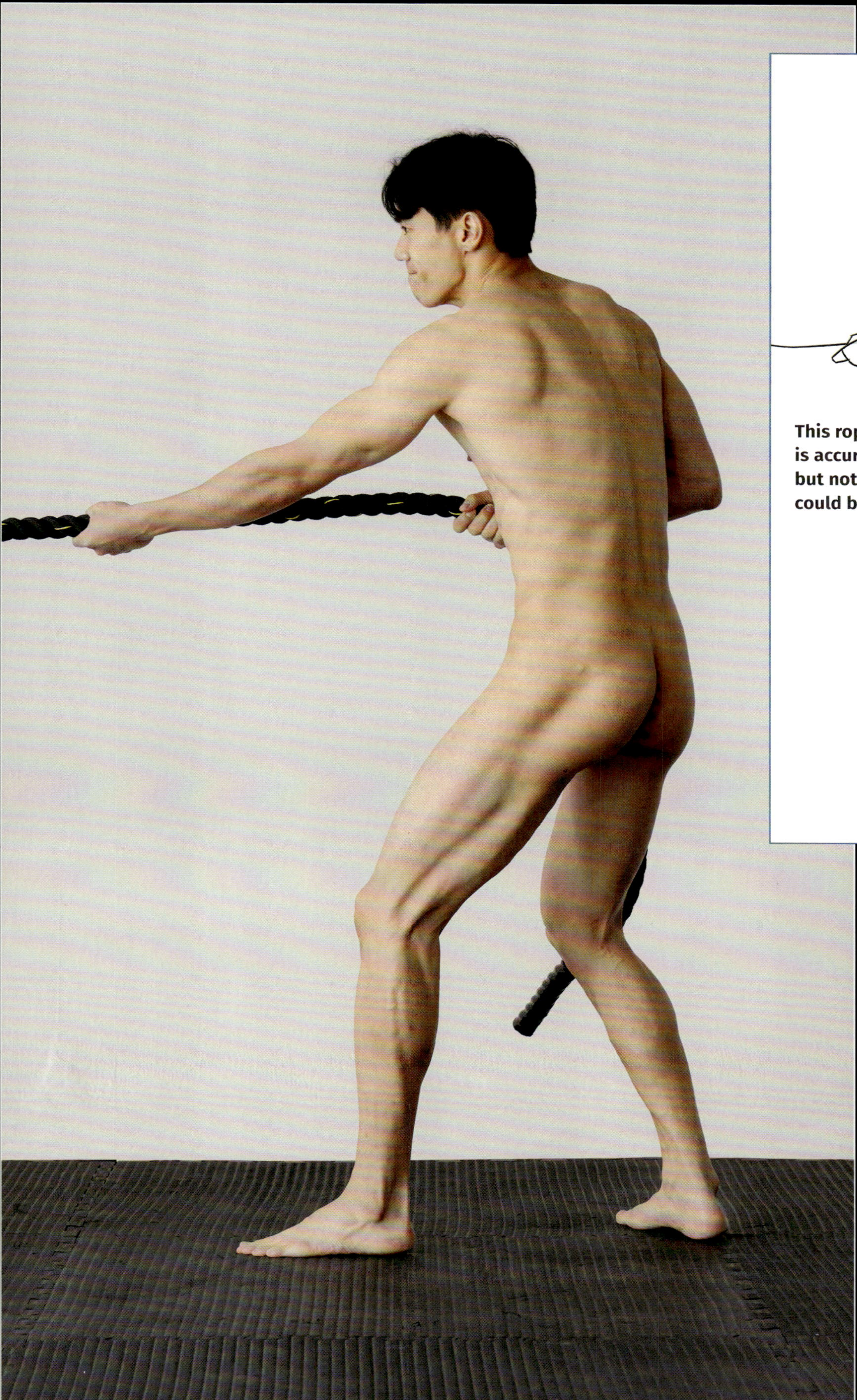

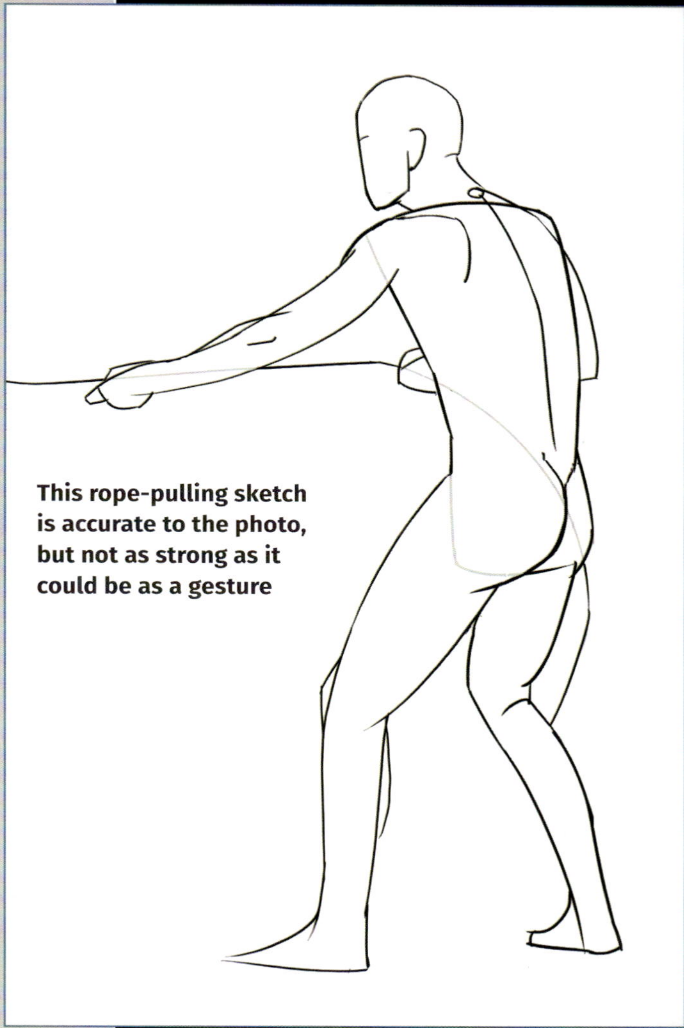

This rope-pulling sketch is accurate to the photo, but not as strong as it could be as a gesture

Try to draw similar schema based on some of the poses in this book. You can see what this might look like in the image above. I have bent the lines to fit this particular pose and we can see that even without all the details it still reads quite clearly to us. The pose is mostly a large backwards C-curve and the main idea to capture is the pulling force on the rope.

However, without all of the exciting details, you might notice that the pose itself feels a bit stiff. Not bad at all, but perhaps lacking some dynamism. However, with the pose stated in such simple lines, it is easy for us to play around with it.

Let's see if we can emphasize that main gesture of pulling on the rope. First it's important to understand the effect of the forces at play in communicating this idea of *pulling*. We need to know what it is we are exaggerating! The only true way to understand these forces is to observe our model in action. Let's look at the whole movement and see if we can observe any patterns we can play with. We might notice that as the movement progresses from a neutral to a strong movement, the main C-curve of the back becomes tighter and more rounded. This is an incredibly useful observation as it gives us something to work with when distilling the character of this movement.

The force in this gesture is pulling in the direction of the arrows, curving the body

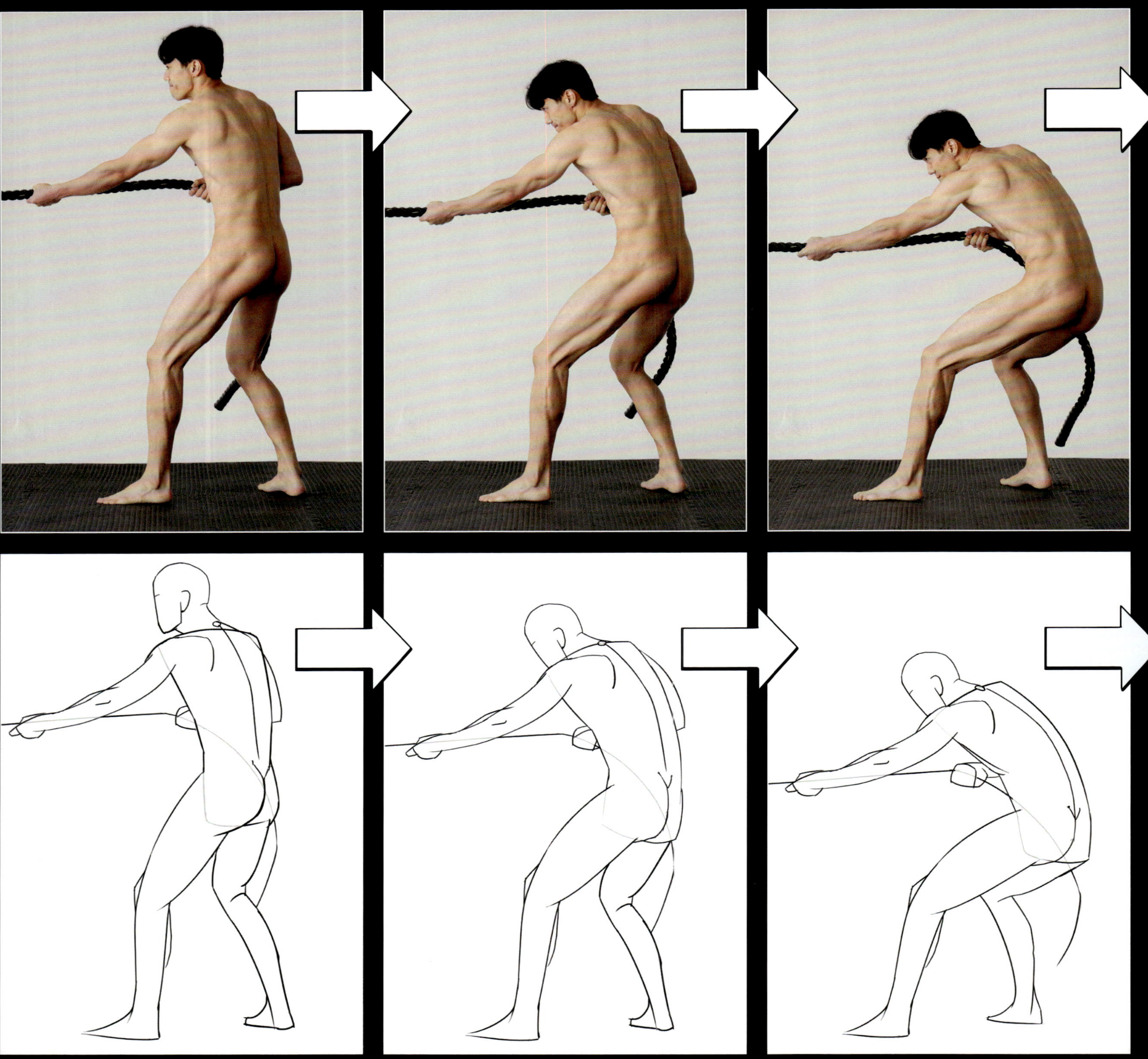

One idea that this pose echoes is a rubber band being stretched. Just like in the pose, as we pull on the rubber band, increasing the force it experiences, its curve becomes tighter and tighter. These kinds of visual analogies can often be helpful when trying to understand a pose and the forces at play, so try to think of them as you draw. It can be fun and a huge help.

The pose's gesture is almost like a rubber band being stretched

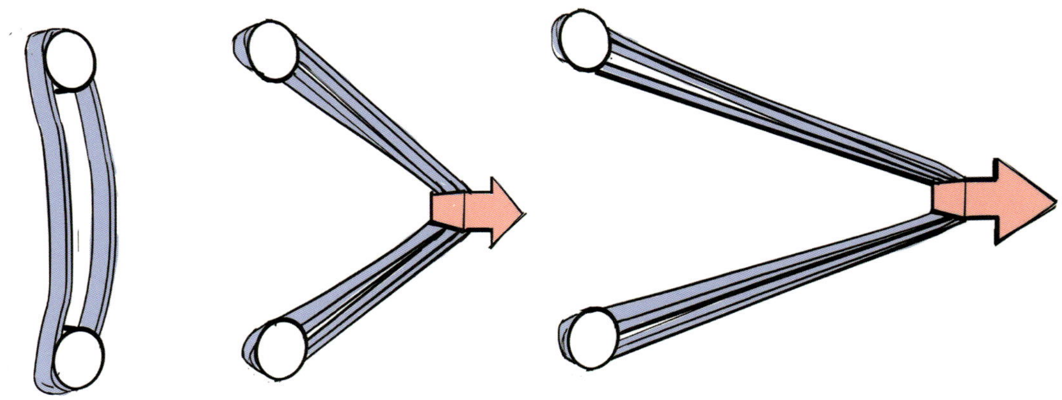

Let's see what happens if we try to push this gesture a bit further. We can tighten up the curve of the spine by pulling the hips further back. In the image below, you can see how much more dynamism is achieved with this slight adjustment.

Keep in mind that this is only one solution to the pose and there are as many ways to interpret it as there are artists who see it; there are no wrong answers here, only ideas we are trying to express. The real goal of this type of drawing is to get you involved in your drawing beyond simple reproduction. Ask yourself: 'What is this pose about? How can I heighten that quality in my own work?' It becomes increasingly important to grasp this basic idea when we want to not only reproduce the figure in front of us but heighten or exaggerate its movement. Consider this as you move through the poses in this book. Make little sketches to practise your gesture drawing. Have fun with it!

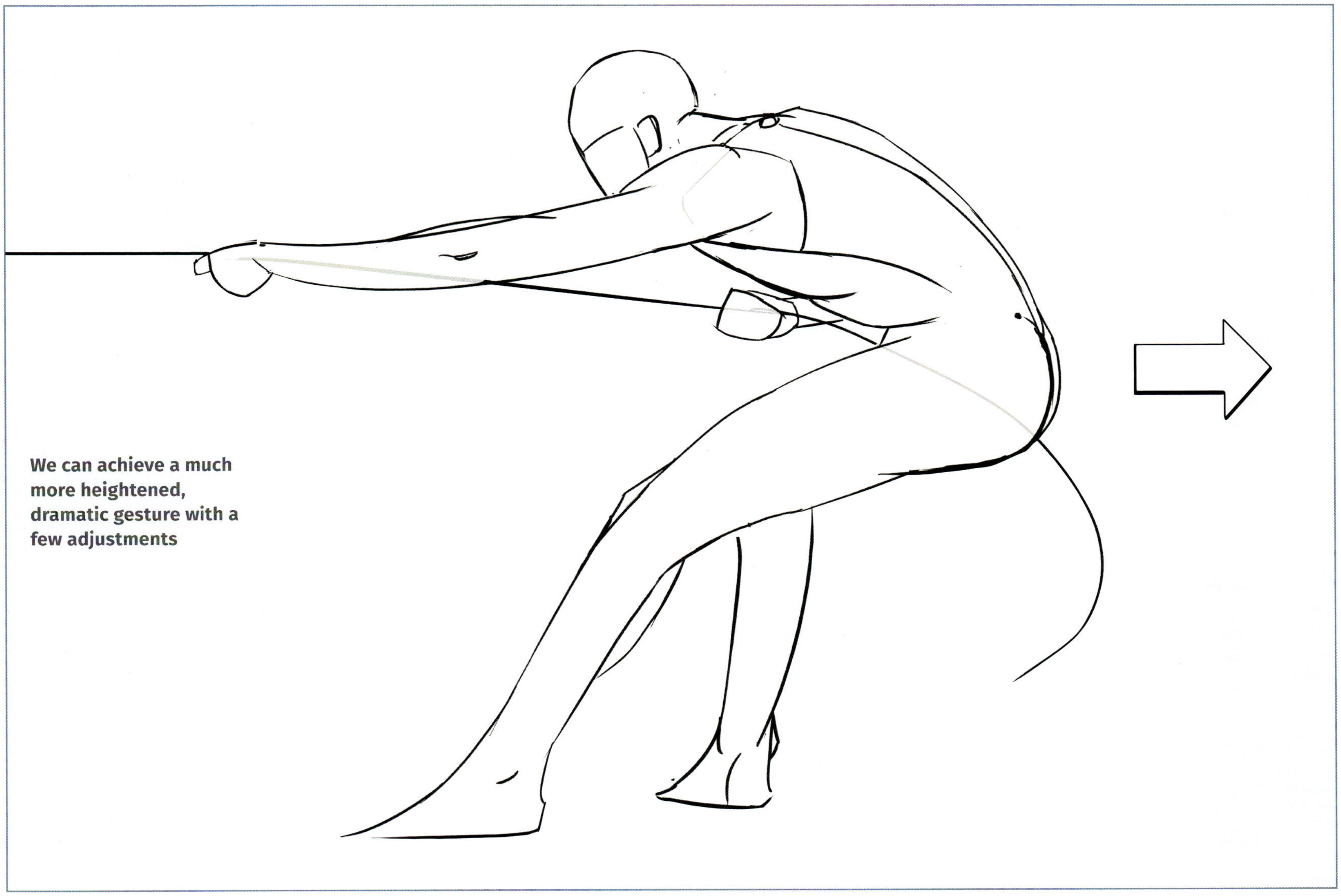

We can achieve a much more heightened, dramatic gesture with a few adjustments

Three main stages of motion

When trying to understand a particular movement and how we can use it to its fullest potential in our stories and art, it is helpful to categorize the various stages of a pose. Understanding poses in this way helps us decide how we might use them to communicate the elements of the story we are trying to tell, and know the best parts of the pose for our particular image or story.

Let's have a look at the simple movement of a punch to see these stages at play. In general, there are three main stages to most poses: the wind-up, the action, and the follow-through.

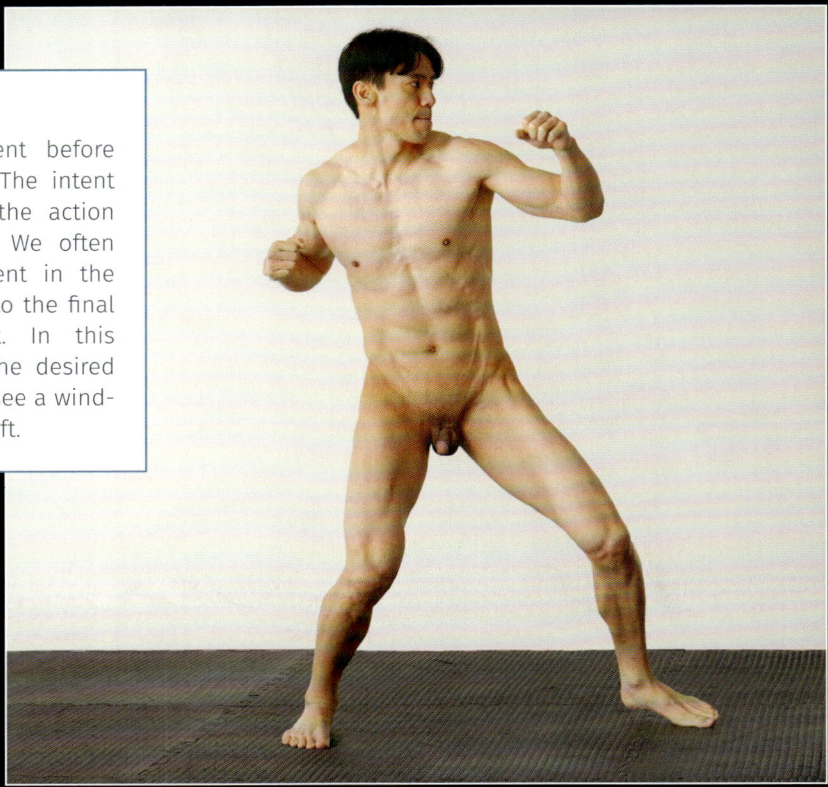

1. The wind-up
This is the moment before the action occurs. The intent is being set and the action is being prepared. We often observe a movement in the opposite direction to the final desired movement. In this case, a punch is the desired movement and we see a wind-up rotation to the left.

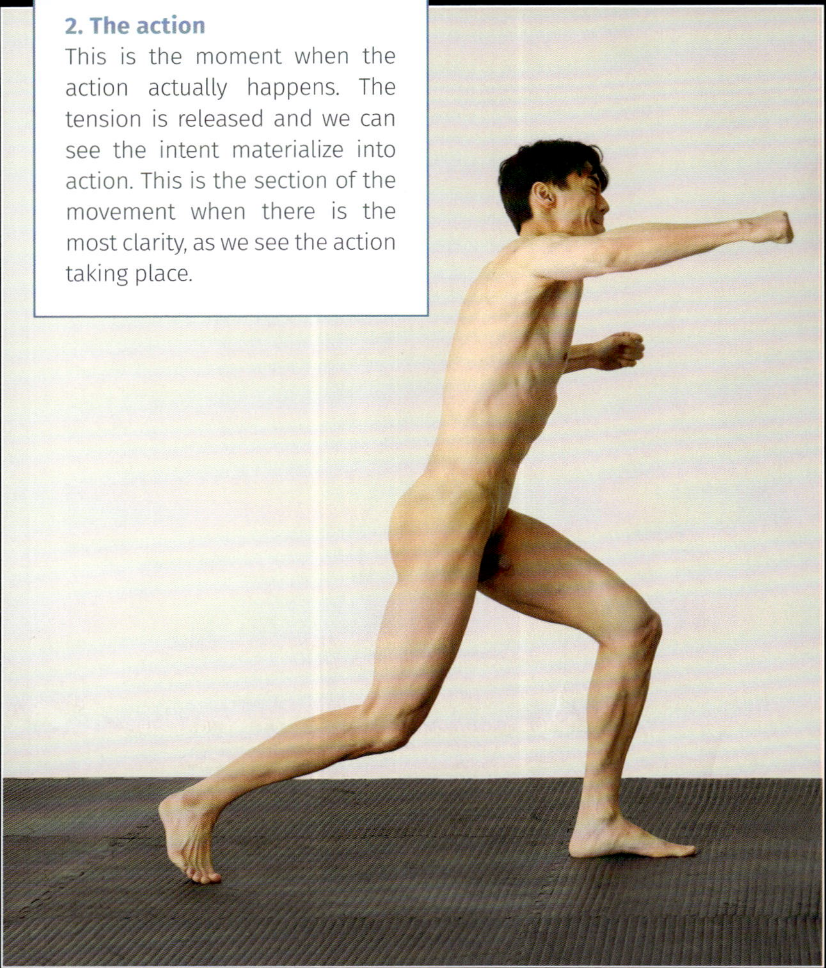

2. The action
This is the moment when the action actually happens. The tension is released and we can see the intent materialize into action. This is the section of the movement when there is the most clarity, as we see the action taking place.

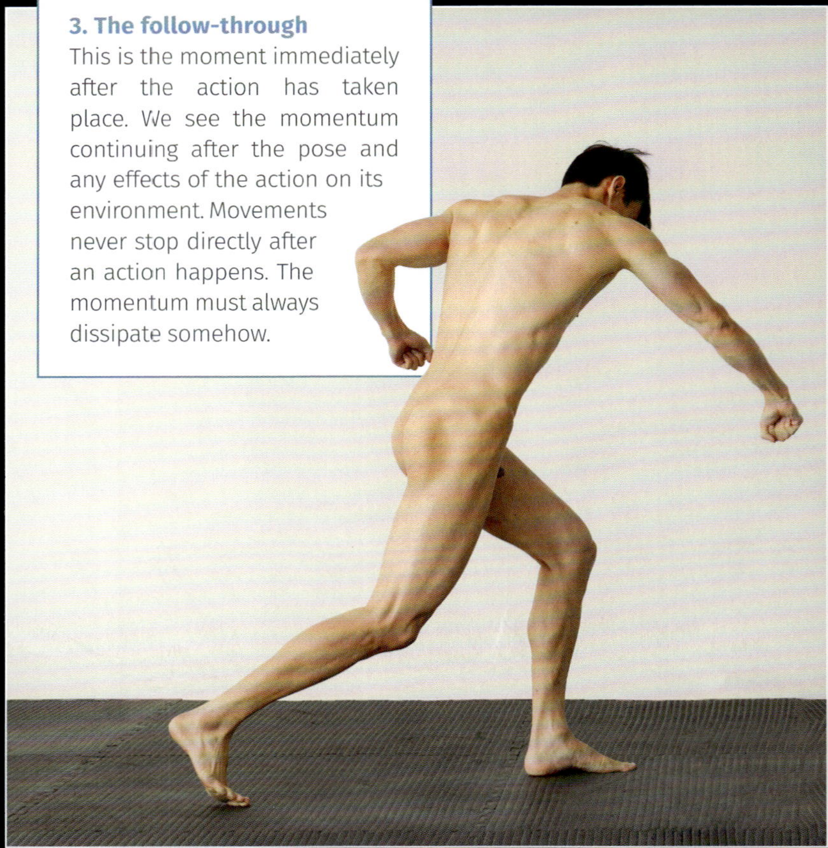

3. The follow-through
This is the moment immediately after the action has taken place. We see the momentum continuing after the pose and any effects of the action on its environment. Movements never stop directly after an action happens. The momentum must always dissipate somehow.

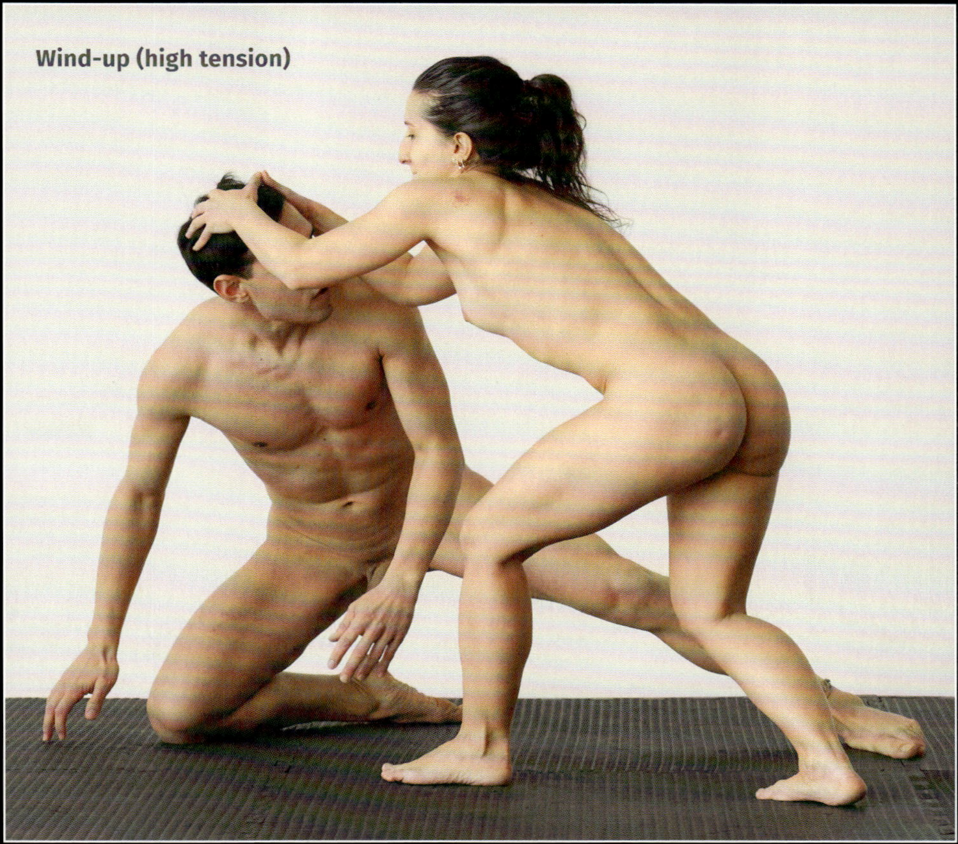

All of these various stages offer us unique and different opportunities for storytelling, so the stage we depict should be carefully considered. The stages are not all created equal and we are often limited in how much of a movement we can represent.

If our main goal is drama, the wind-up and follow-through are generally the two more dramatic stages of the three. The reason for this is that the wind-up has a tension in the mystery of it. We can see the intent of the pose but we do not know what will happen next. Will it be successful? How powerful will it be? These questions create anticipation and drama. With the follow-through it is the opposite – we see the full aftermath of the motion in all its gloriously dramatic effect.

With the moment of actual action, the main thing we gain is clarity on how an action happened, but this clarity sucks the mystery out of the moment. Without the effect on the environment provided by the follow-through, it is hard to get strong drama out of the action itself. Due to this, artists throughout history have often chosen to depict moments immediately before or after an action rather than the actual event.

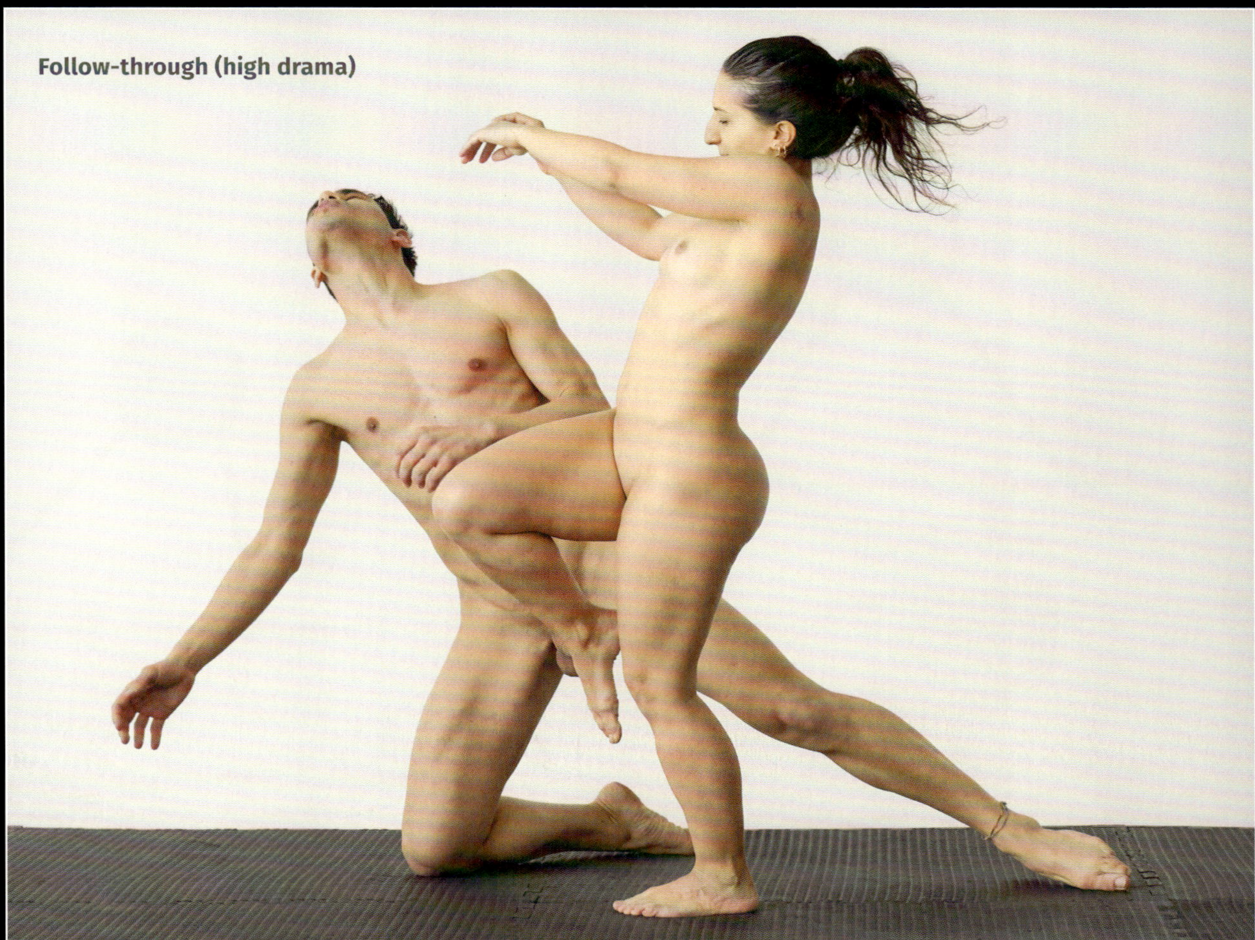

Balance and movement

As we have previously discussed, the human figure is fundamentally a machine of locomotion. It enables us to create and react to forces in our environment. As we look towards analysing the full figure in motion, we have to first deal with the most fundamental force we interact with every day: gravity.

From the moment we are born, we are always under the influence of gravity. It is easy to forget that dealing with this force was ever a conscious difficulty, but it once was for all of us. On average, a child will take a year and a half to tackle this force confidently enough to walk! This is forgotten as we age and develop a keen and innate sense of balance. It is often forgotten when we come to creating our artwork, too.

Gravity and balance are so fundamental and universal that our audience will notice errors instantly, so it's important we understand them well. The first thing we can say about gravity is fairly obvious: it always goes straight down.

But how and why is this useful to us? The best way to understand this is to look at the simplest setup the body can have: perfect static balance. In the first example below, we can see an arrow showing the direction of gravity (straight down) and a diagram indicating the body's balance. The most important elements are the centre of gravity (blue circle) and the two feet making contact with the ground. These two contact points create what we can imagine as a 'rectangle of balance'. As long as the body's centre of gravity stays inside this shape, our figure will be balanced.

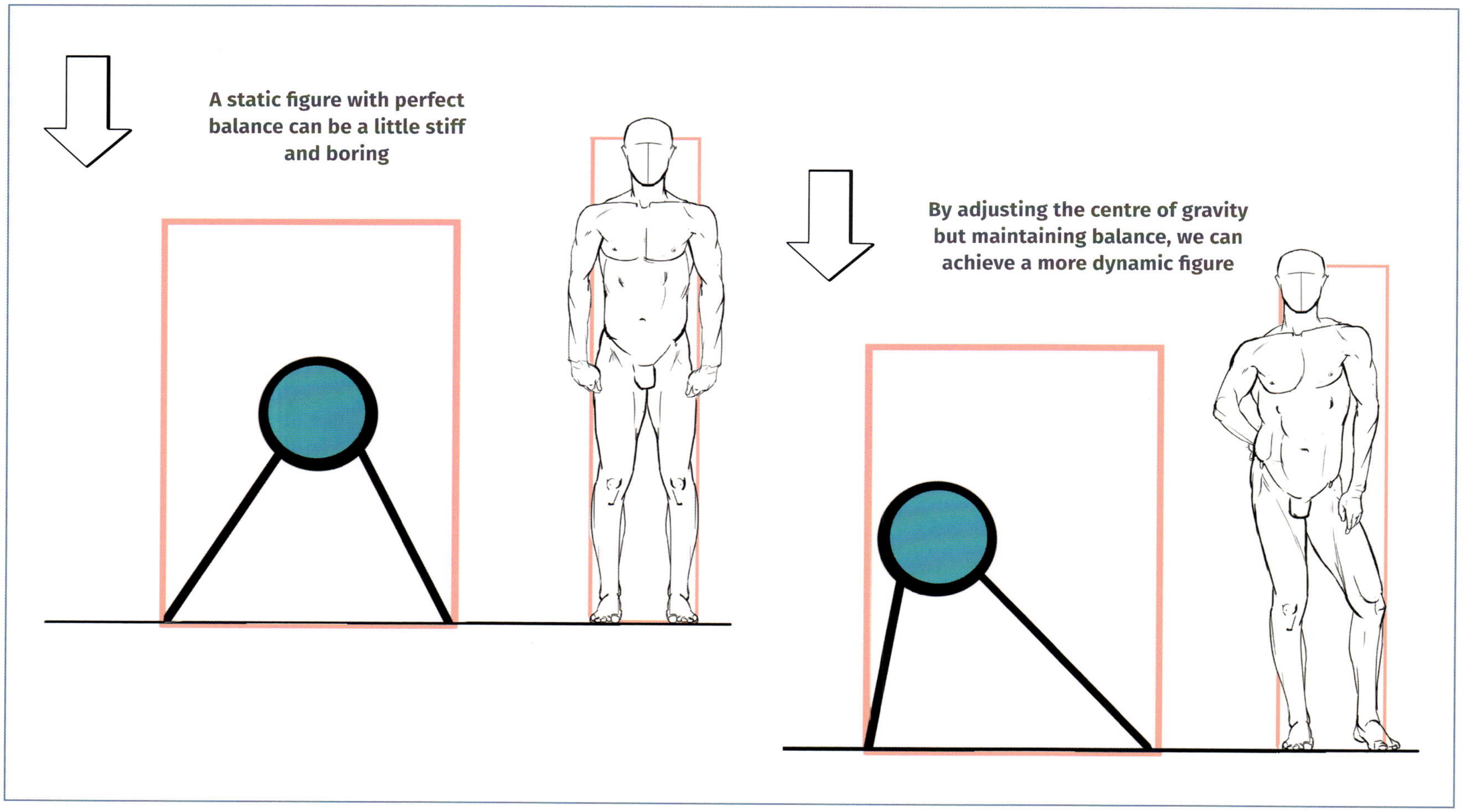

In the first example, the centre of gravity lies directly between the feet. This immediately achieves perfect balance, which is easy, but may be quite boring. If we want to add some dynamism to our drawing, we might move this centre of mass around, perhaps to the edge of the rectangle as shown in the second example.

This gives us a slightly more exciting pose, which is less static but still balanced. In fact, we have landed on a classic pose in figurative art, called *contrapposto*. This pose was most famously used in Michelangelo's *David* (as we saw on page 7), and is one of the most popular poses throughout art history, so loved for its dynamic balance.

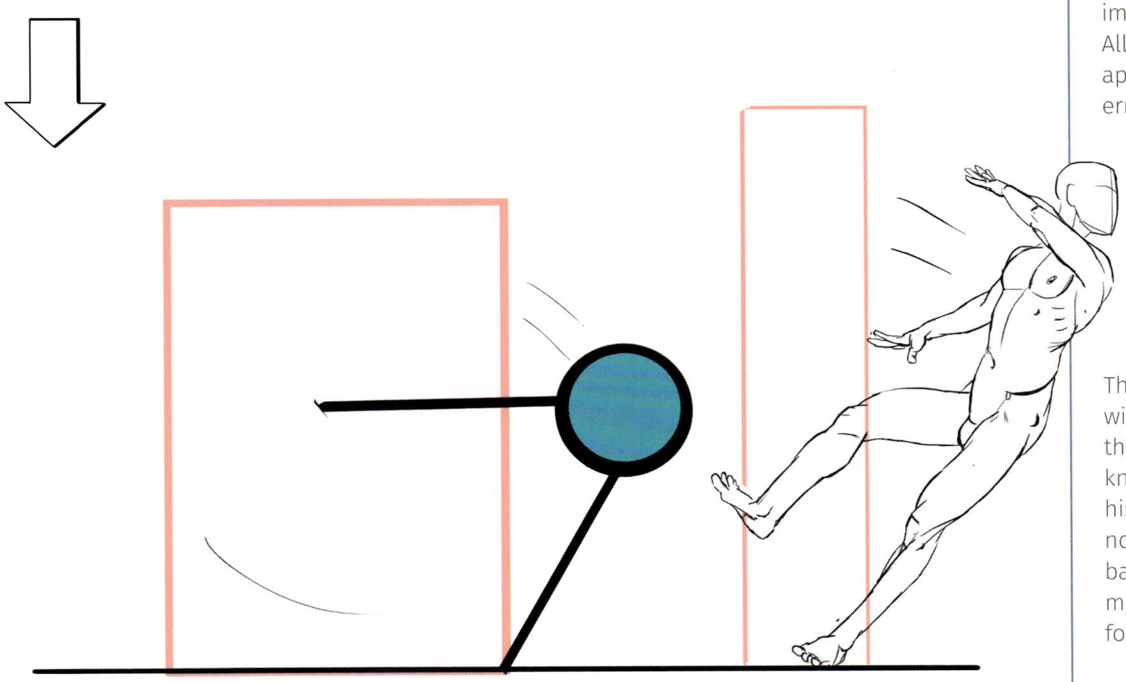

We can harness a lack of balance to create movement in our figures

But what happens when we leave the safety of the rectangle of balance? As you can see in the left image, the result is not so great for our little friend. All sense of balance is lost and our figure starts to appear as if he is falling. This is an extremely common error in figure-drawing classes, where we are often striving to depict static models and balance is desired. However, as with many things in art, there are no hard rules, only principles and effects. The effect of this imbalance is that our figure is no longer static, but *moving*. This is the most fundamental idea for implying movement in images: *imbalance = movement*.

This movement is not good news for our figure, who will probably hurt himself falling like that. However, this isn't the first time he has been off-balance. He knows that all he needs to do is catch himself with his foot and he's back to being balanced. You might notice that this action is strikingly similar to walking backwards. If we were to turn our figure around and maintain the same elements, he would be walking forwards – a movement familiar to all of us.

This is fundamentally all that is going on when we move. We are constantly falling and catching ourselves. As long as we maintain this imbalance, we continue to move. When we return to balance, we stop moving.

Movement is simply a process of going off-balance and catching ourselves

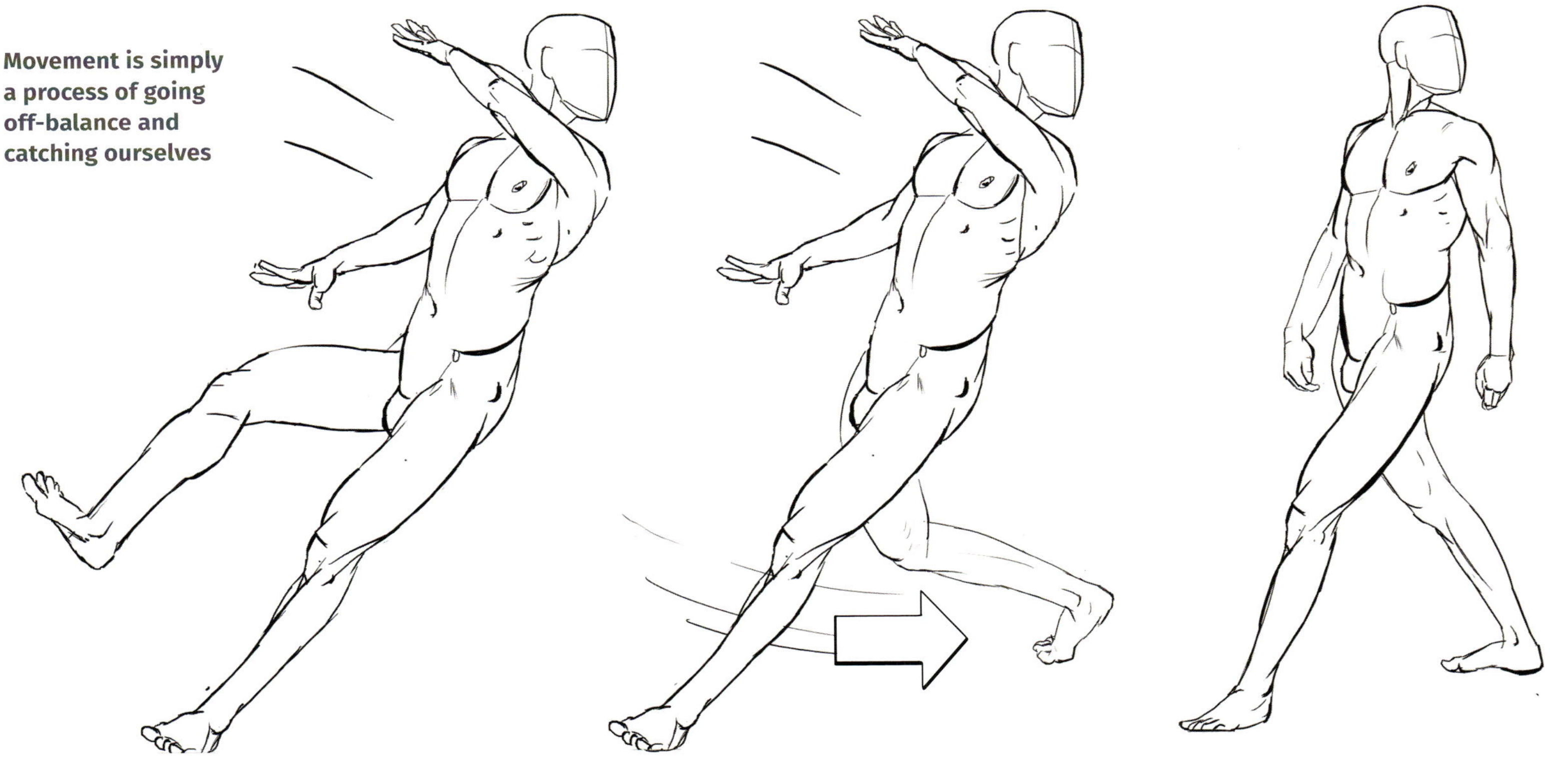

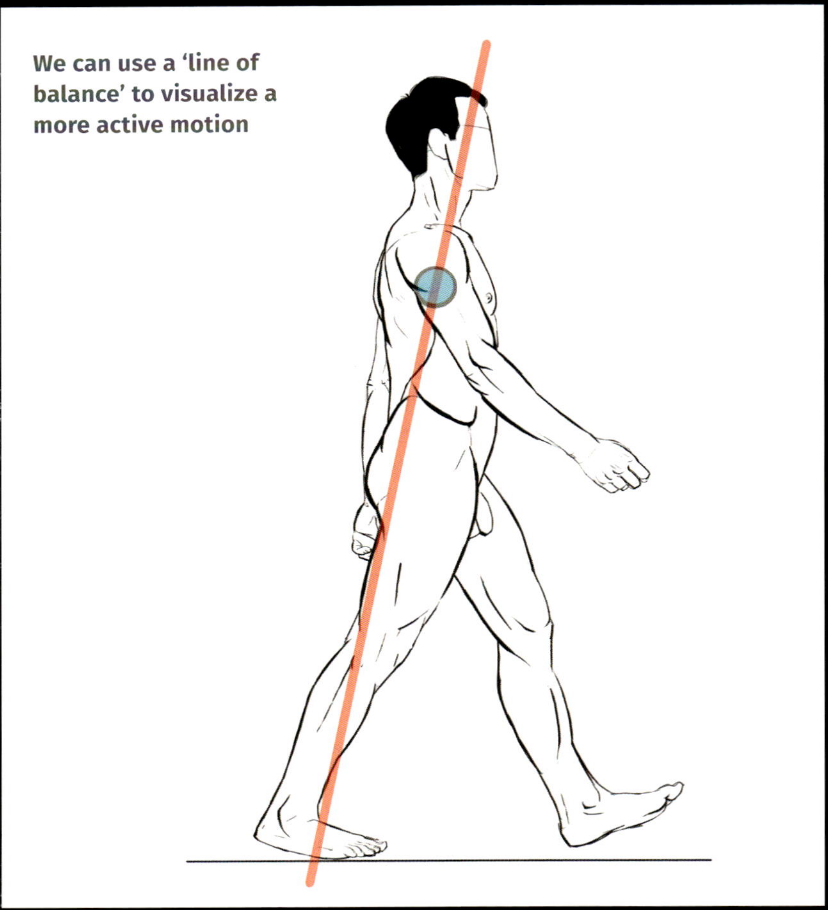

As we are focused on studying movement in this book, let's abandon our static rectangle and replace it with something we can call a 'line of balance'. This line connects the body's centre of gravity to the point of contact with the ground. In the case of the example on the left, the element that will catch the figure's 'fall' is his front foot, resulting in a walking motion.

Below we see a model moving from walking to running, and all the elements we have talked about so far are present. The line of balance starts perfectly vertical in the static pose and begins to tilt as the model starts to move. An interesting relationship also starts to emerge. As the model begins to run, moving faster, the line of balance becomes more diagonal. This relationship is incredibly useful to us as artists. The more extreme we make this diagonal, the more extreme the movement we imply!

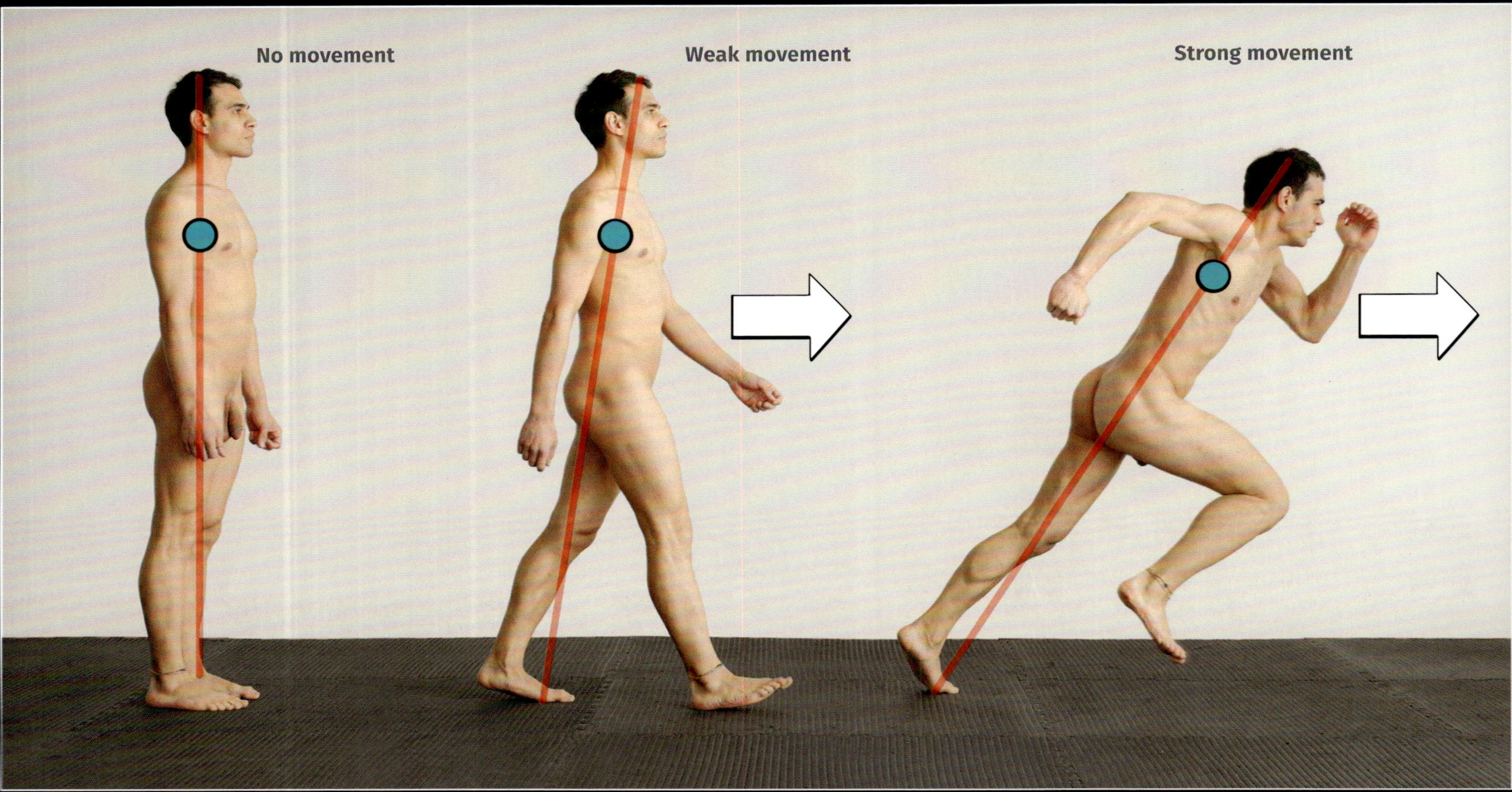

This drawing, taken directly from a photograph, is a bit stiff

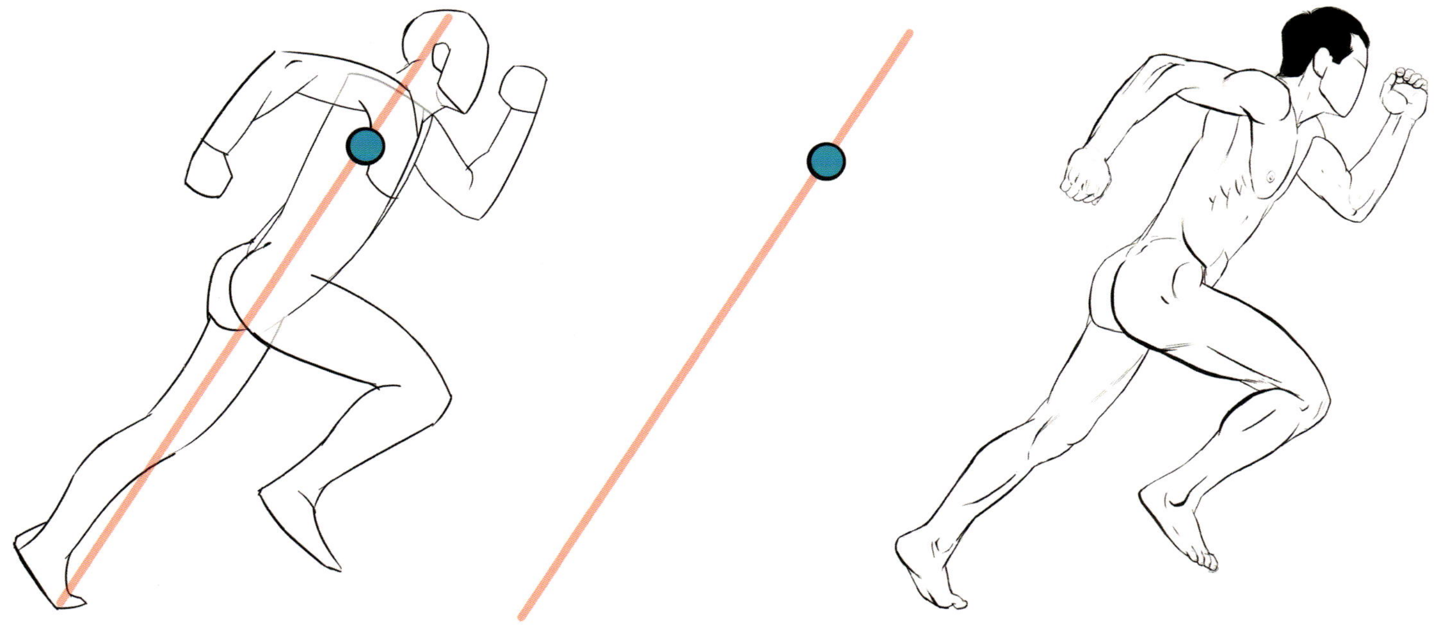

Exaggerating the line of action's tilt creates a more dynamic movement

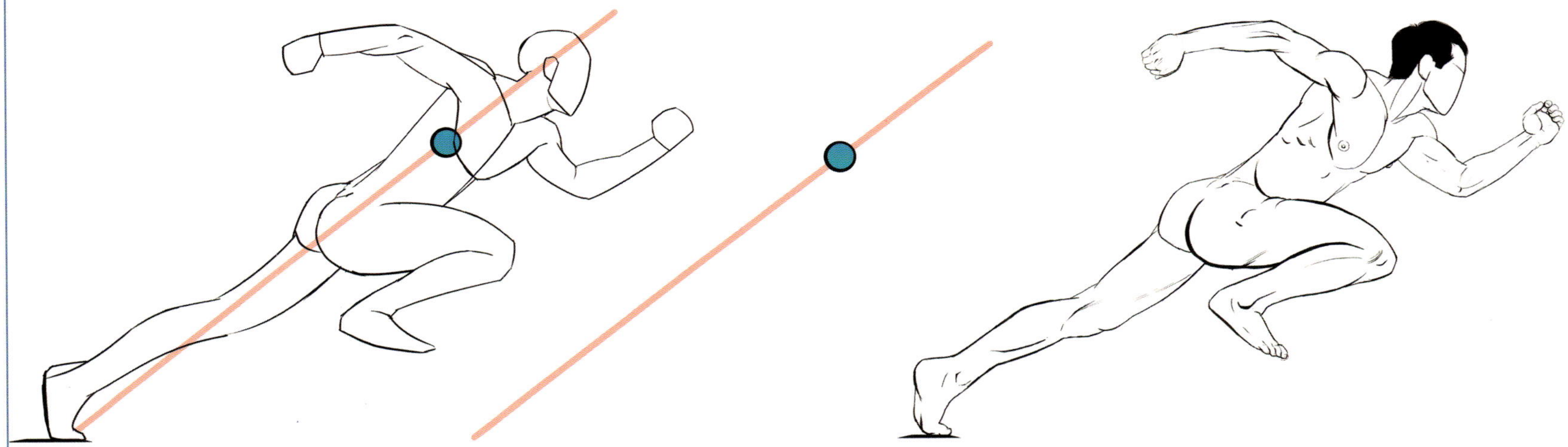

We can use this relationship to our major advantage when trying to depict movement in our own work. In the top drawings above, I have simply traced the figure's gesture directly from a photograph. From this, you can hopefully see why artists tend not to want to be restricted by their references! There is definitely movement here, but it is stiff, which is often the case with even the best models. Nature simply does not translate directly to a drawing.

If we want to capture the spirit and feeling of a movement, we can do better, like in the second example. The main thing I have done here is increase the tilt of the line of balance. You can see just how much more dynamism can be achieved with this simple adjustment. This book is largely focused on real-life references, which are the foundation of everything, but don't forget to experiment, exaggerate, and have fun. The reason to learn about nature and its relationships is to heighten them in our art.

Three major masses

As we move away from the individual movement of parts and begin to focus on how the body moves as a whole, we need to establish a hierarchy of importance of the parts in how they contribute to this movement. Not all parts have an equal effect. When our goal is to understand dynamic movement, it is imperative that we first understand the three most important masses of the body for all movements: the skull, ribcage, and pelvis.

These three masses are the source of most of the movements of the body. For the rib cage and pelvis, this is because they are the heaviest parts of the body, and thus have the most powerful muscles attached to them. Though smaller, the head contains the sense organs, and so is most often leading the movement and displaying the intent driving the movement. Careful attention to these three forms is the most important way to understand any movement.

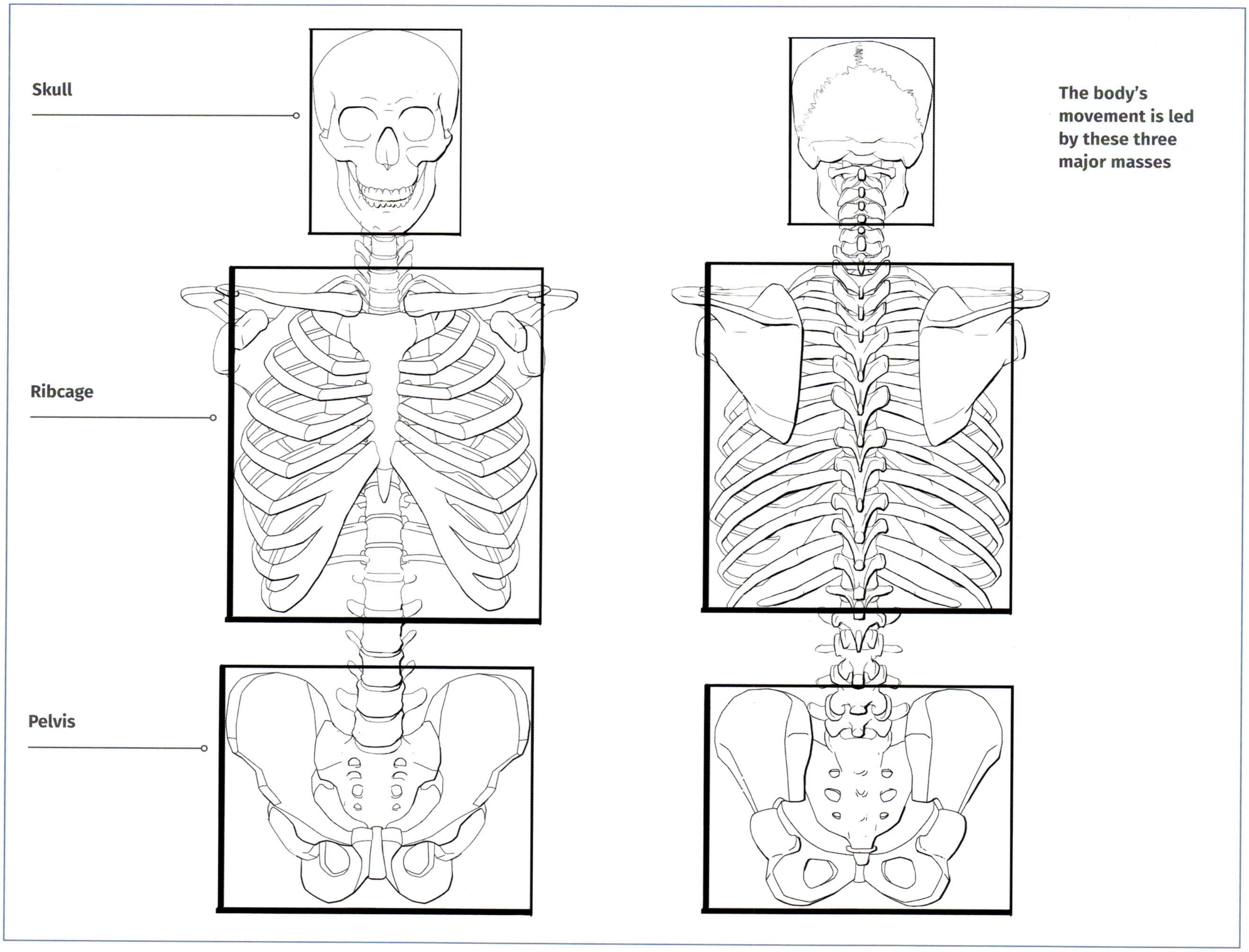

Since we are primarily interested in how these masses influence figure movement, it can be helpful to simplify them into box forms, connected with a wire to represent the spine. Getting this basic 'box person' design clearly worked out in your head is the first step in really understanding these three most fundamental forms, without distracting detail, and can be helpful to do as an initial study of the poses in this book.

Try making up positions from your mind using the box forms. The more comfortably you can do so, the greater your understanding will be. As you approach this, try to think of the head block as leading the rest of the blocks, and have the ribcage and pelvis follow it around.

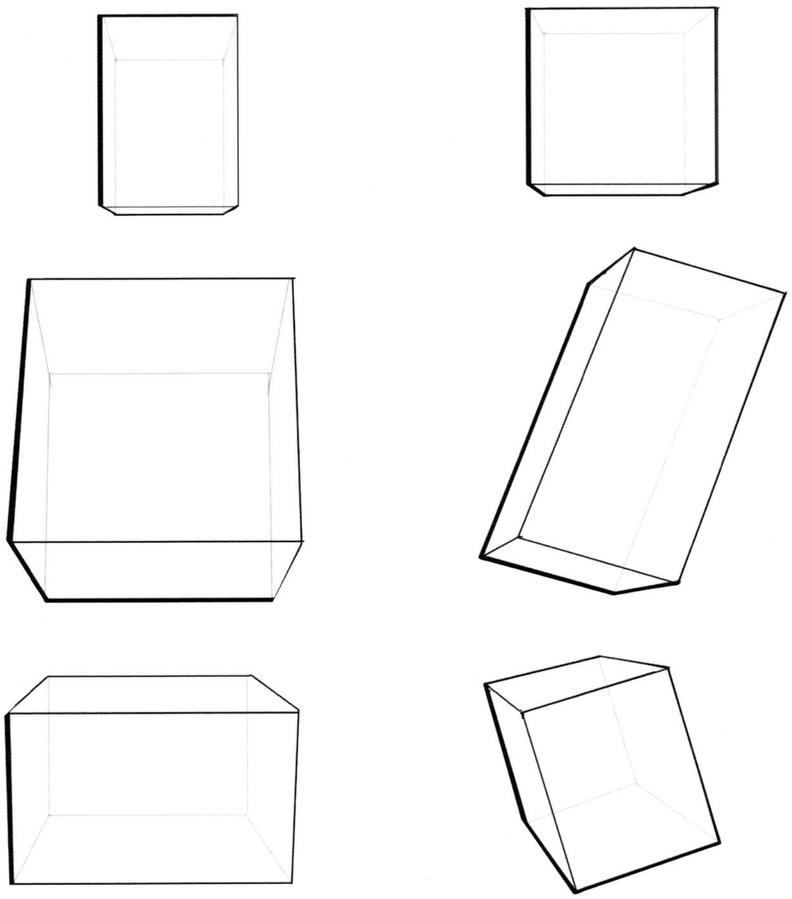

Simplify the three masses into boxes

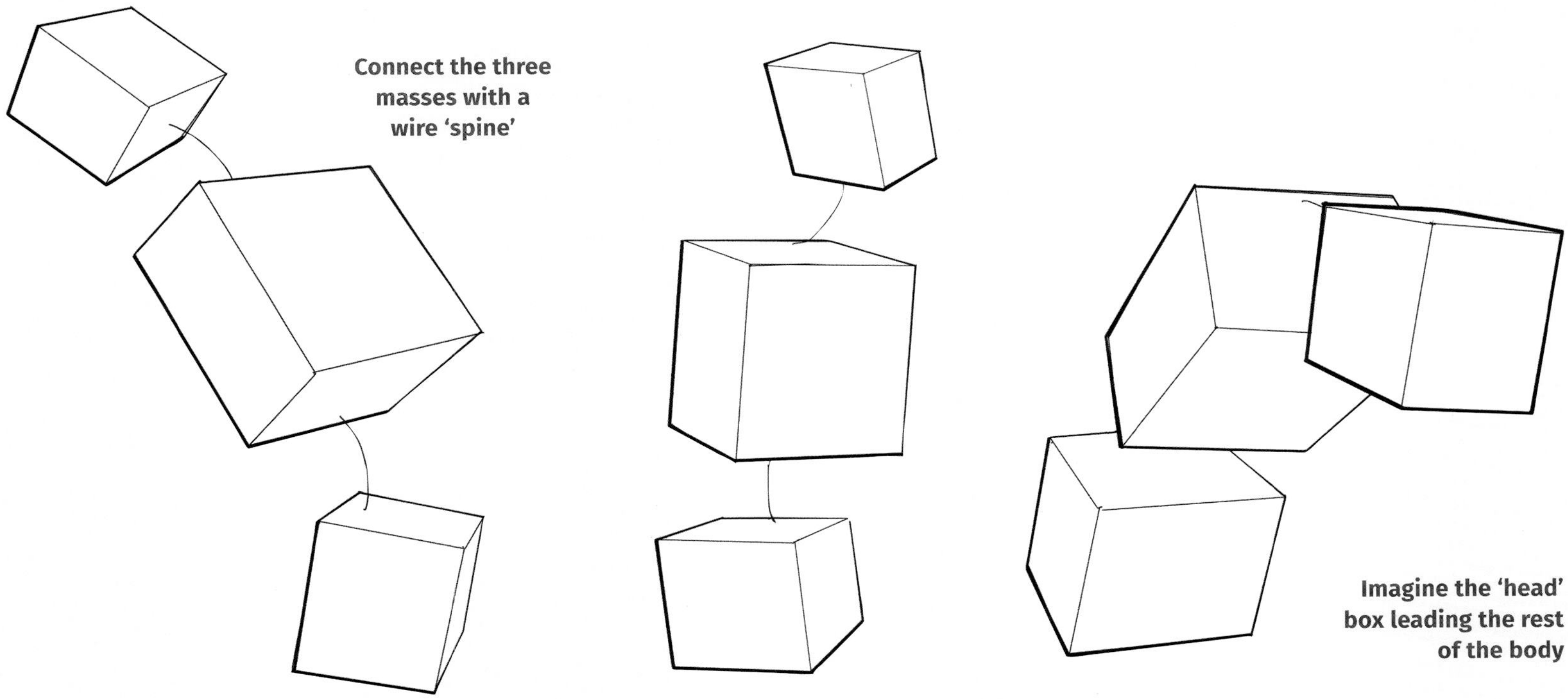

Let's take a look at the simple action of a punch to see the importance and impact of these forms. First we will have our figure execute the move without any momentum (see right). The effect of this is fairly static and uninteresting. That punch is weak, so how can we improve it?

If we look at this pose in real life, shown below, we can study the relationships between the three masses and see what we can take back to our drawing. We can draw the boxes directly from our reference and observe the results.

First, from the box forms, we can see the clear intent in the position of the head, and how it is always leading the movement. Second, we can see that the three masses start leaning to the left, winding up to the action. As the movement is released, the three masses tilt in the other direction, leaning into the punch. Finally, we can see a strong rotation through the entire torso. The torso starts off facing us and actually ends up facing the opposite direction. This rotation is the real core of the movement; the arms only follow along this strong direction, which is caused by the major masses.

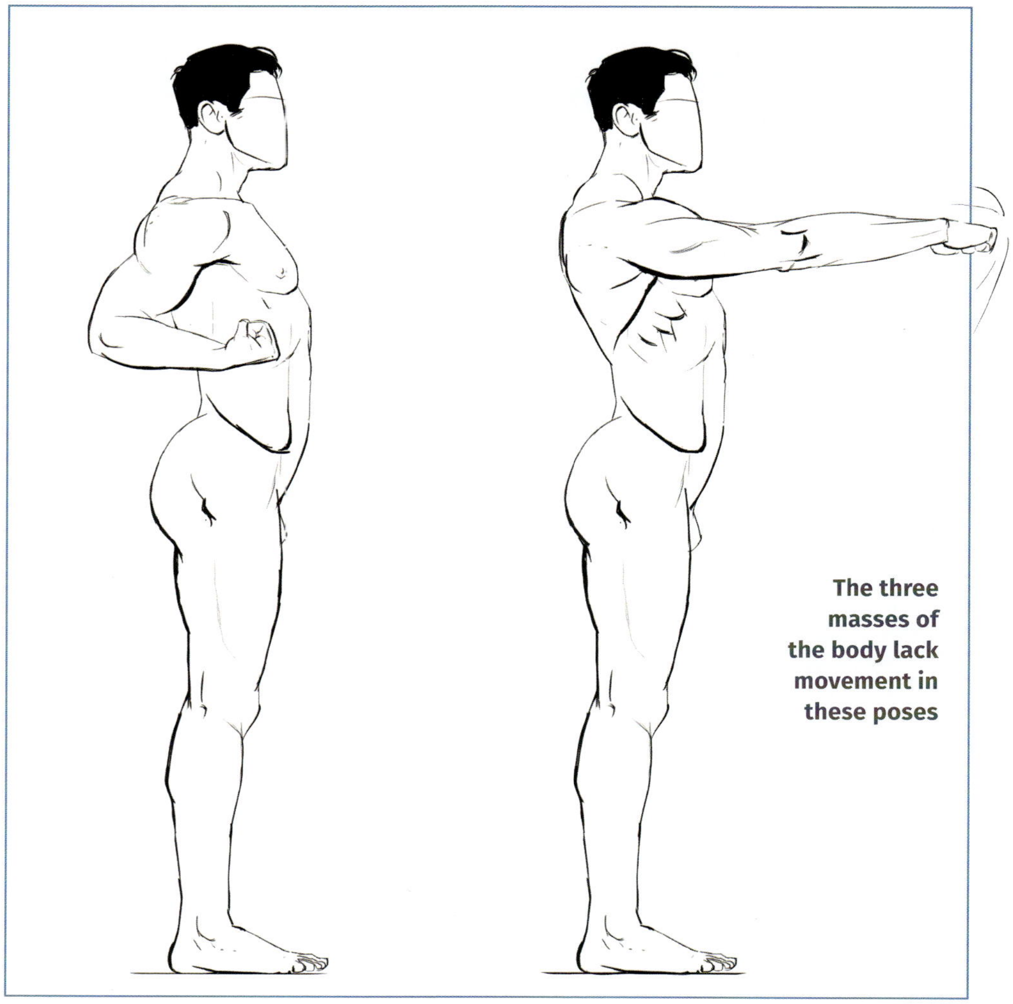

The three masses of the body lack movement in these poses

Applying our box form design to a life model in action

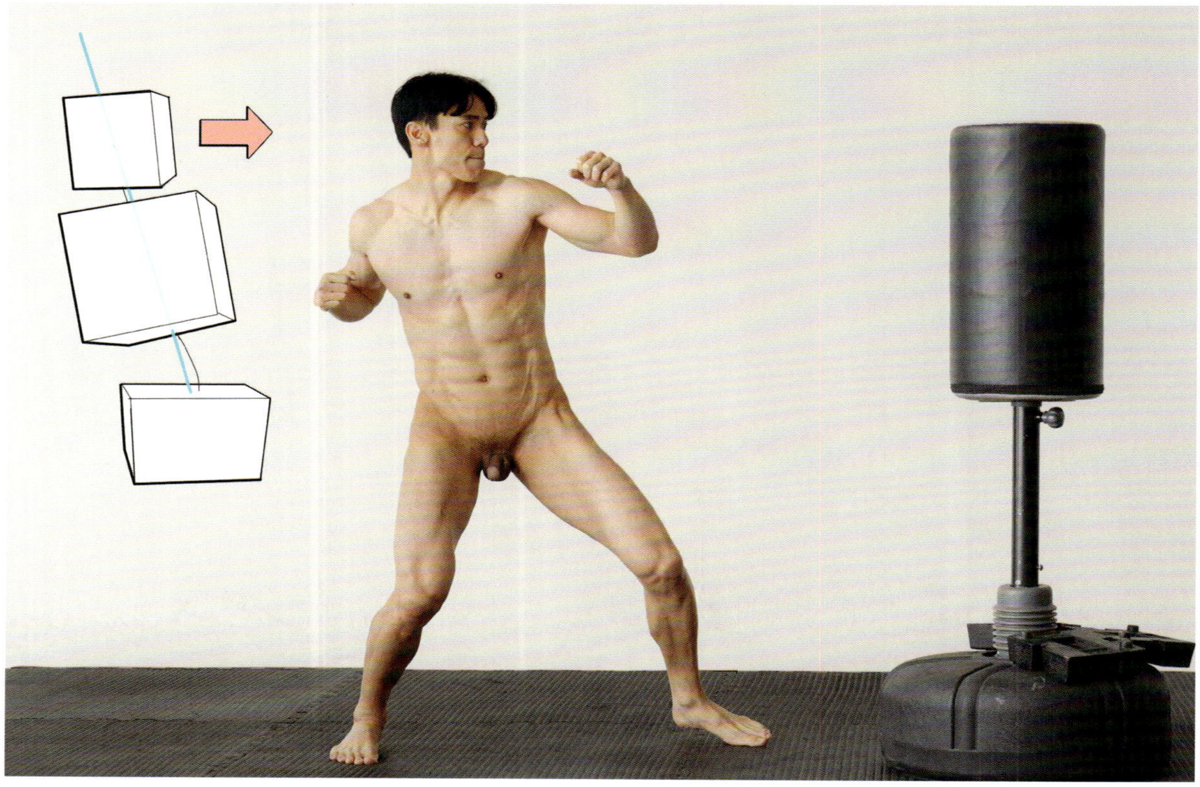

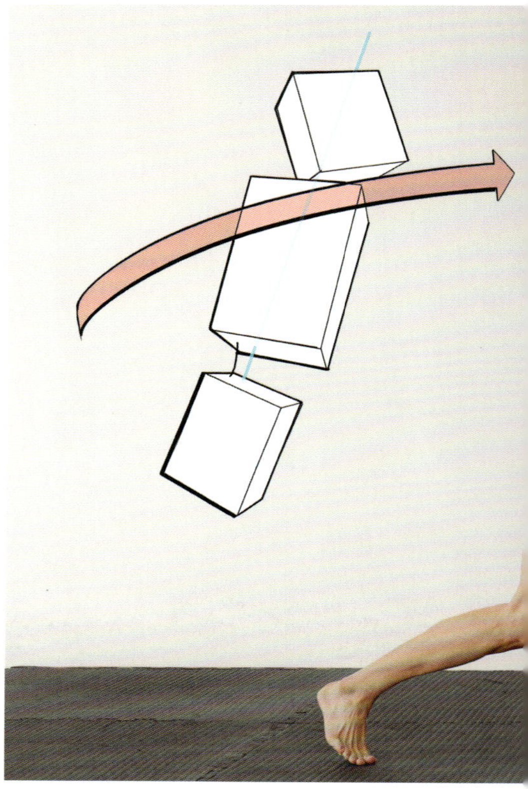

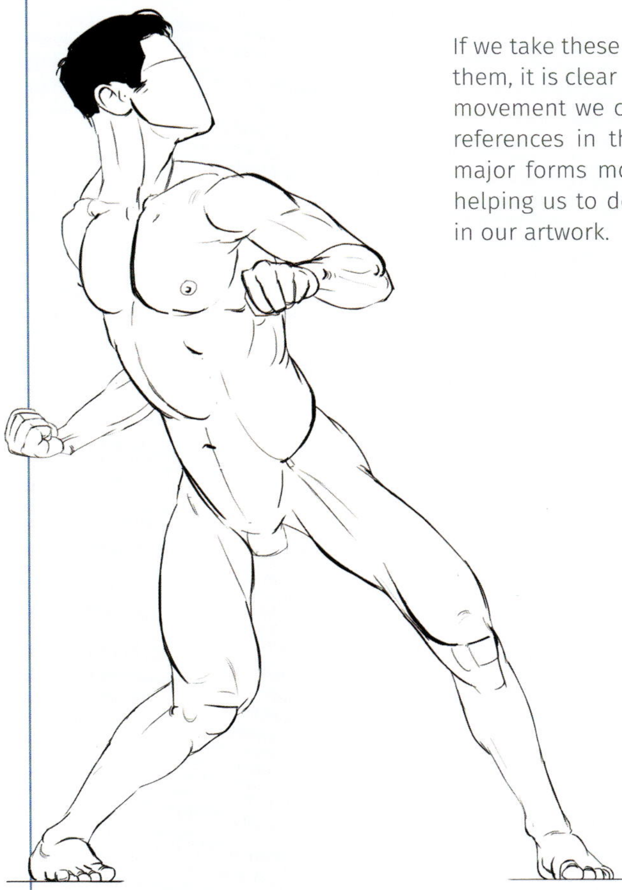

If we take these ideas back to our figure and apply them, it is clear just how much more dramatic of a movement we can achieve. Try to use this book's references in this way; analysing how the three major forms move can be extremely powerful in helping us to design strong, dynamic movements in our artwork.

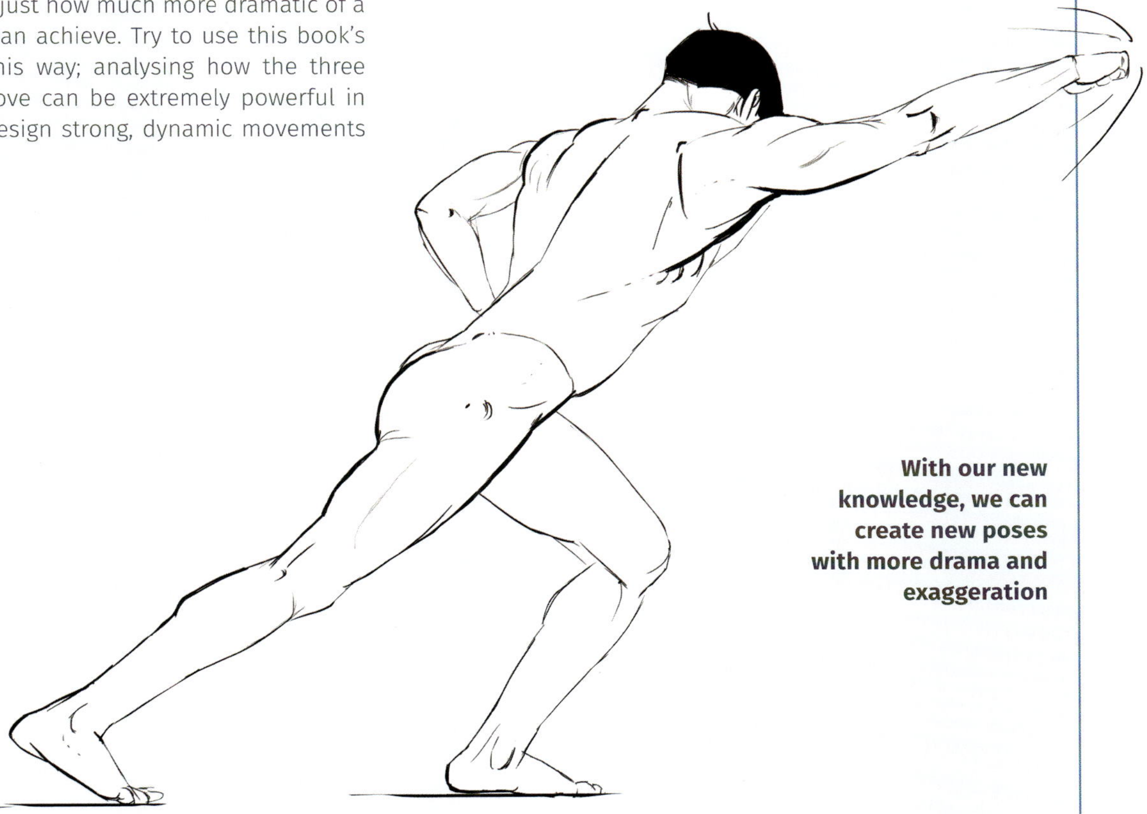

With our new knowledge, we can create new poses with more drama and exaggeration

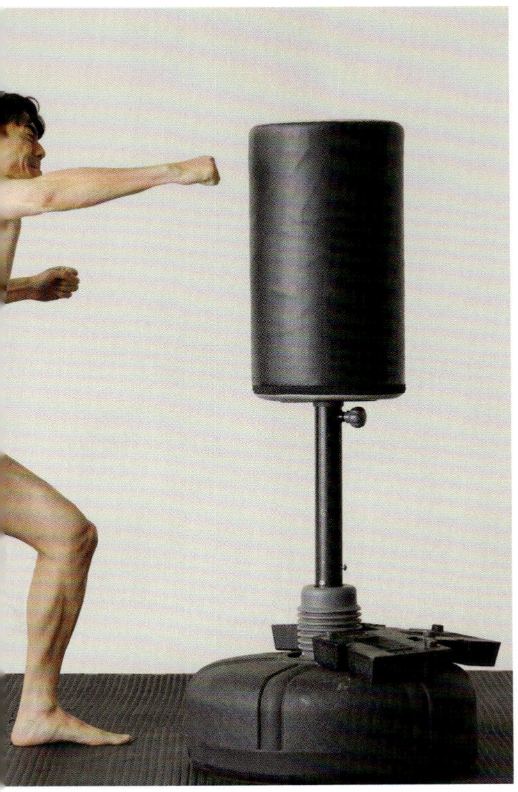

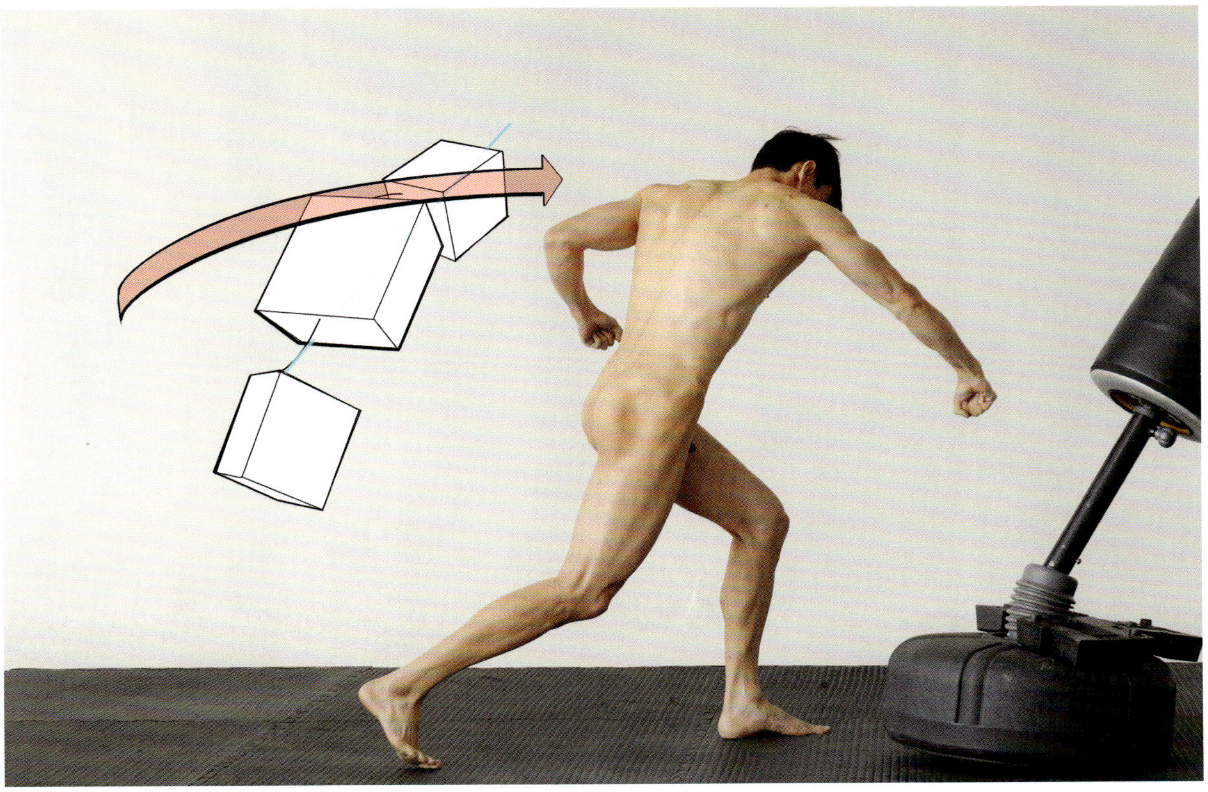

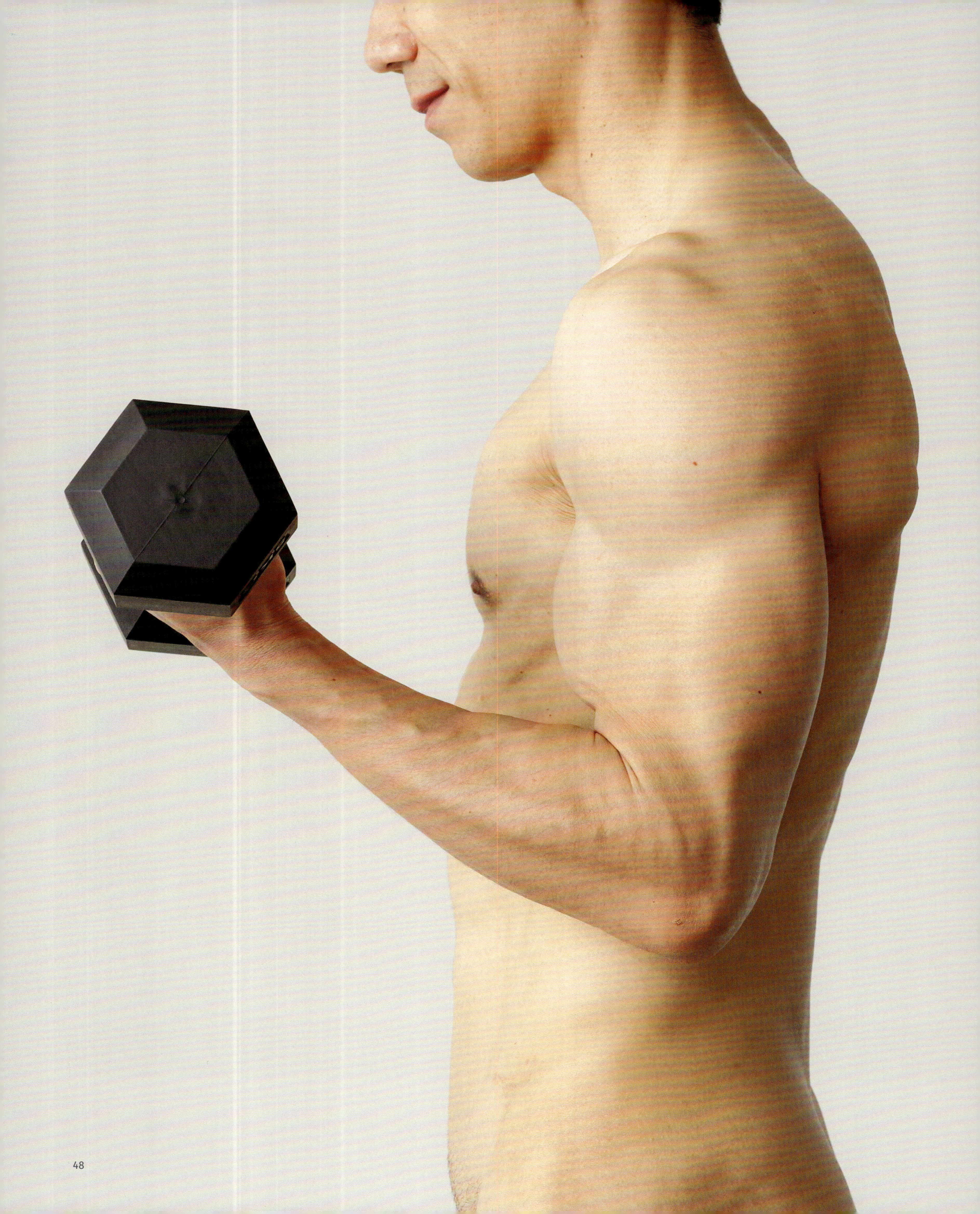

Basic body movements

Shoulder extension to flexion

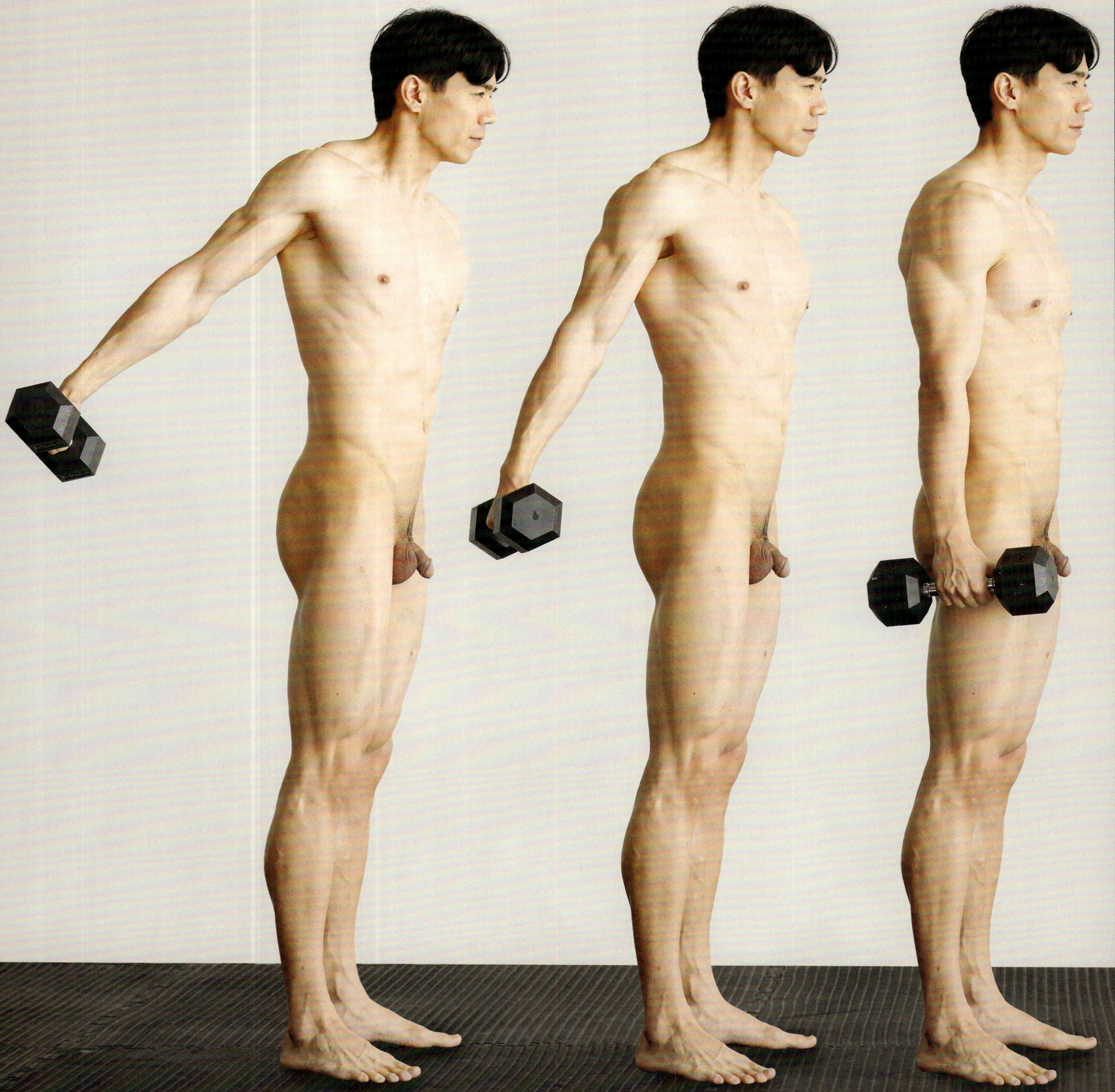

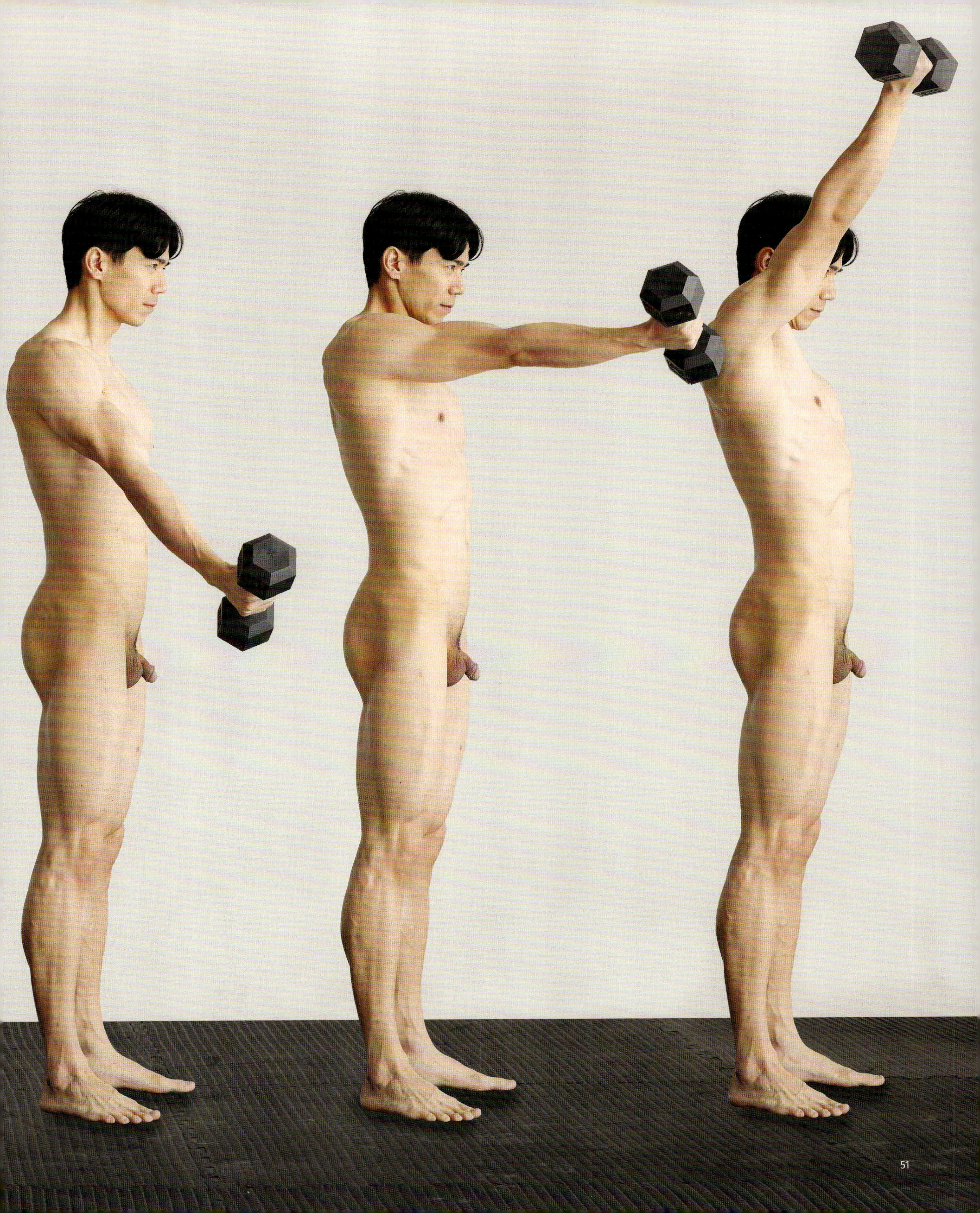

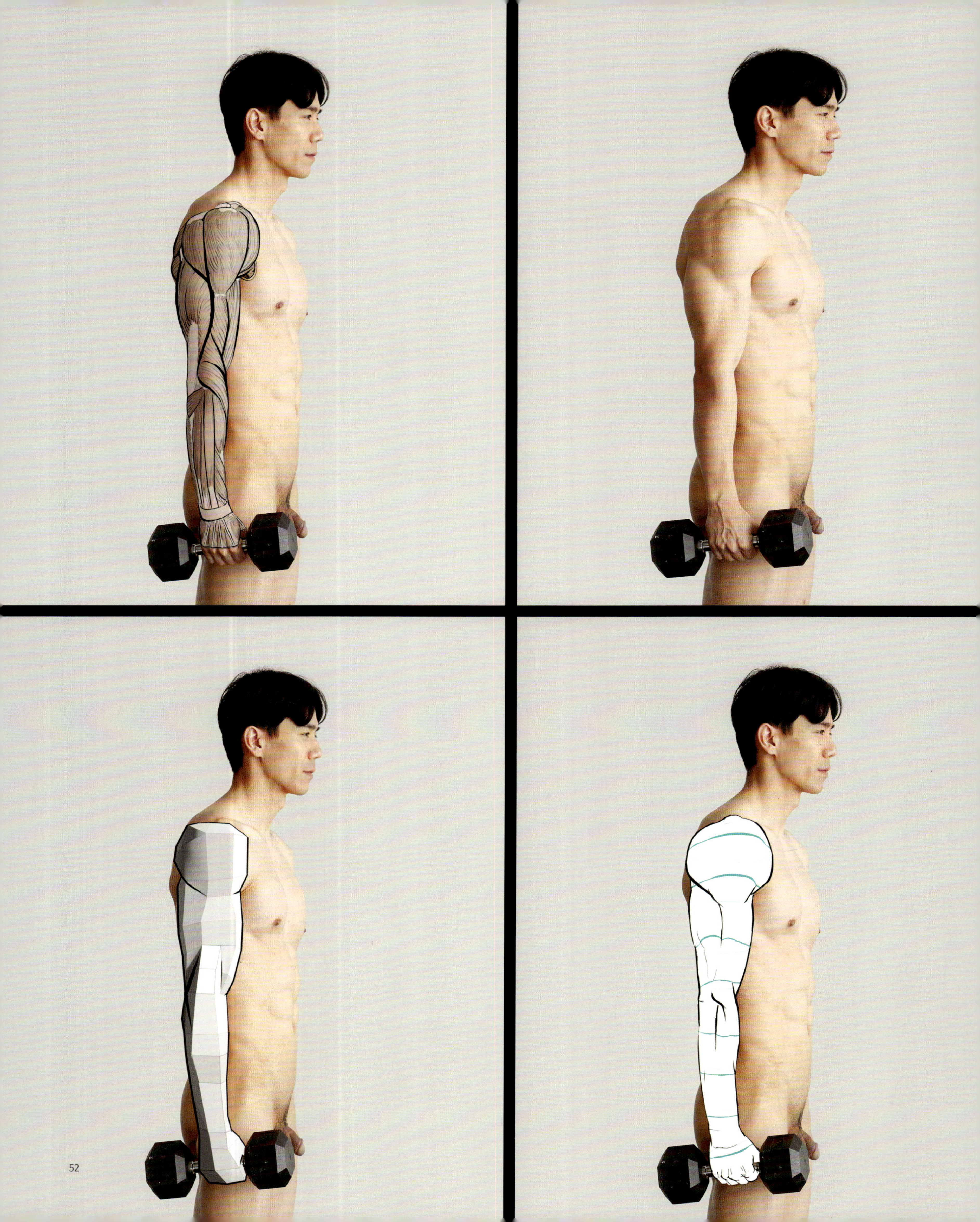

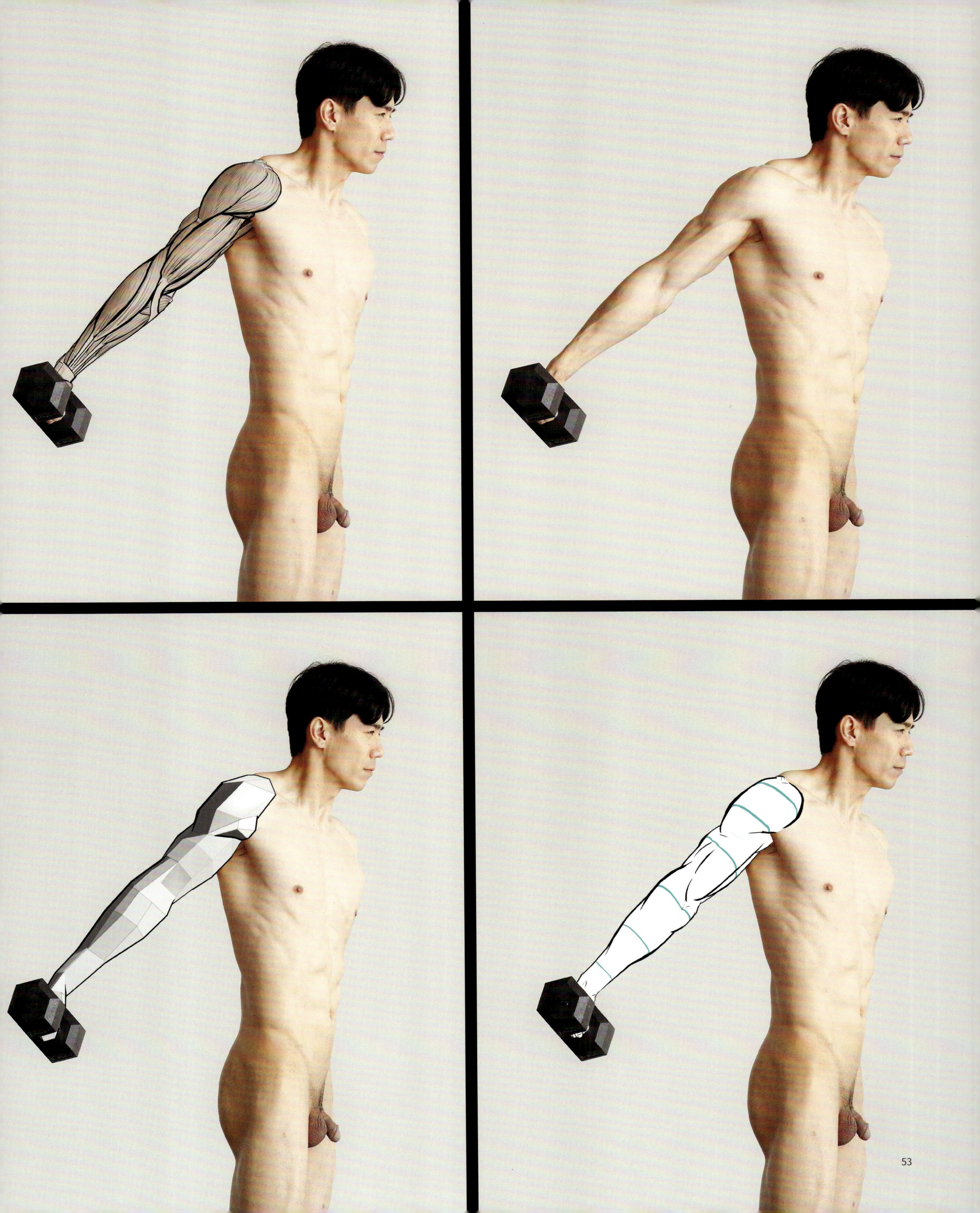

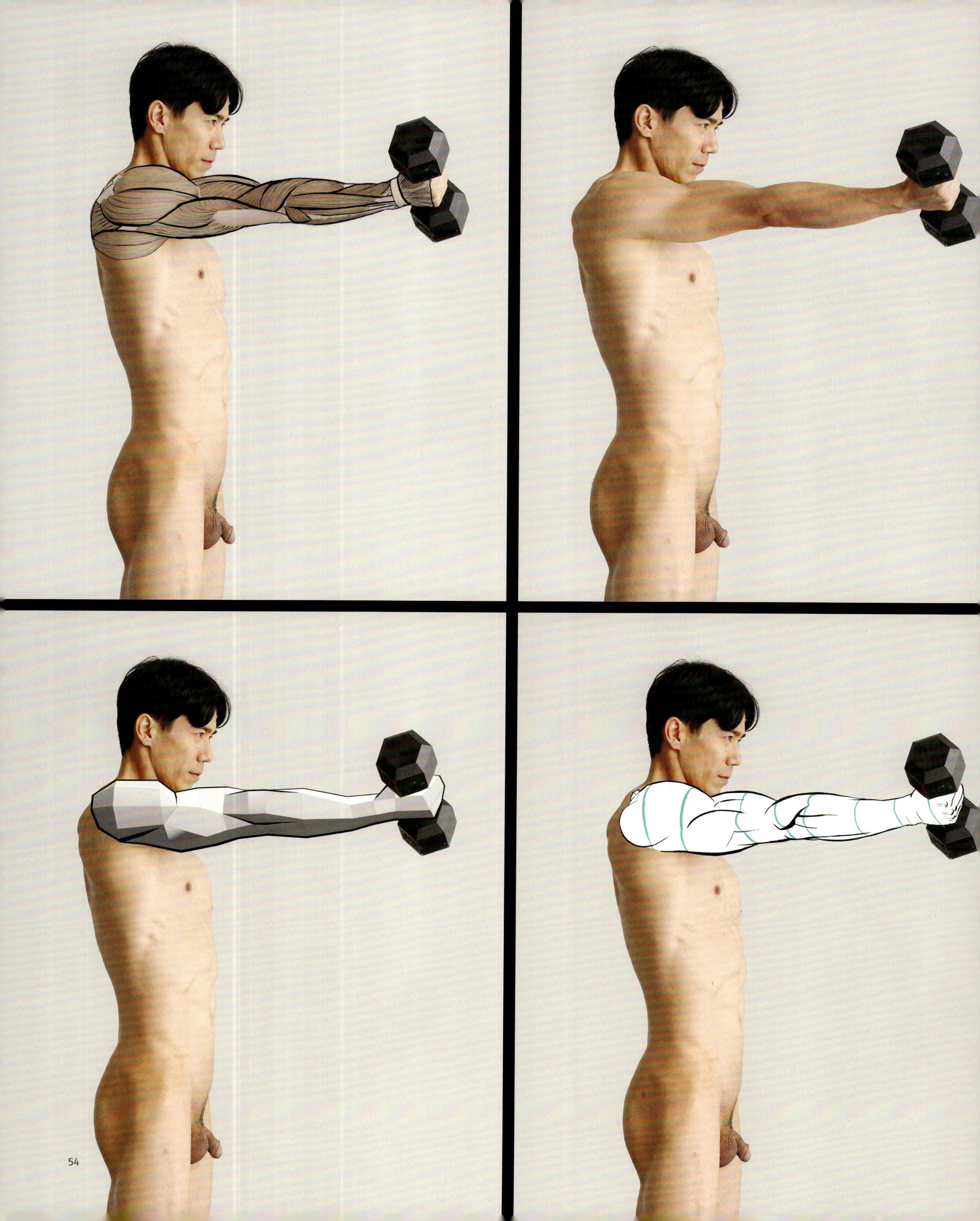

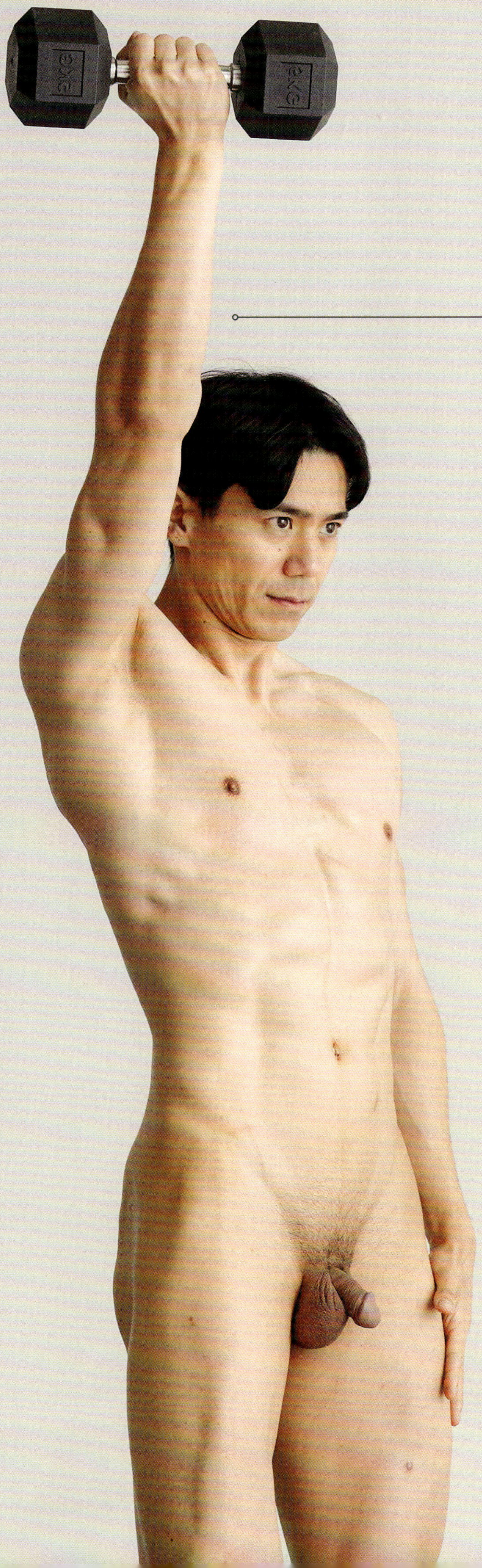

Fully flexed

Arm extension to flexion

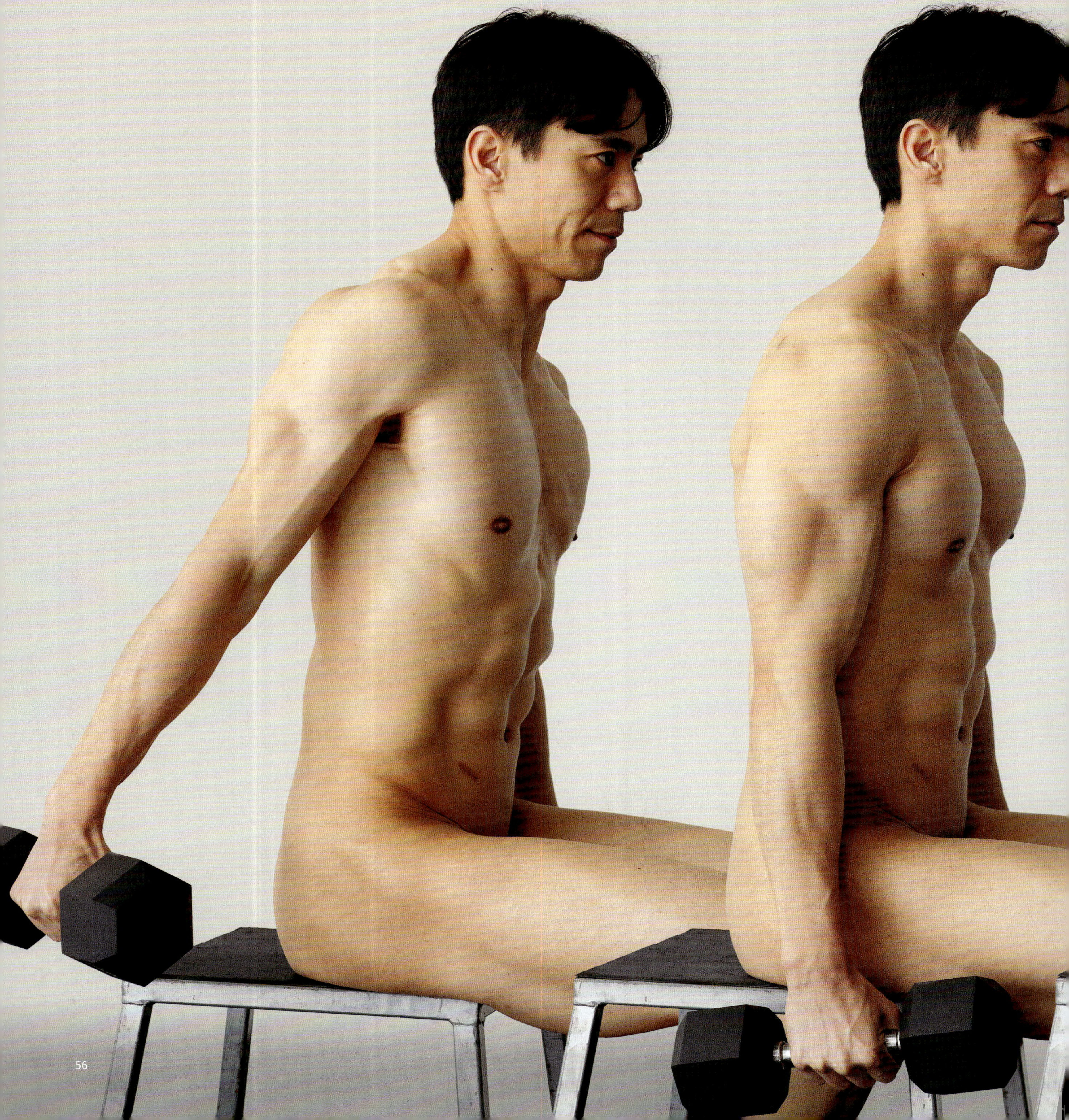

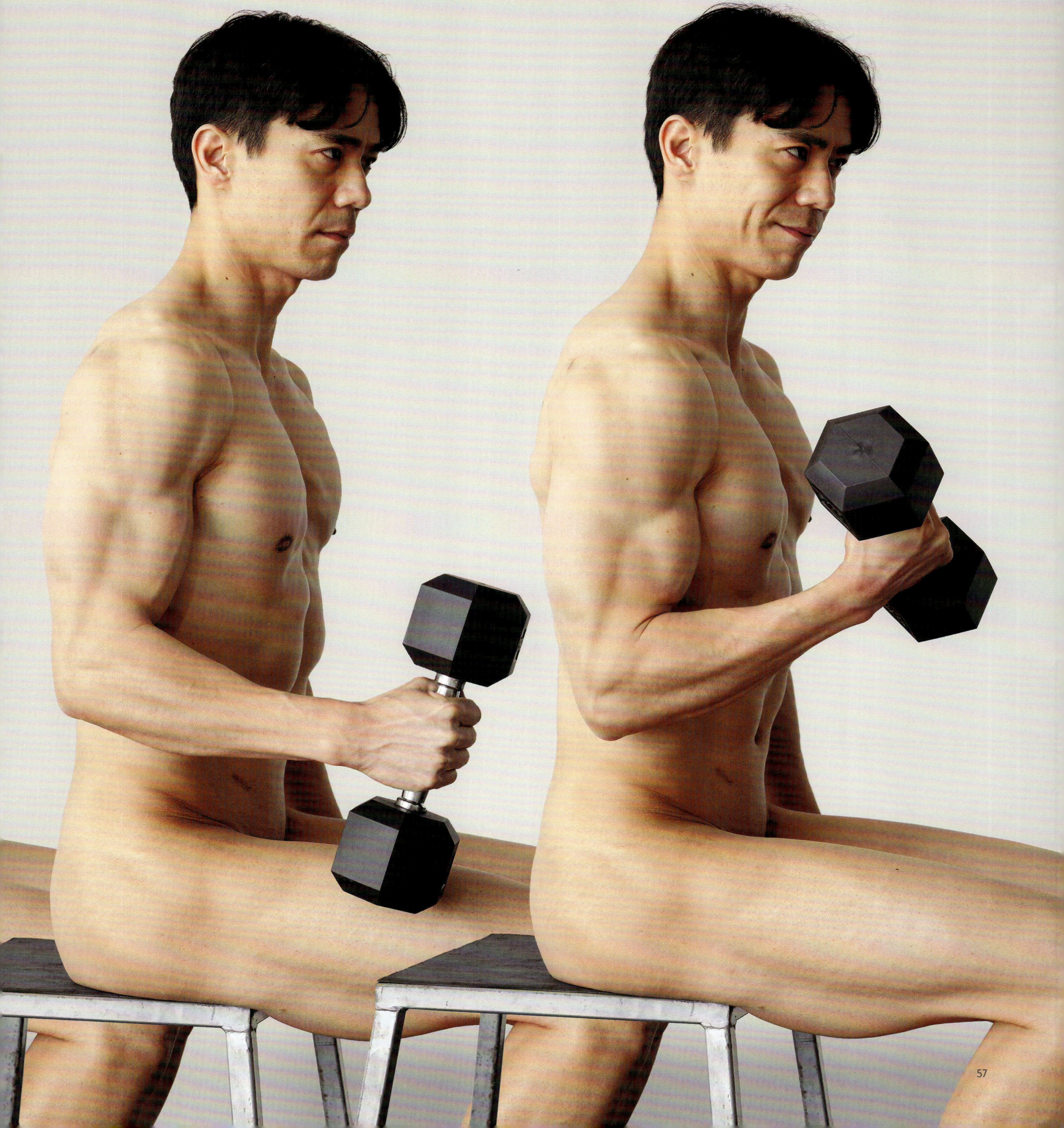

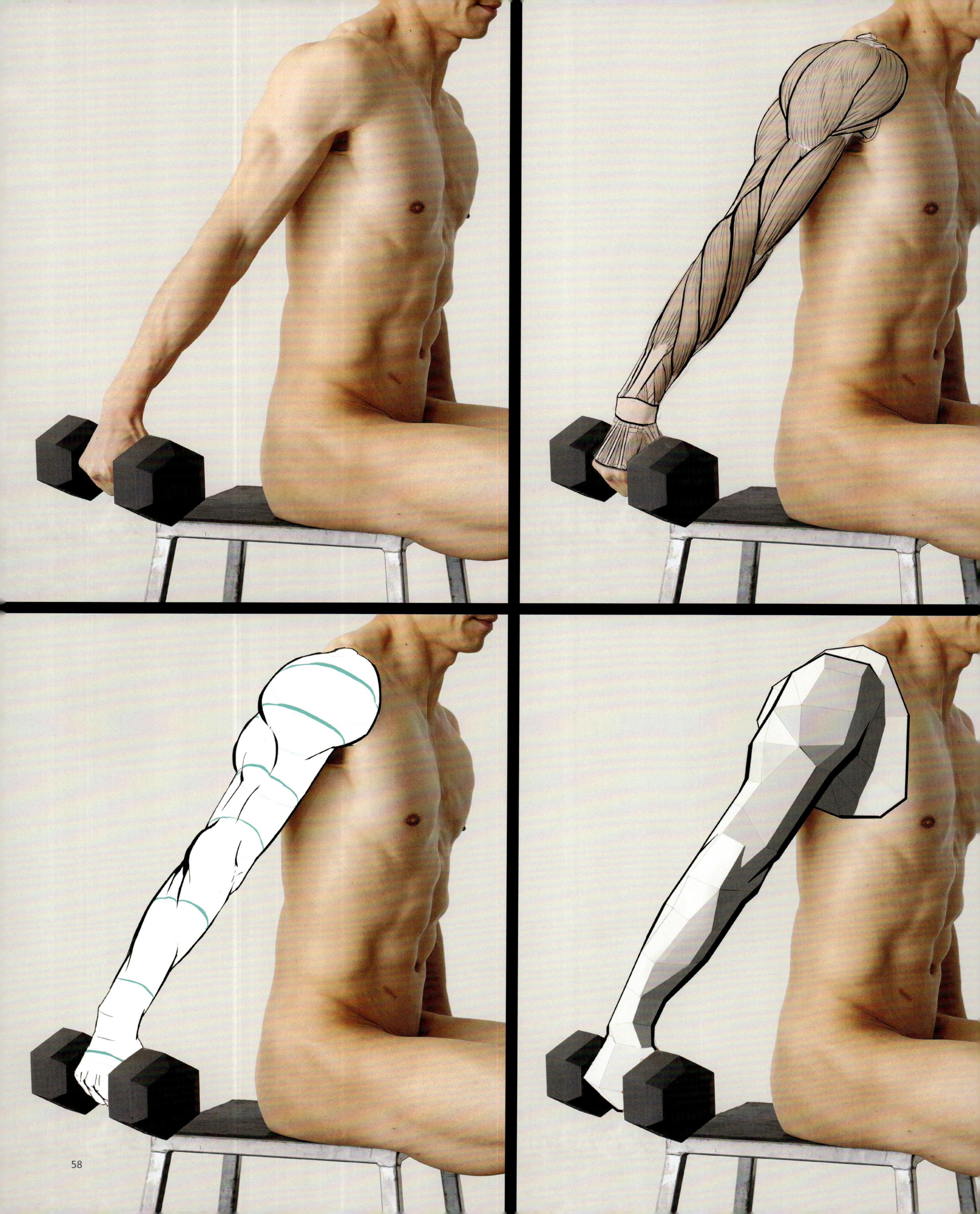

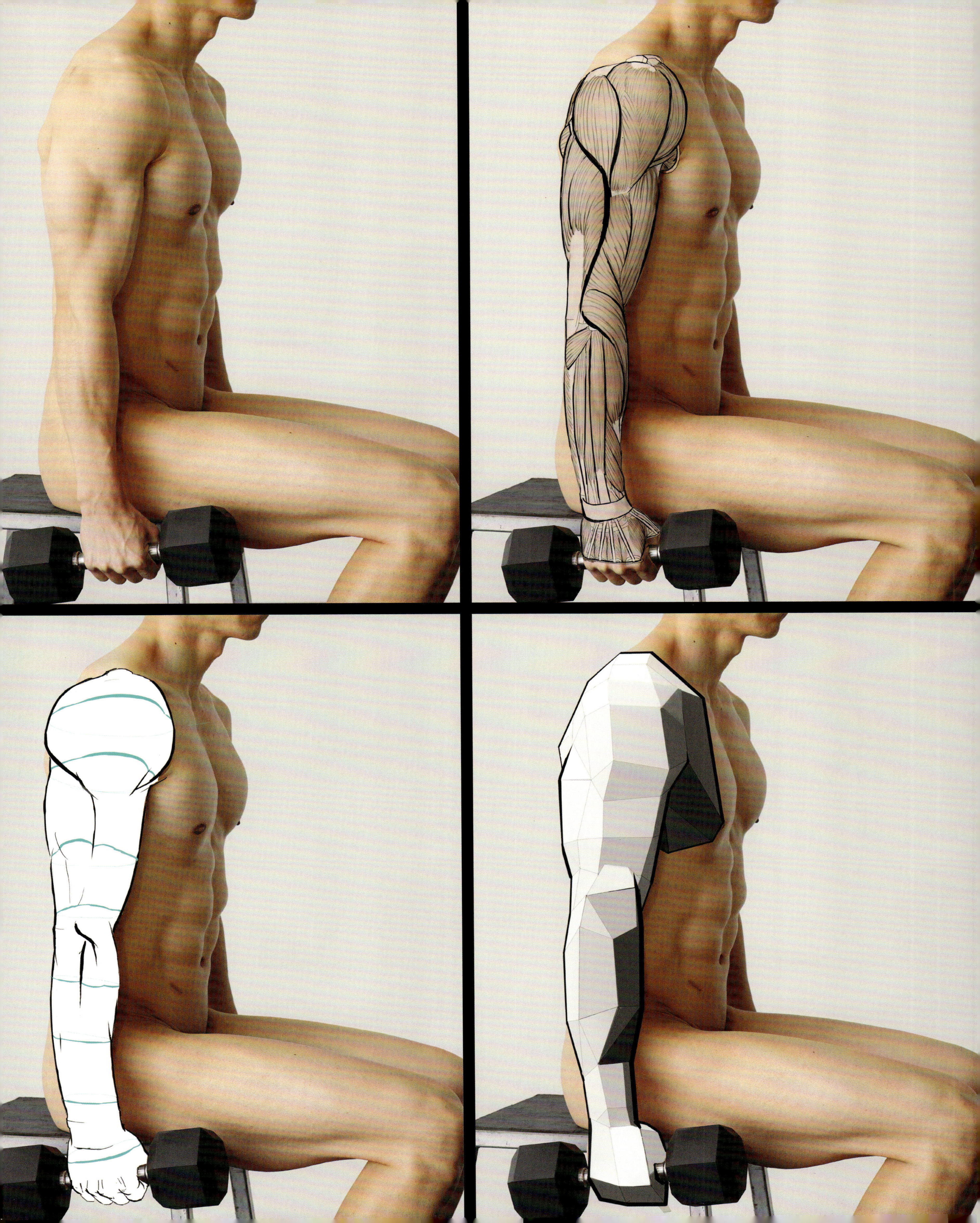

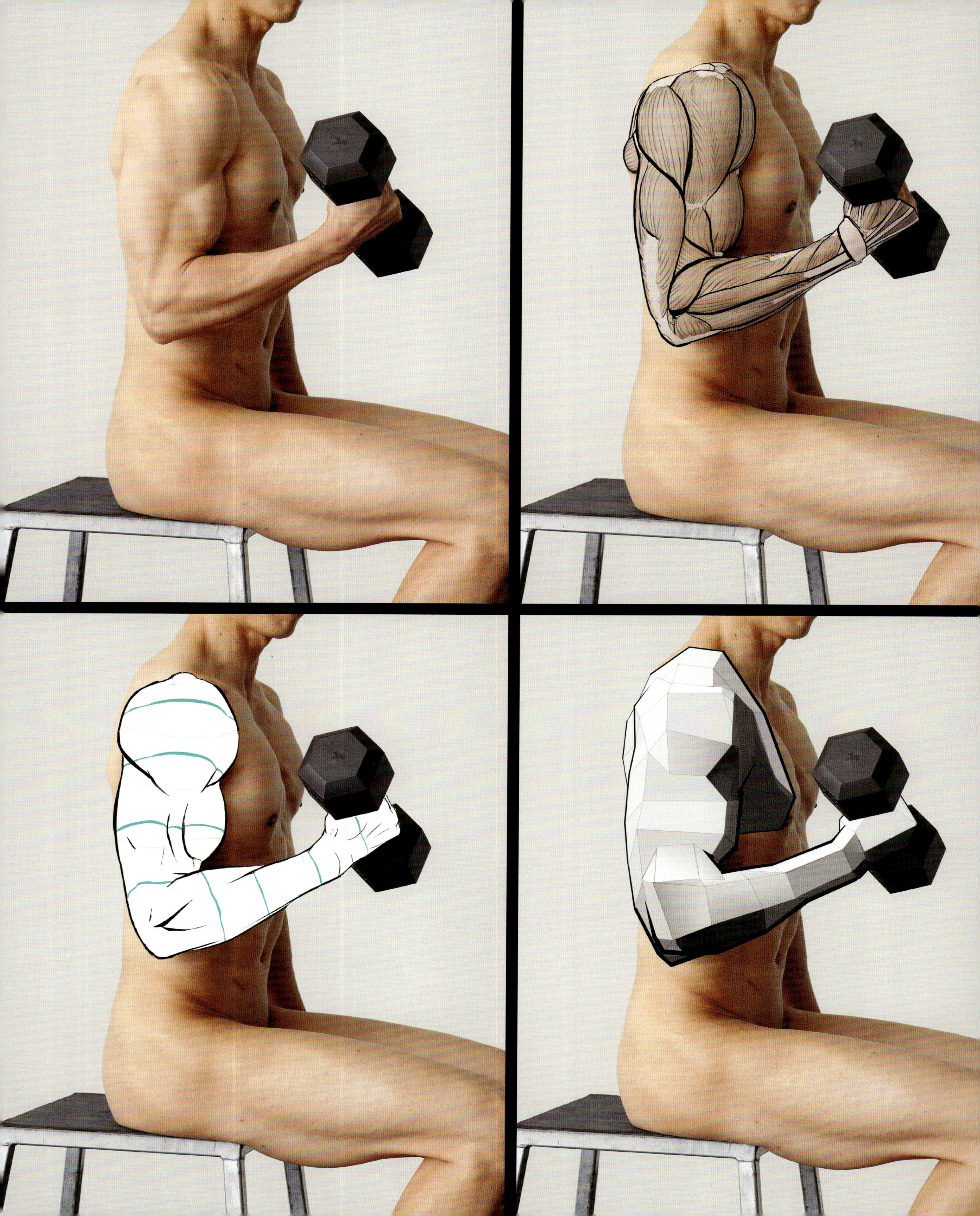

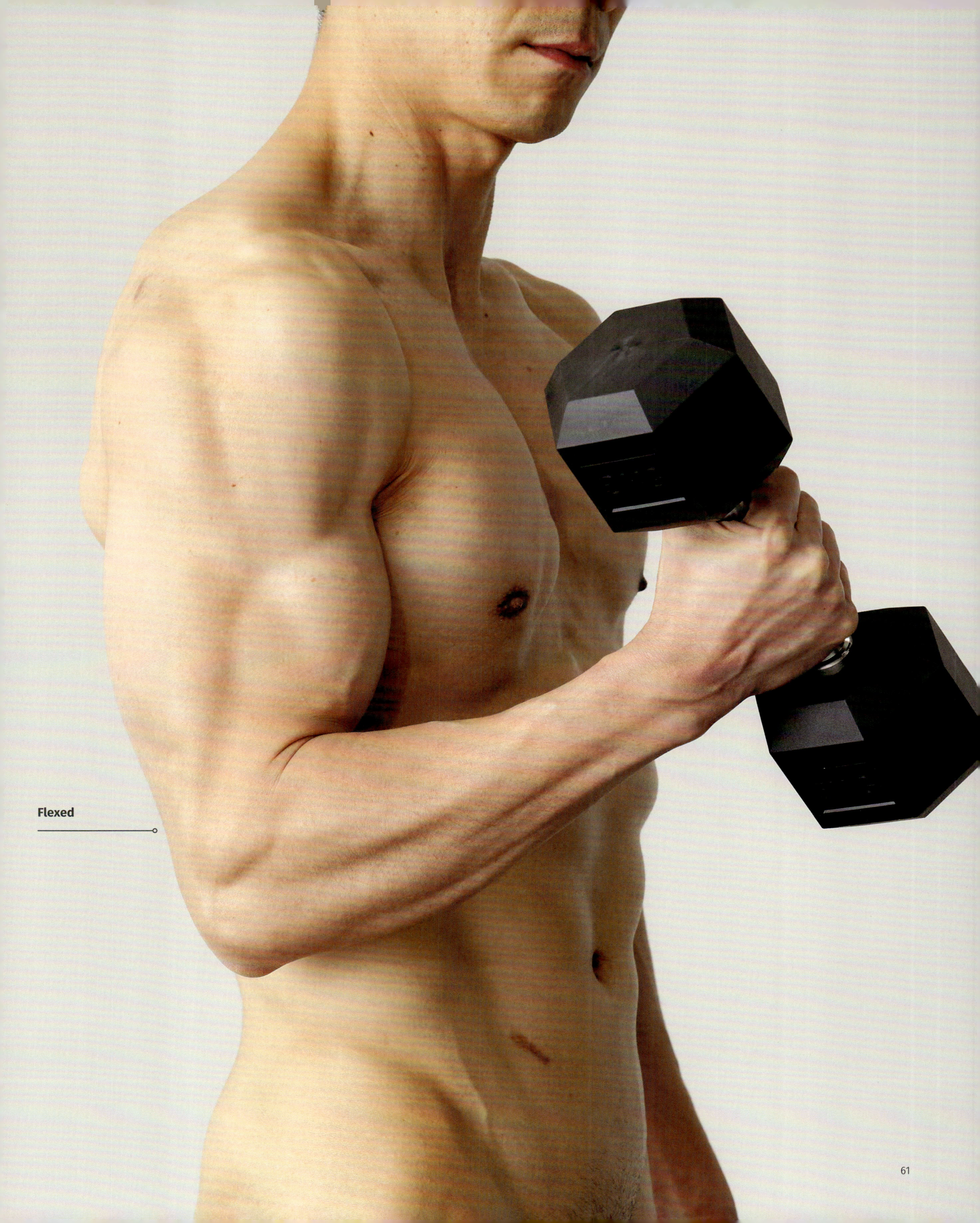
Flexed

Knee extension to flexion

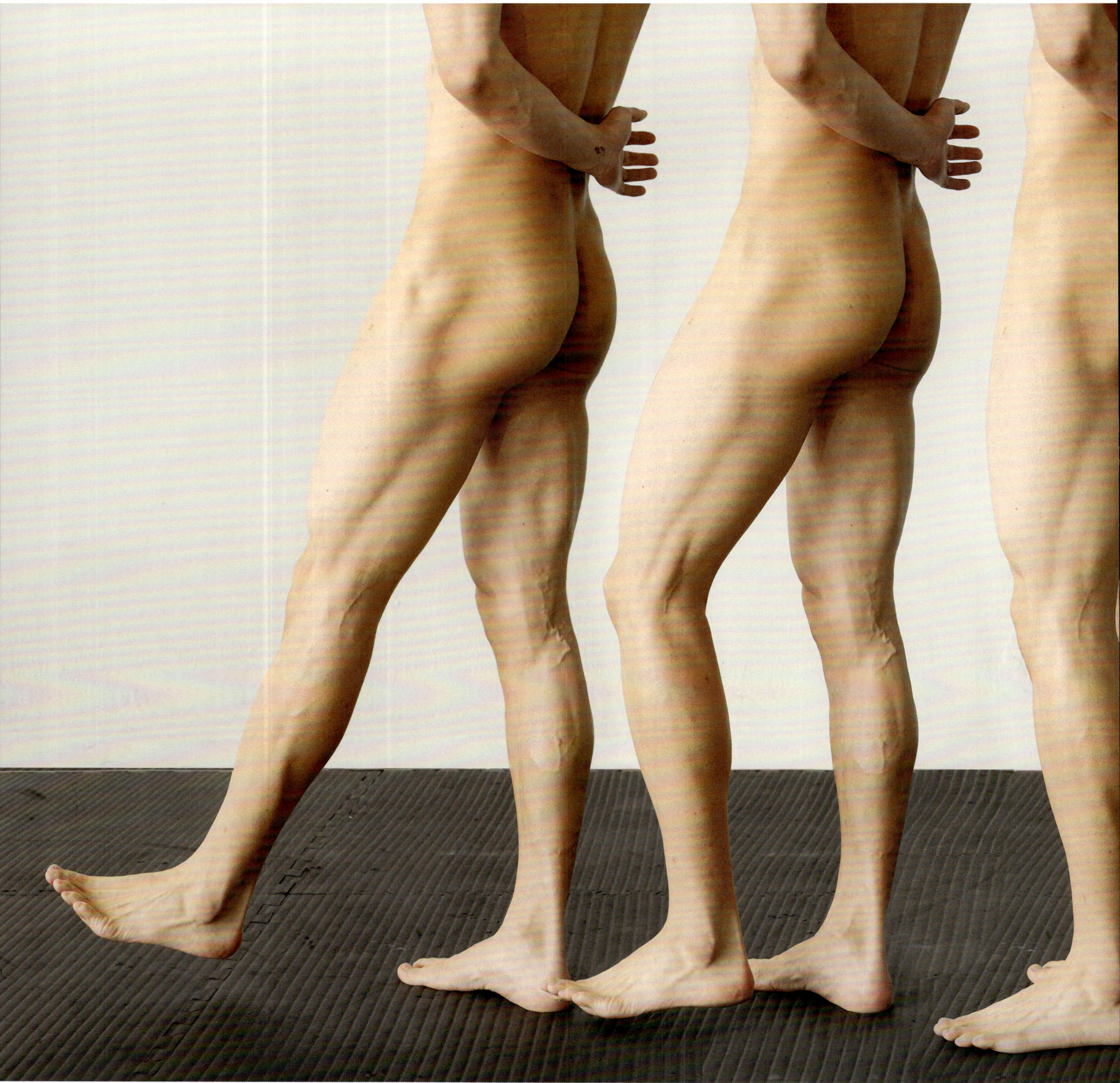

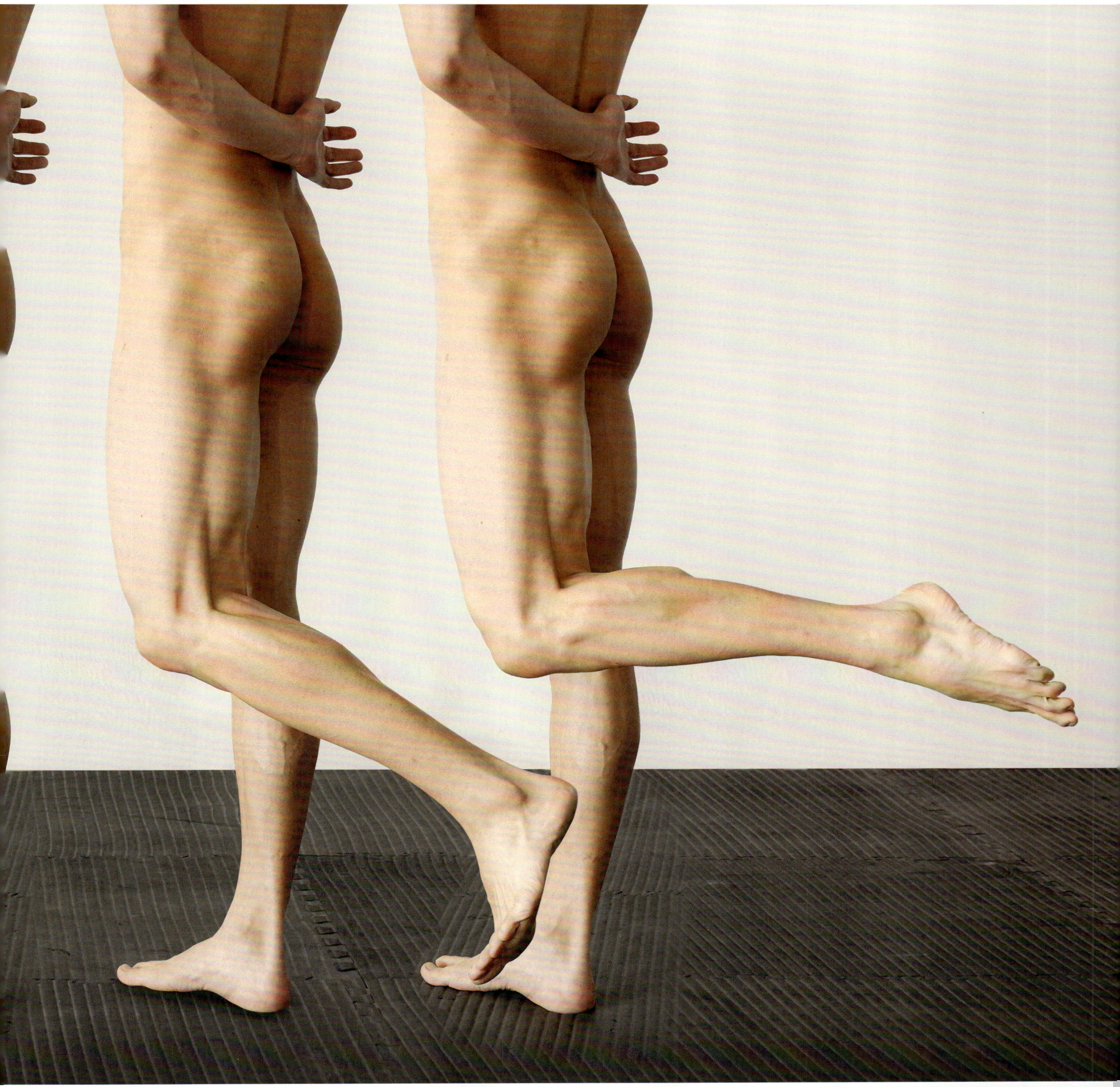

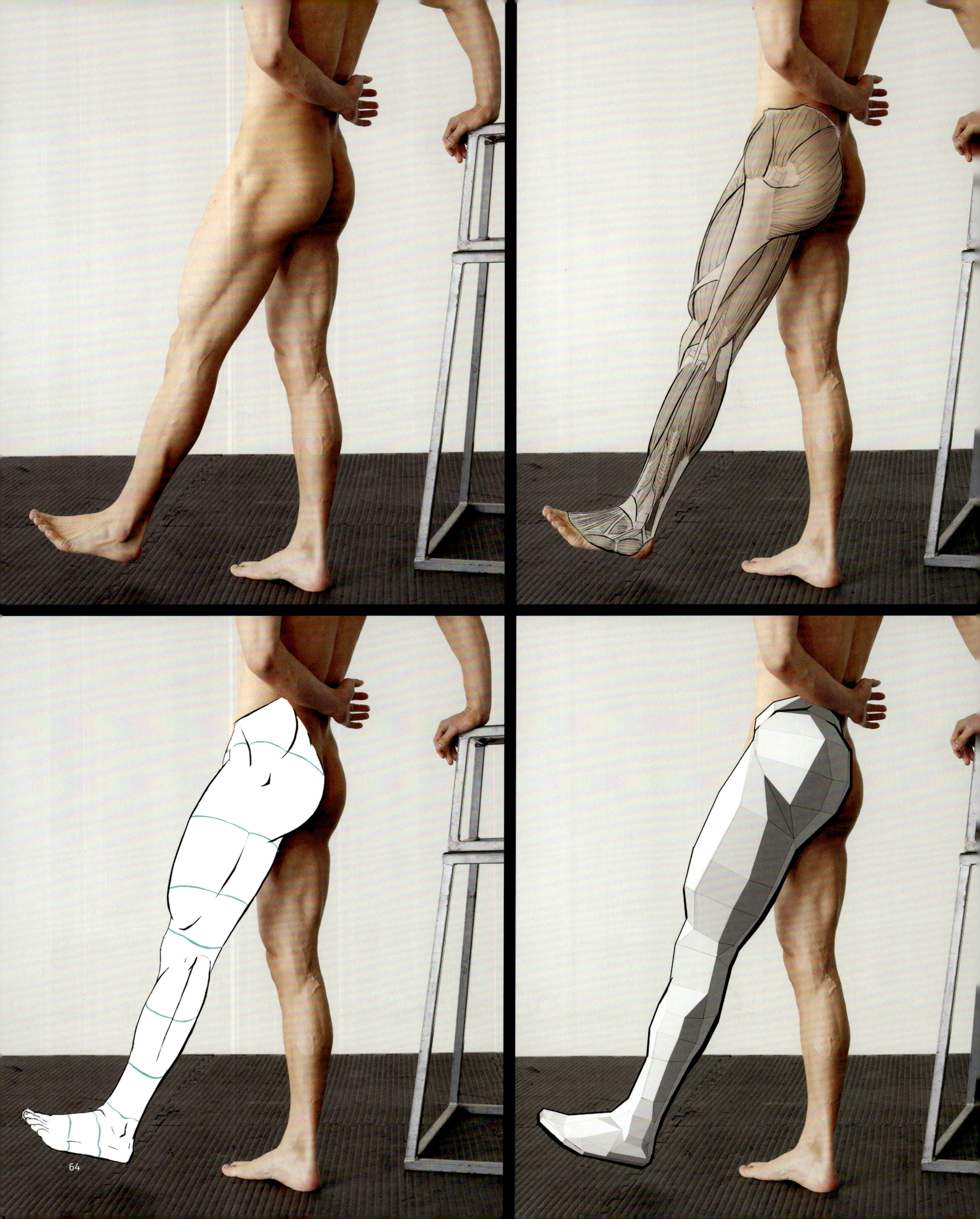

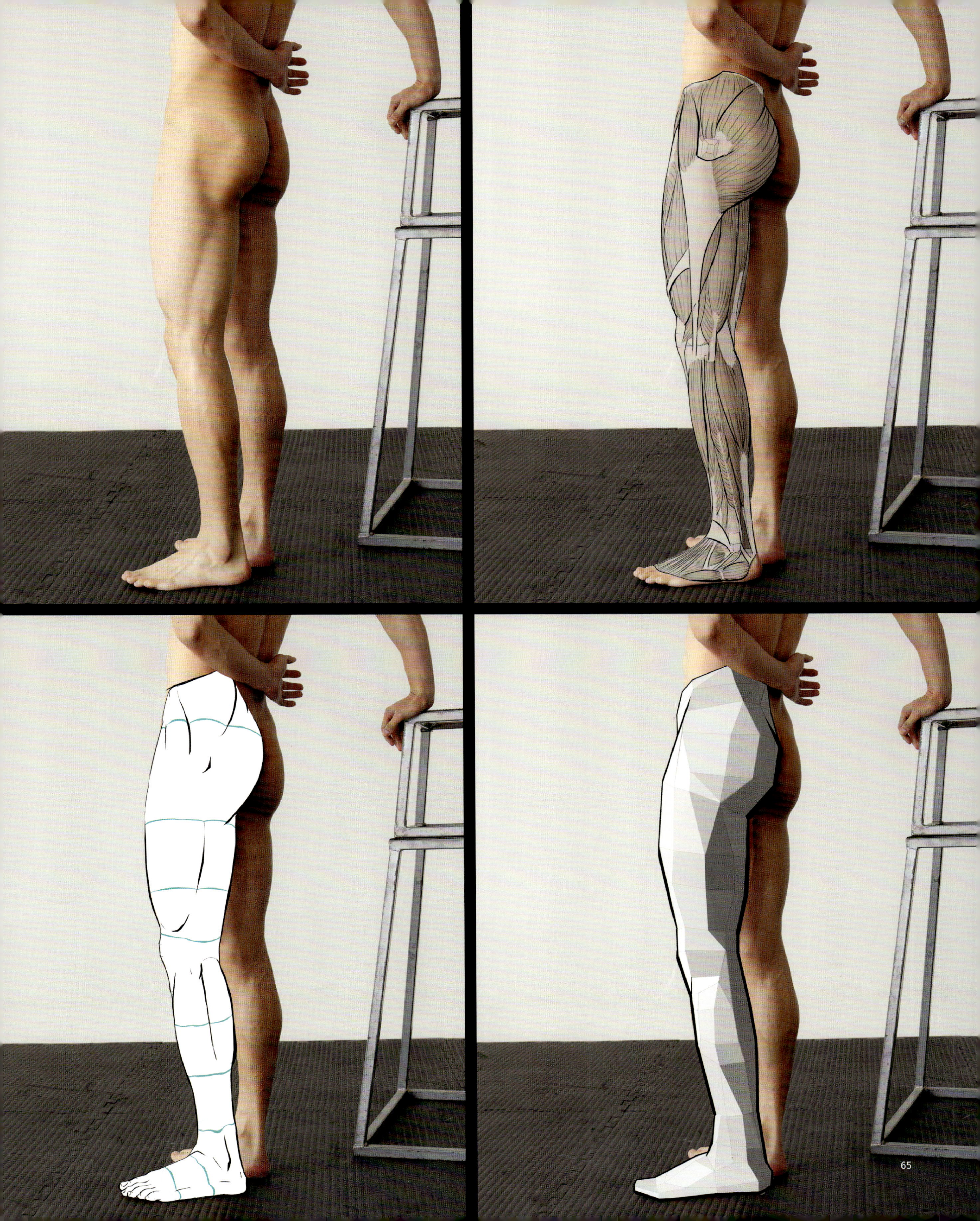

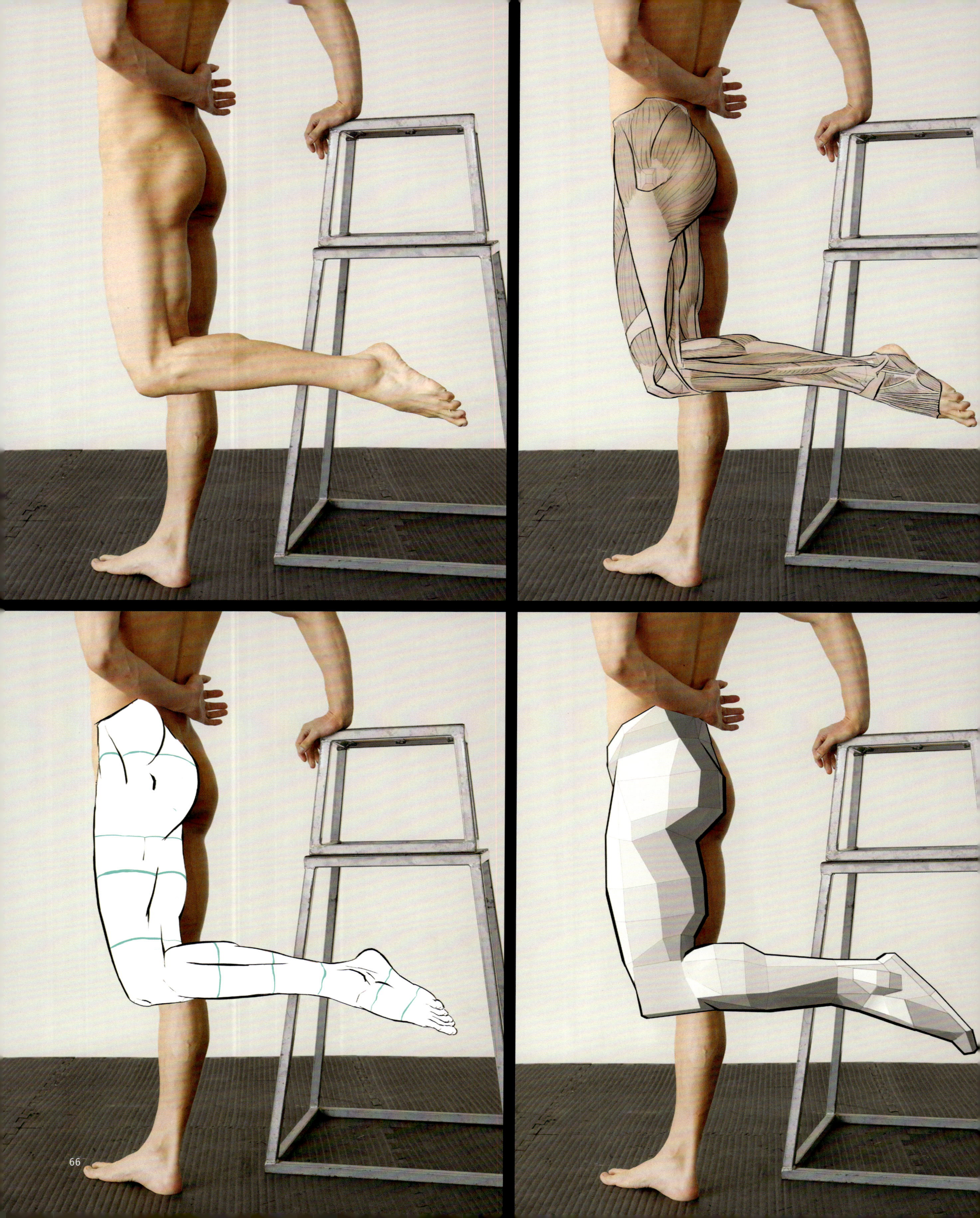

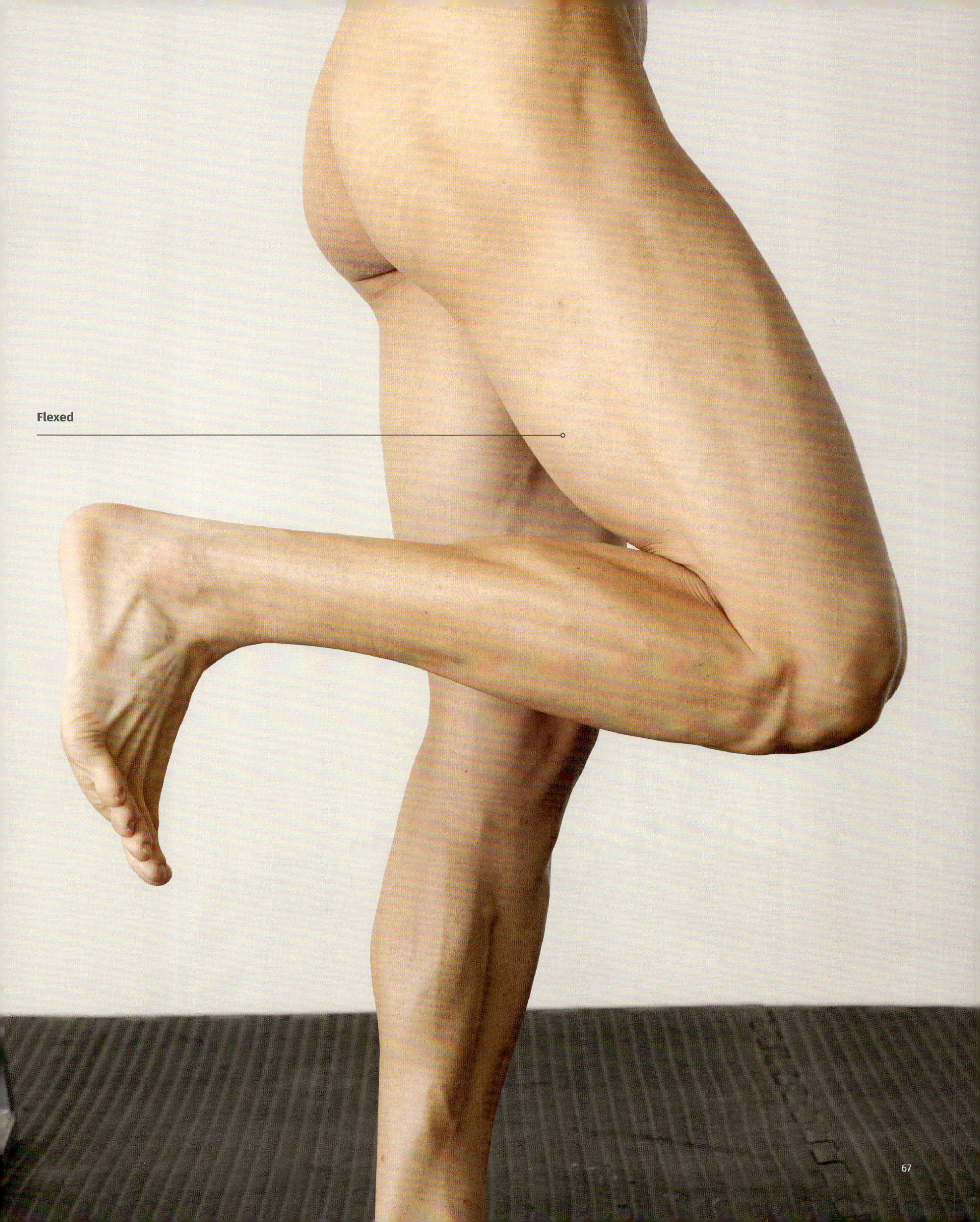
Flexed

Hip flexion to extension

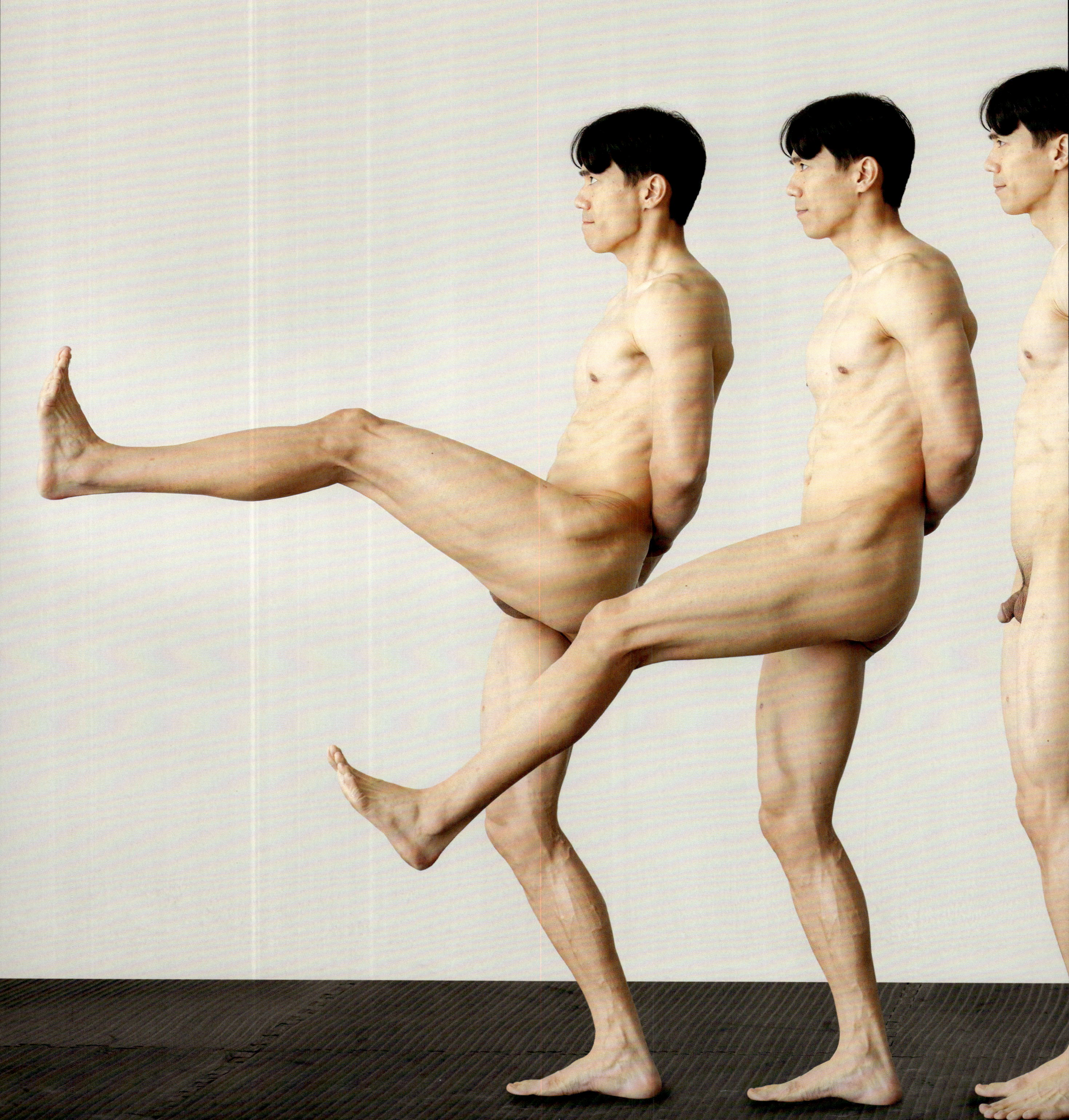

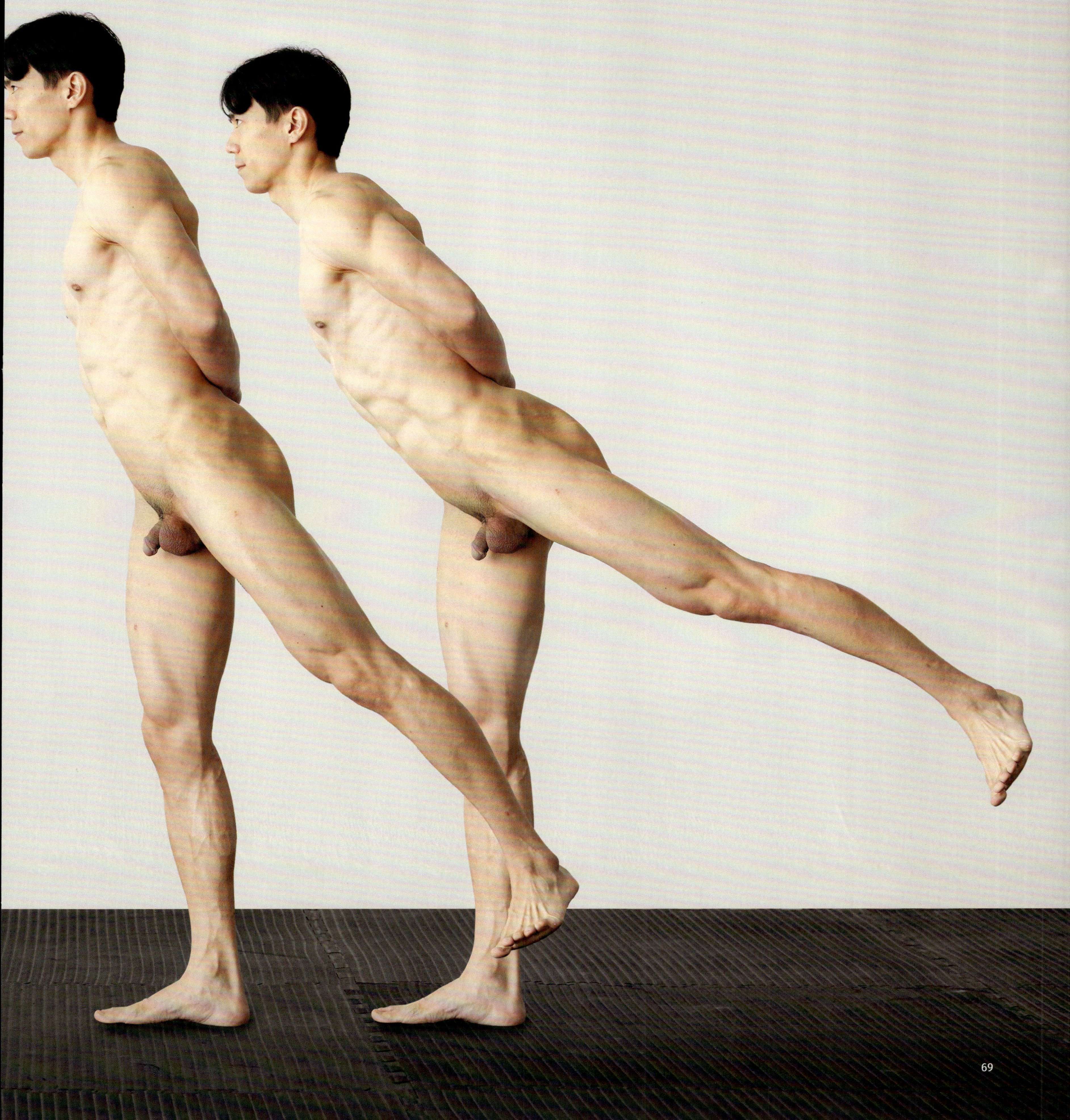

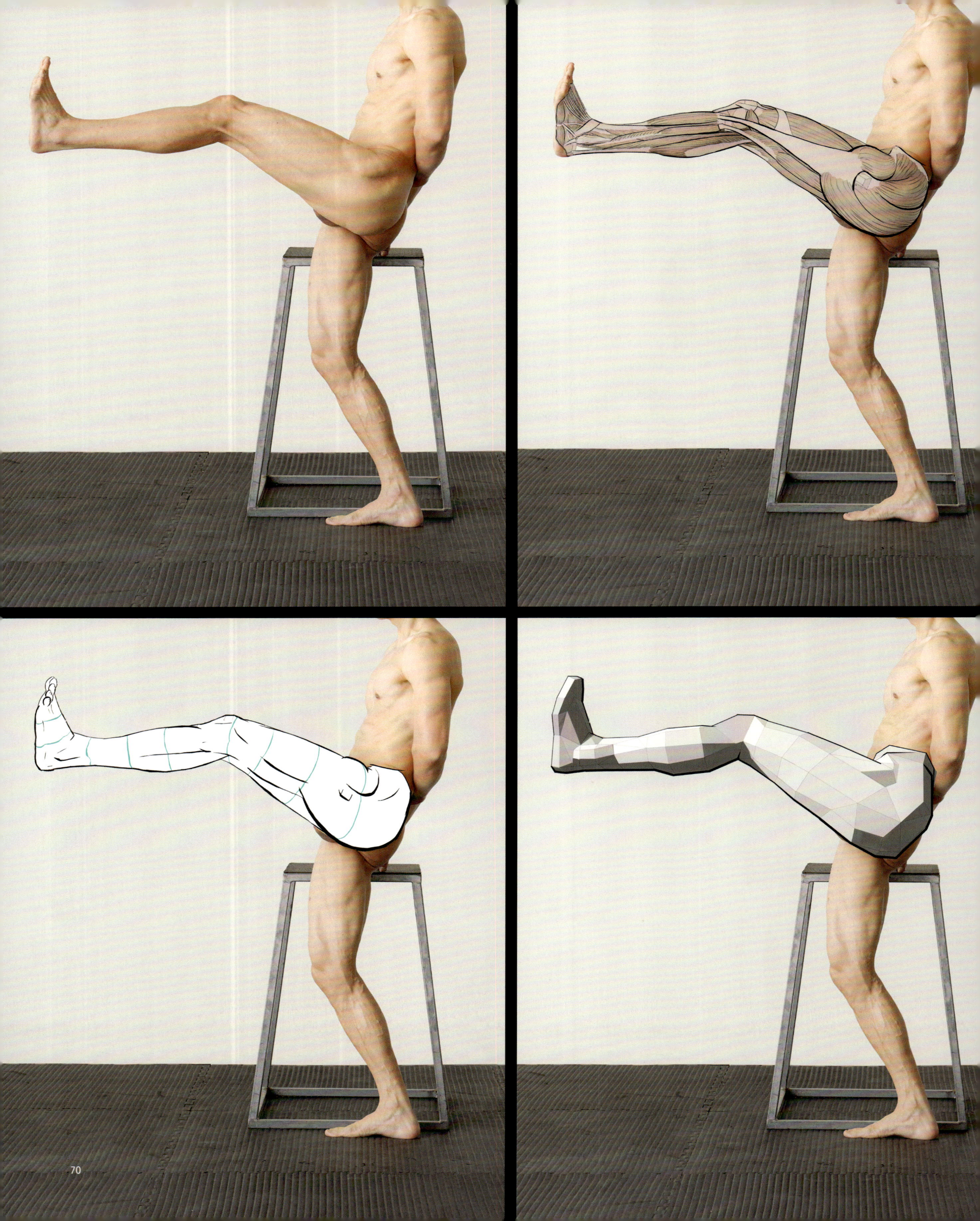

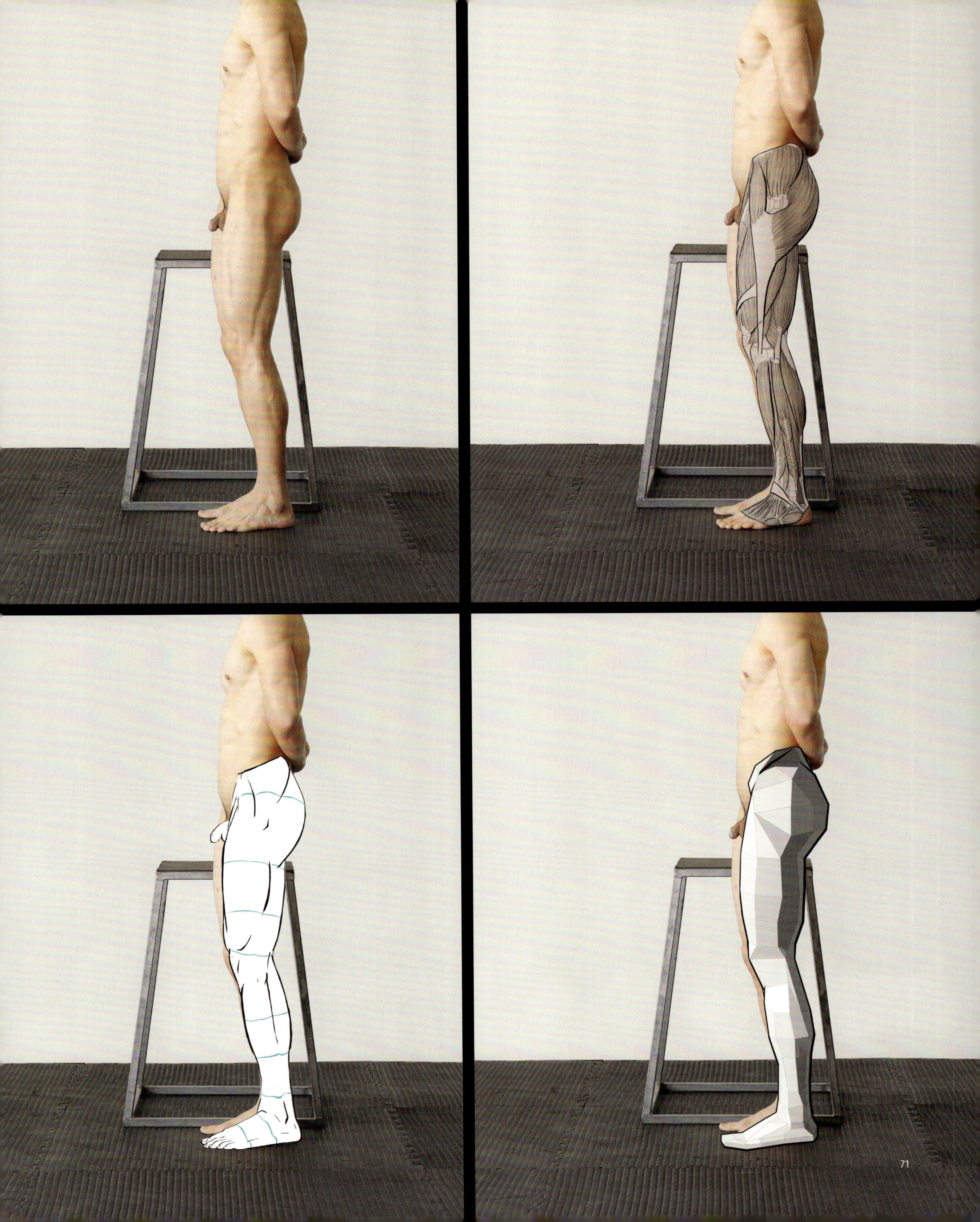

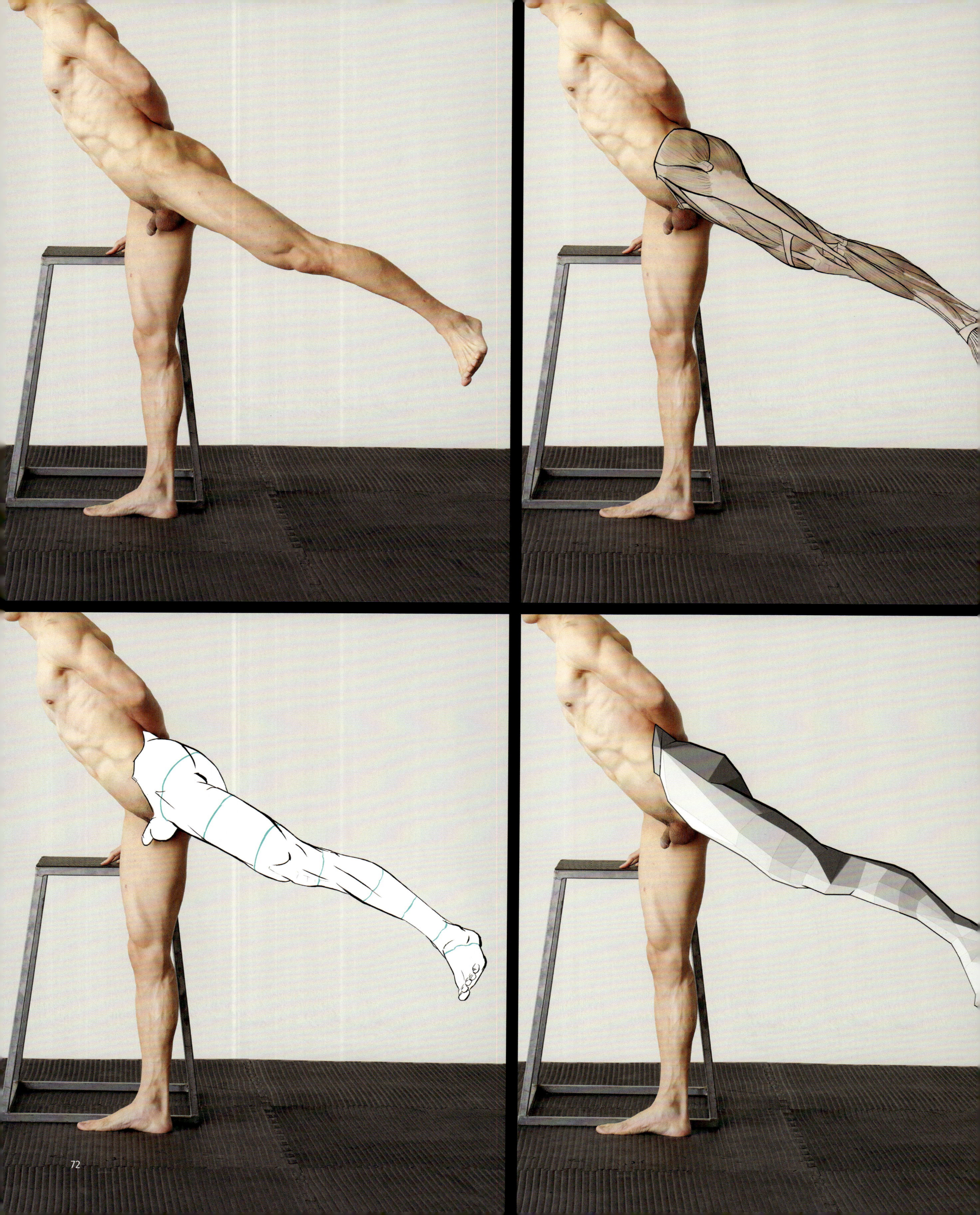

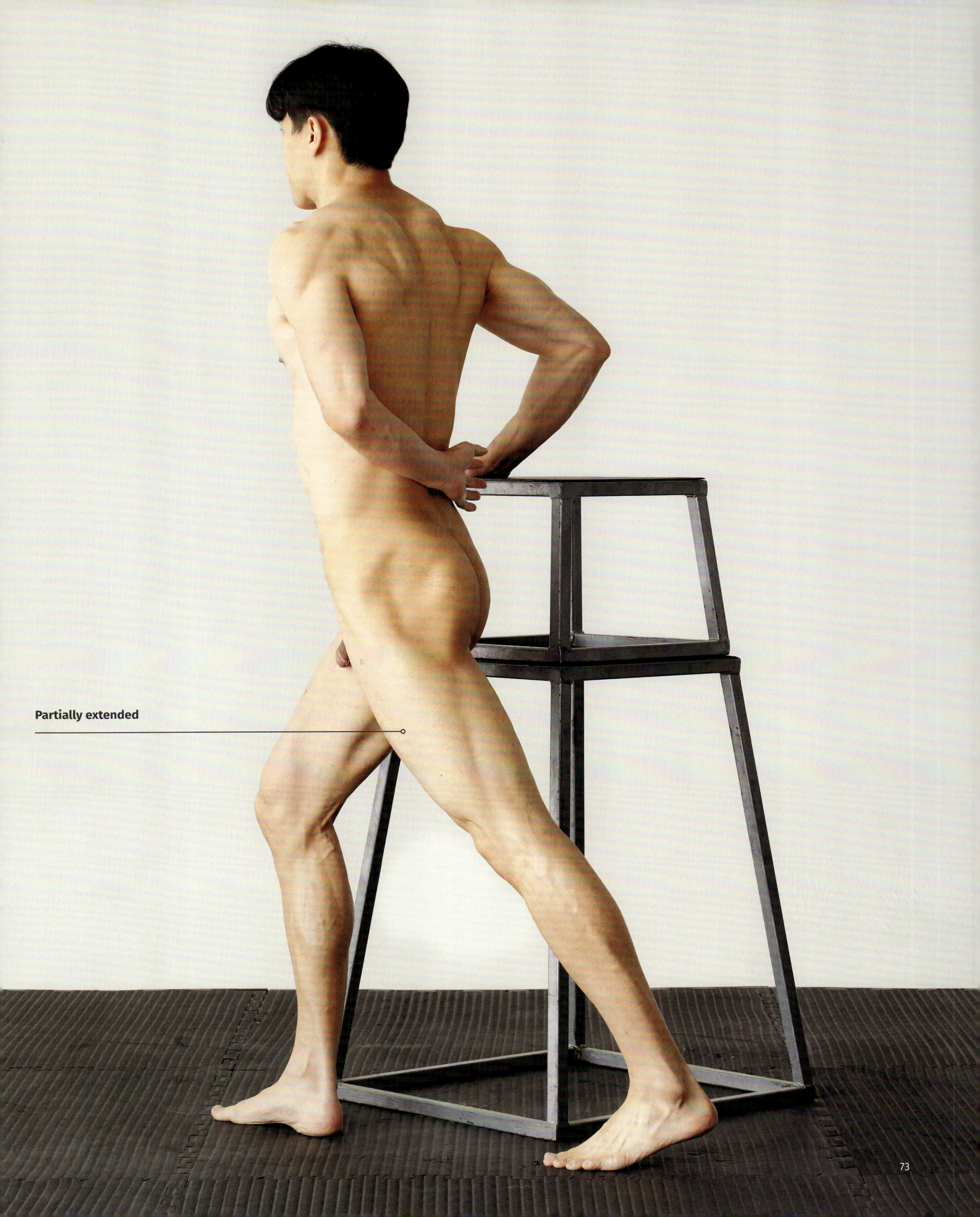
Partially extended

Torso flexion to extension

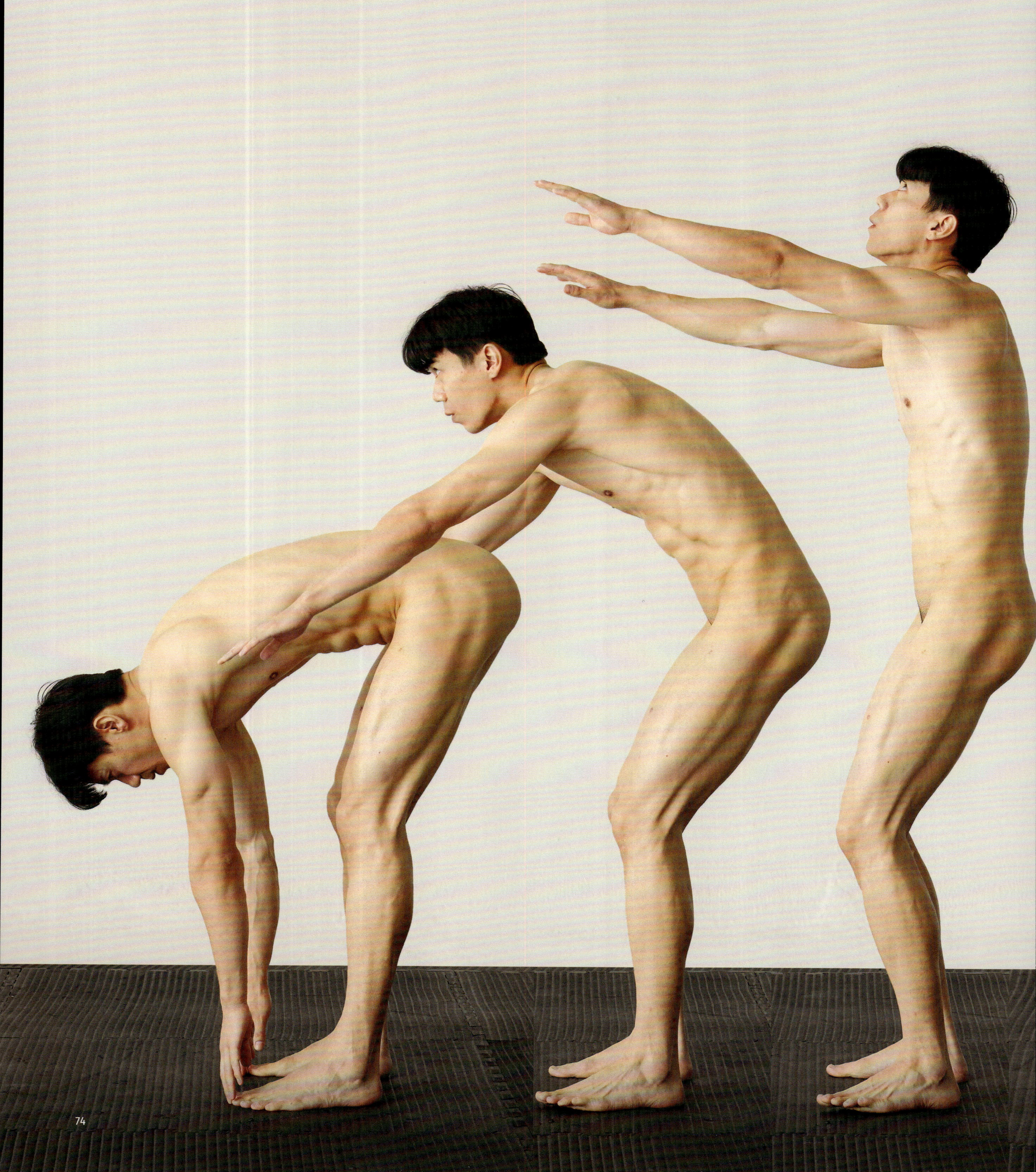

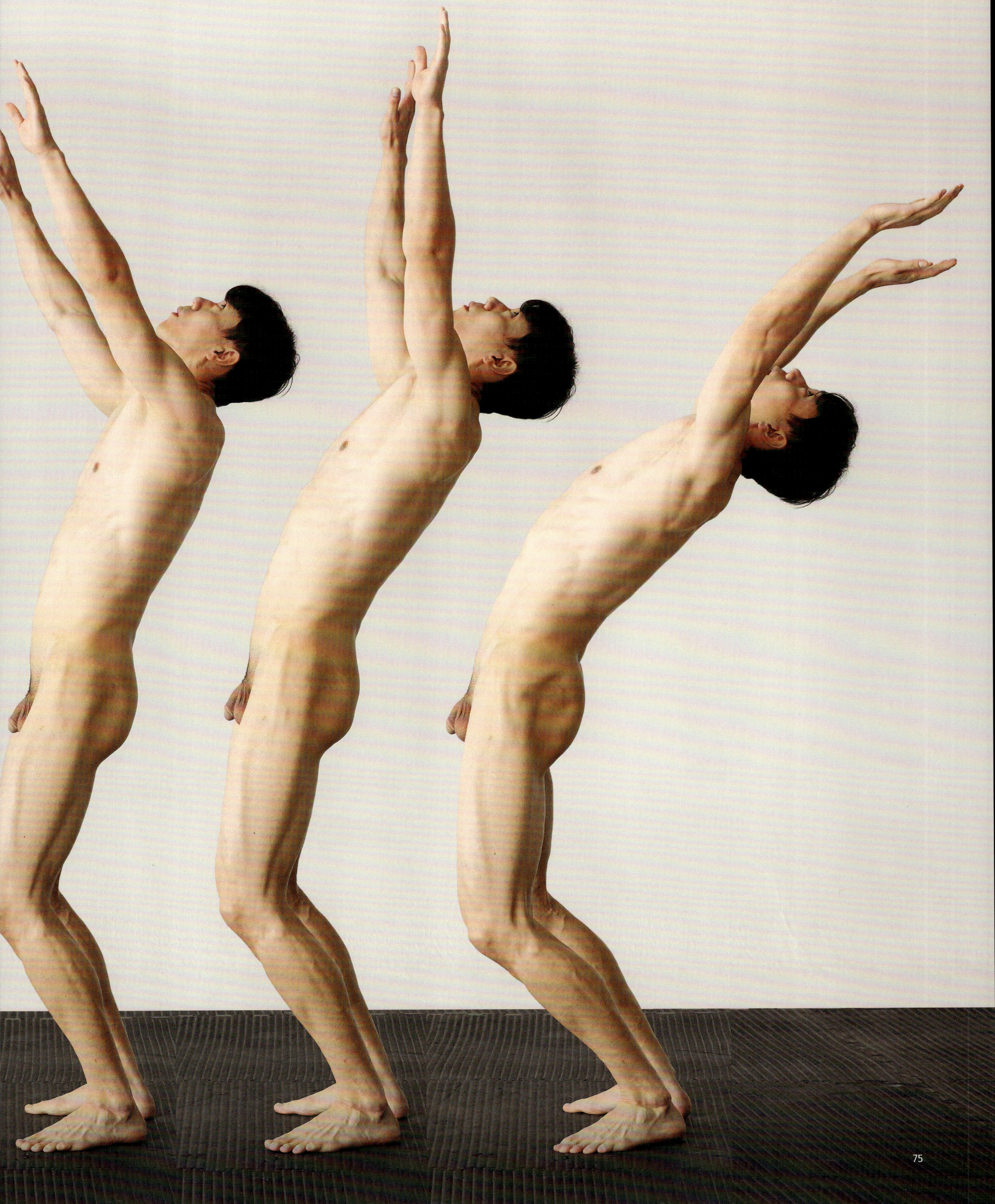

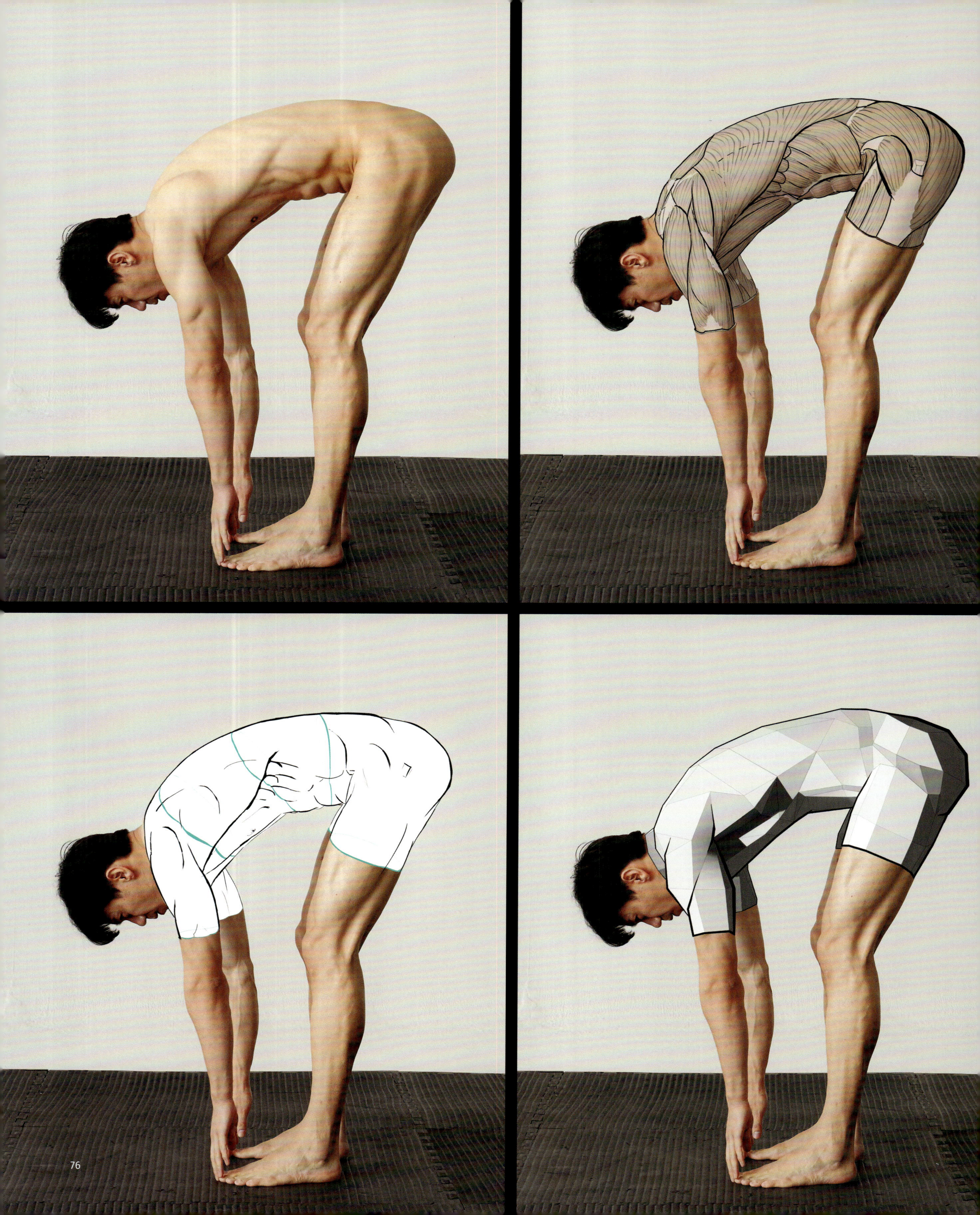

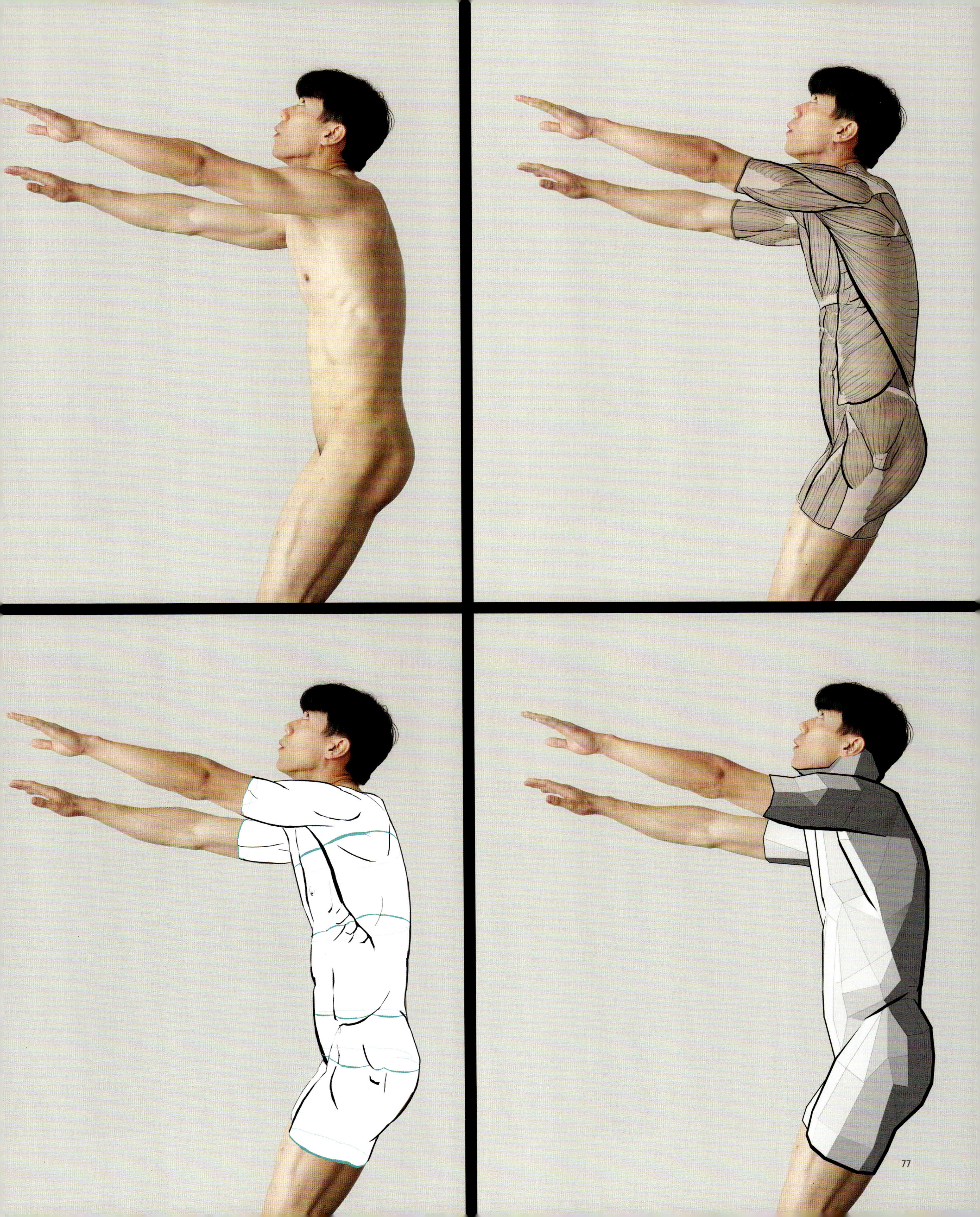

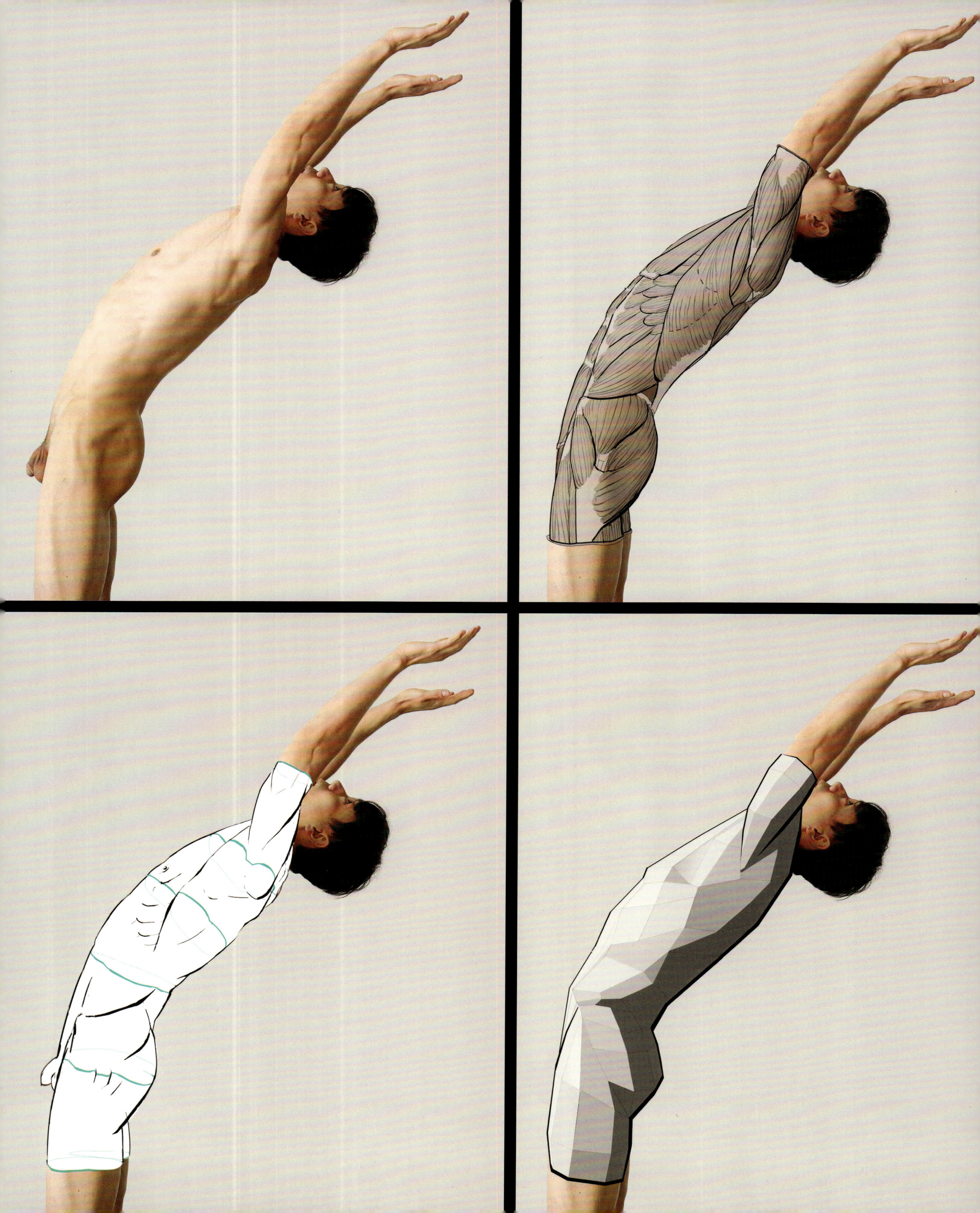

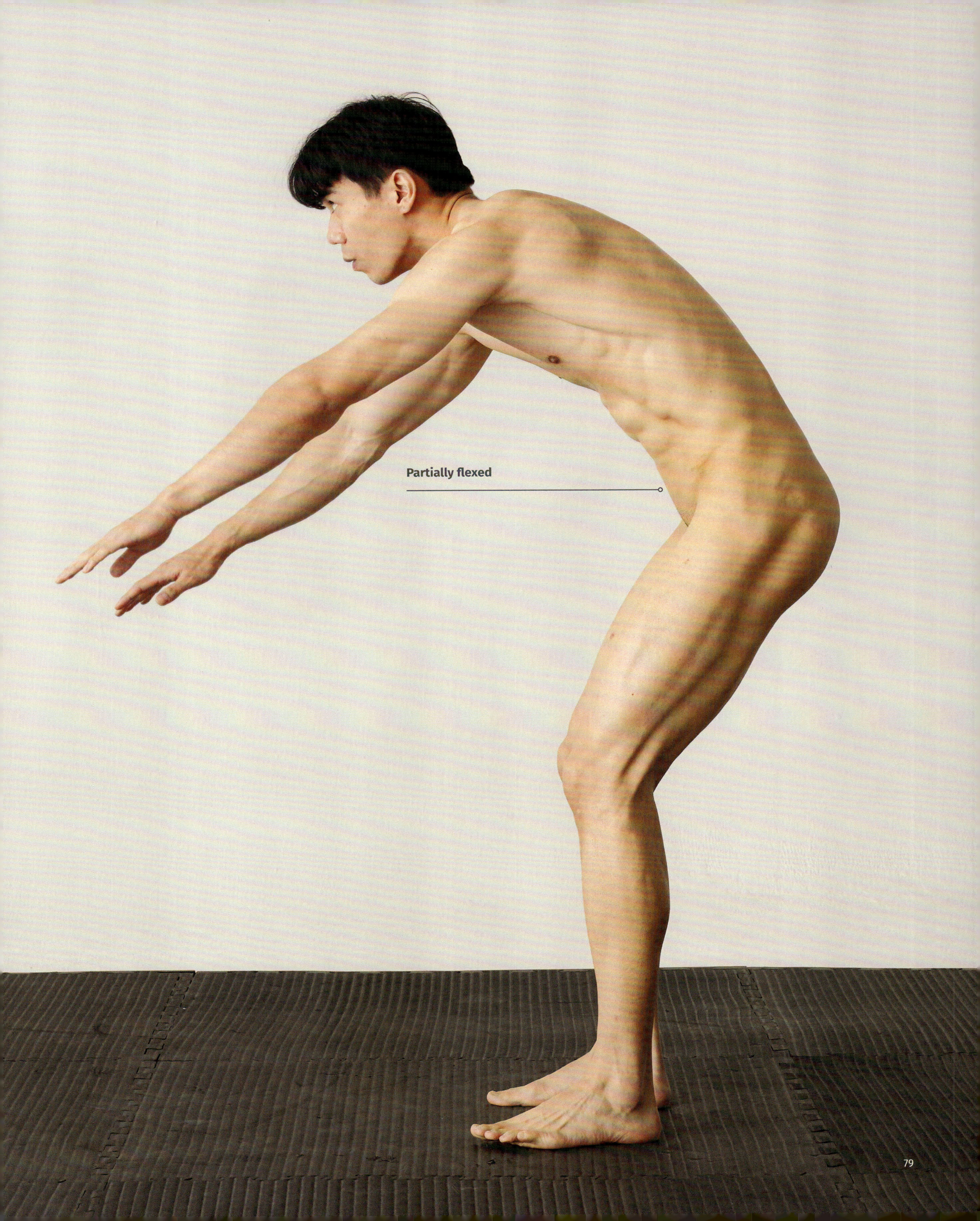
Partially flexed

Neck flexion to extension

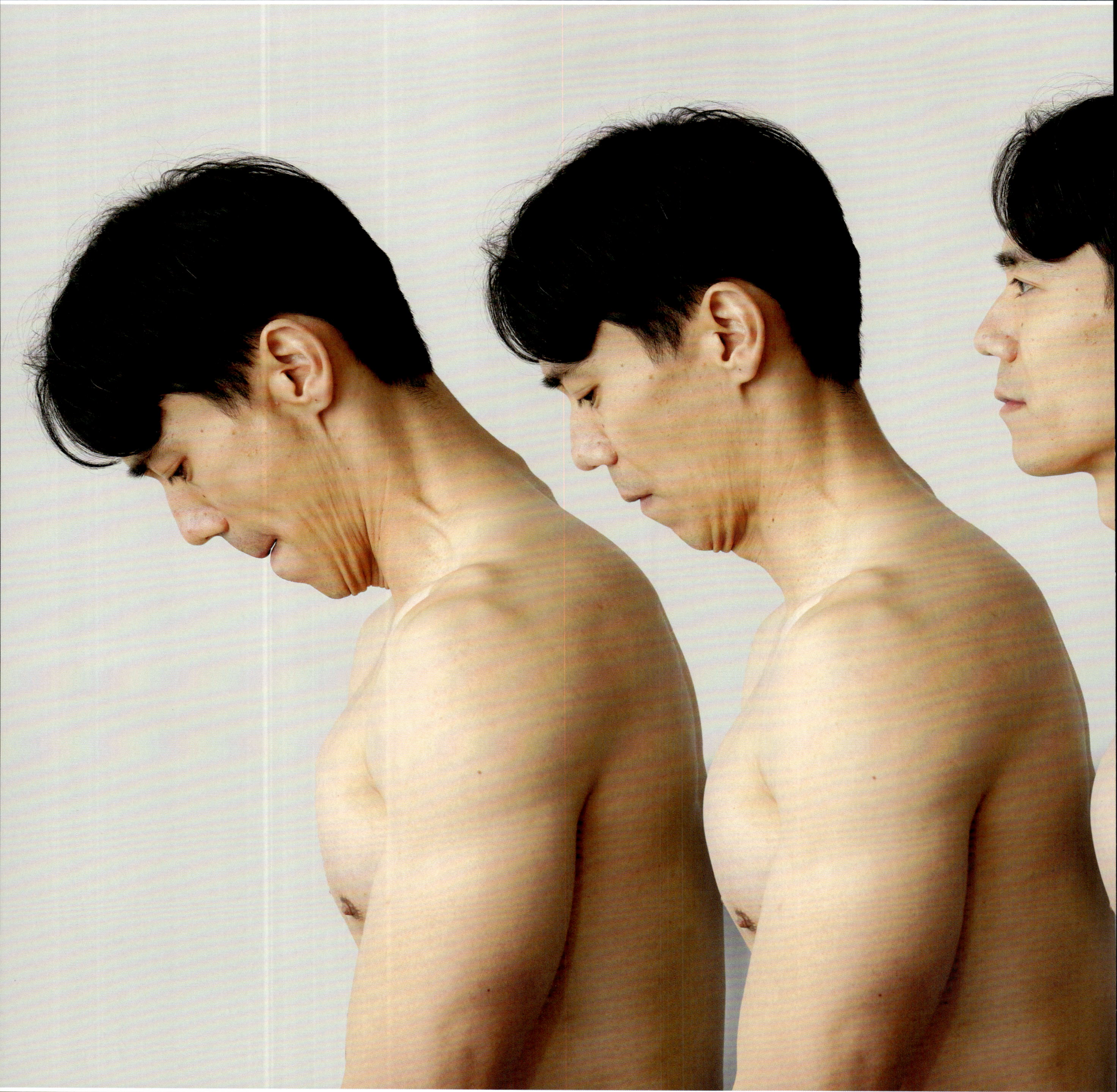

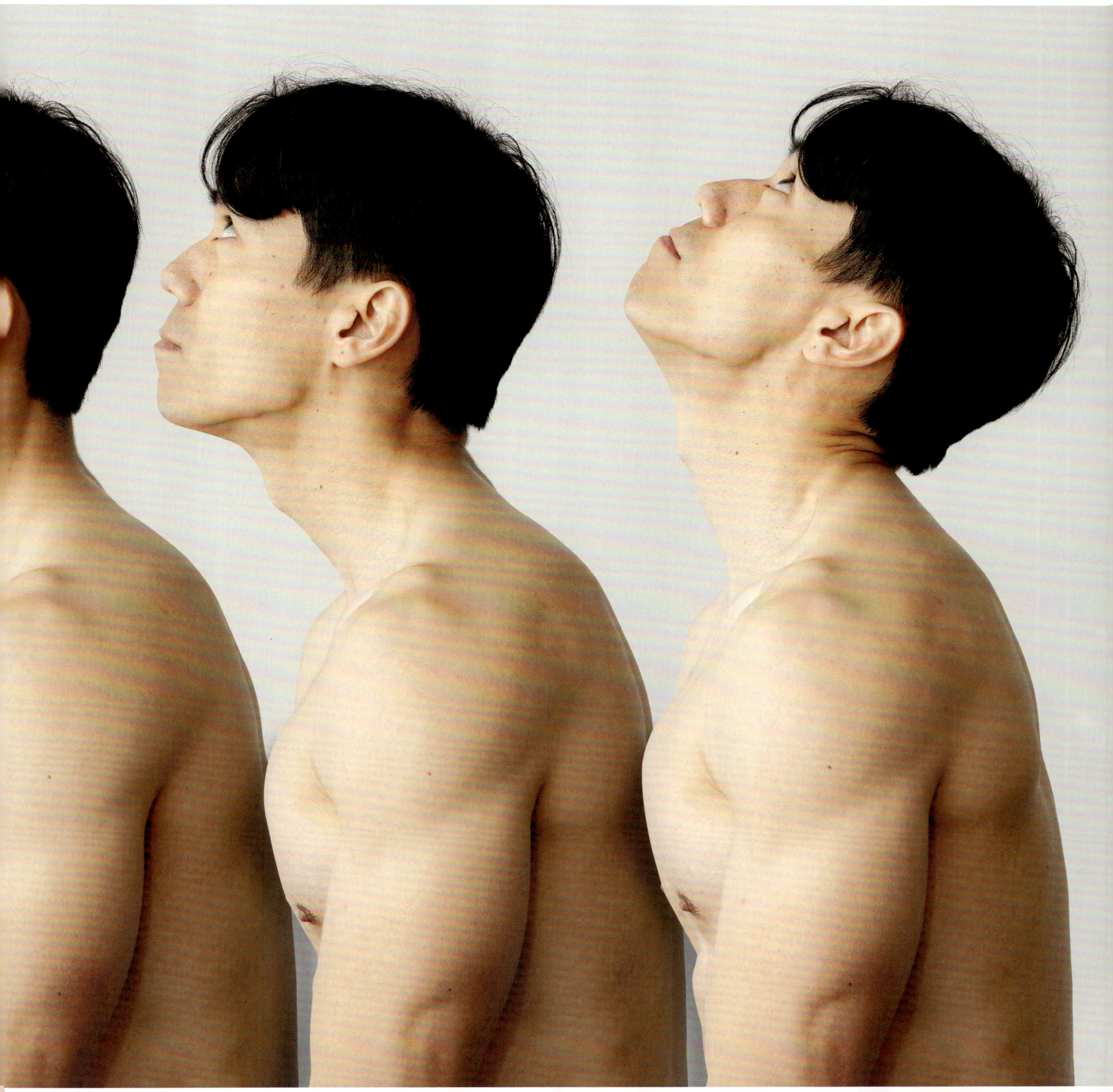

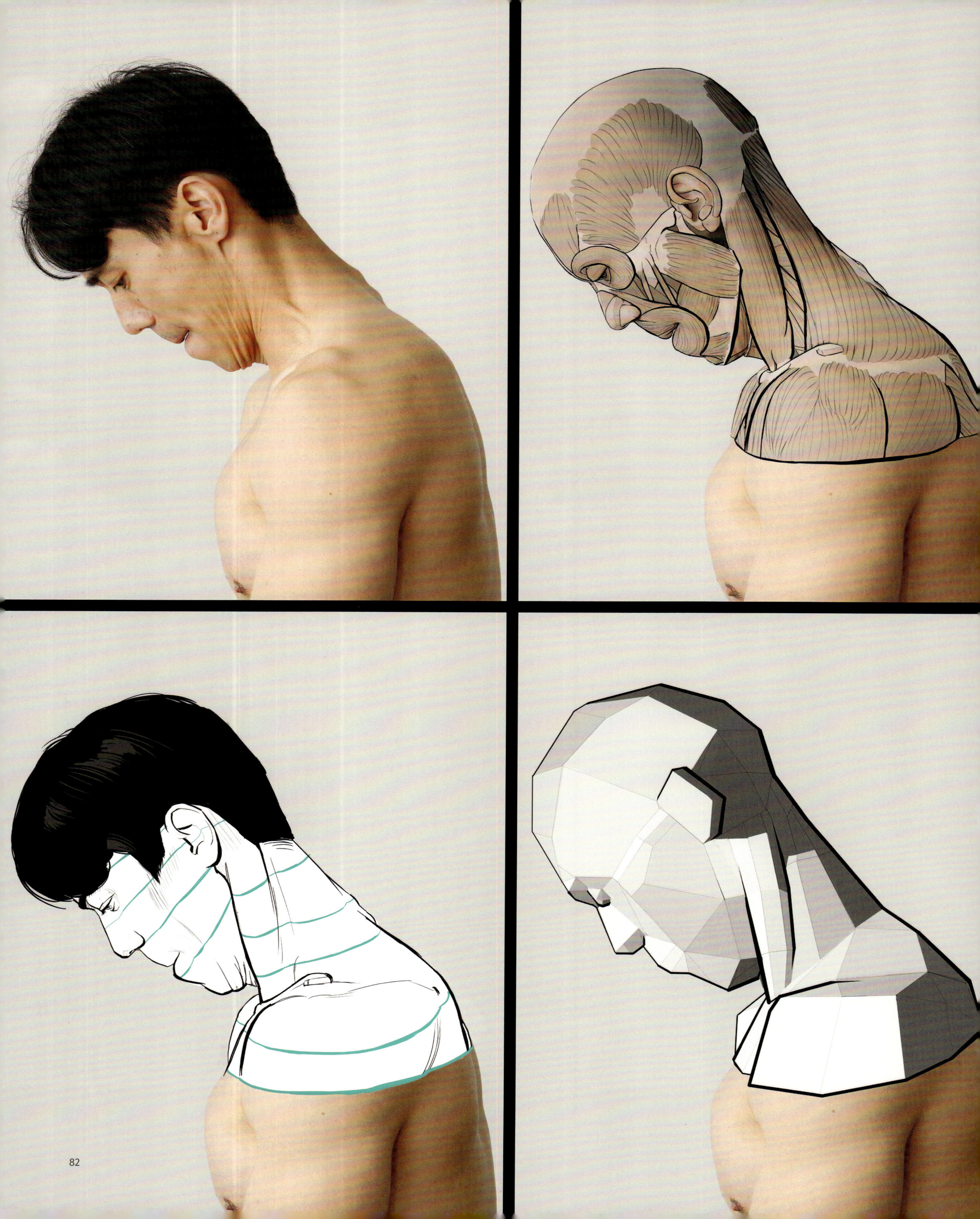

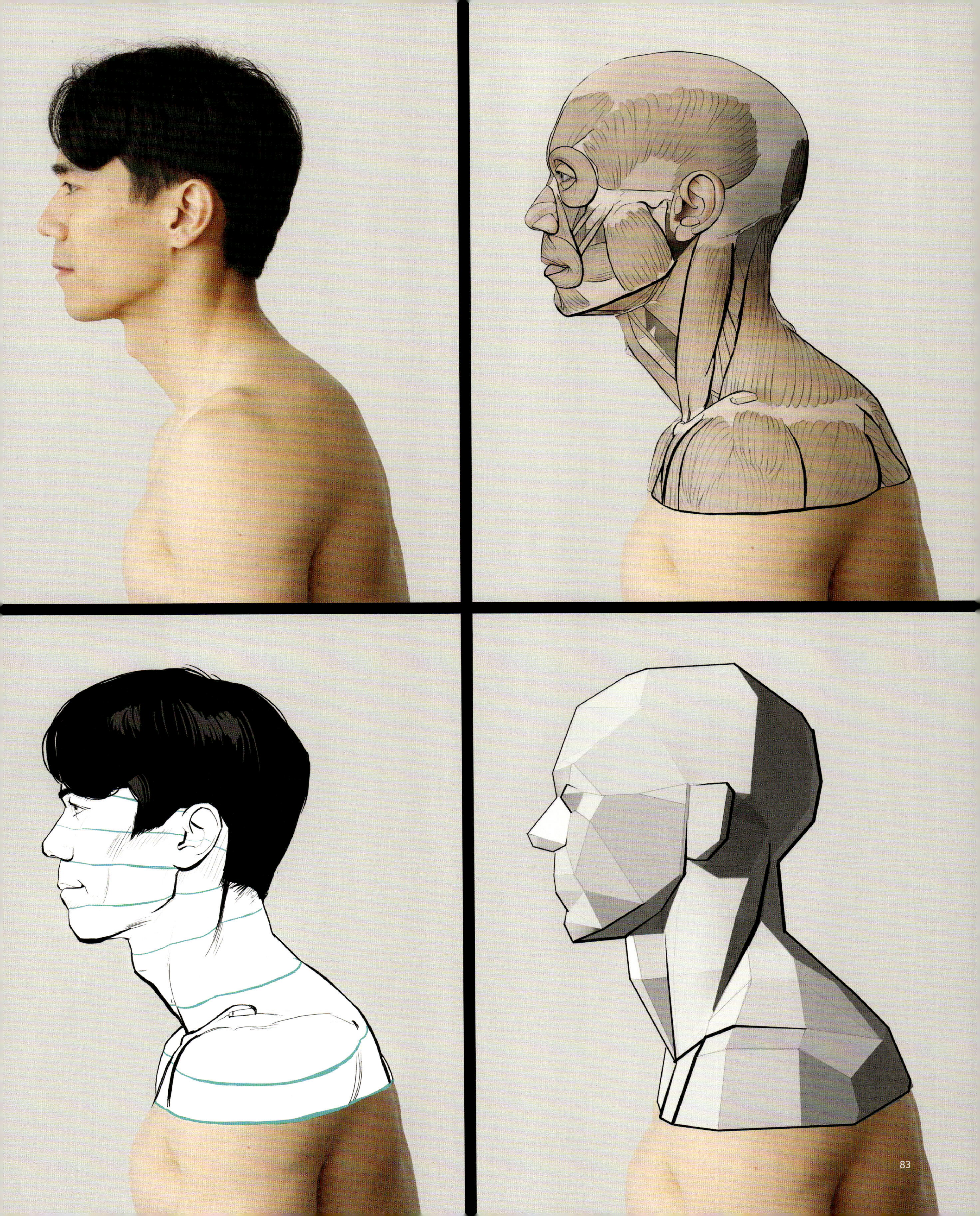

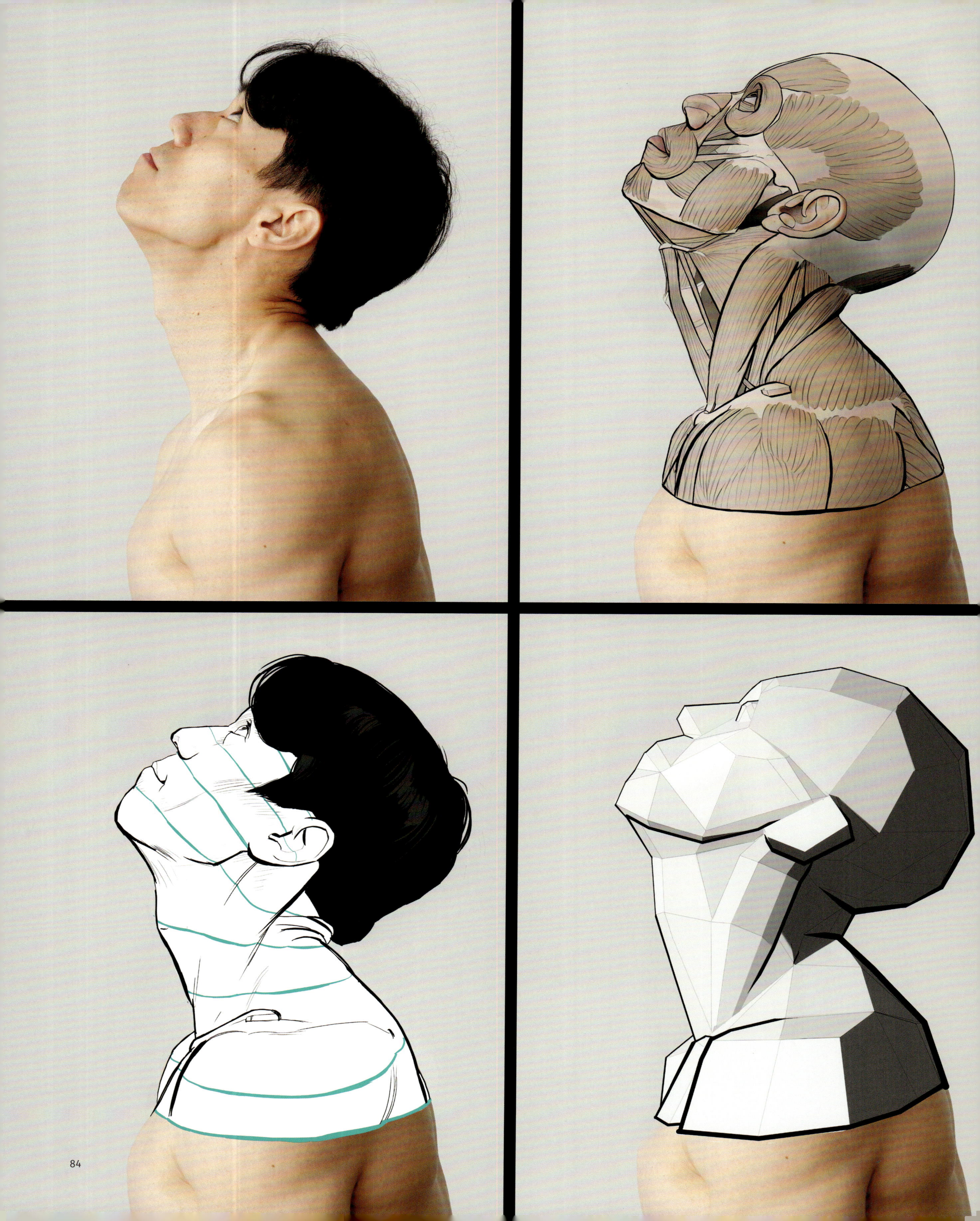

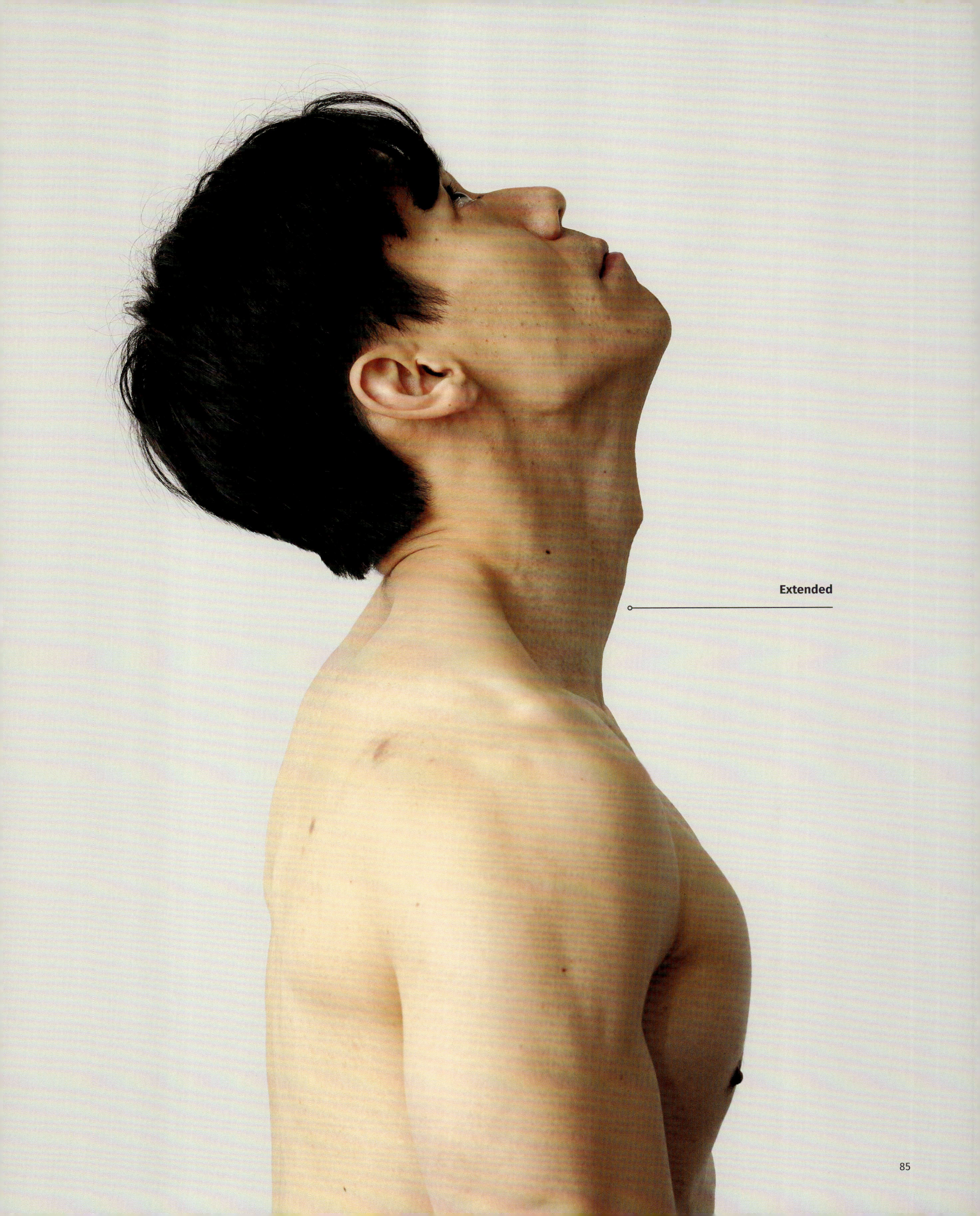
Extended

Arm abduction to adduction

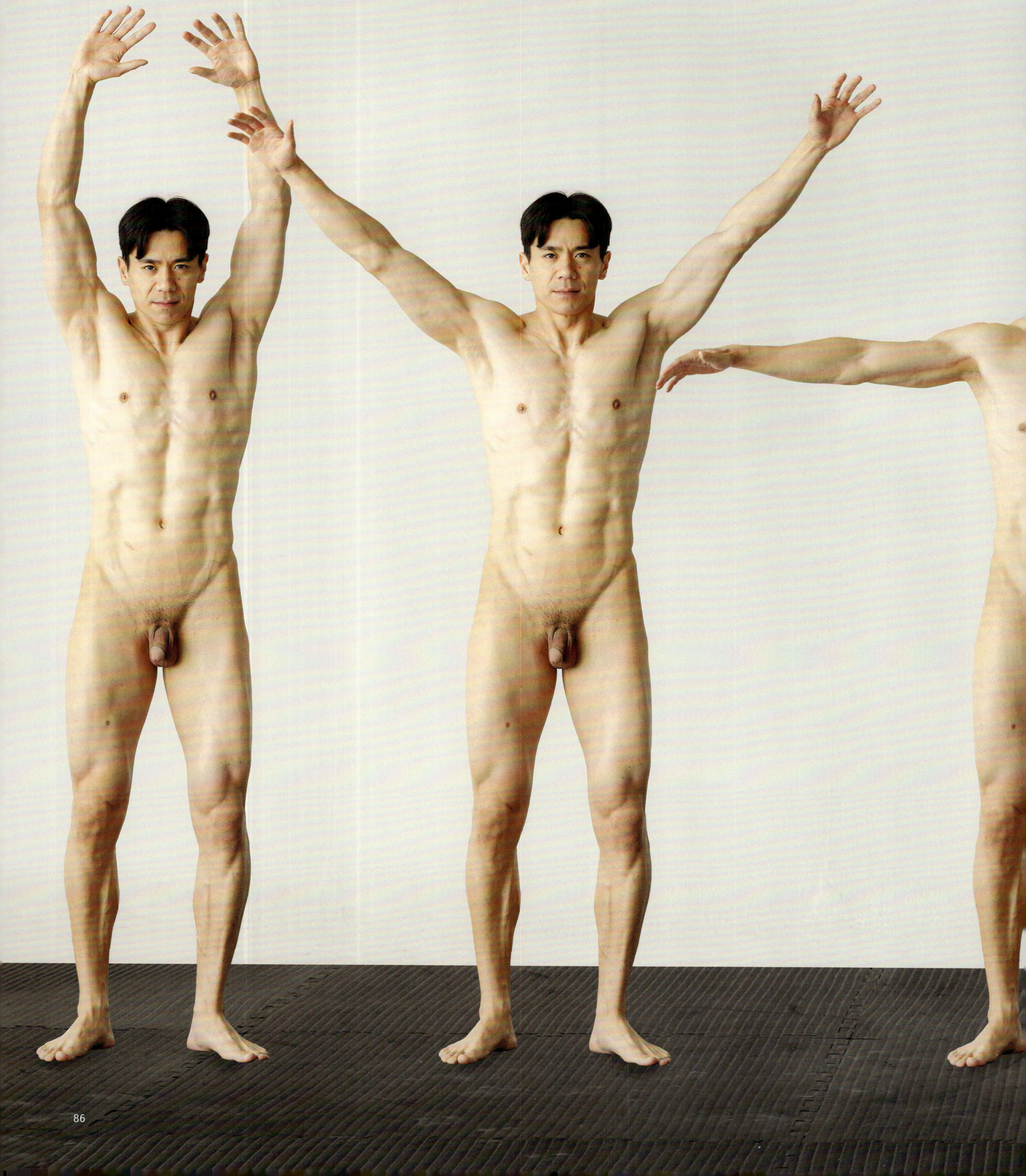

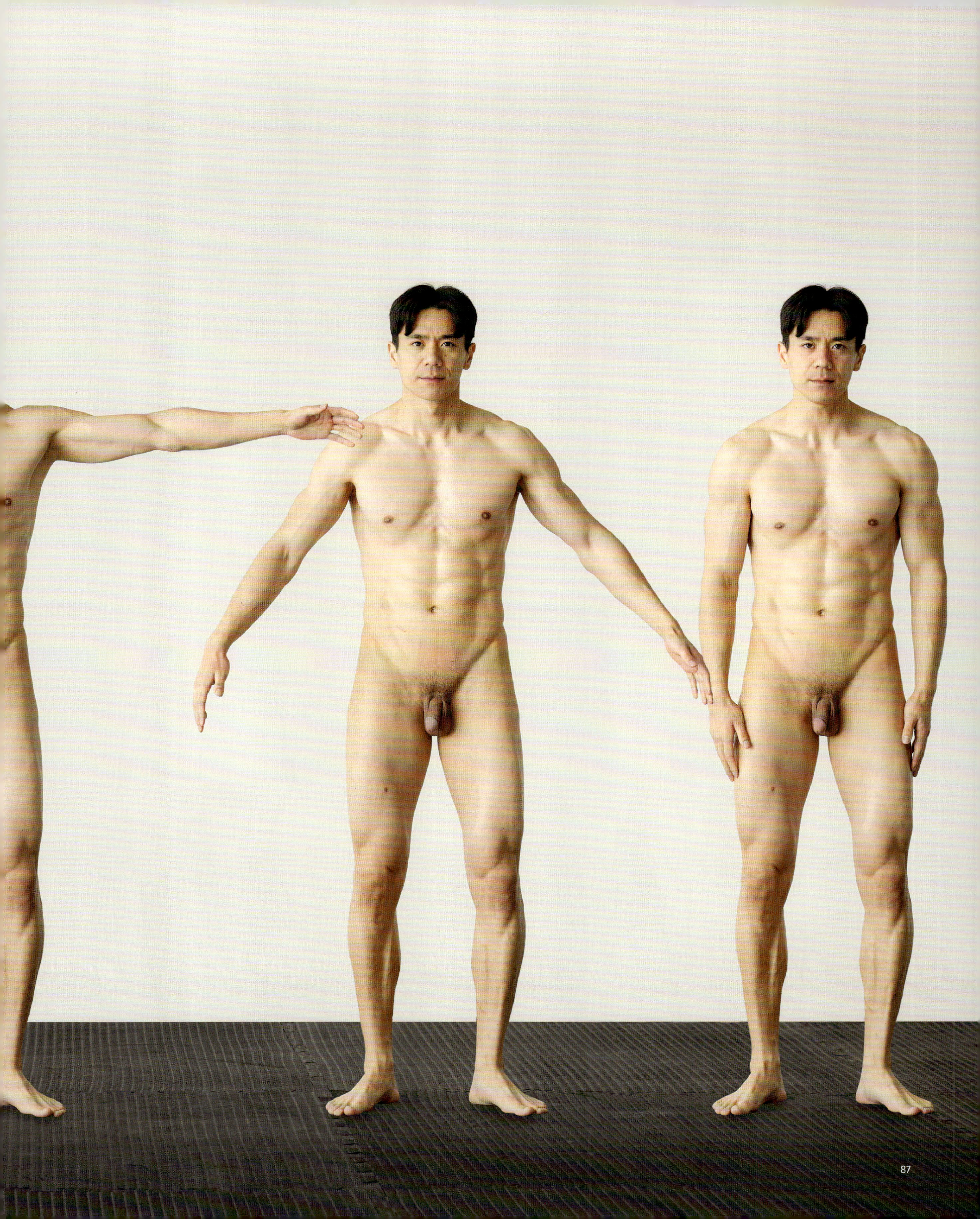

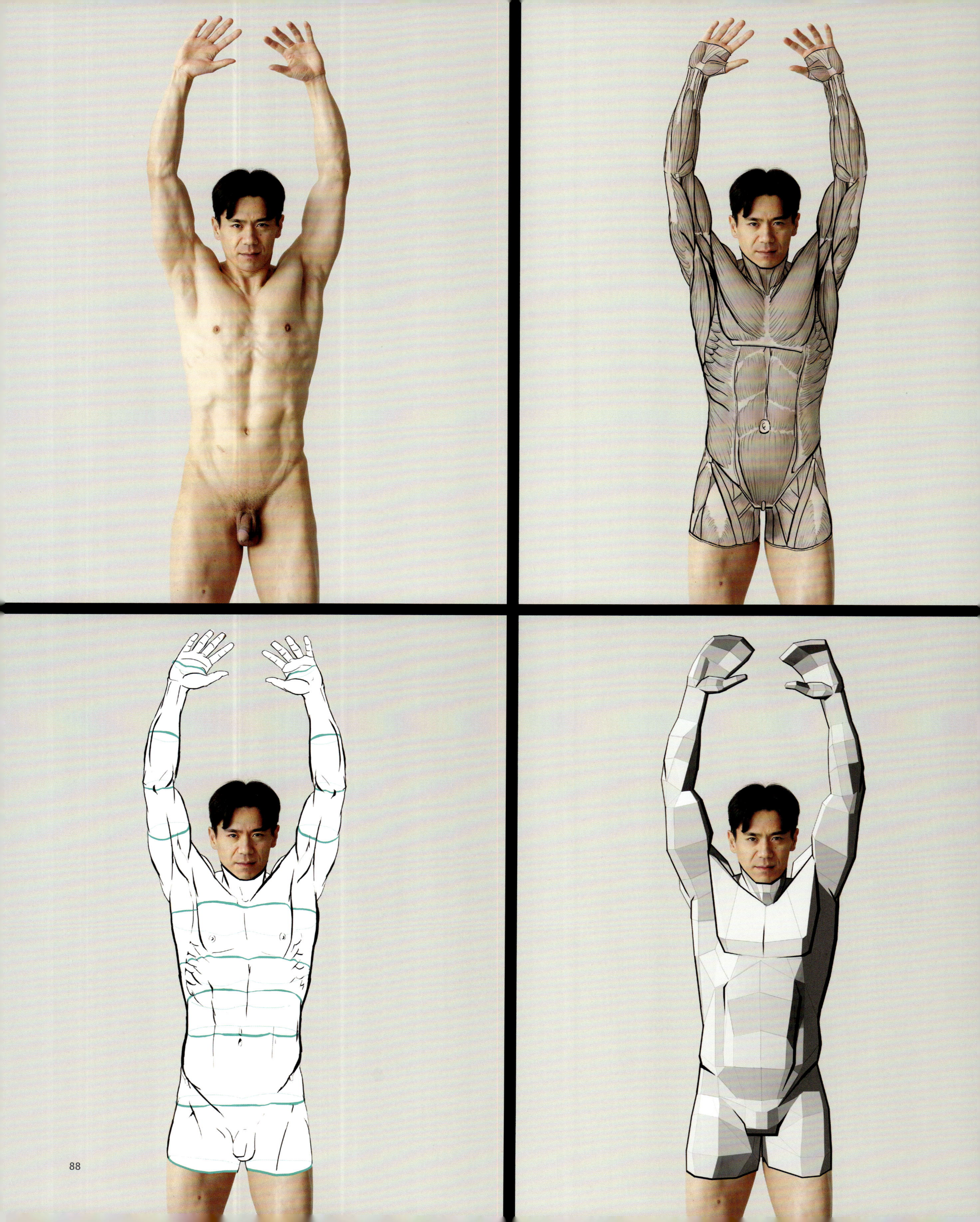

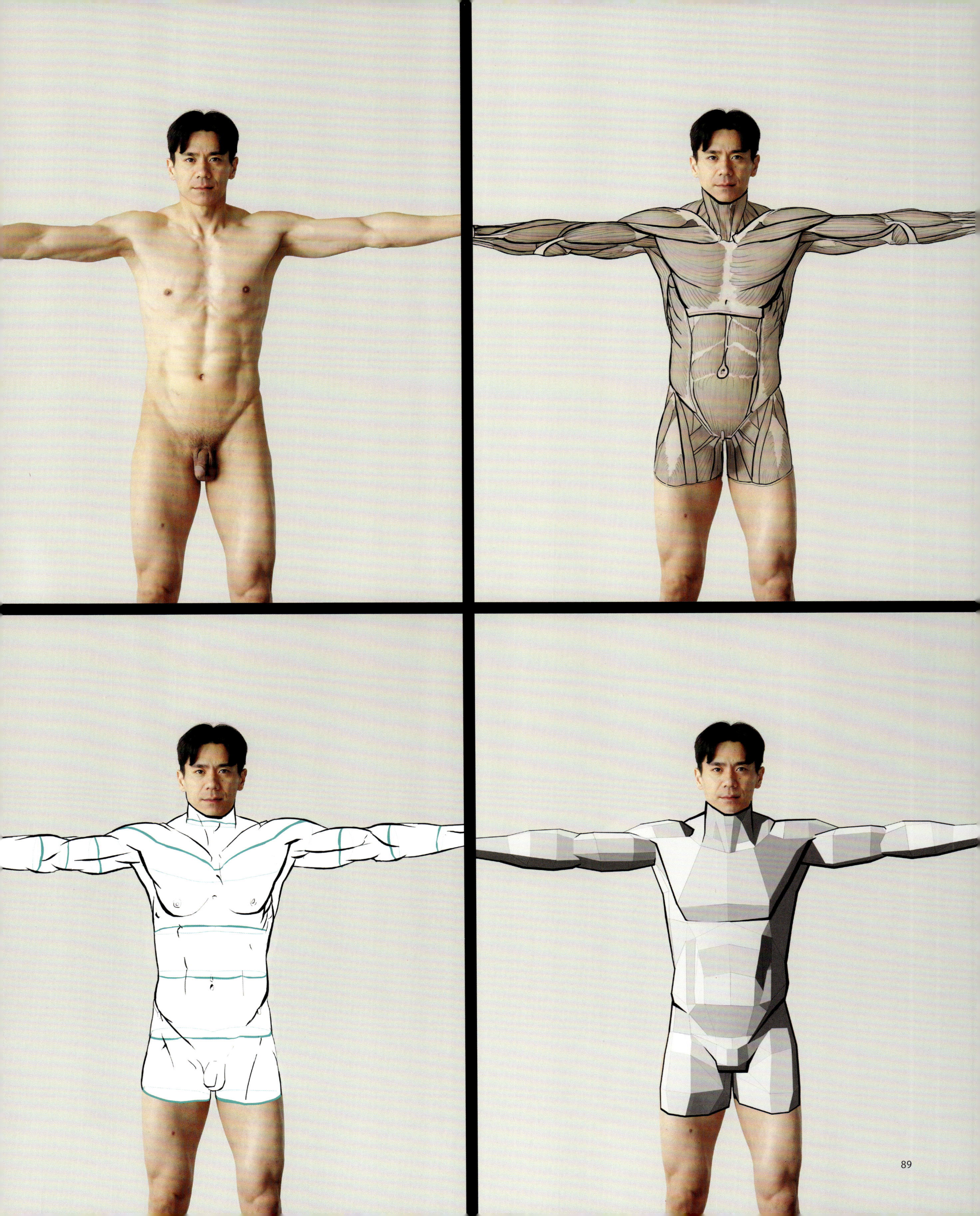

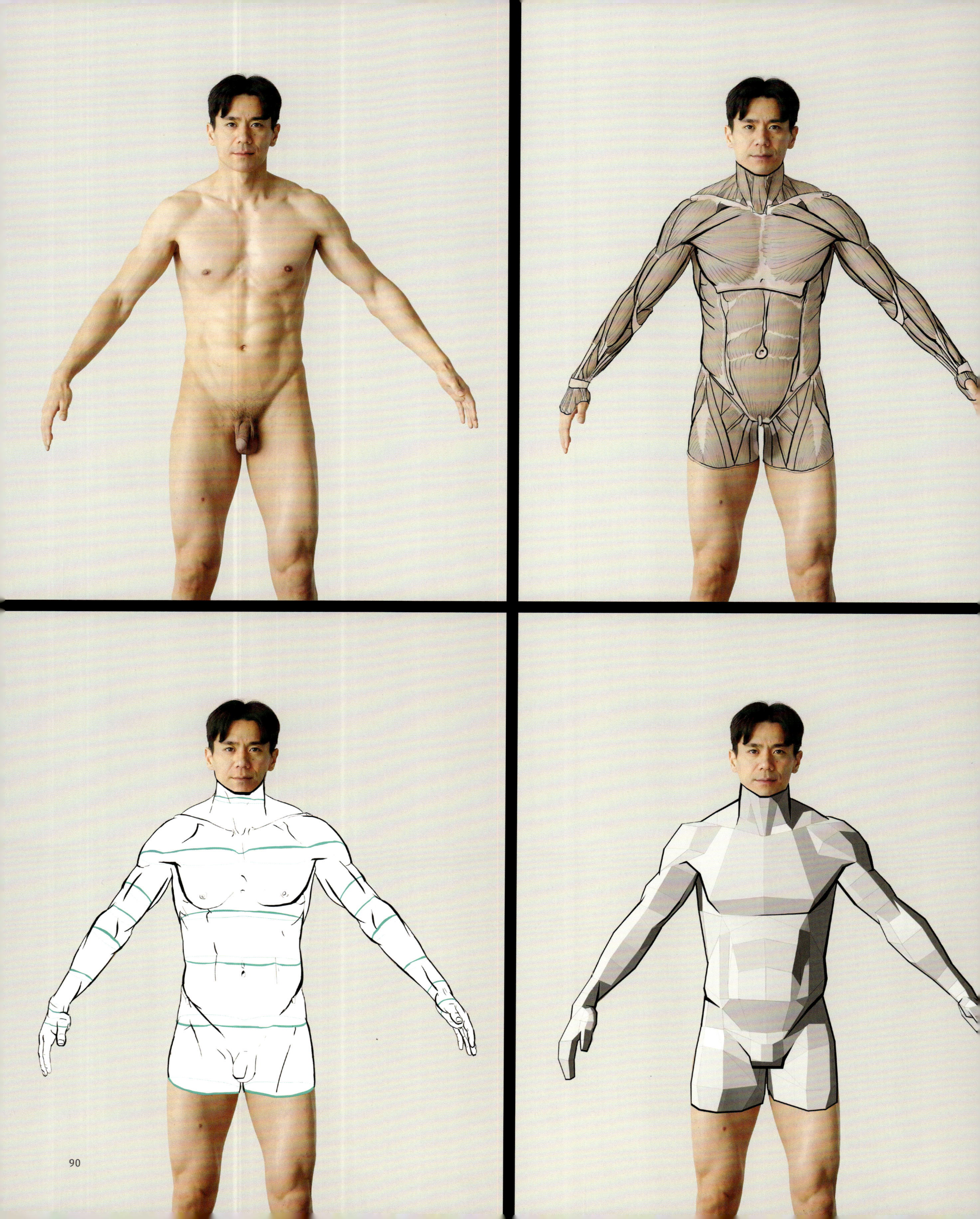

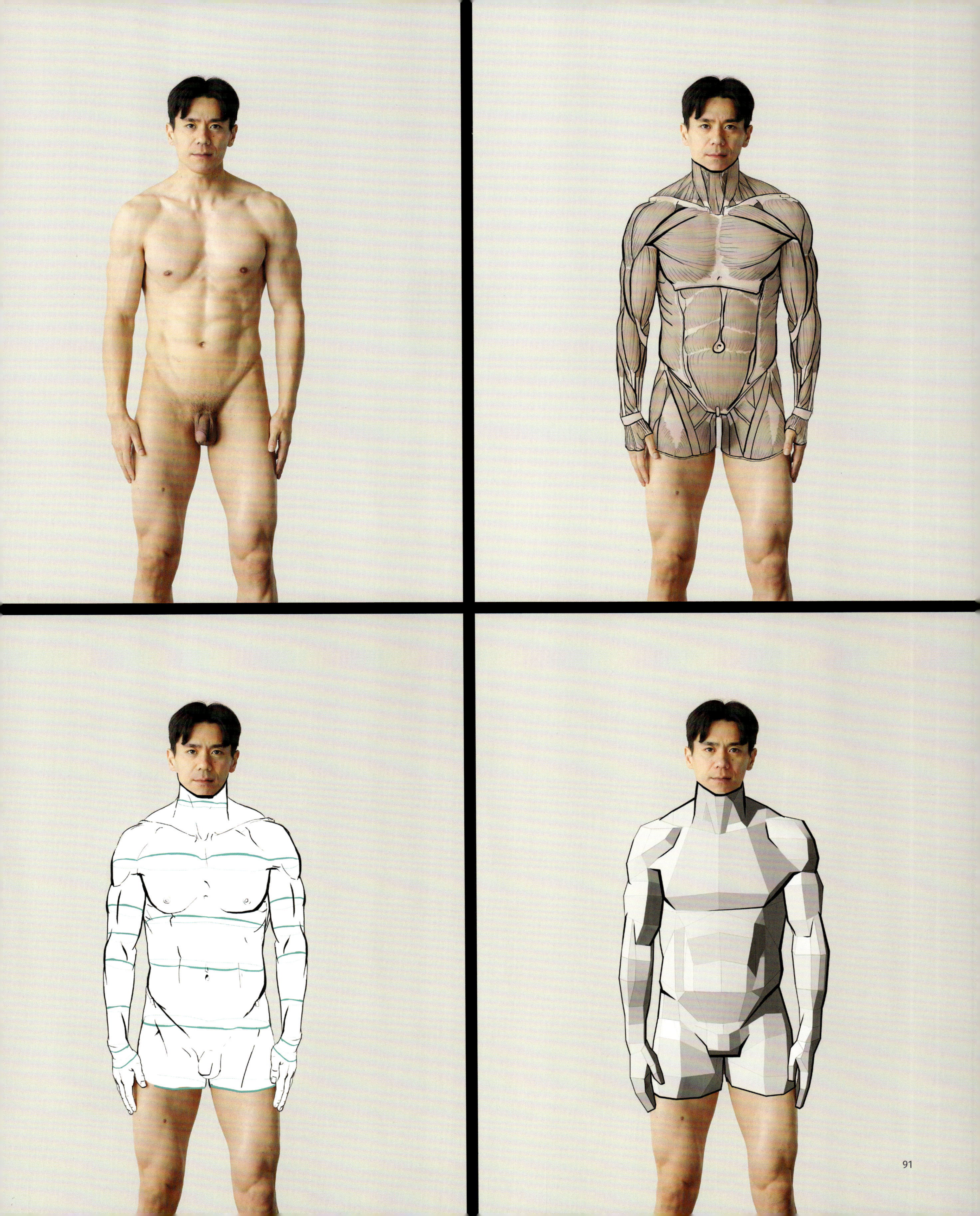

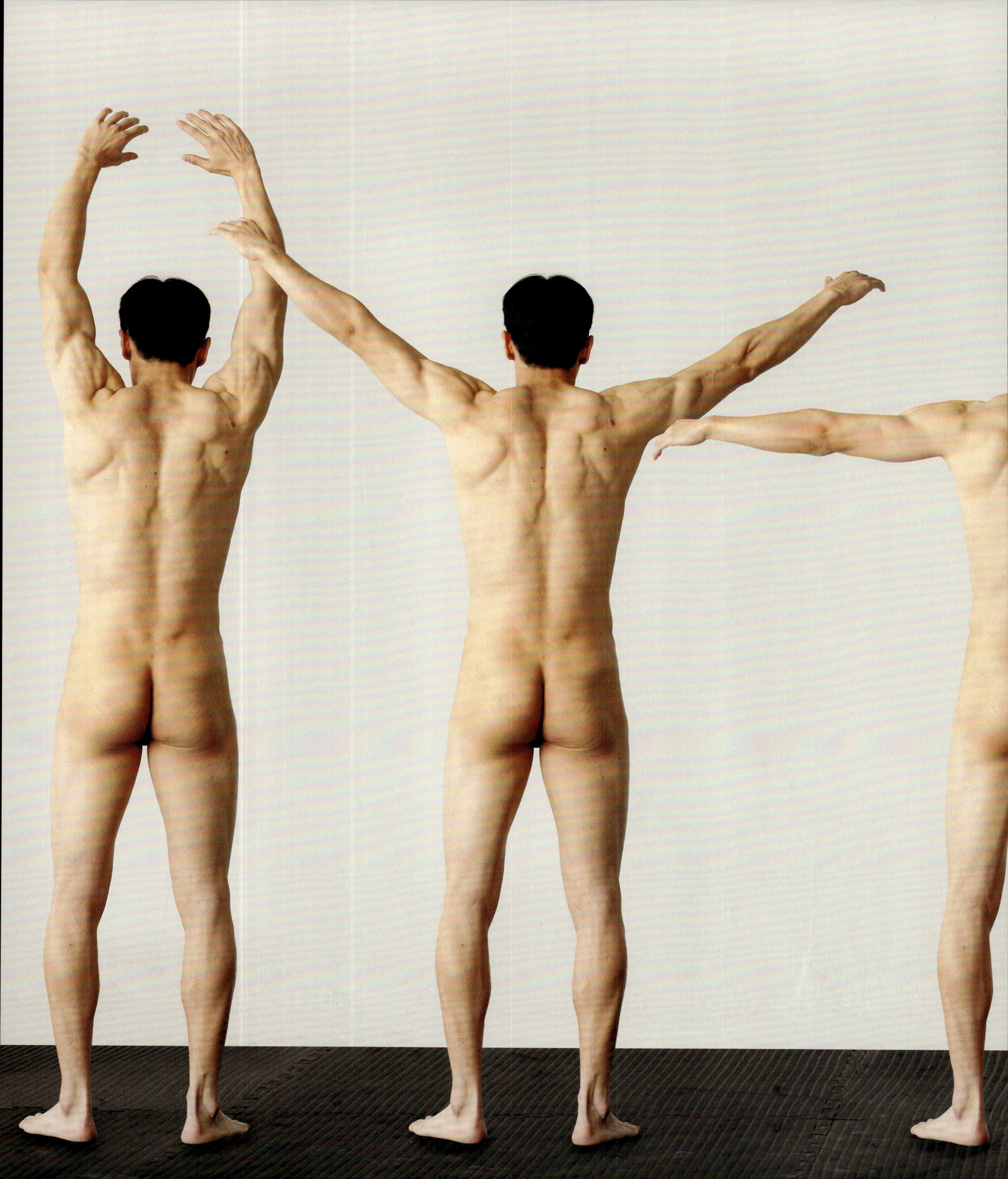

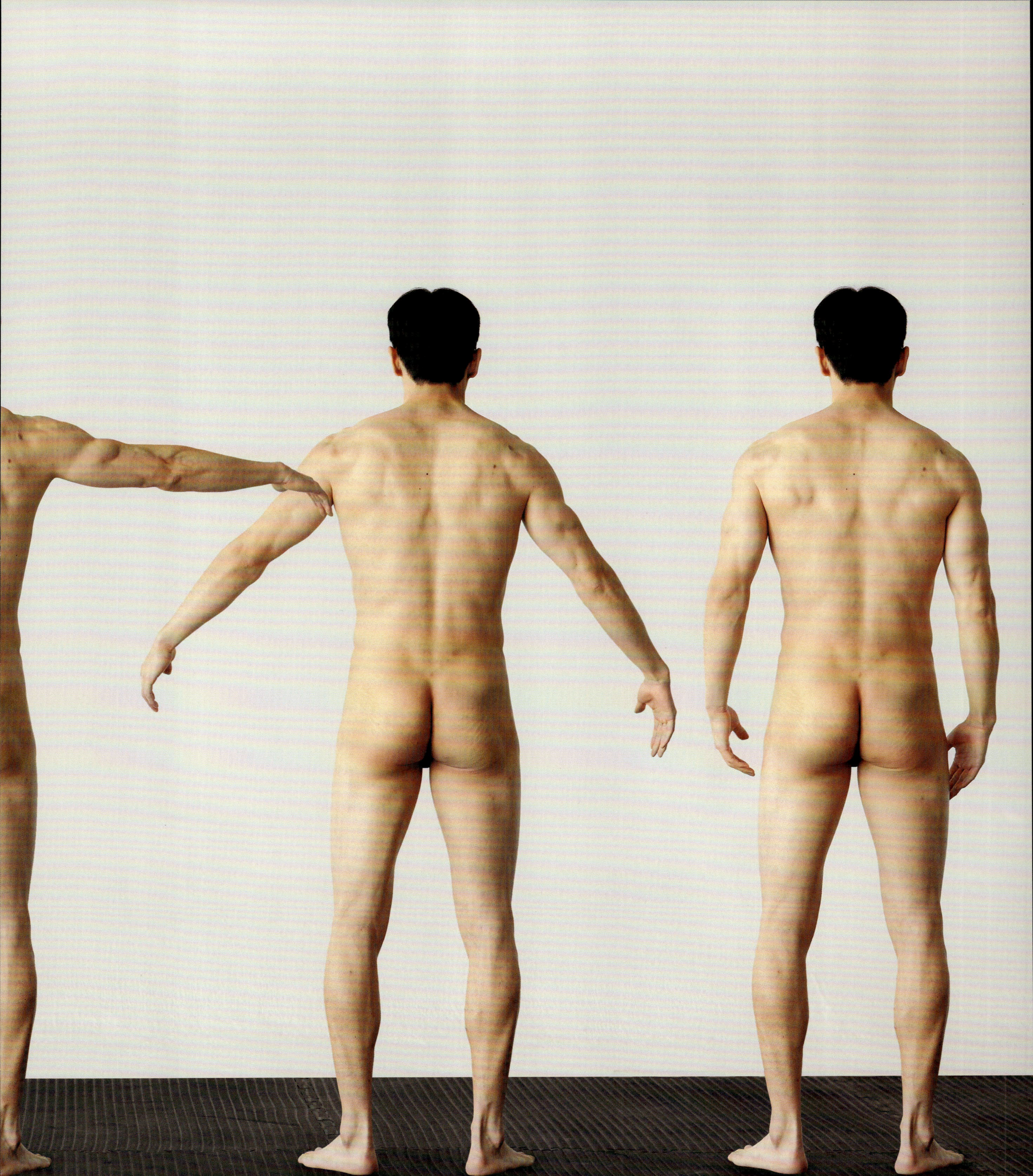

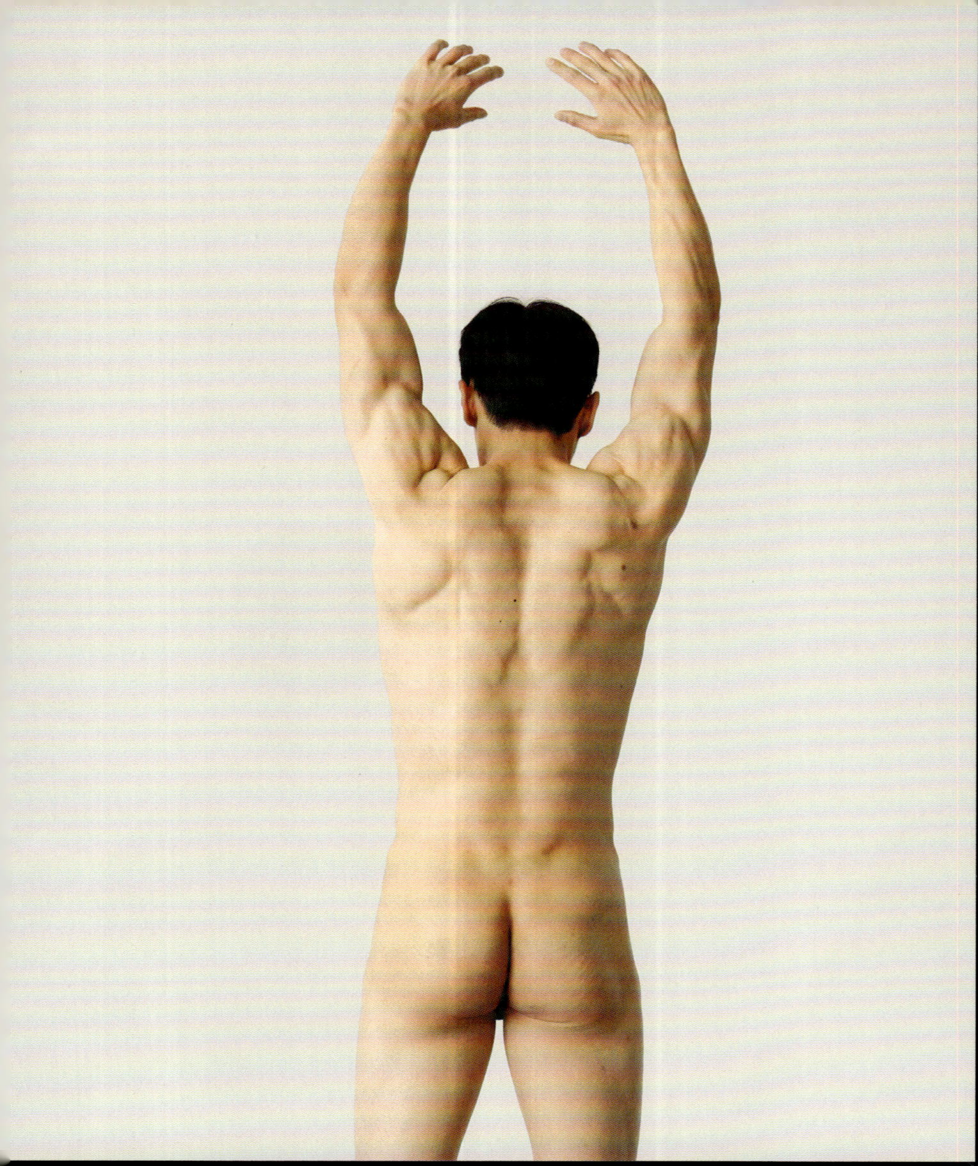

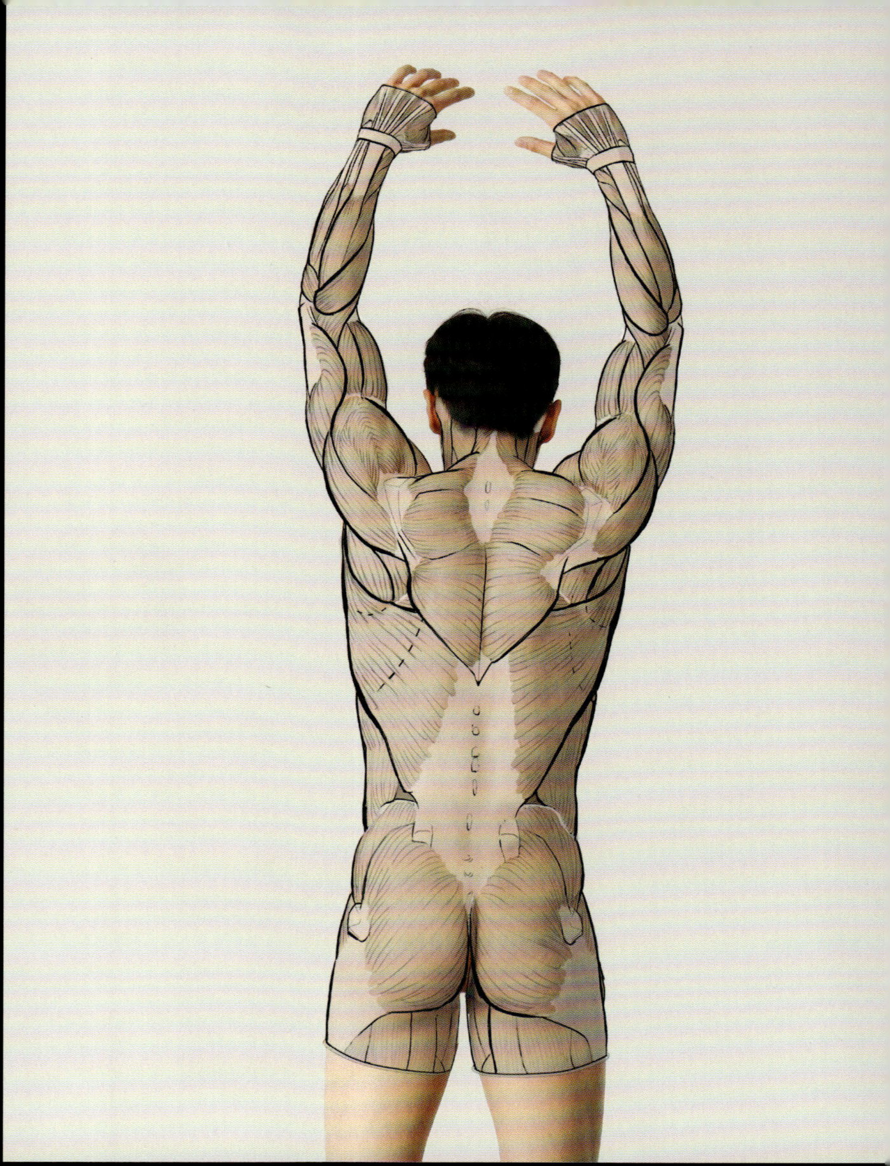

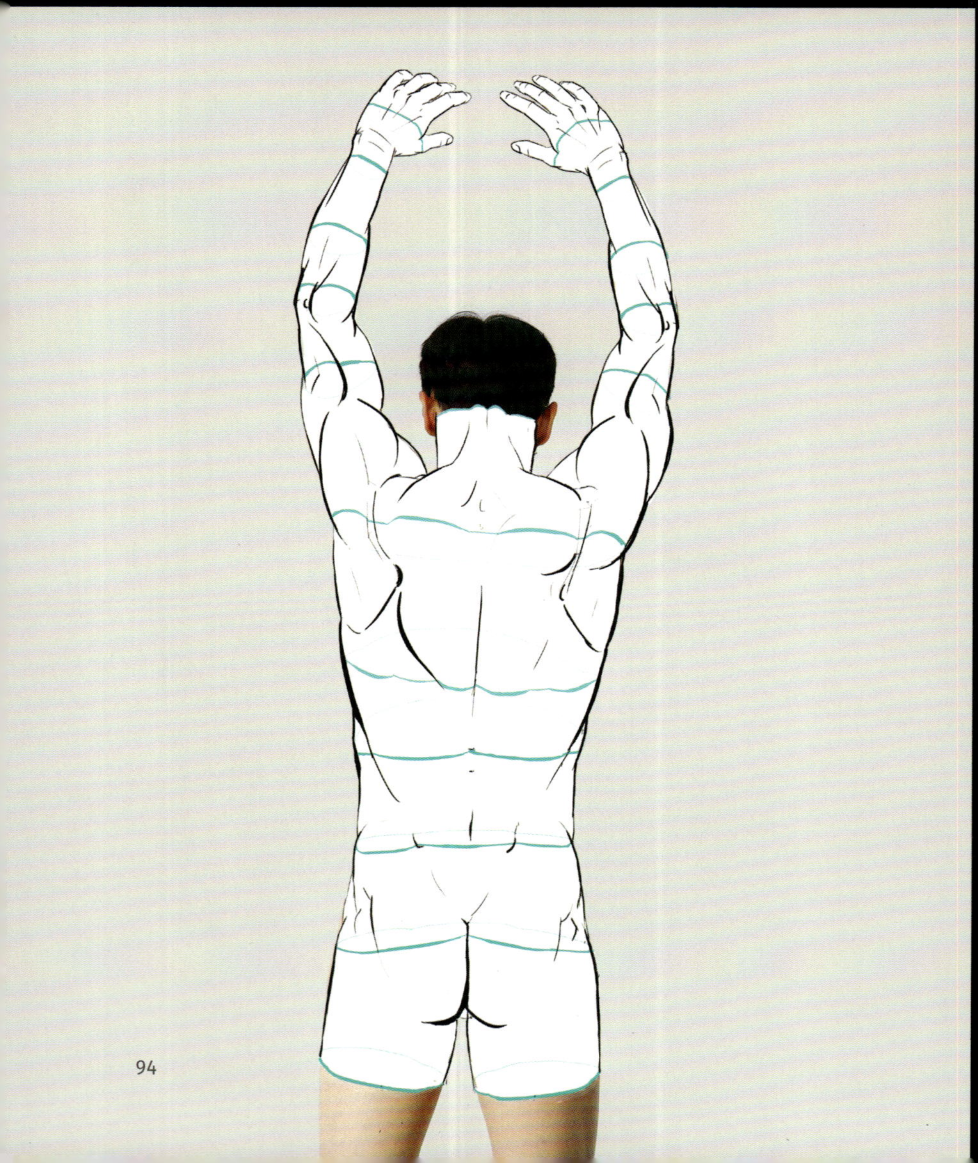

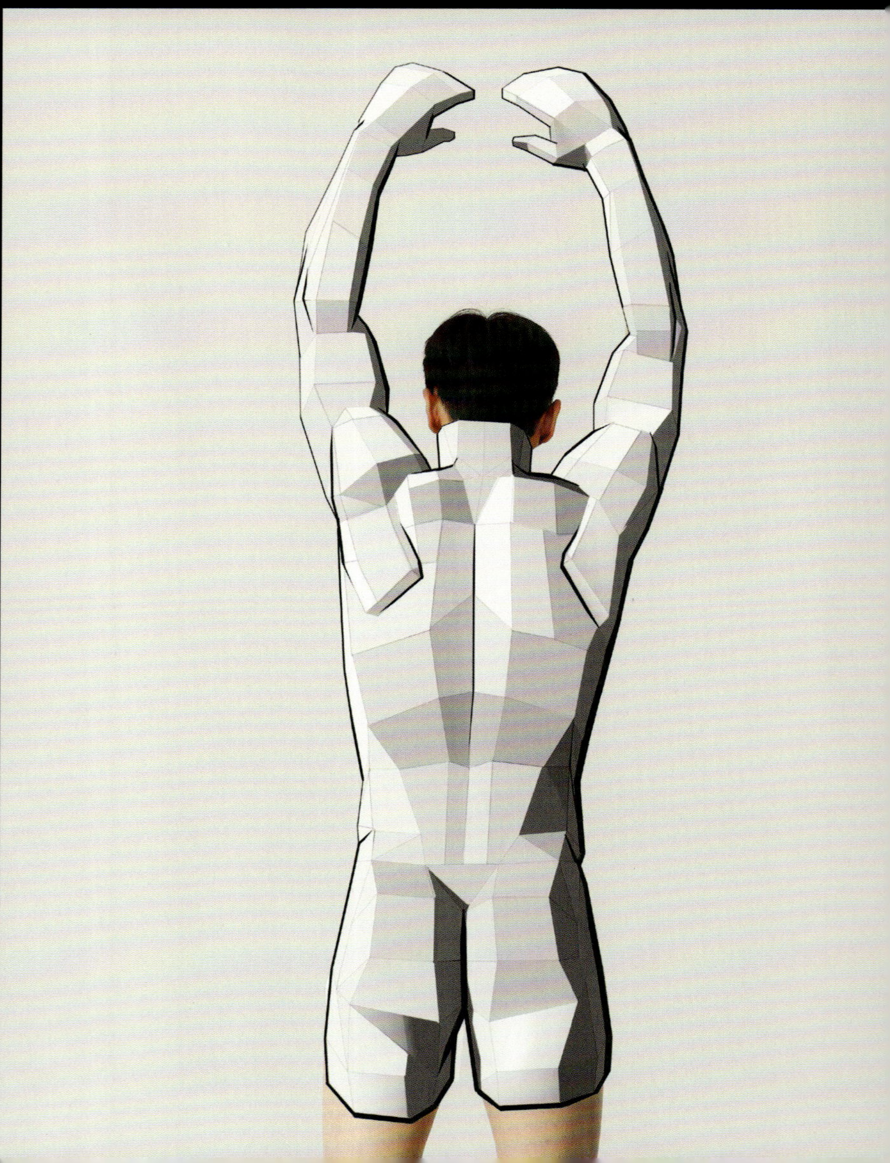

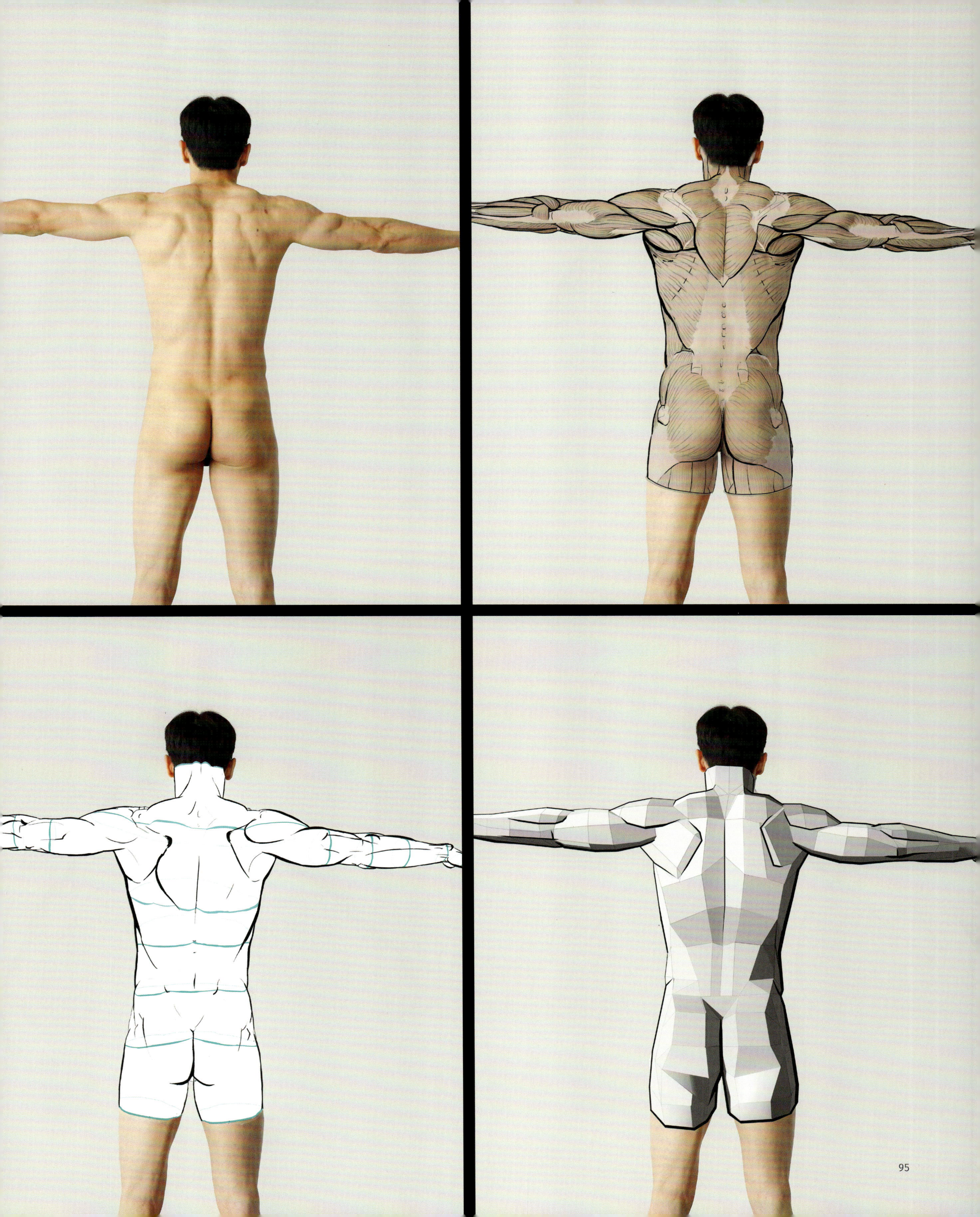

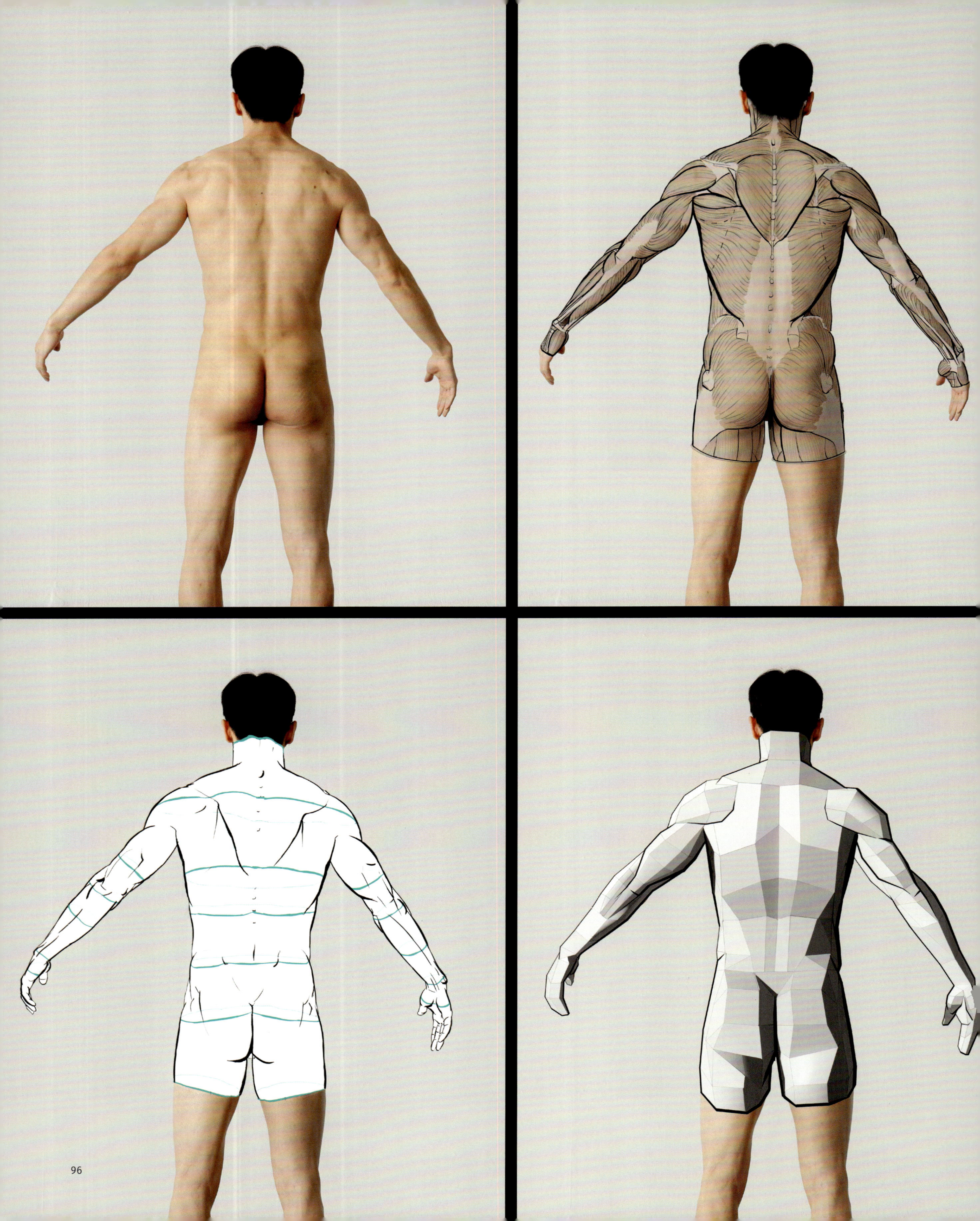

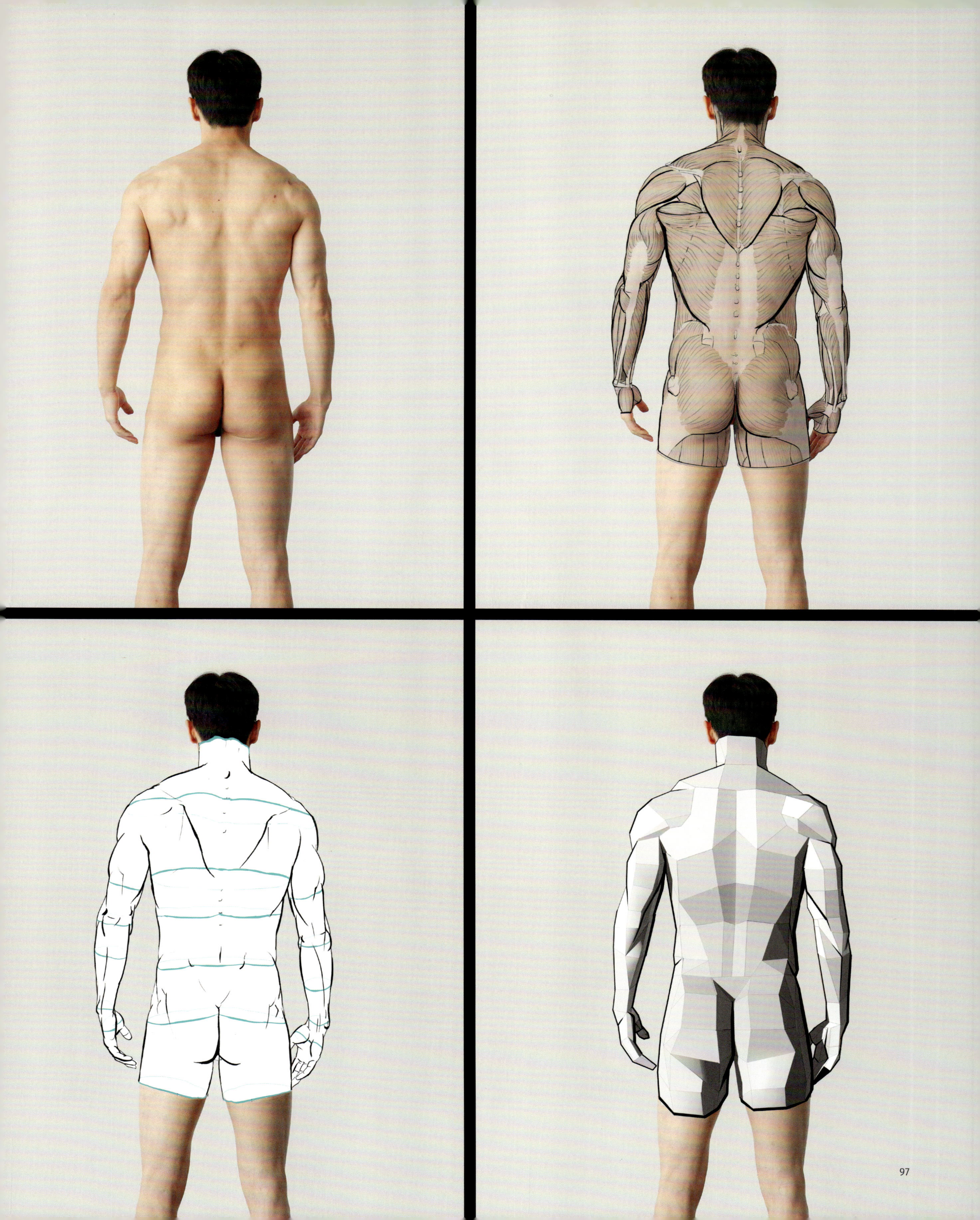

Leg abduction to adduction

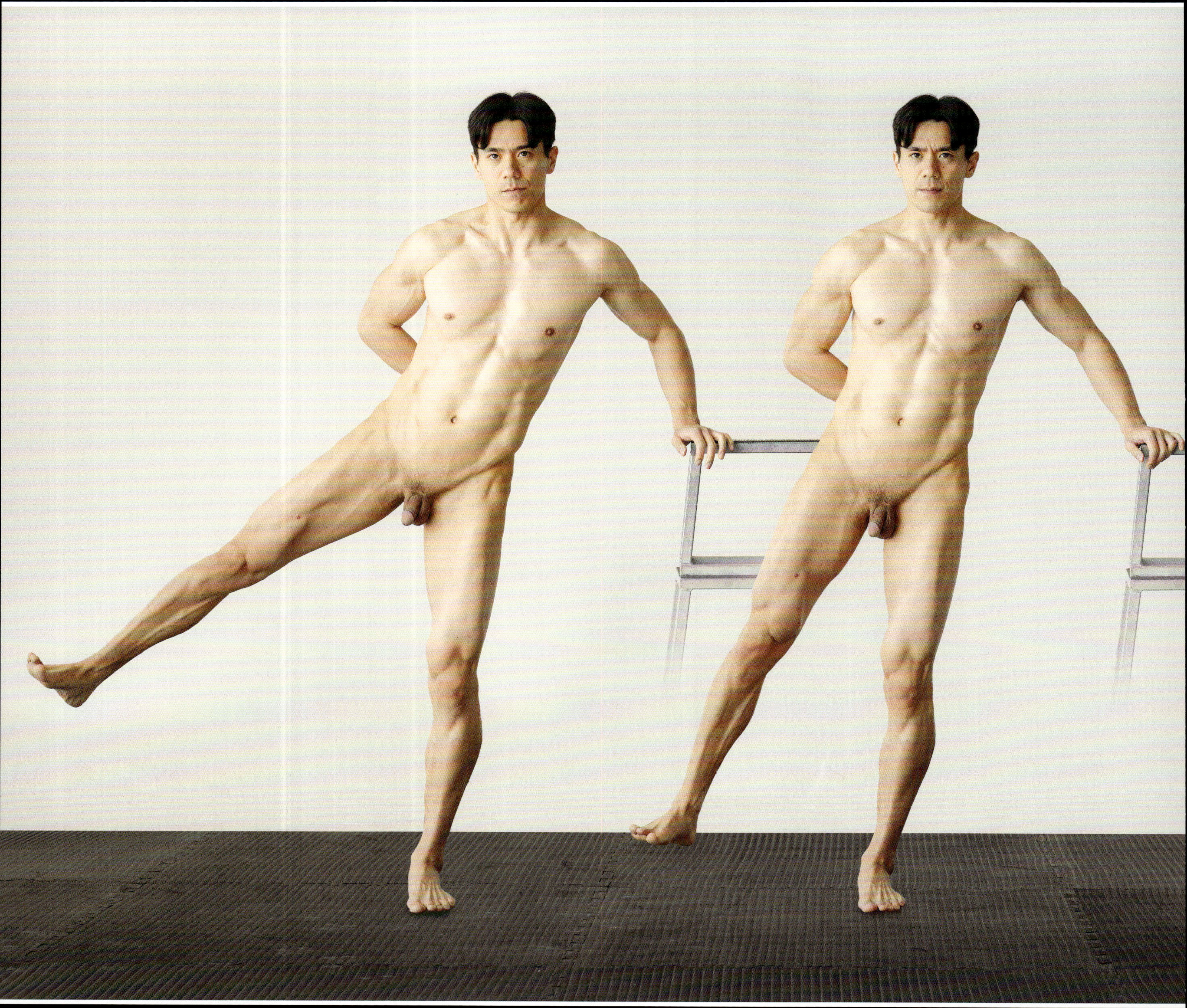

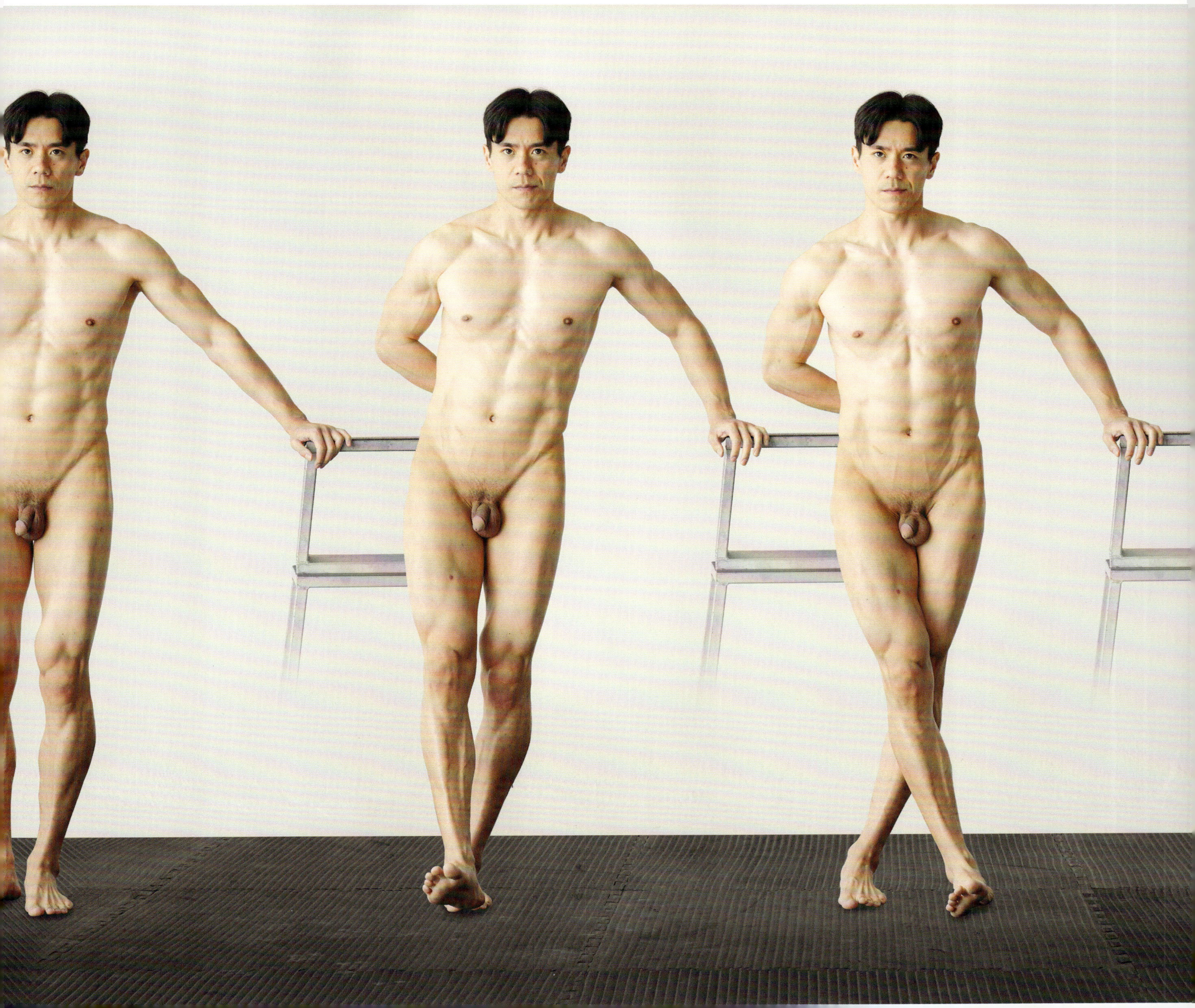

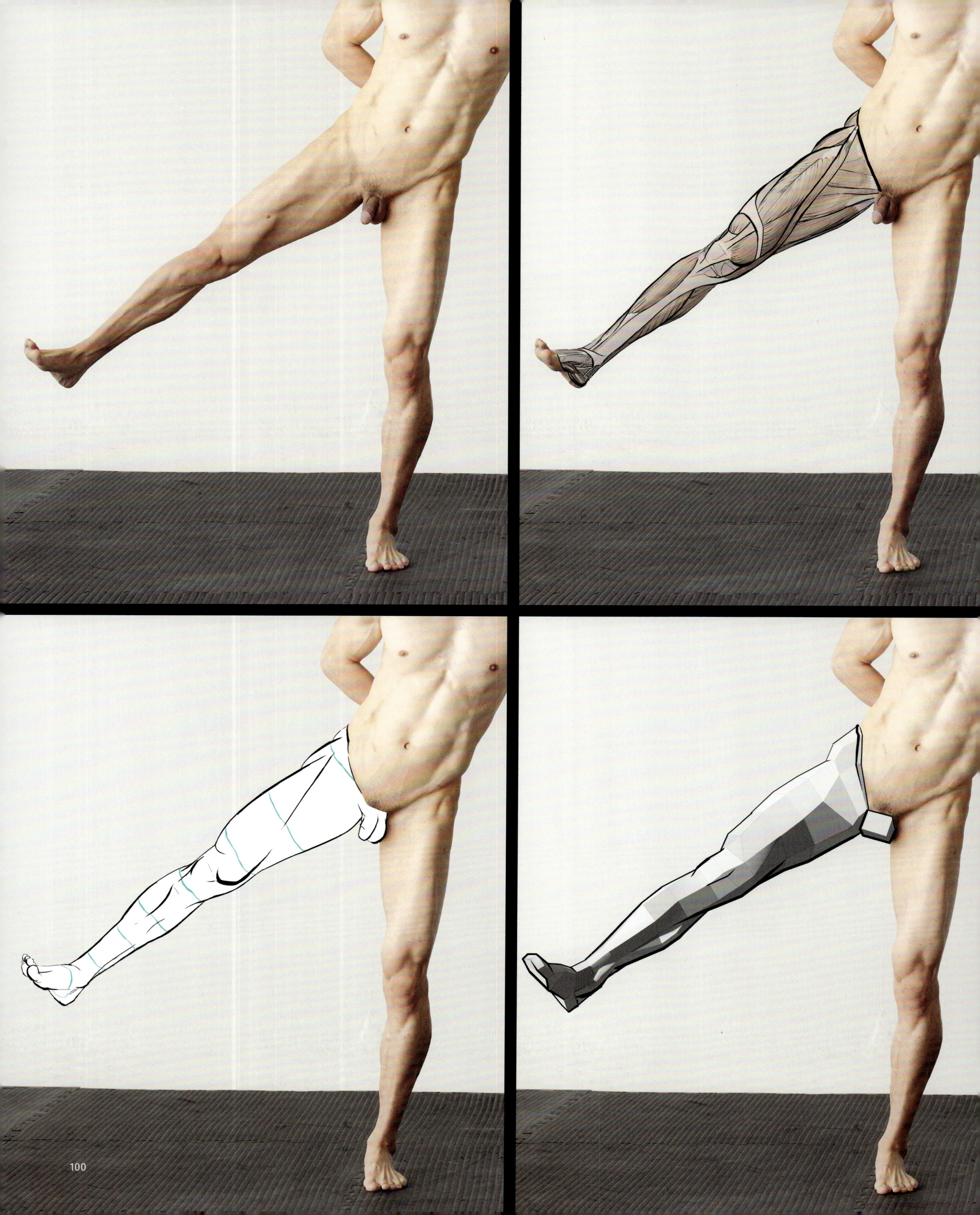

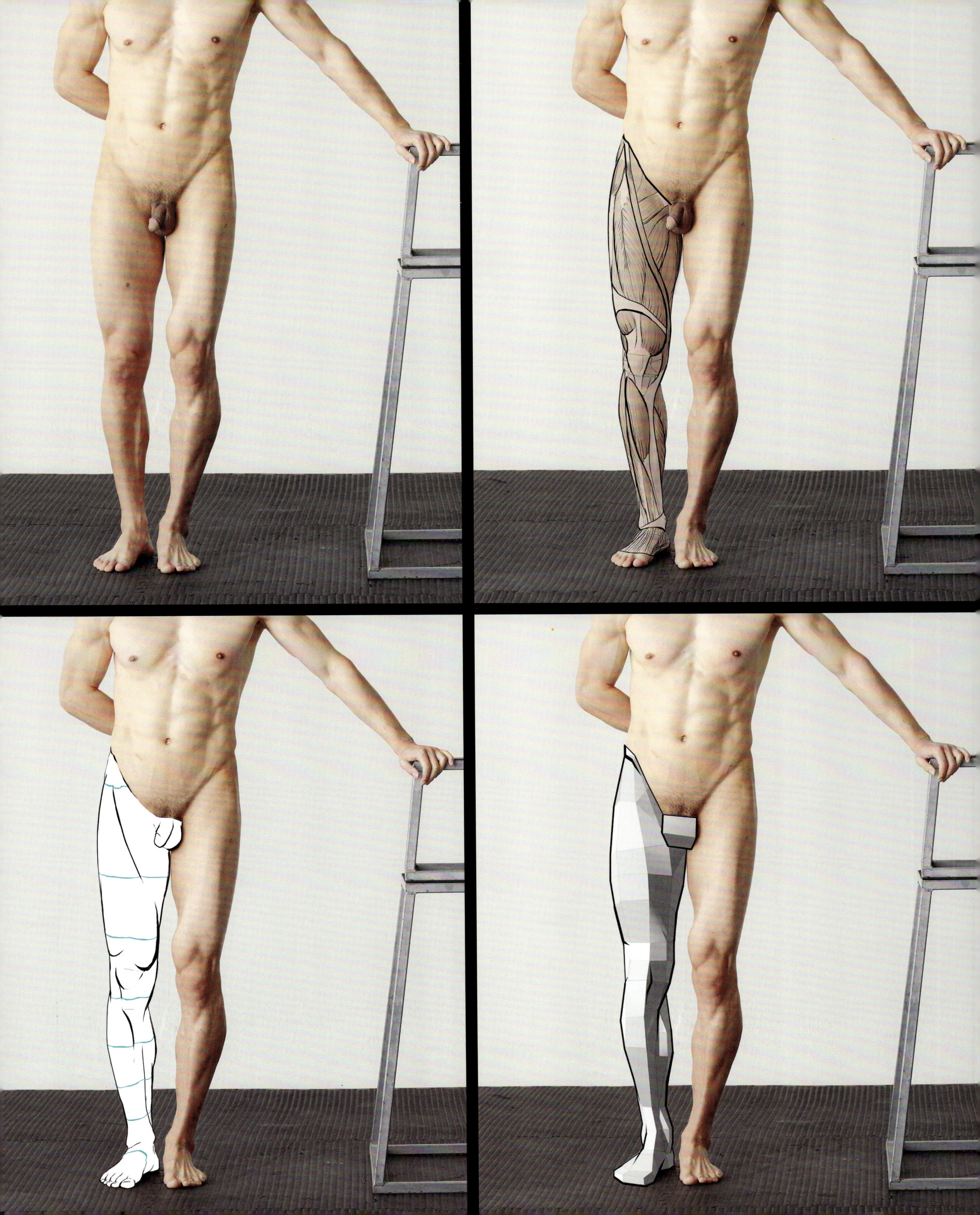

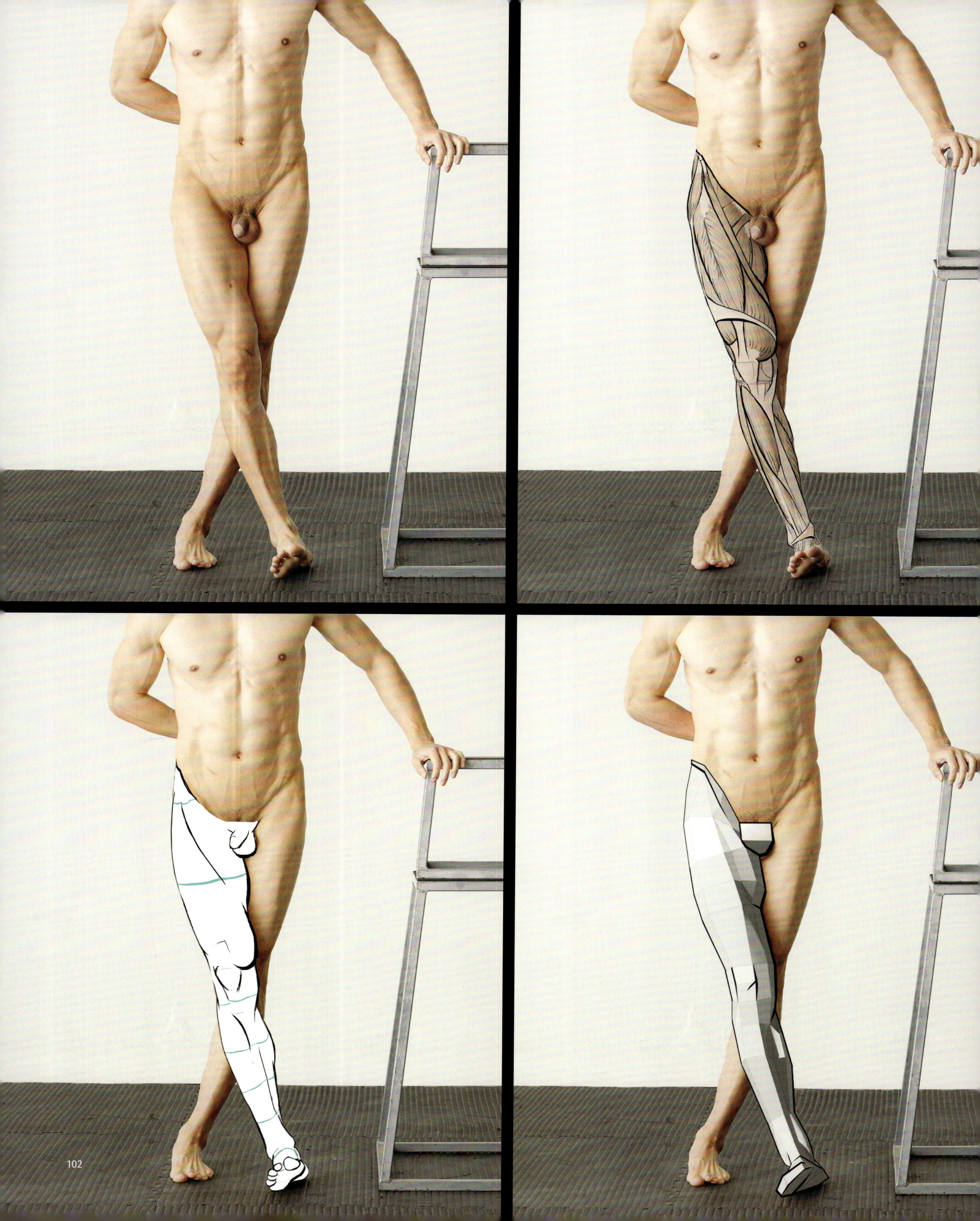

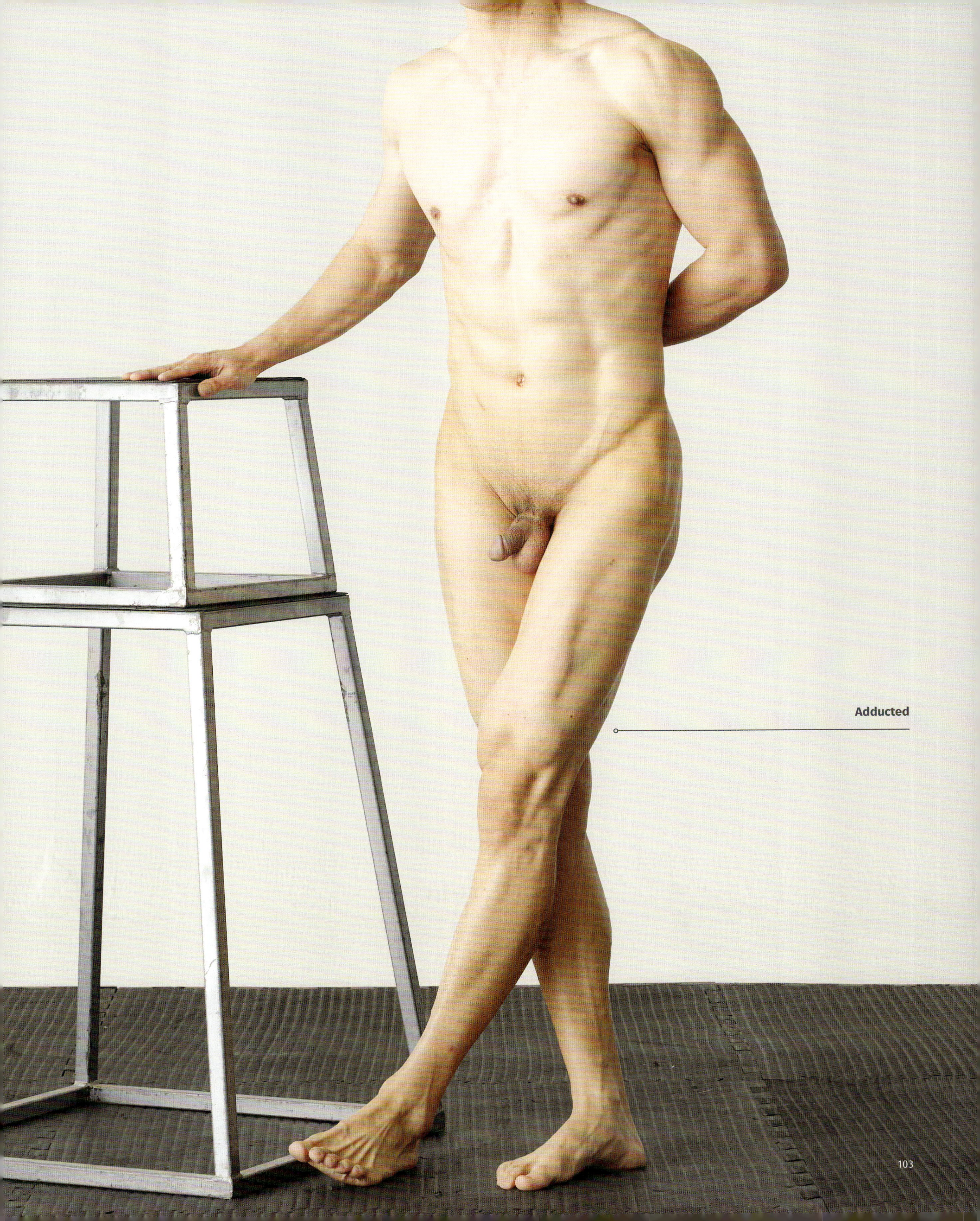
Adducted

Neck rotation

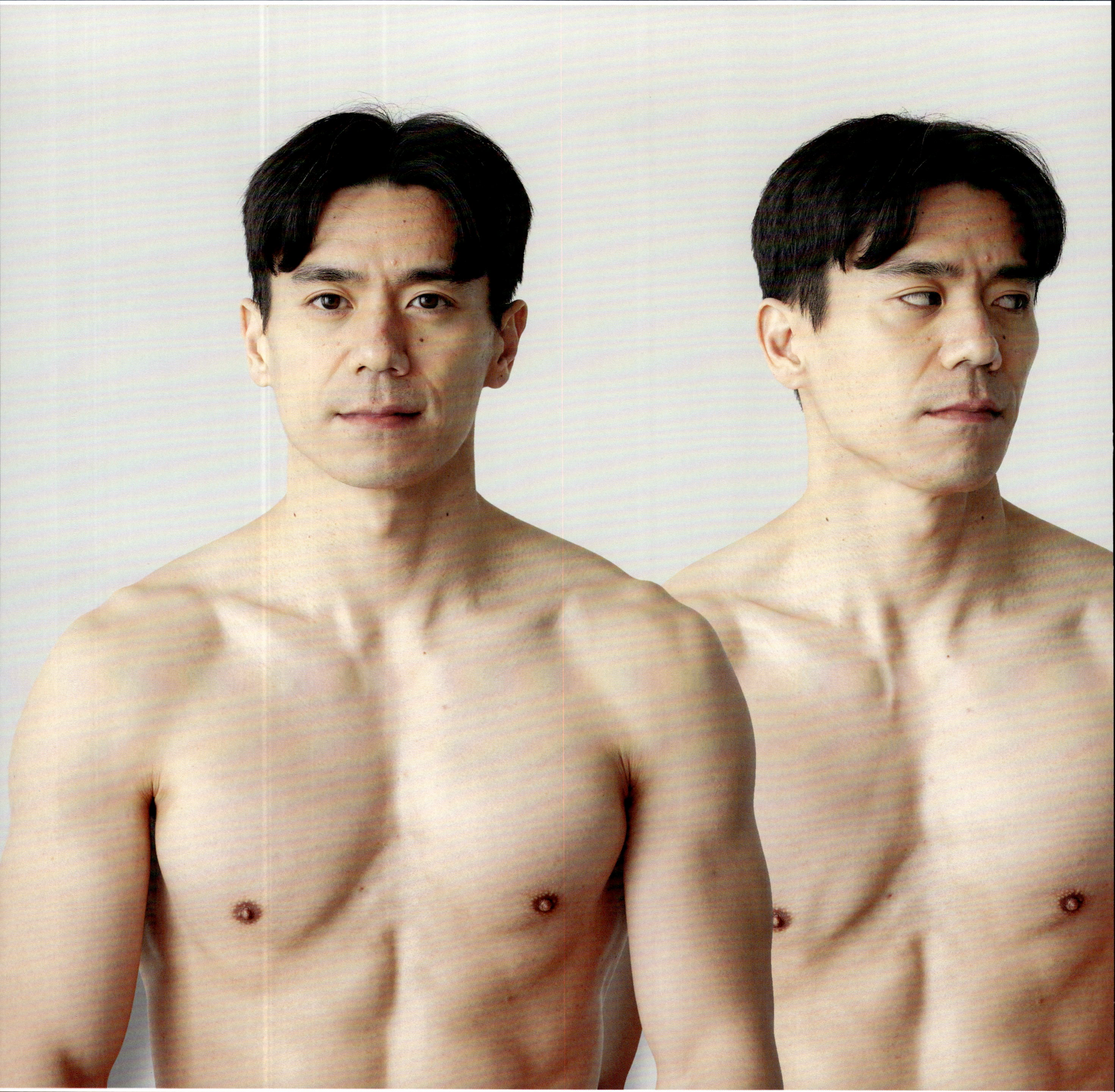

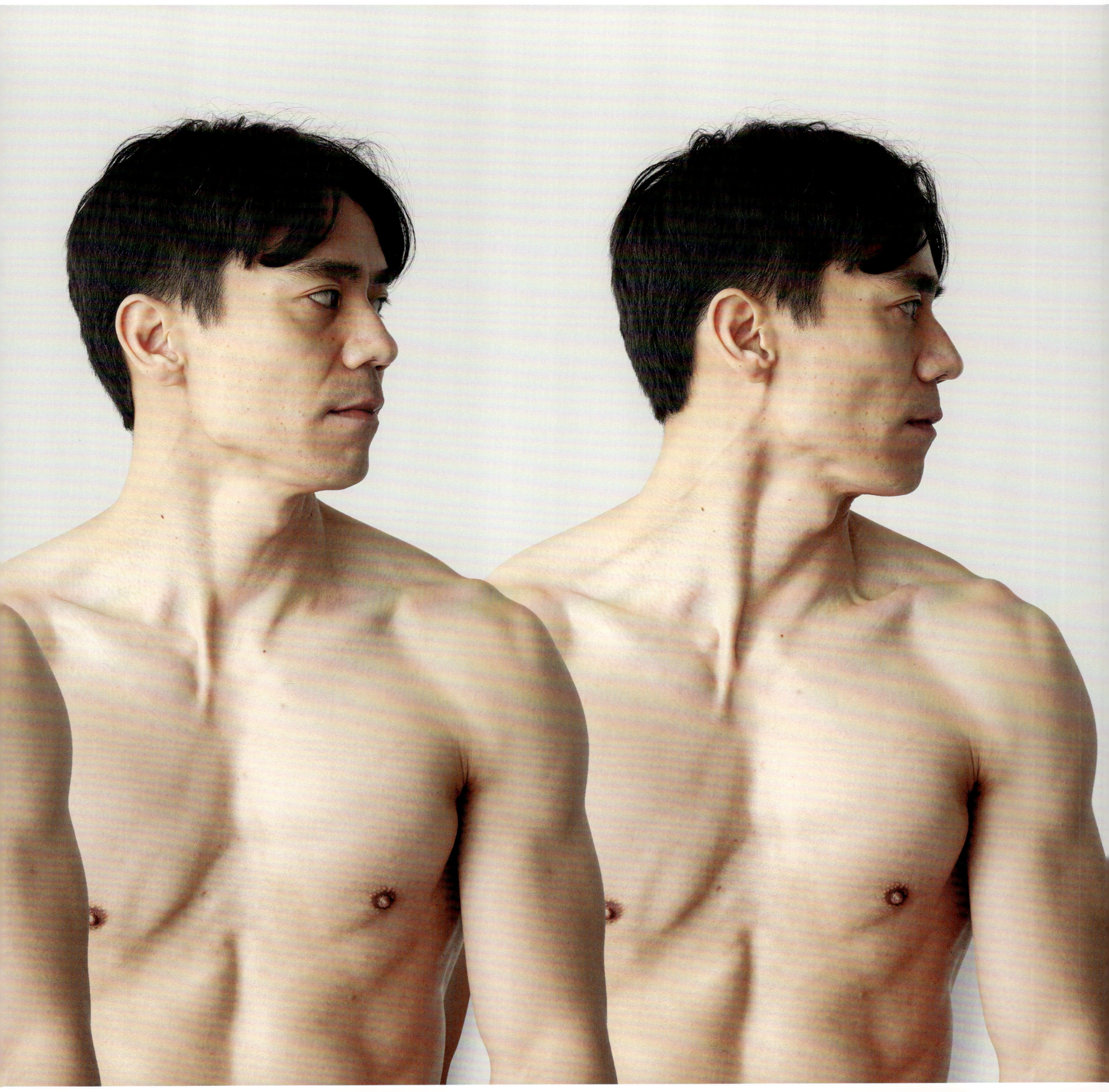

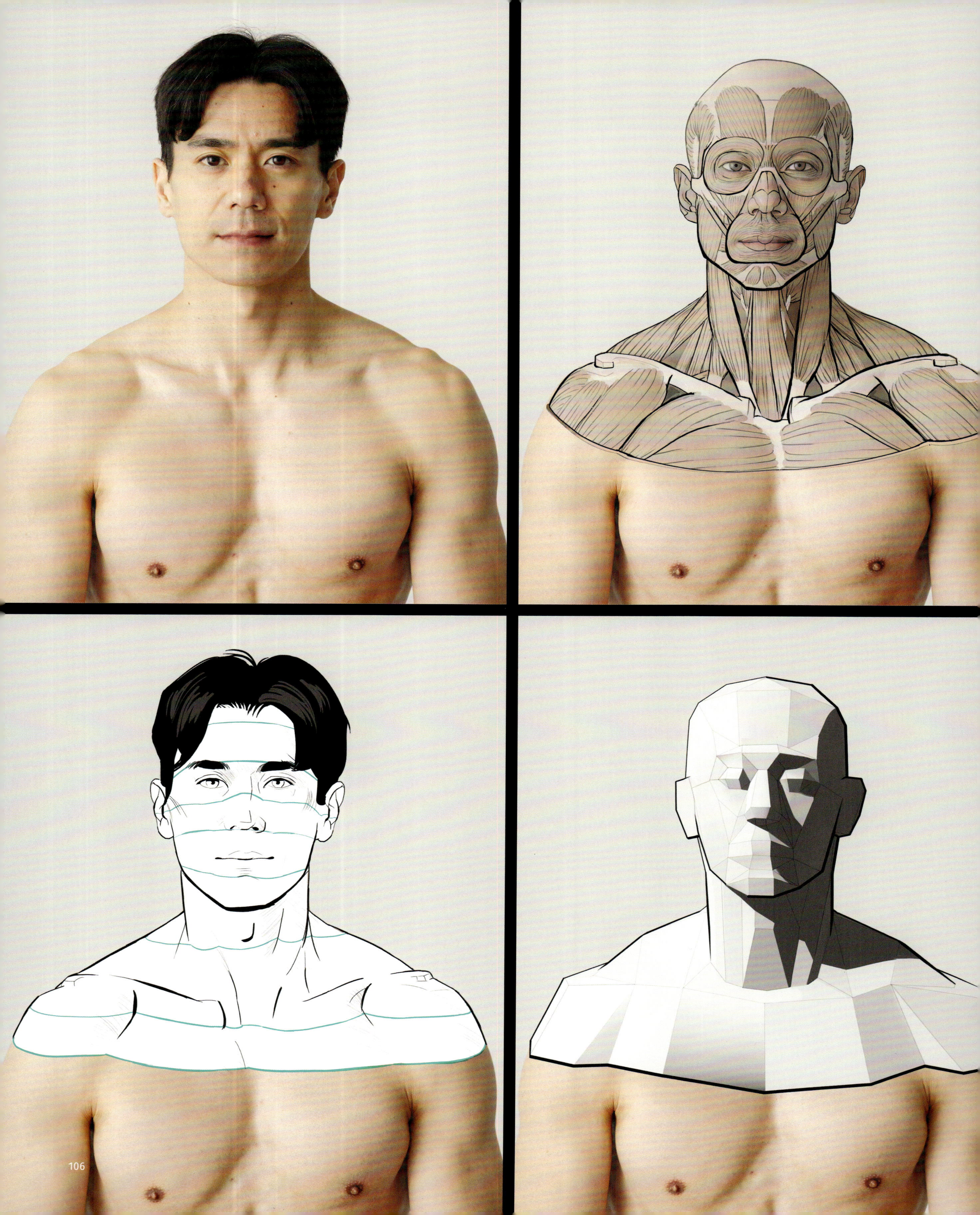

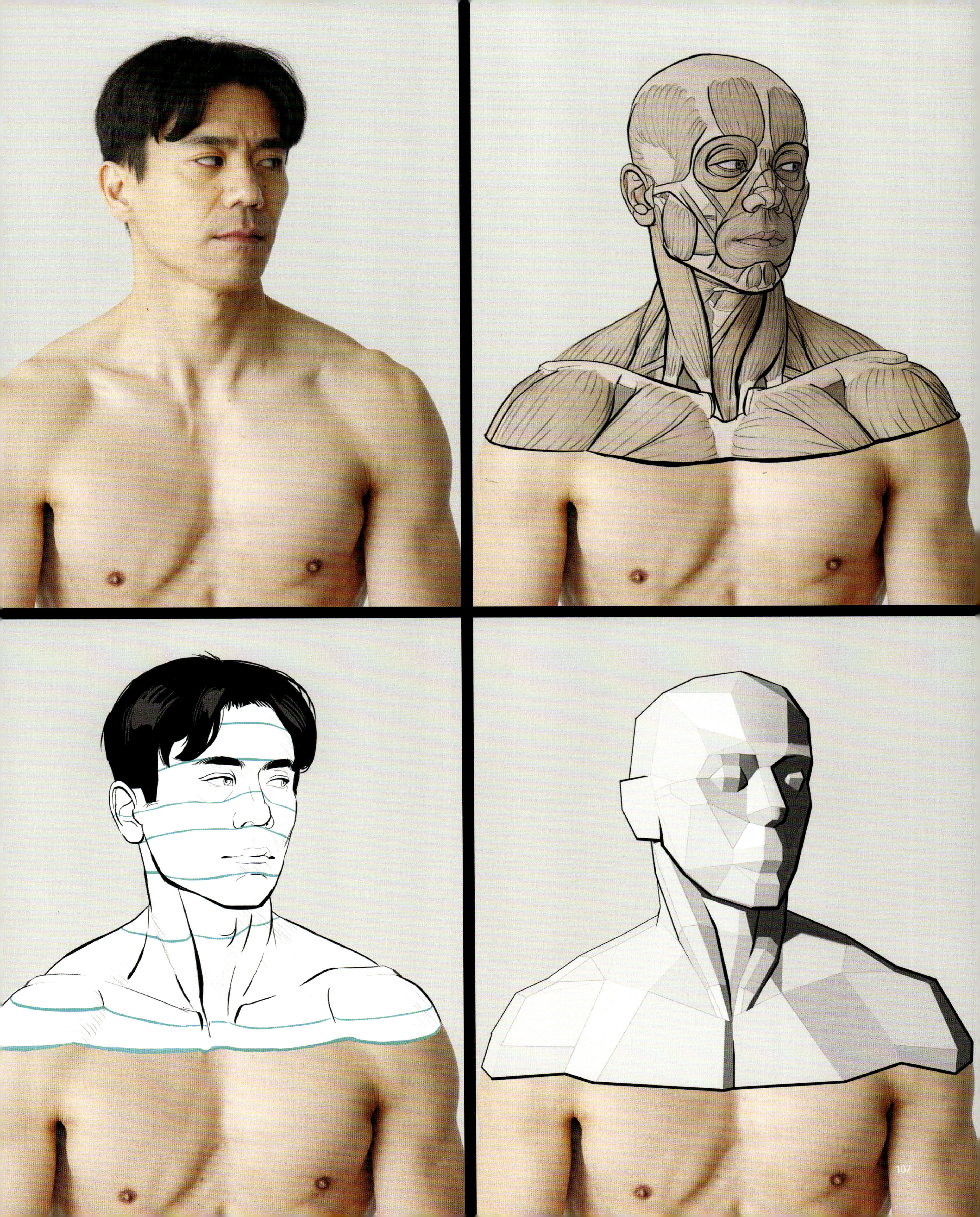

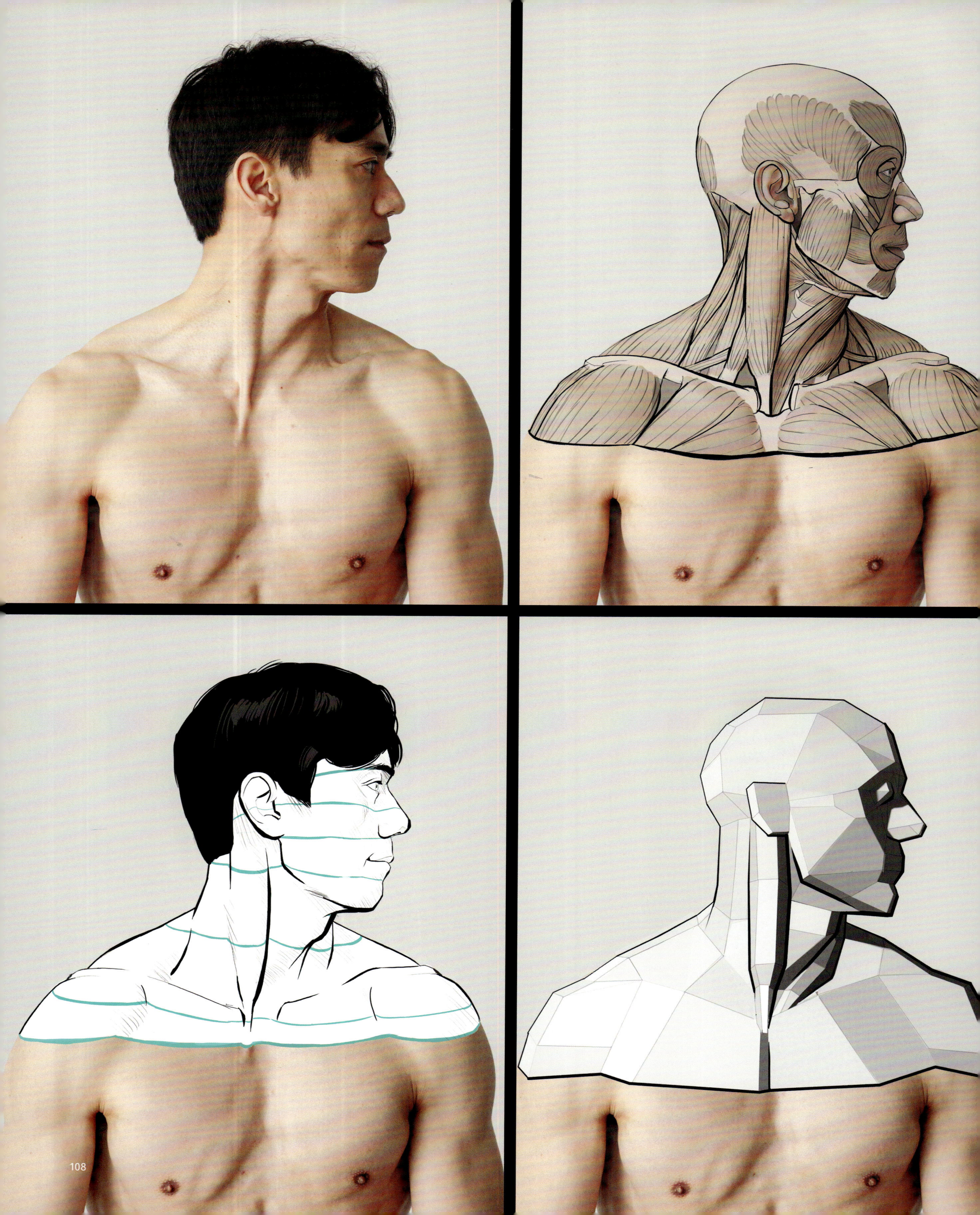

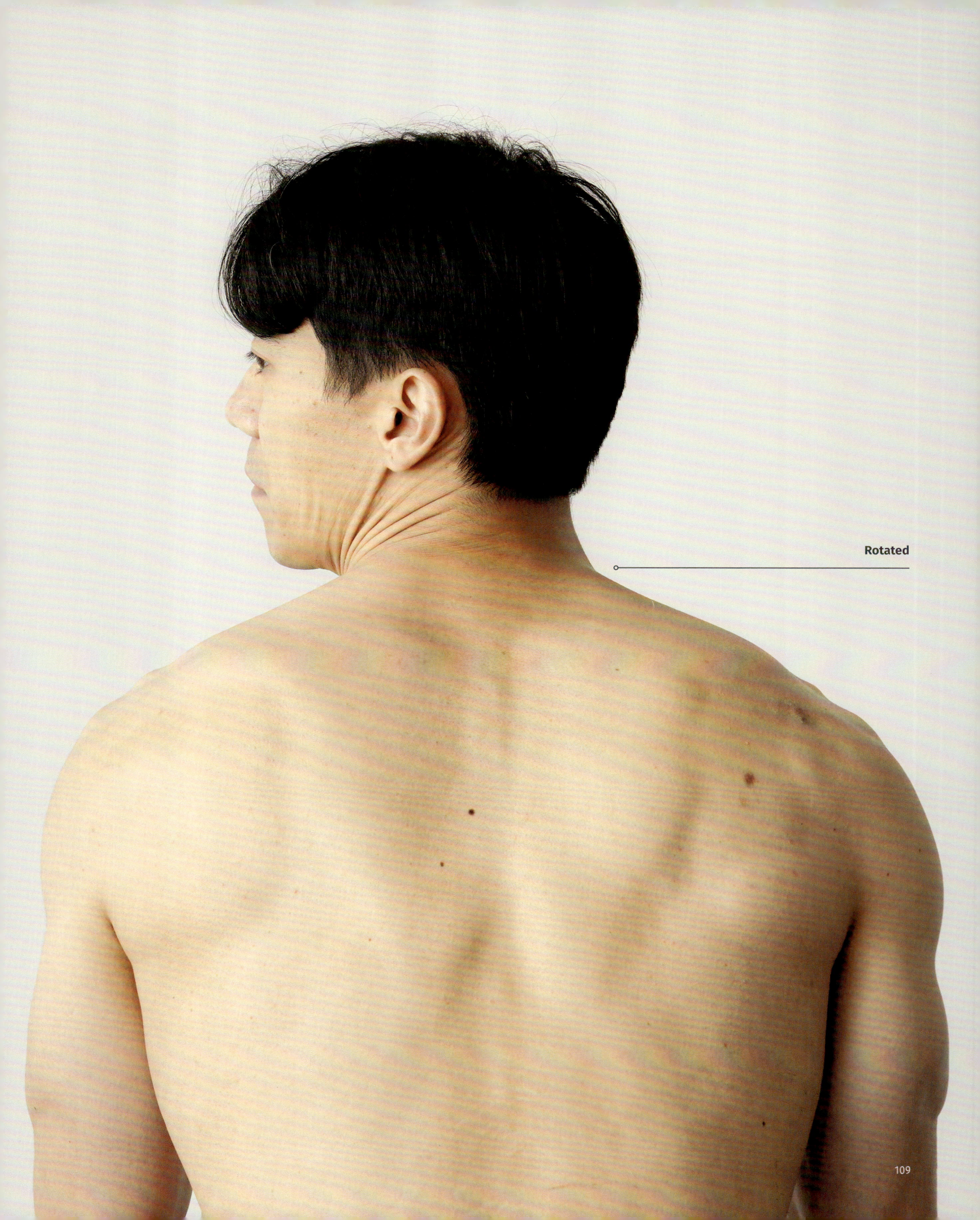
Rotated

Torso rotation

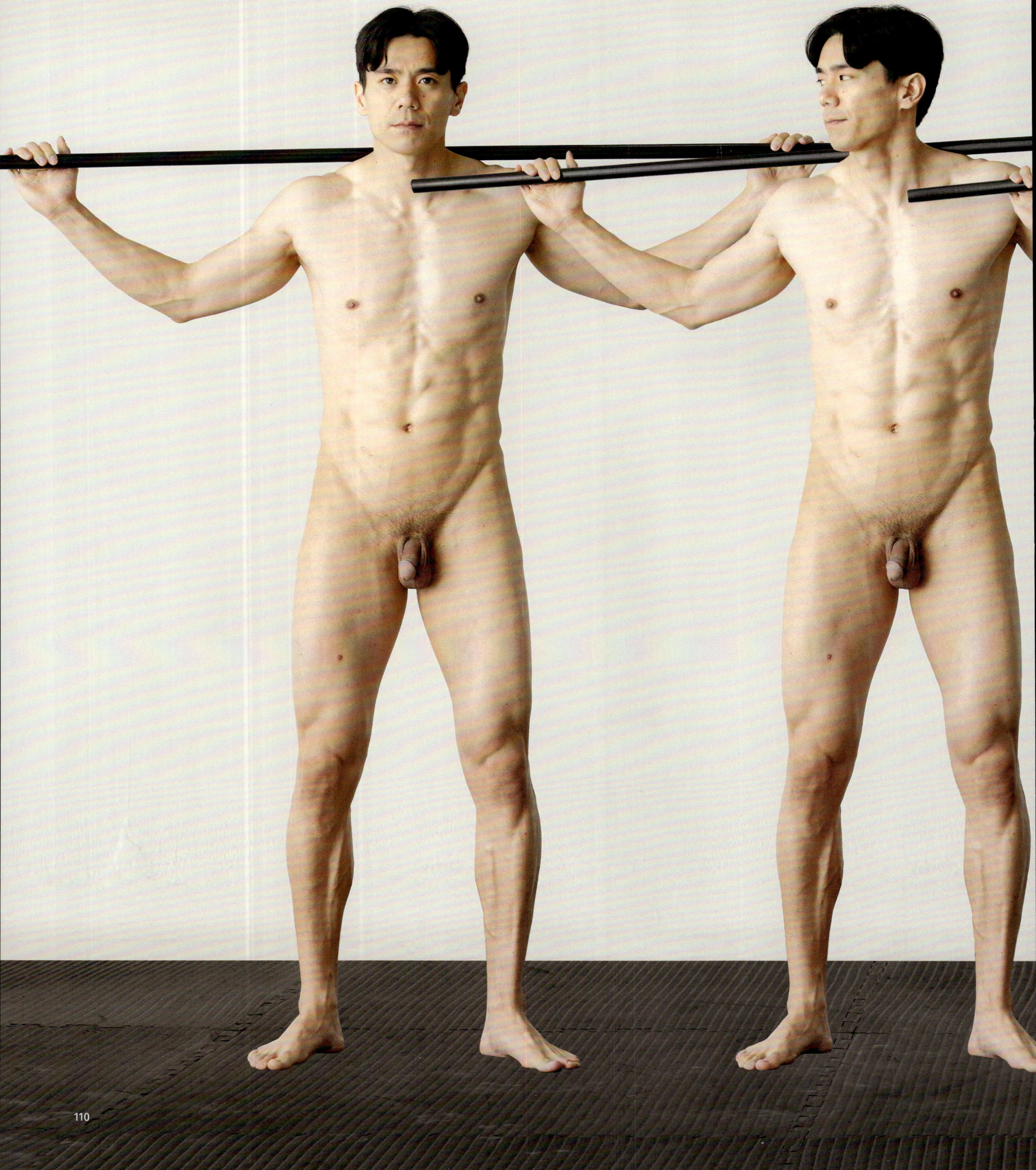

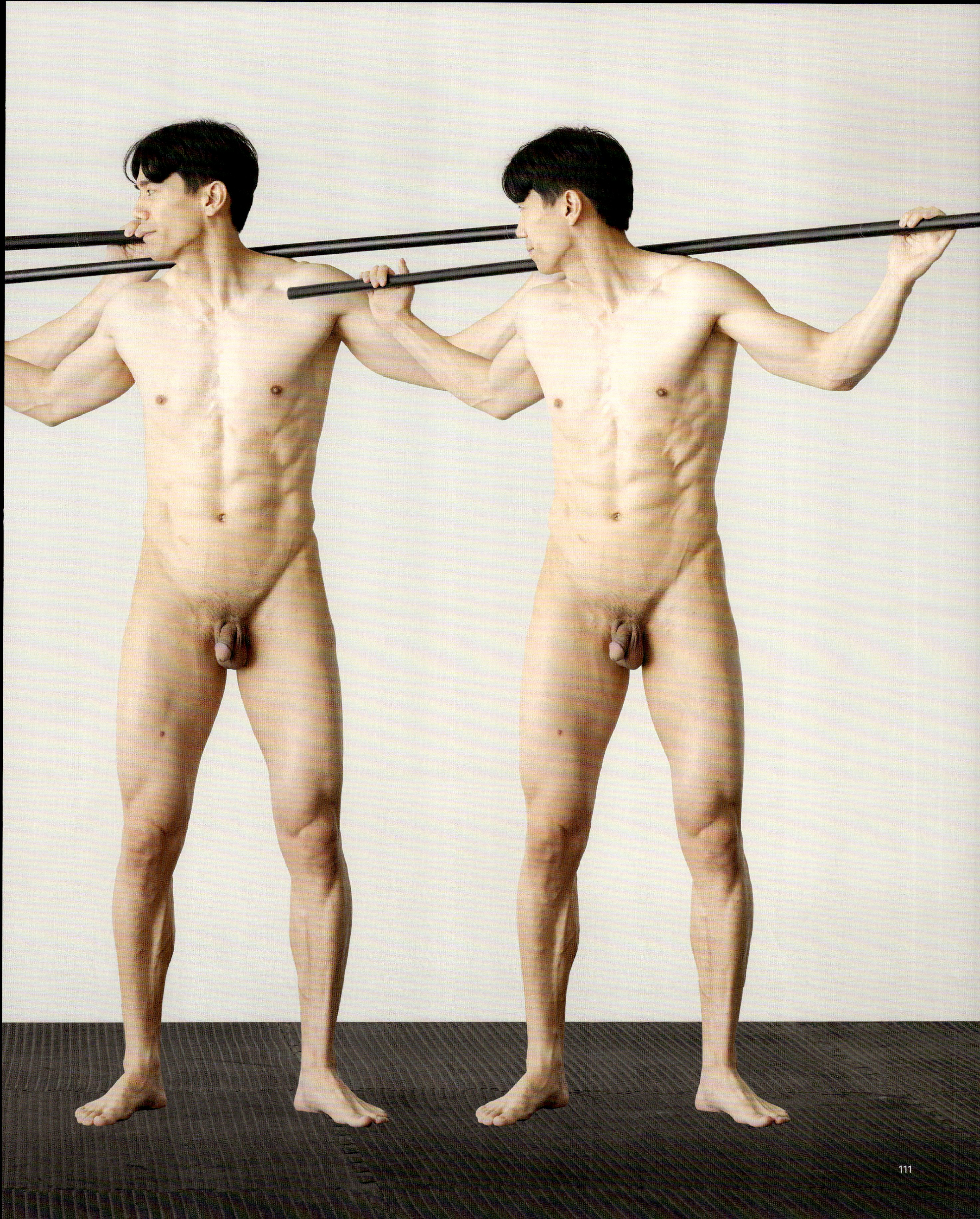

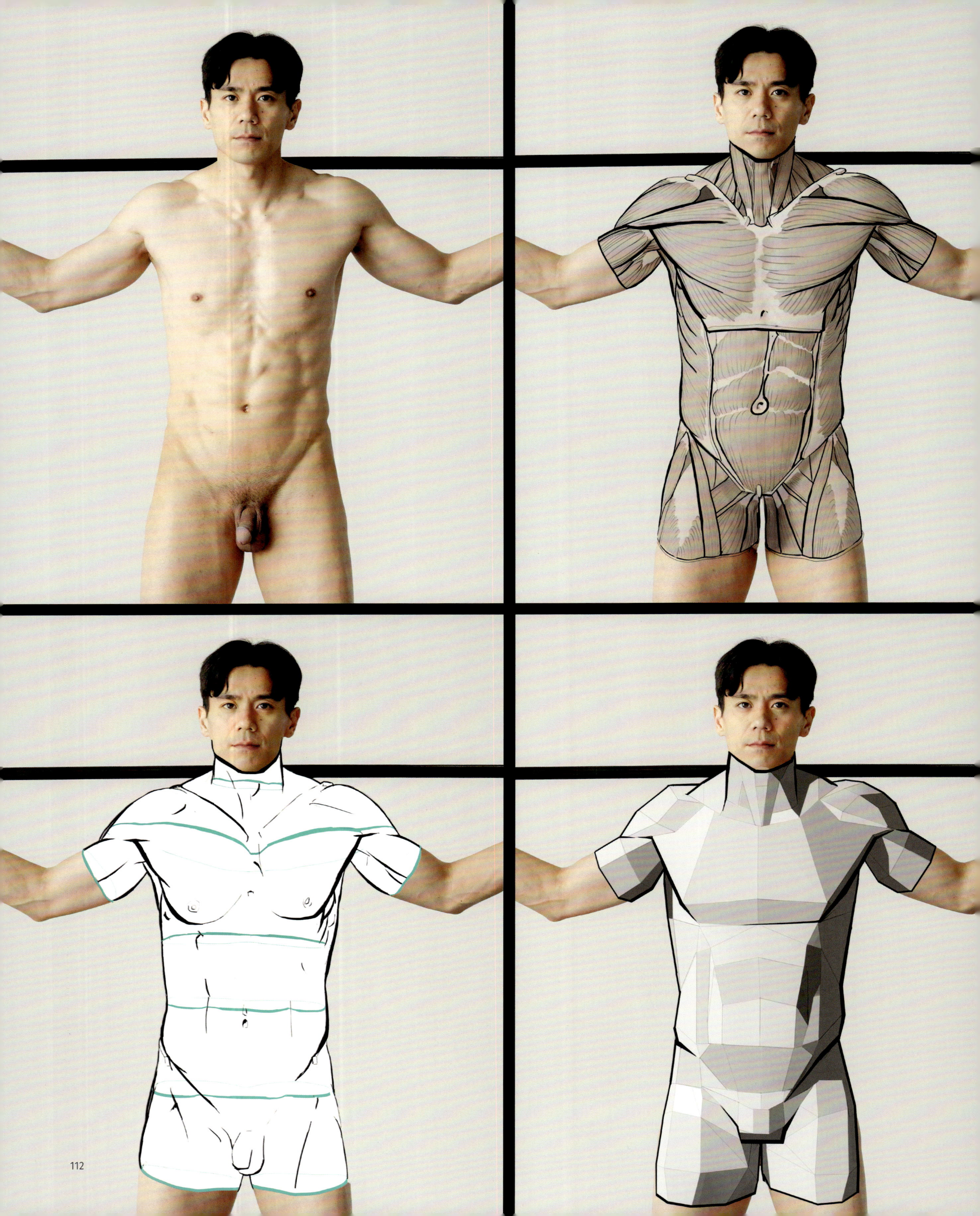

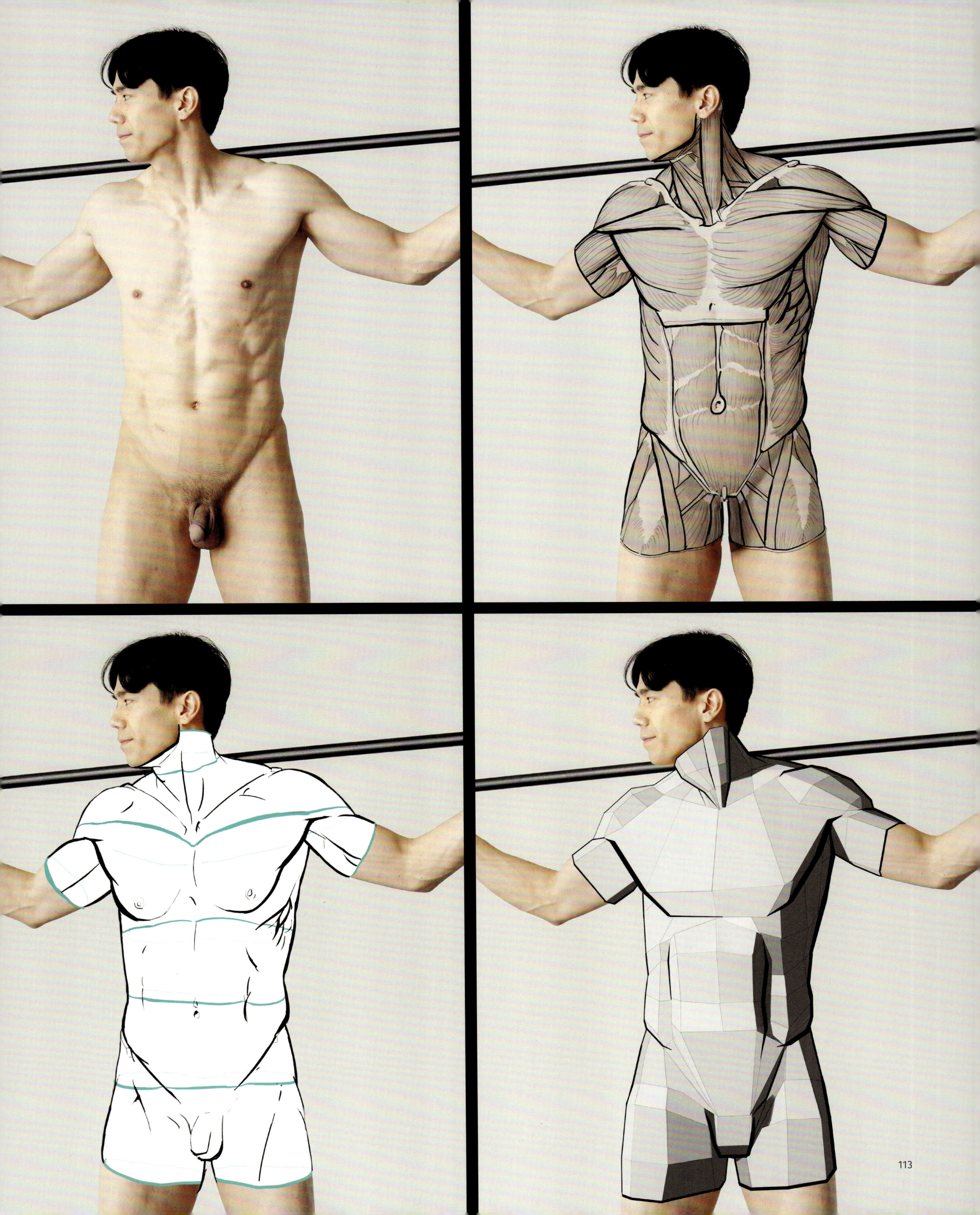

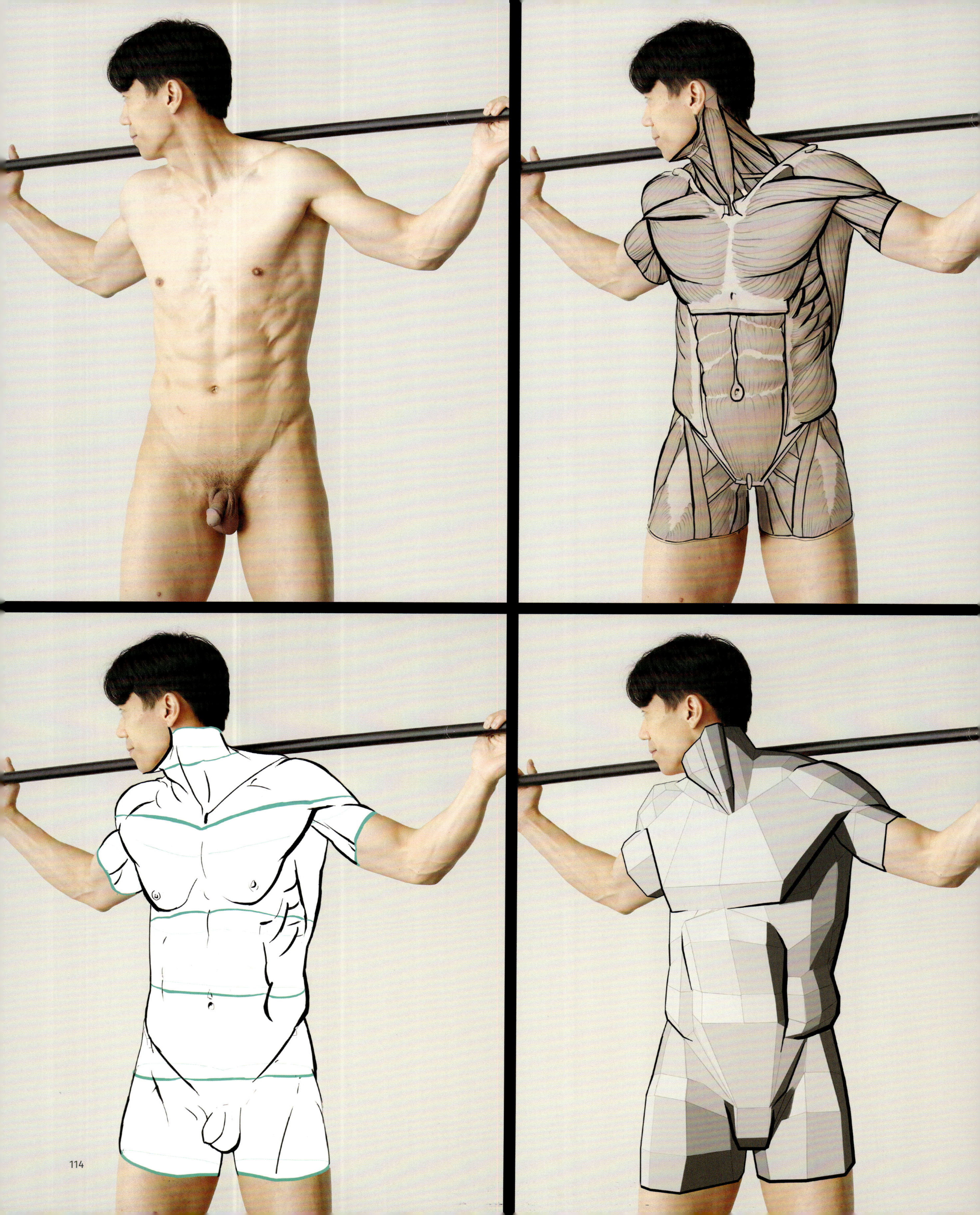

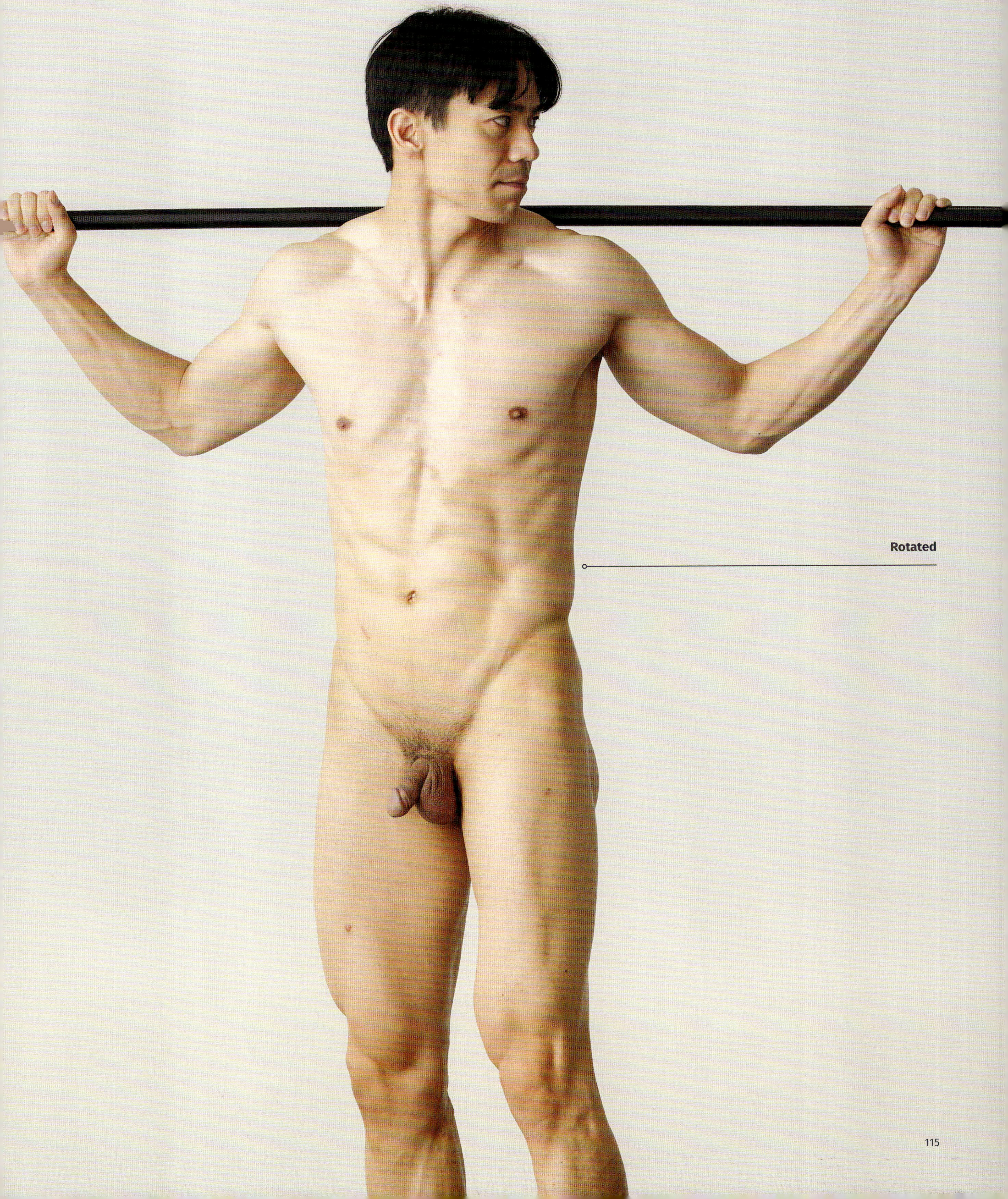
Rotated

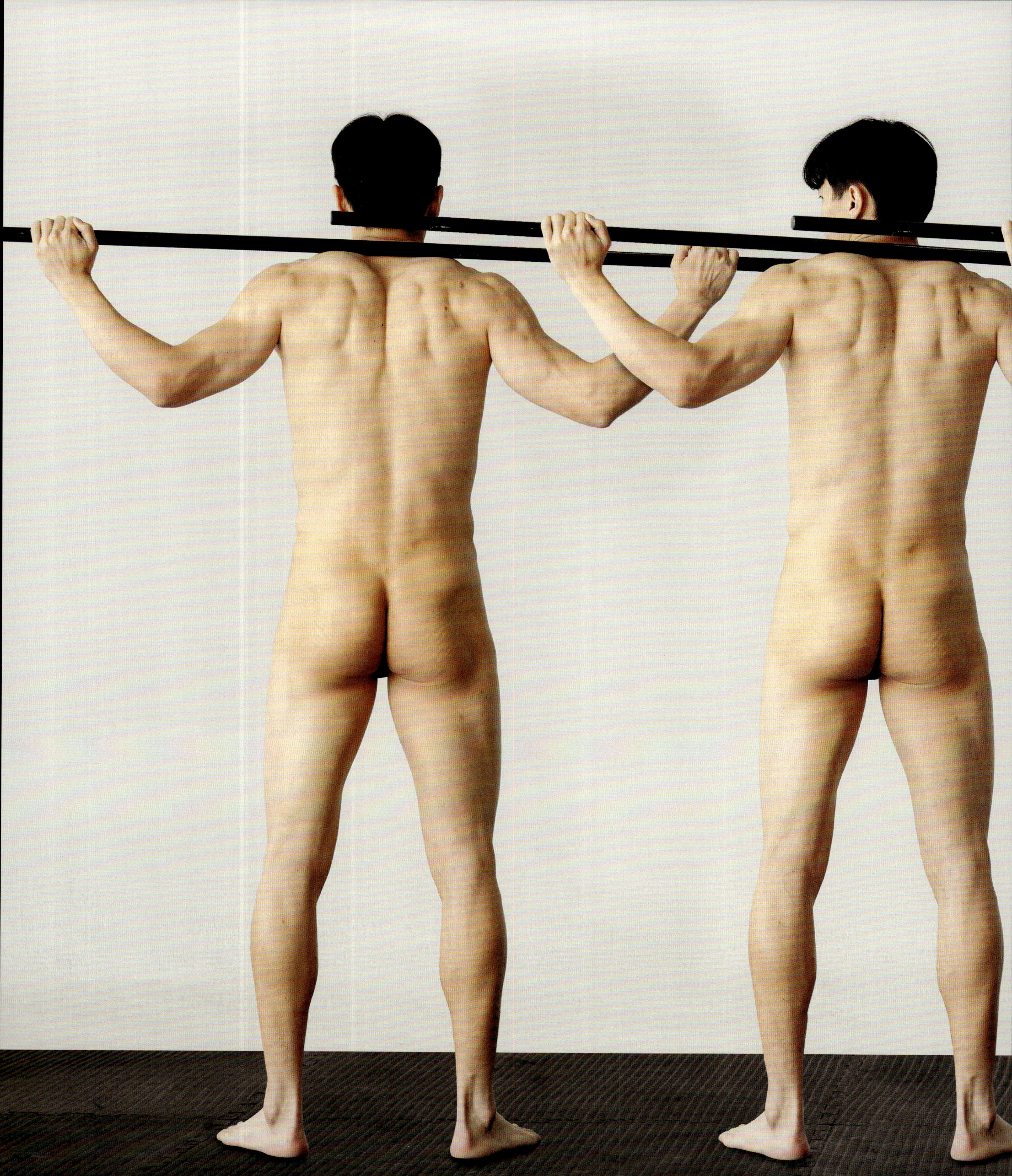

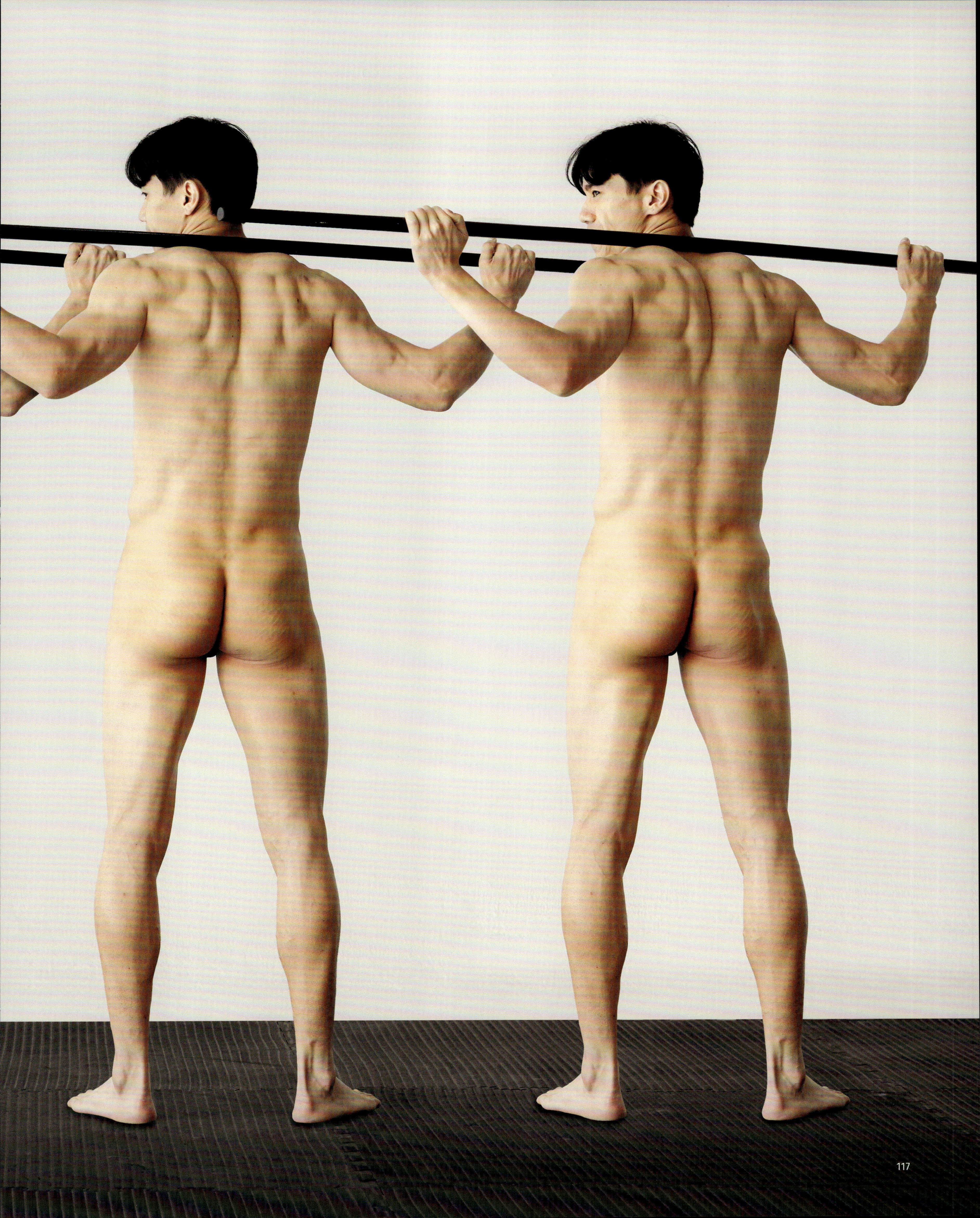

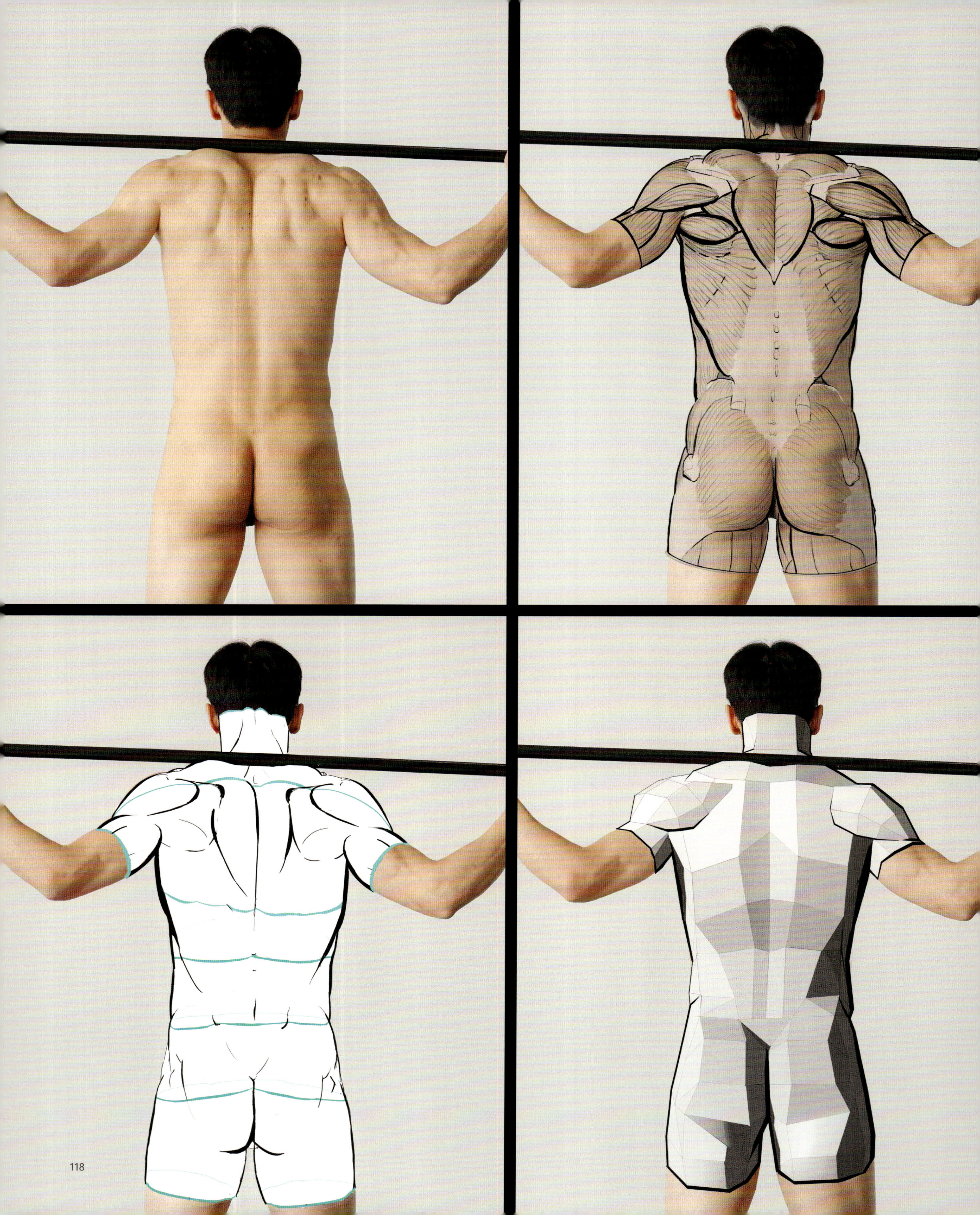

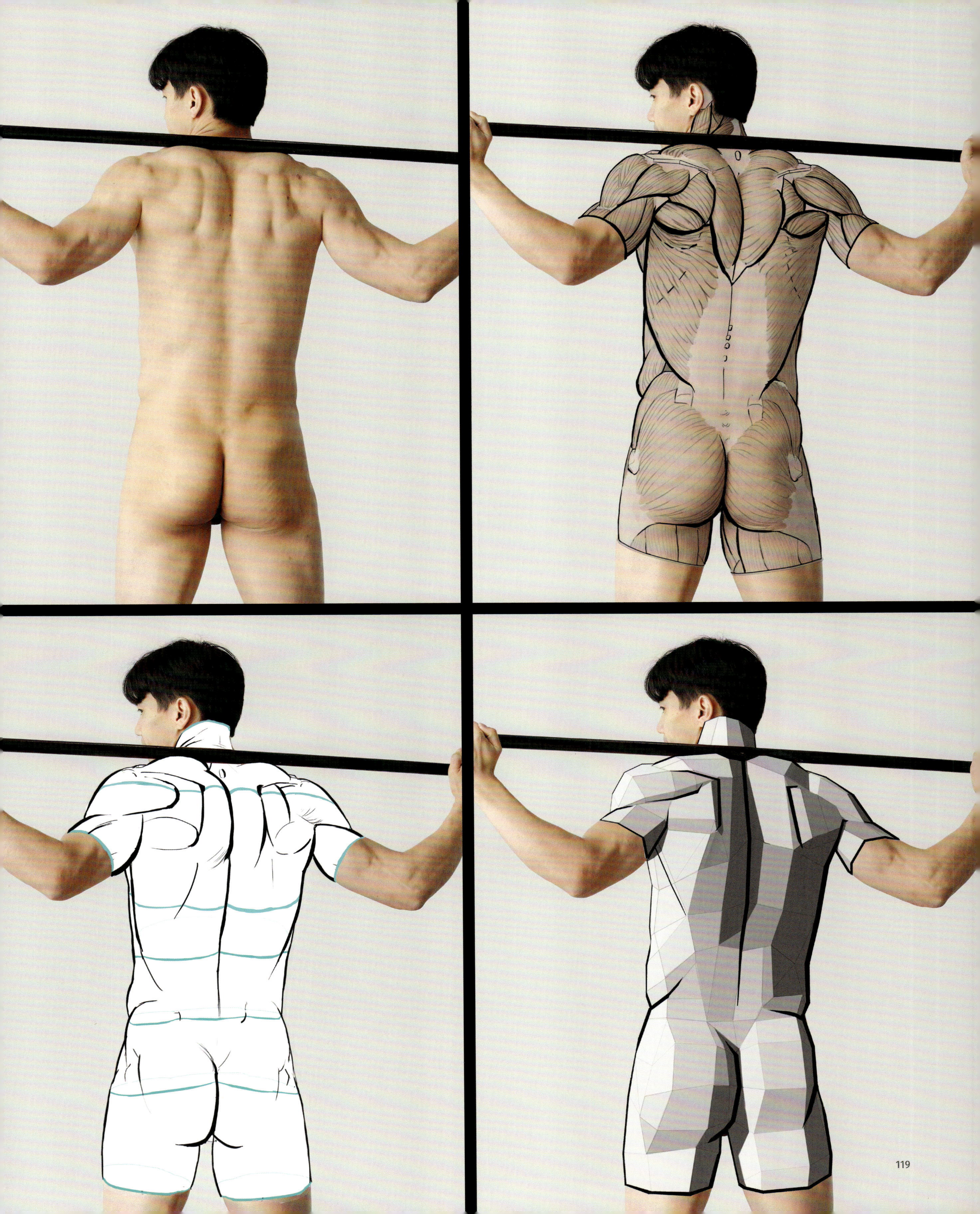

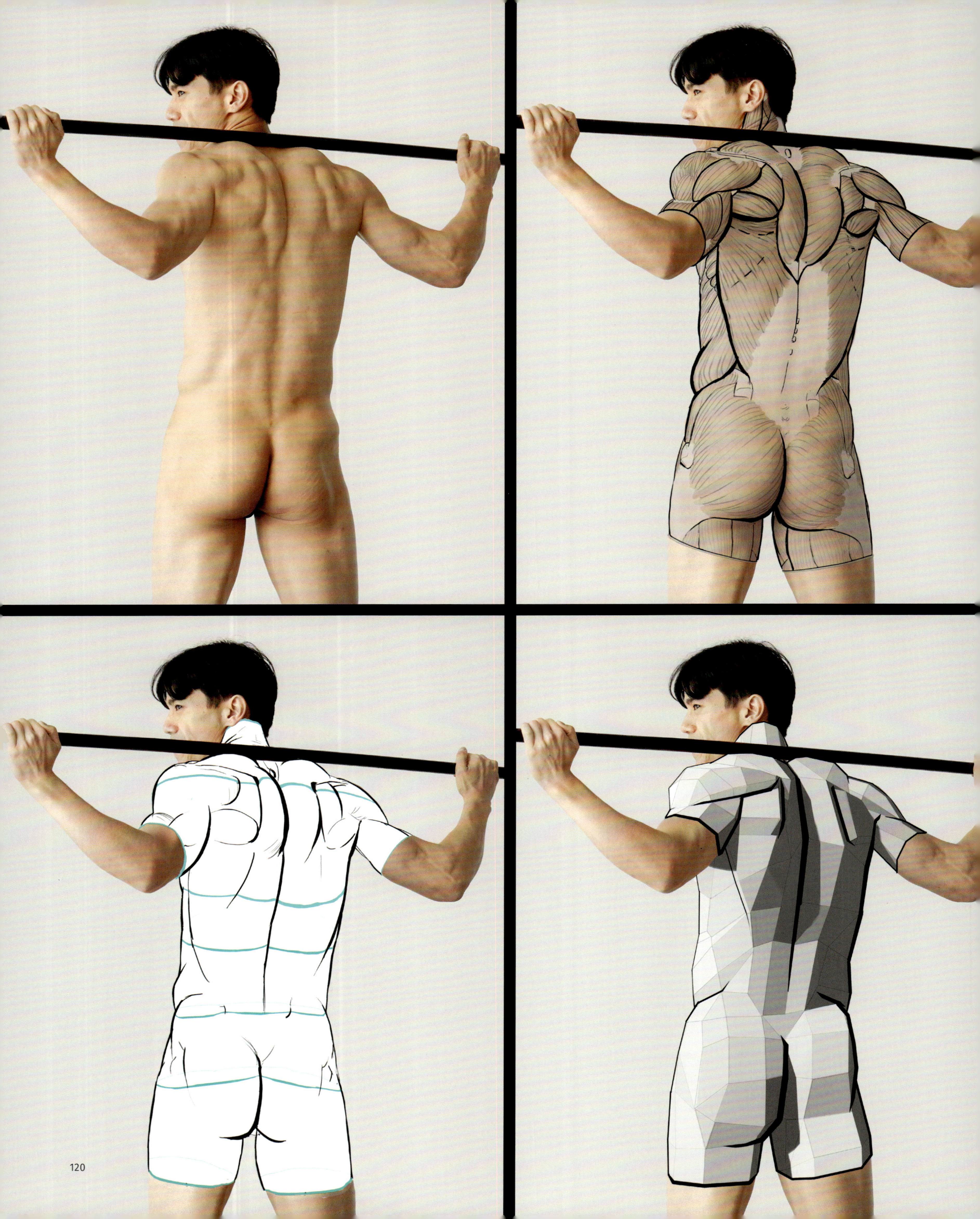

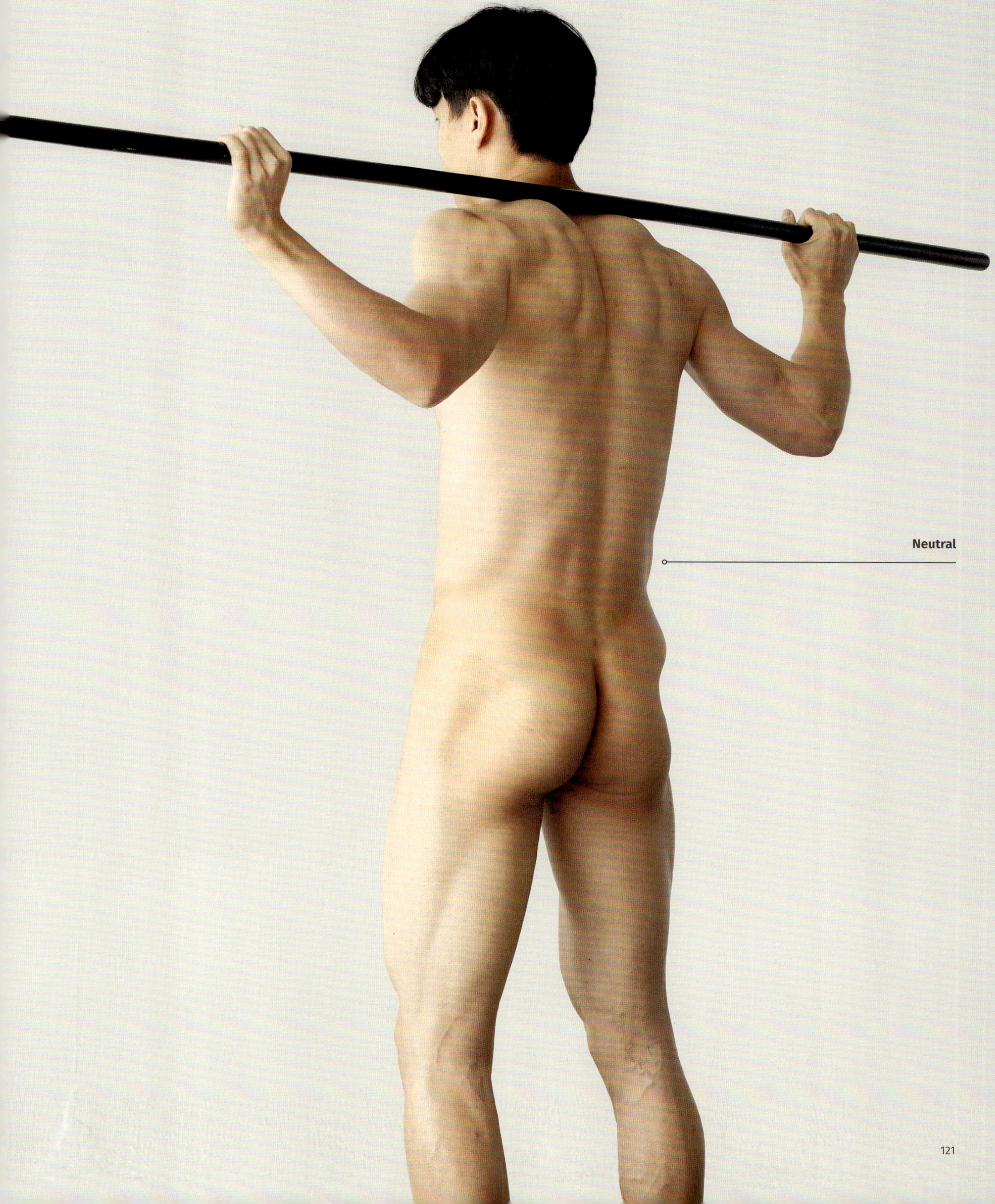
Neutral

Torso lateral bend

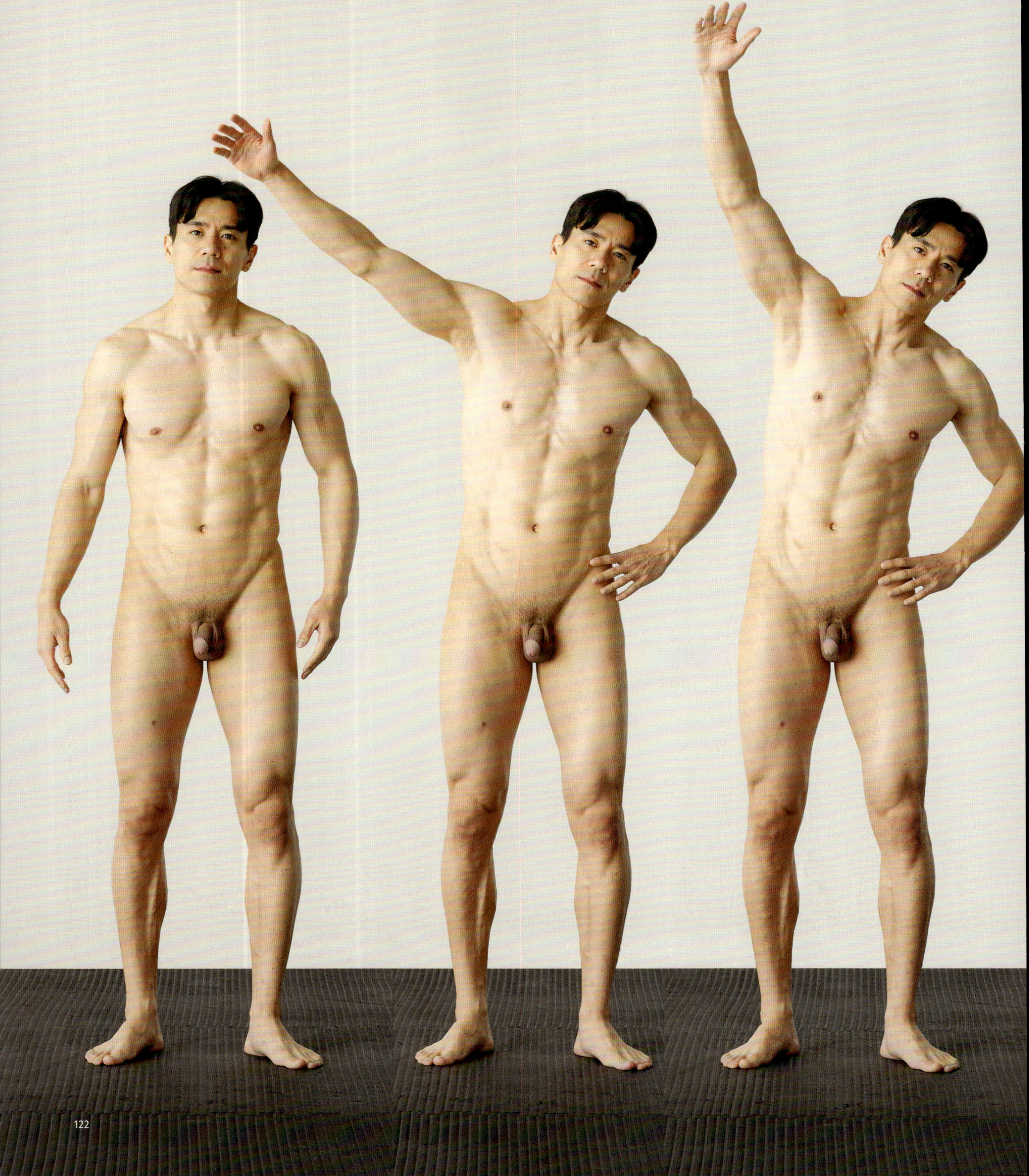

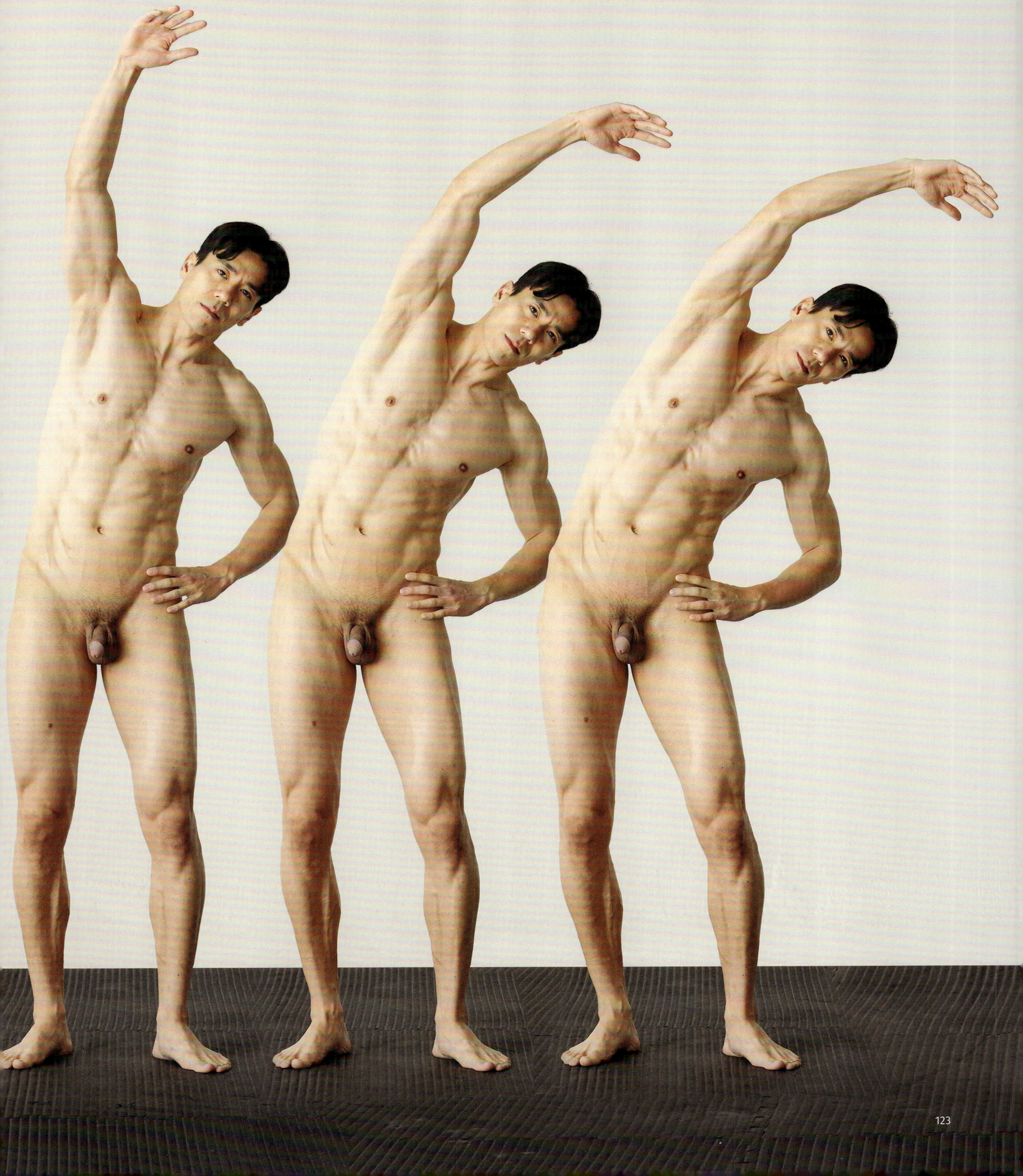

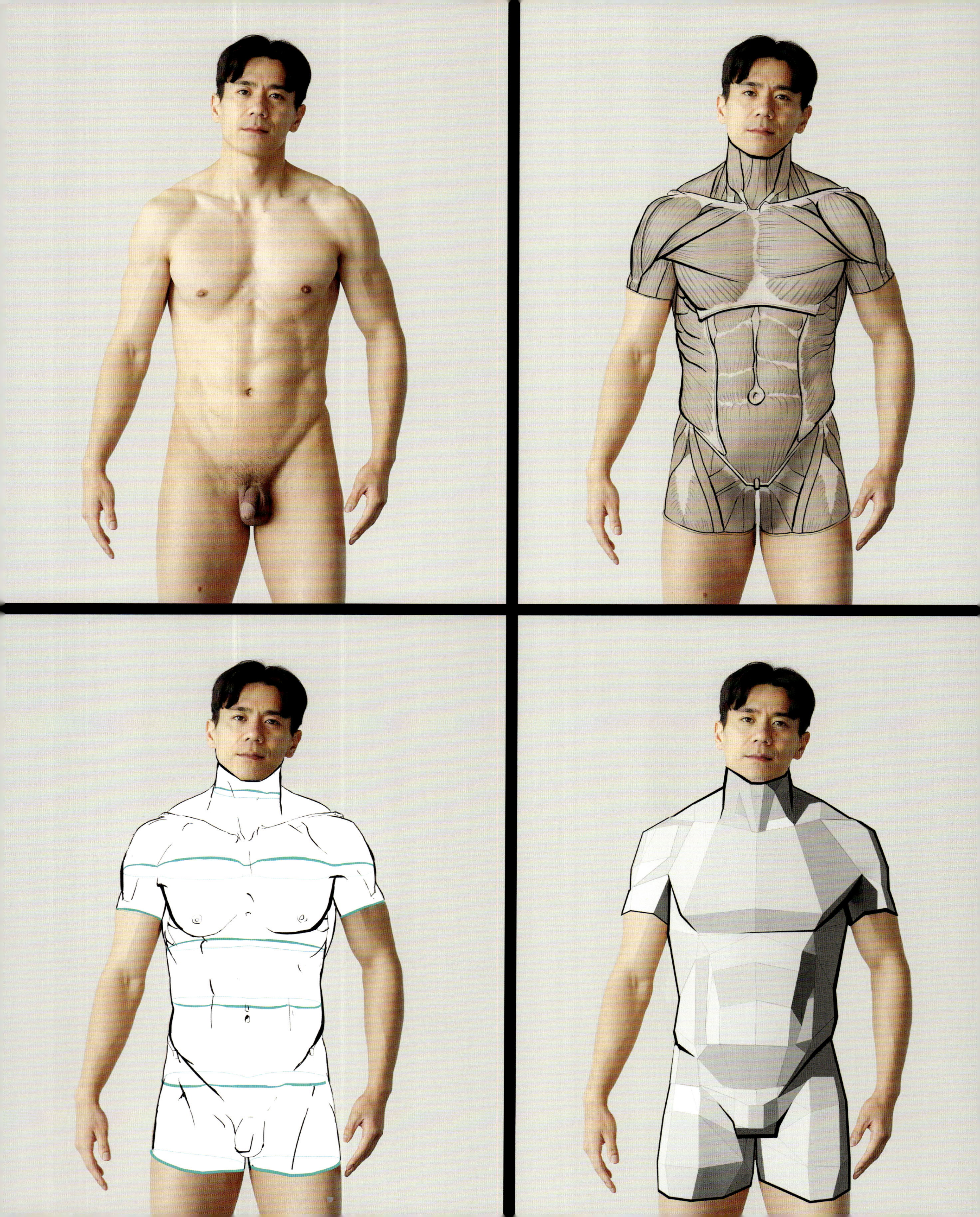

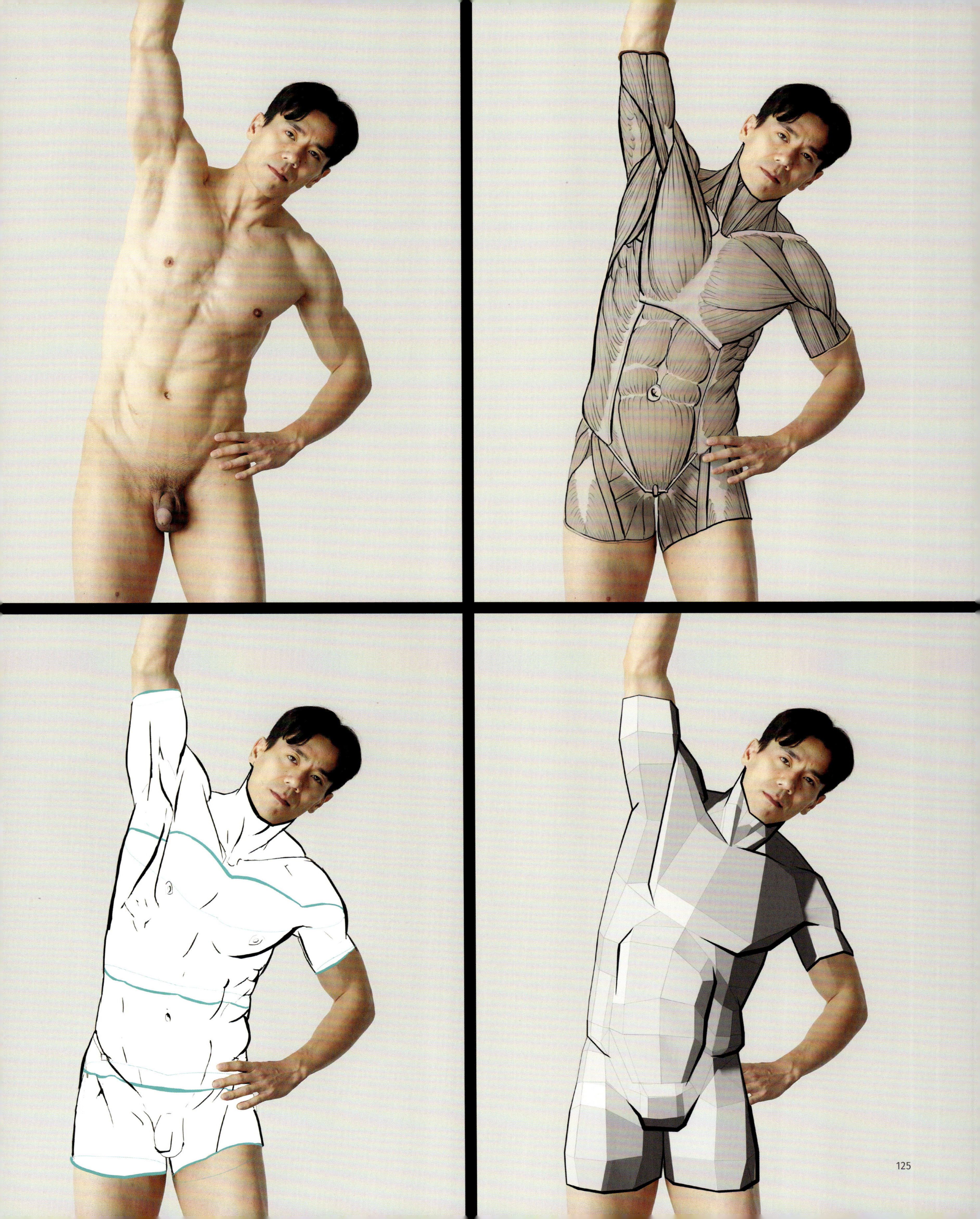

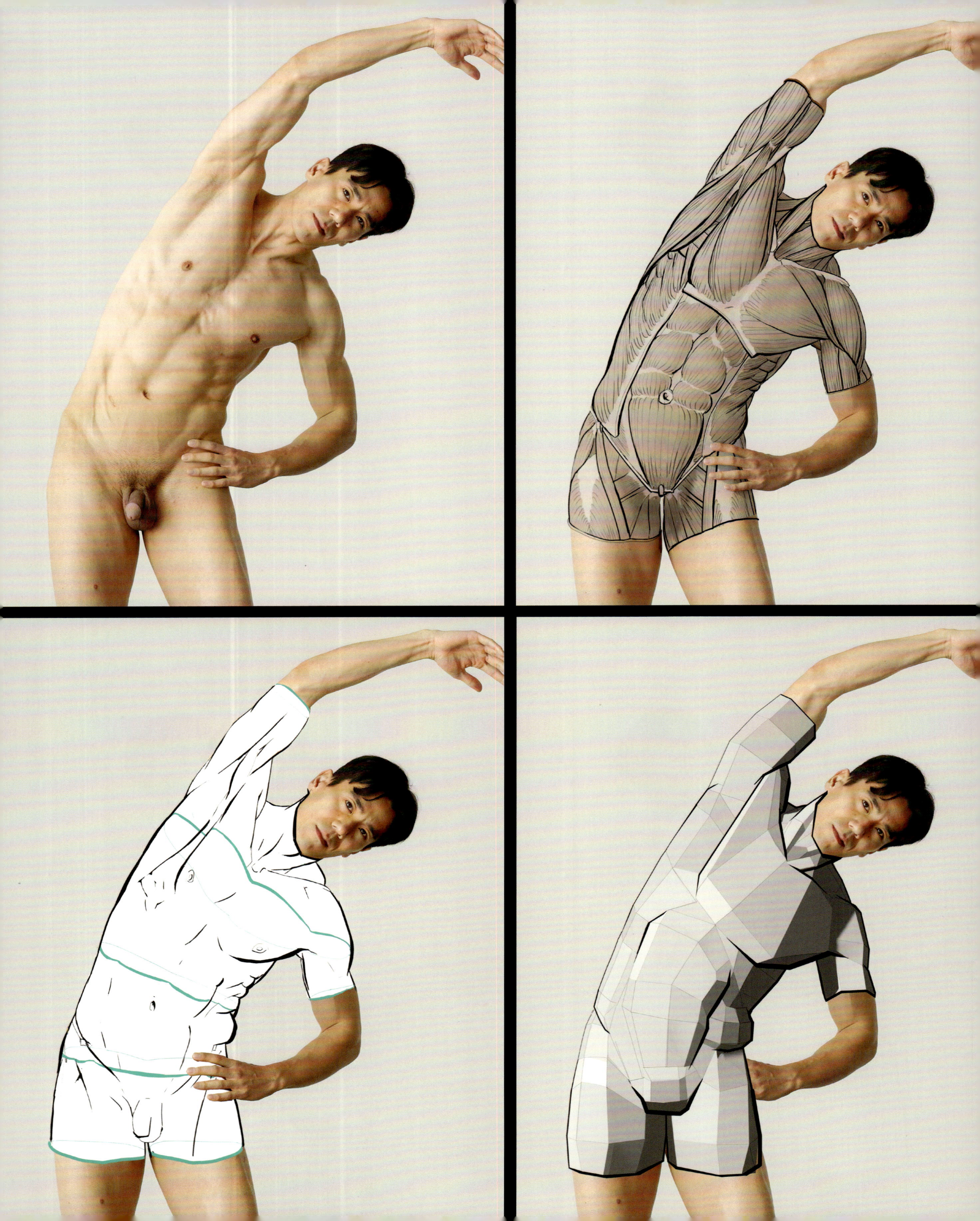

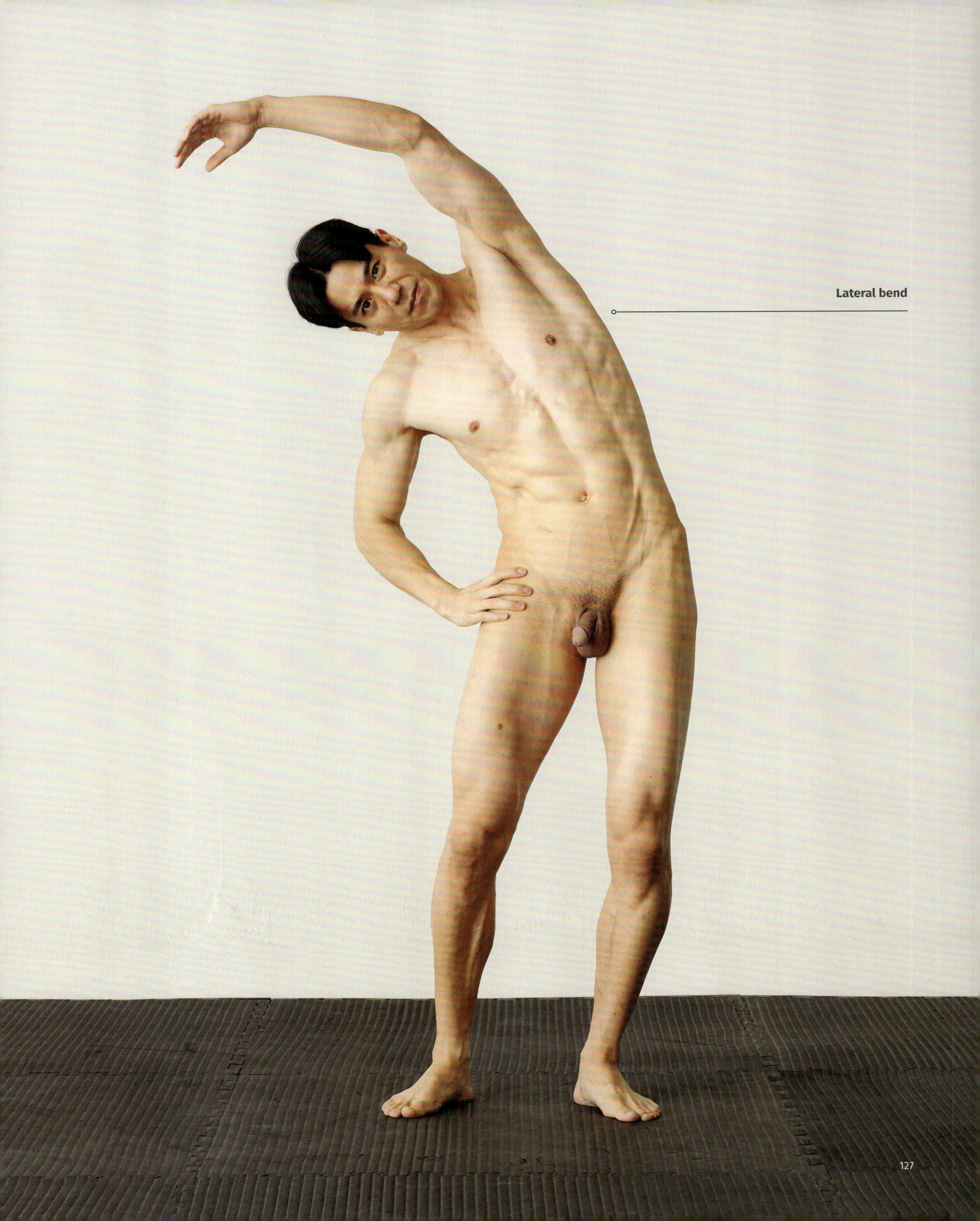
Lateral bend

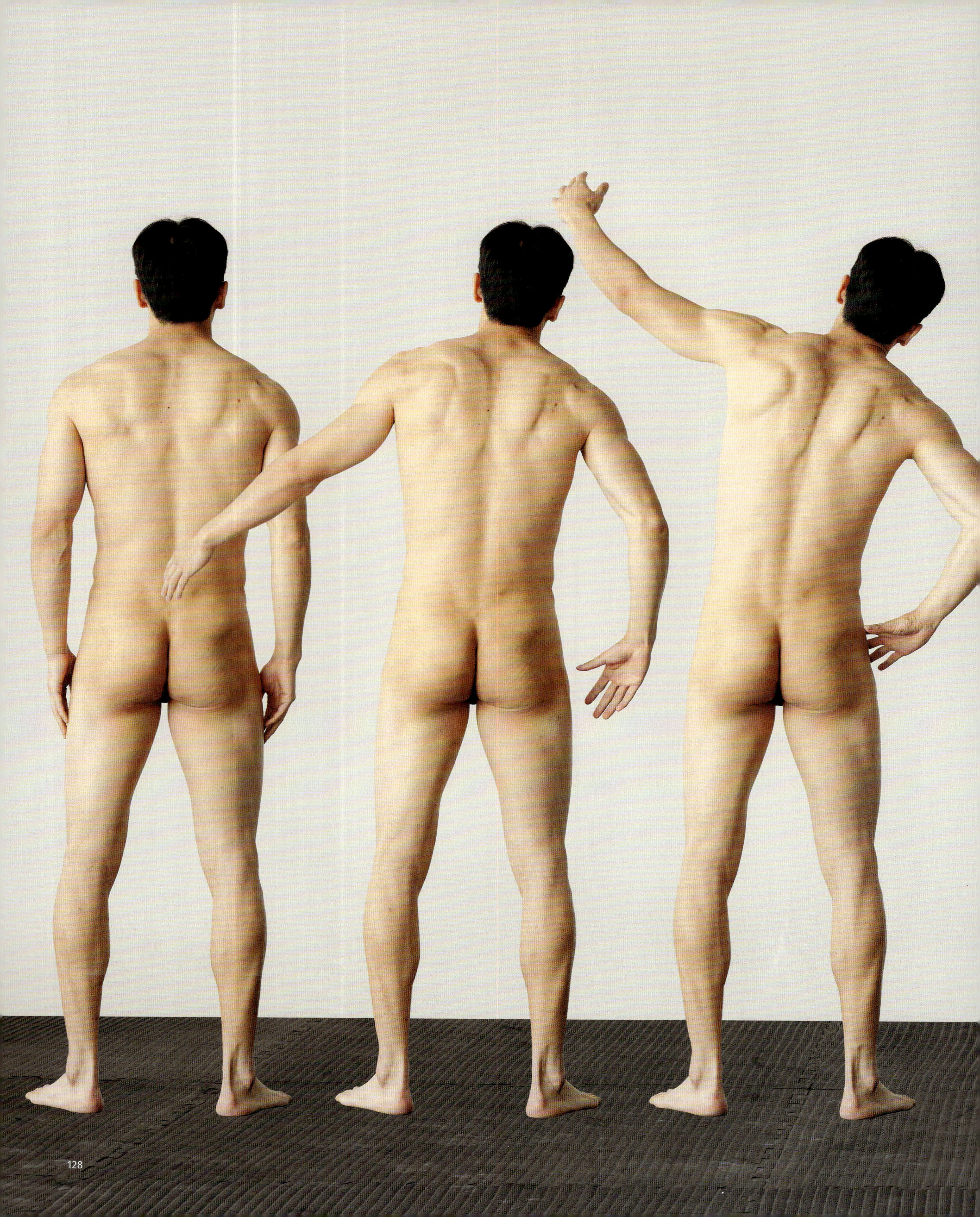

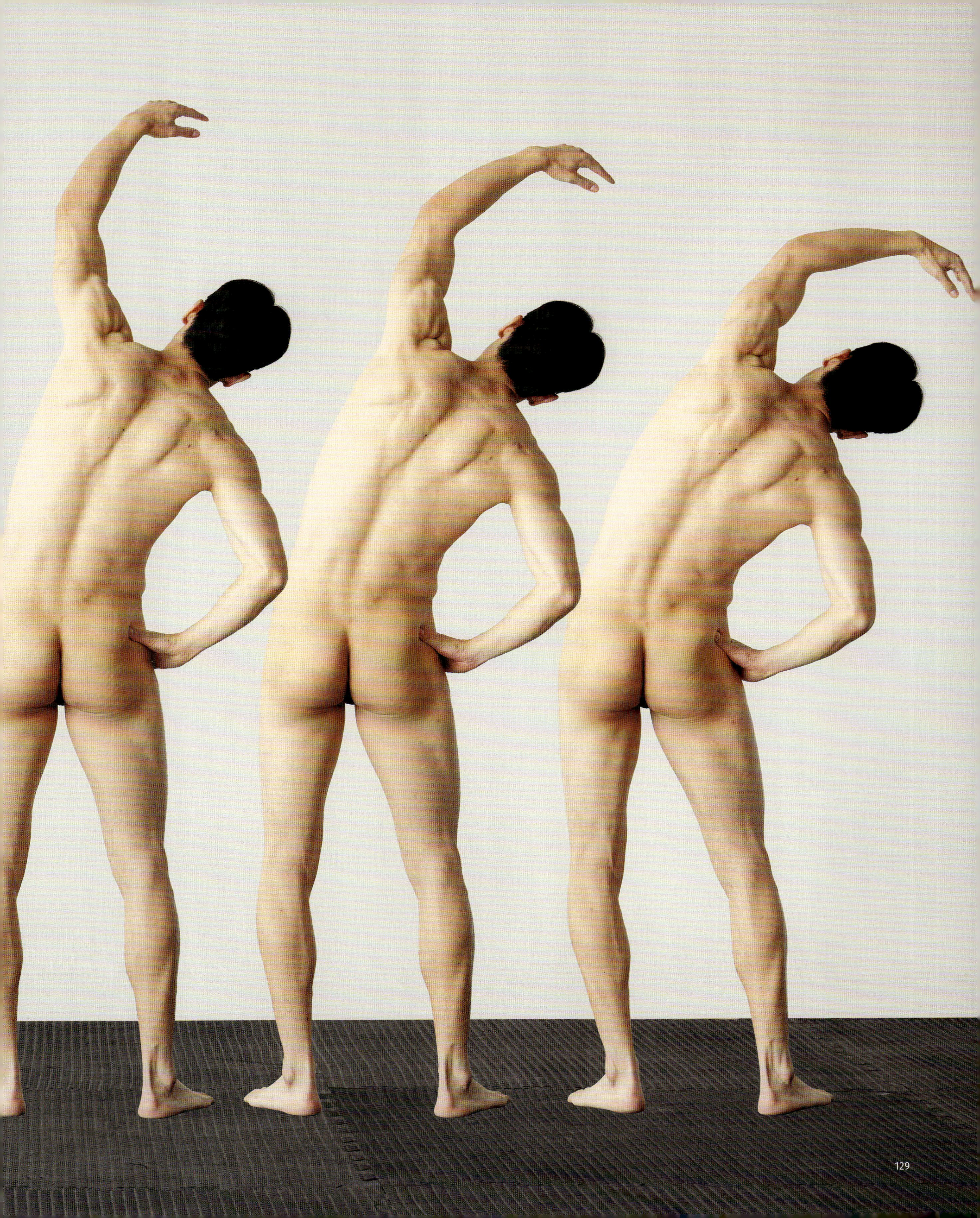

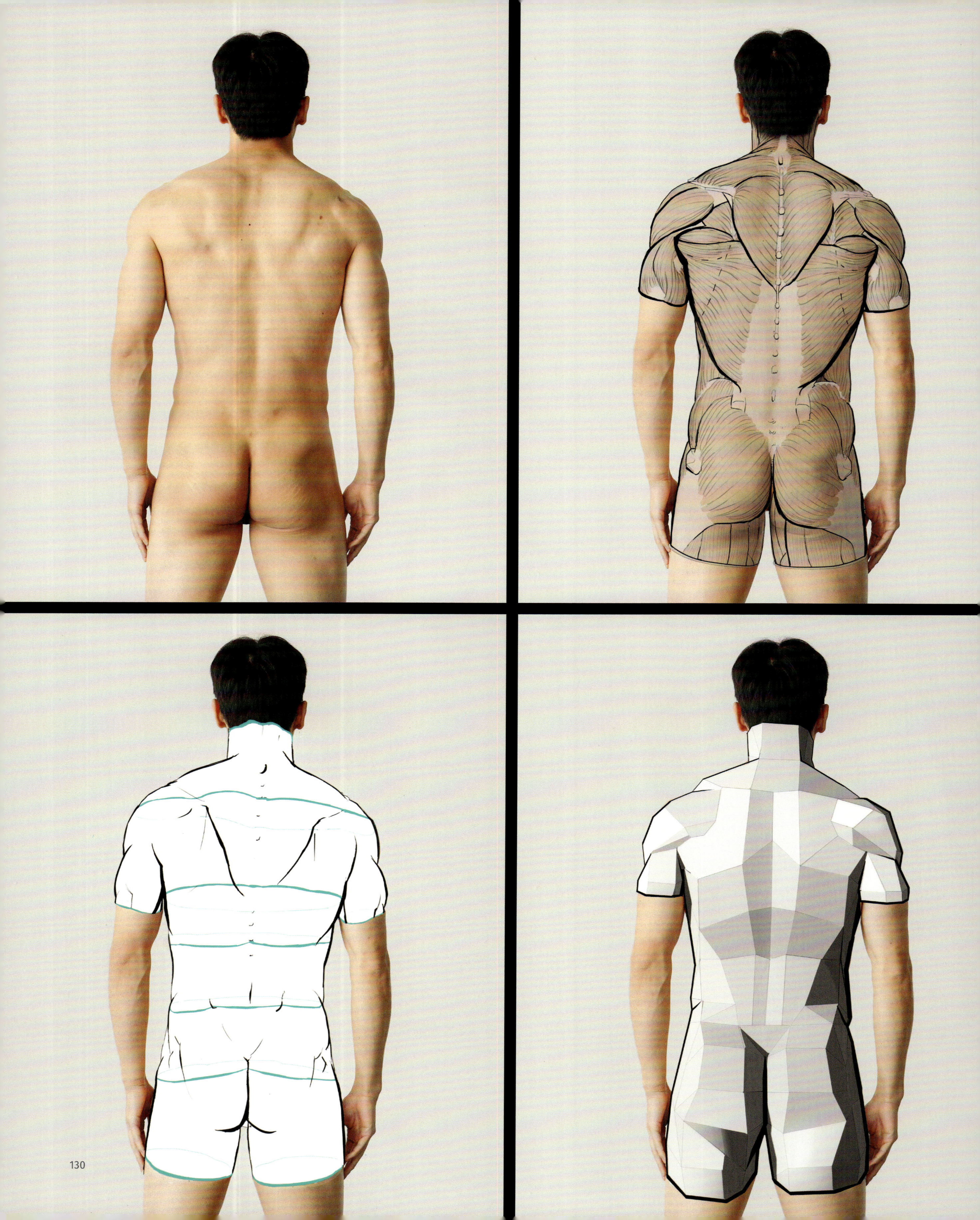

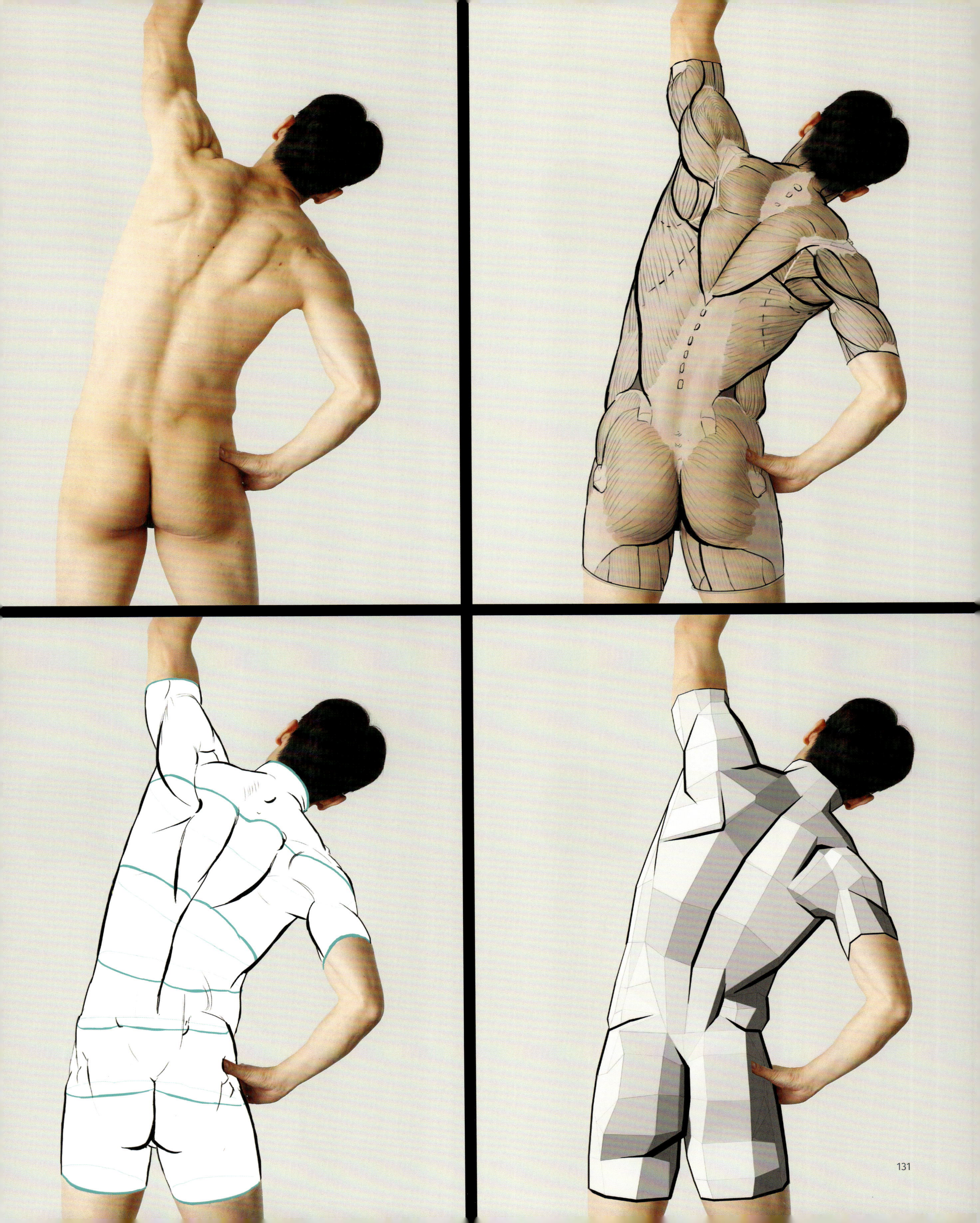

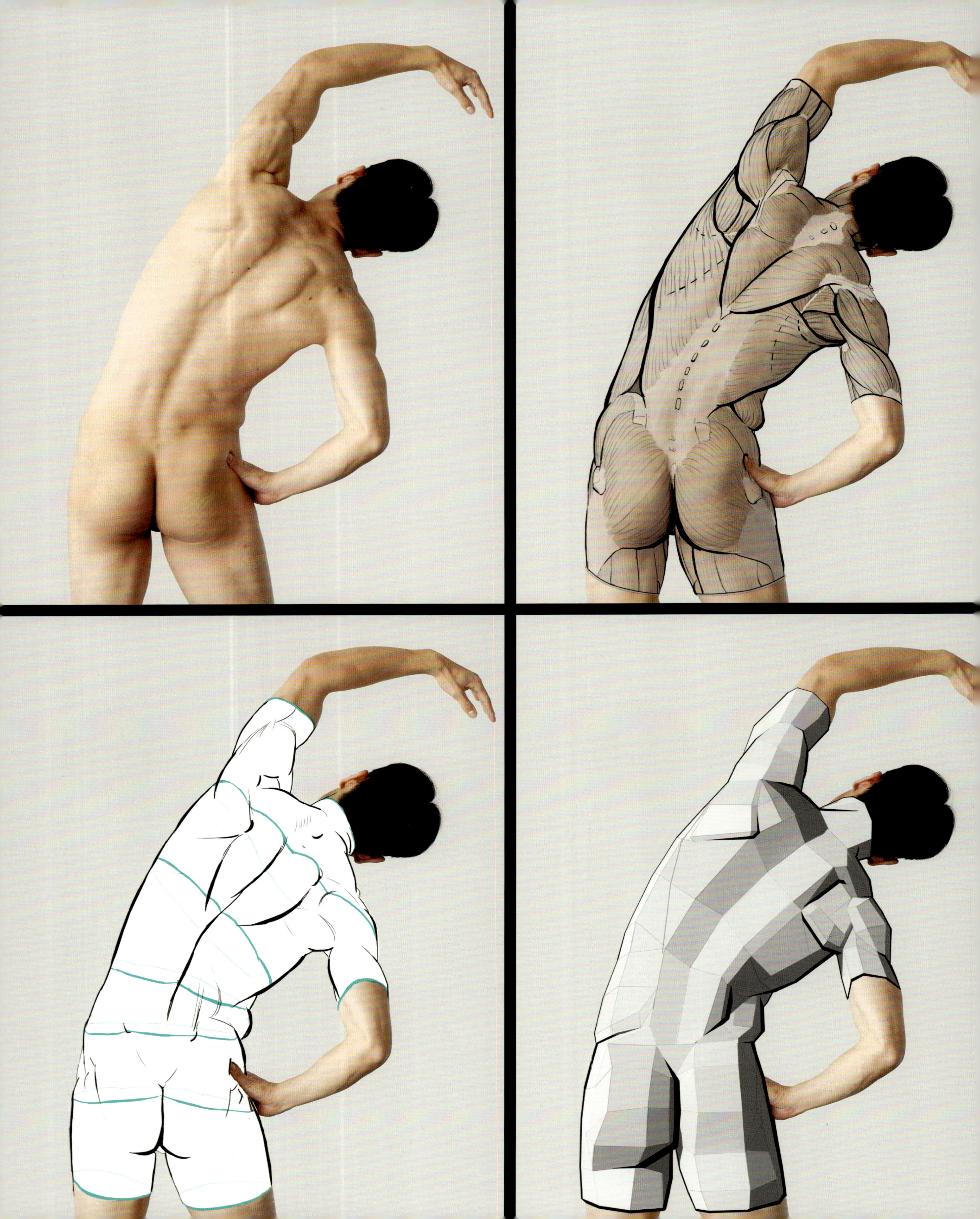

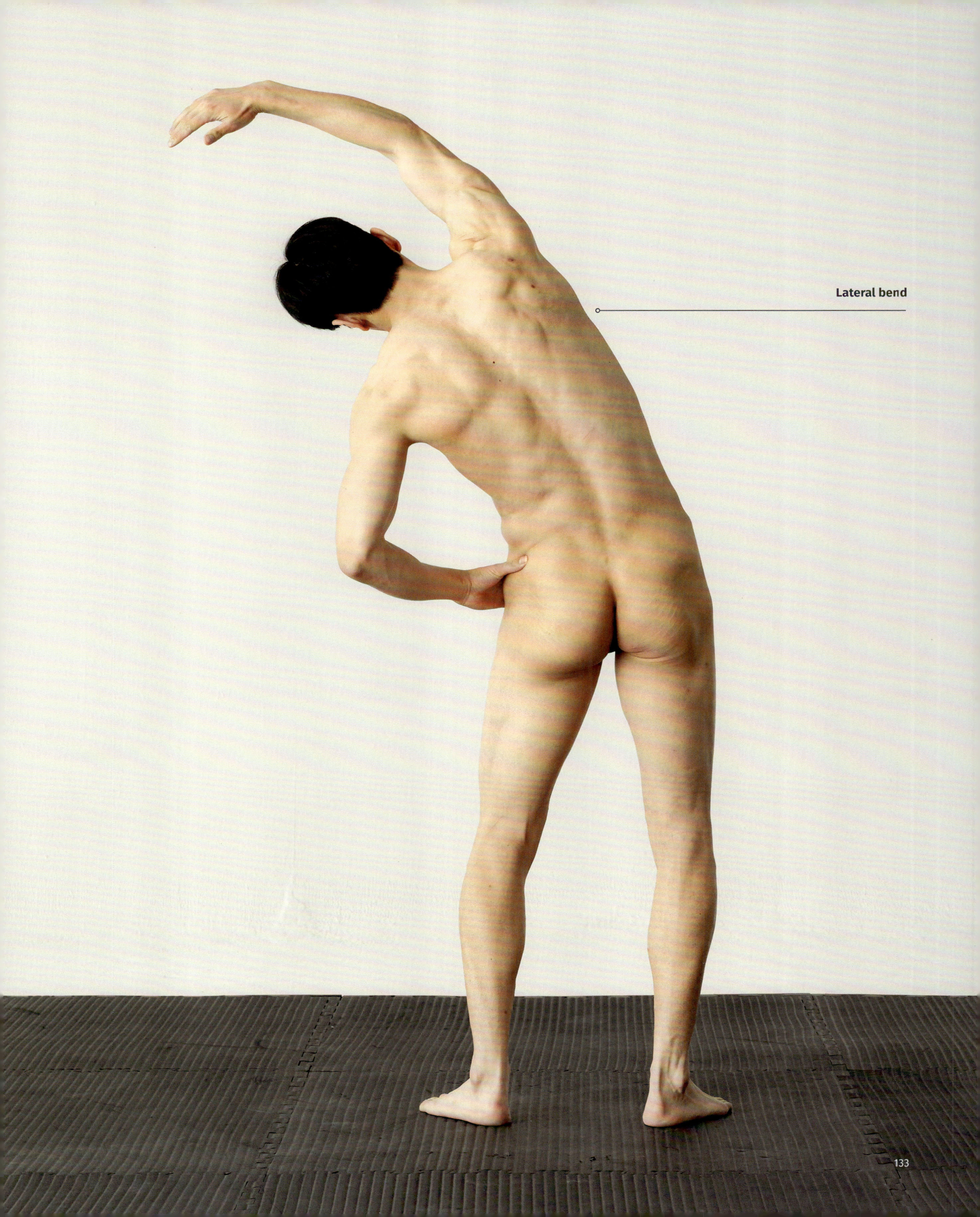
Lateral bend

Forearm pronation to supination

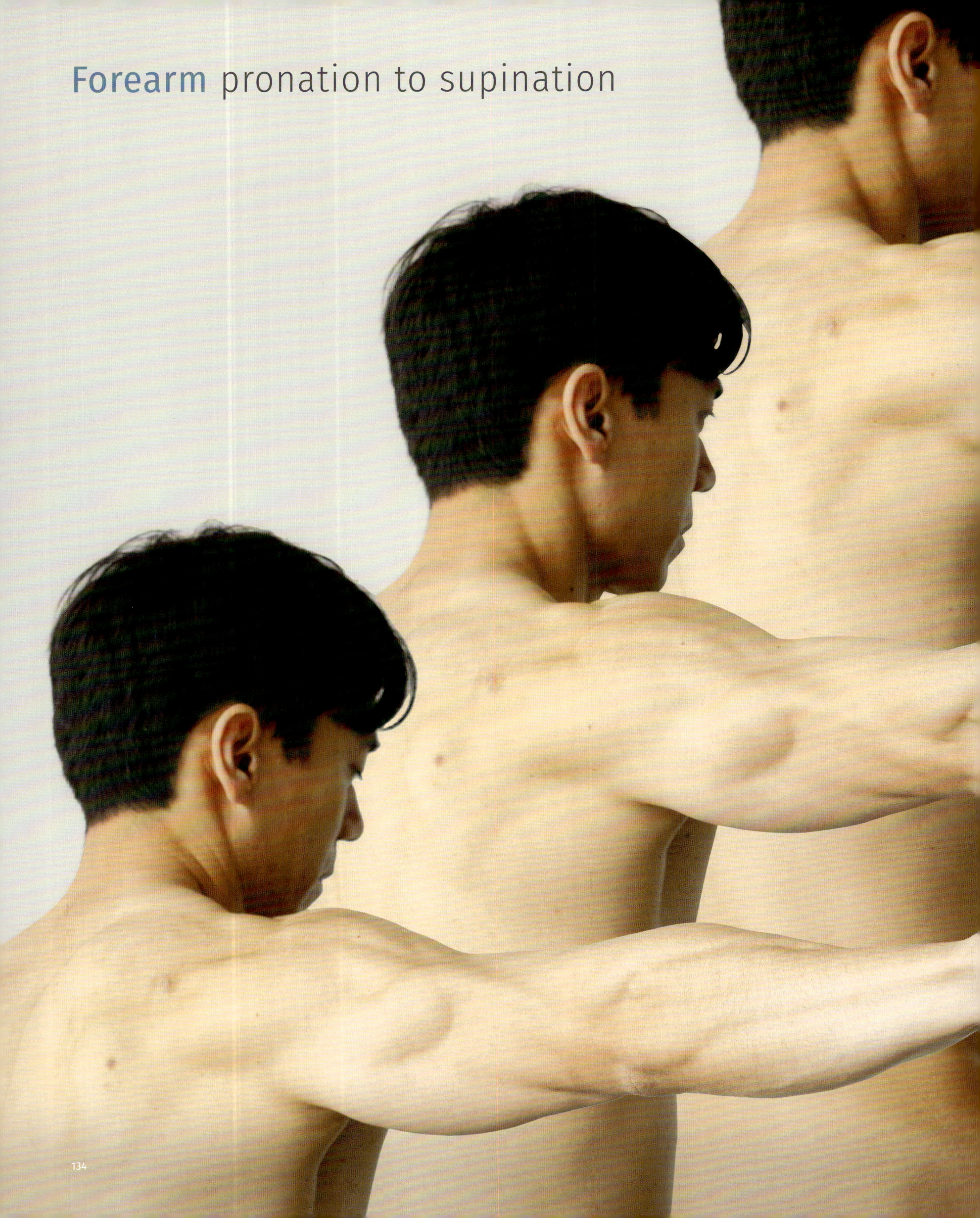

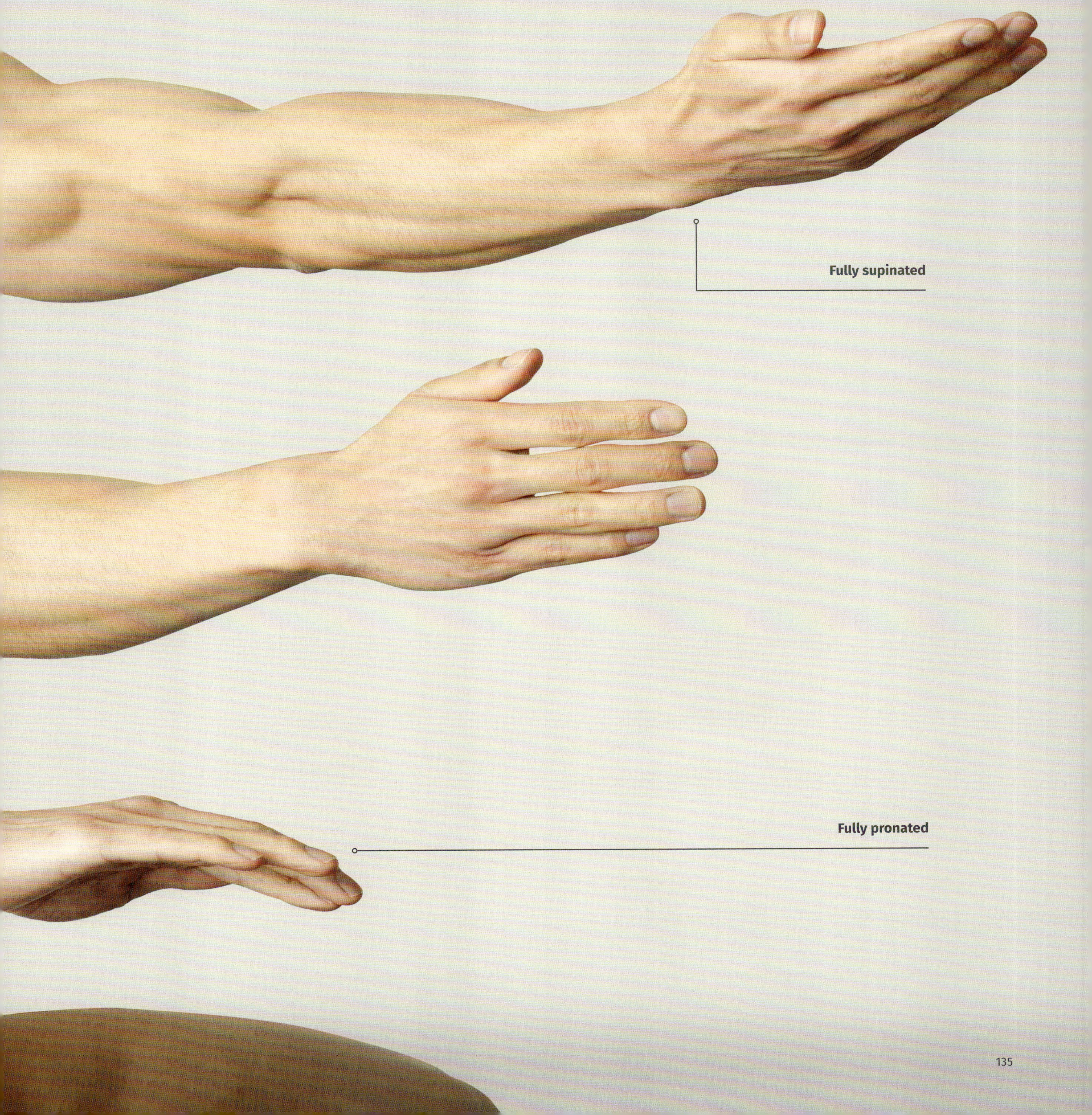

Fully supinated
Fully pronated

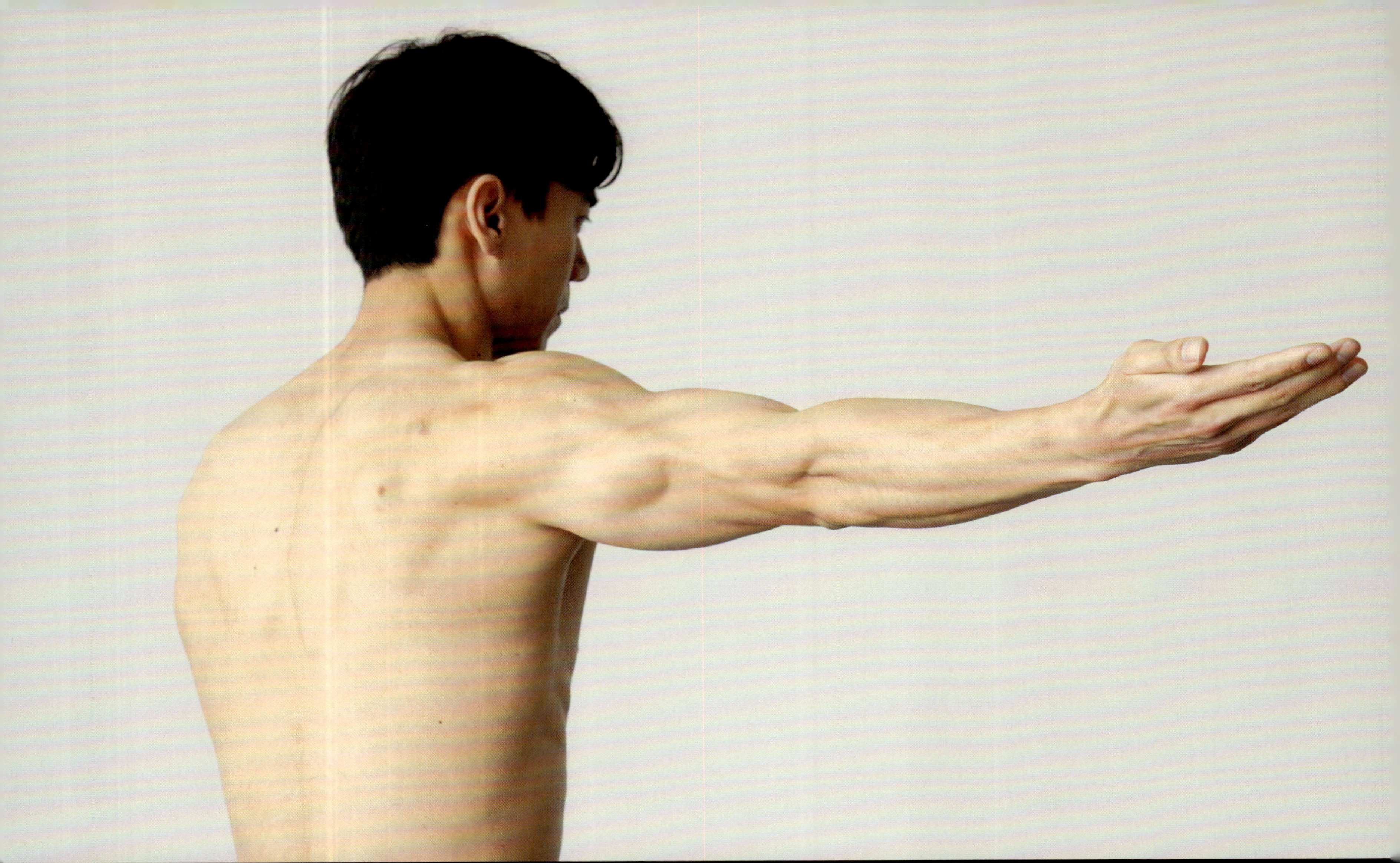

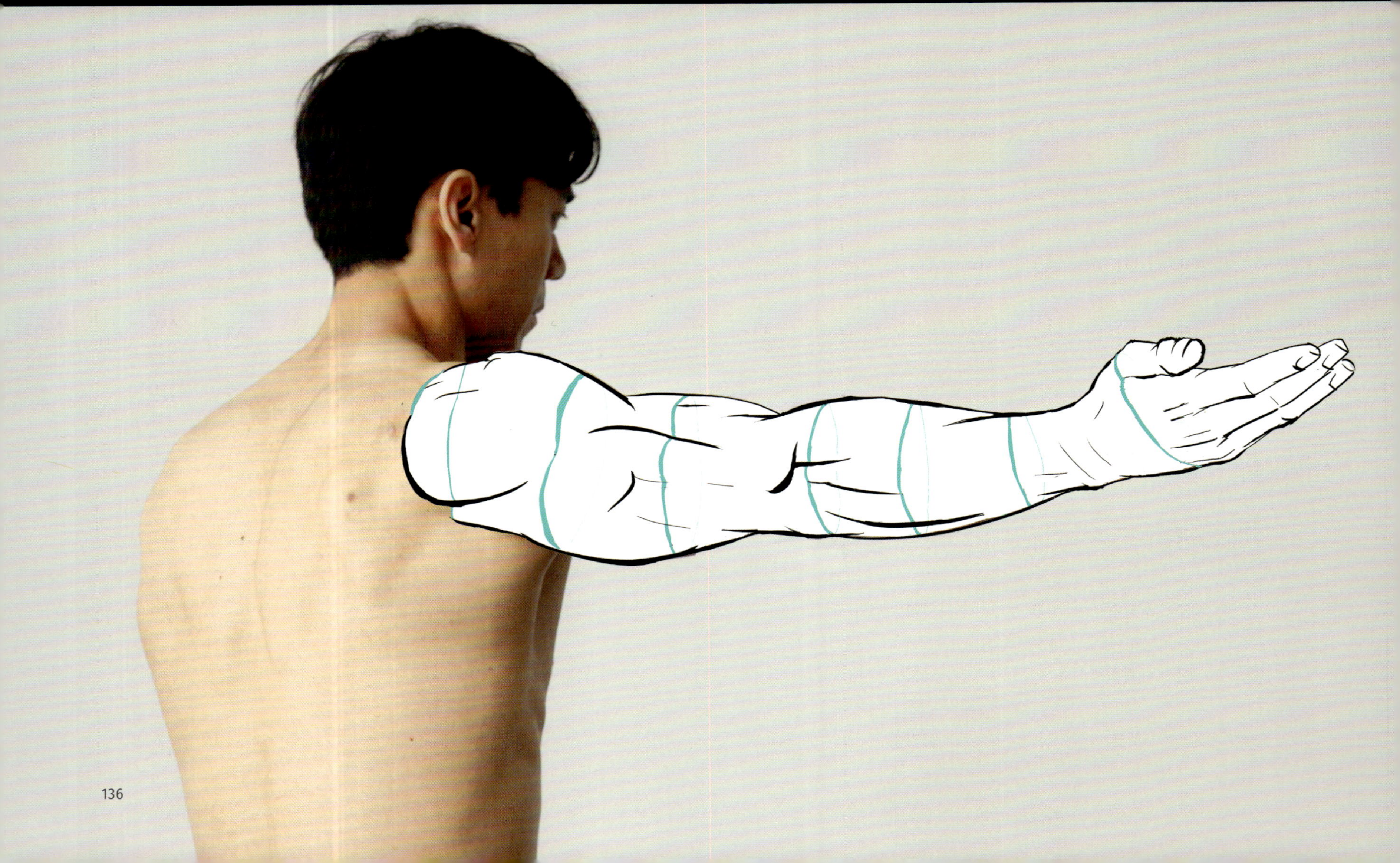

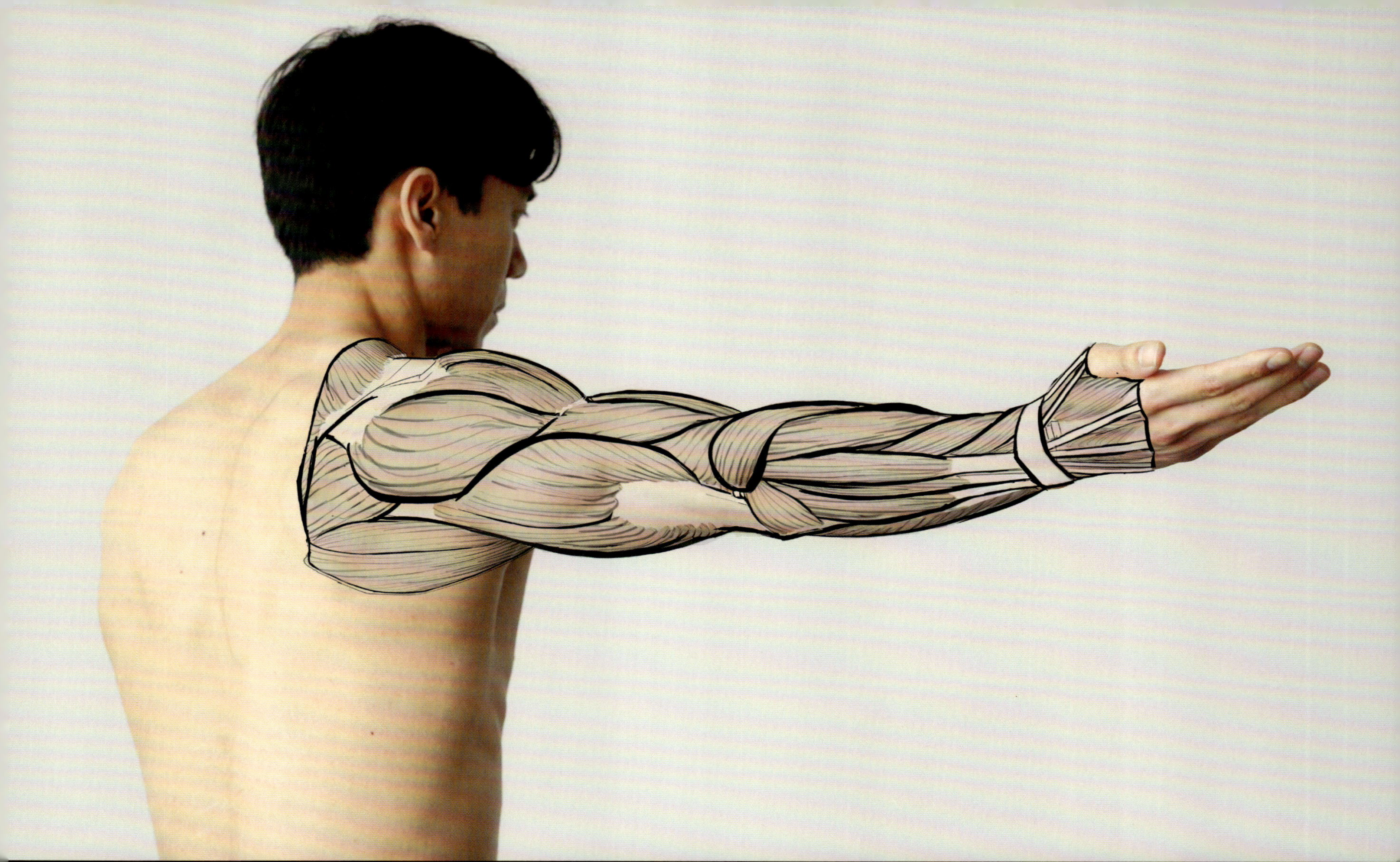

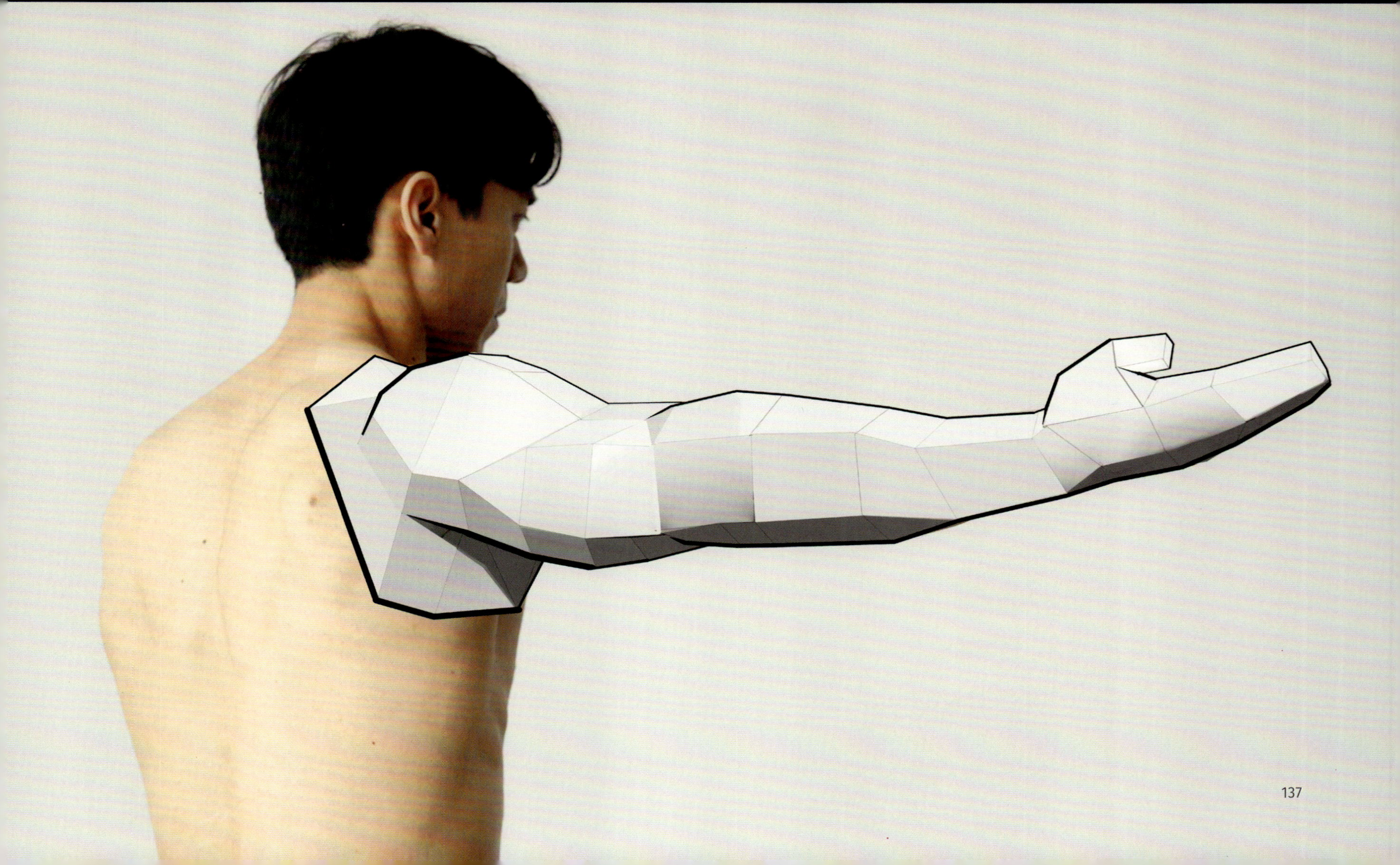

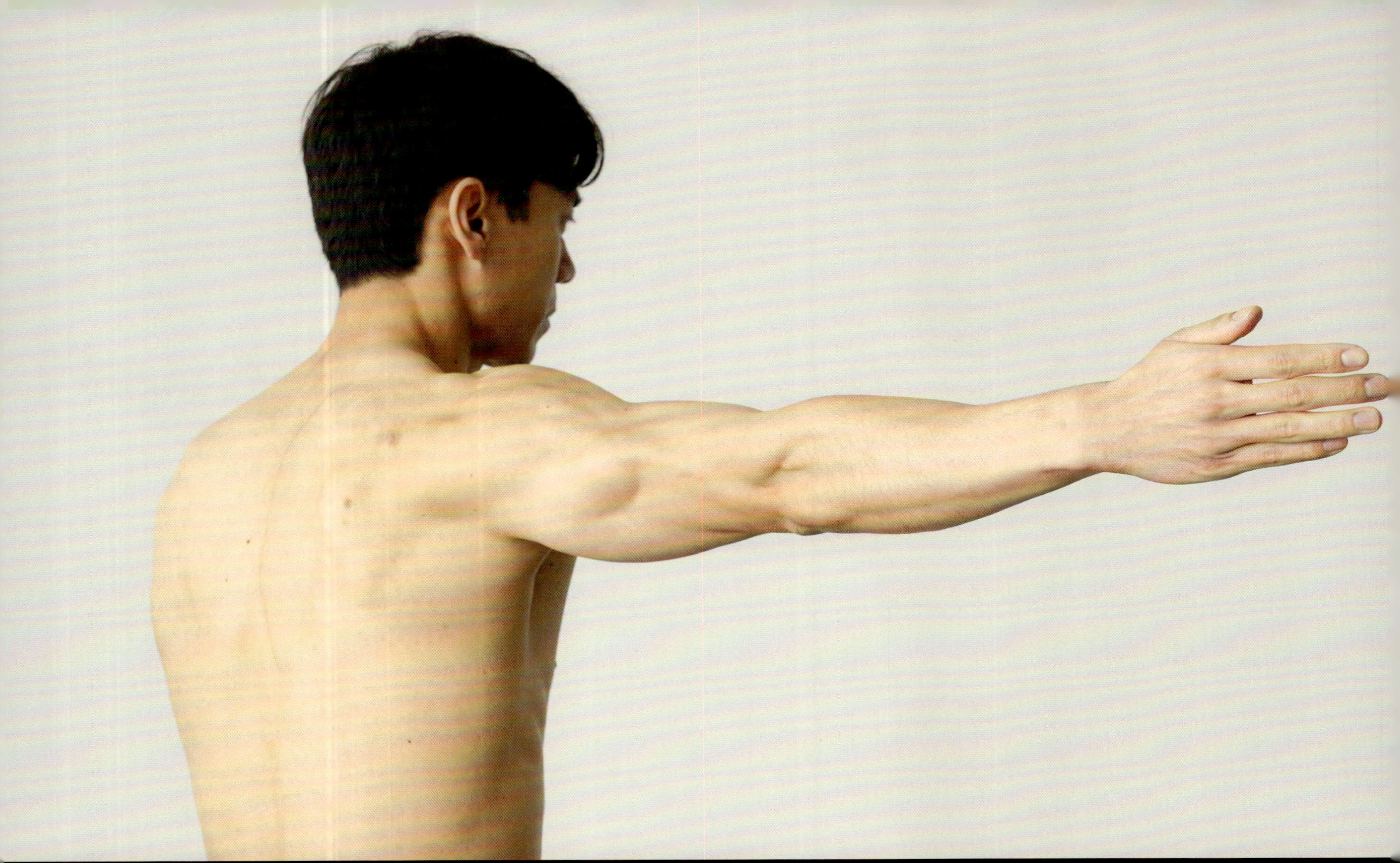

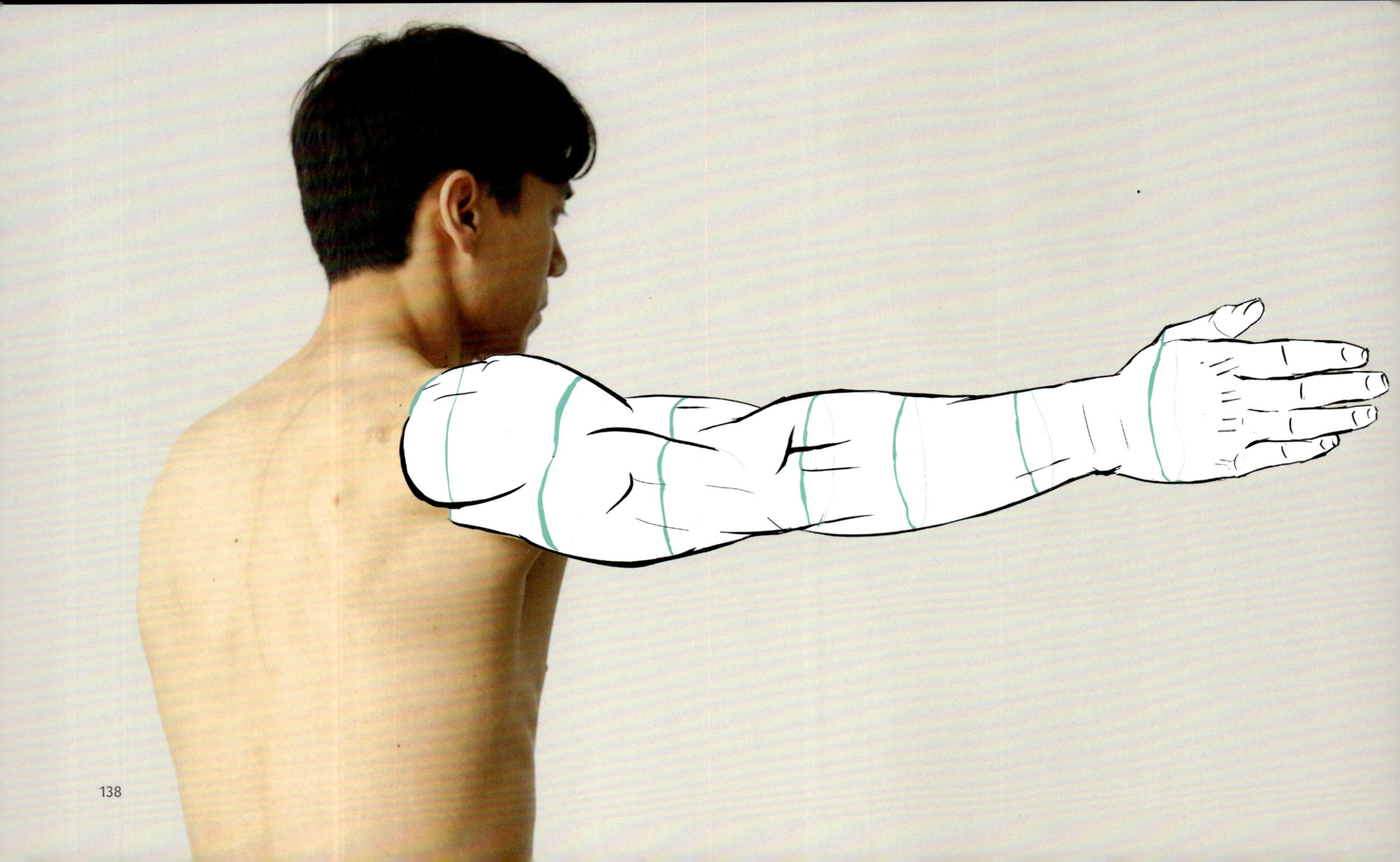

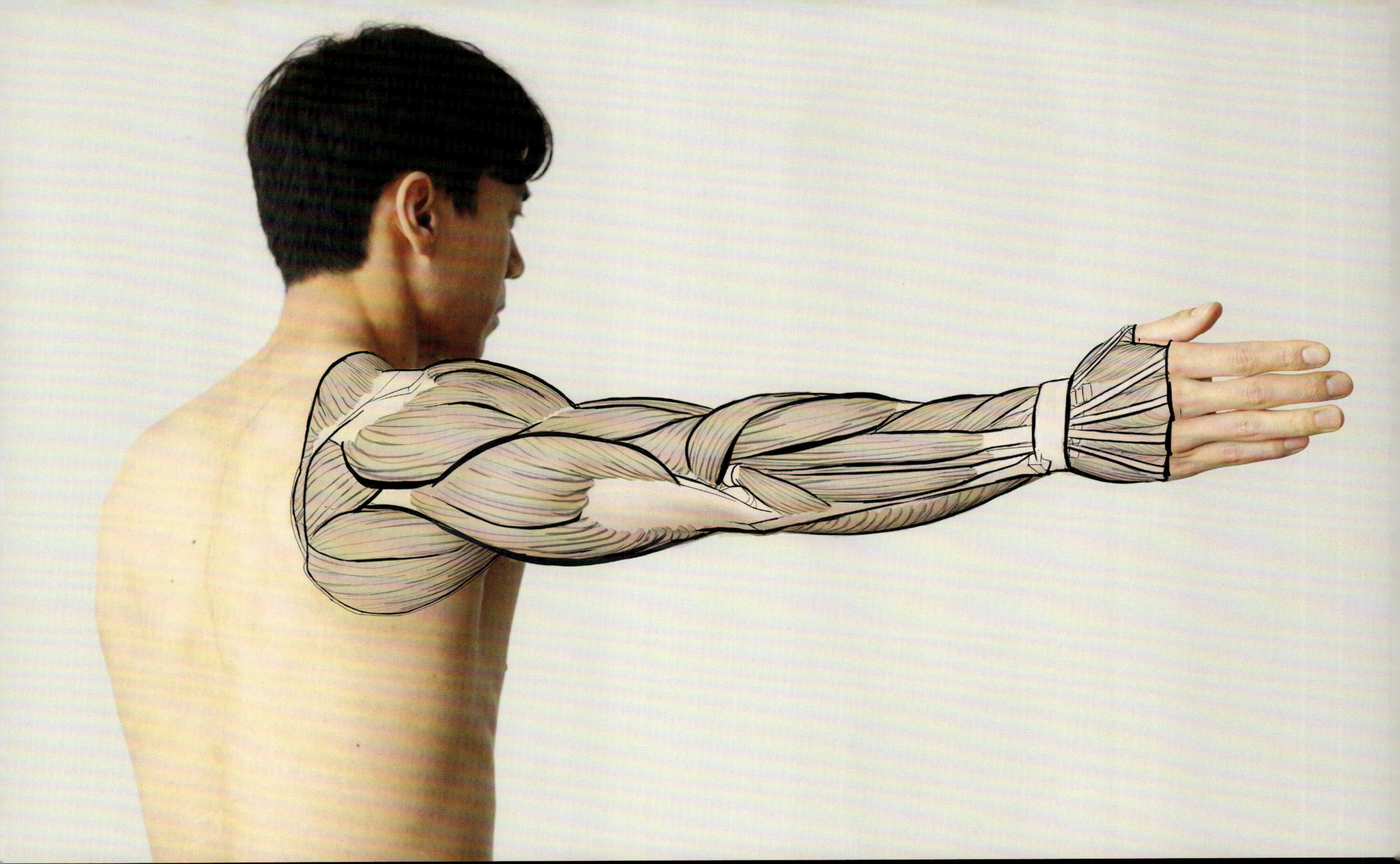

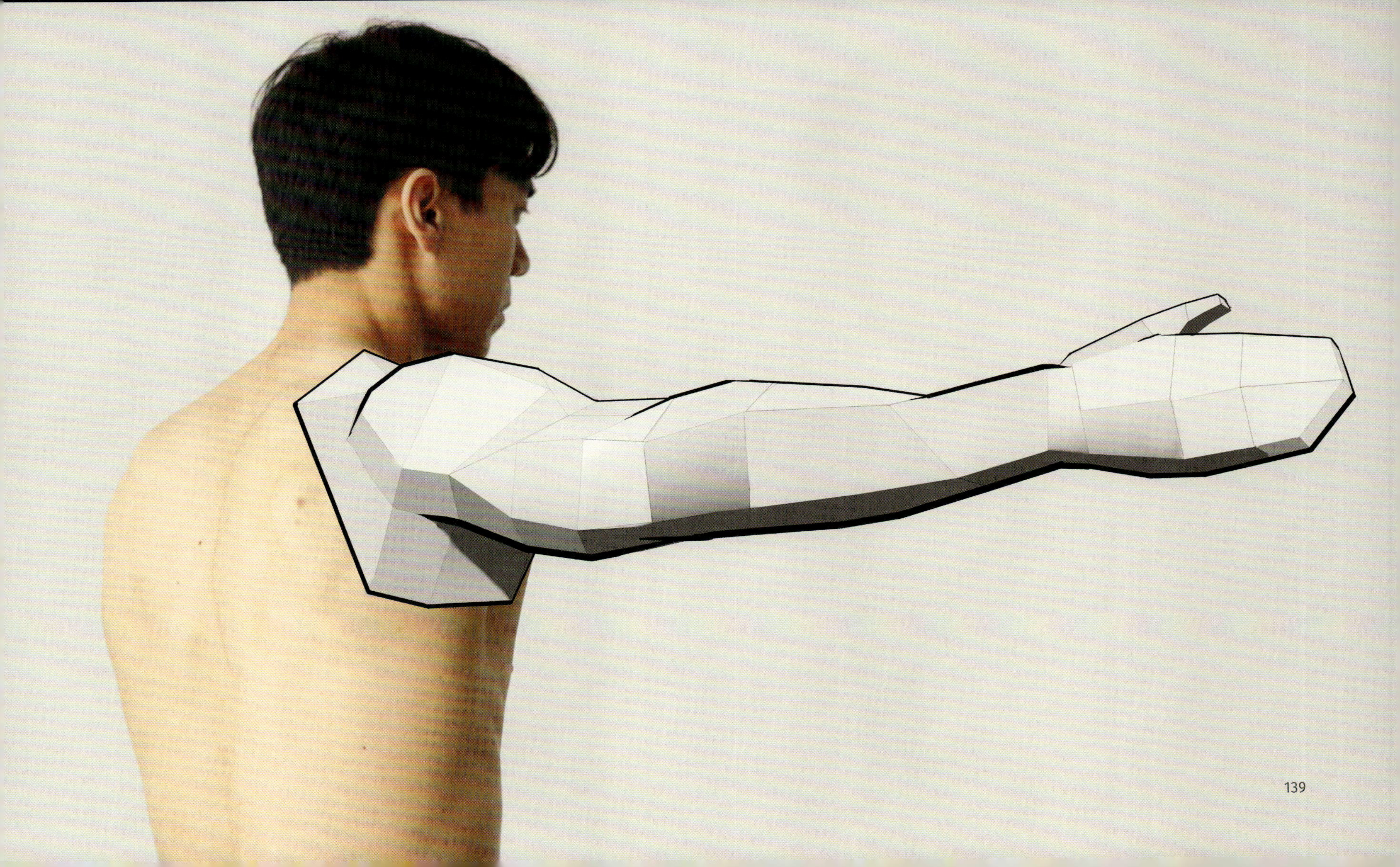

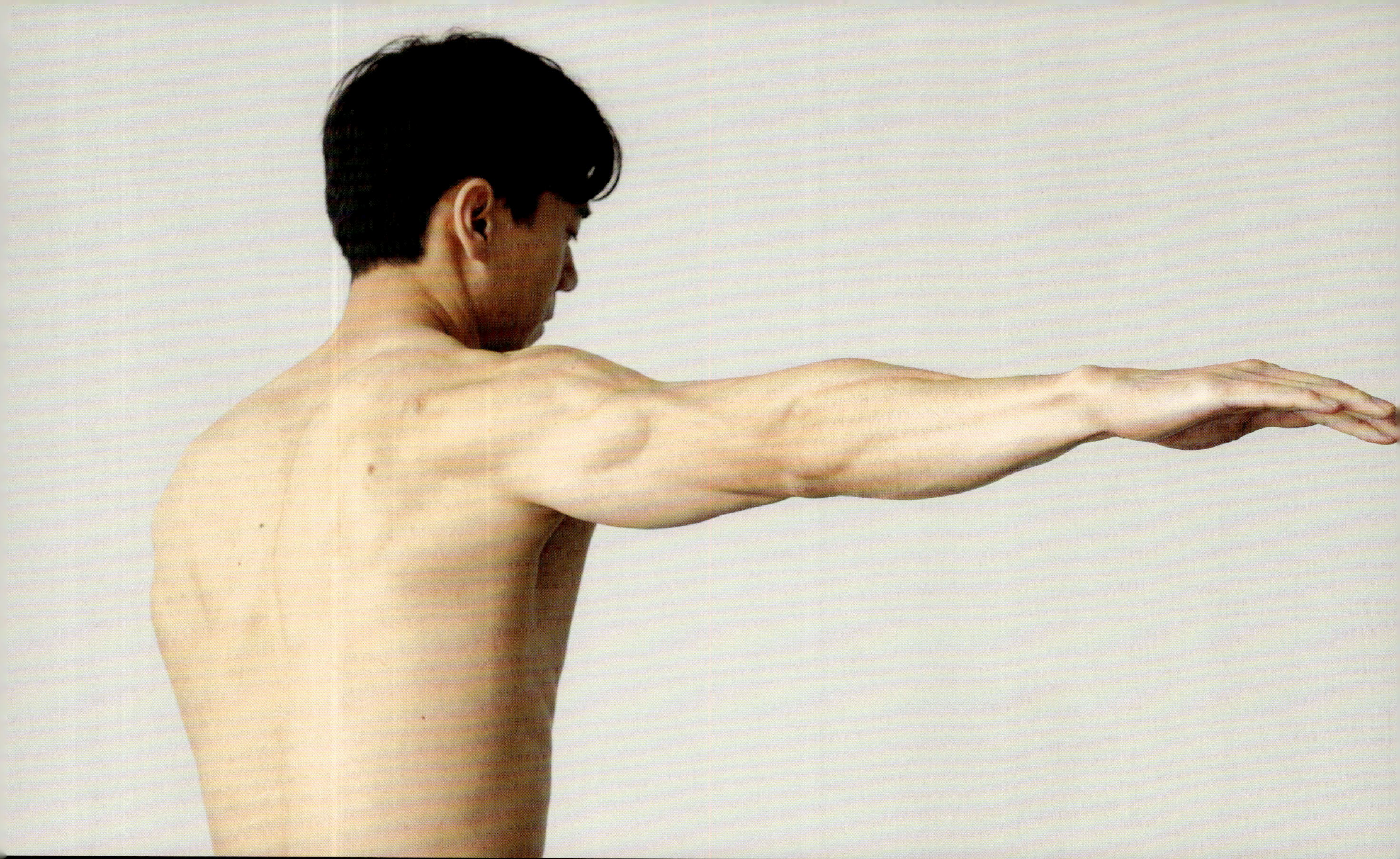

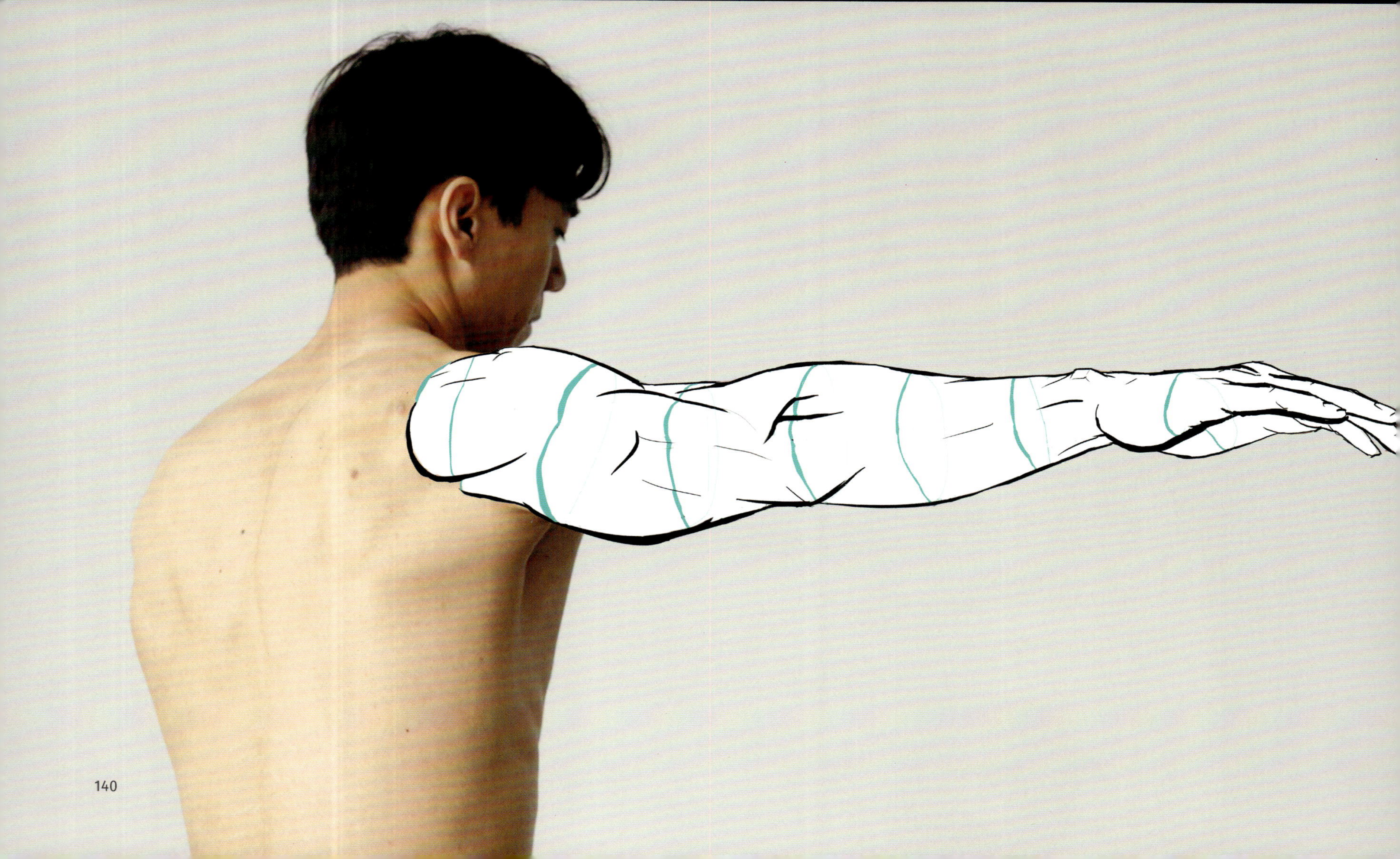

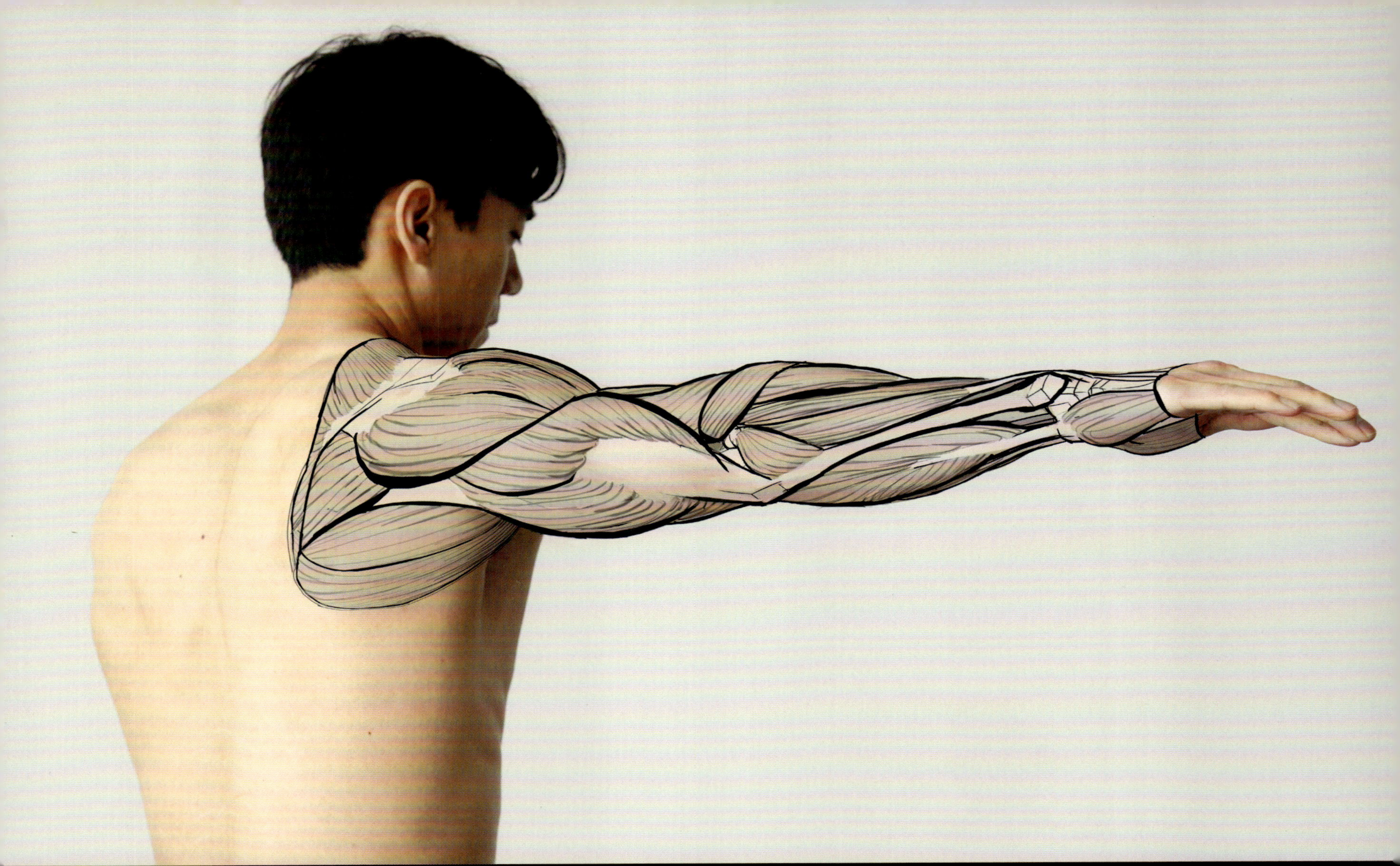

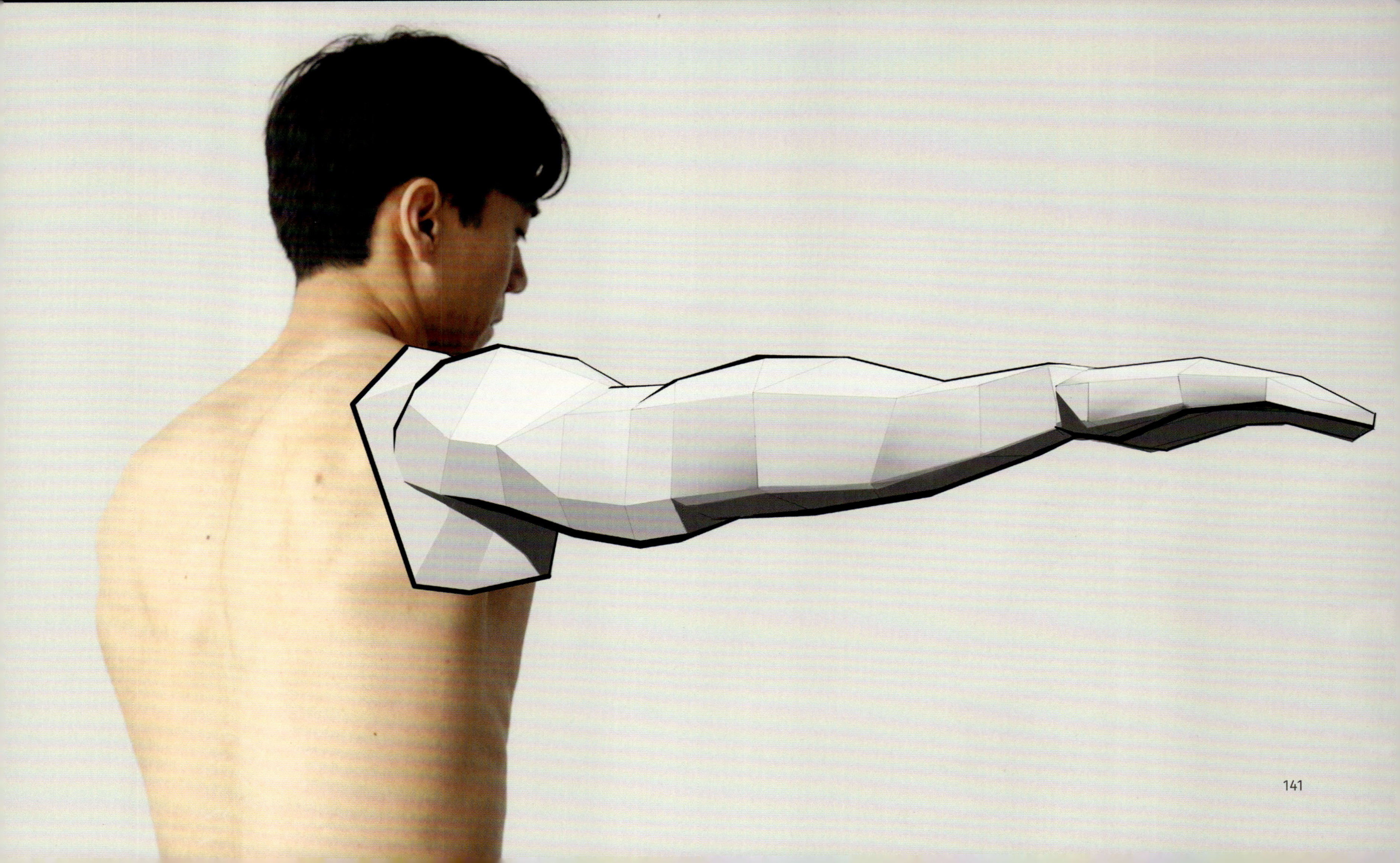

Torso retraction to protraction

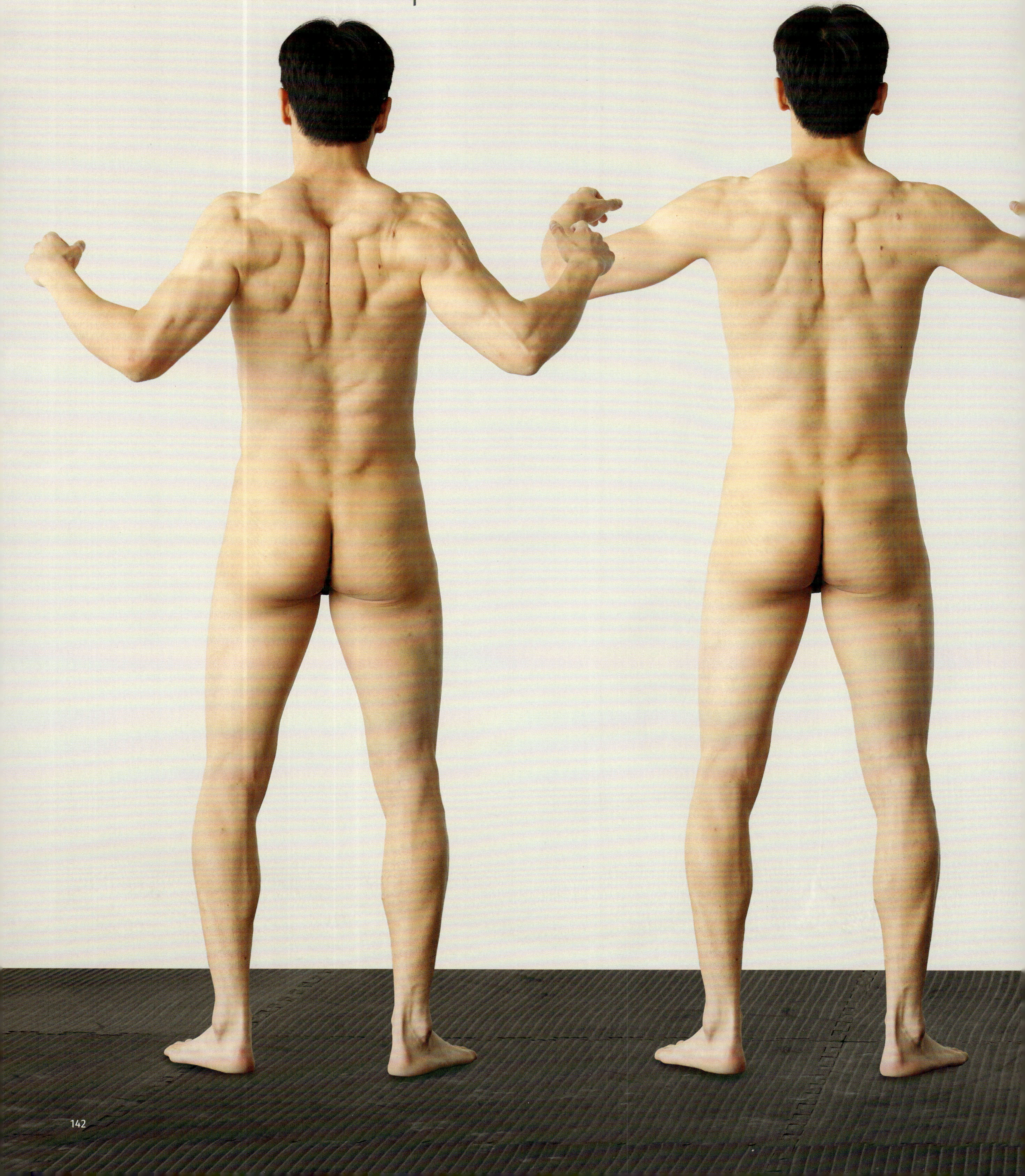

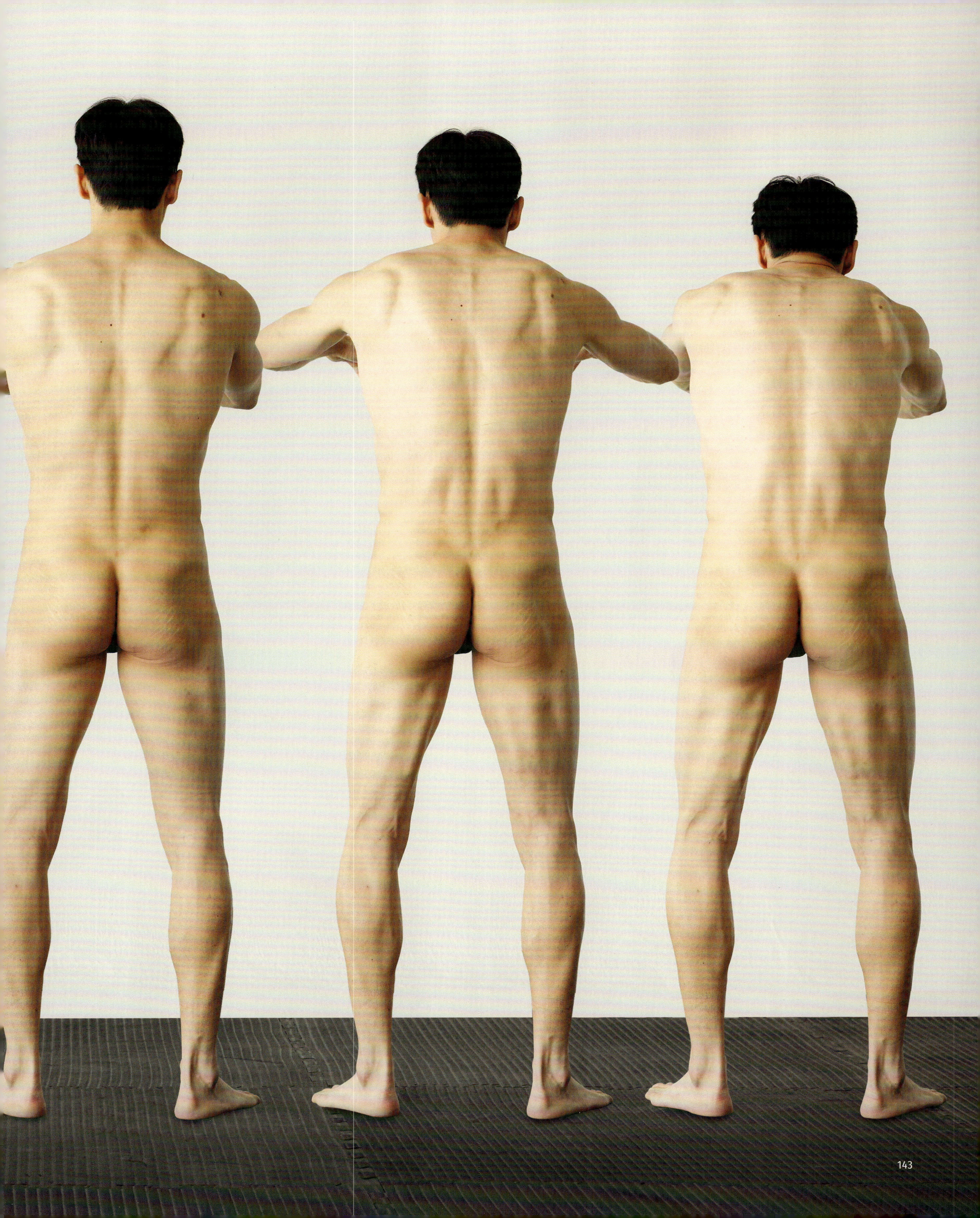

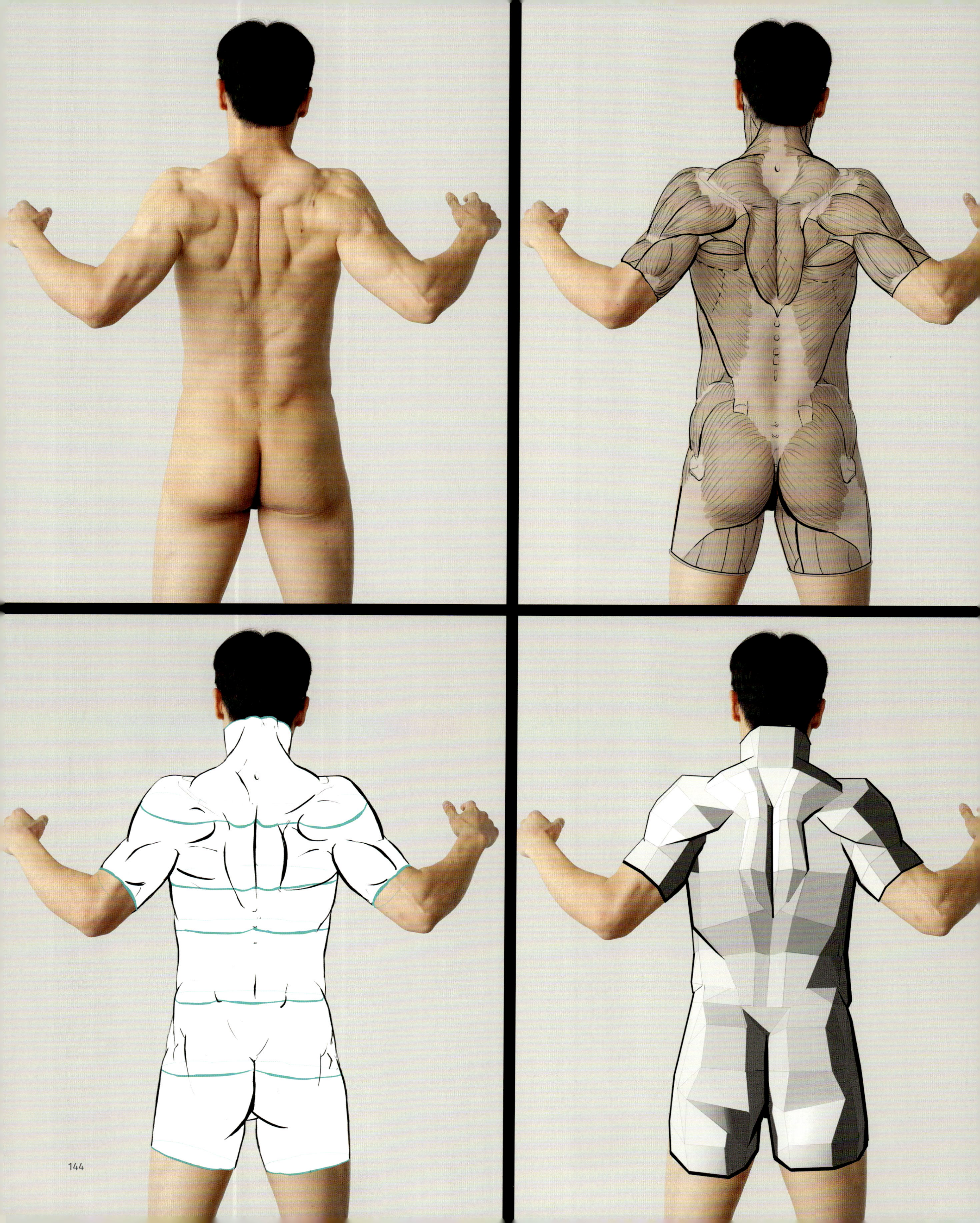

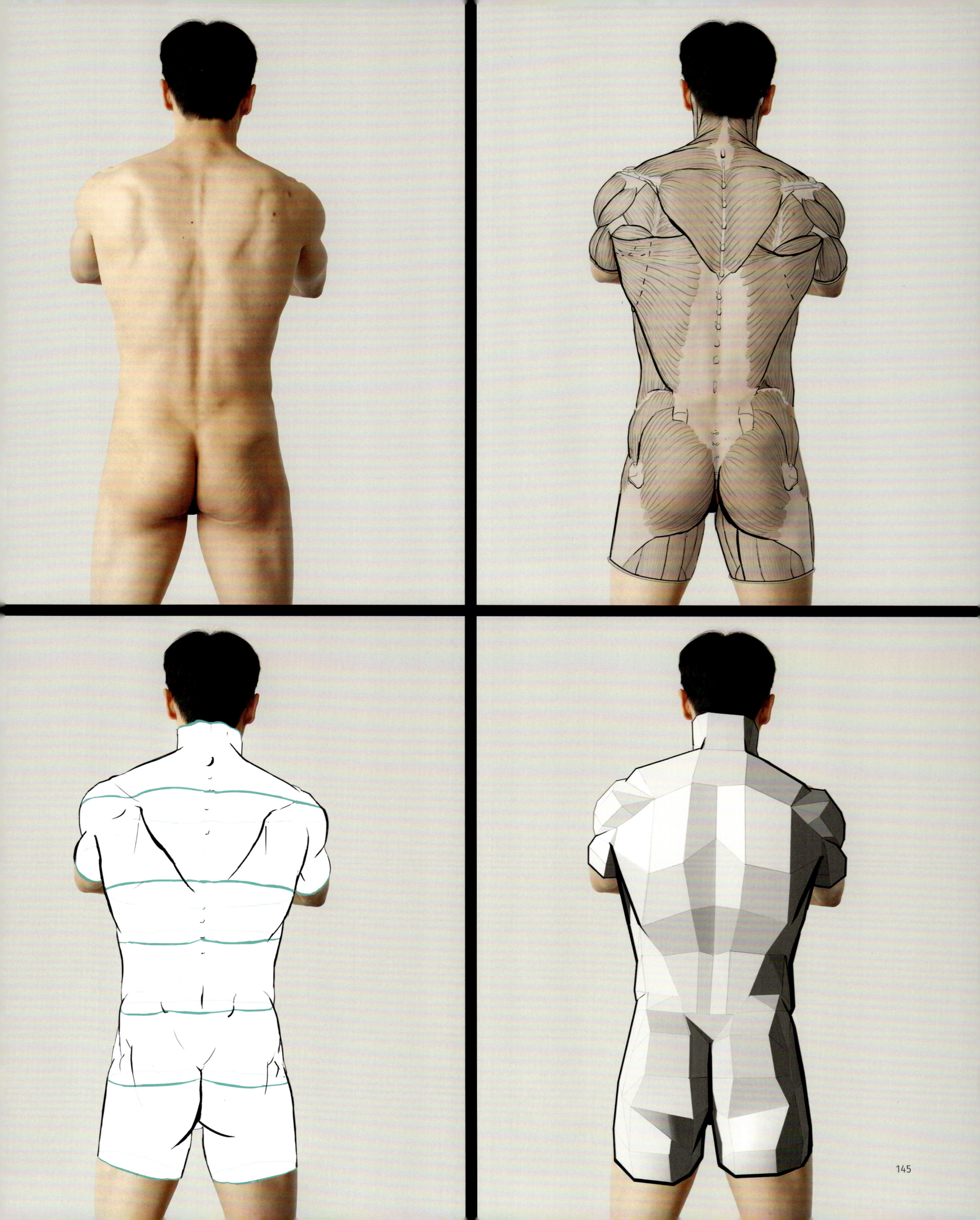

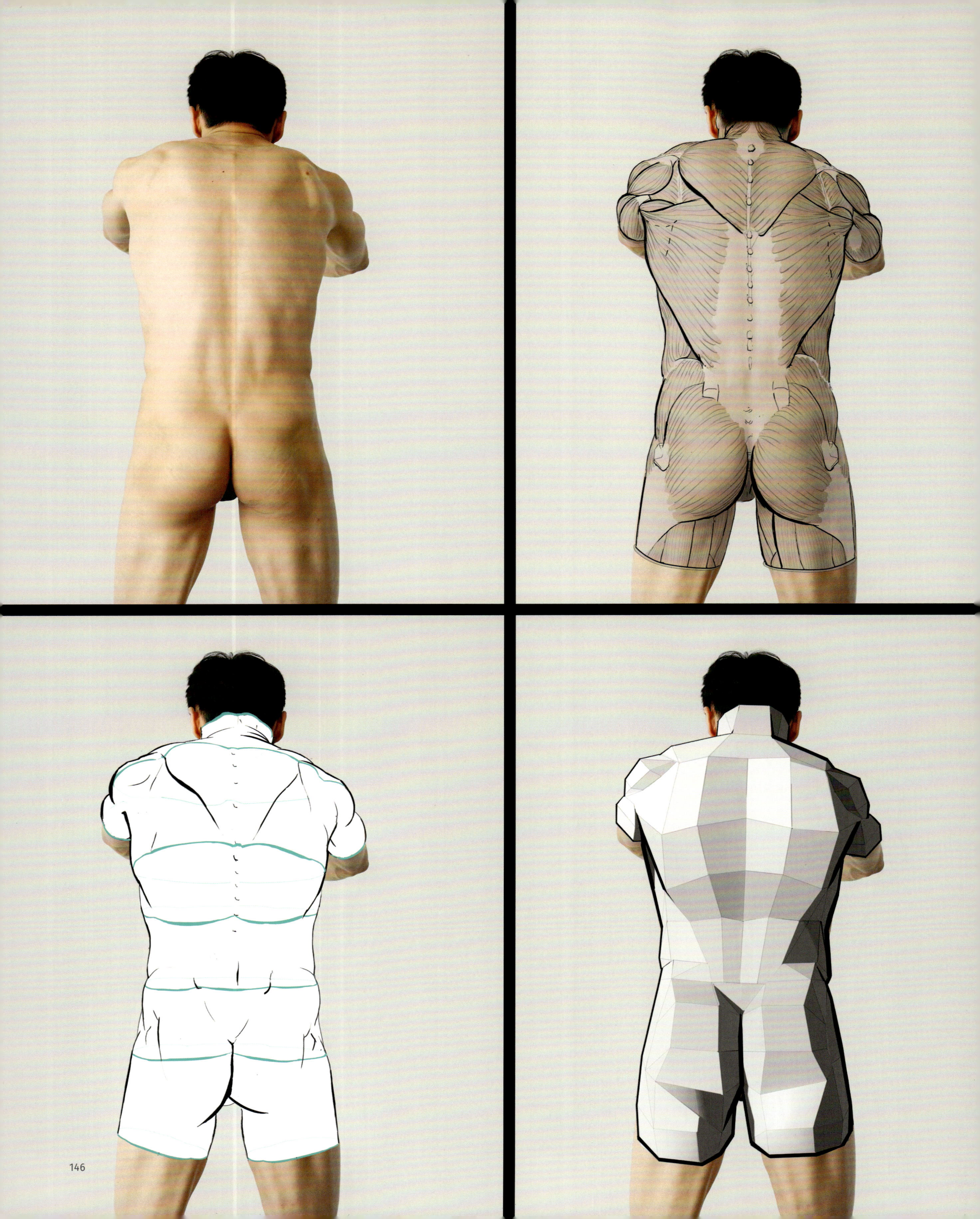

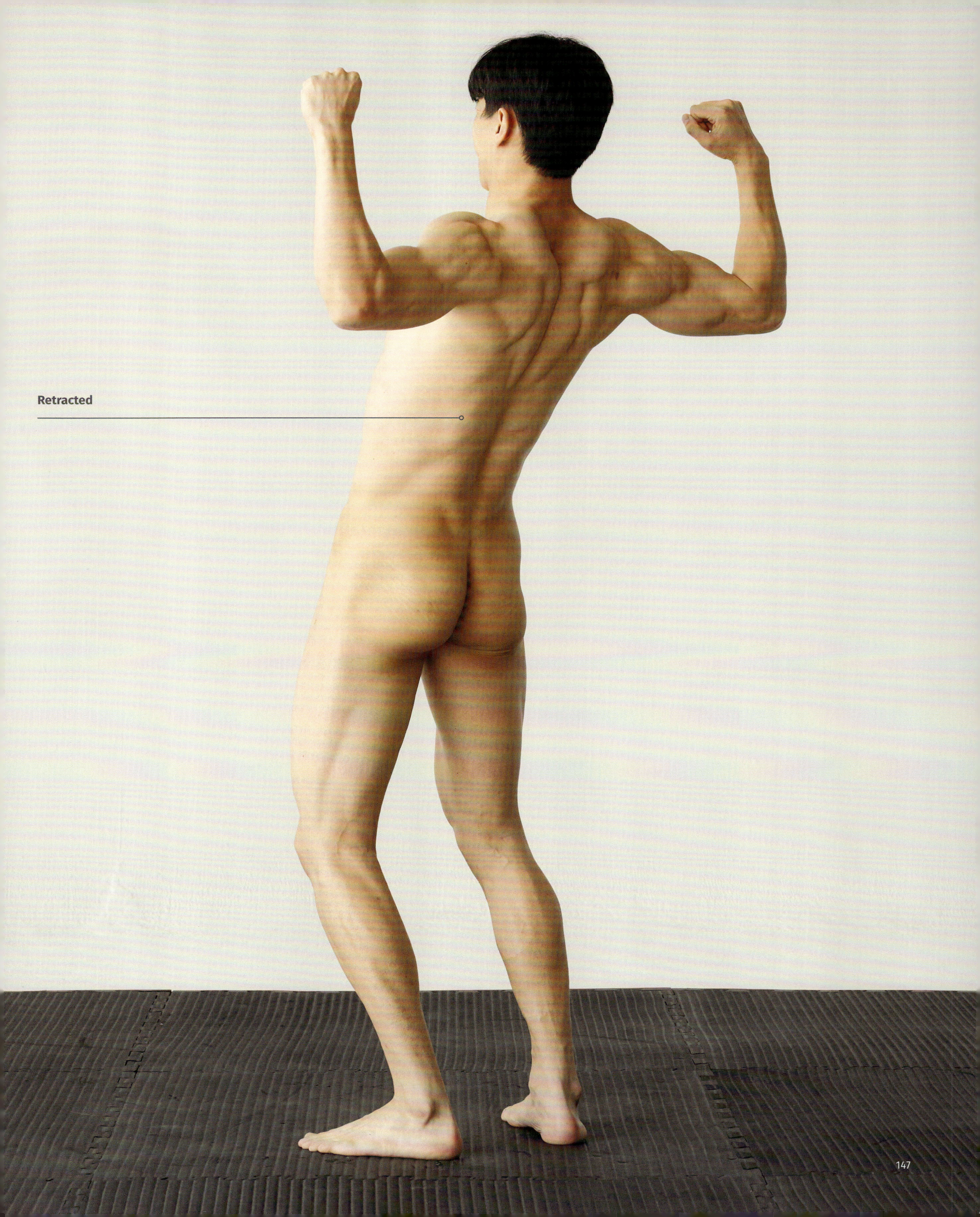
Retracted

Neck lateral bend

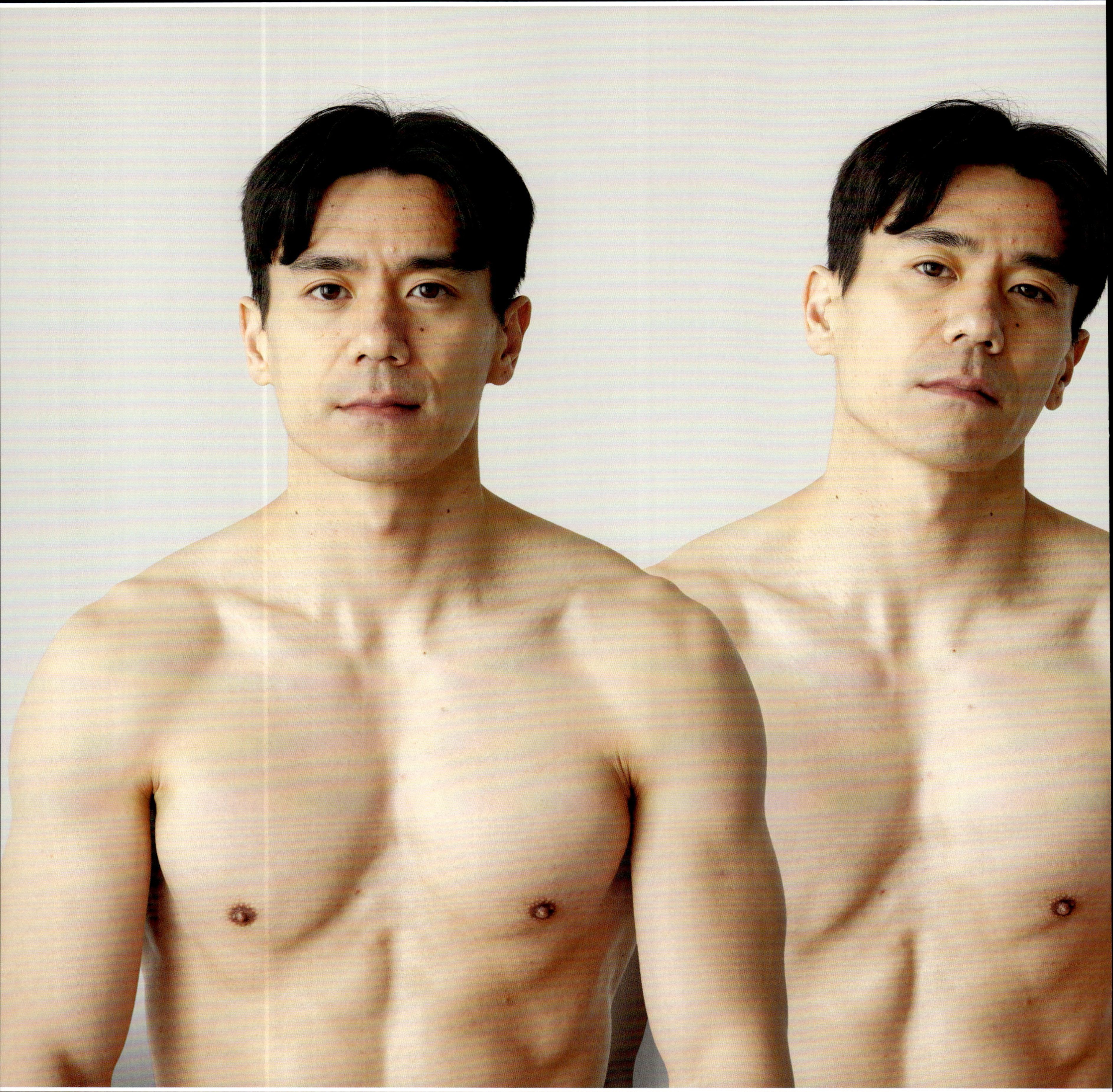

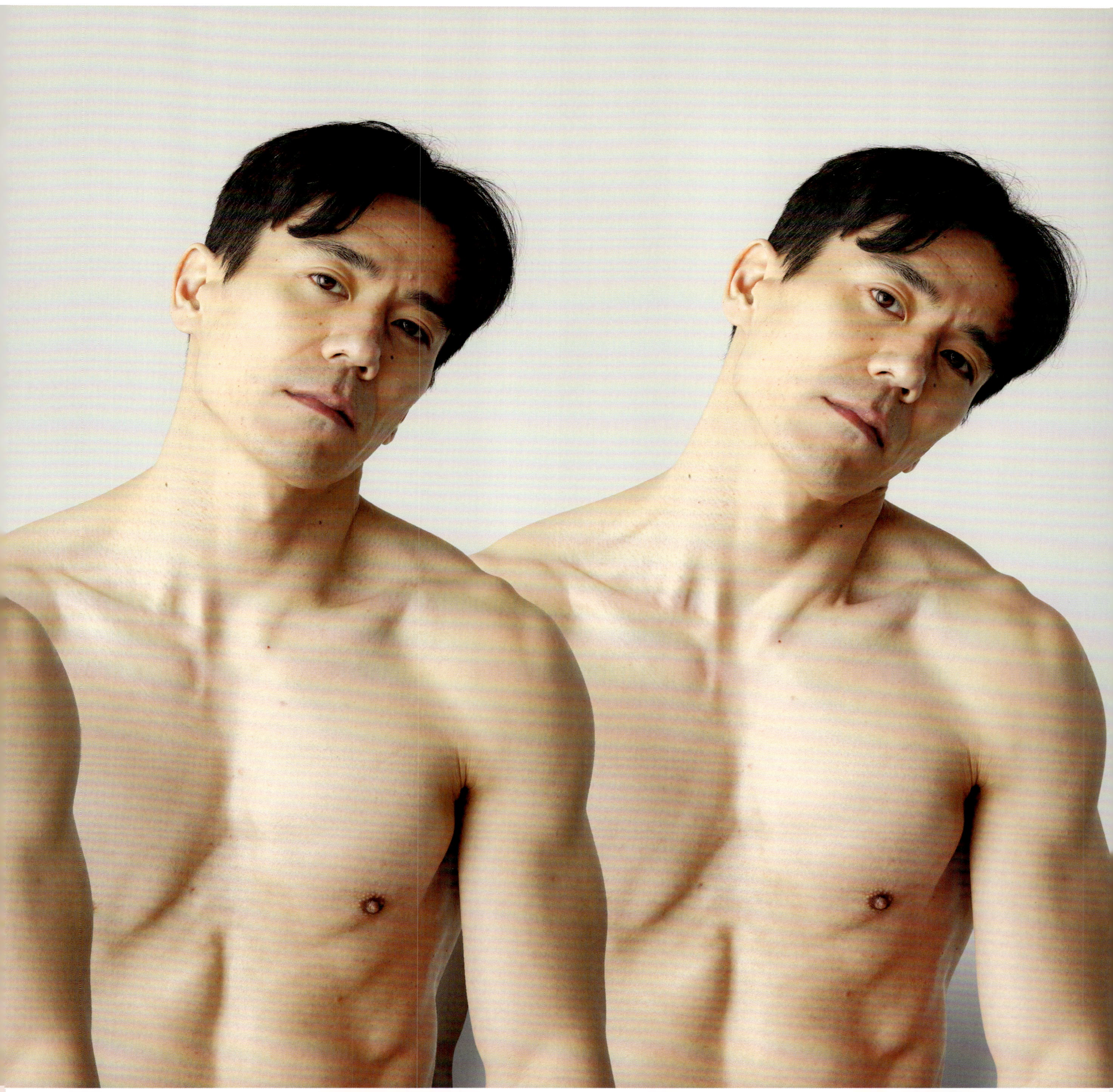

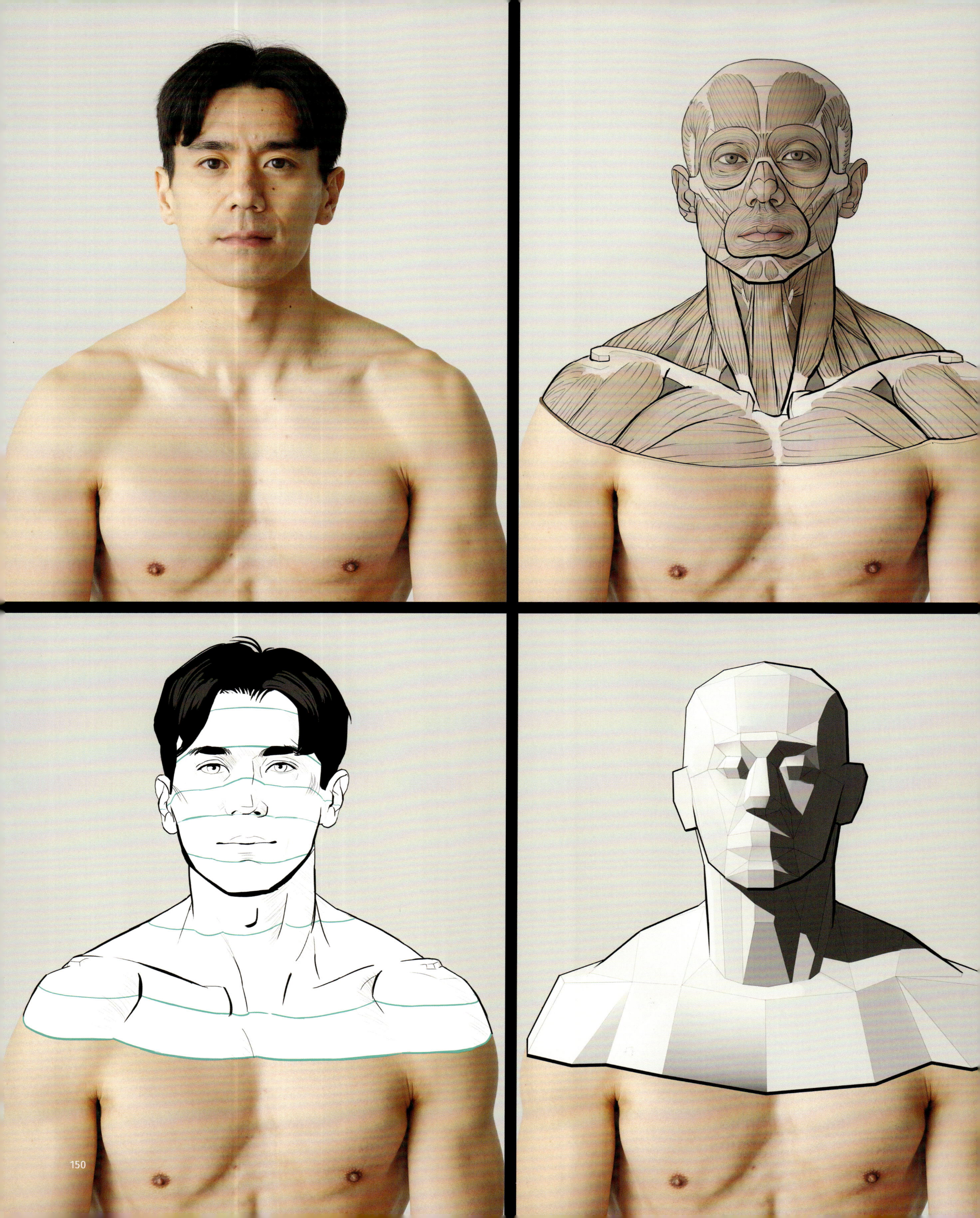

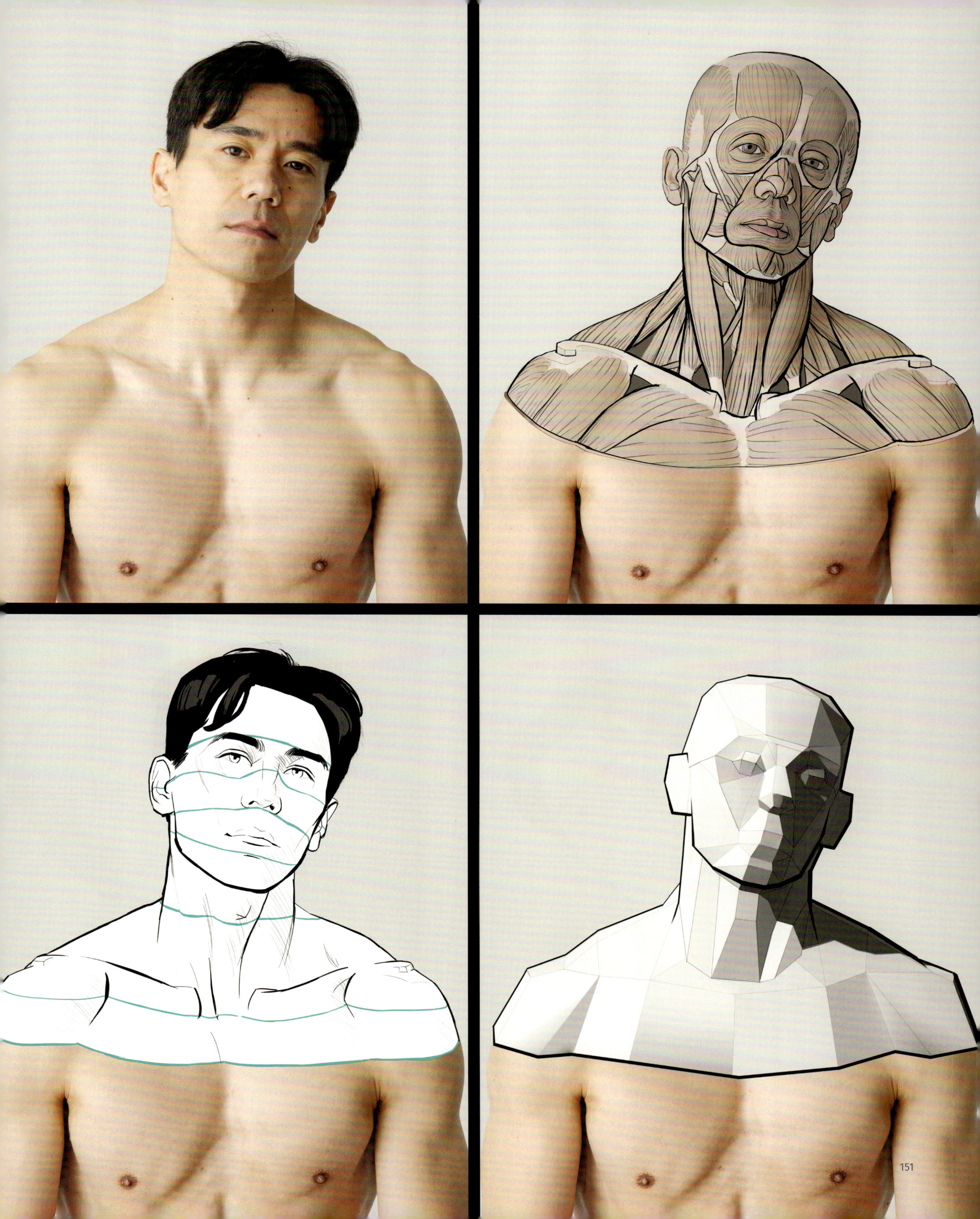

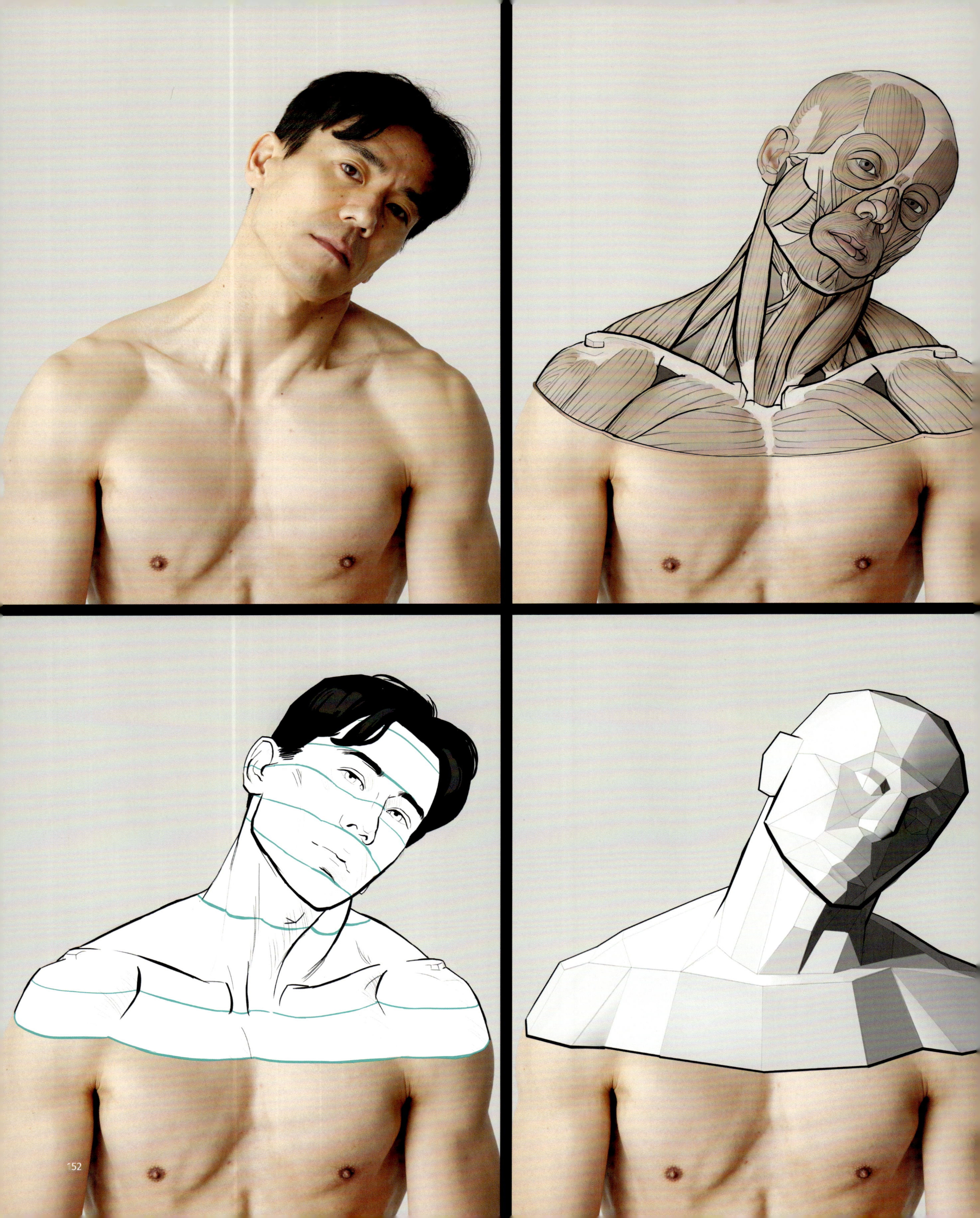

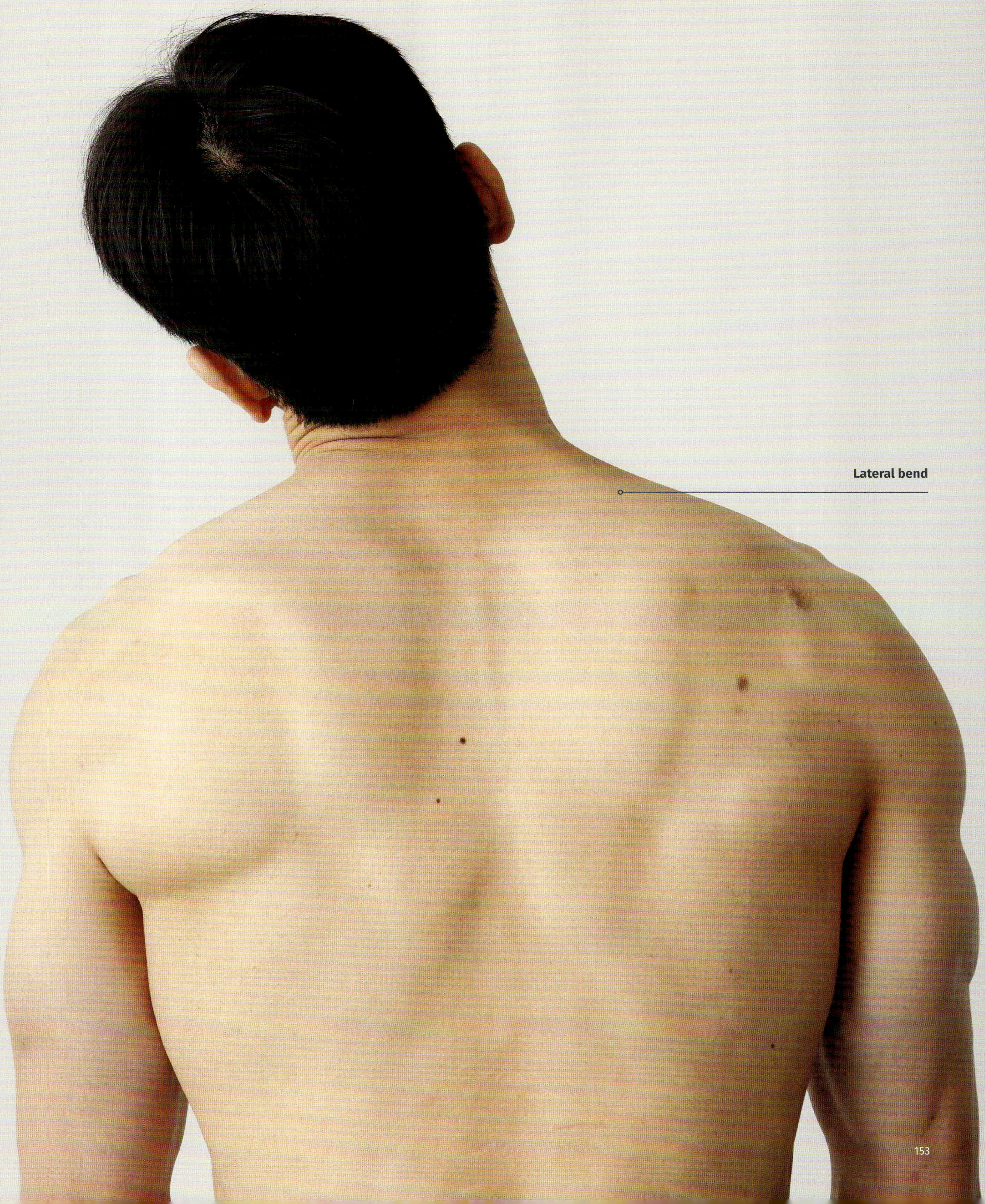
Lateral bend

Jaw opening

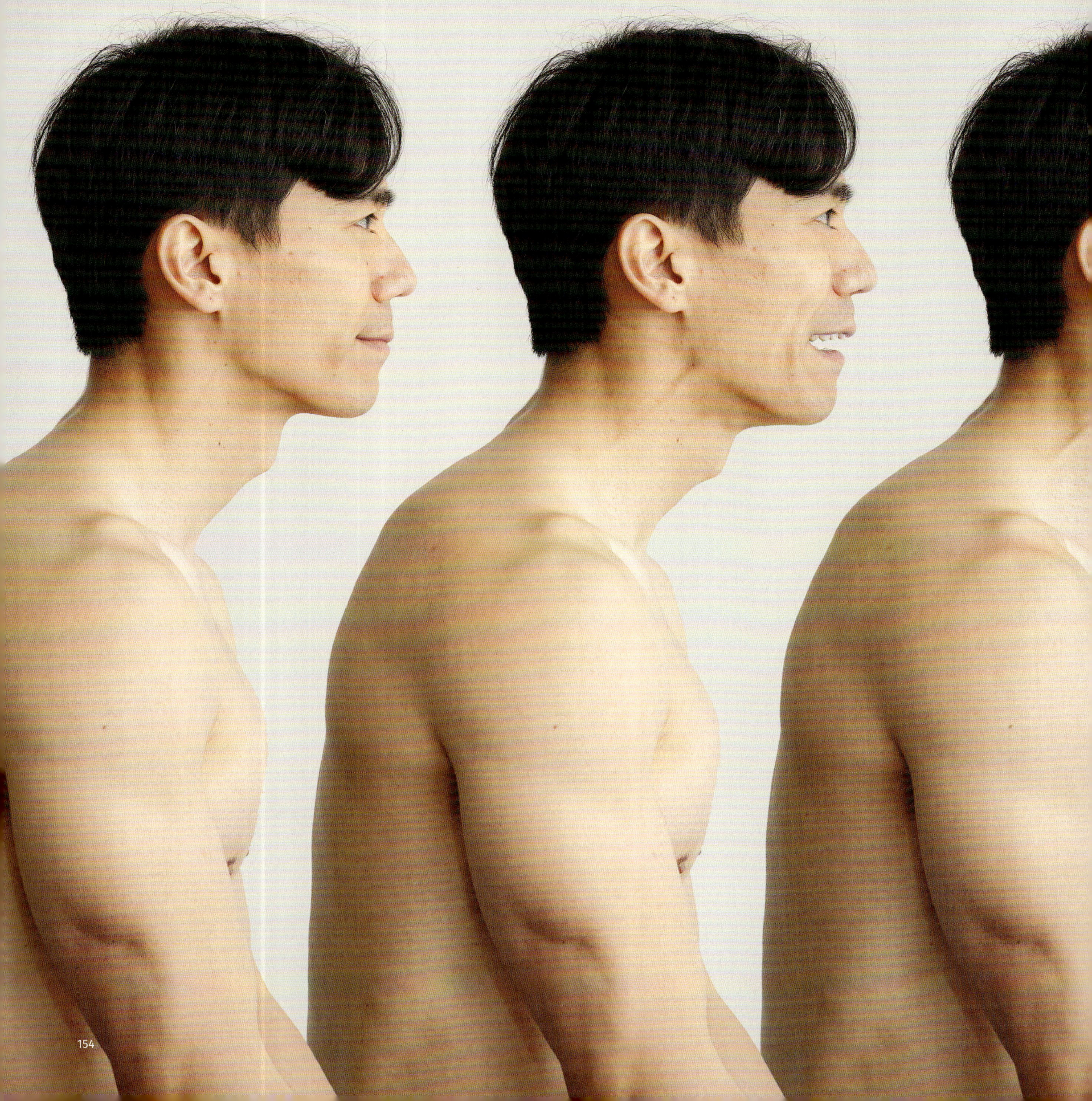

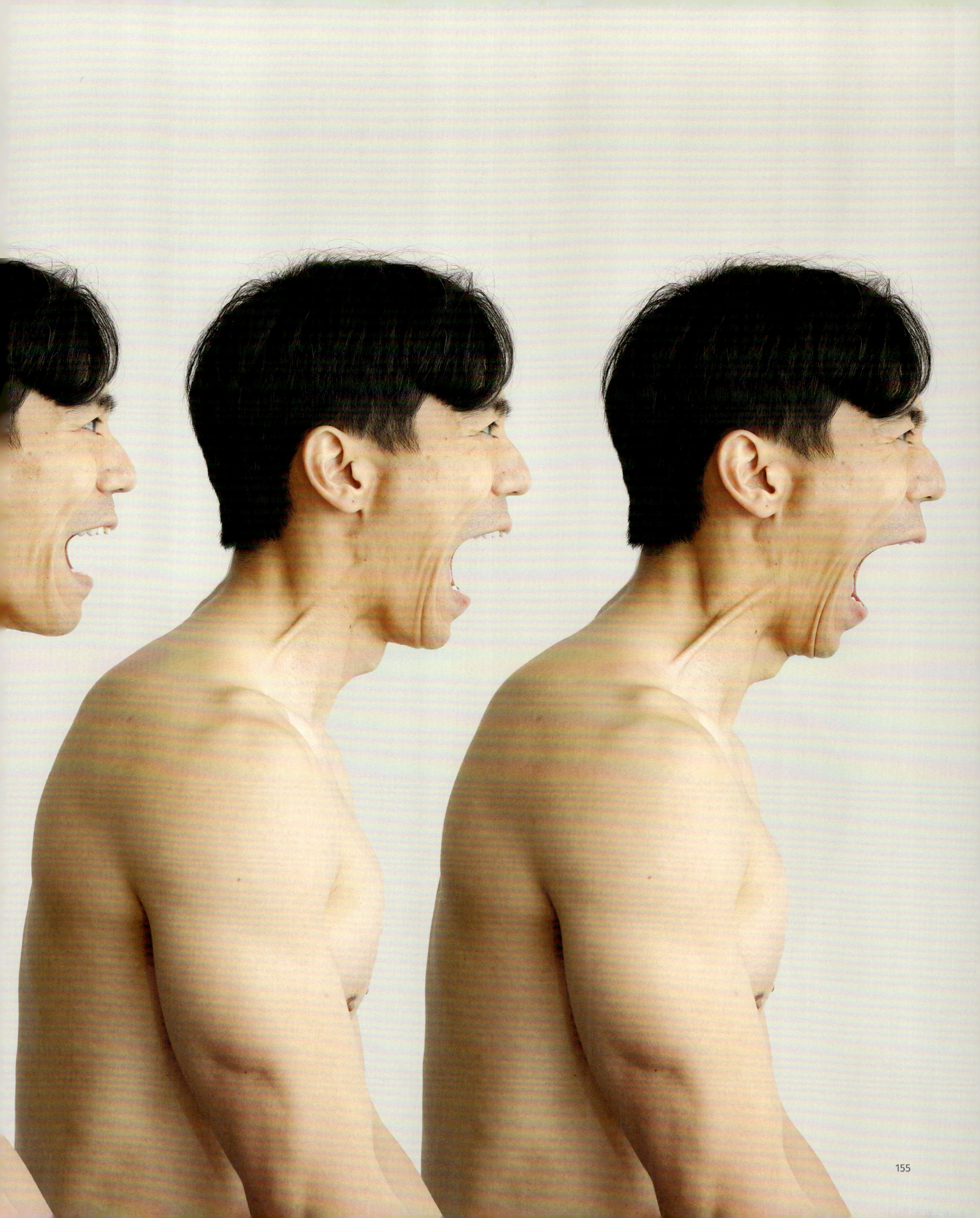

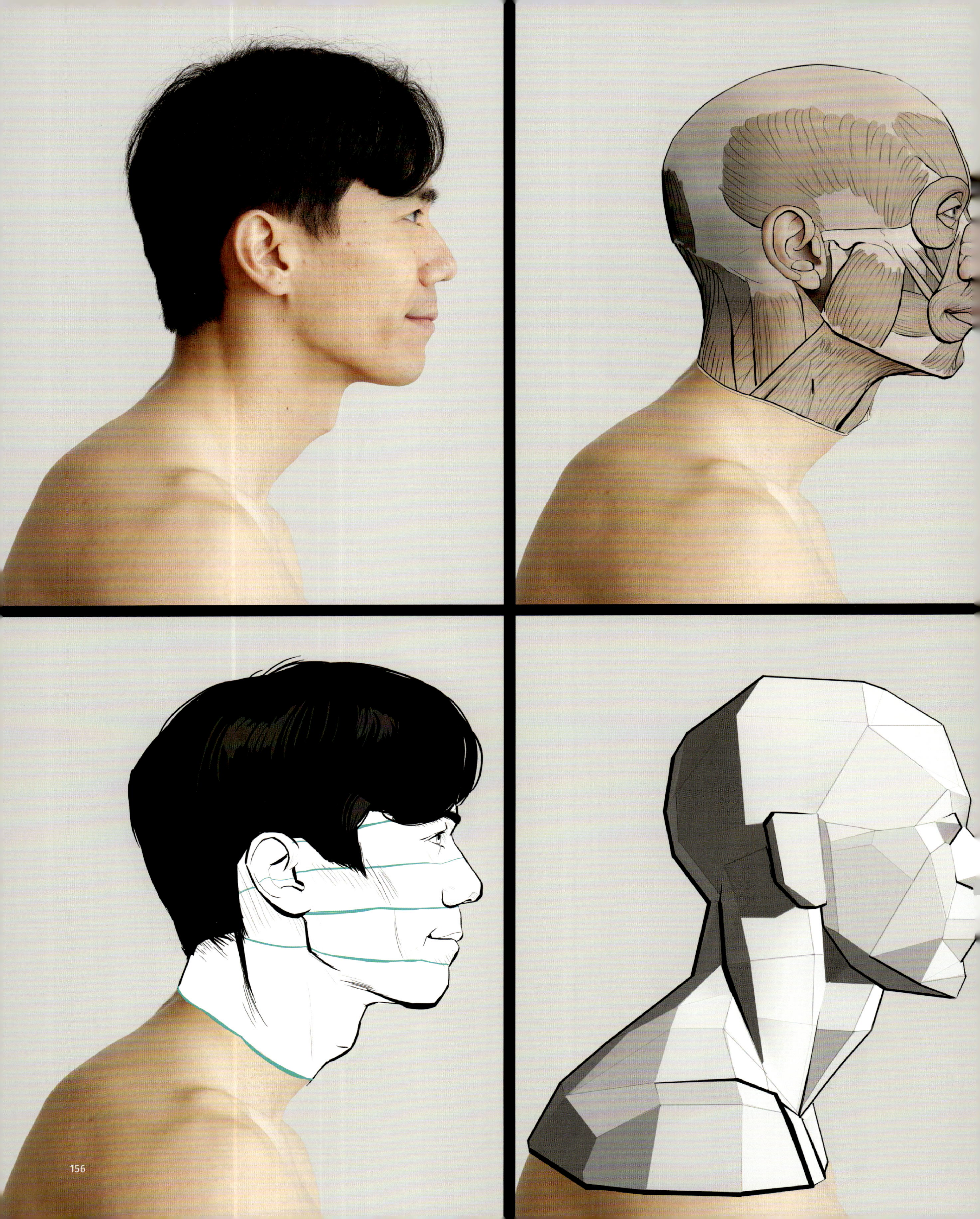

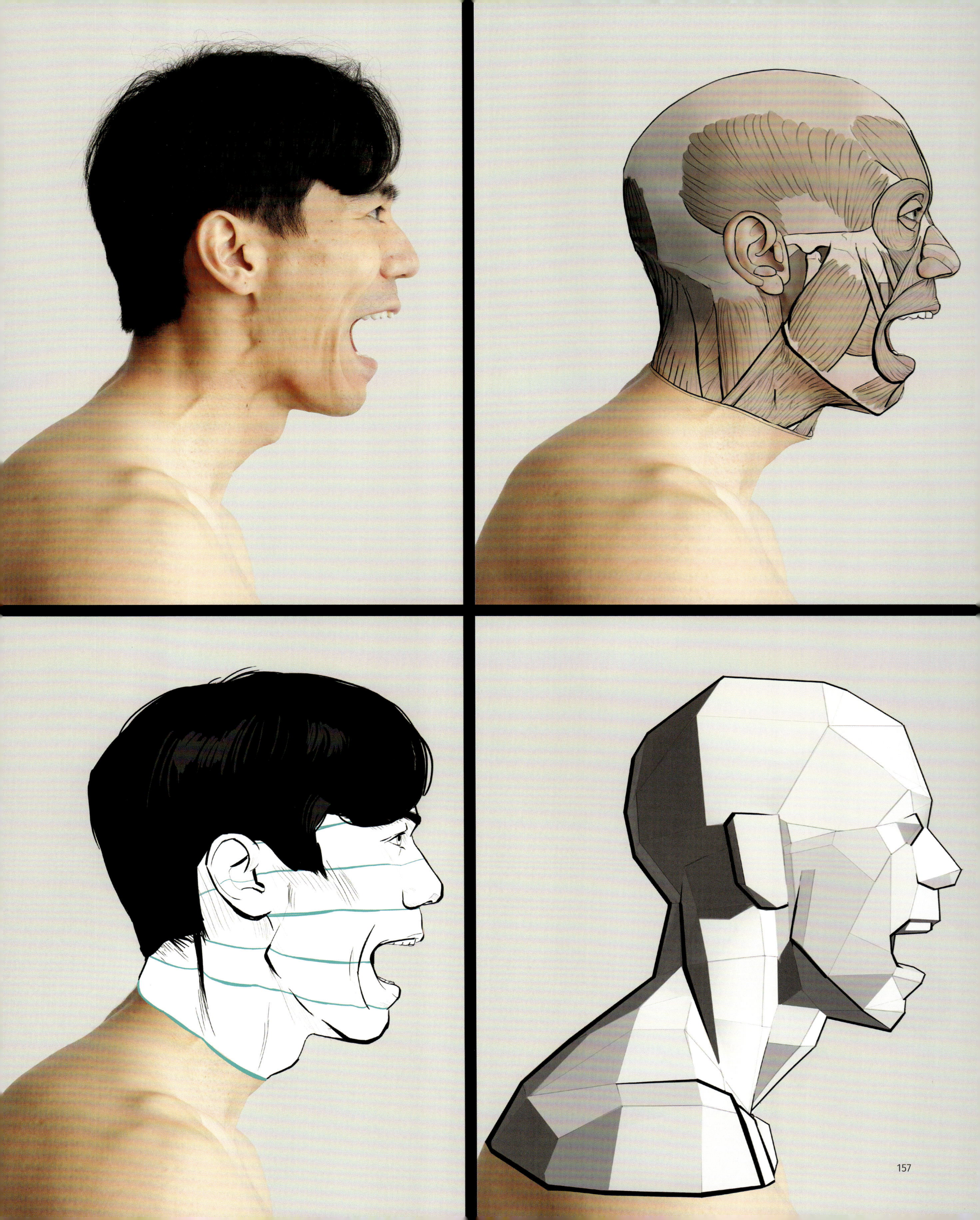

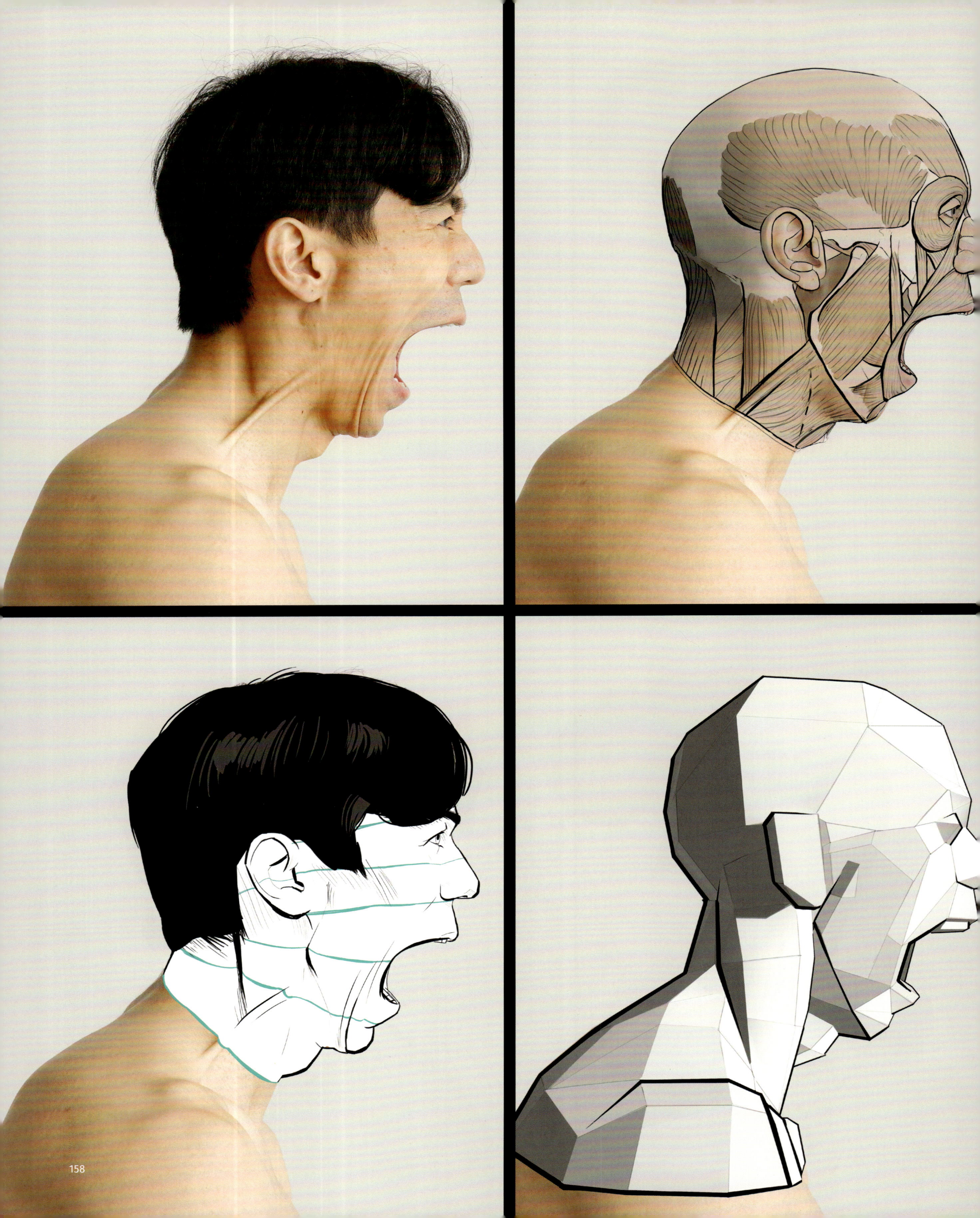

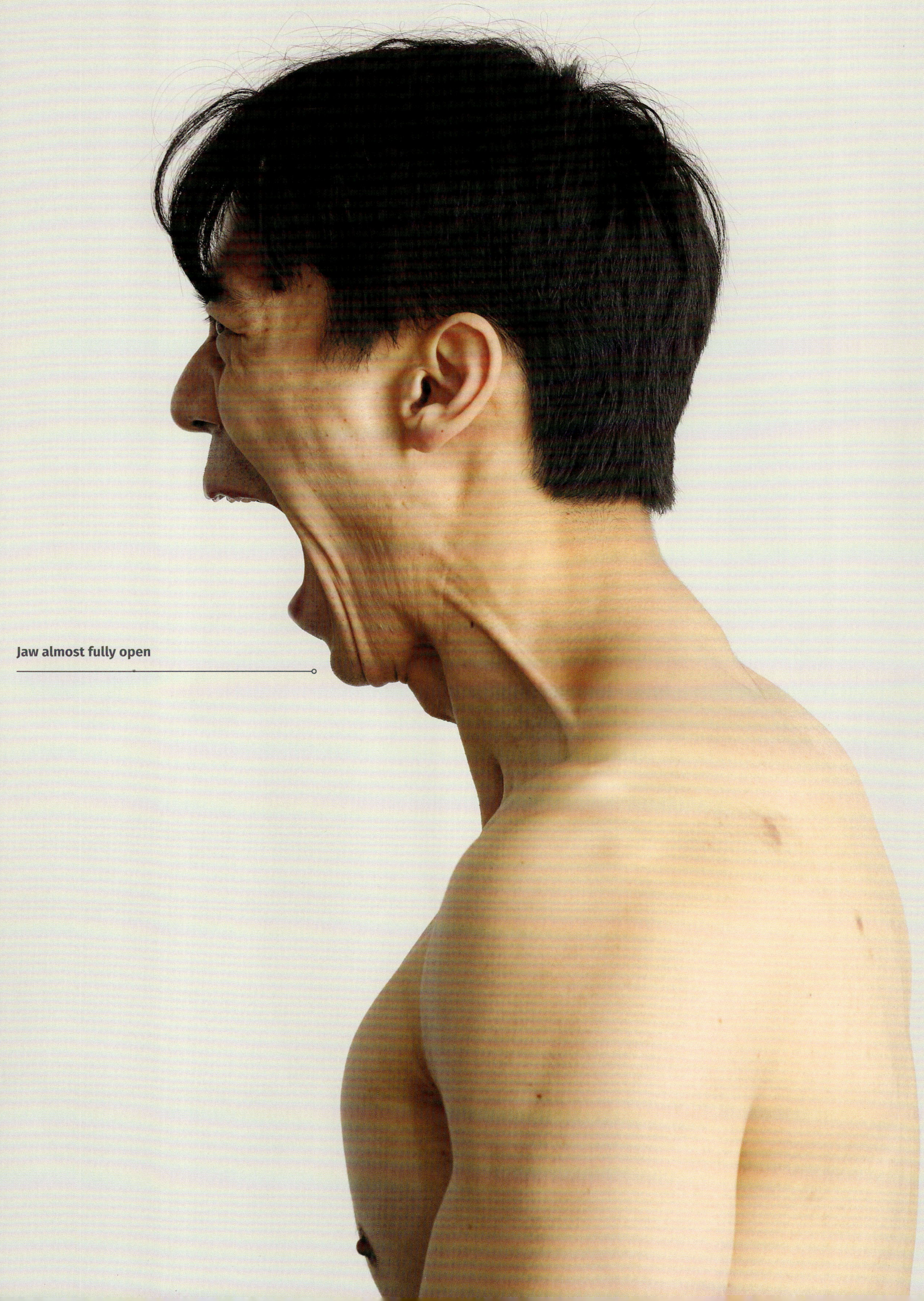
Jaw almost fully open

Shoulders lowering and raising

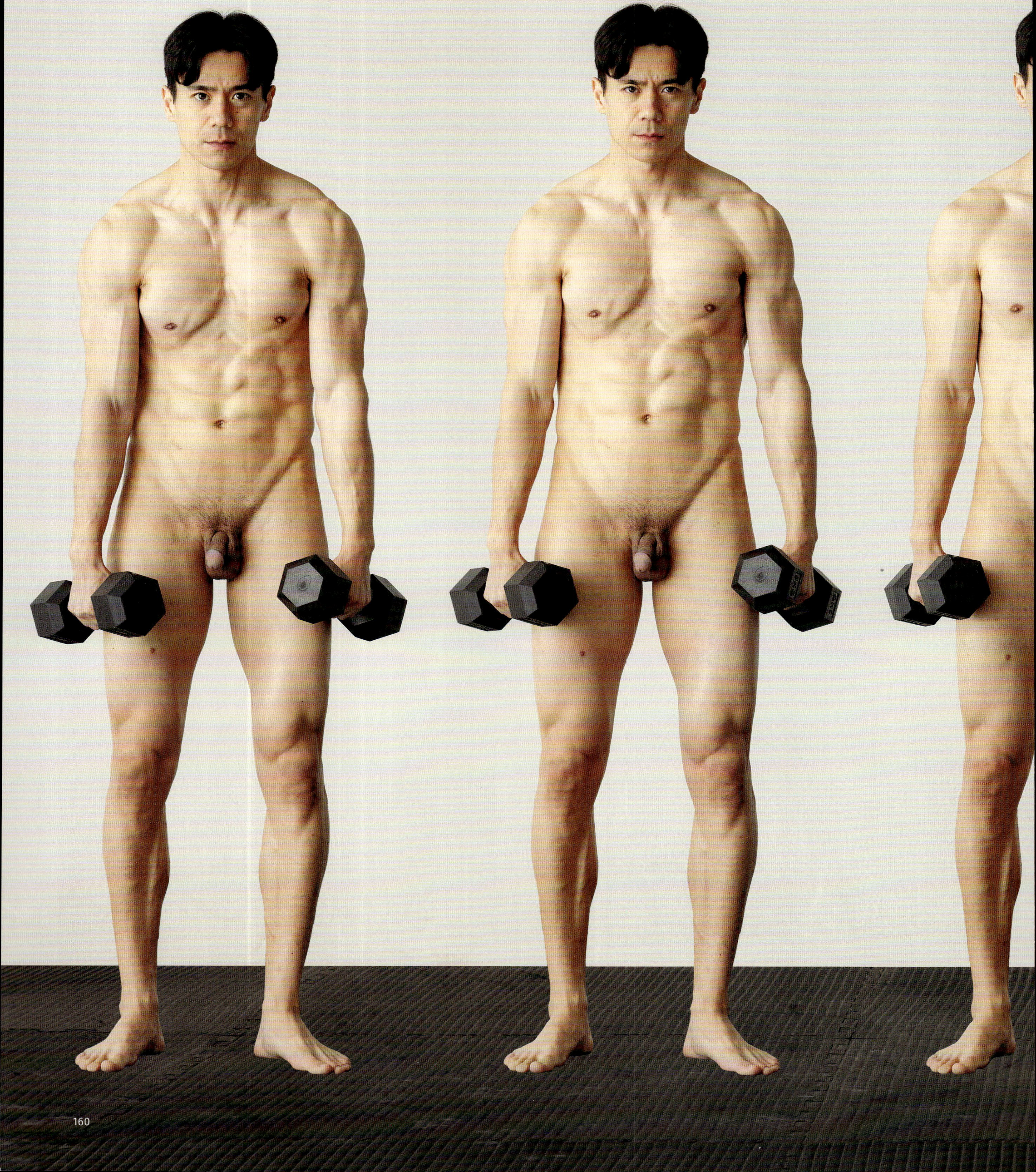

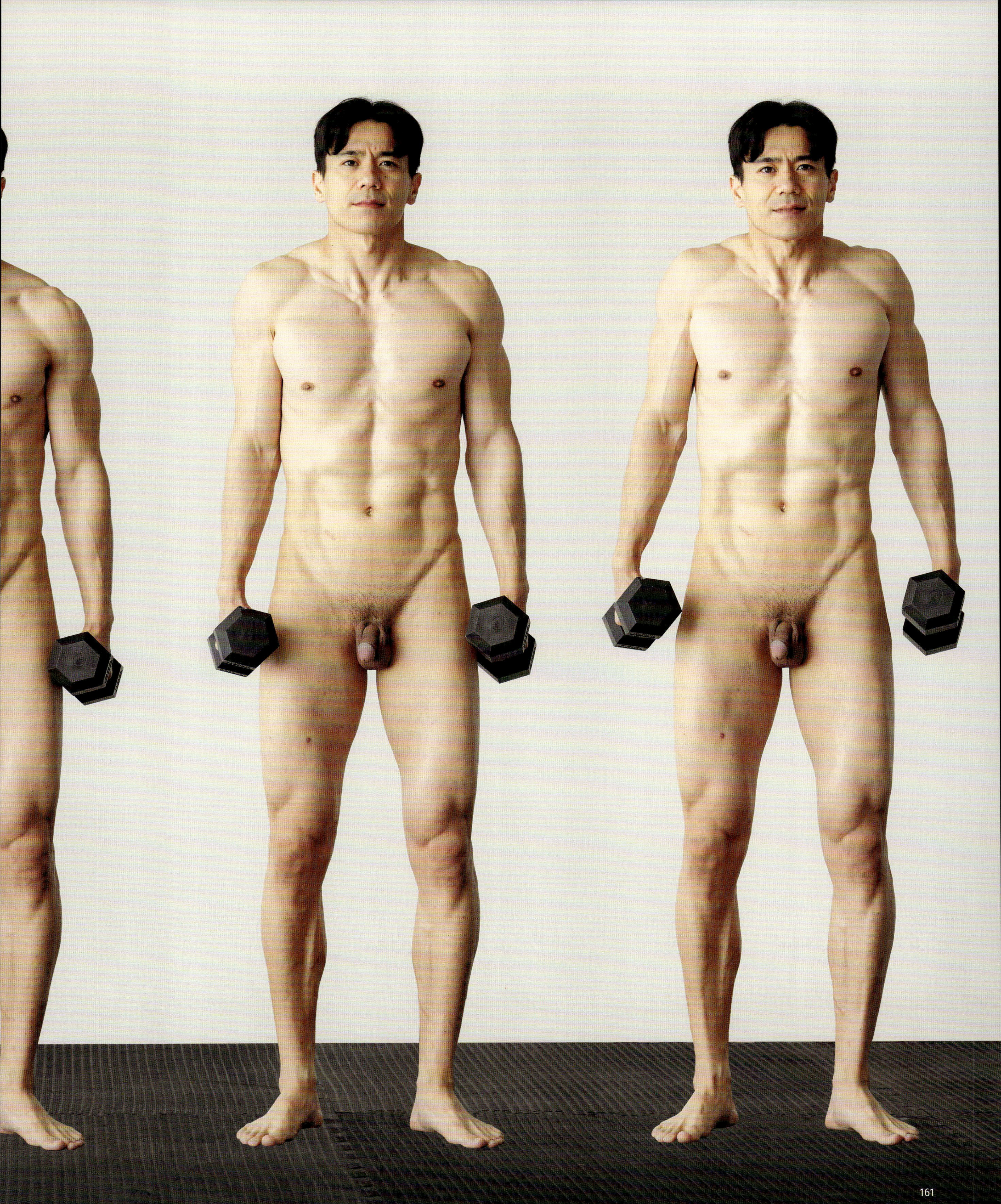

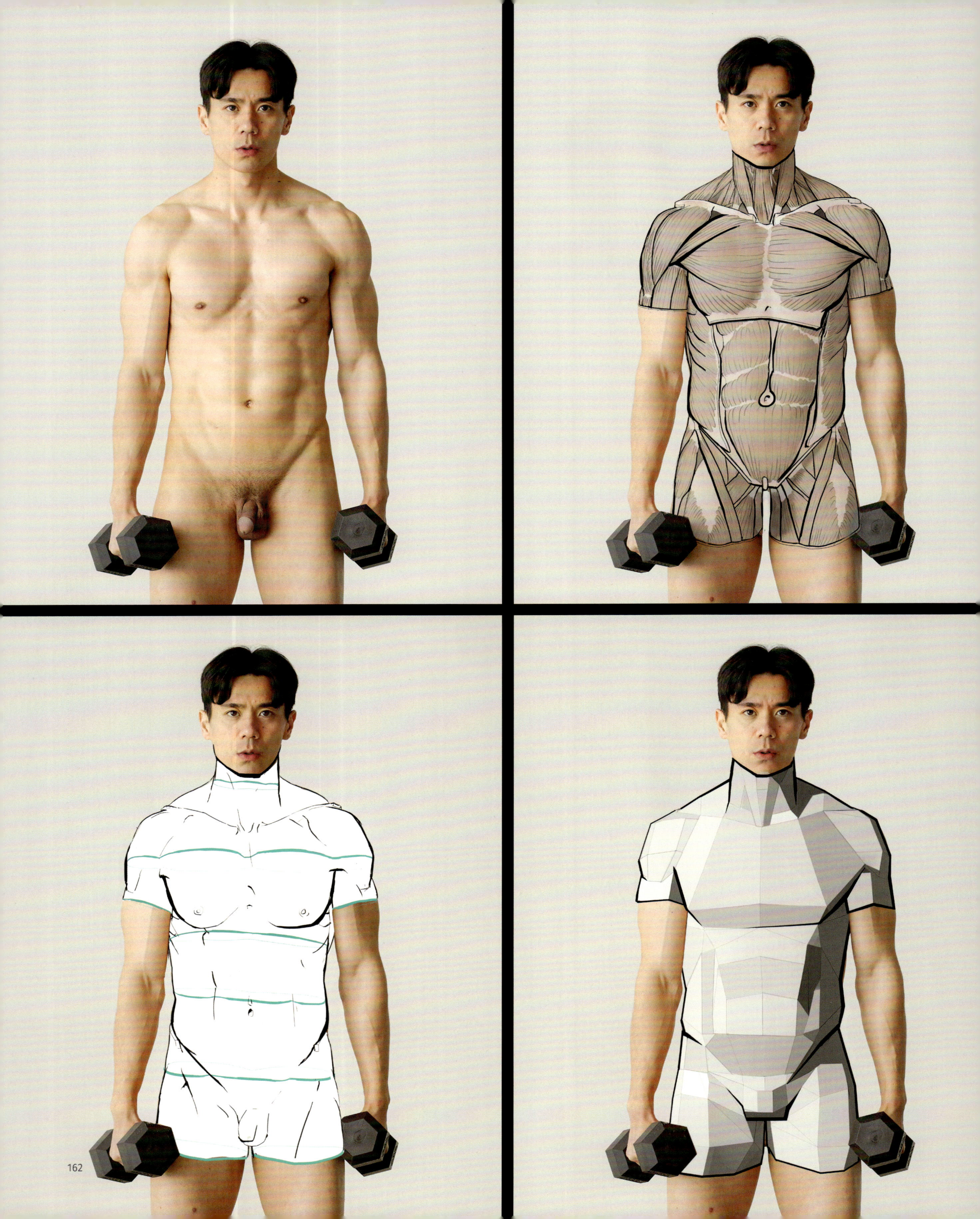

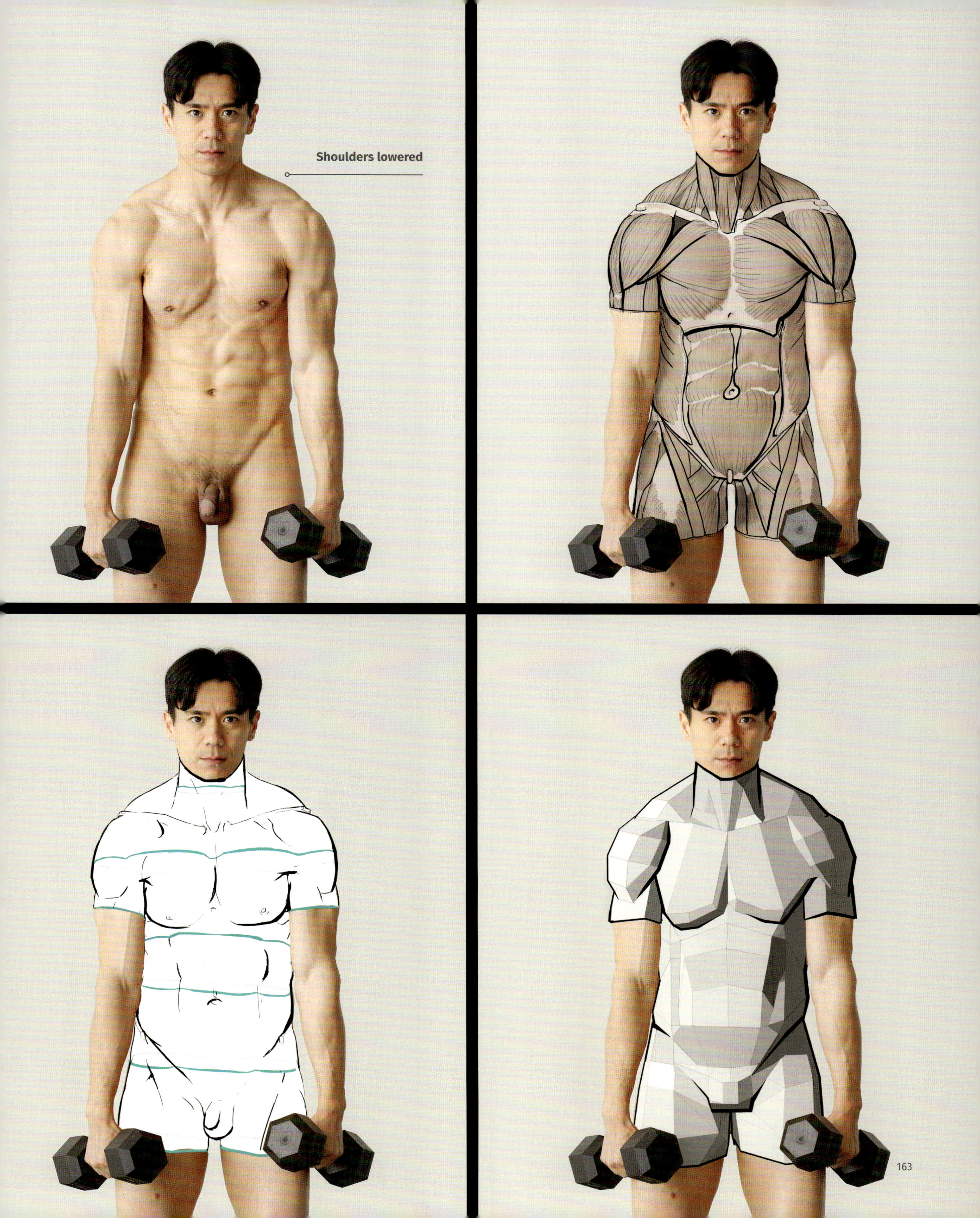
Shoulders lowered

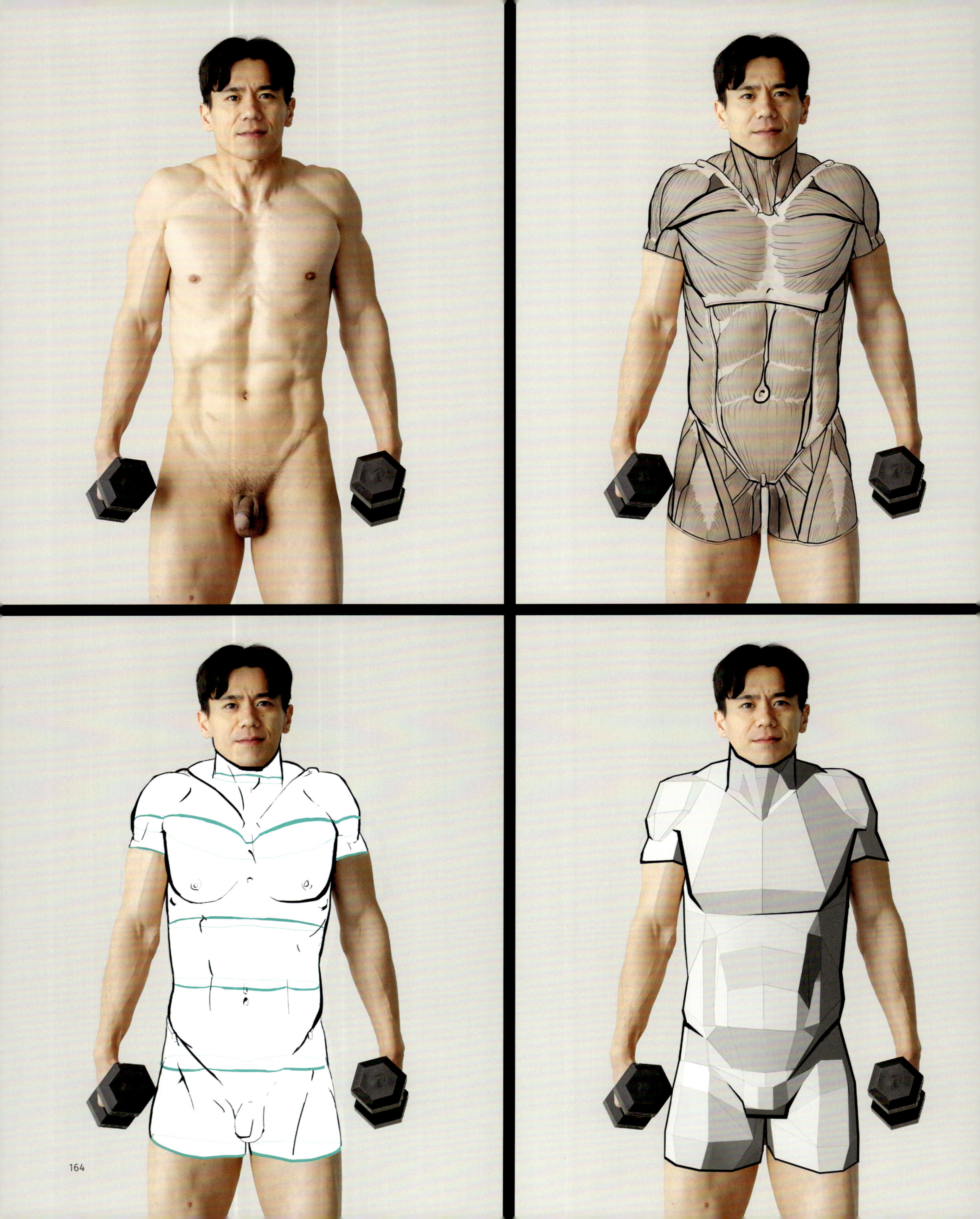

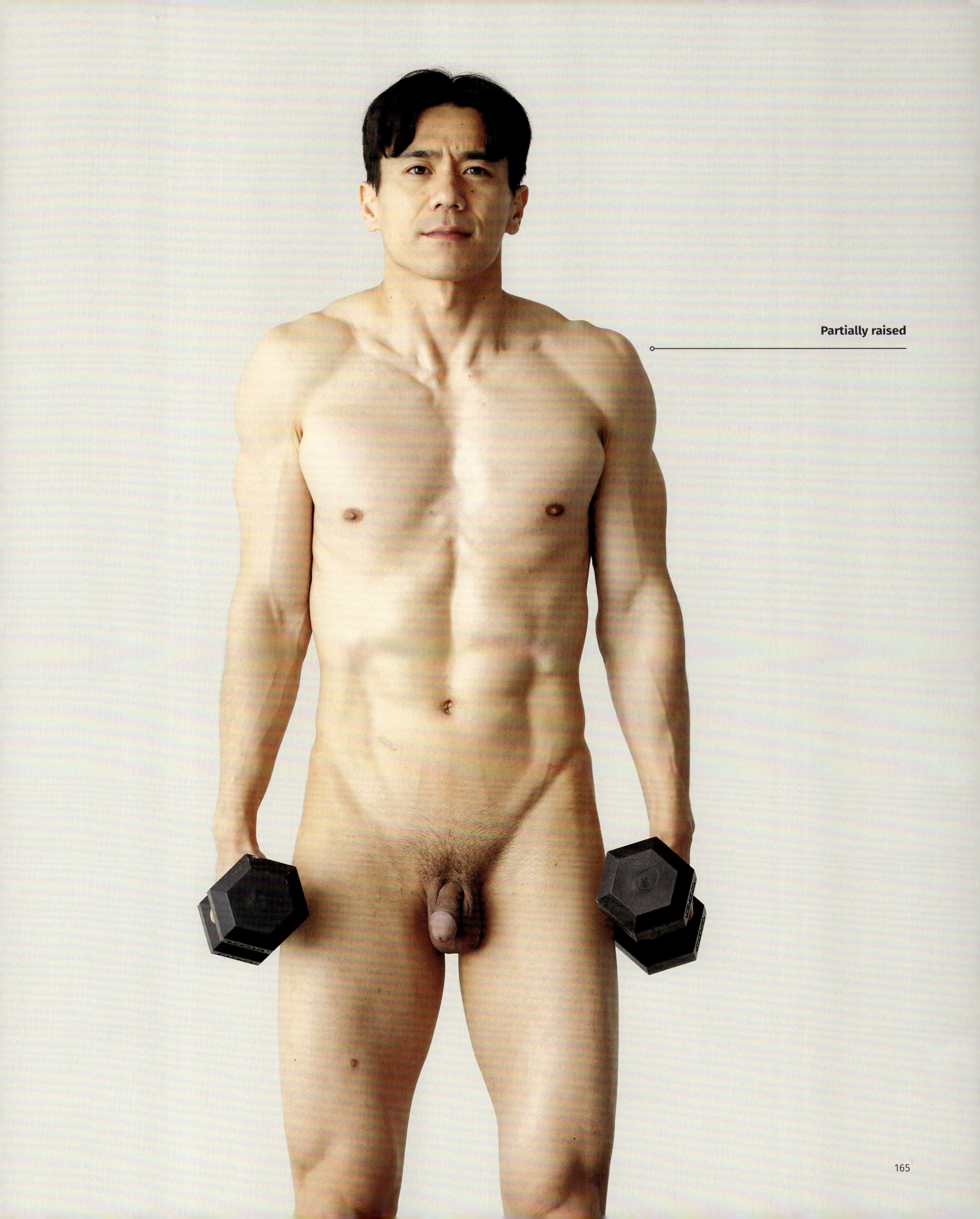
Partially raised

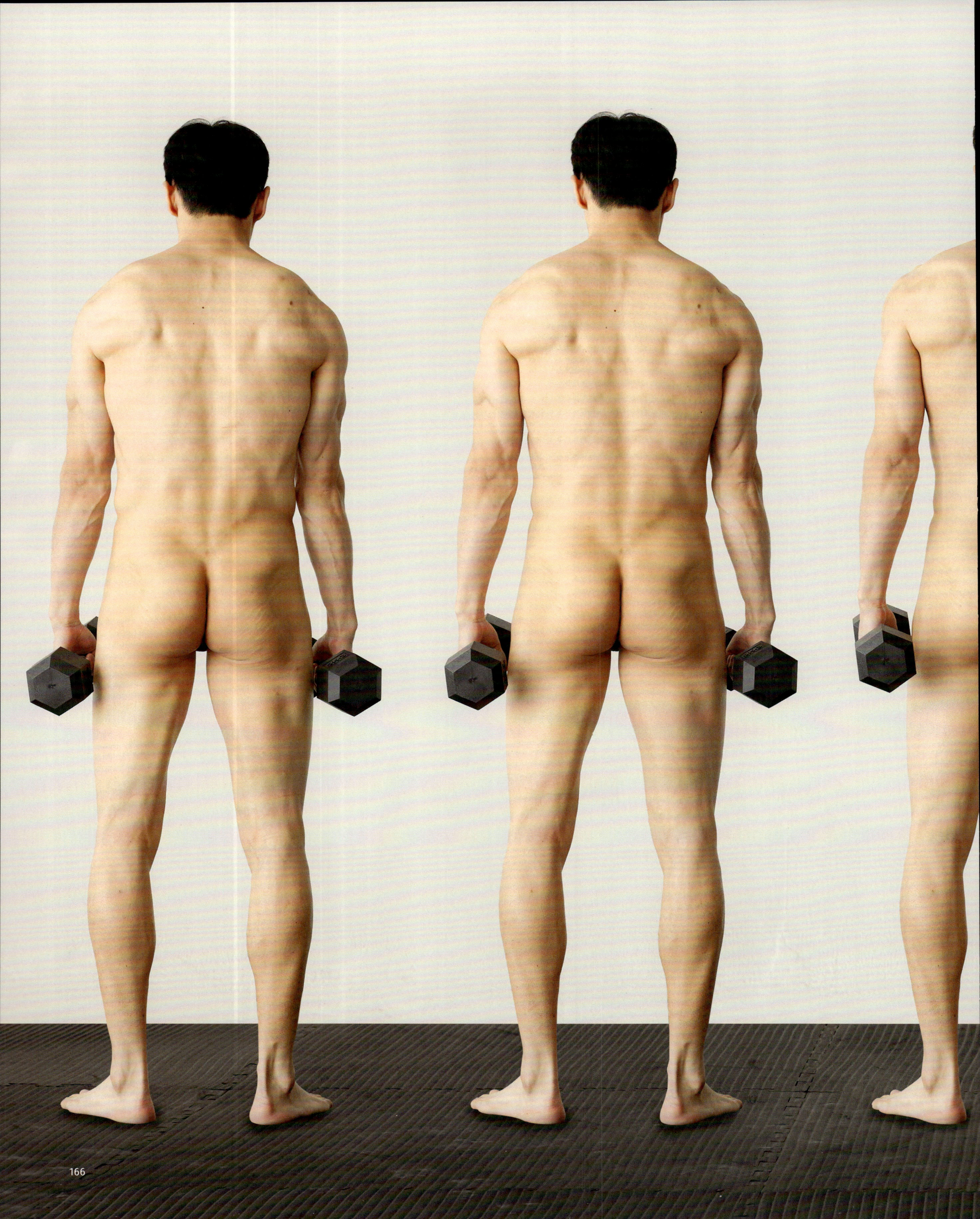

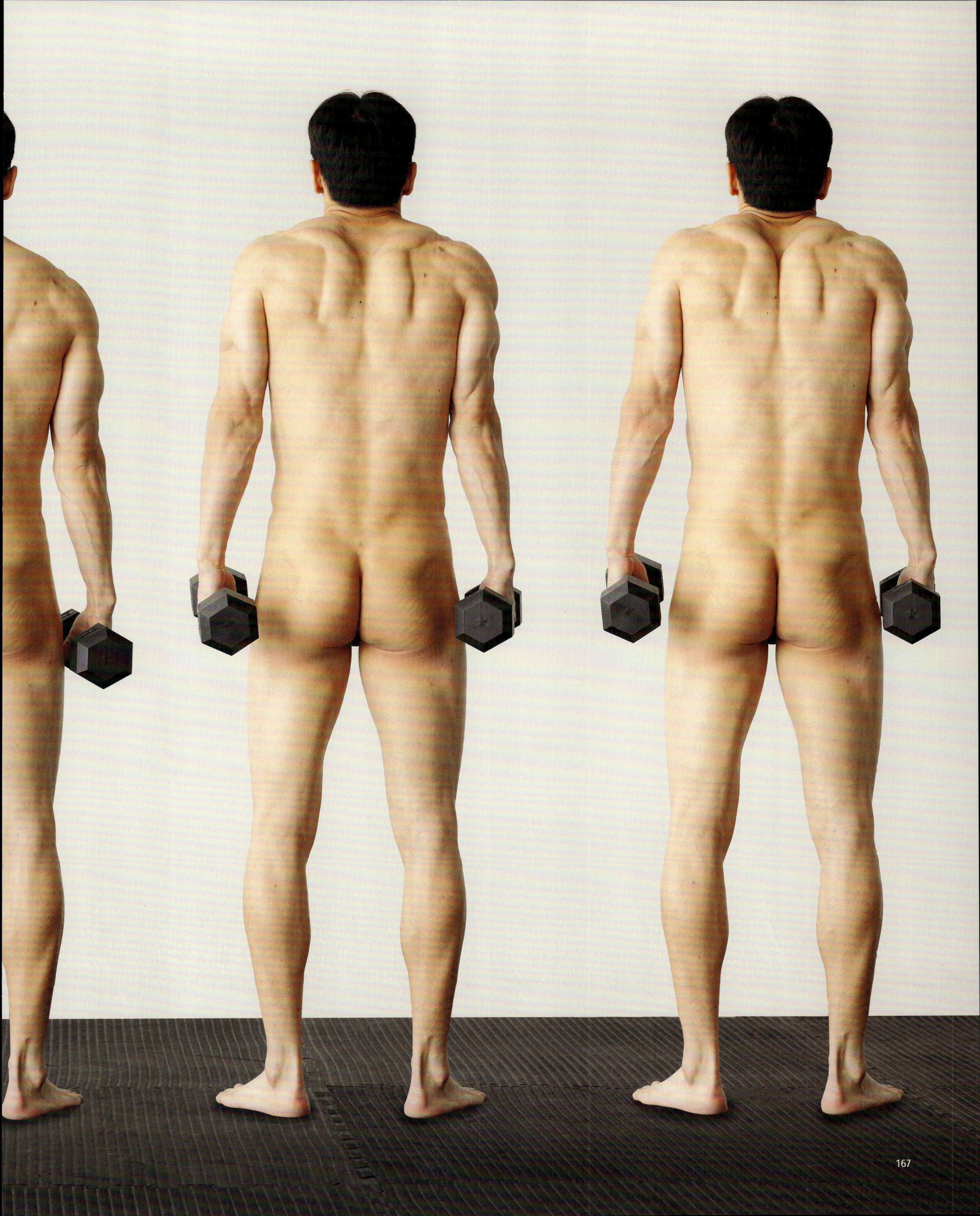

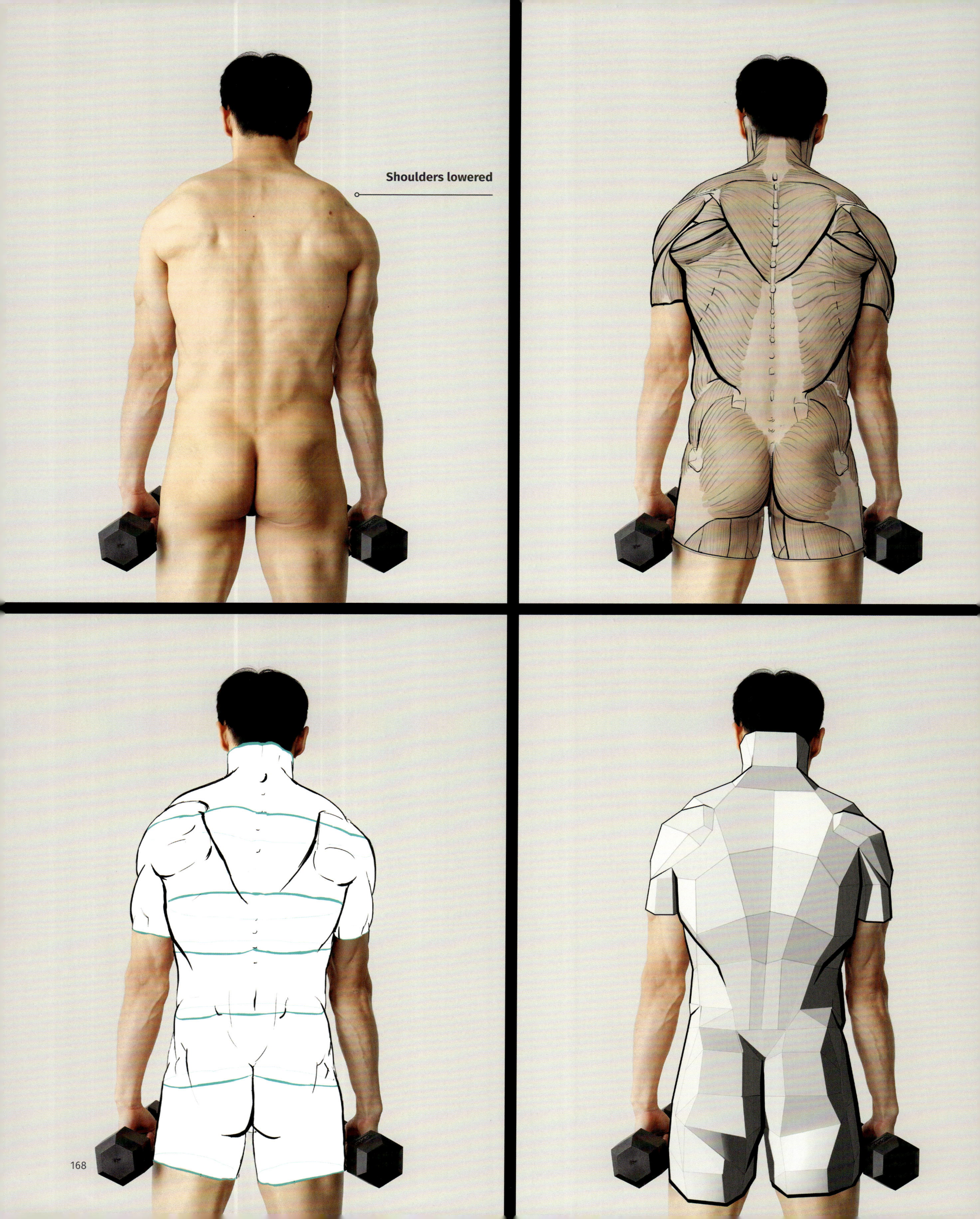
Shoulders lowered

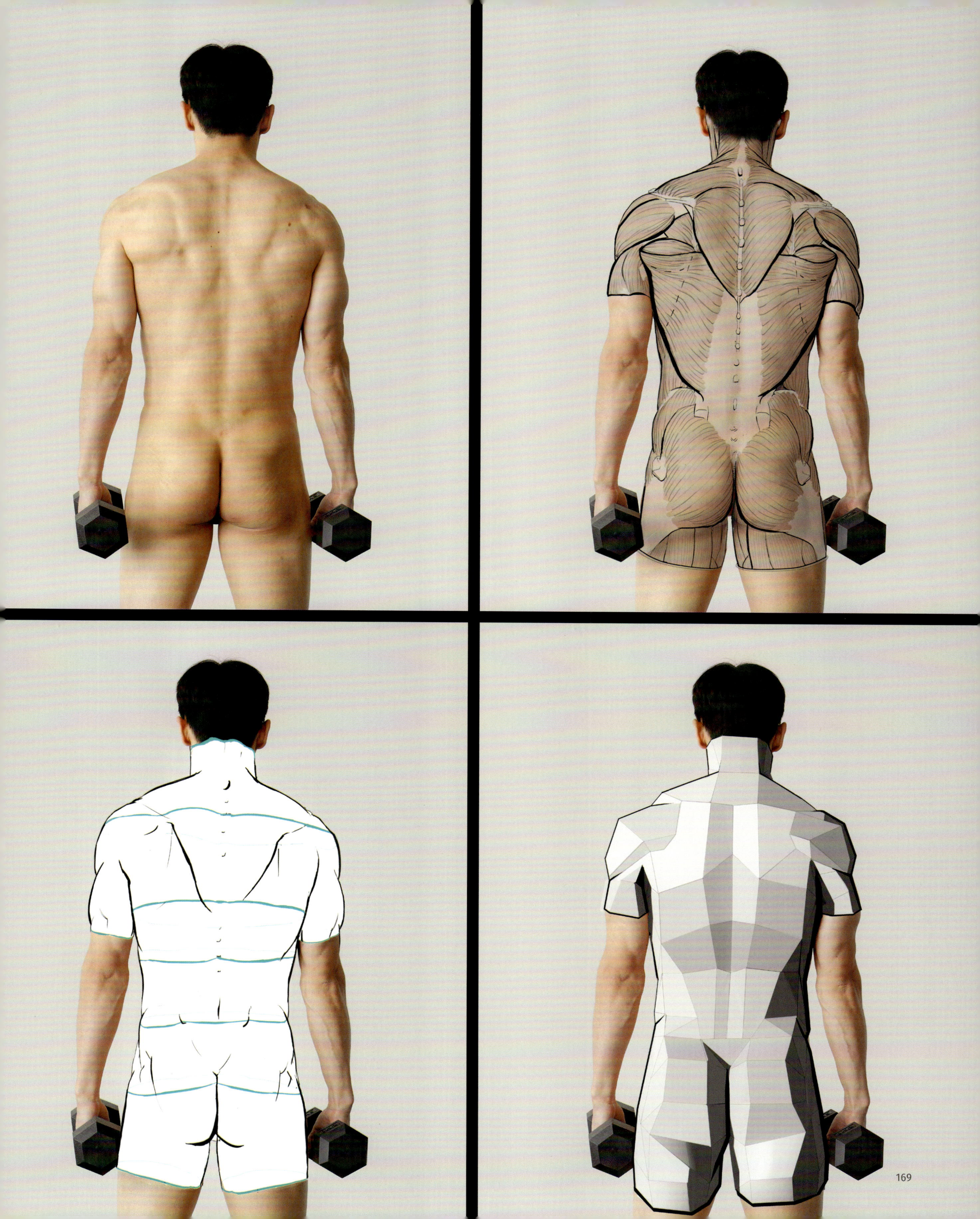

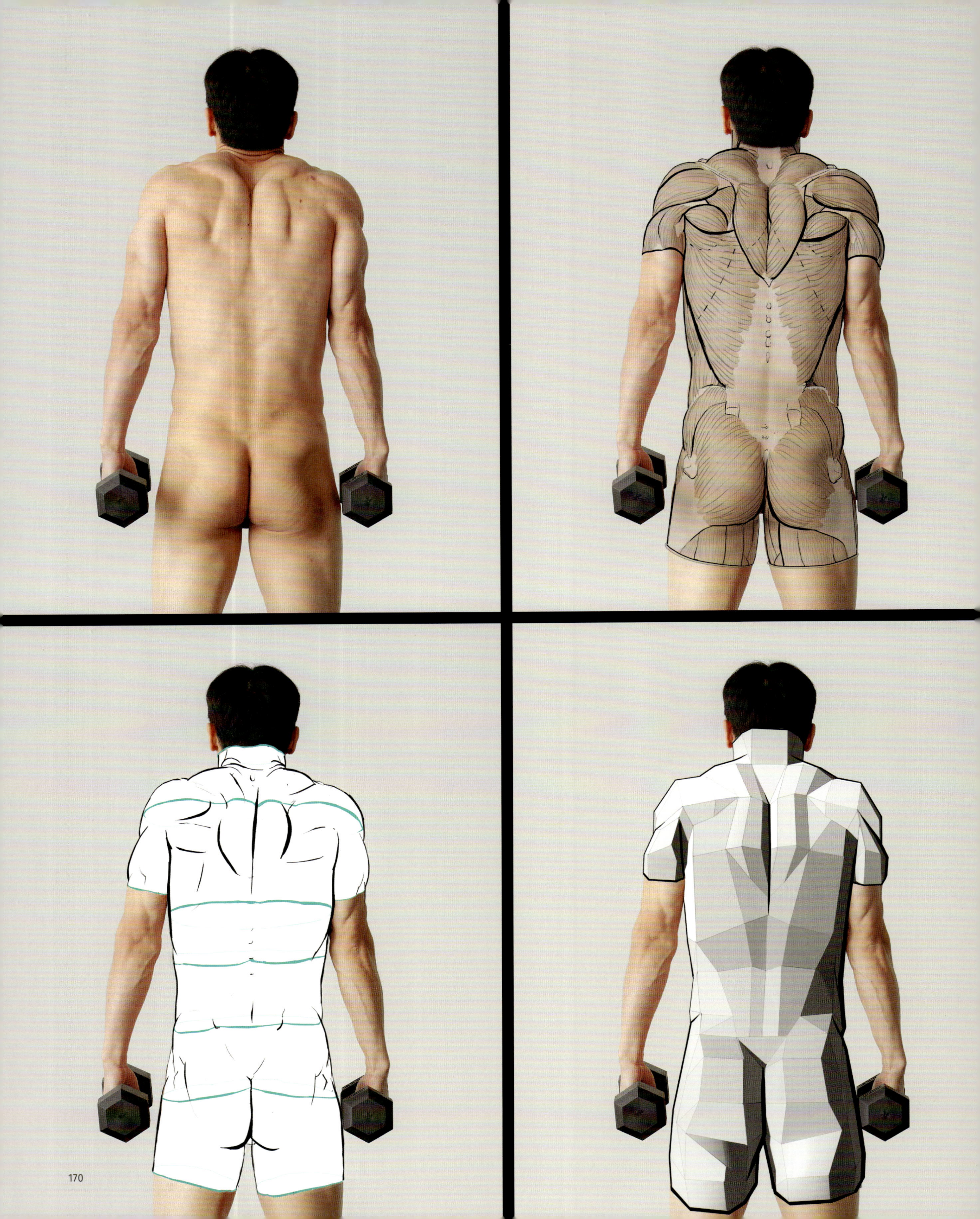

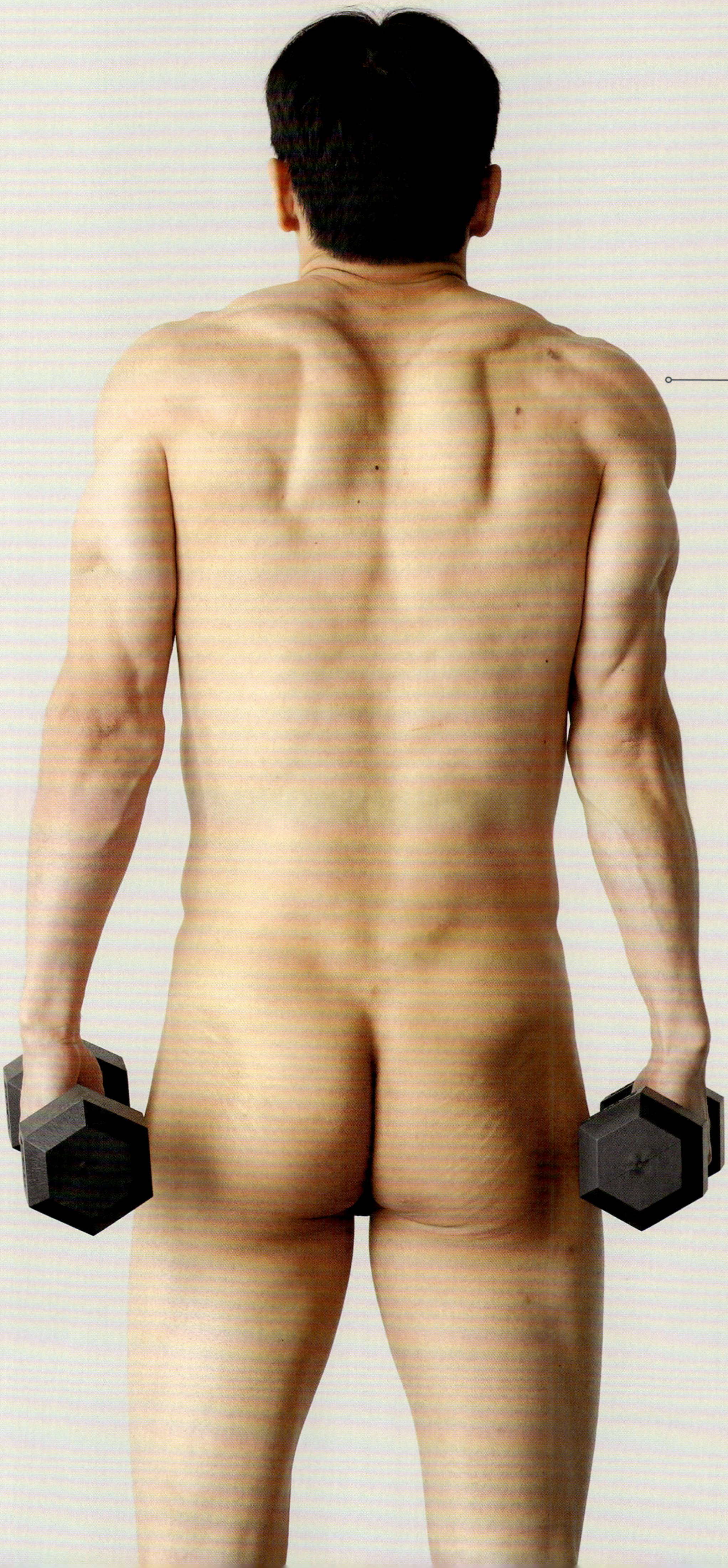
Partially raised

Full-body actions

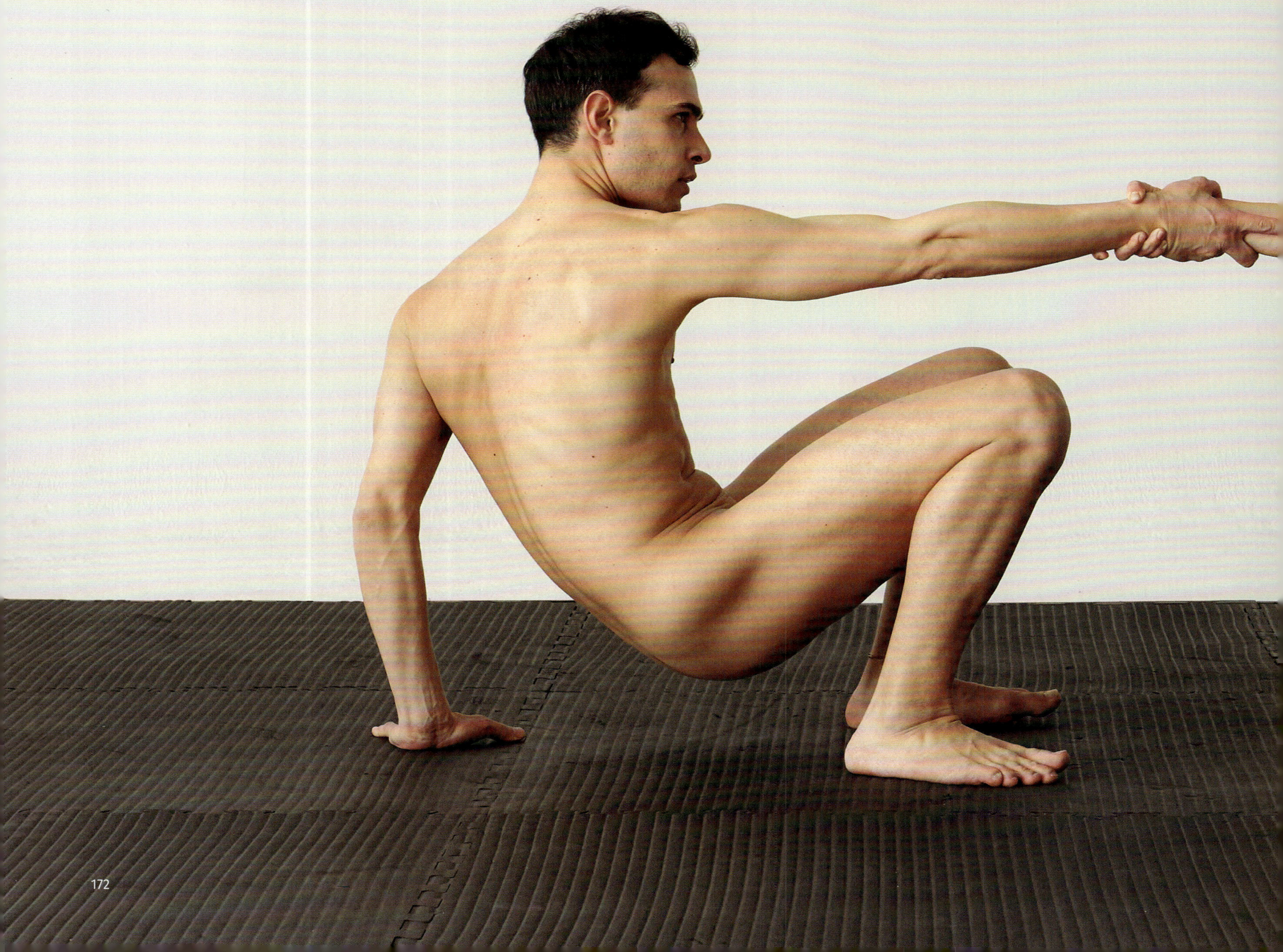

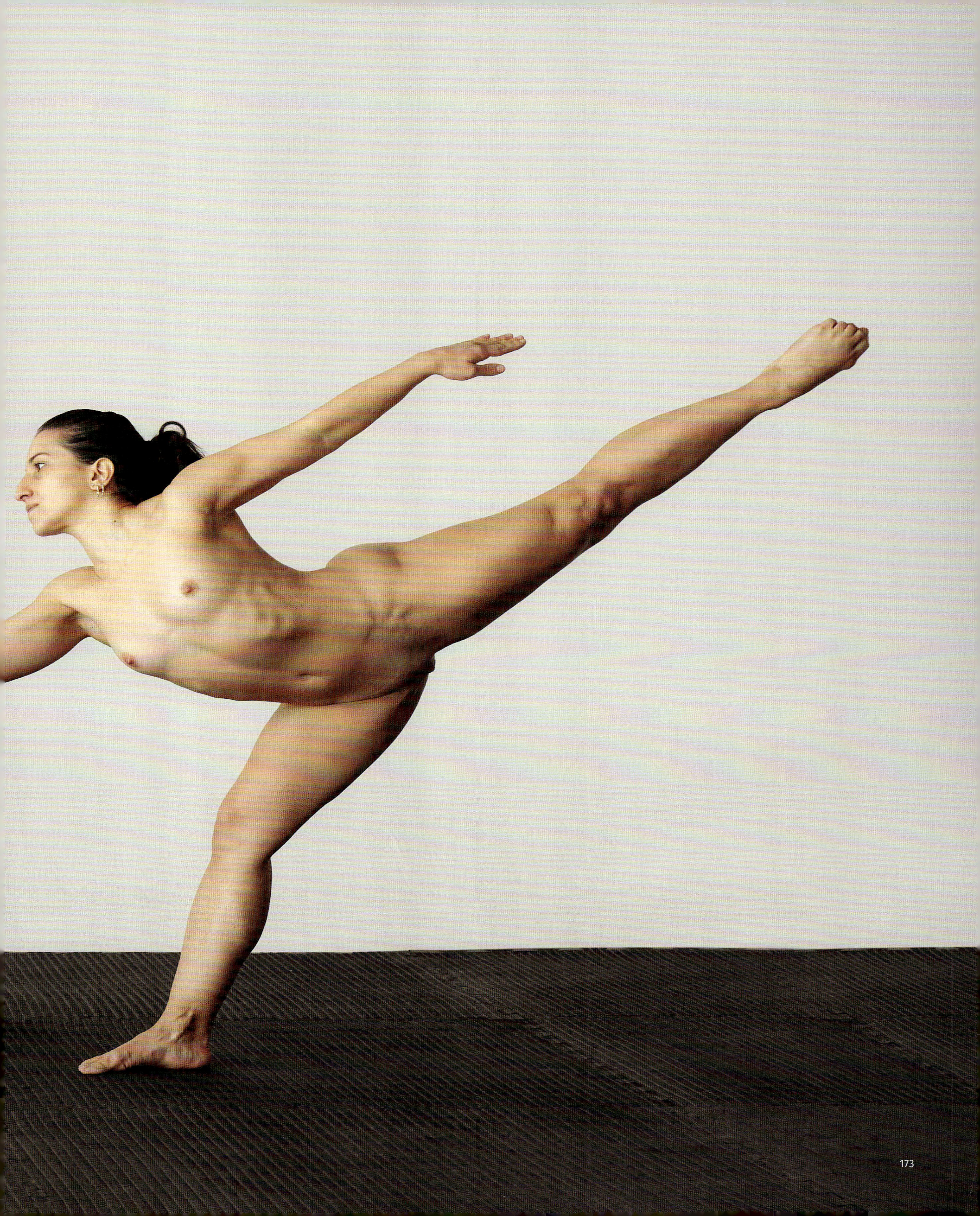

Walking

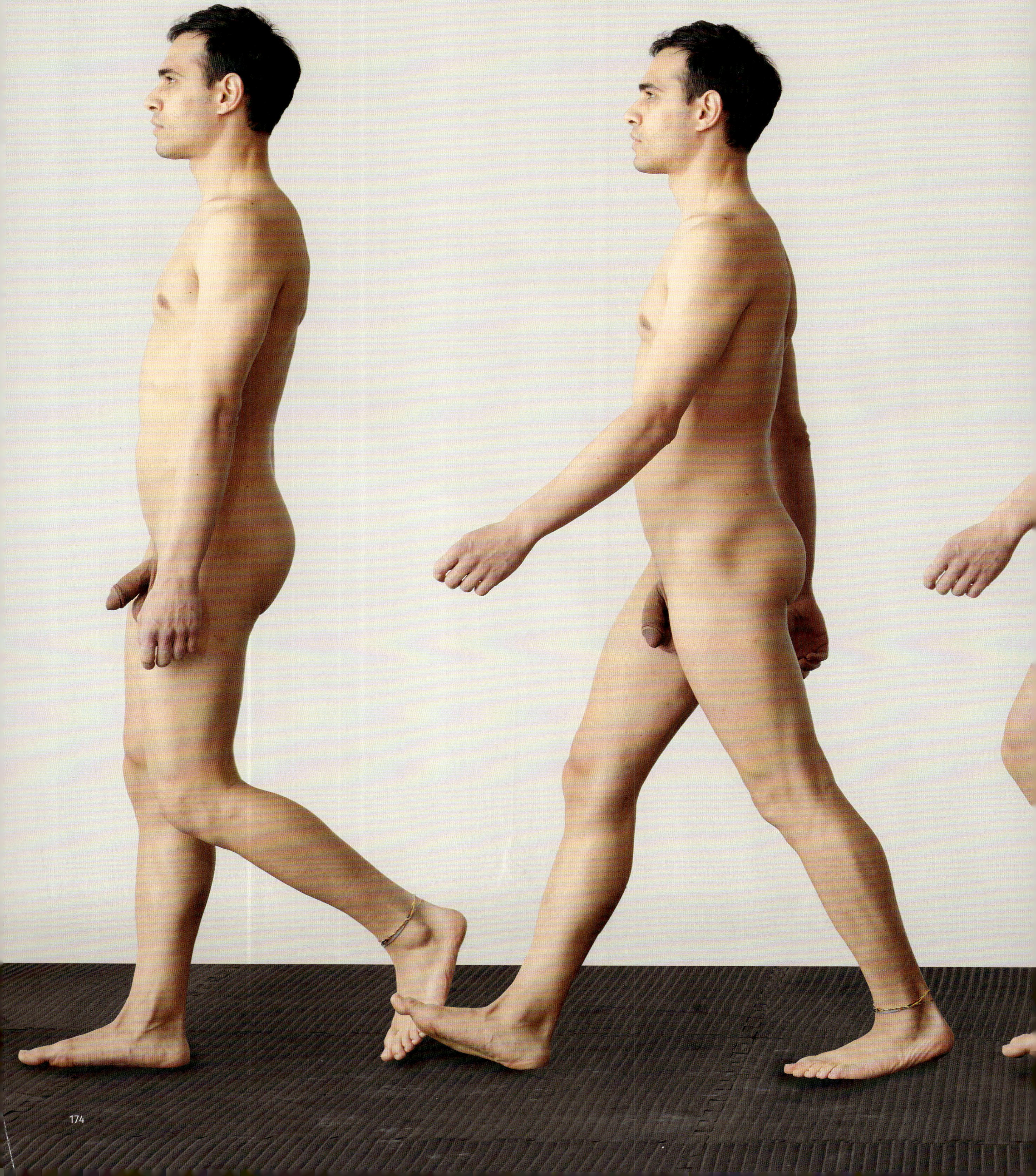

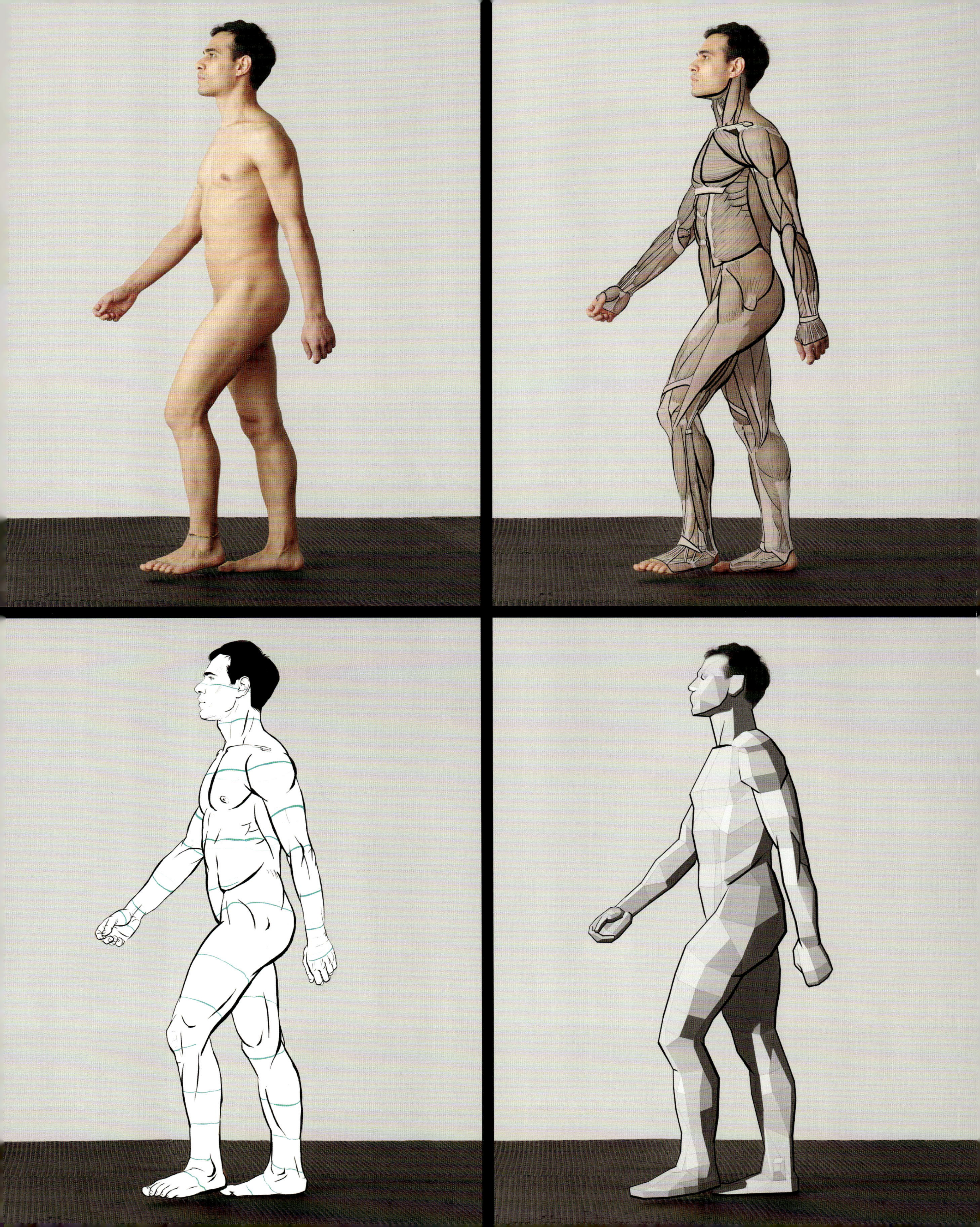

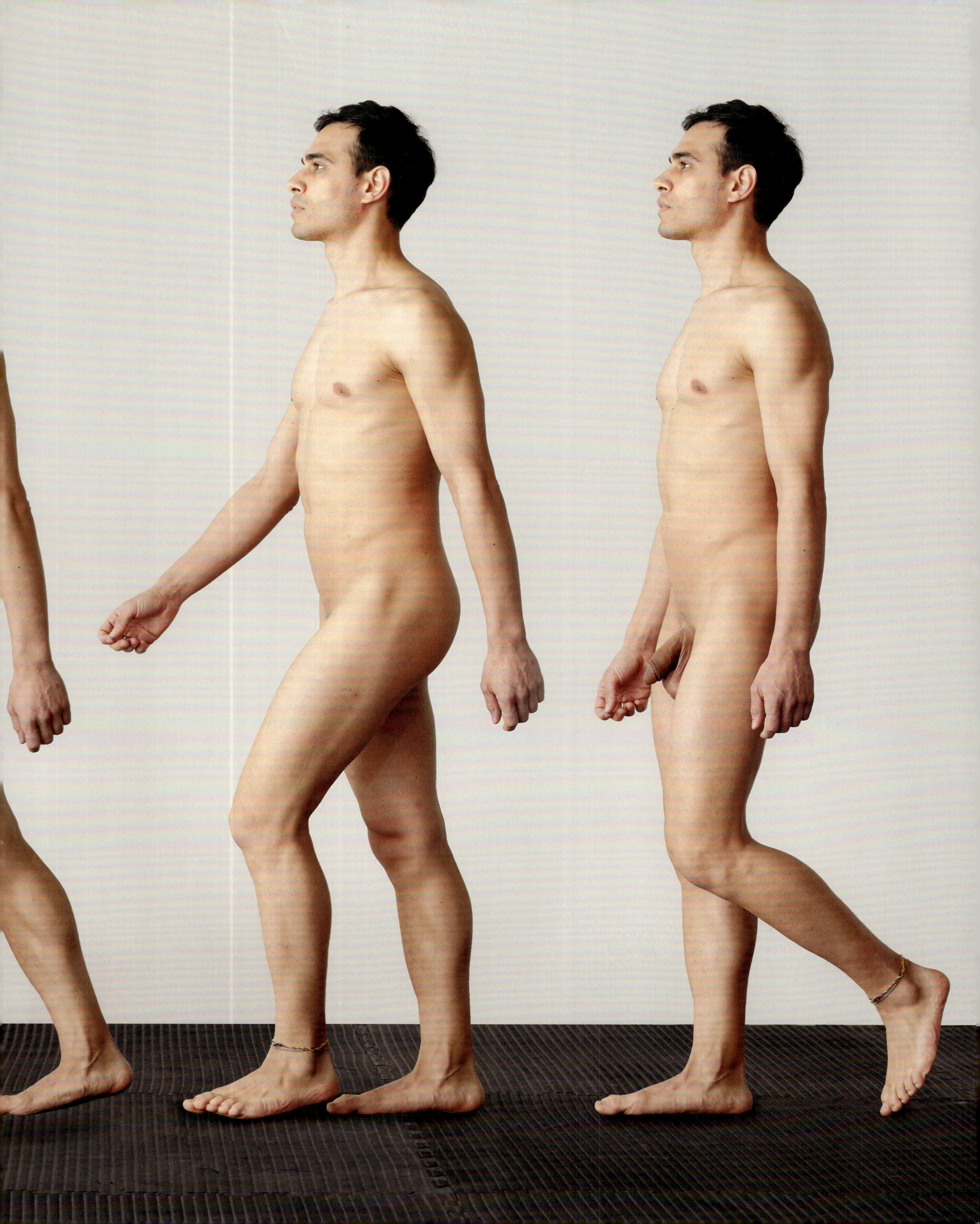

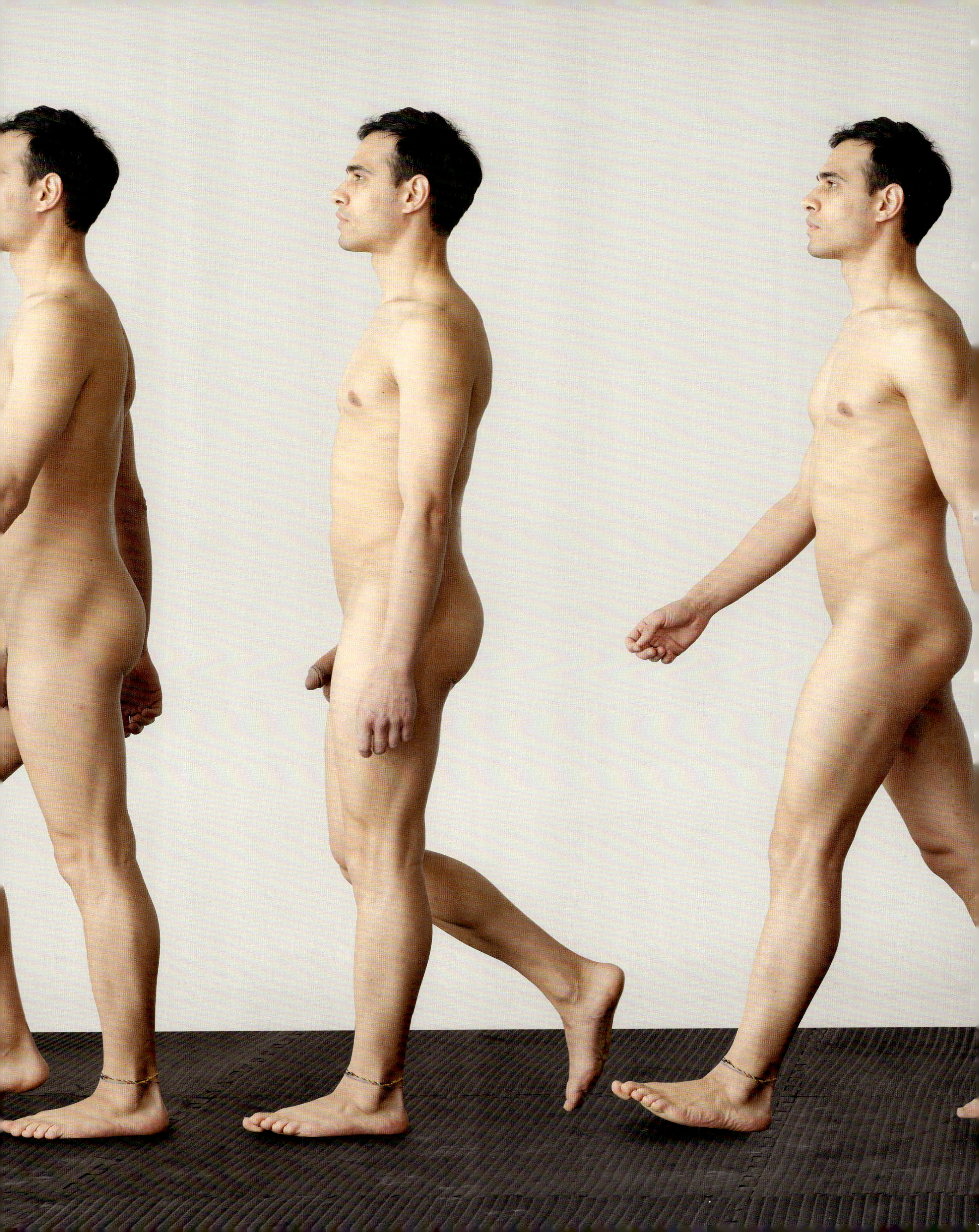

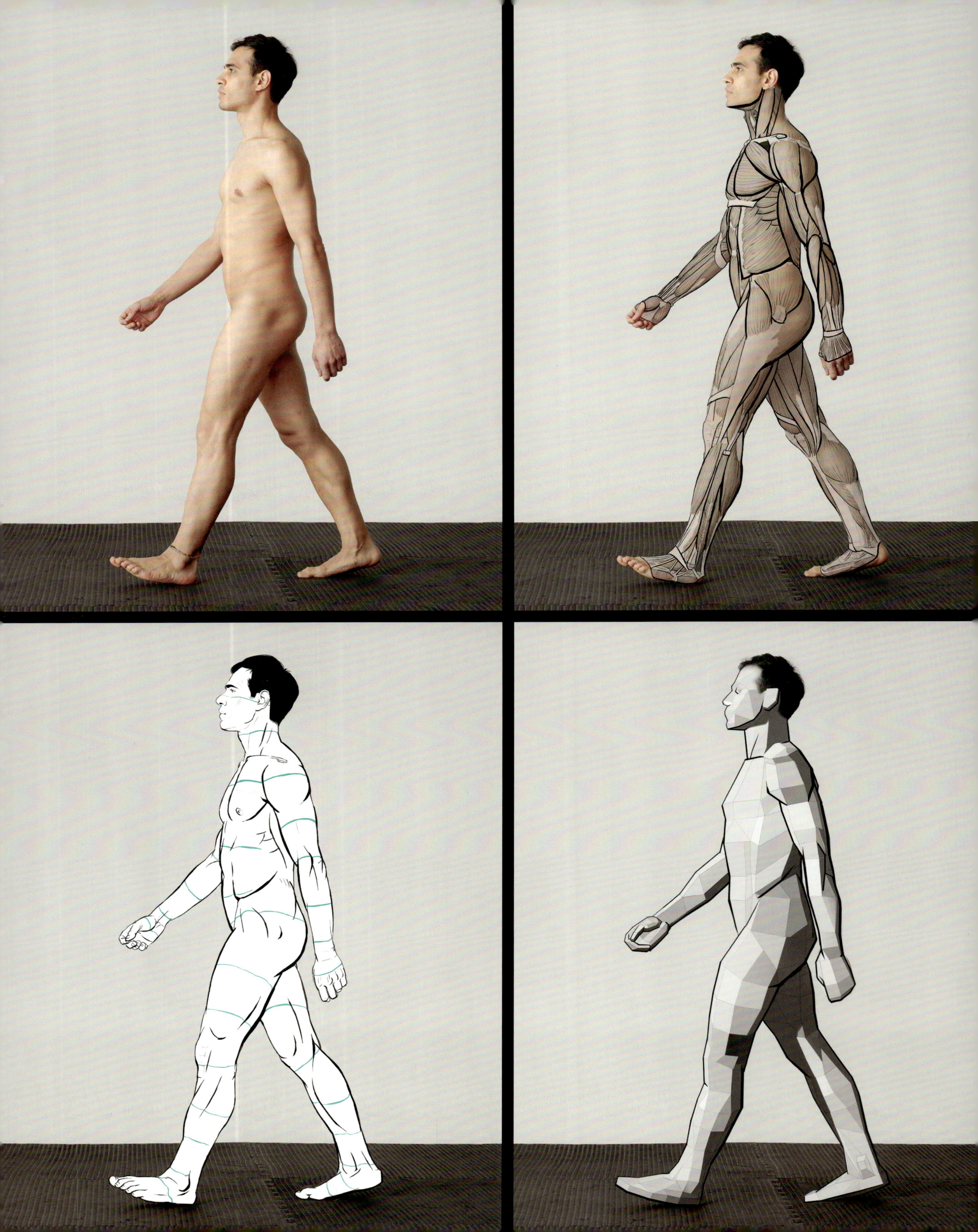

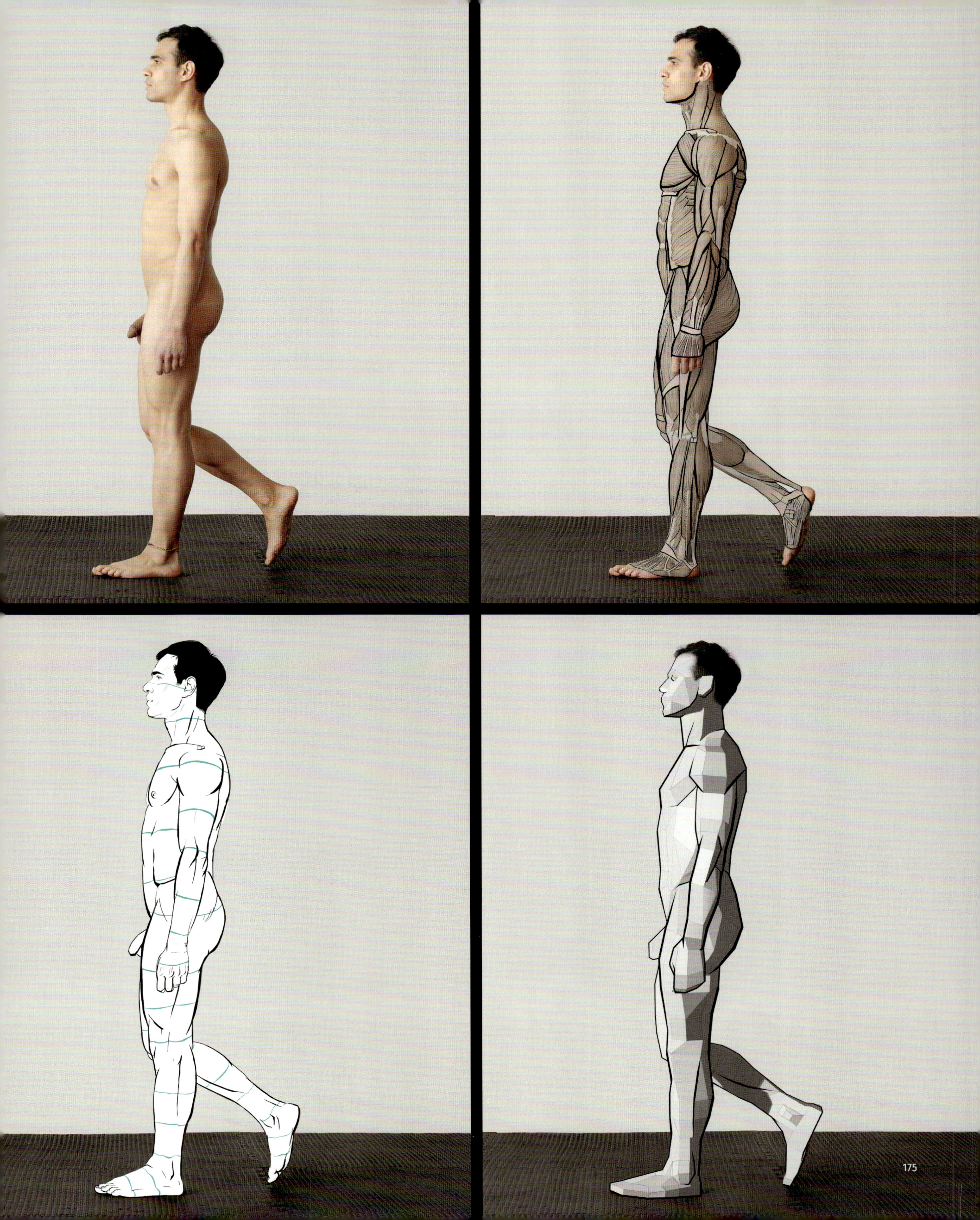

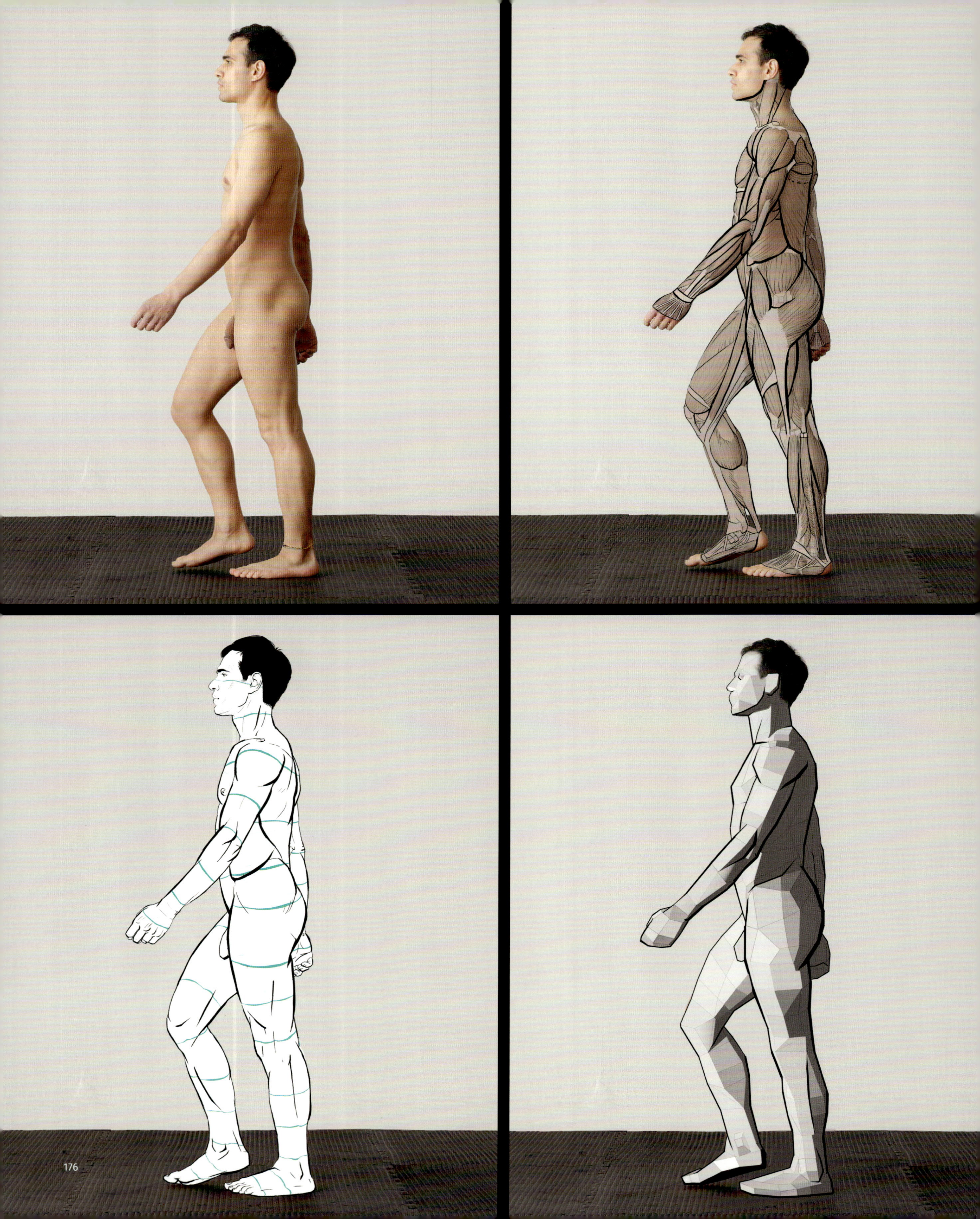

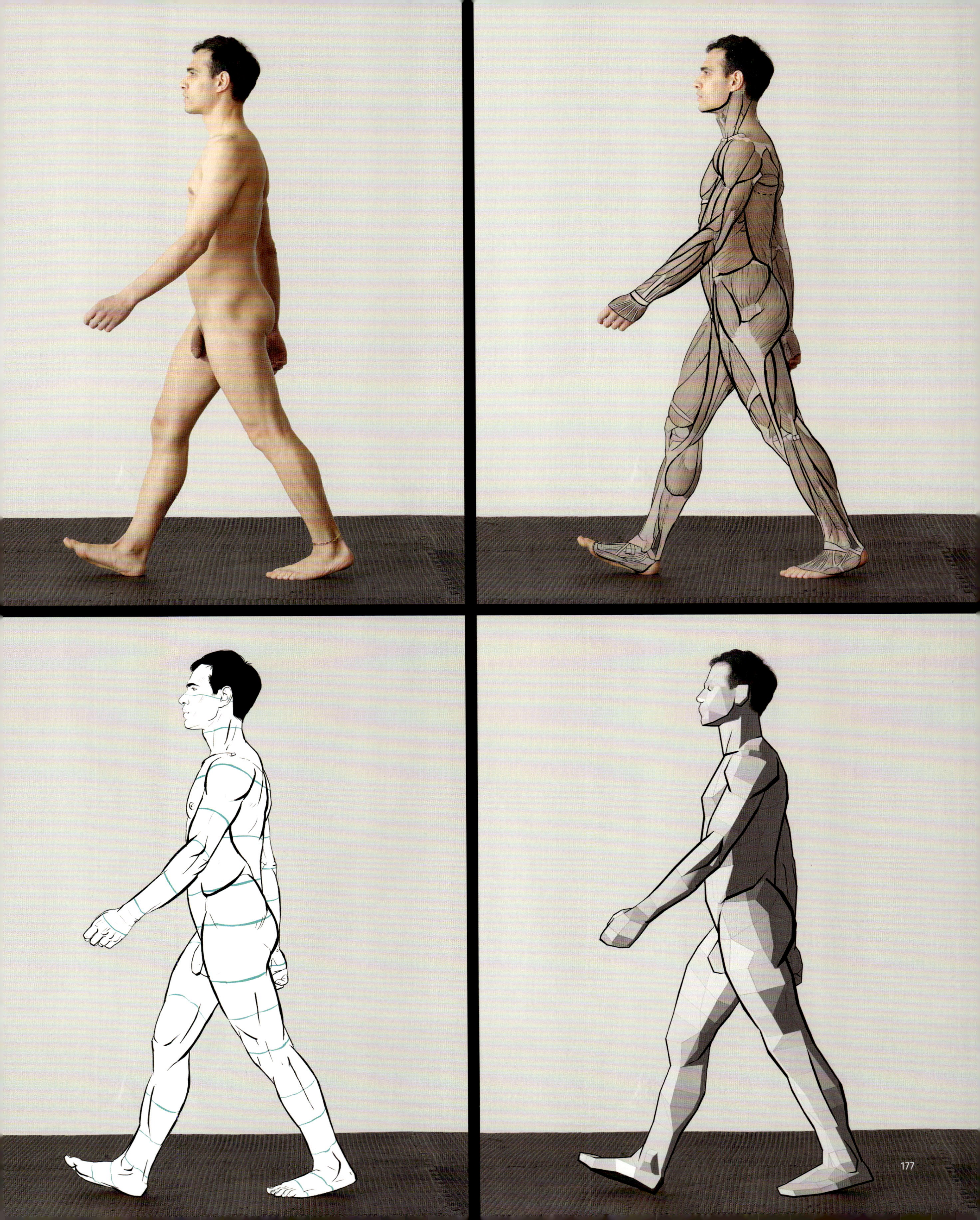

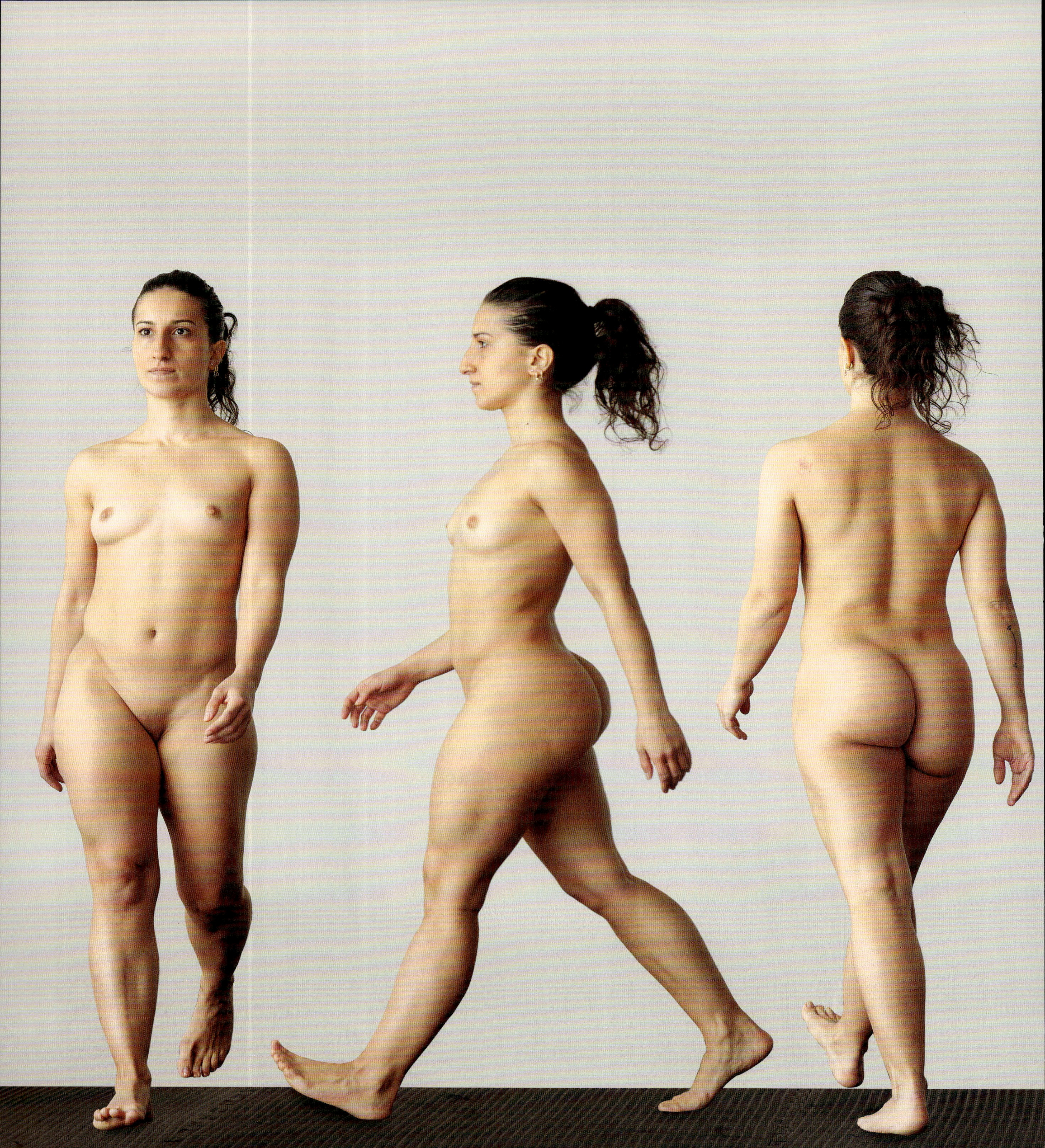

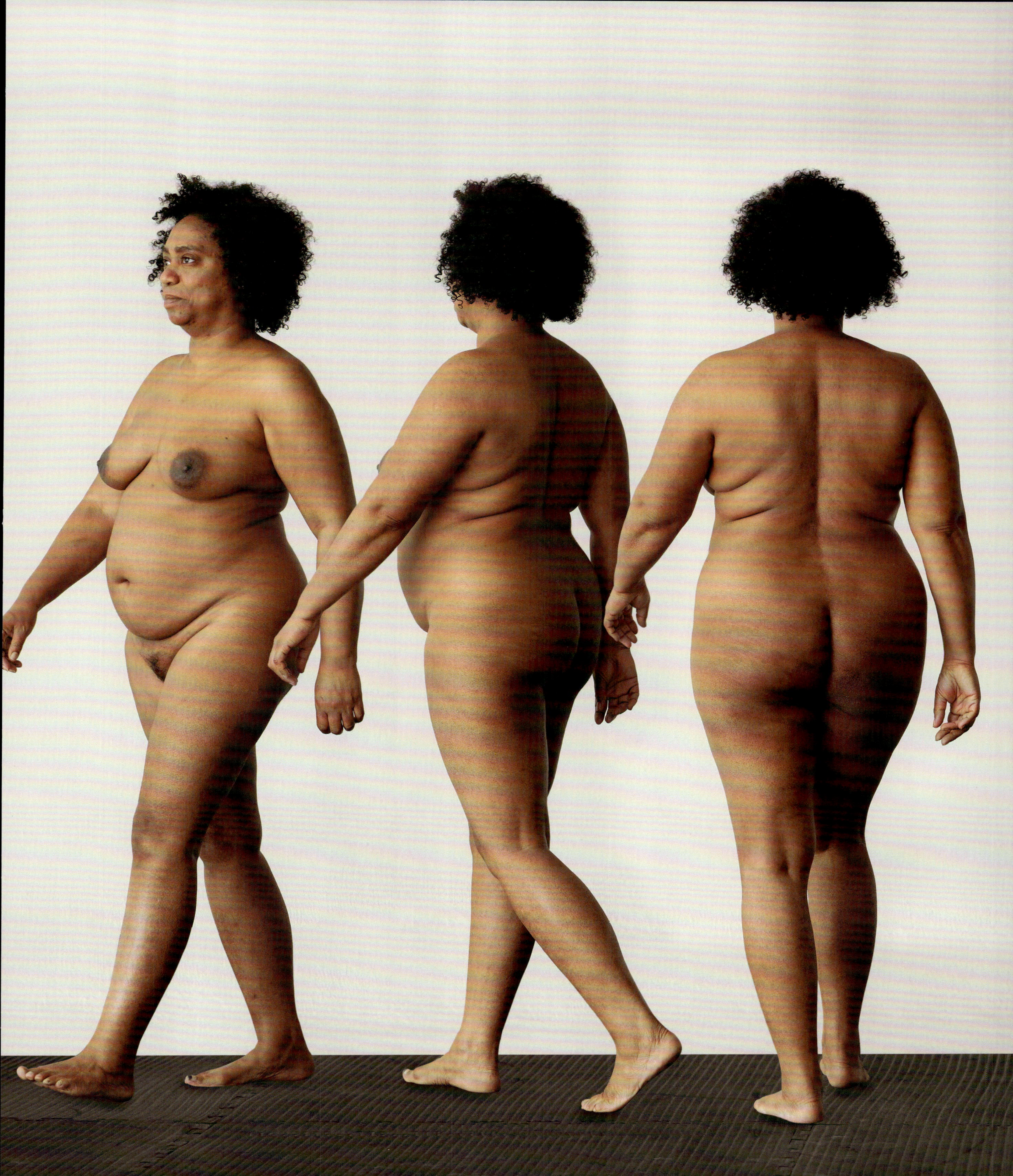

Running

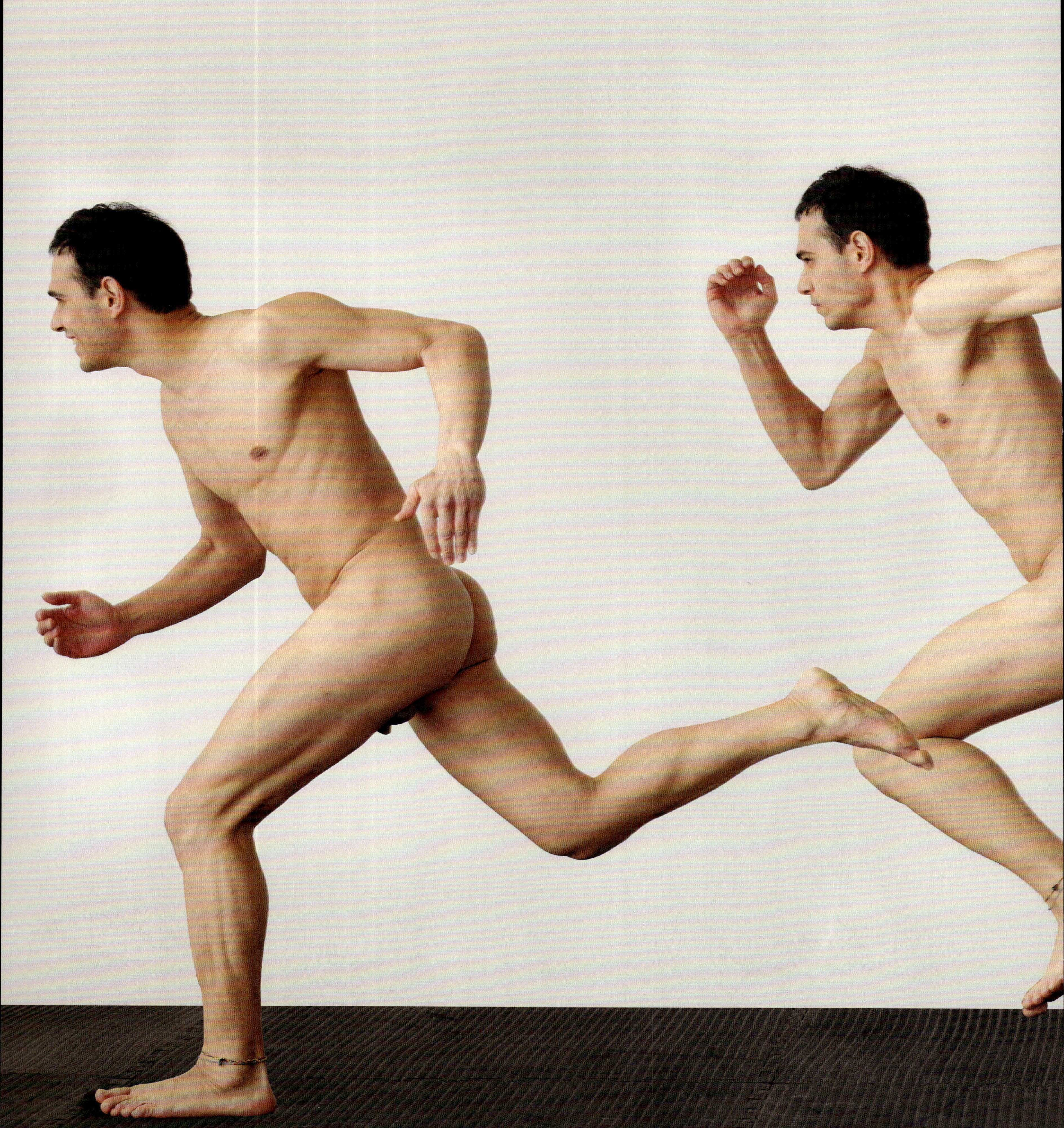

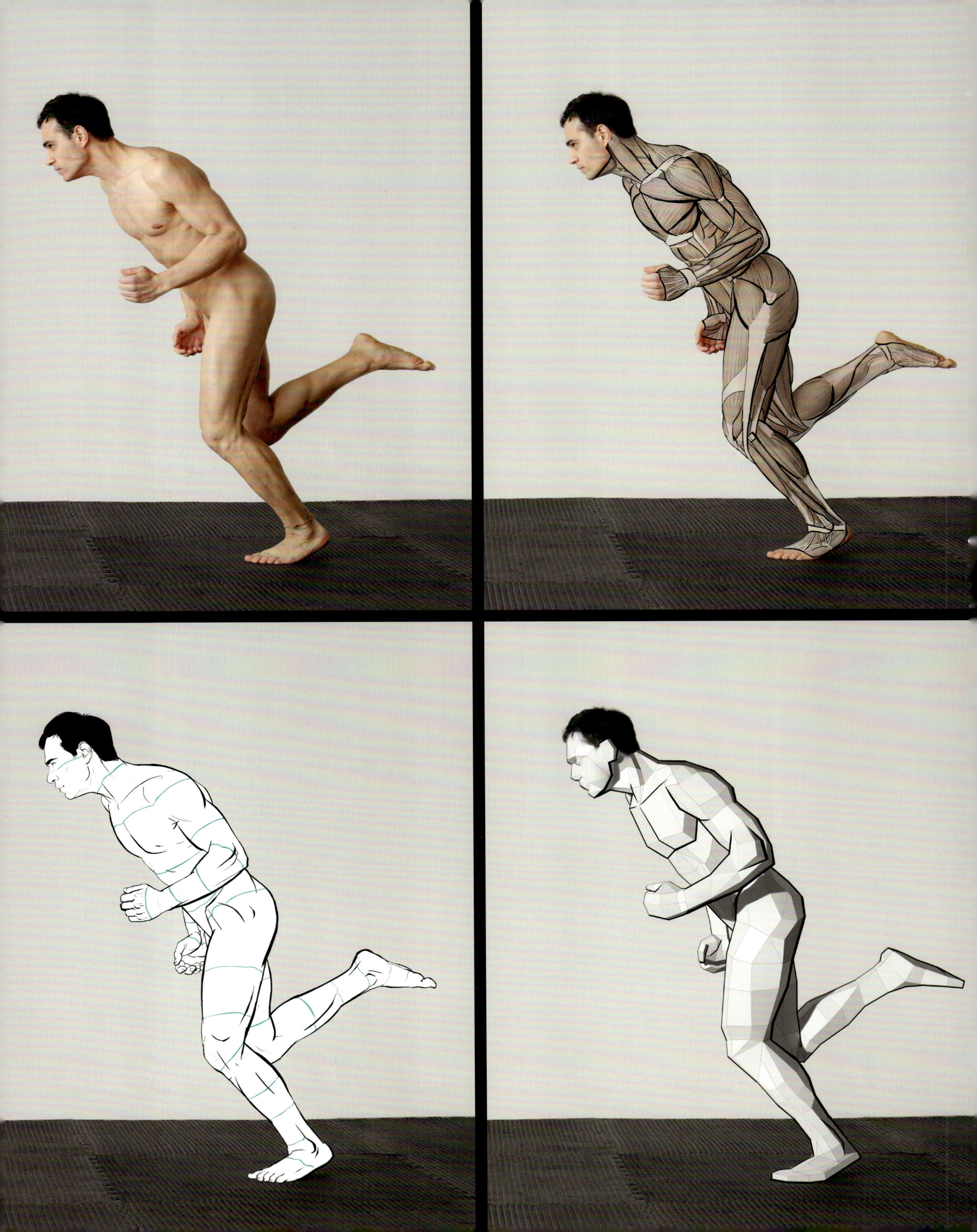

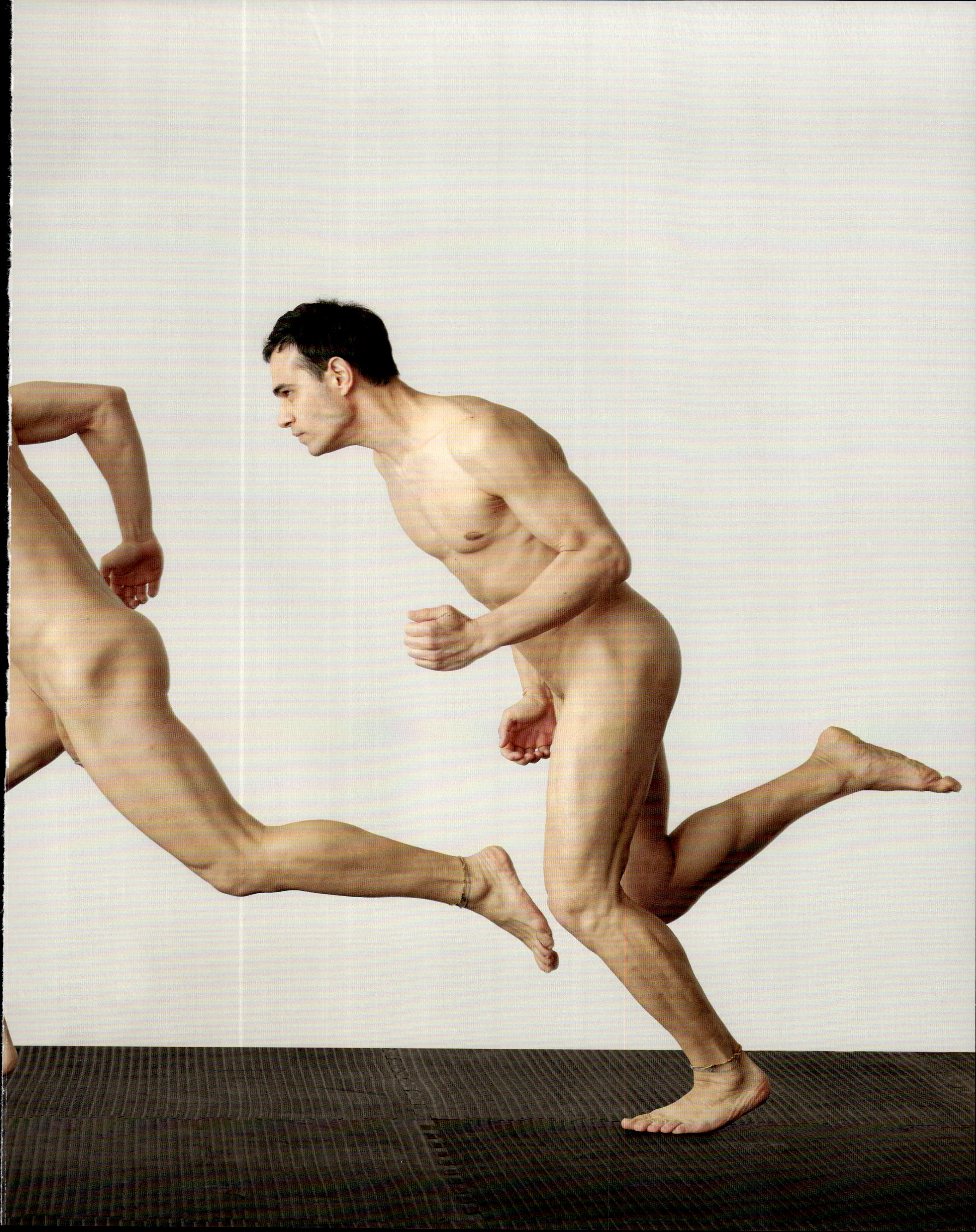

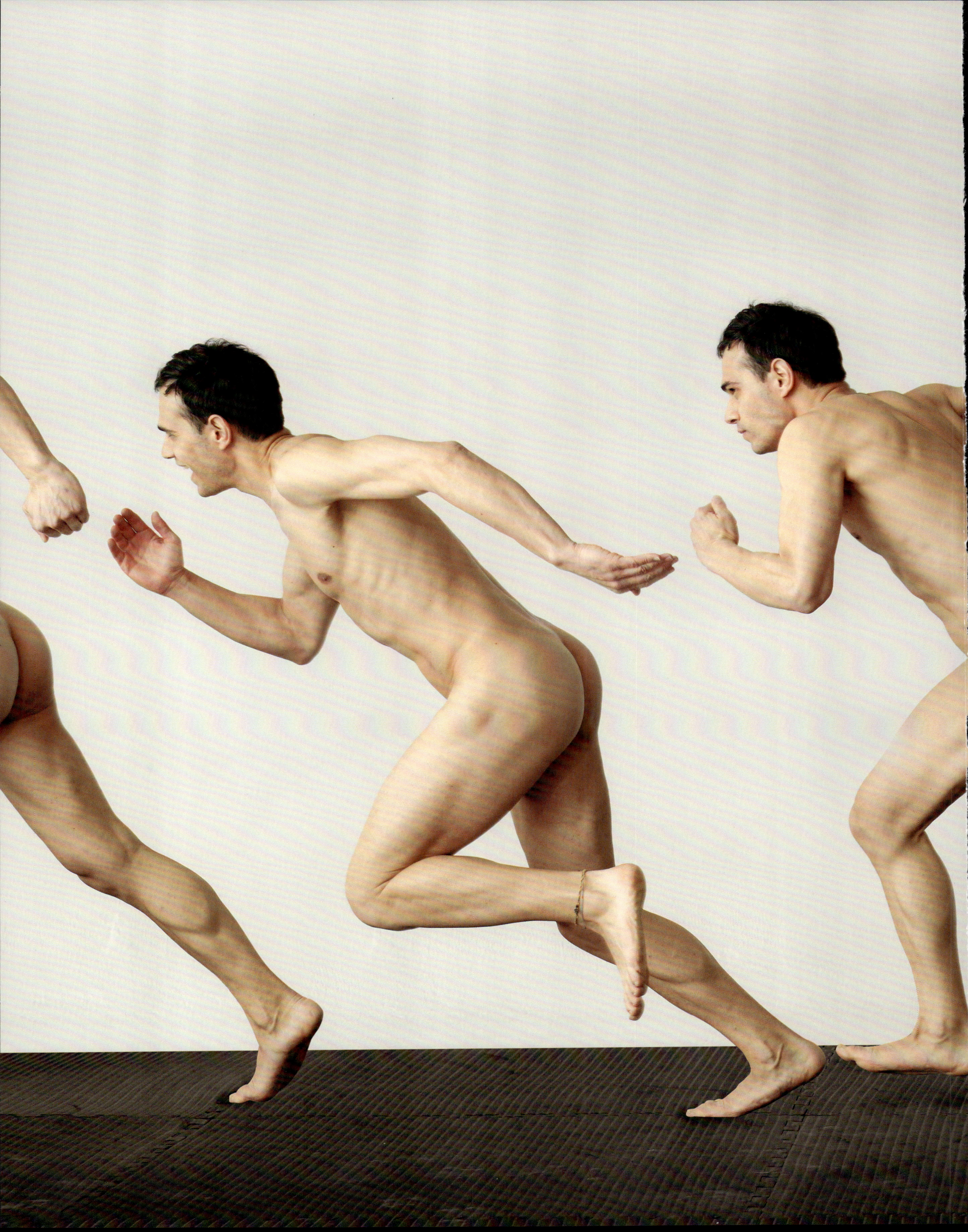

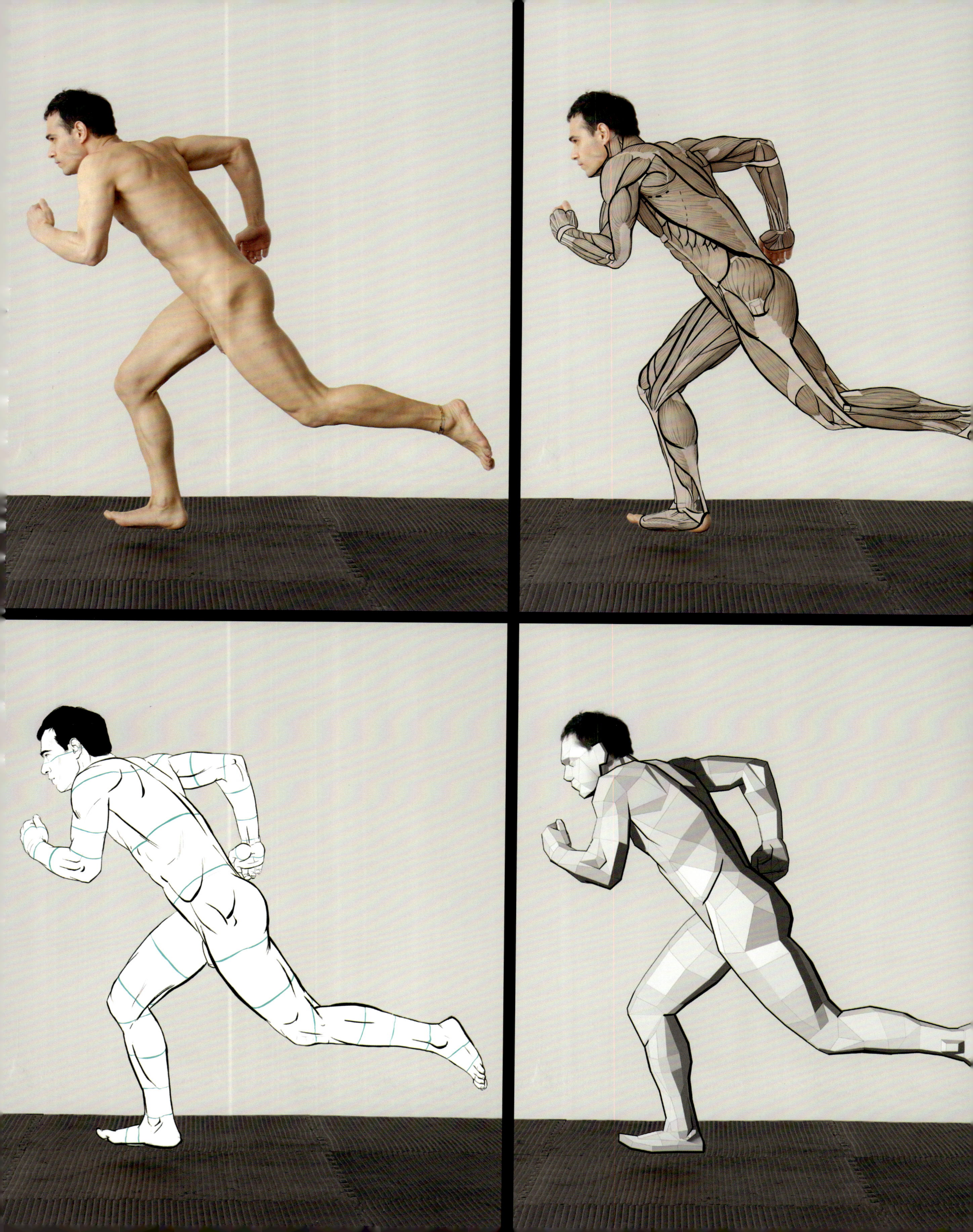

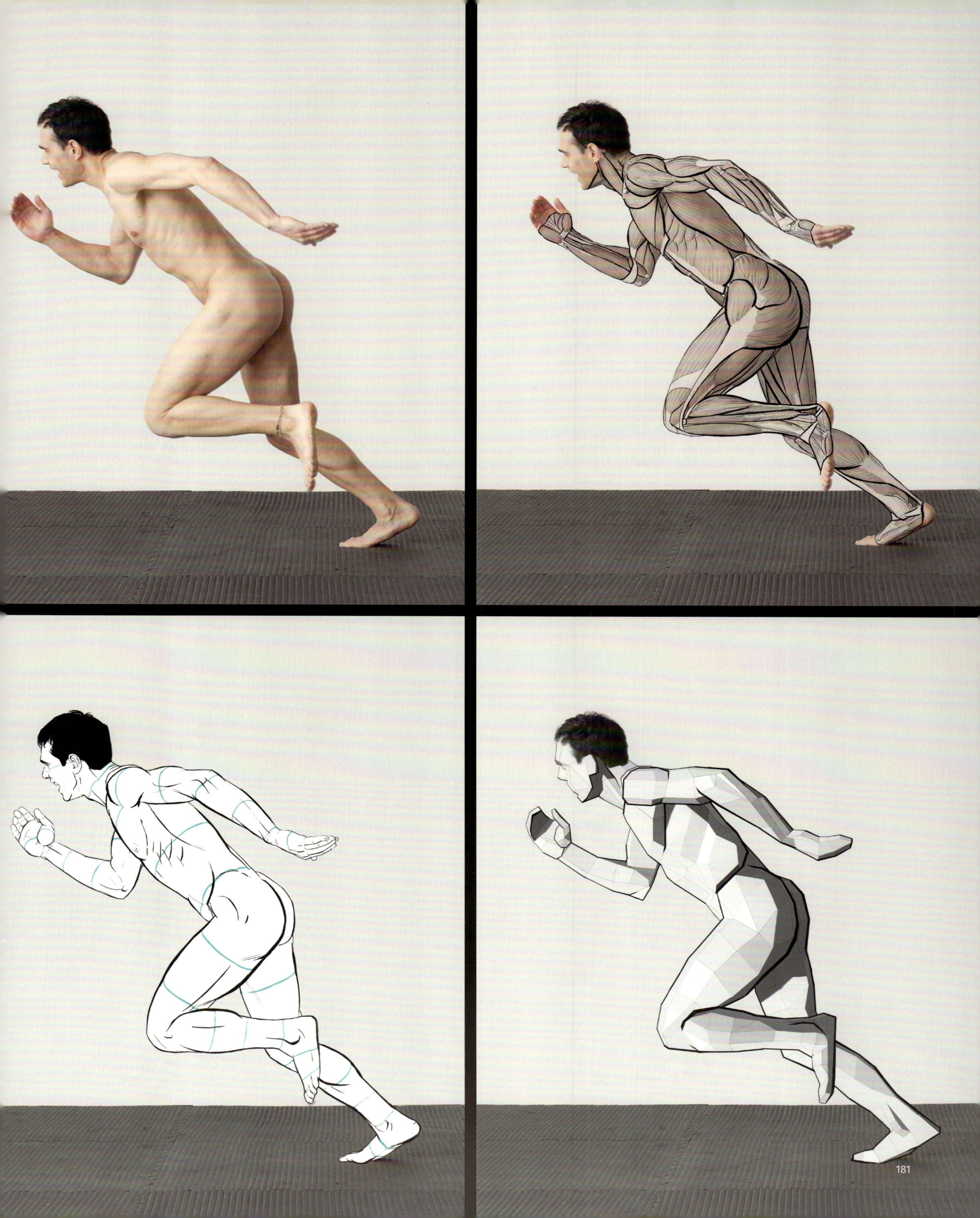

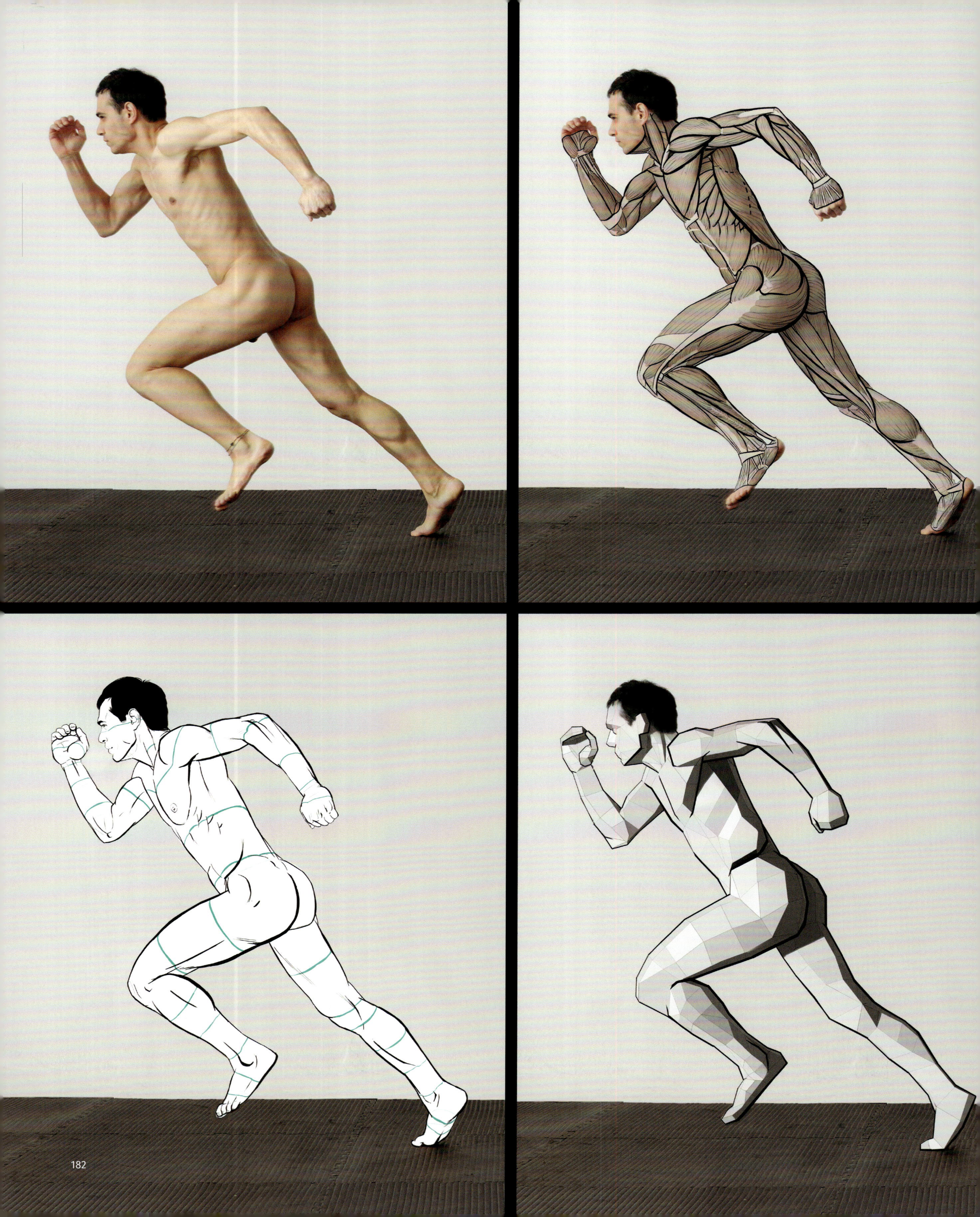

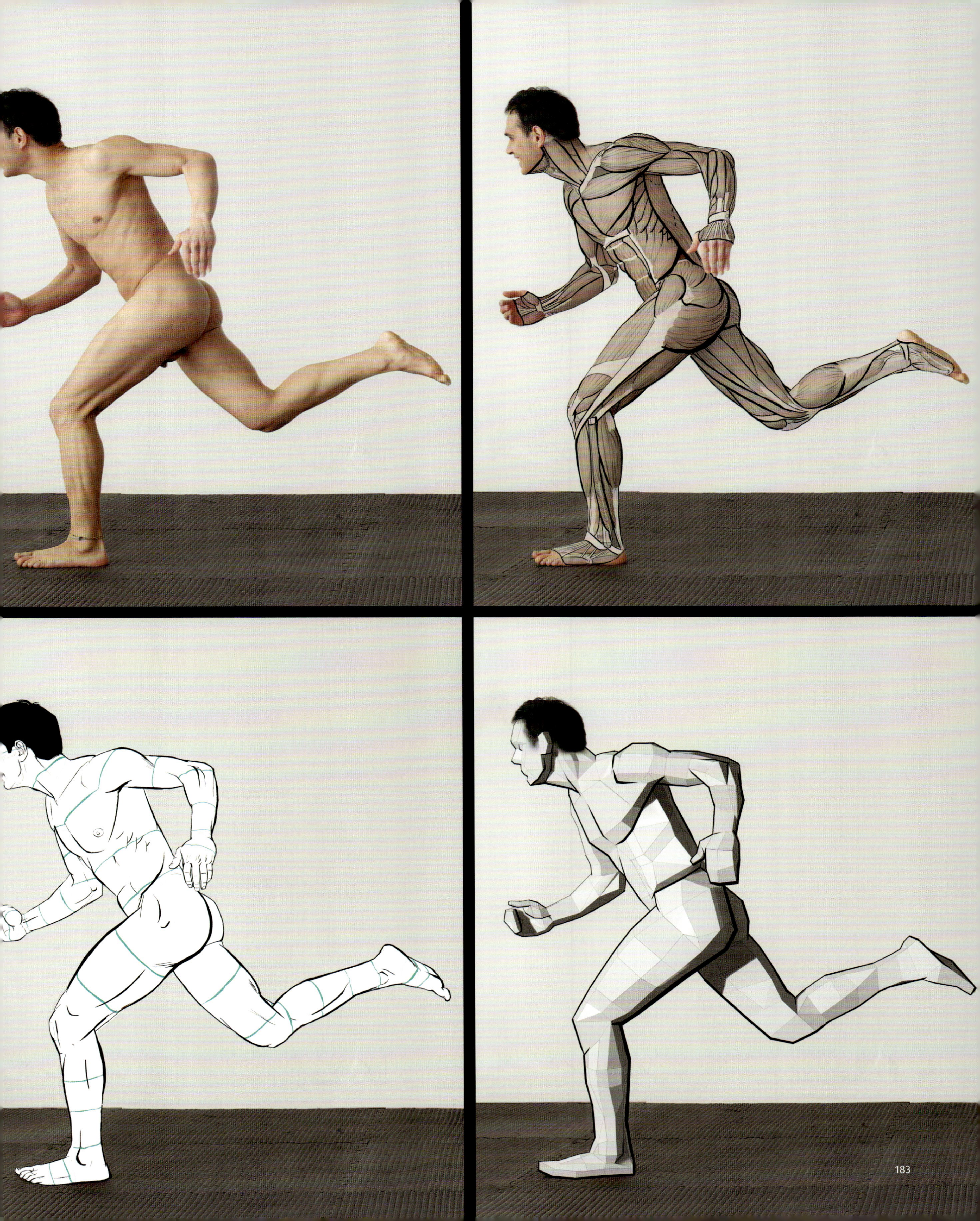

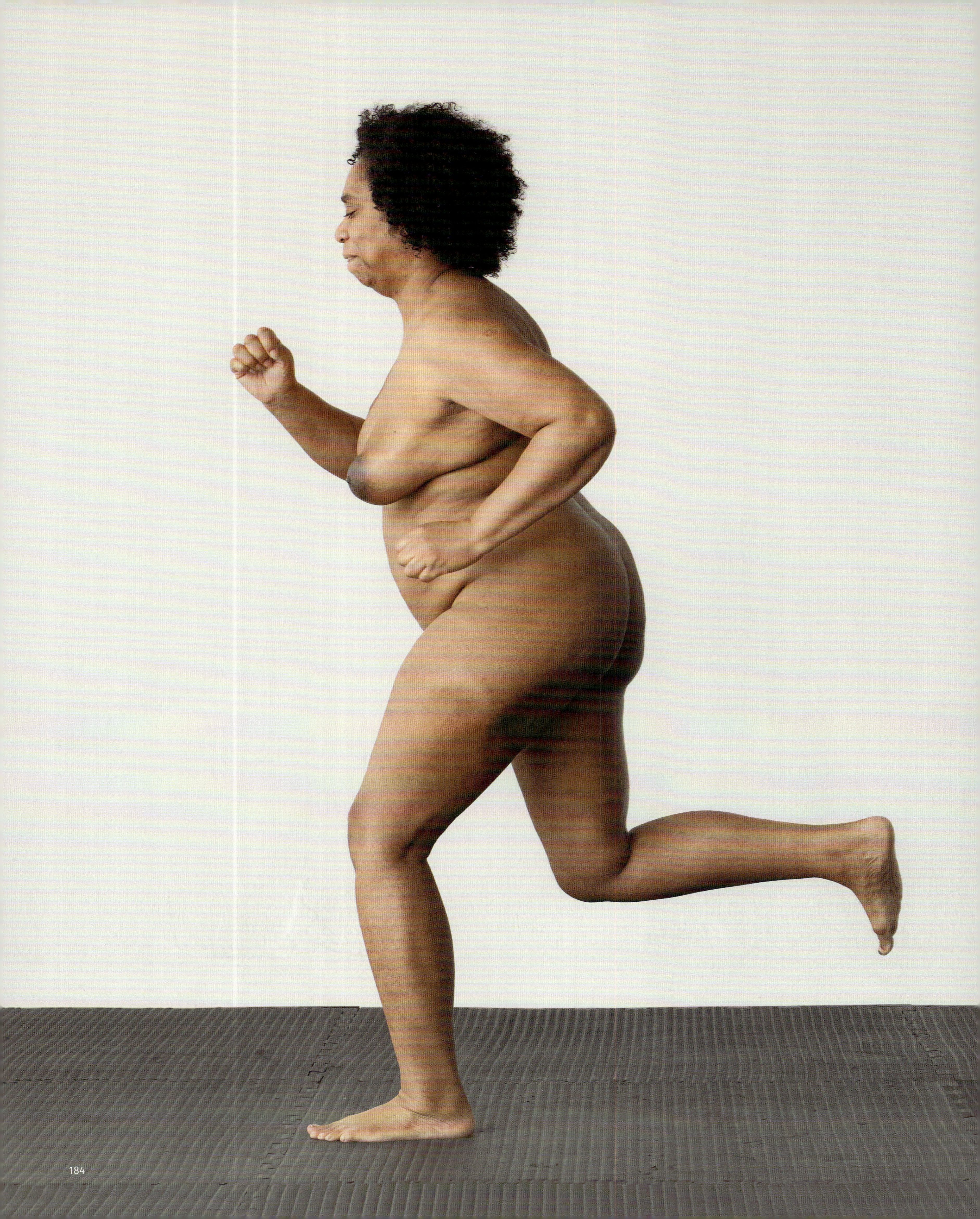

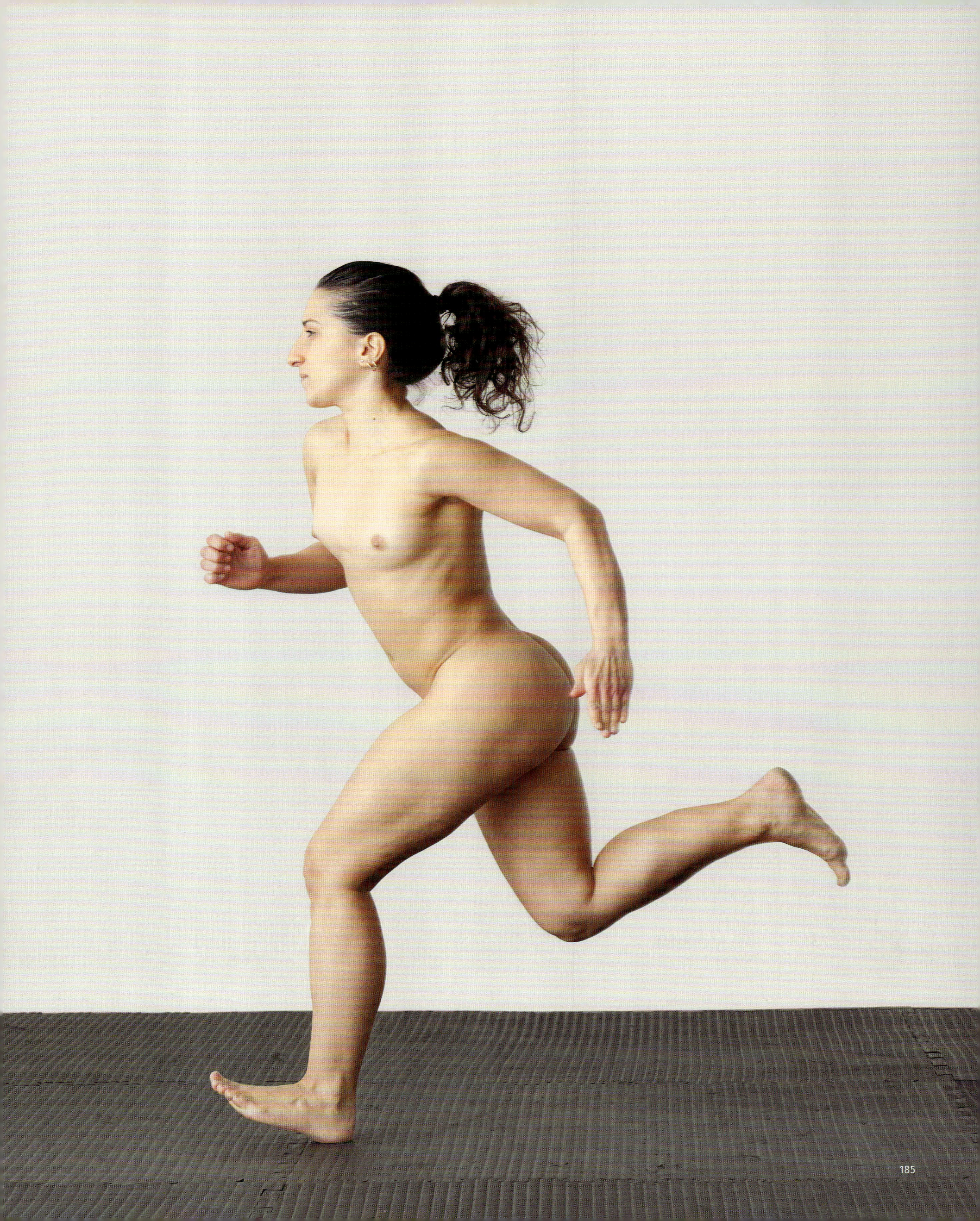

Lifting an object

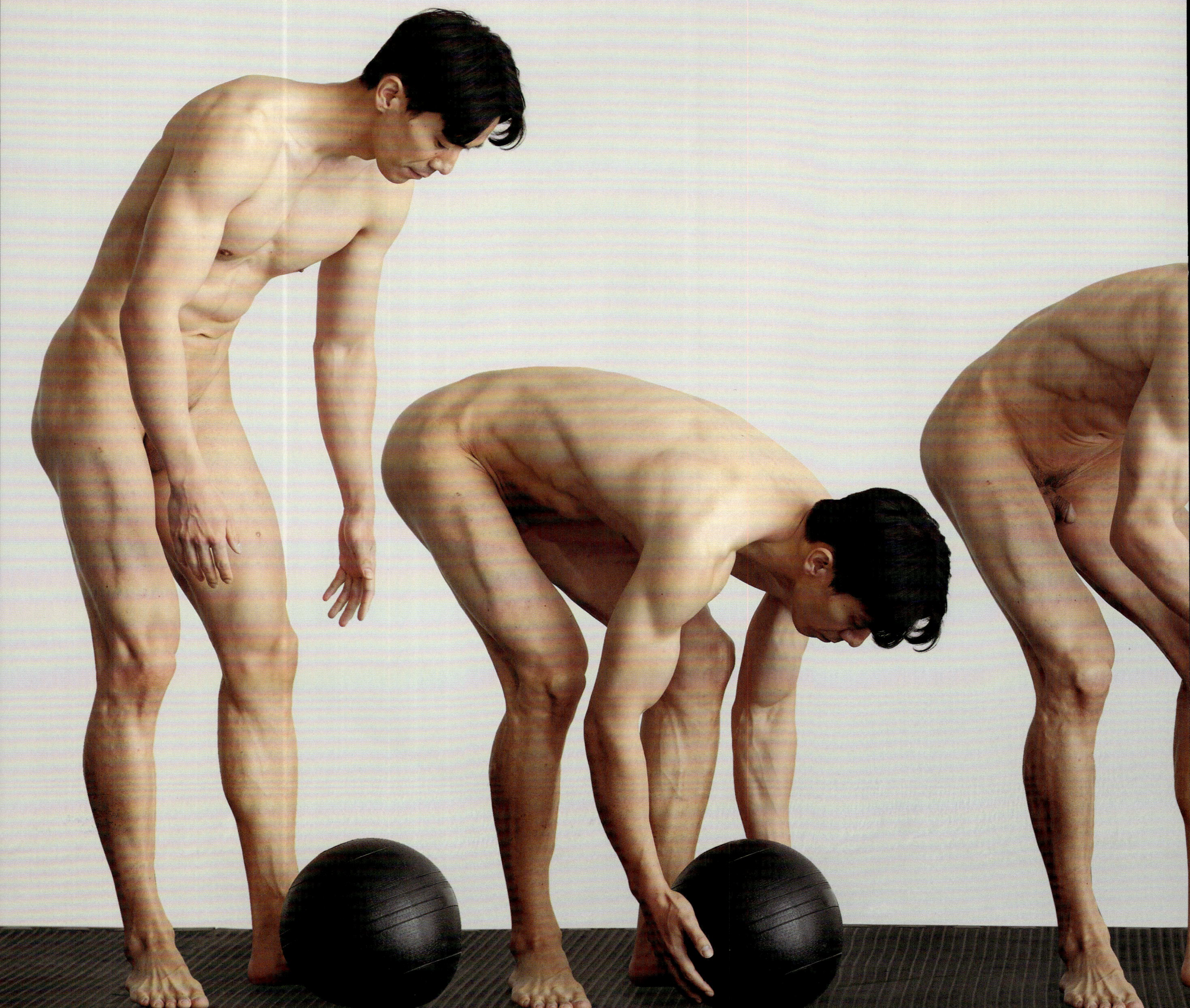

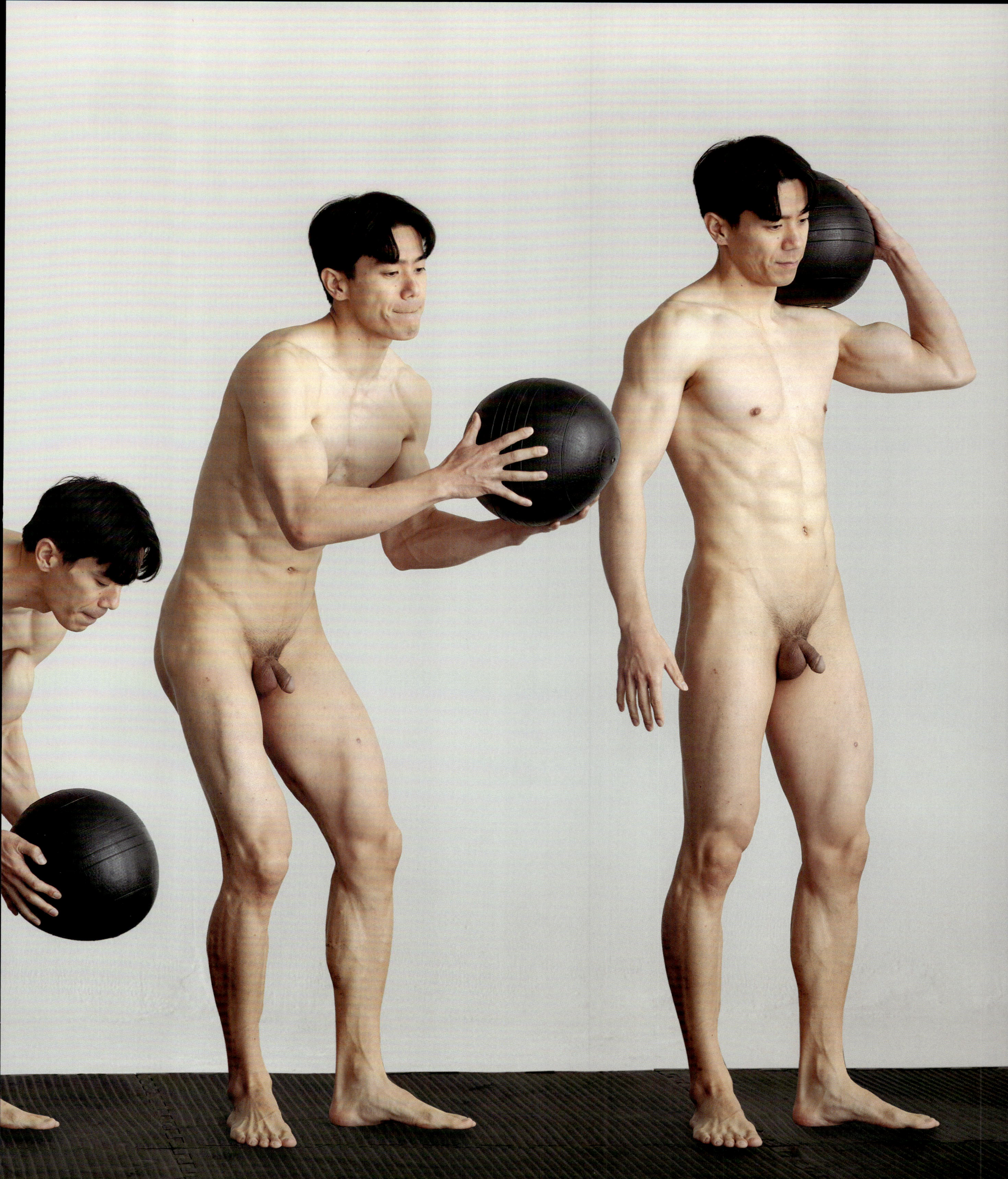

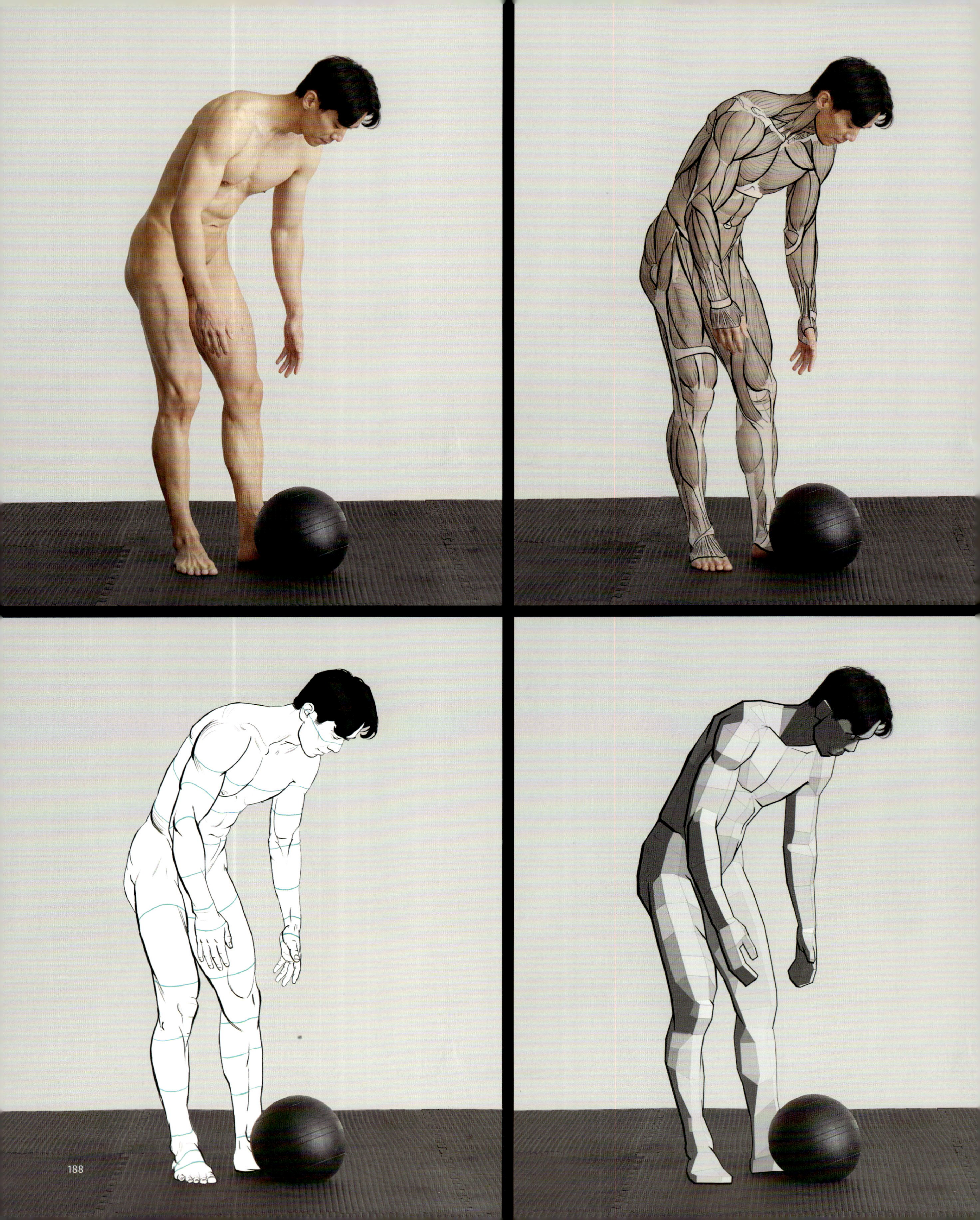

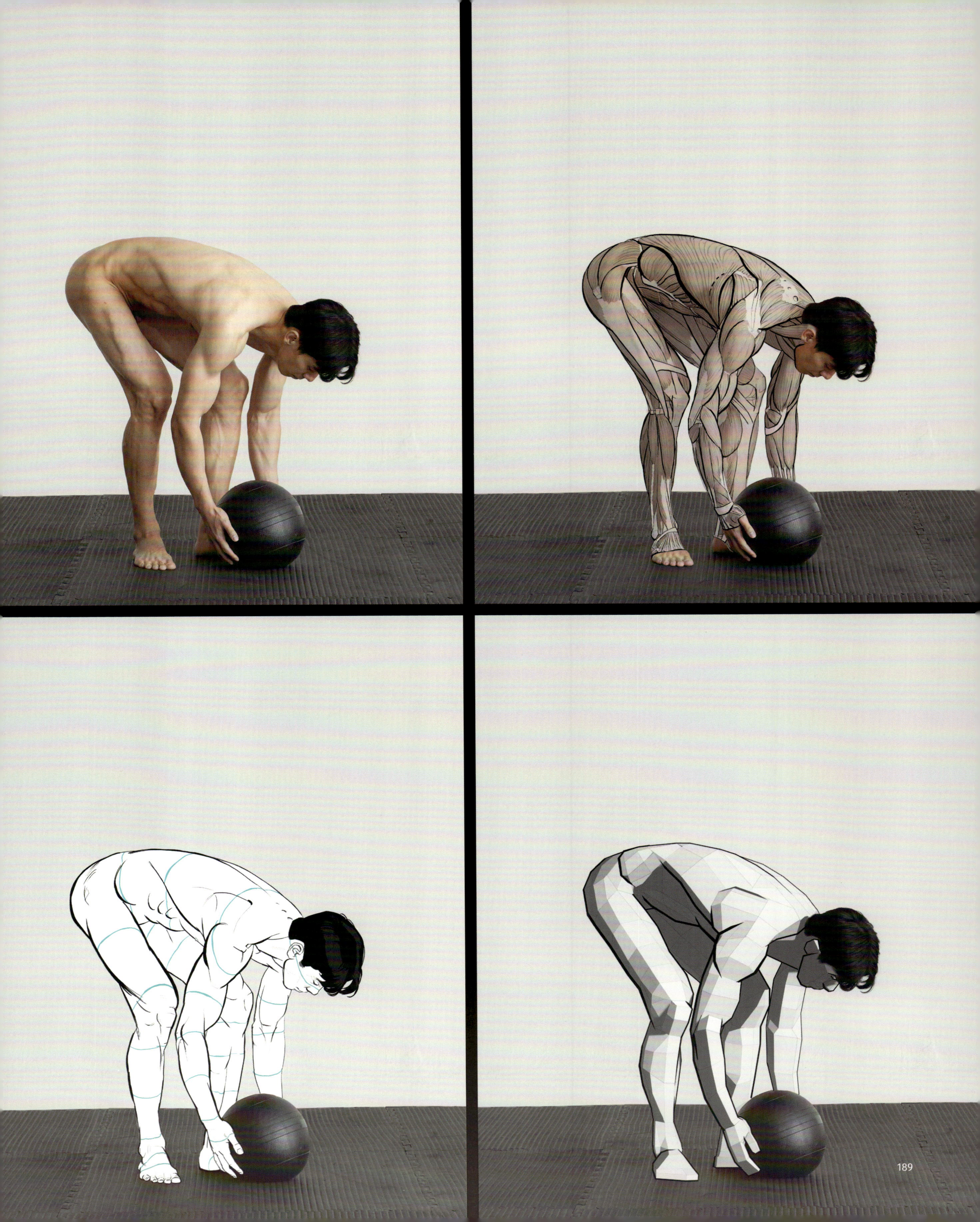

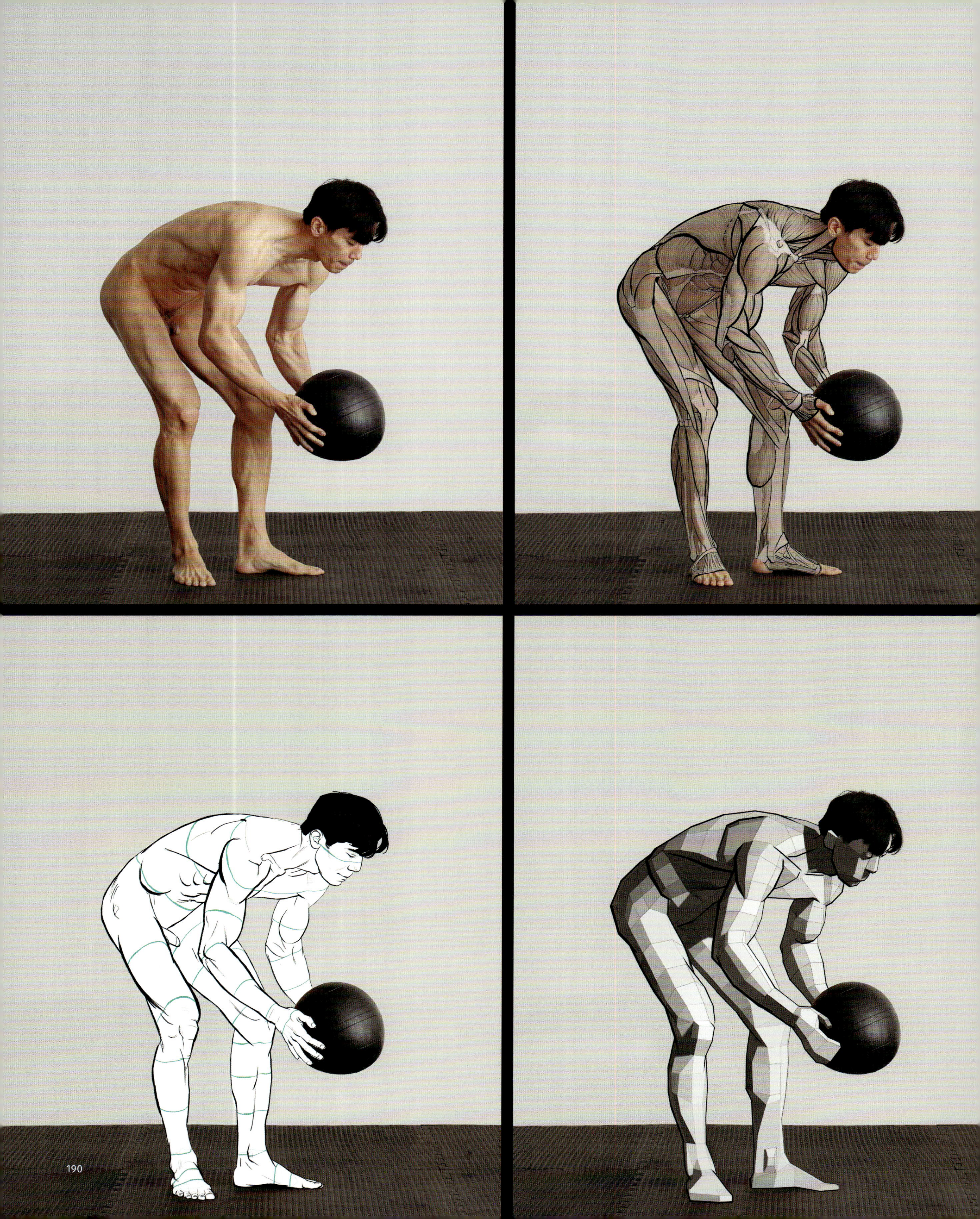

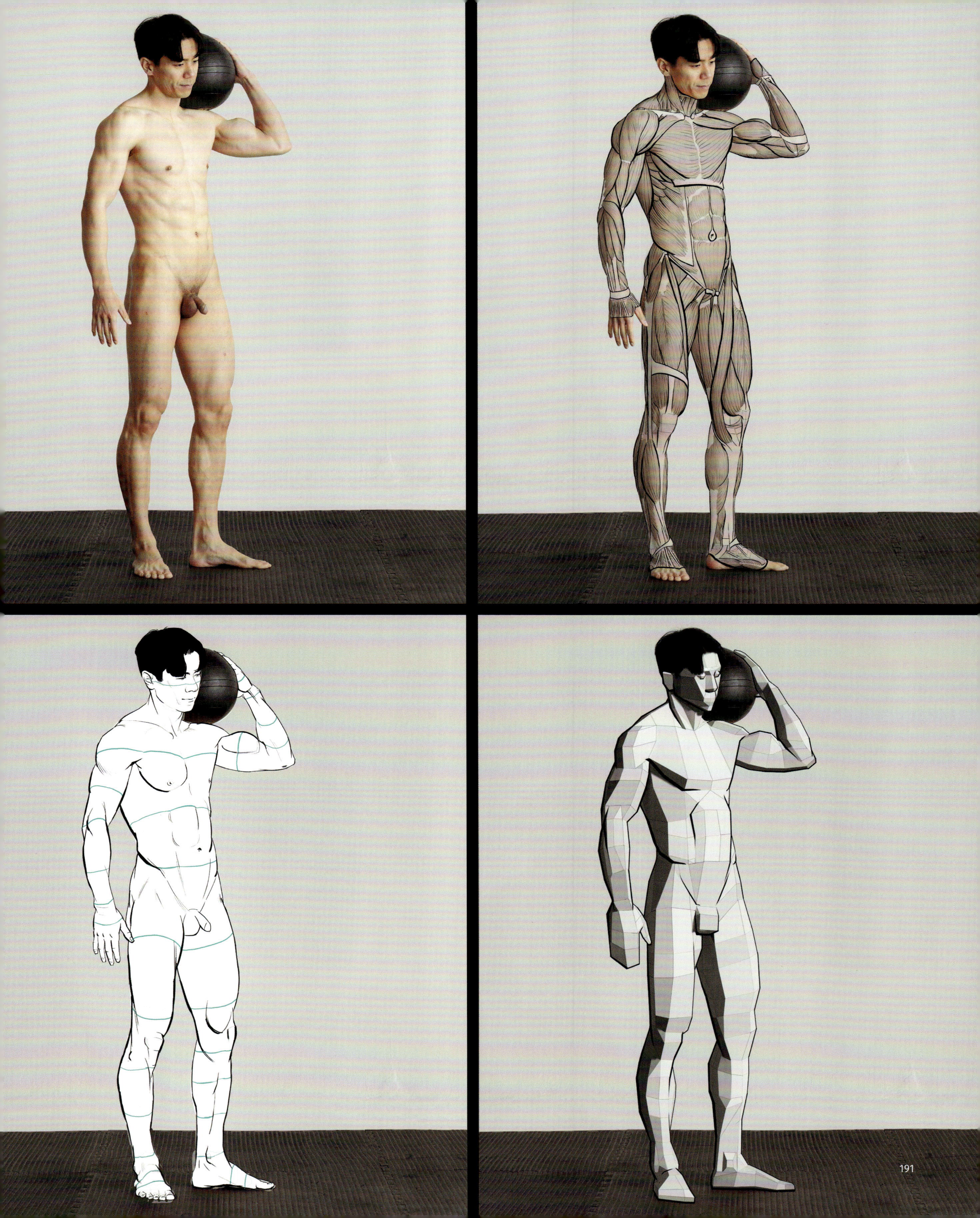

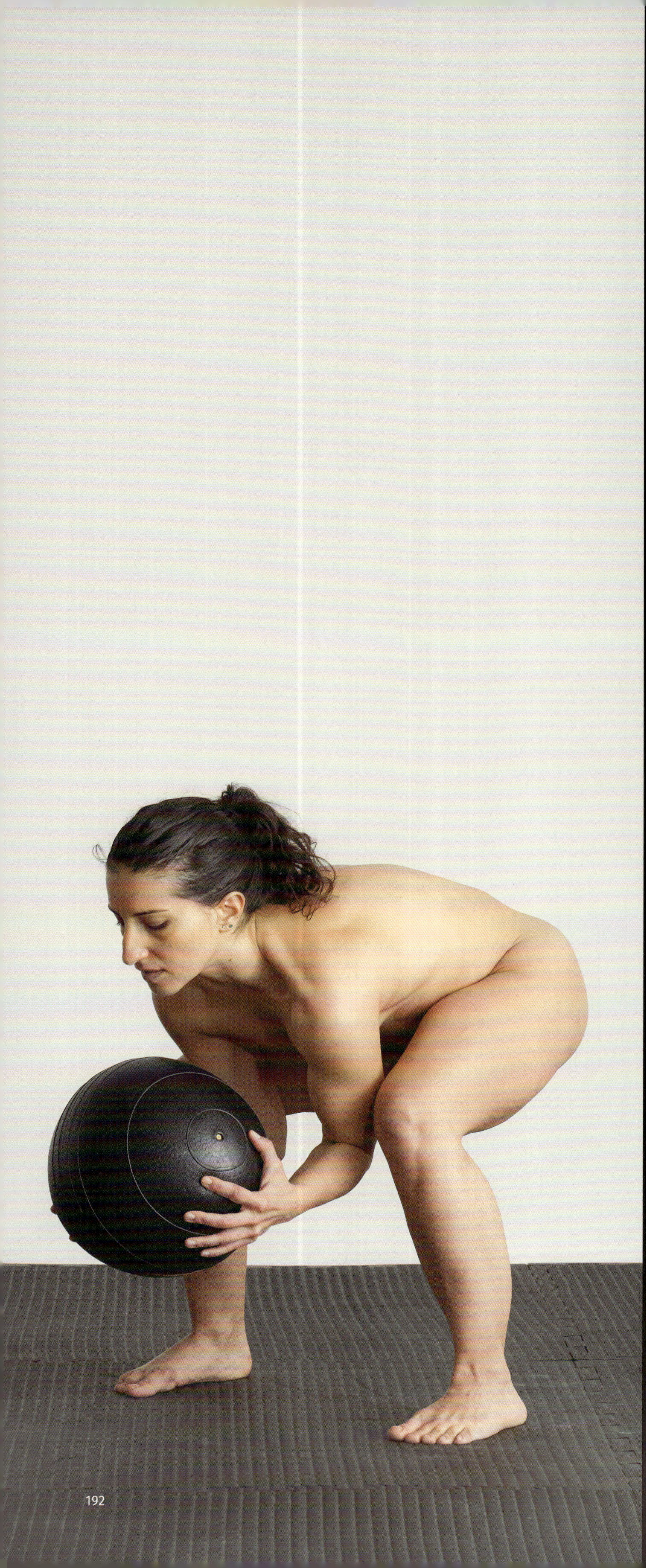

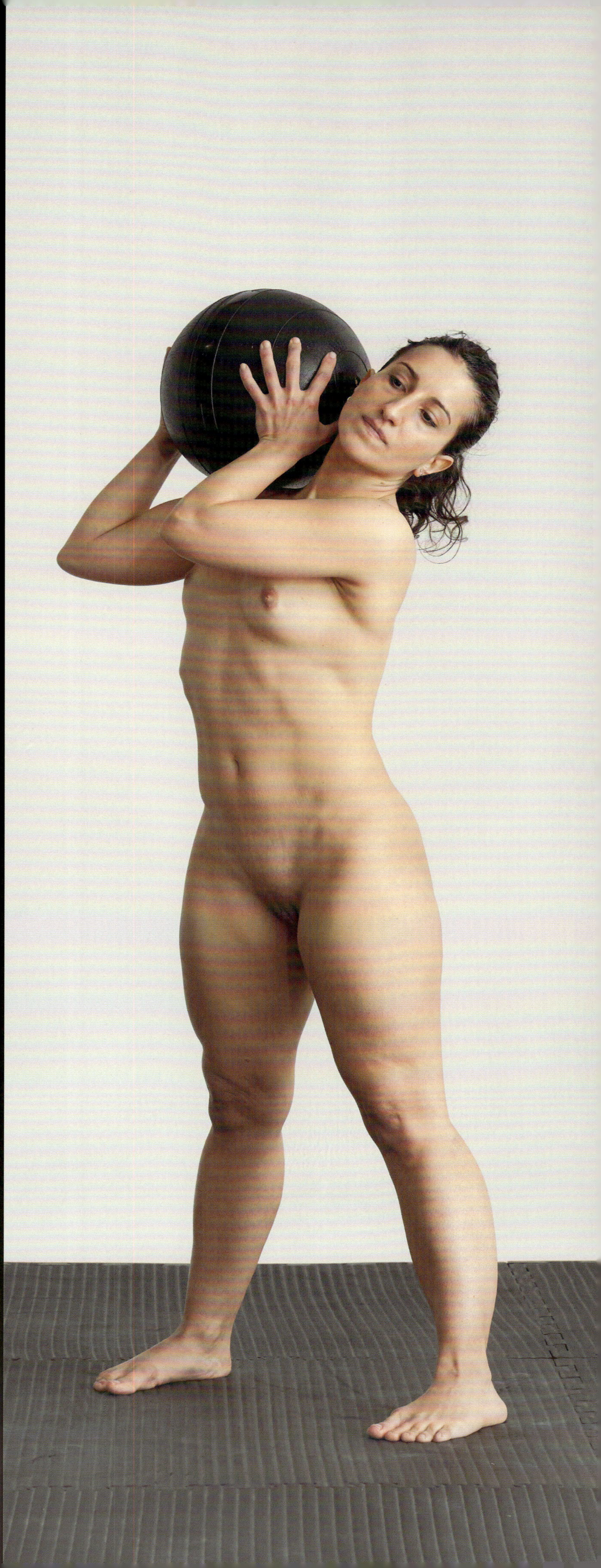

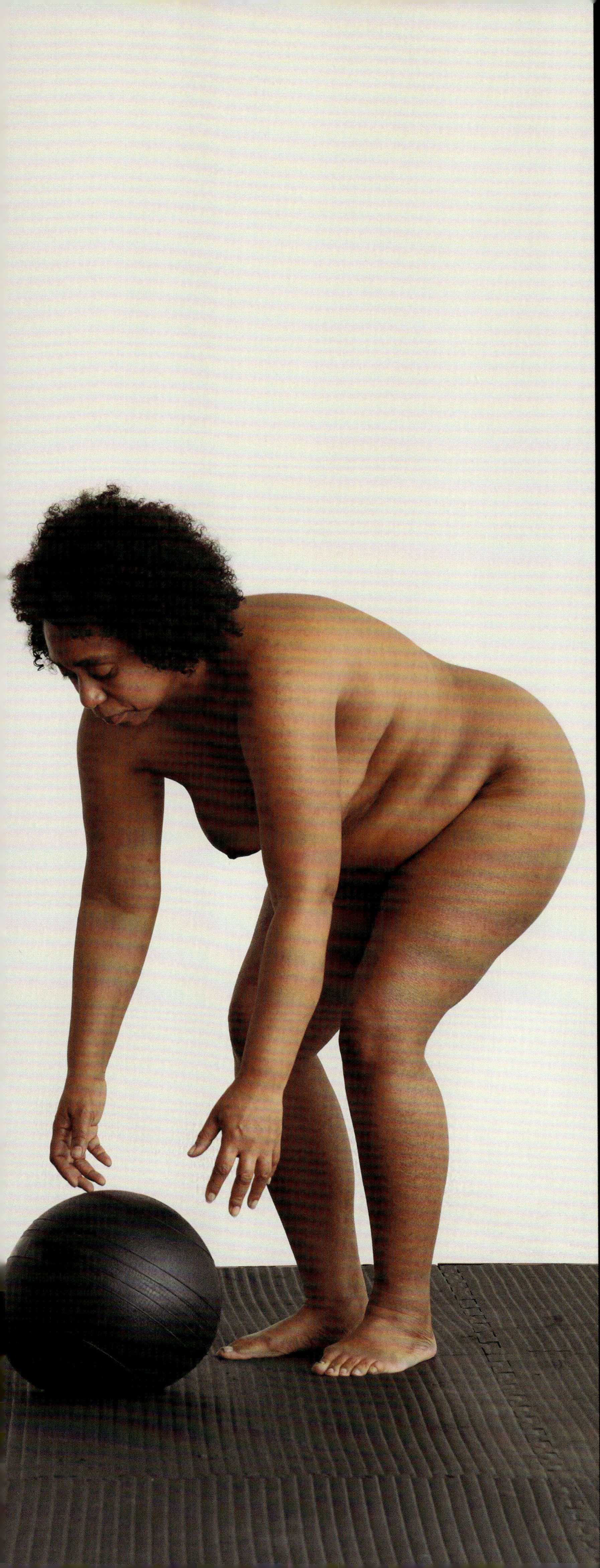

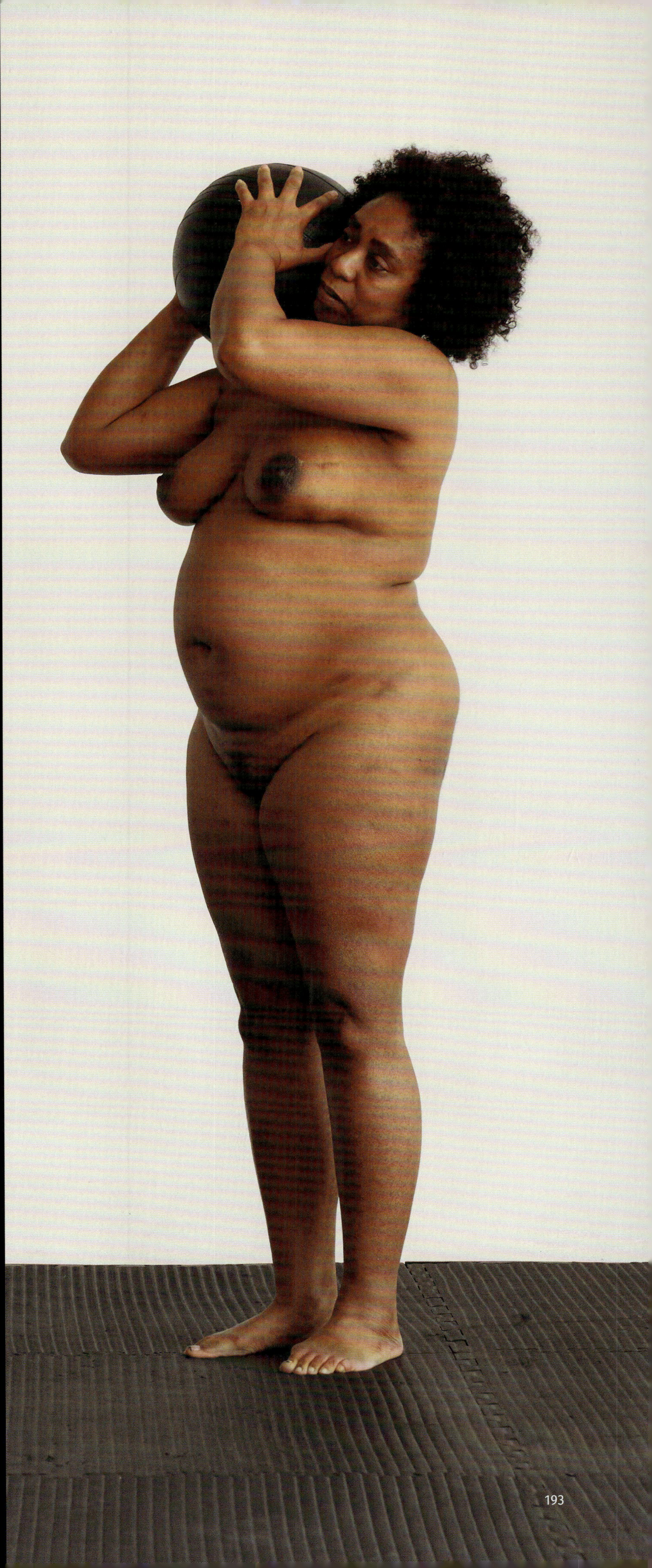

Jumping from a run-up

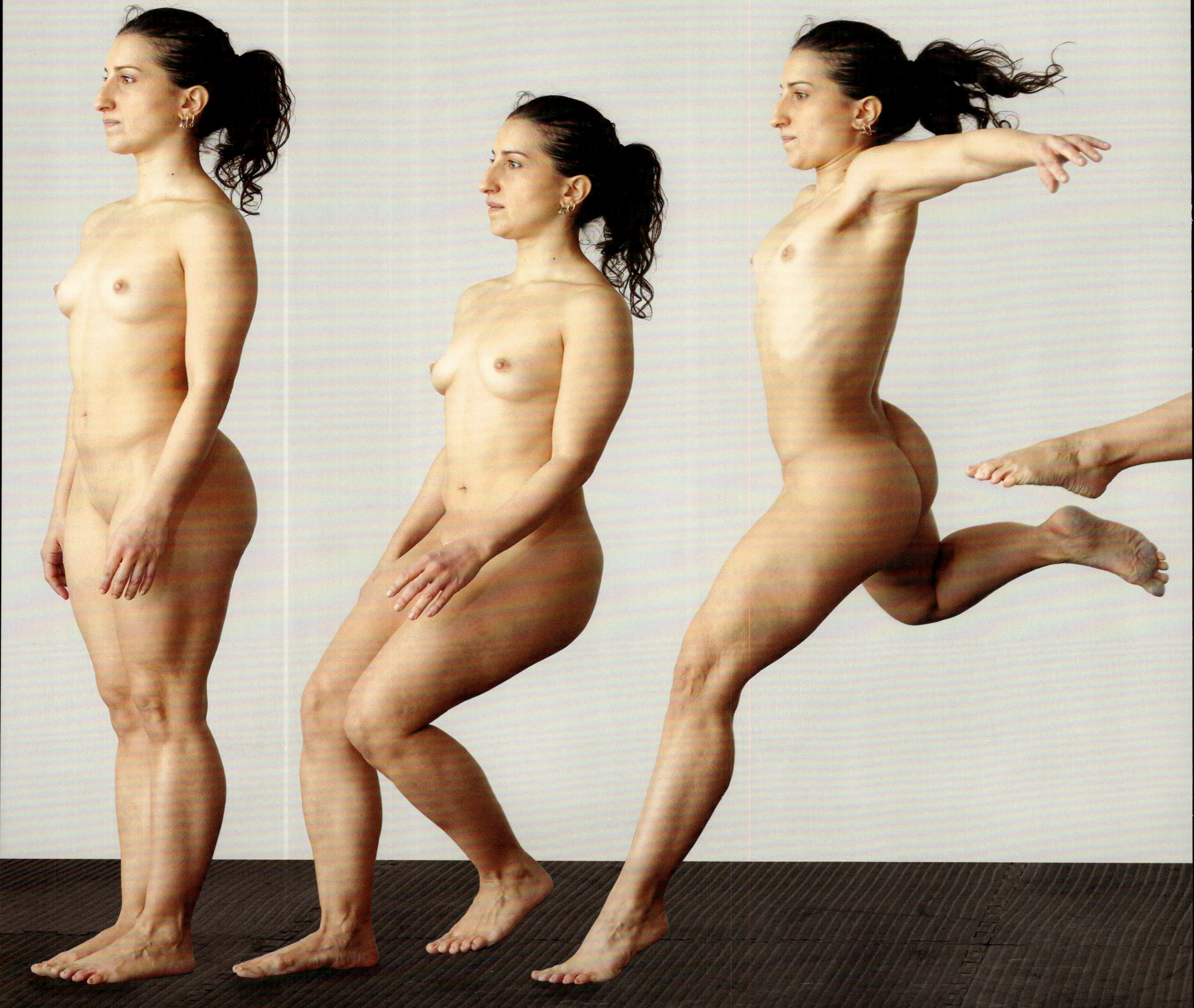

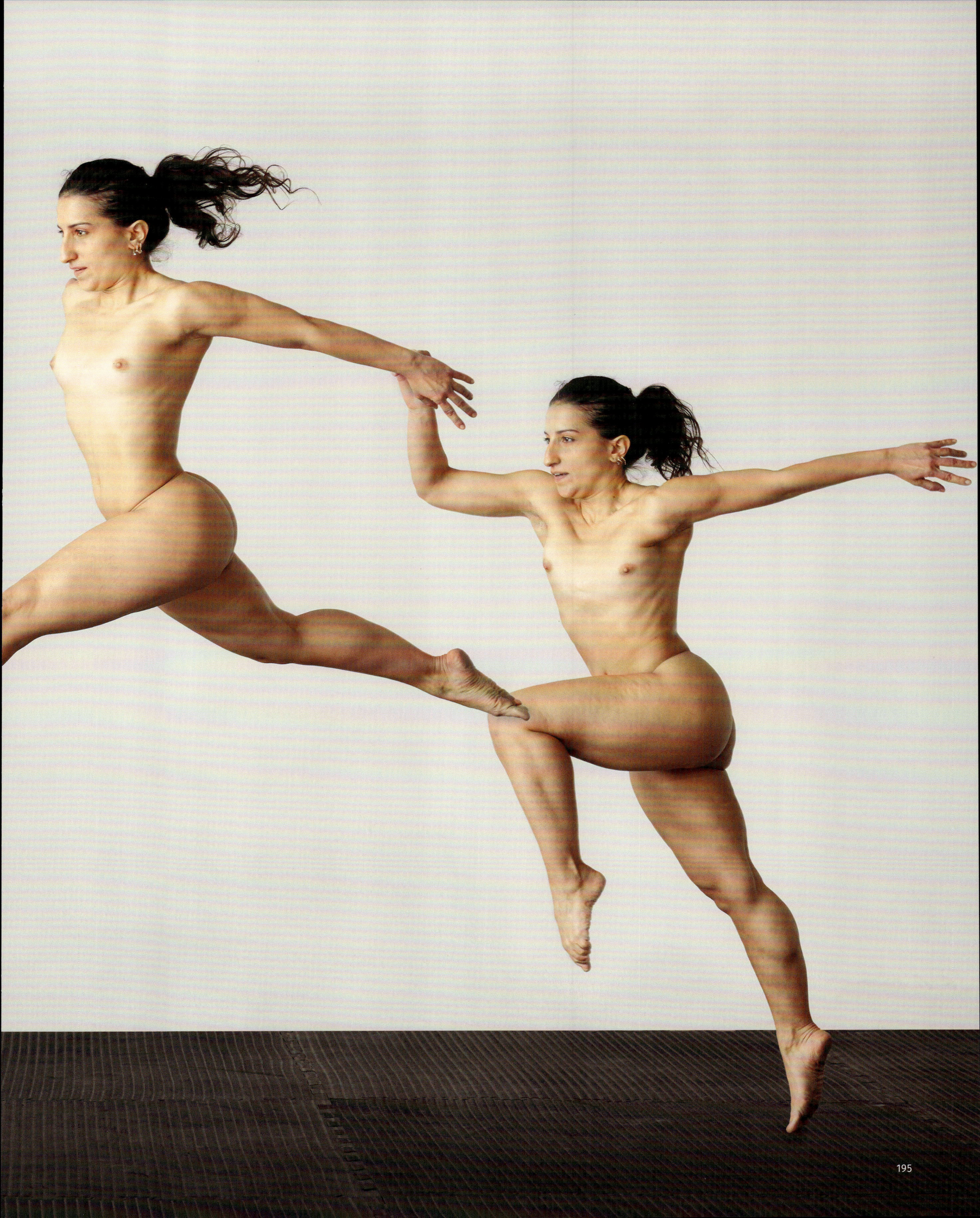

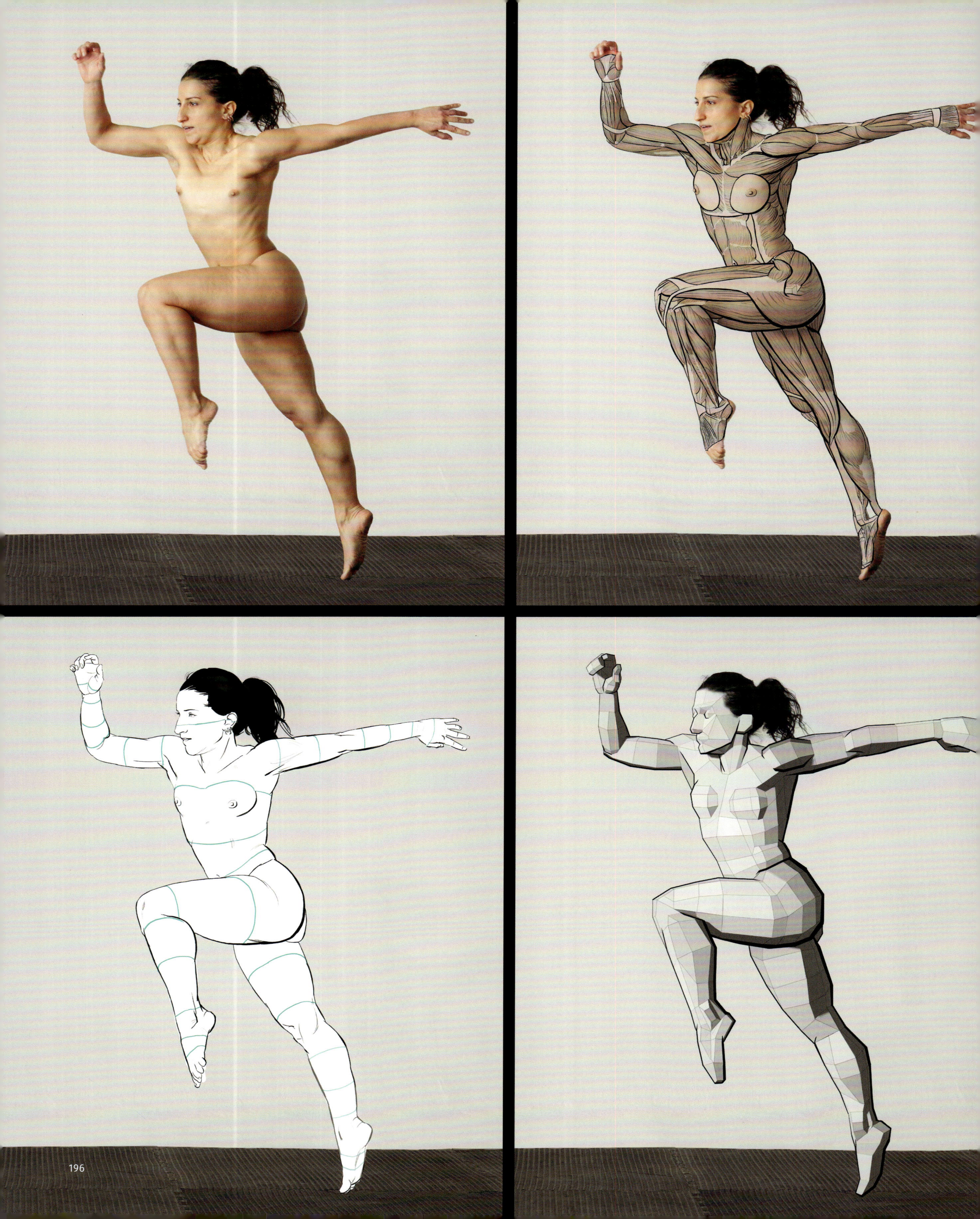

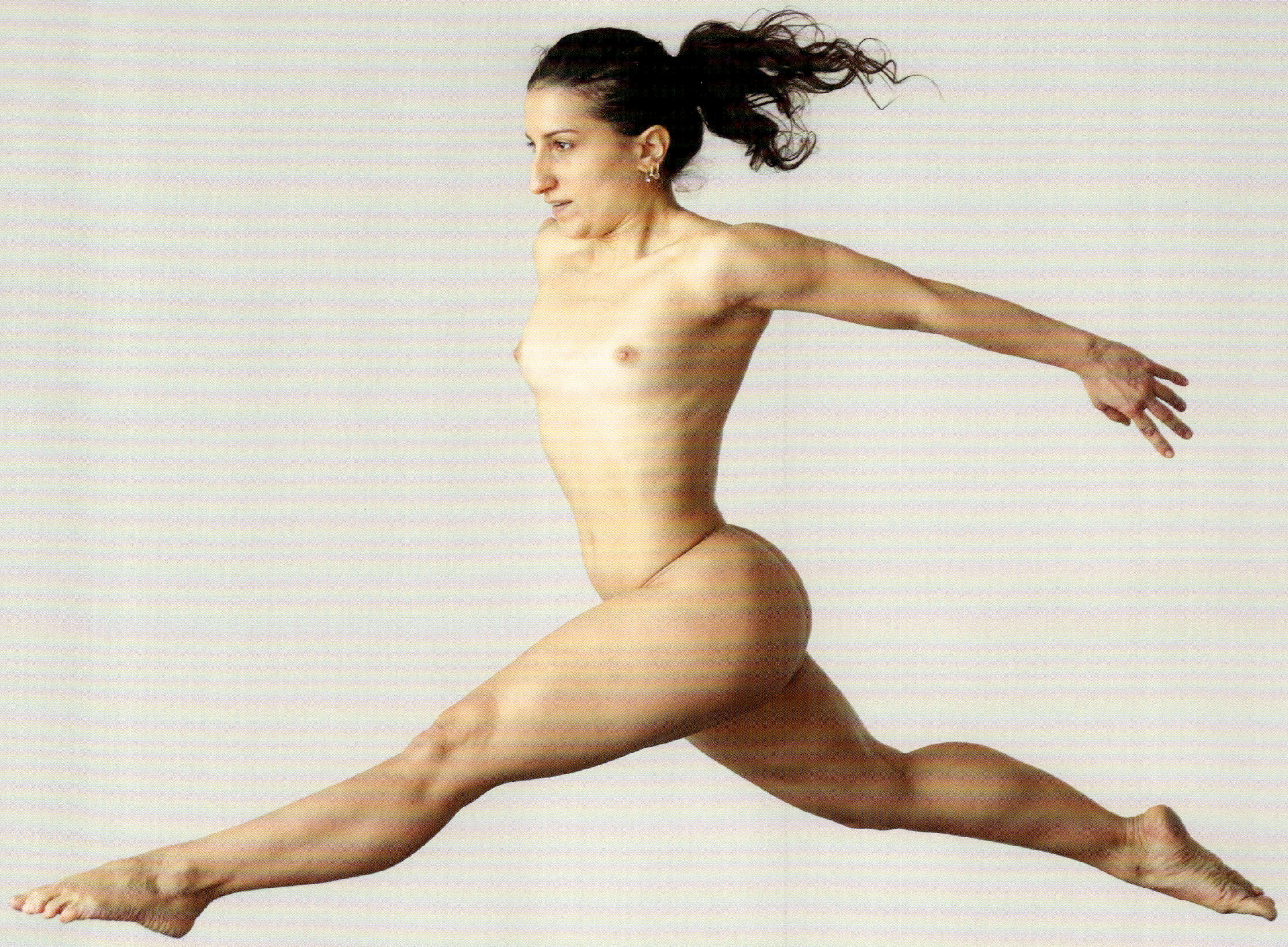

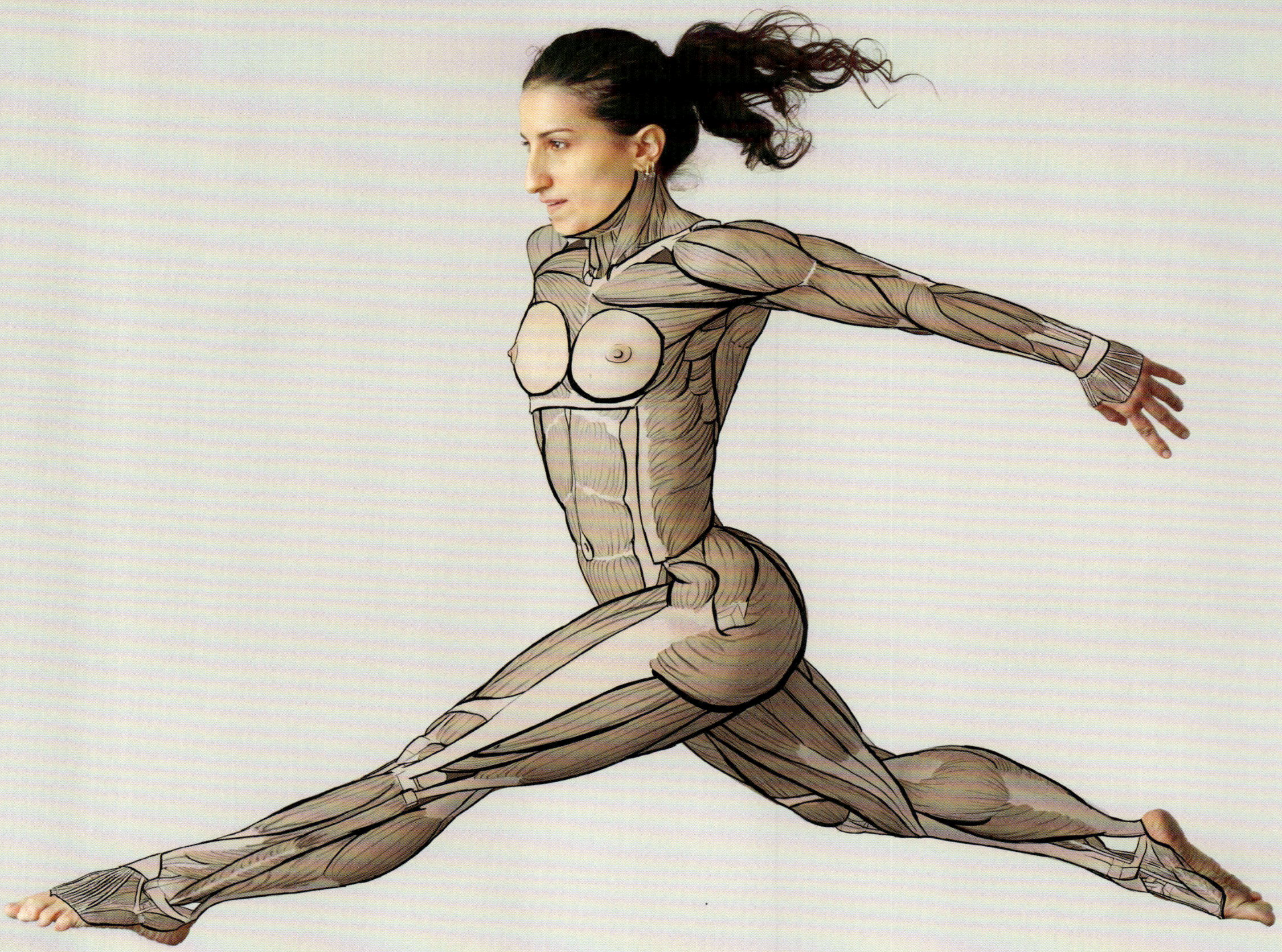

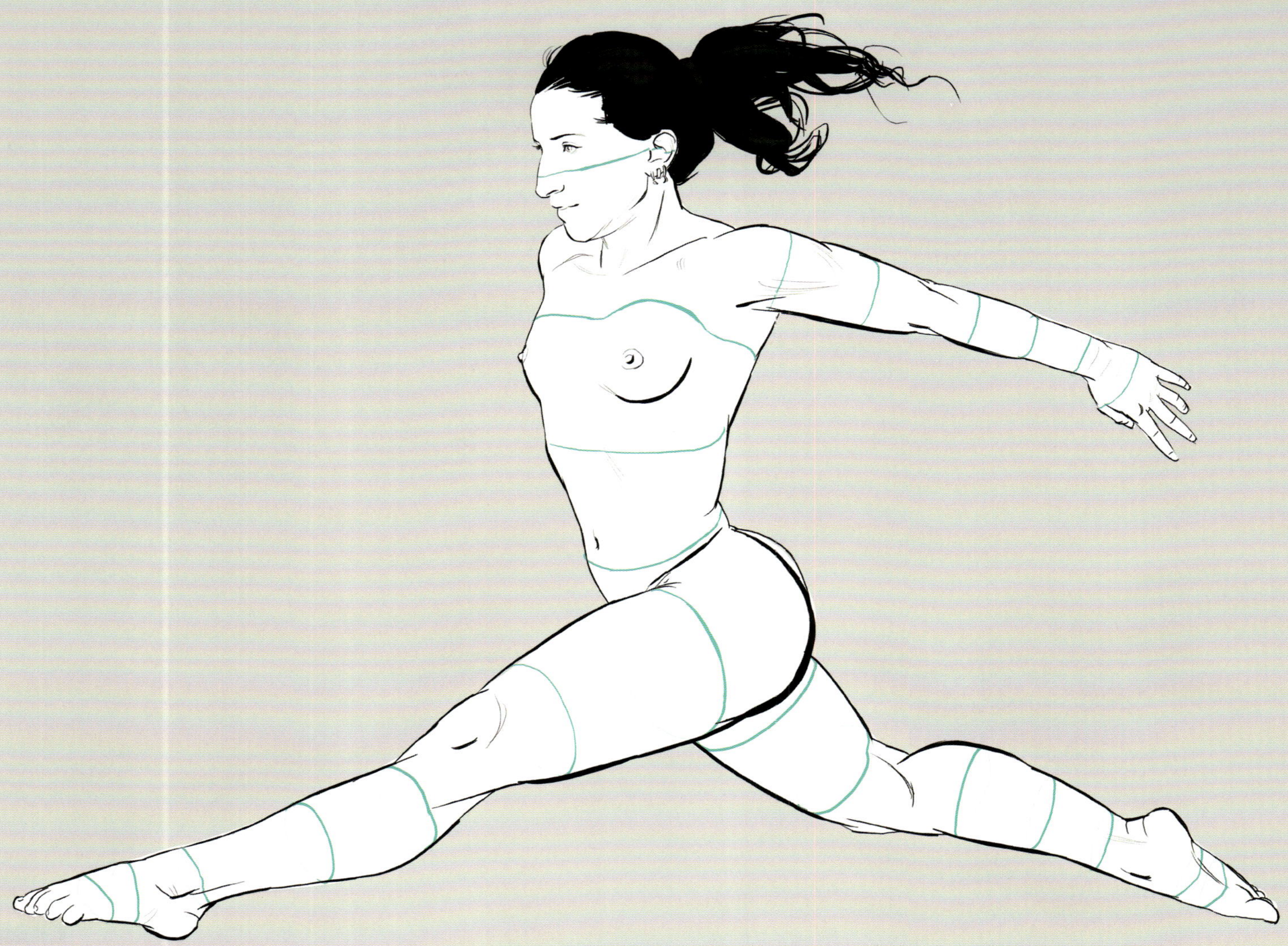

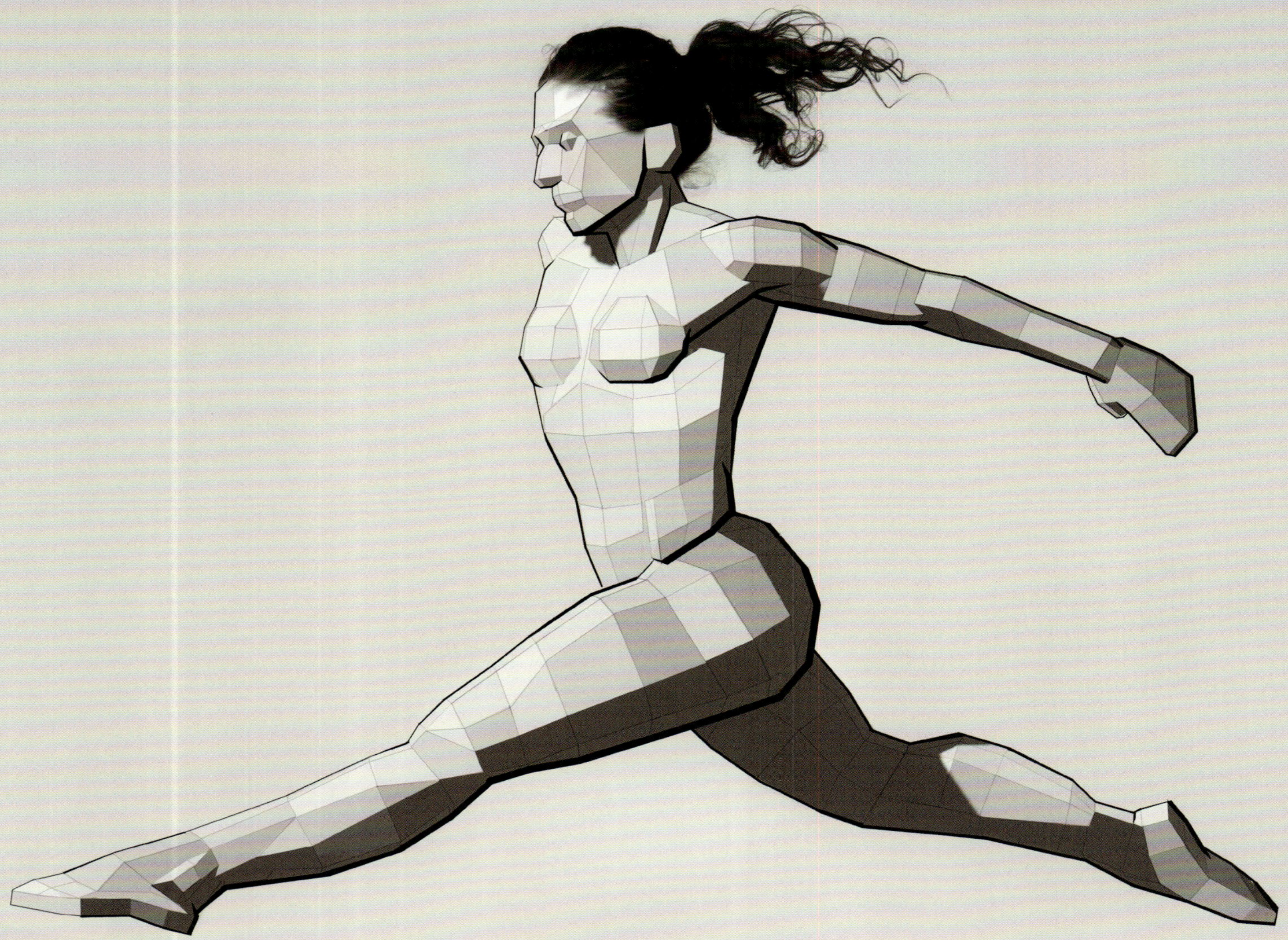

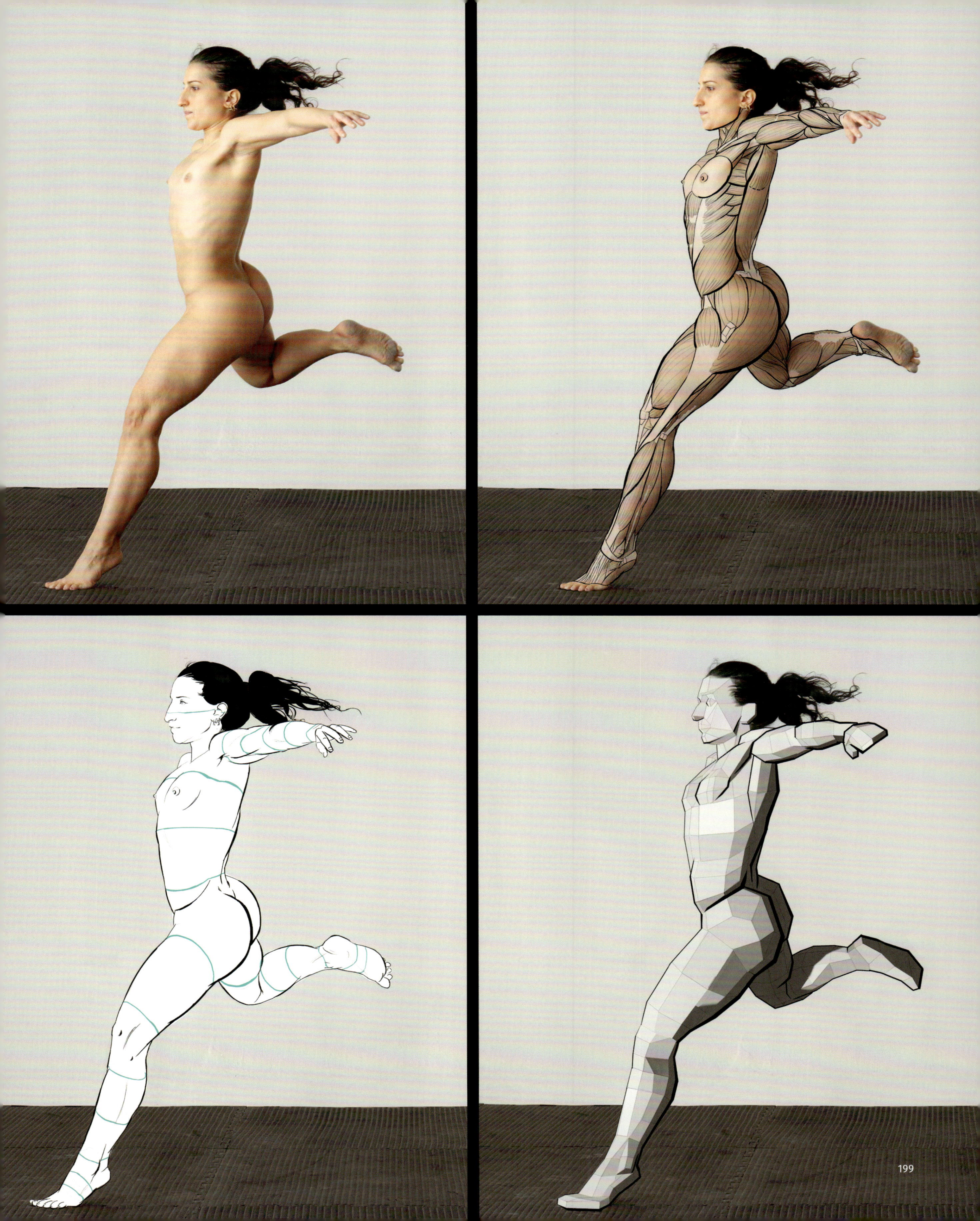

Vaulting over an obstacle

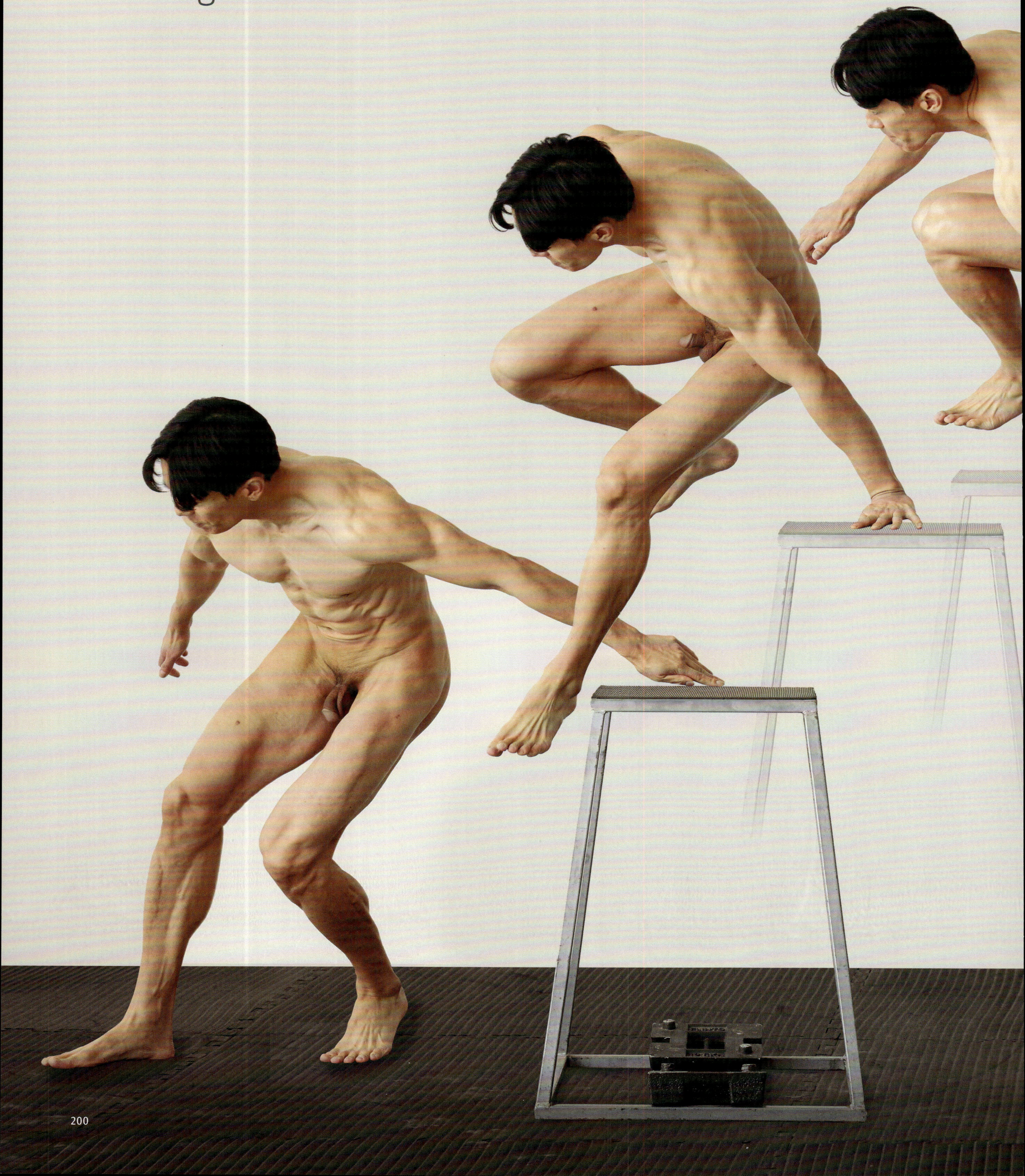

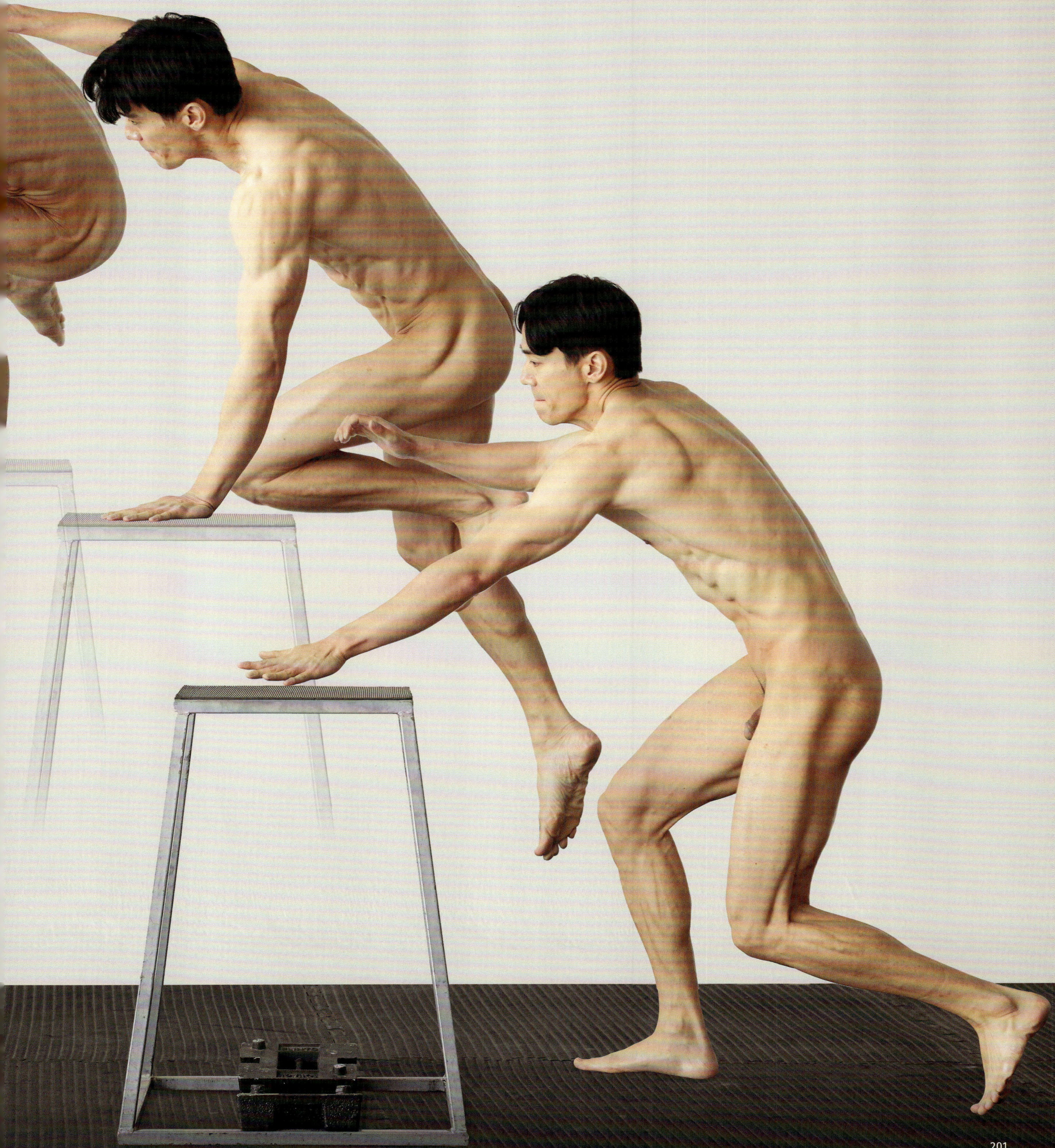

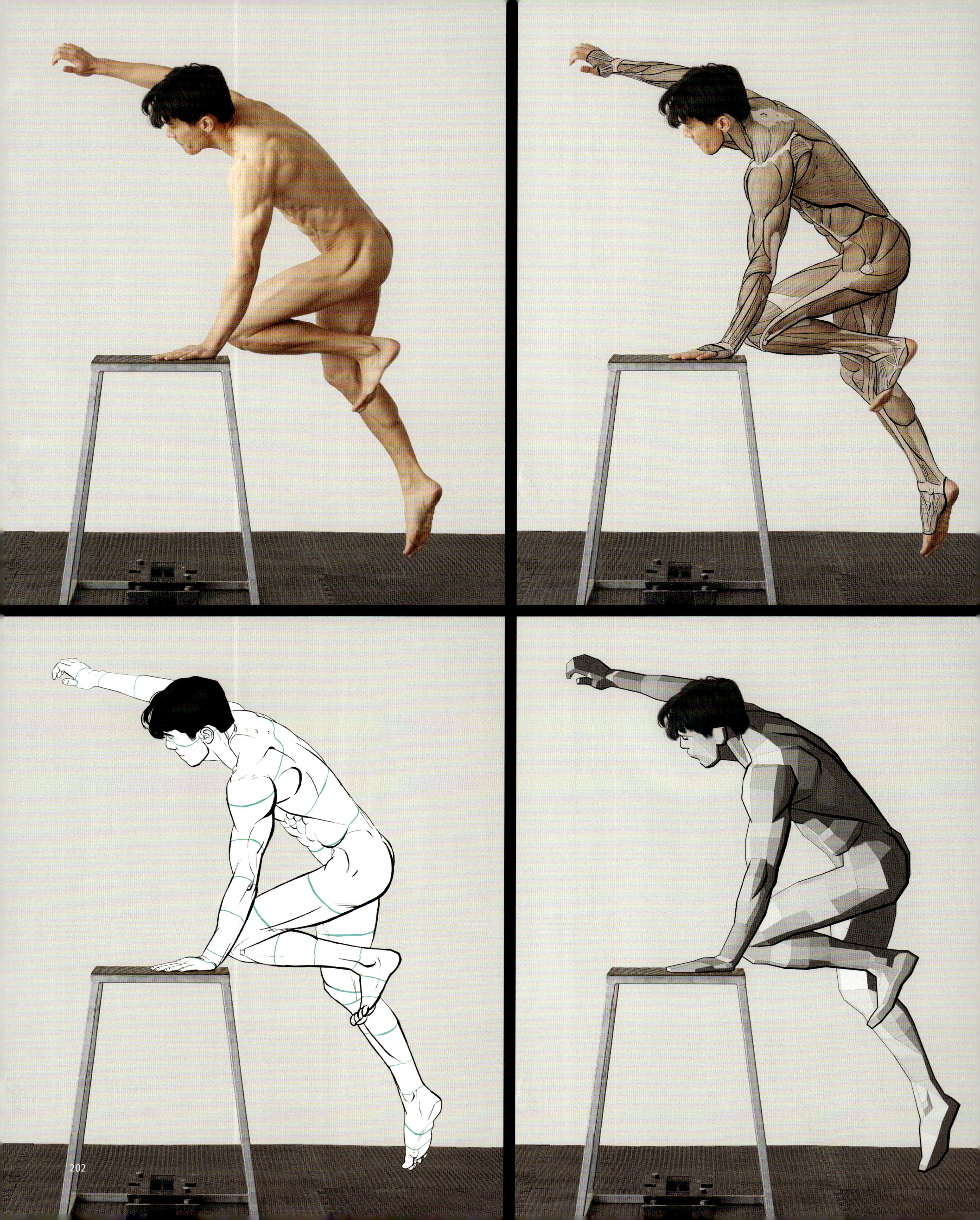

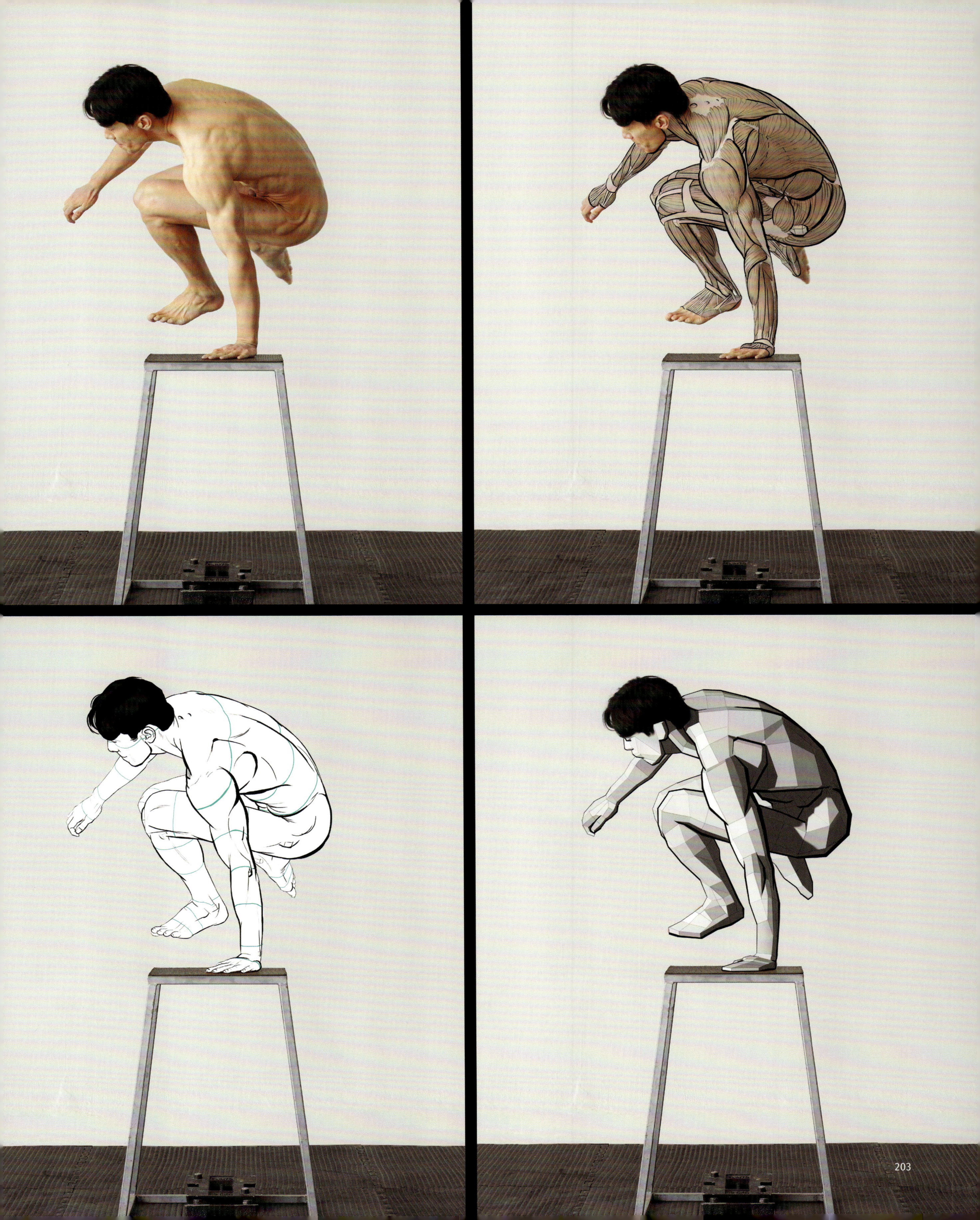

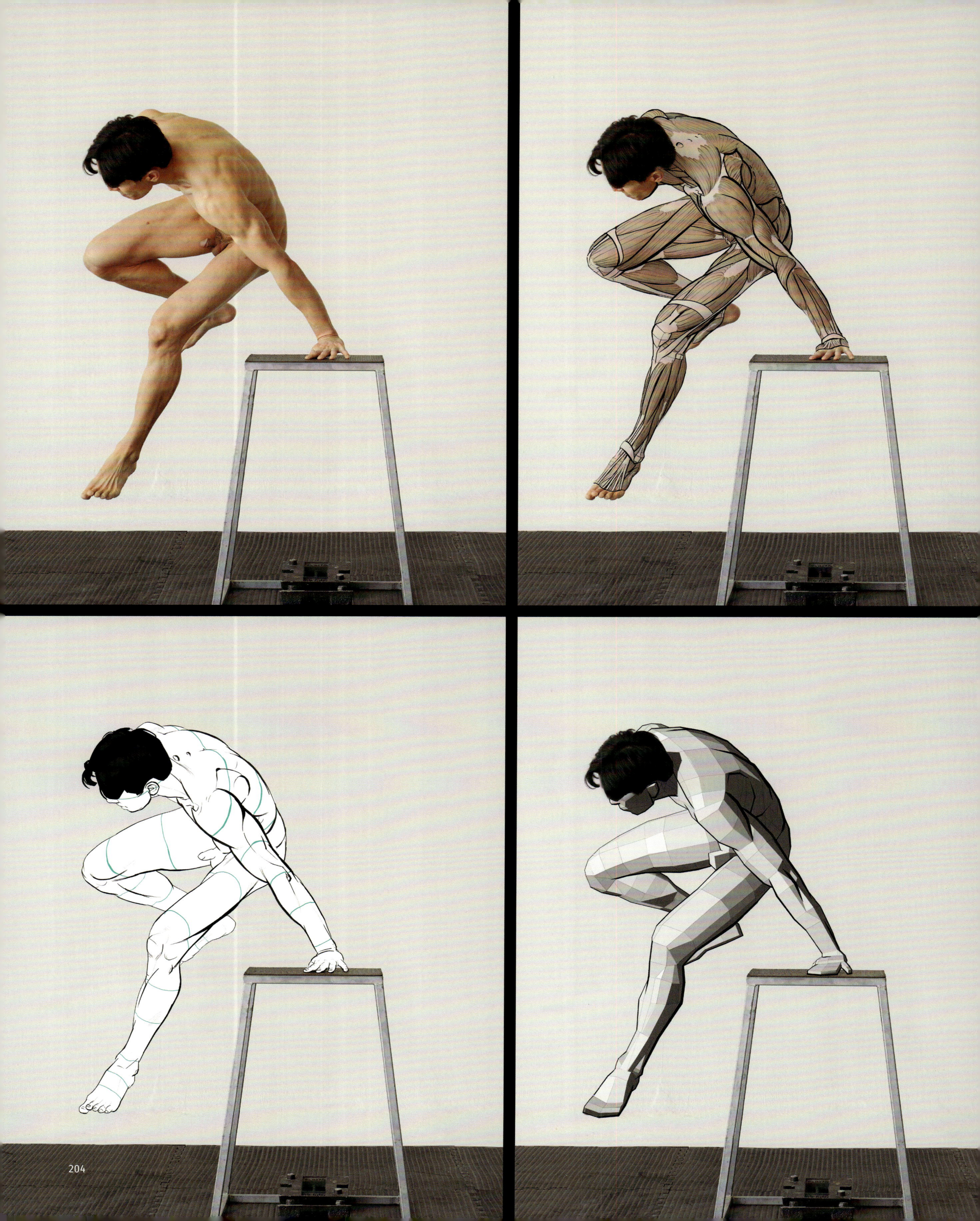

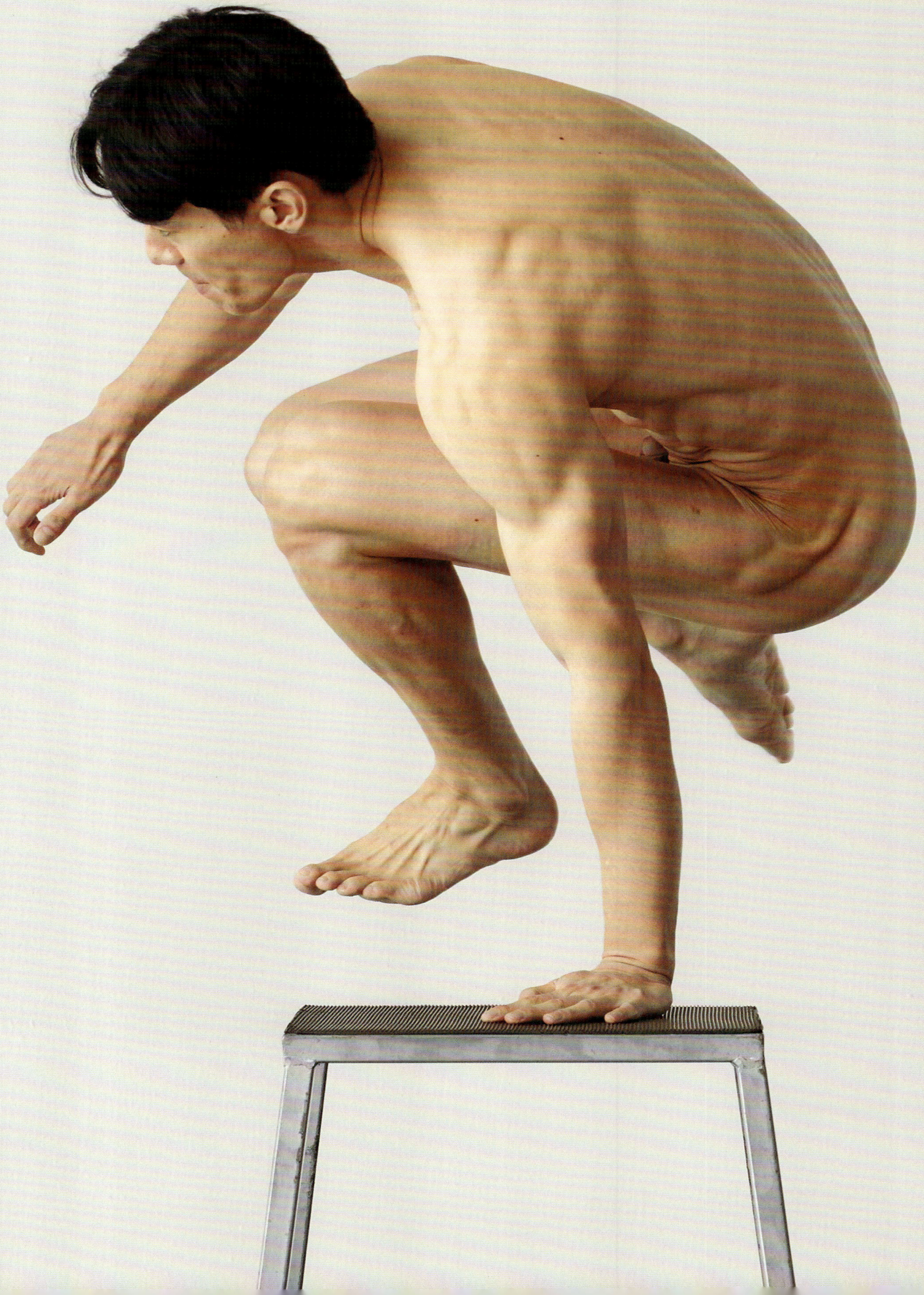

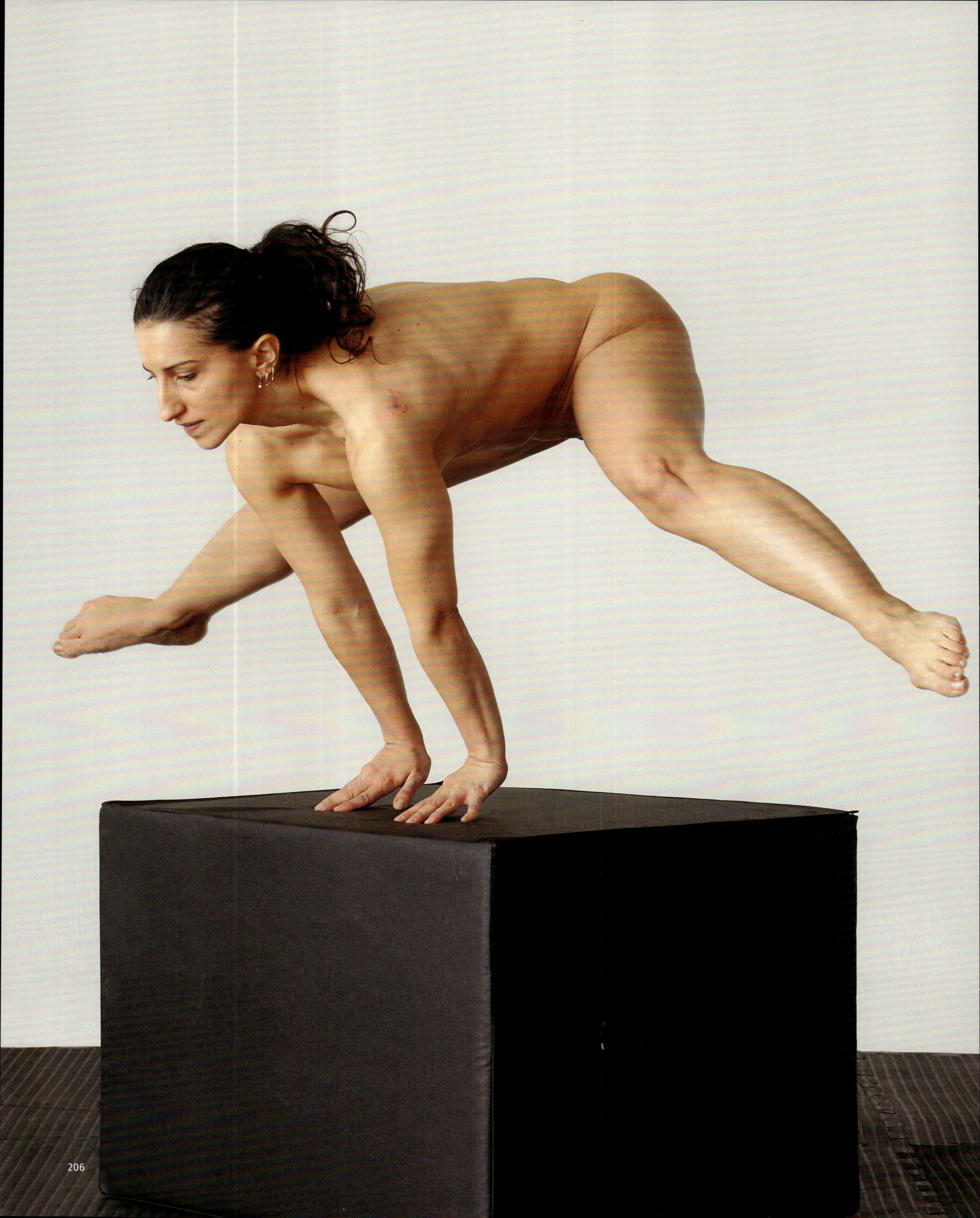

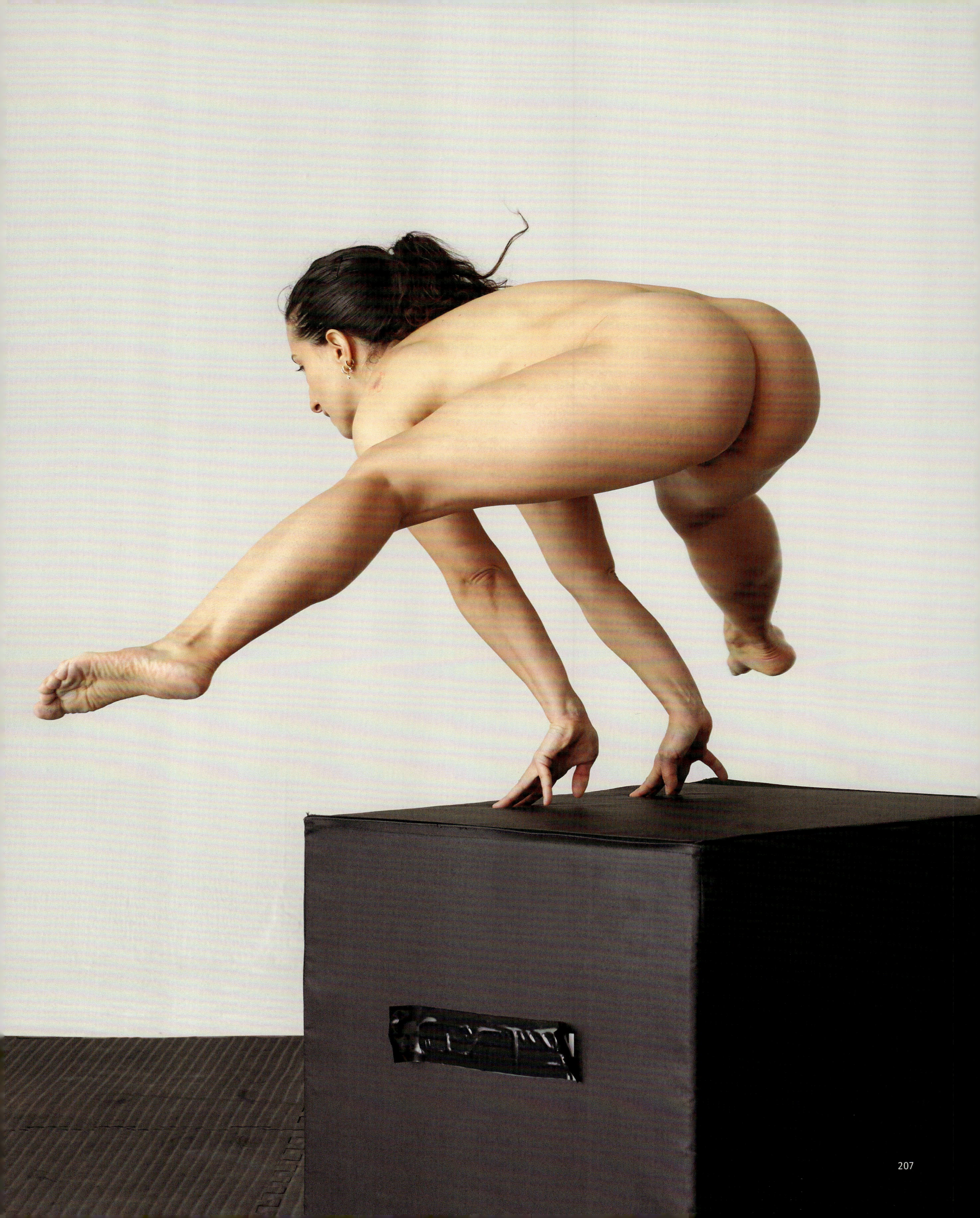

Jumping in place

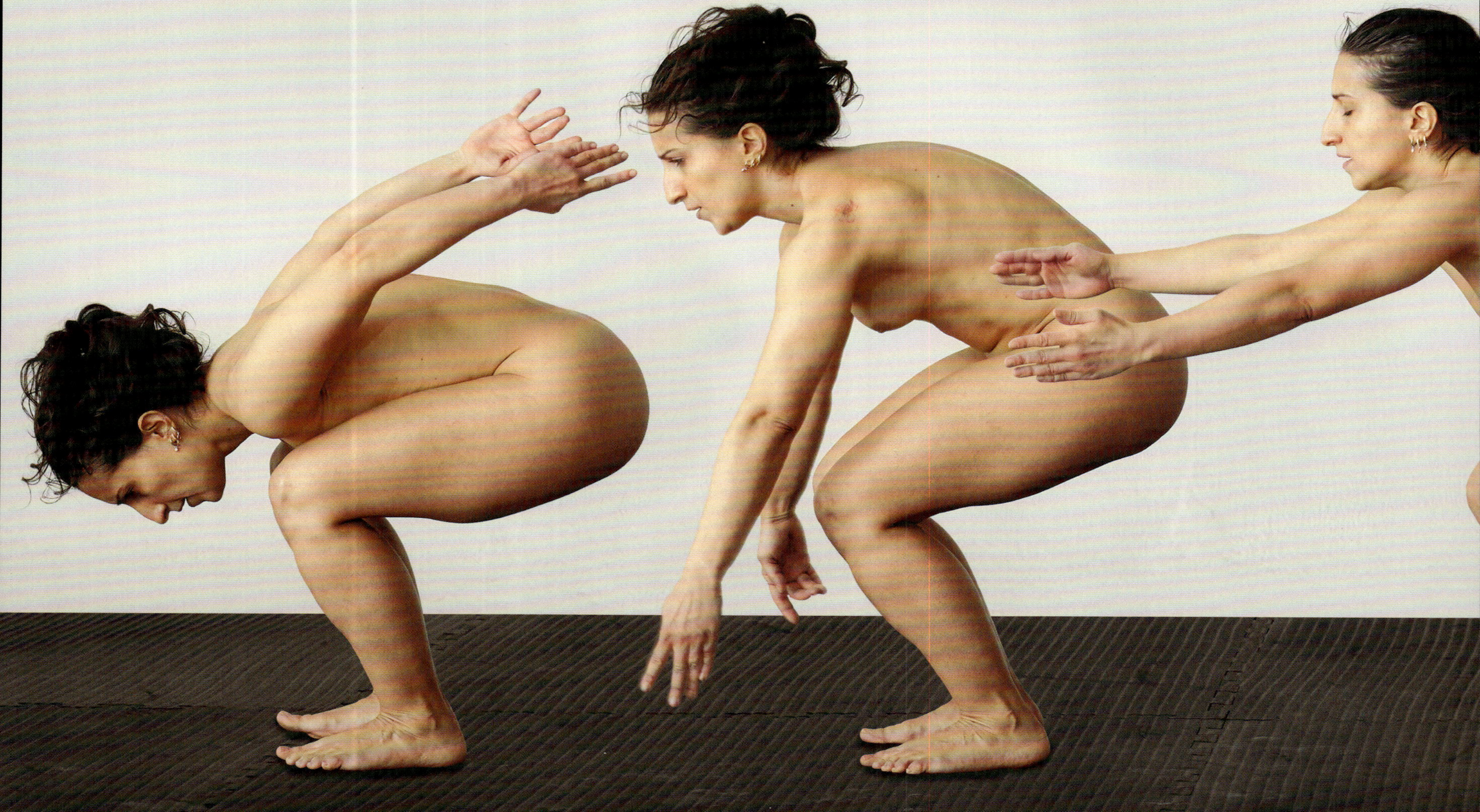

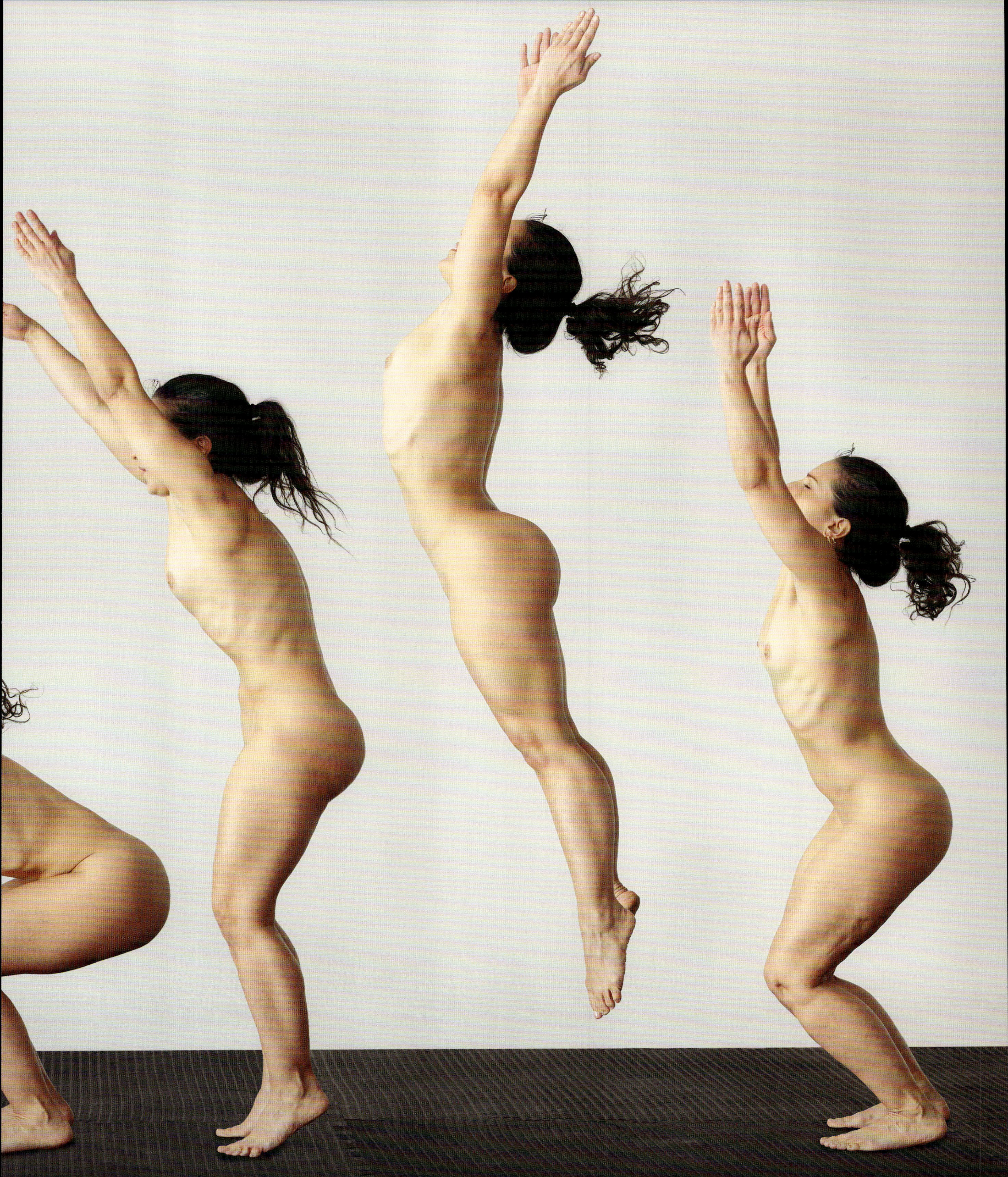

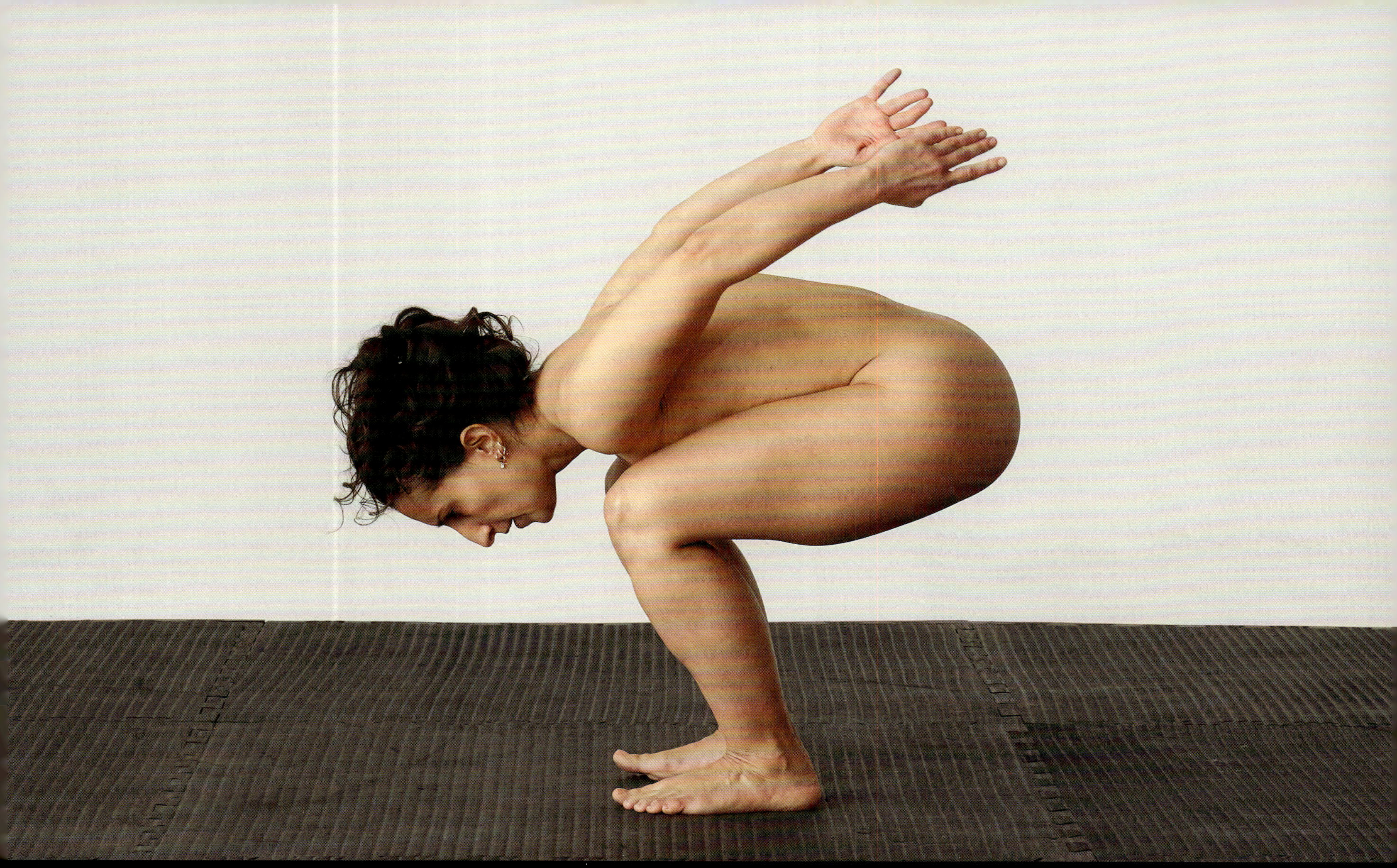

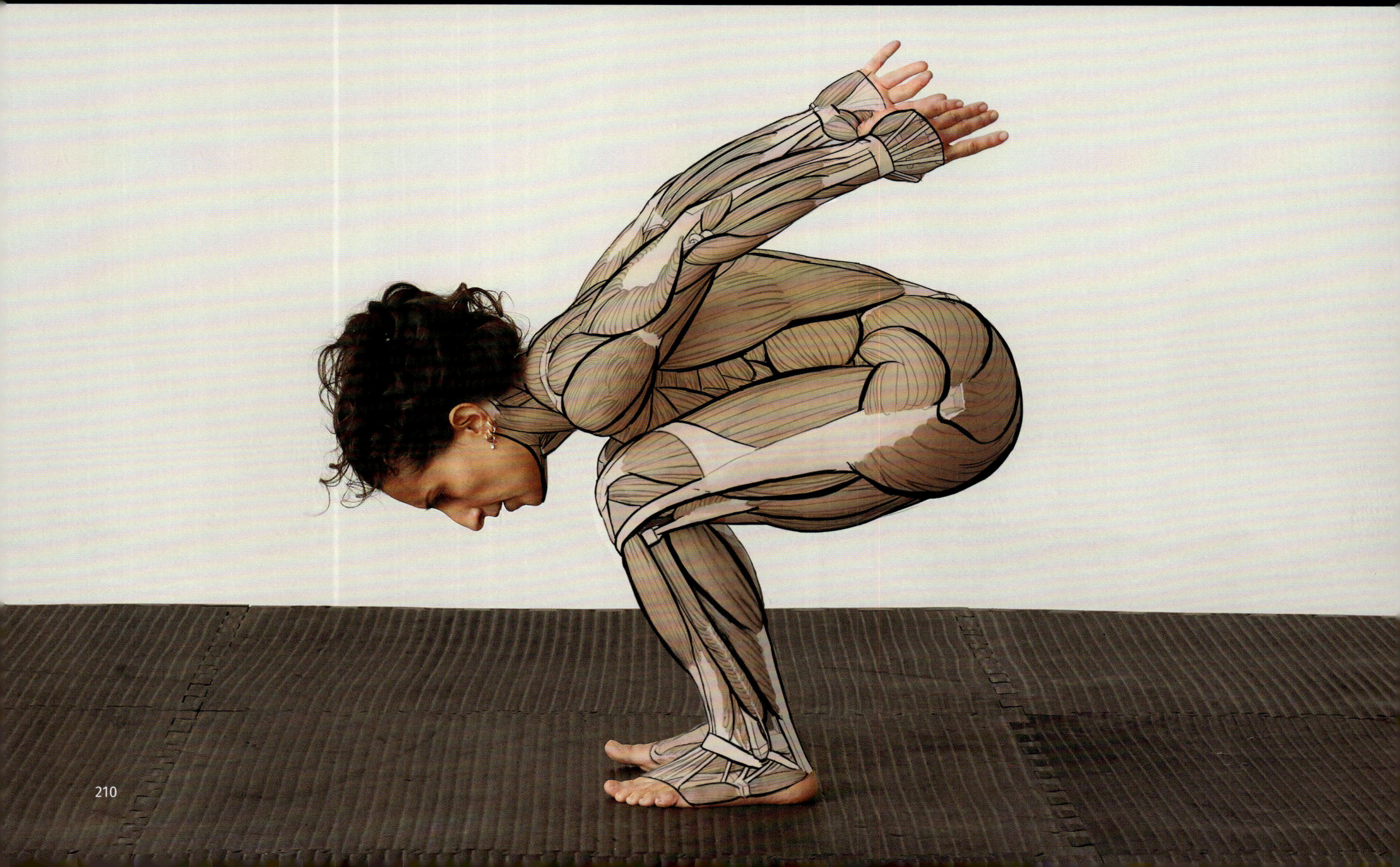

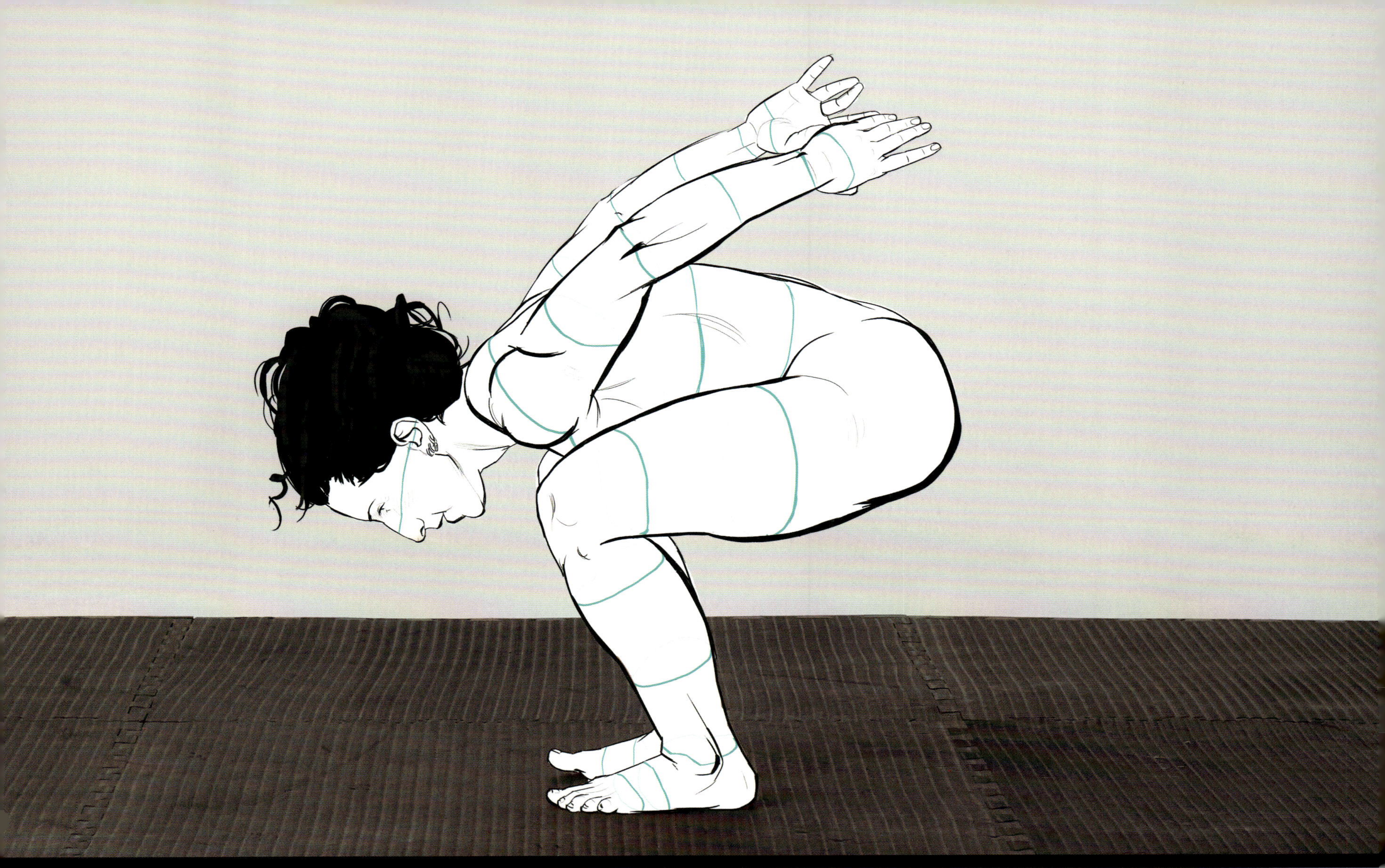

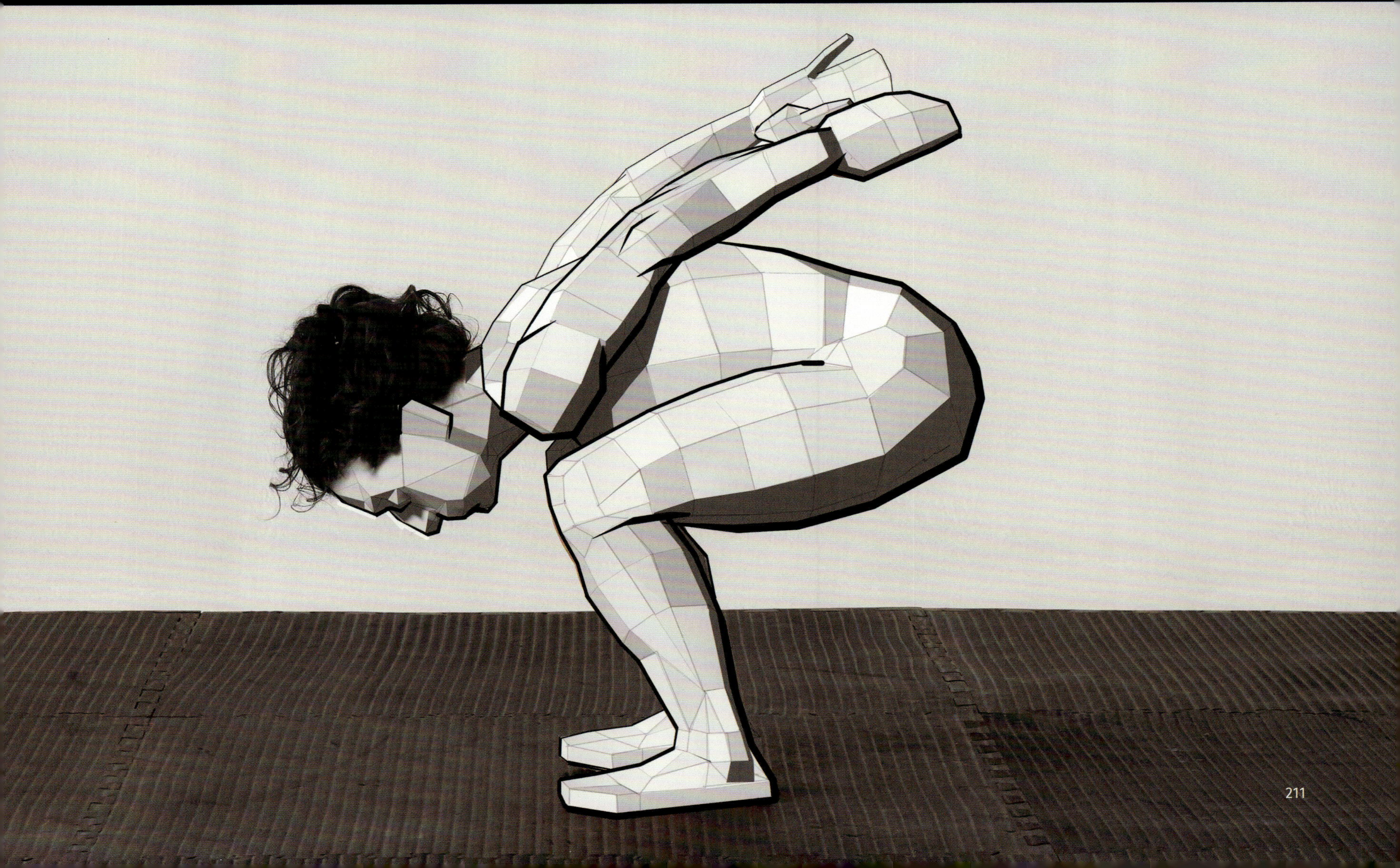

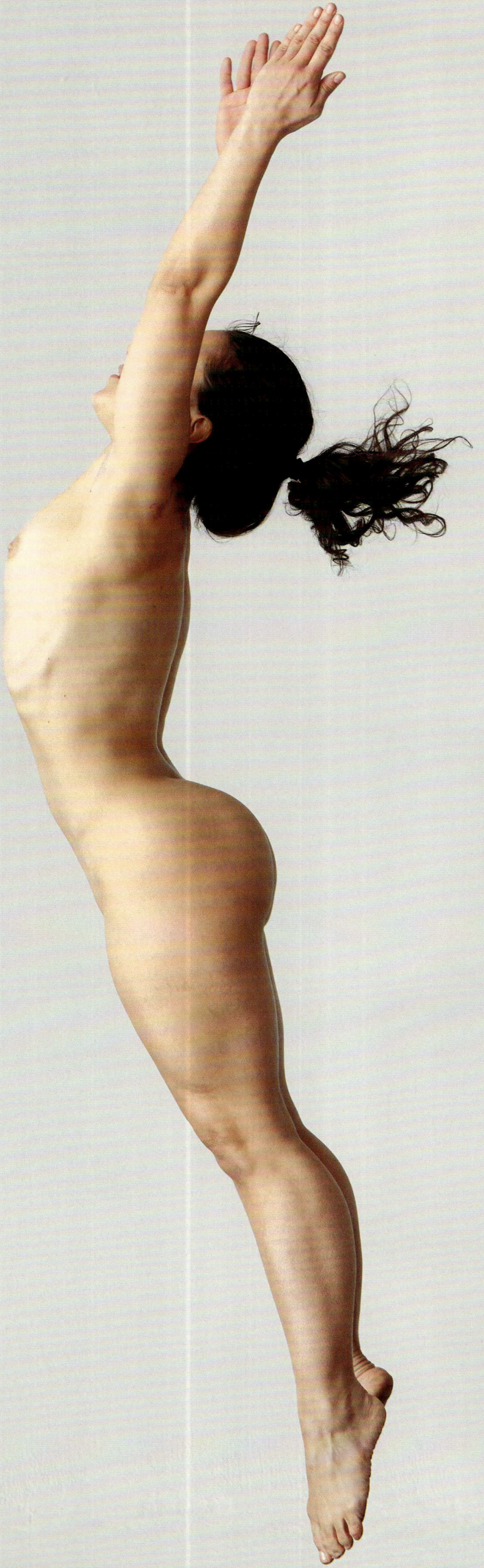

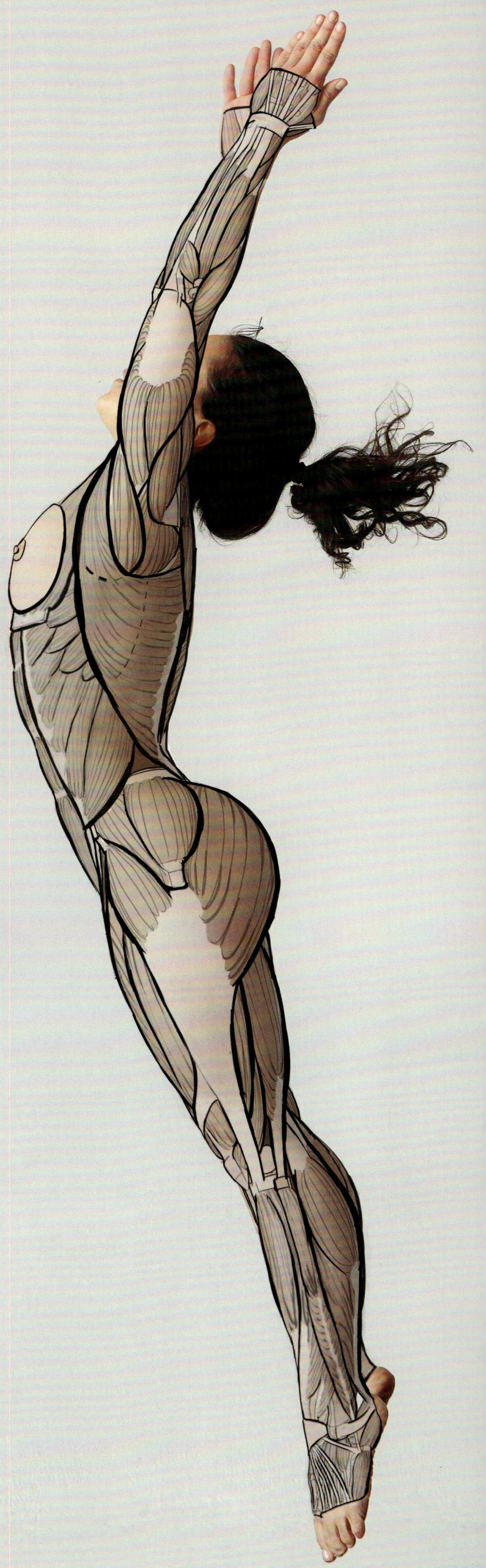

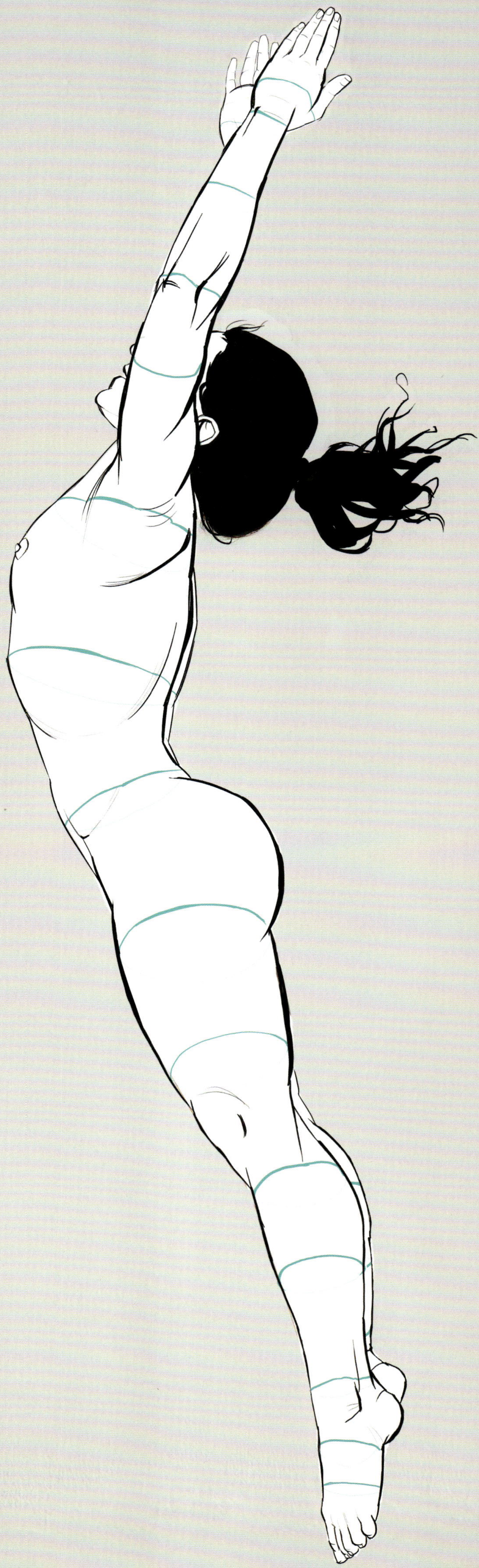

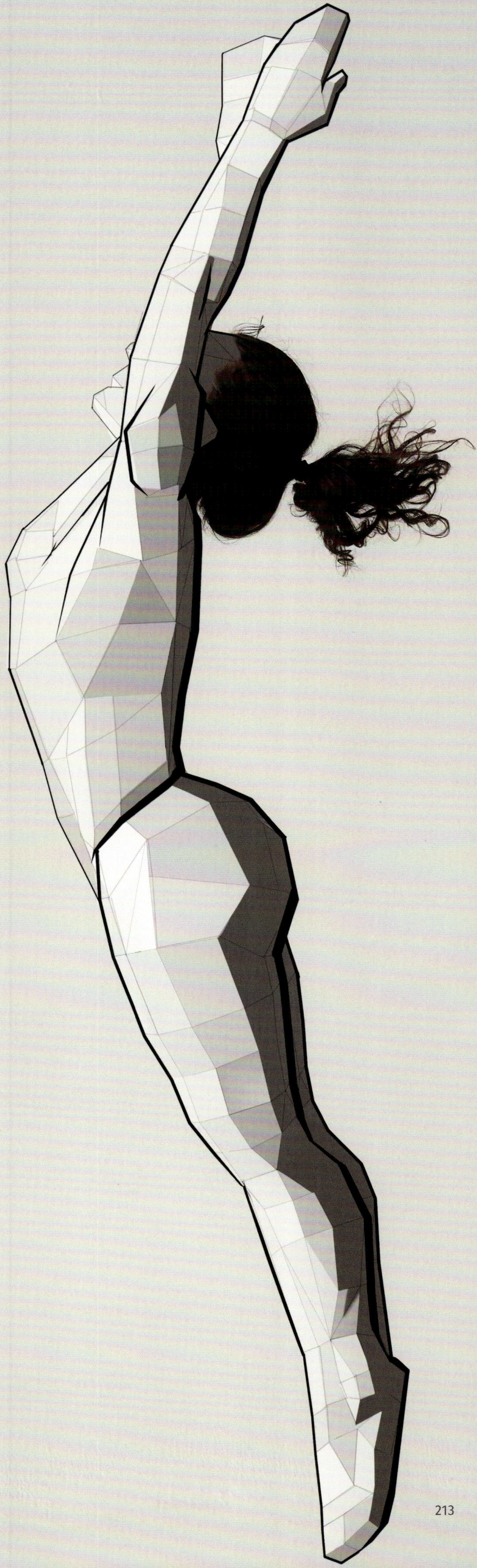

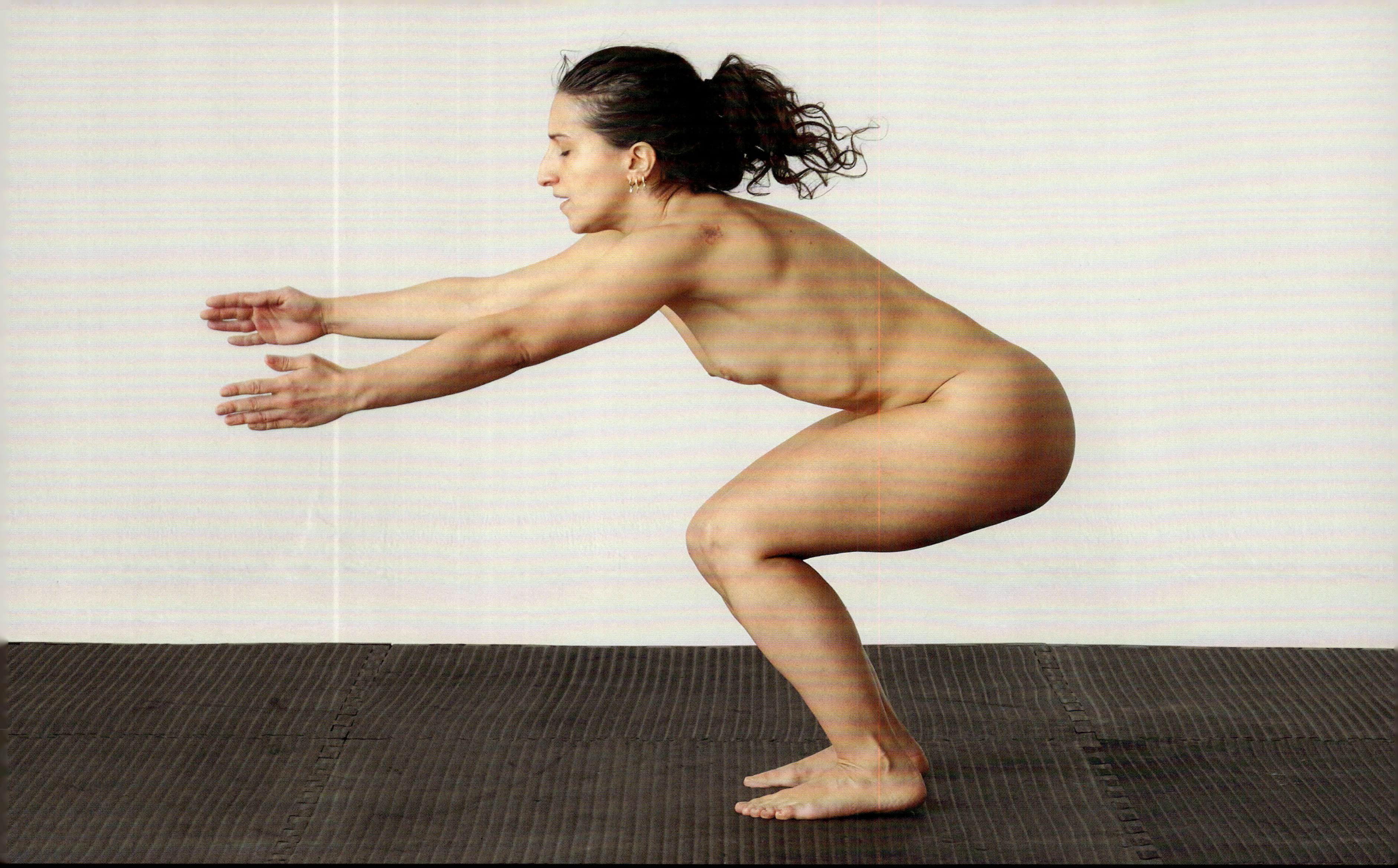

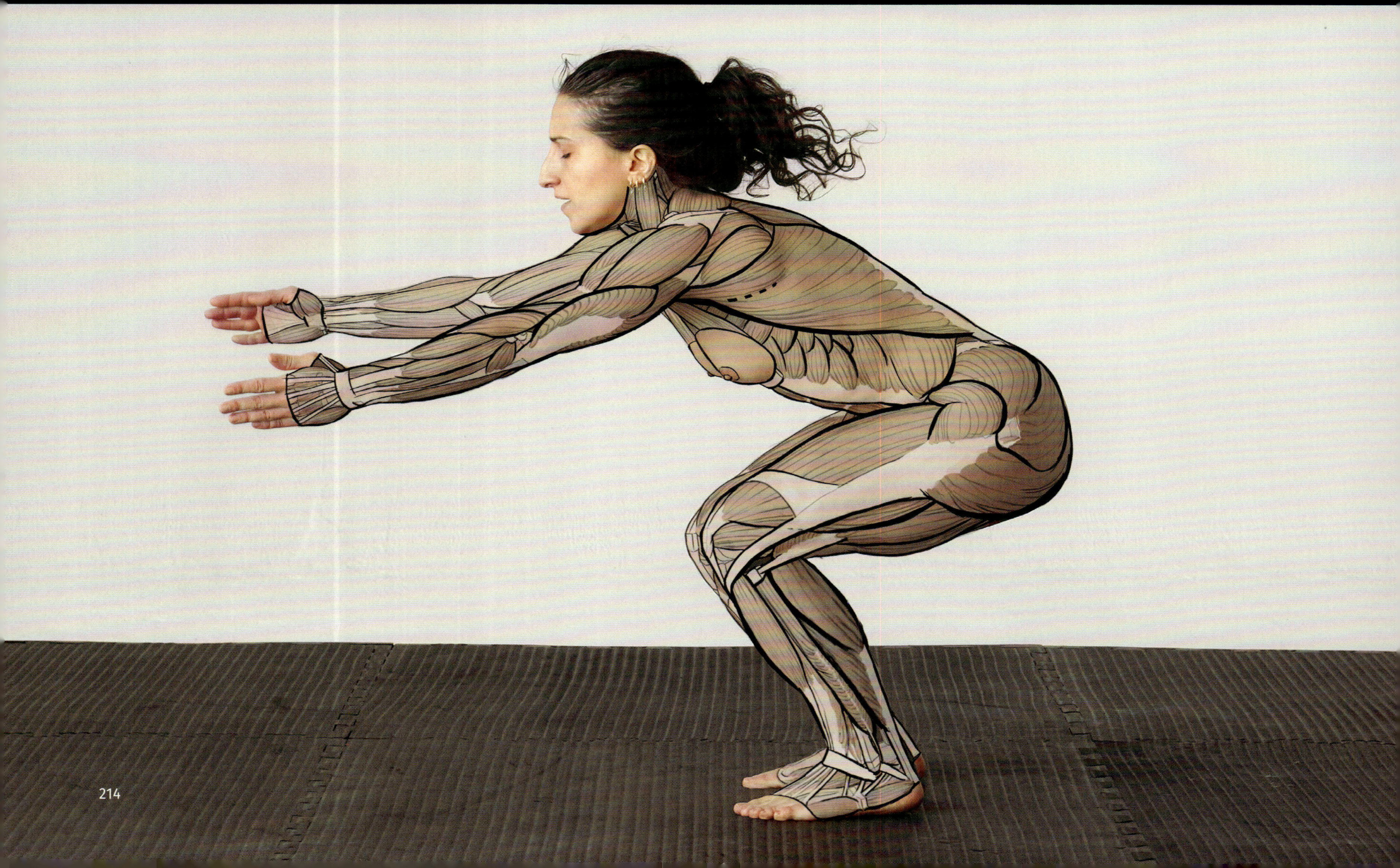

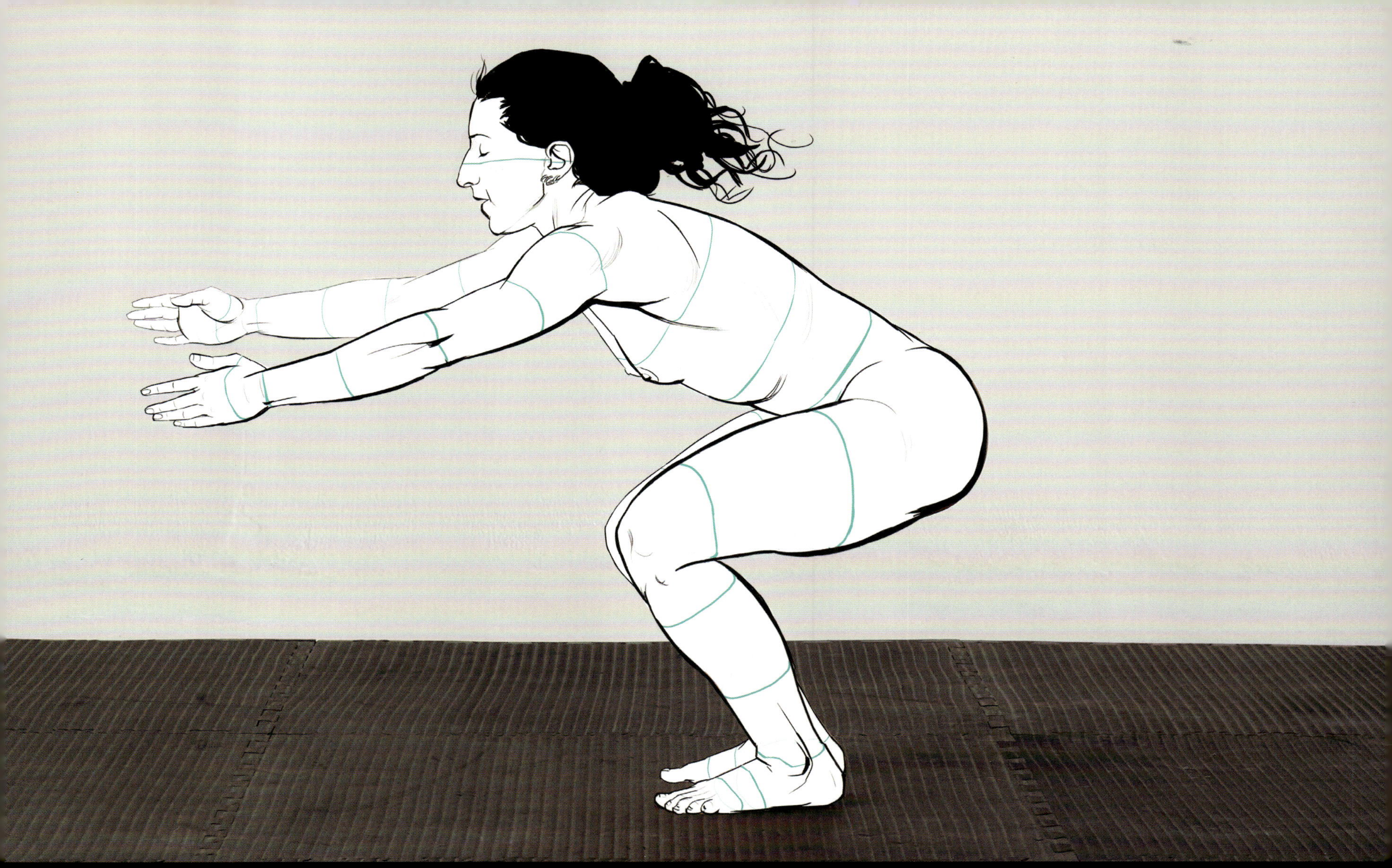

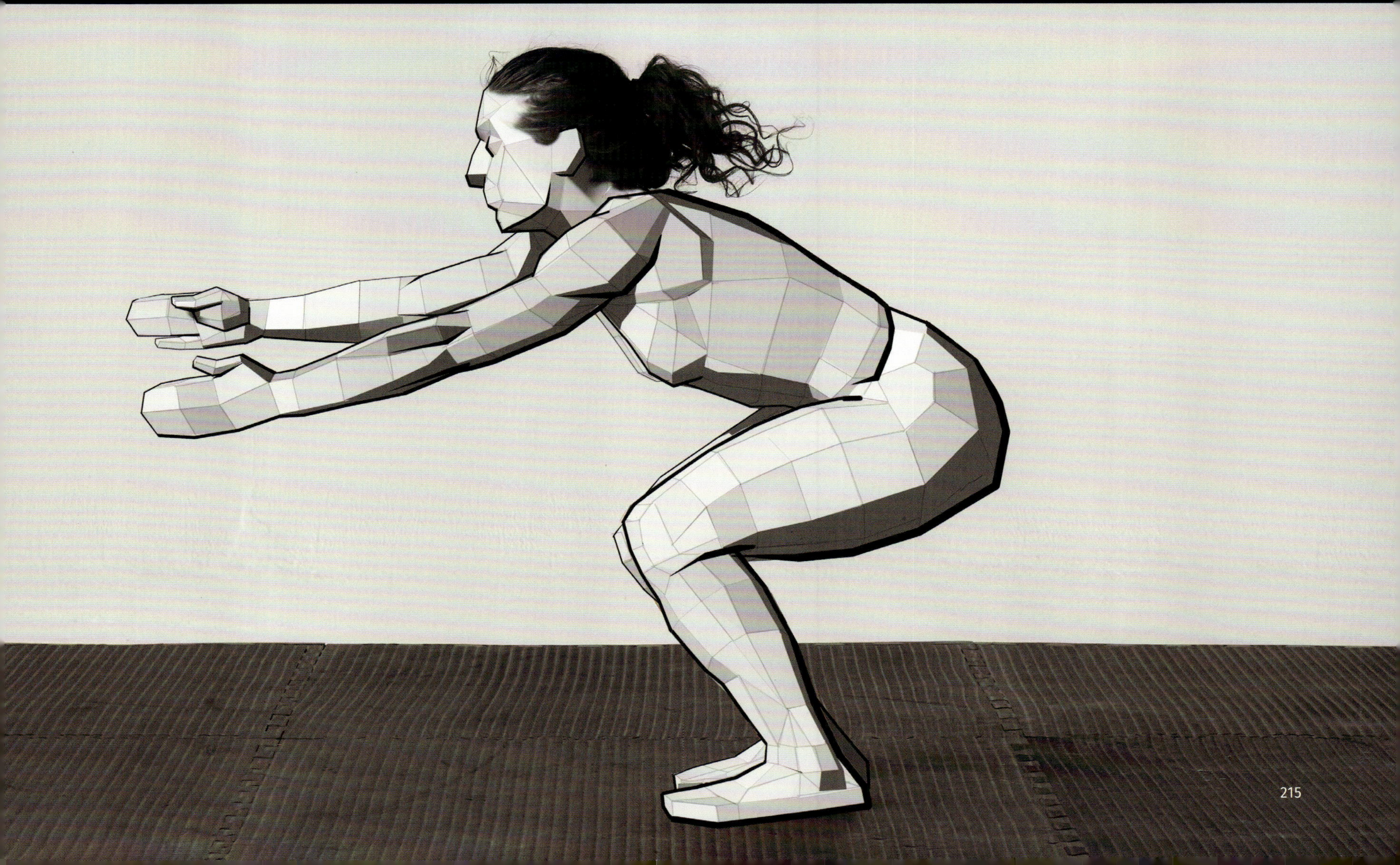

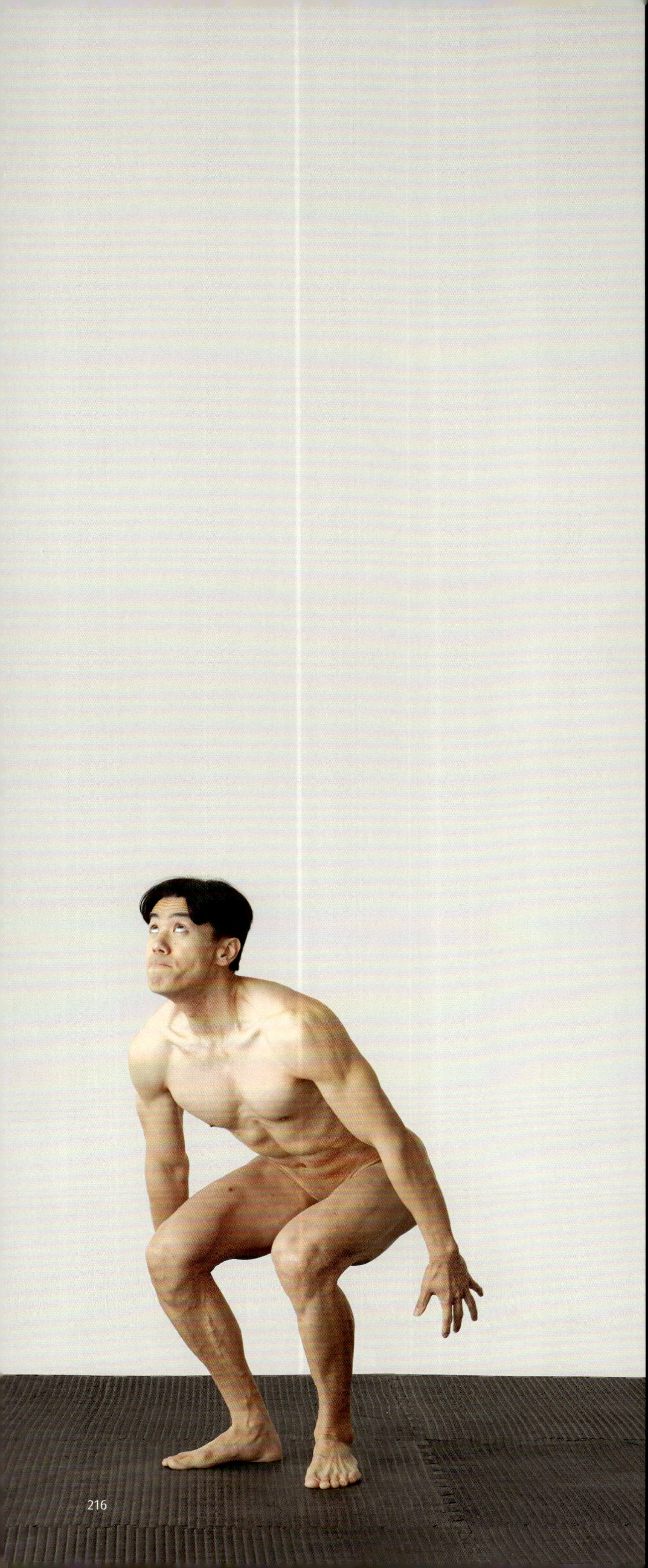

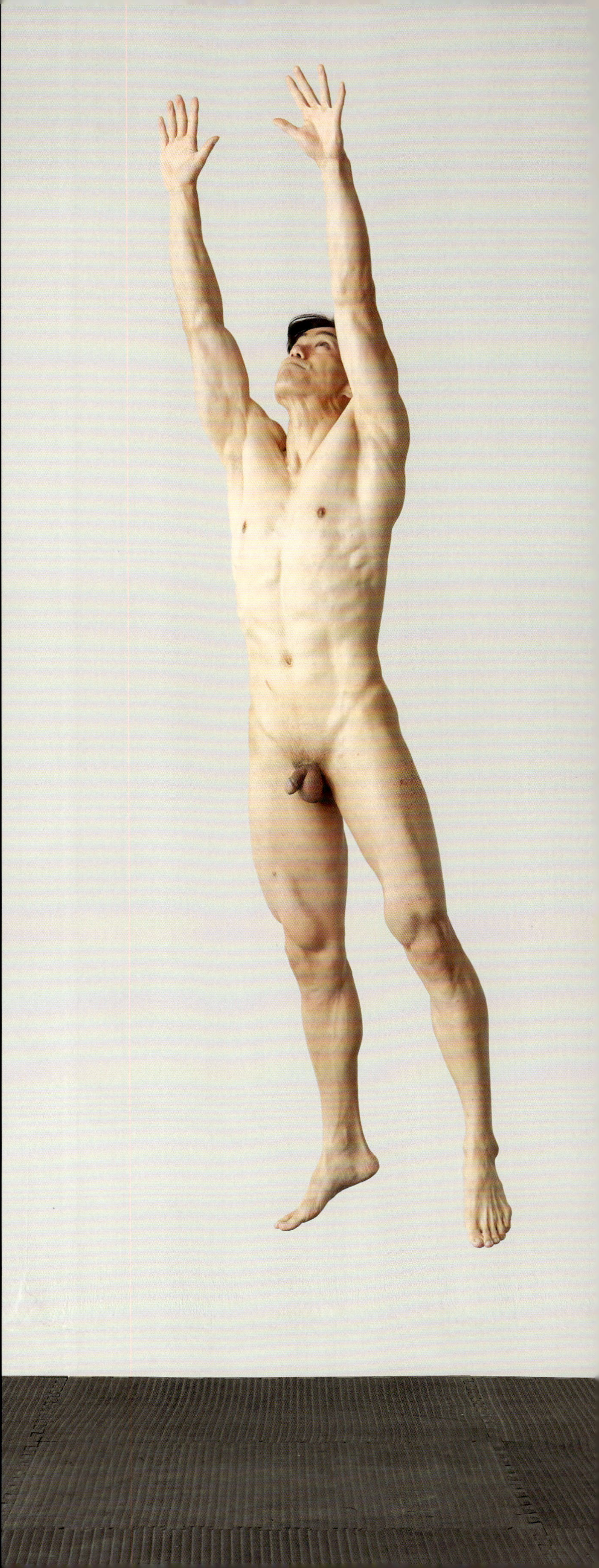

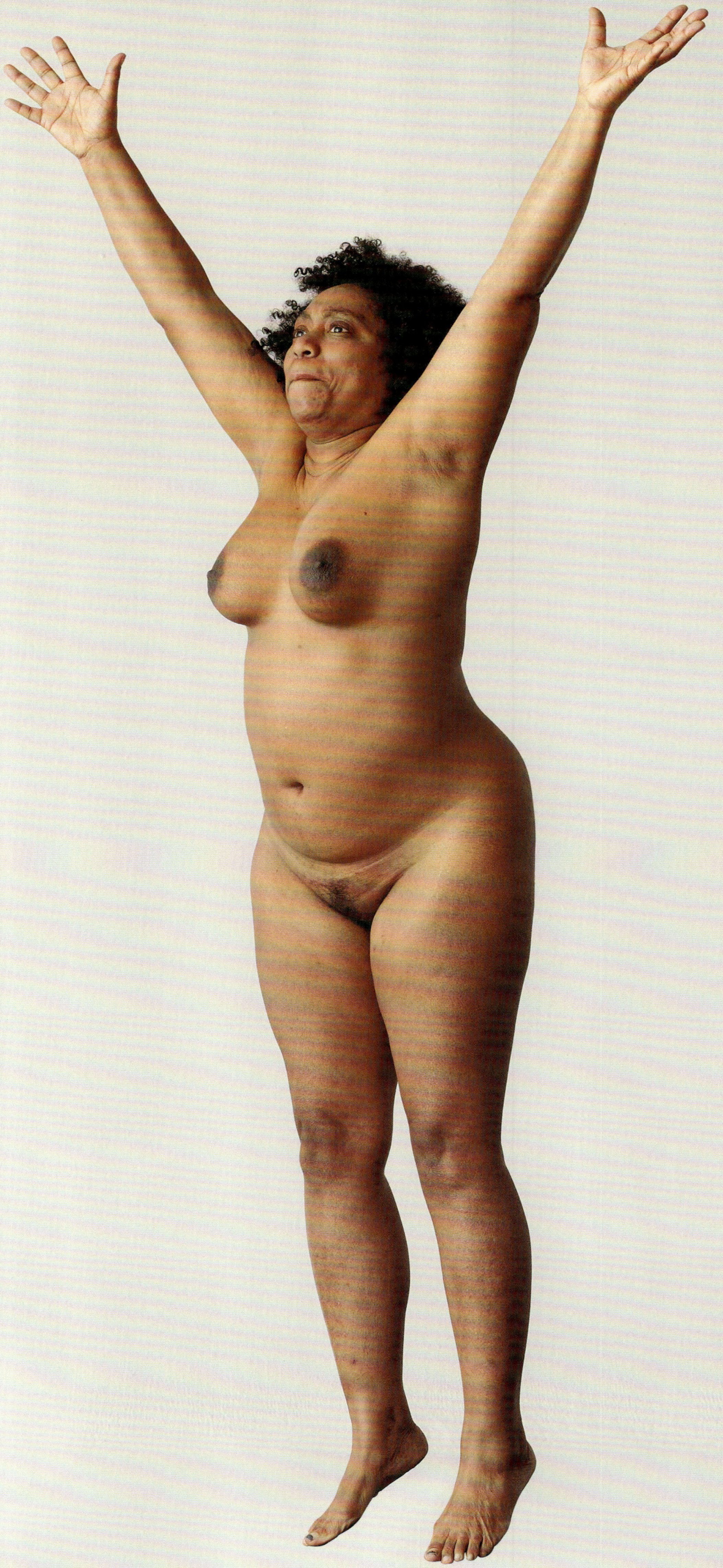

Pulling on a rope

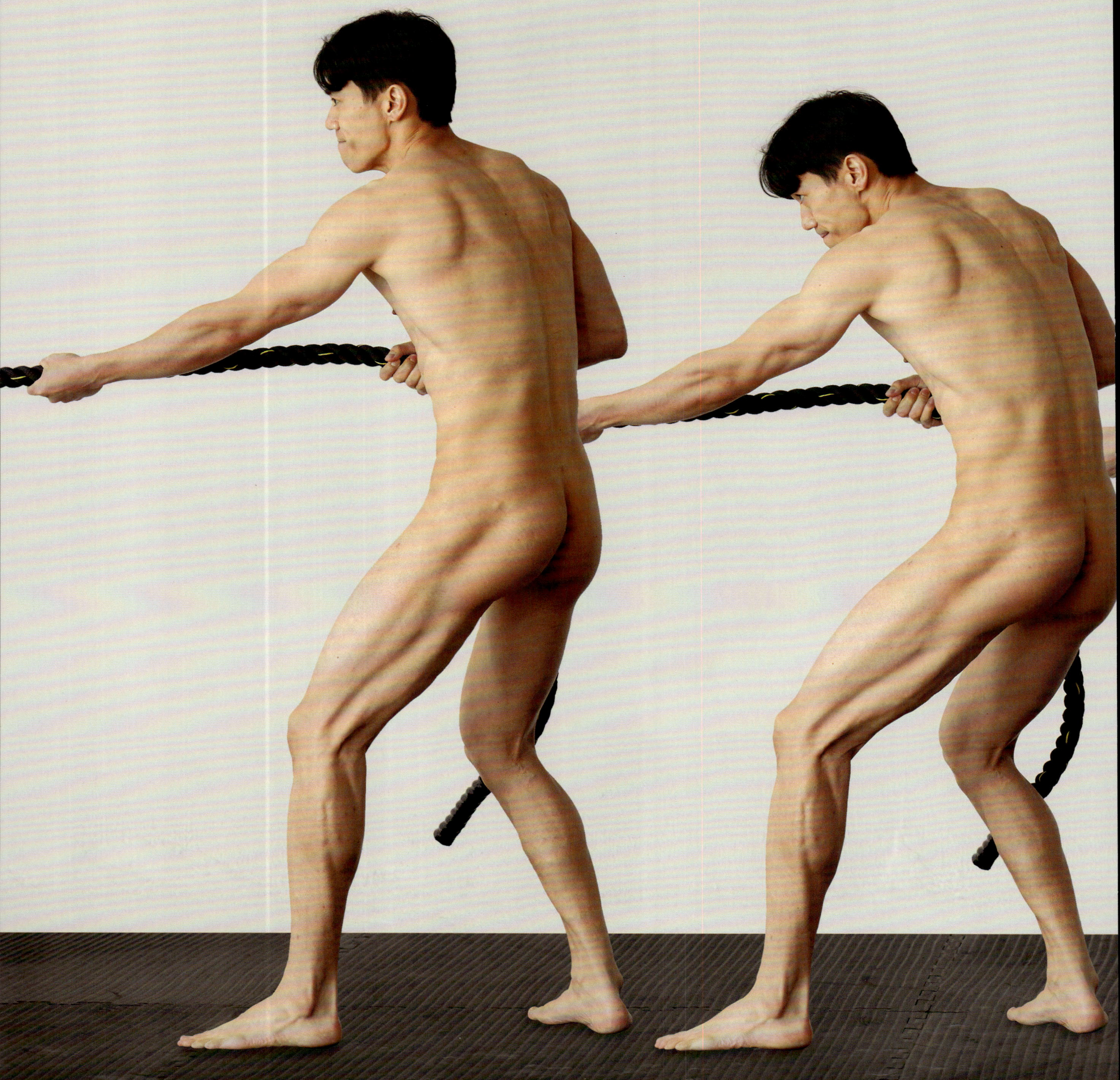

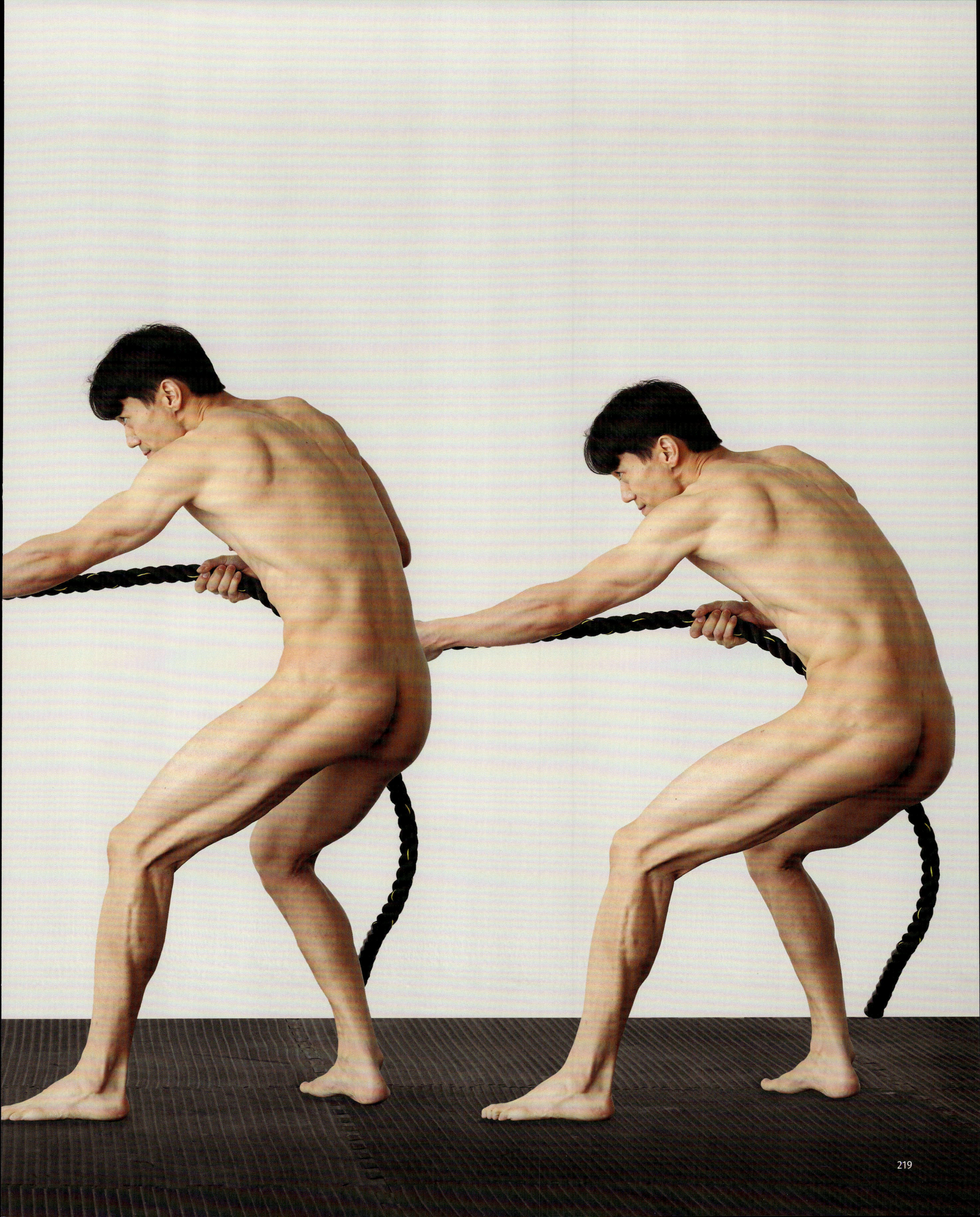

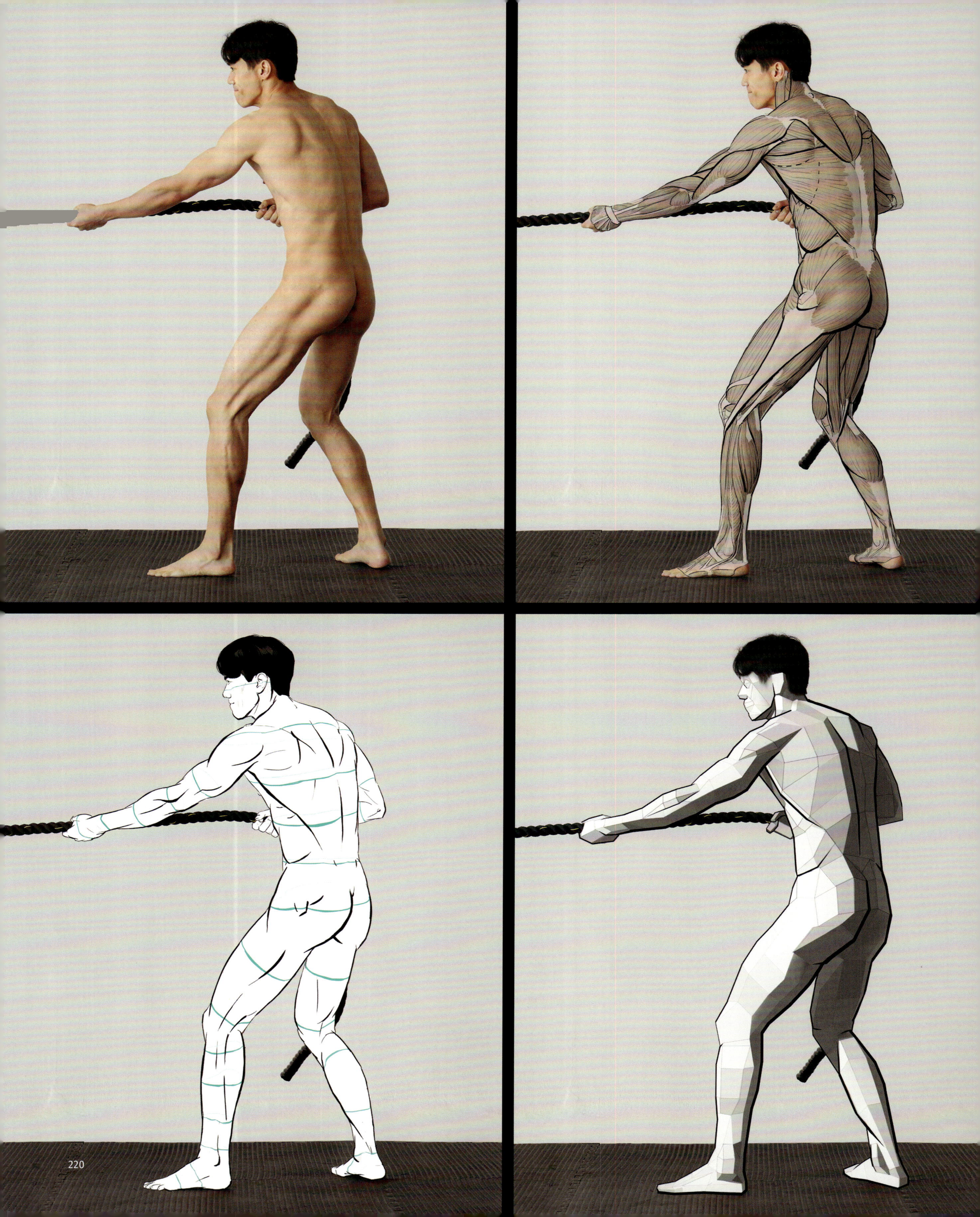

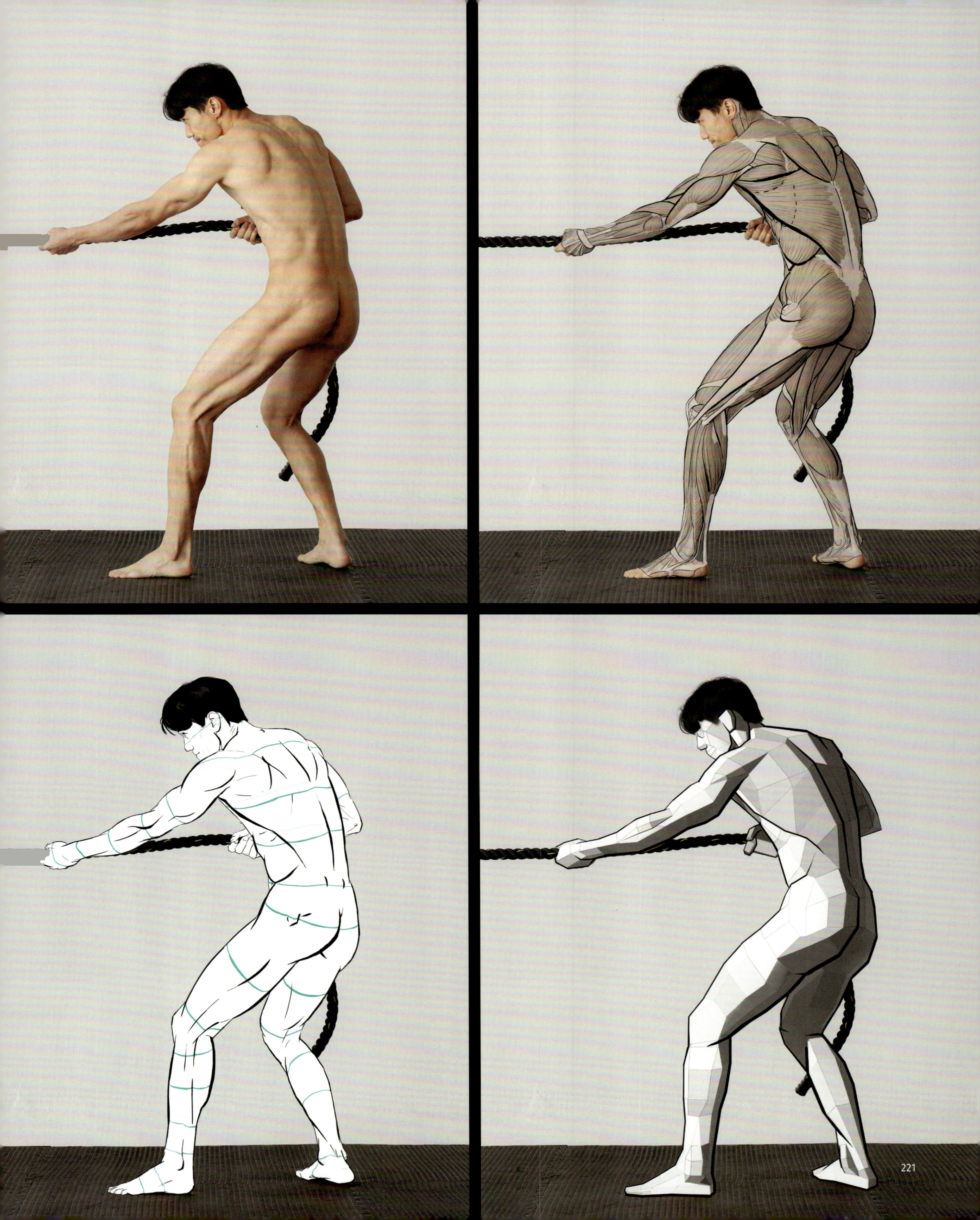

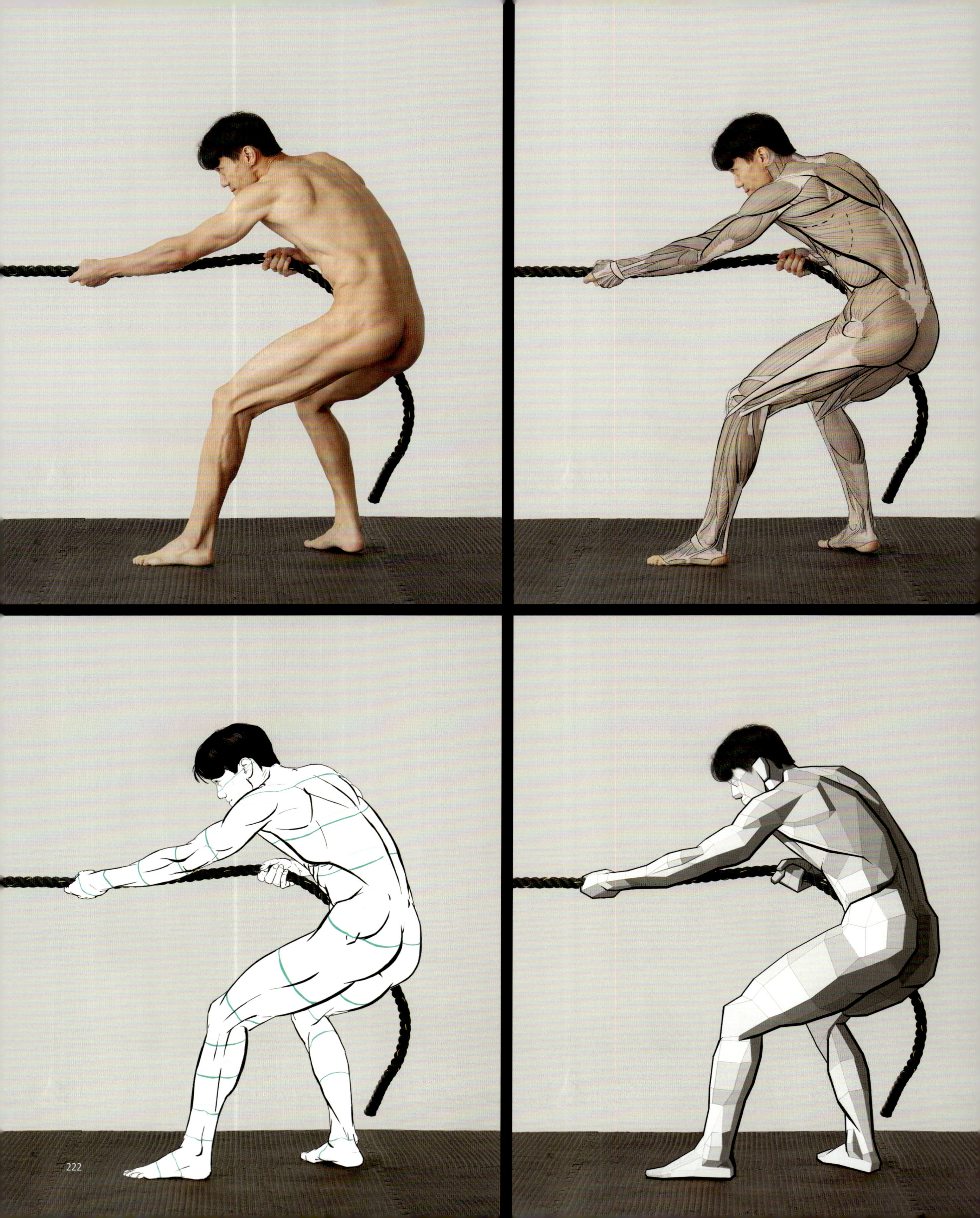

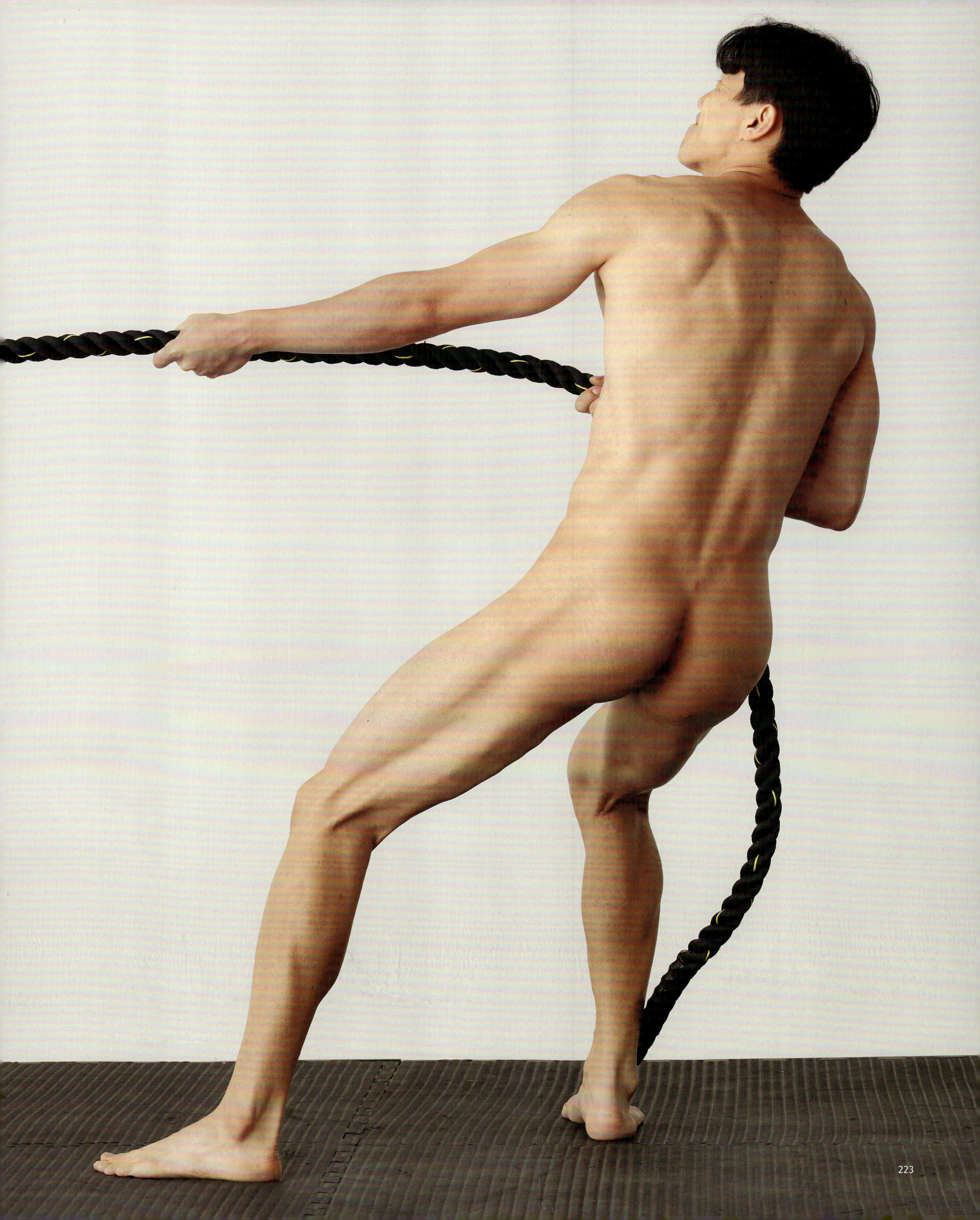

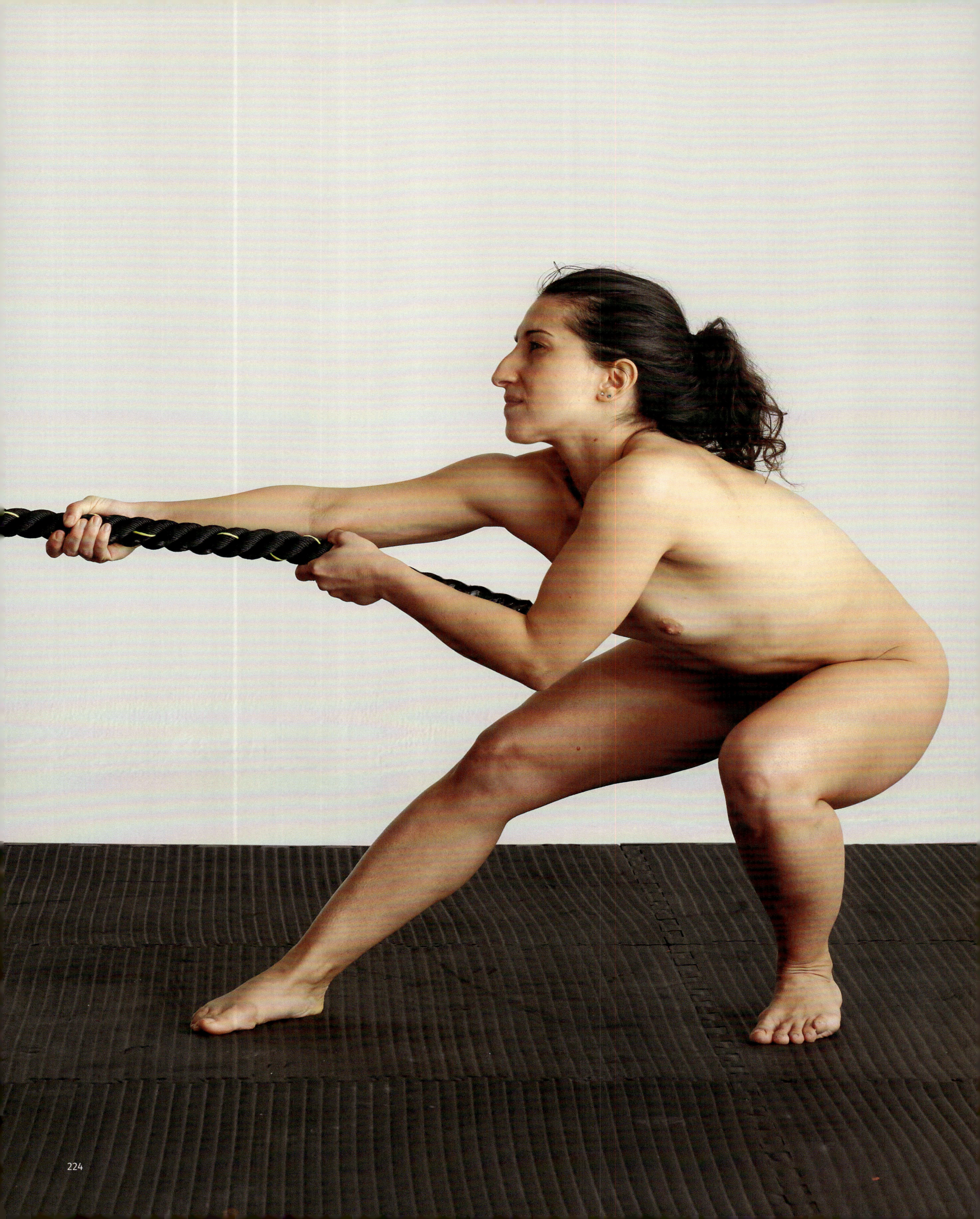

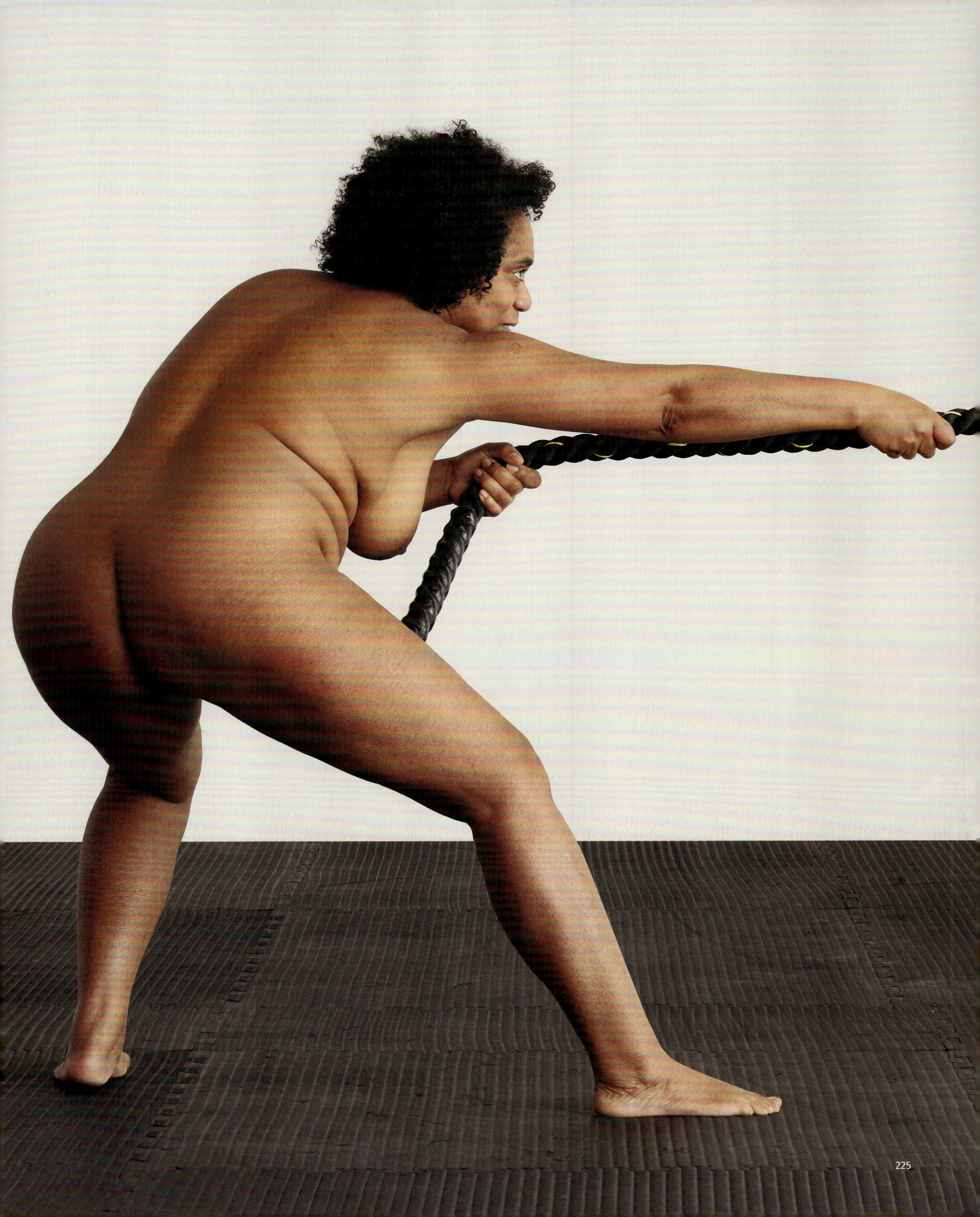

Pushing an object

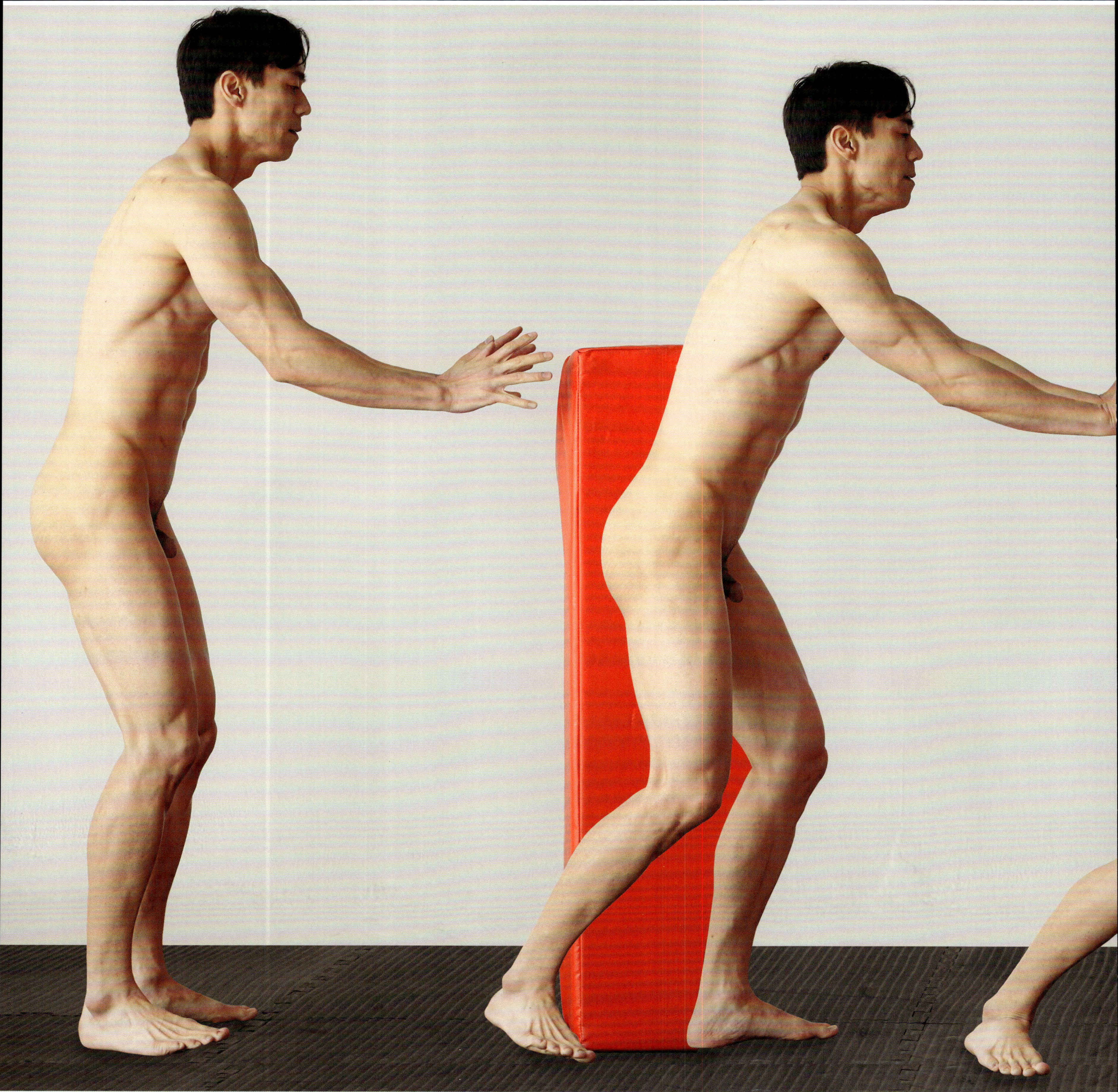

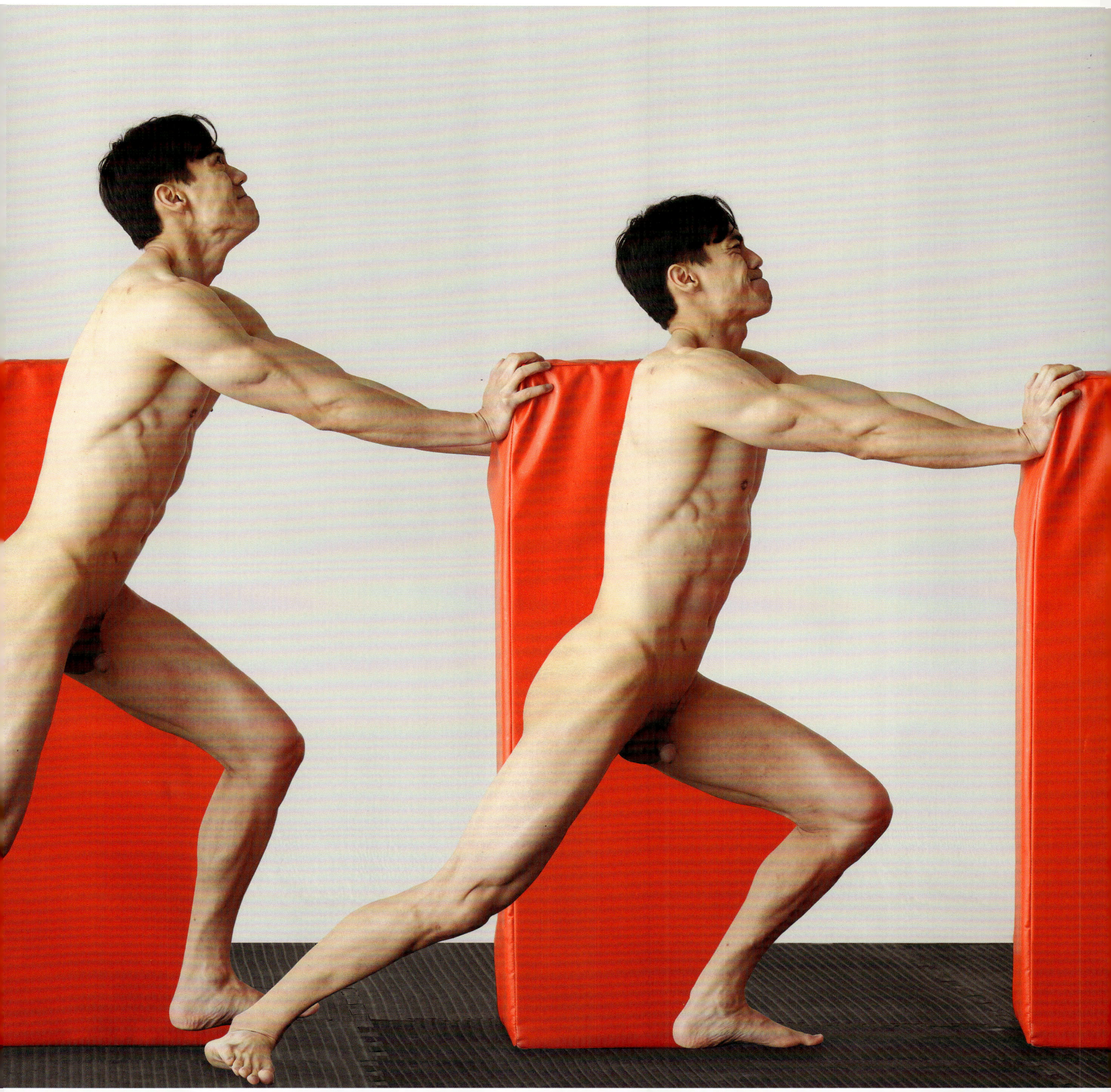

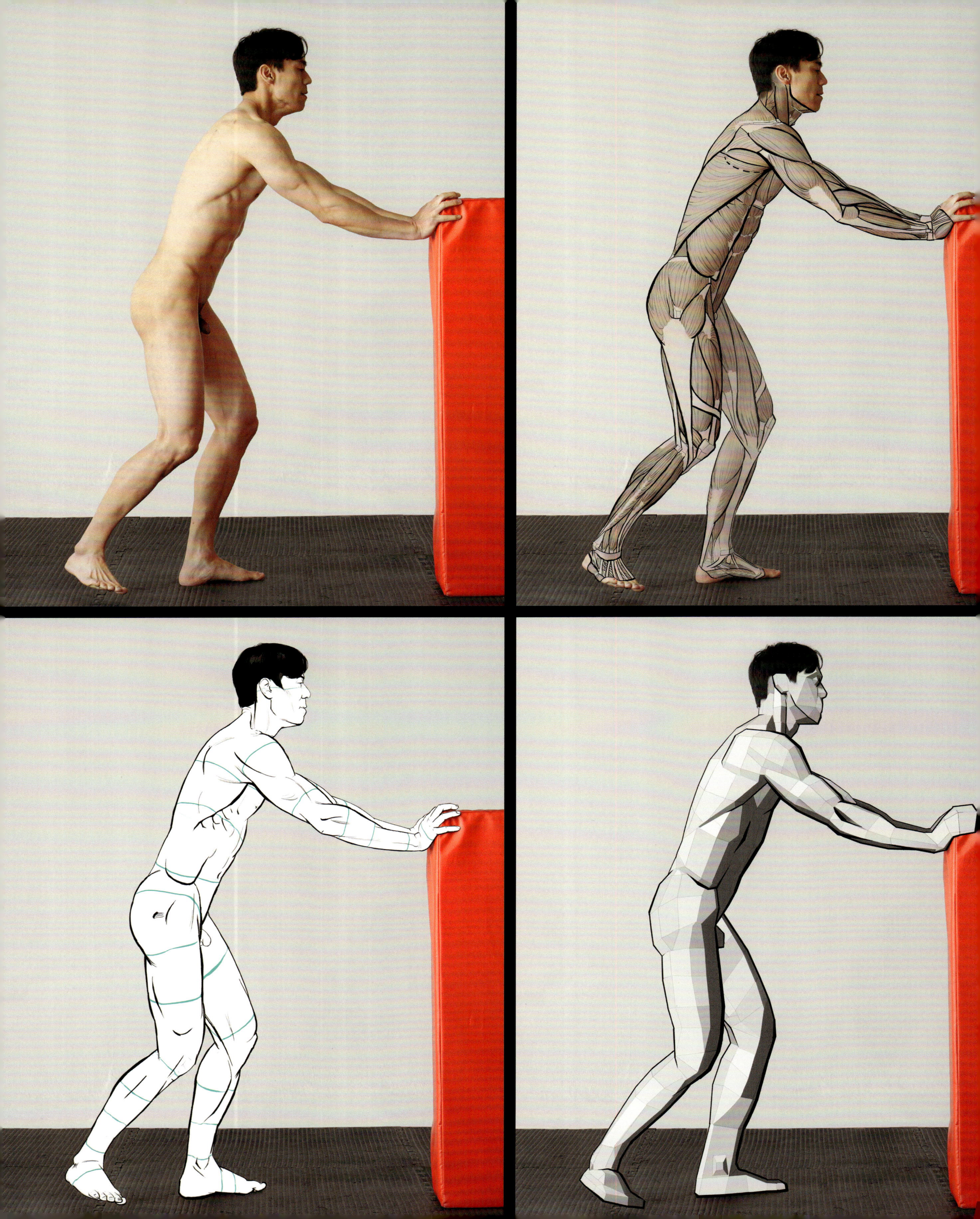

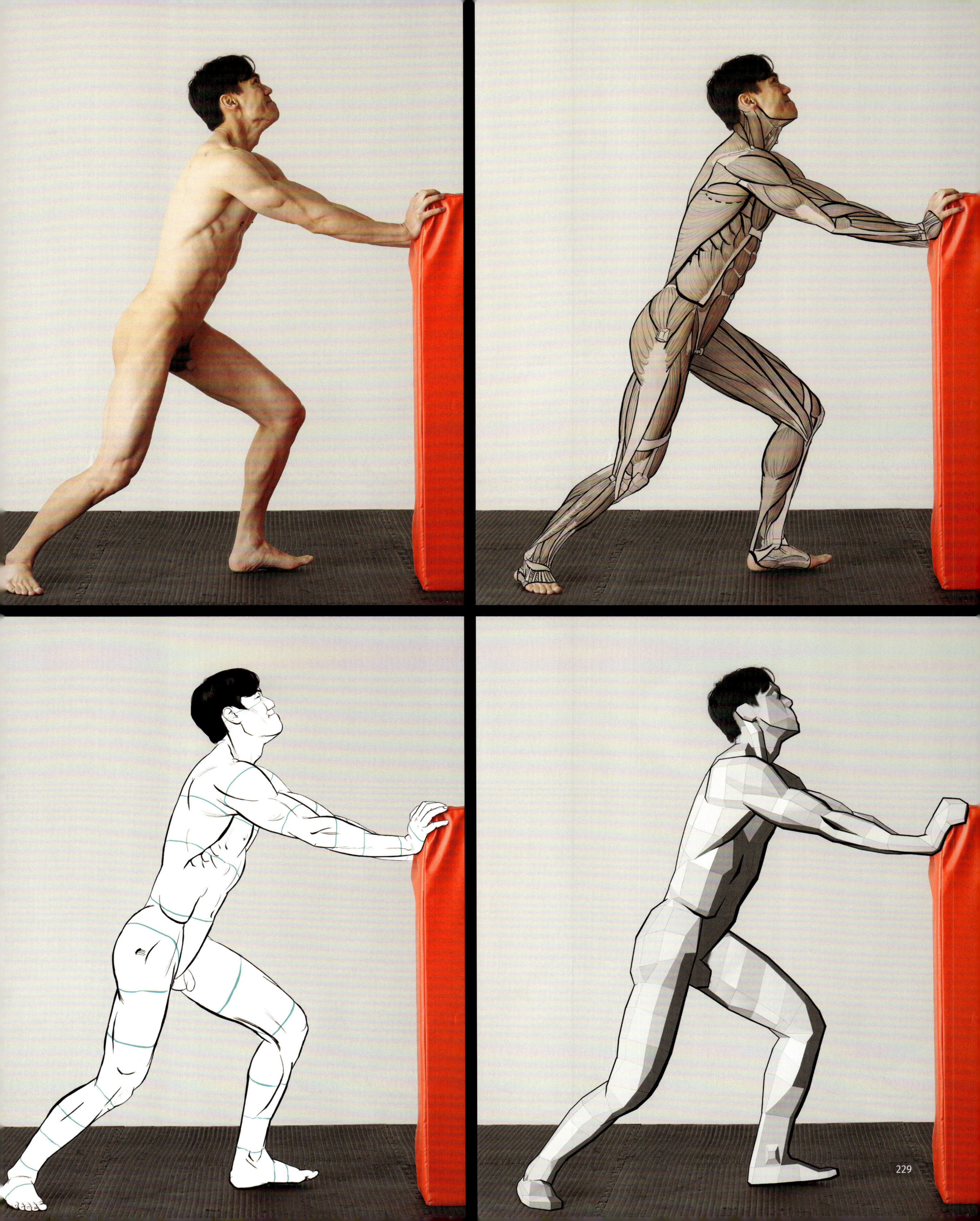

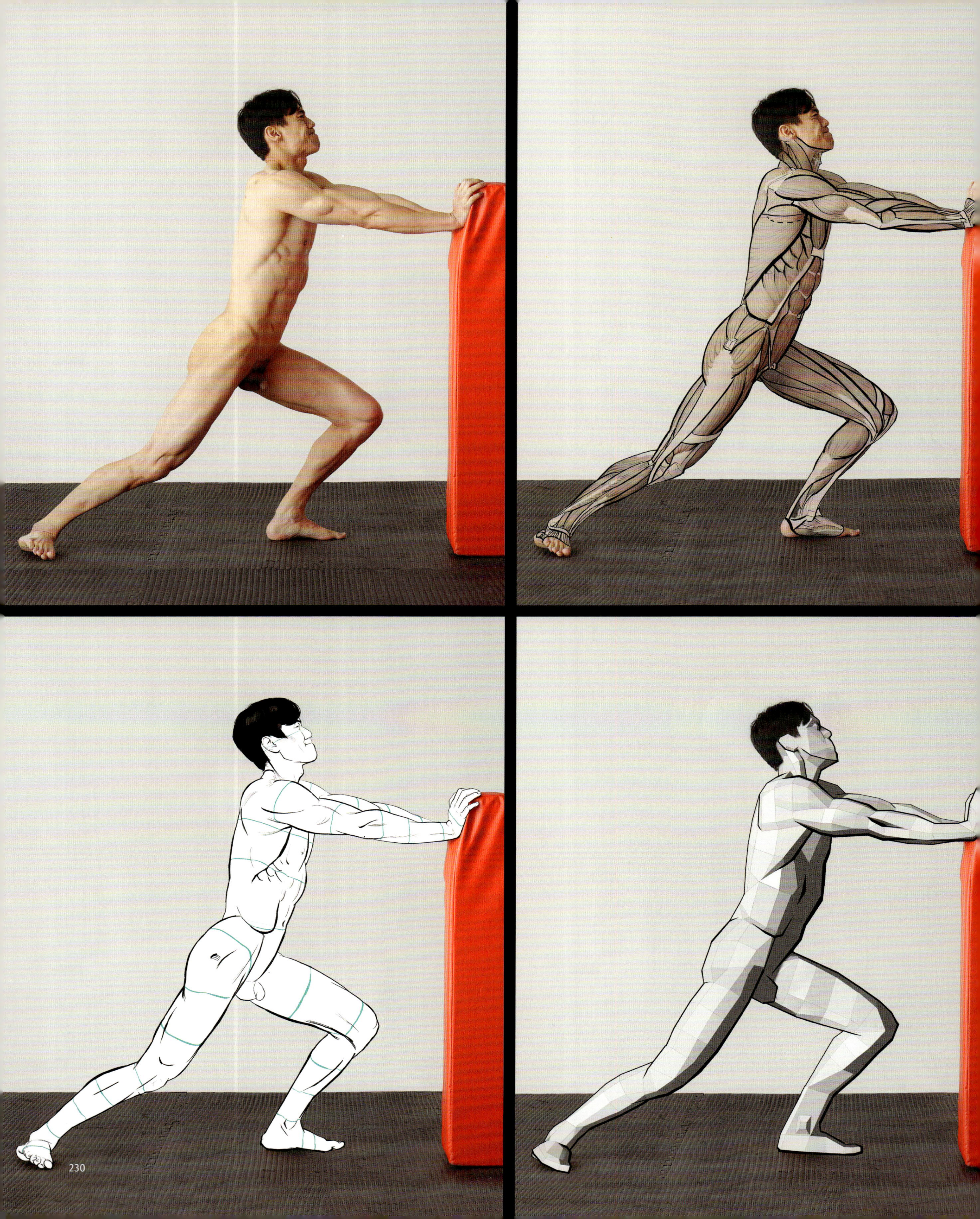

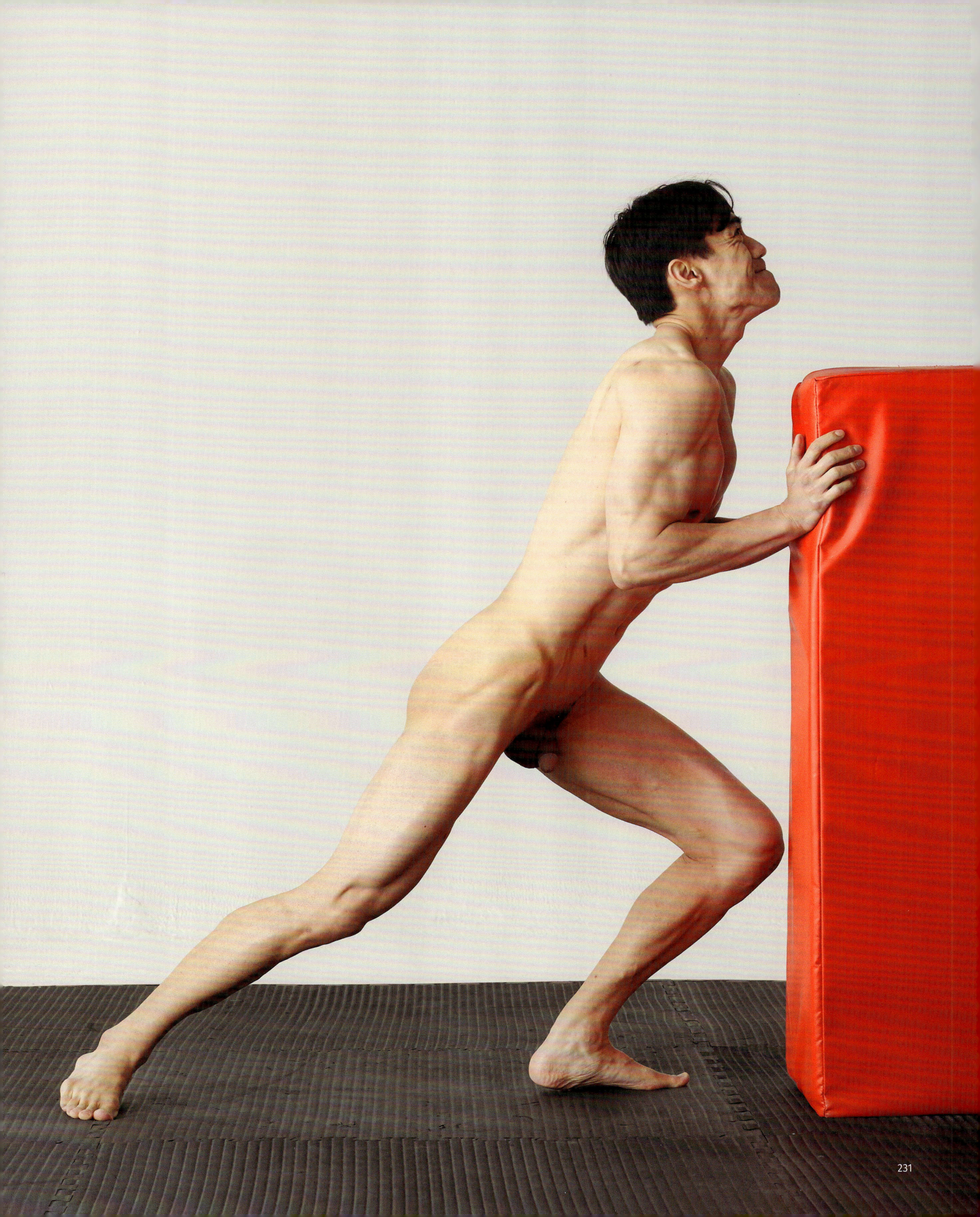

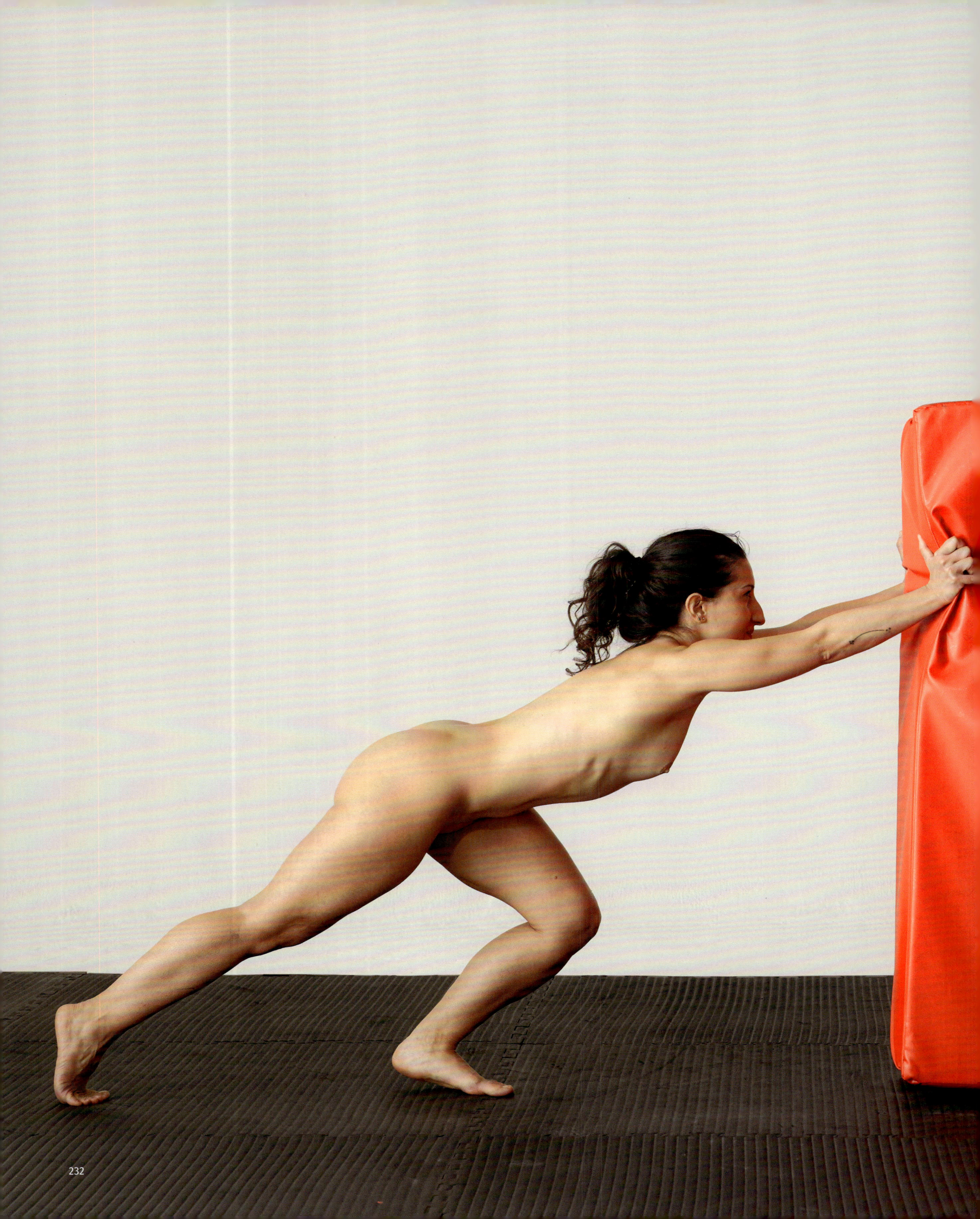

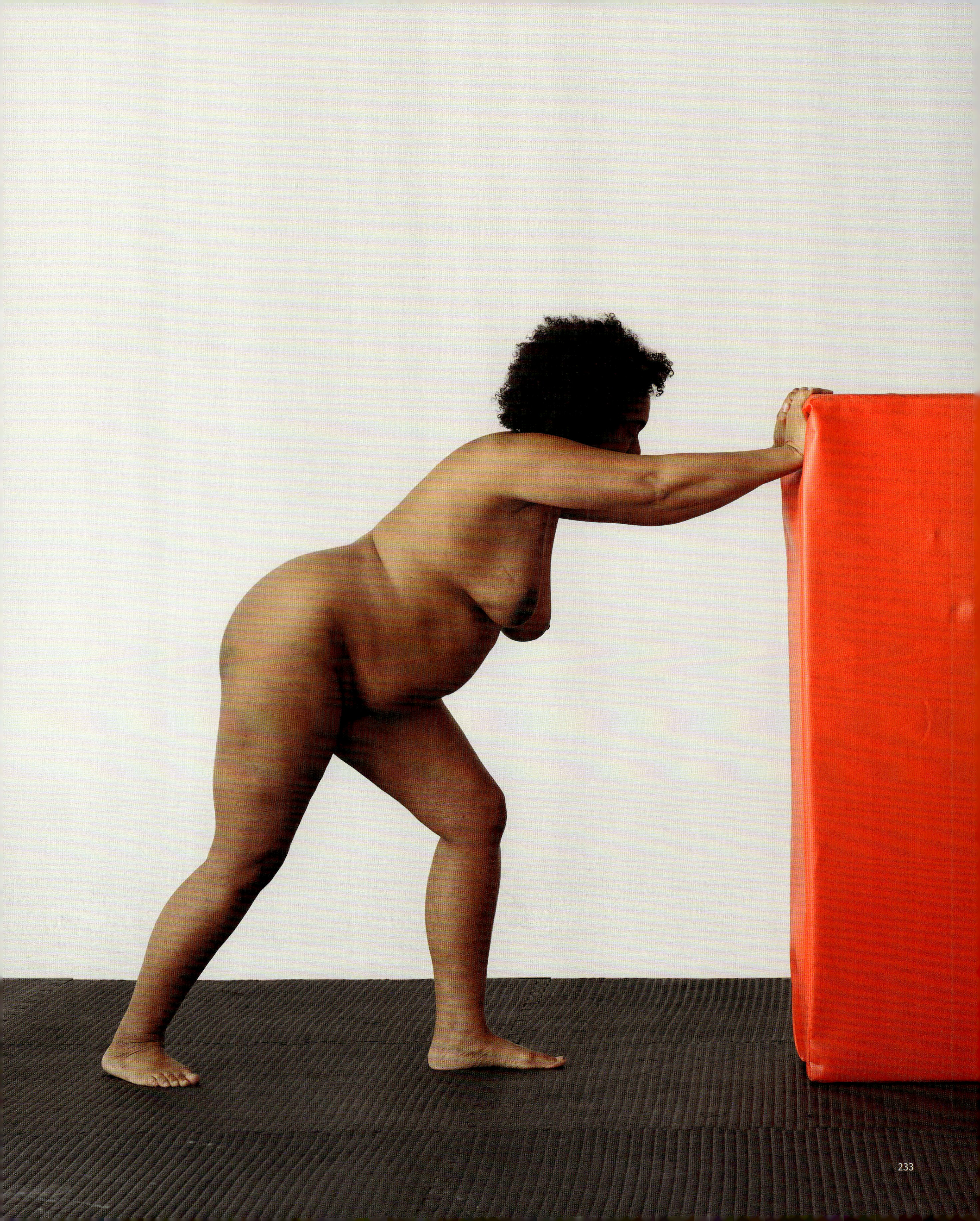

Hitting an object

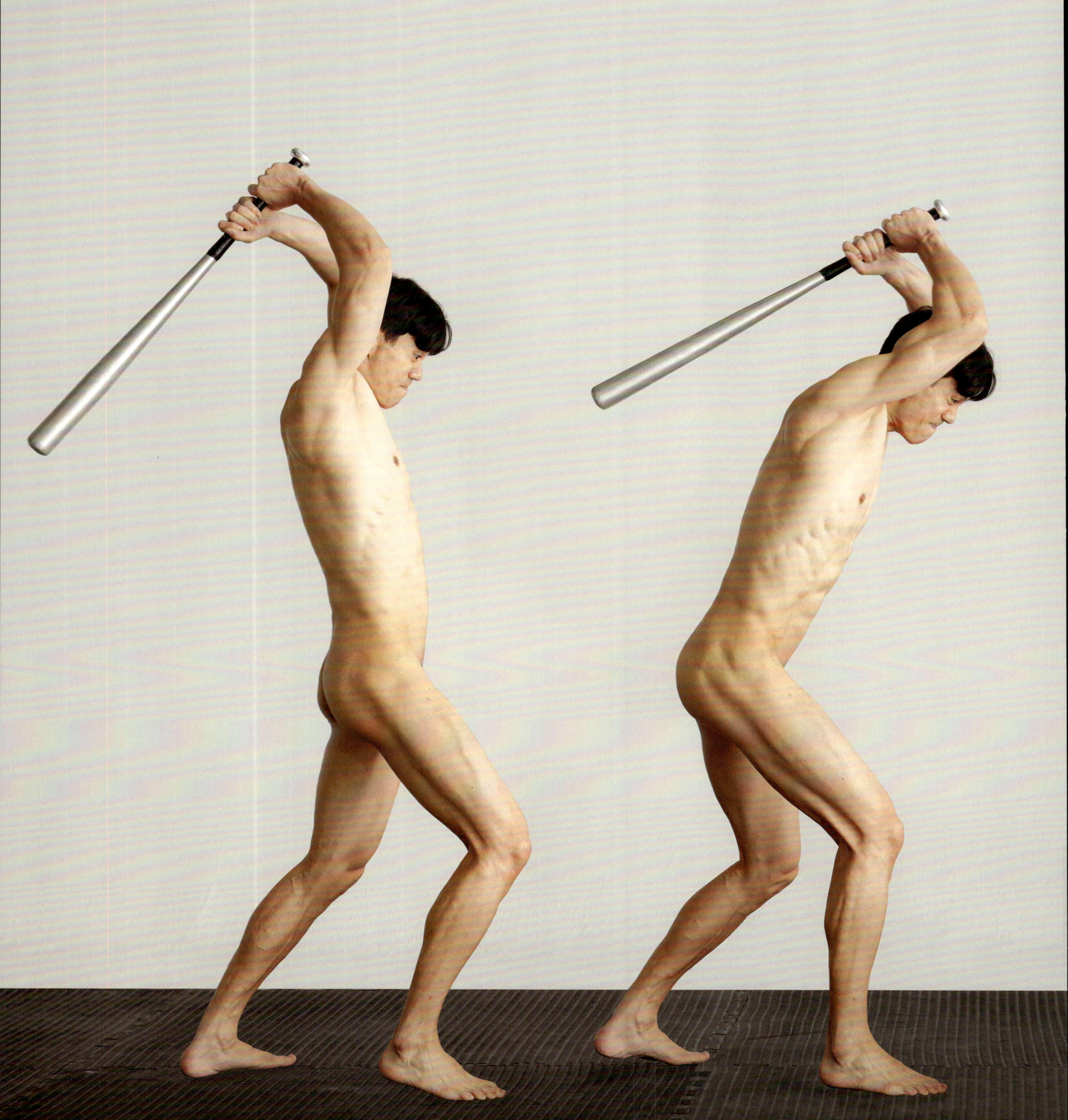

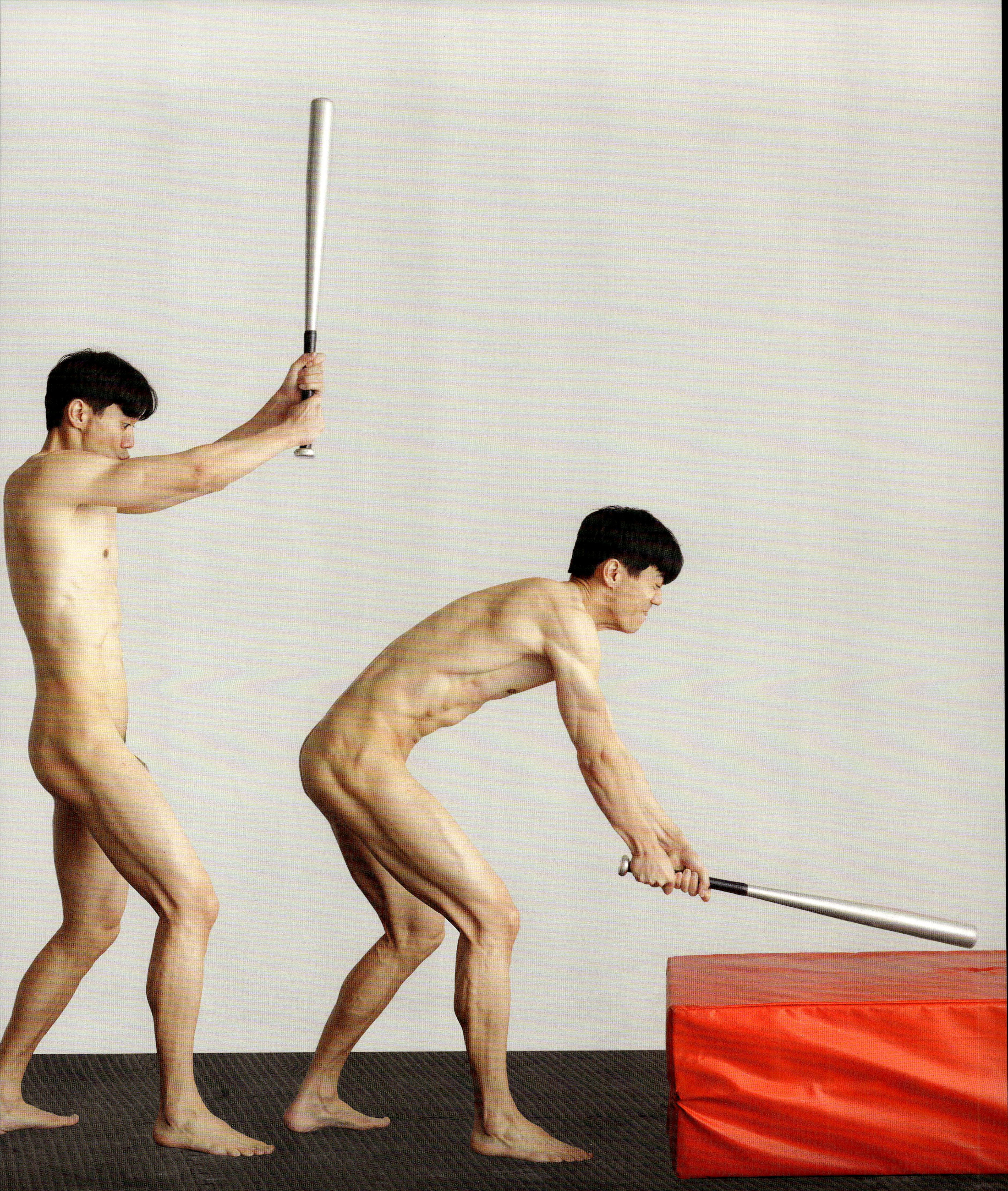

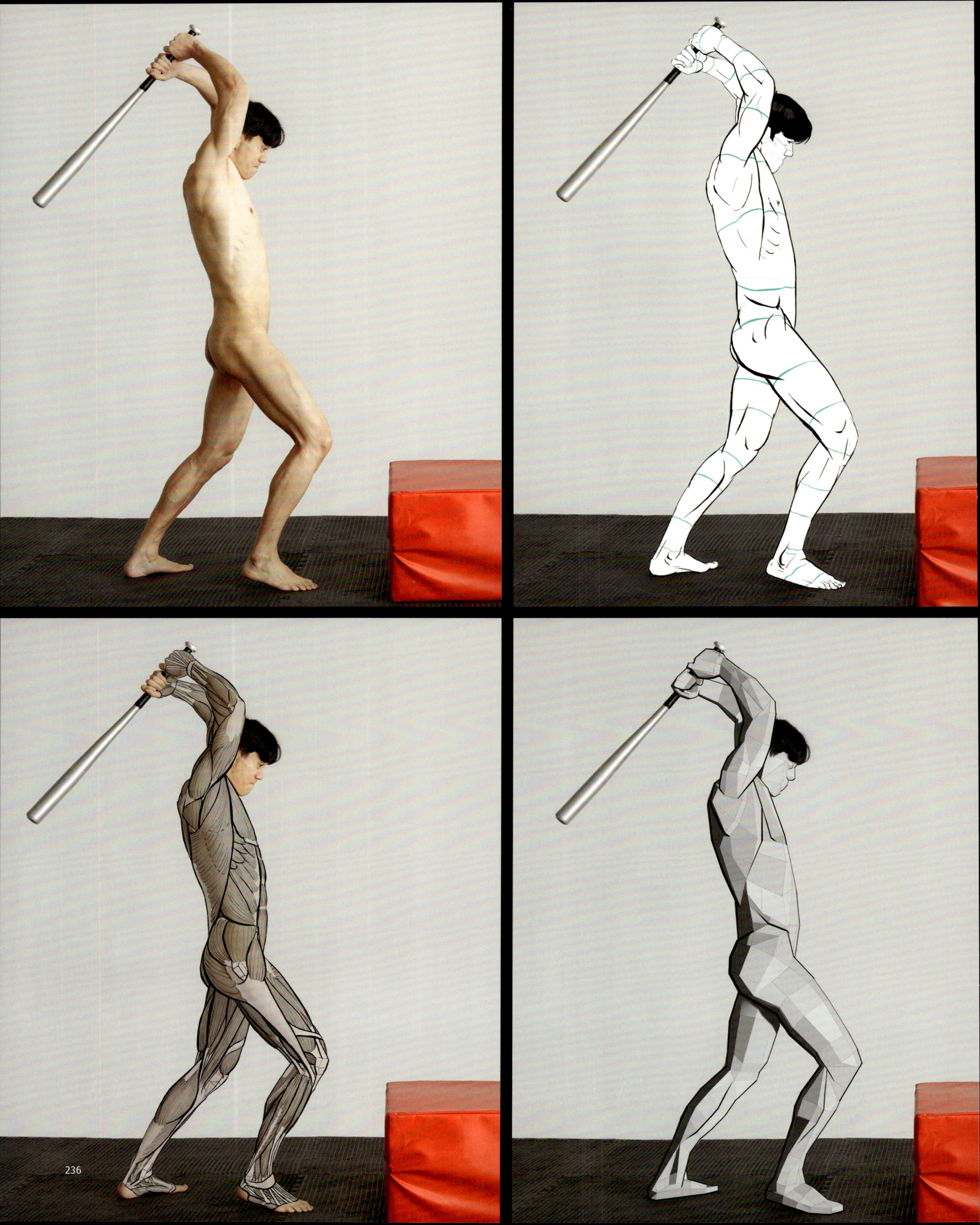

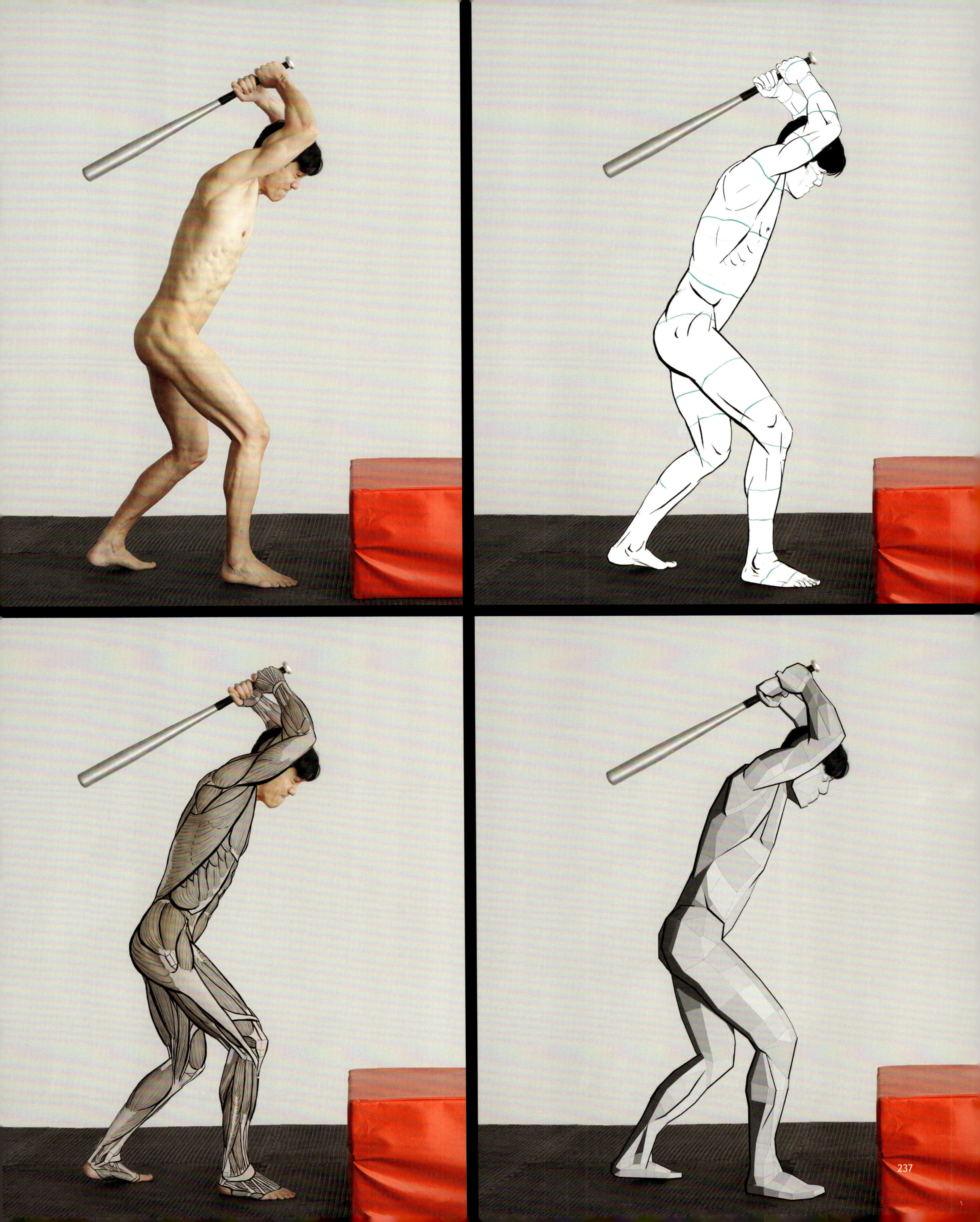

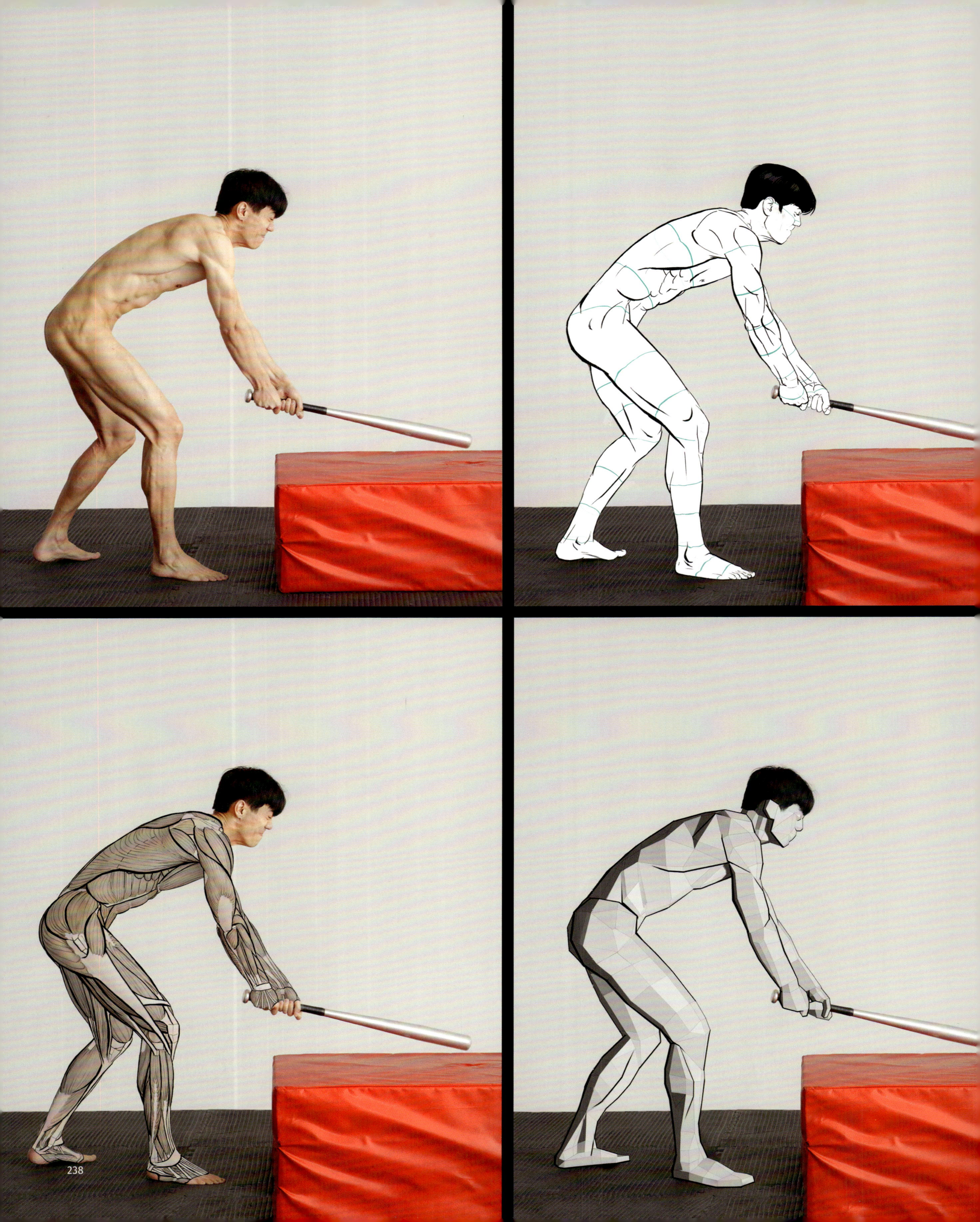

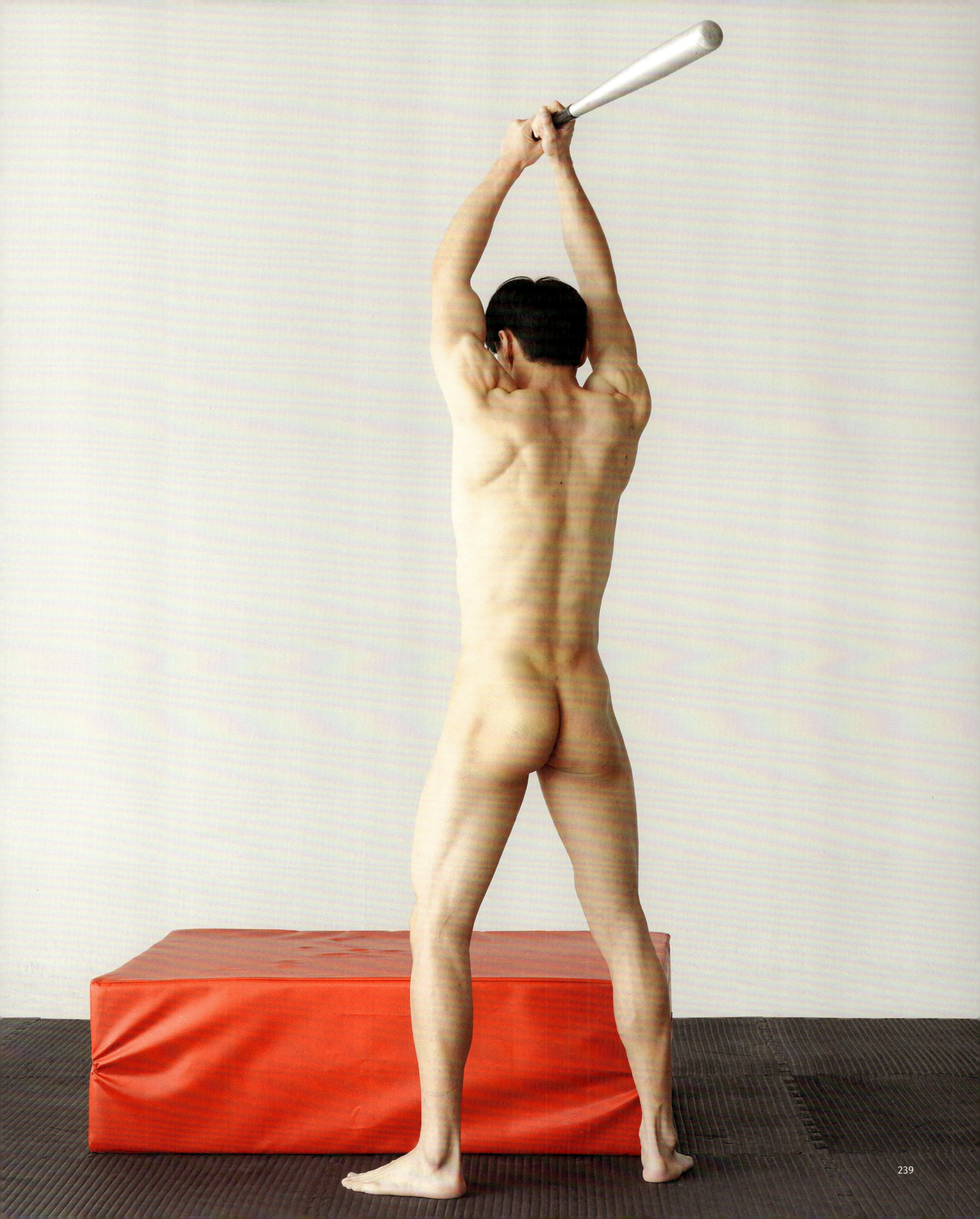

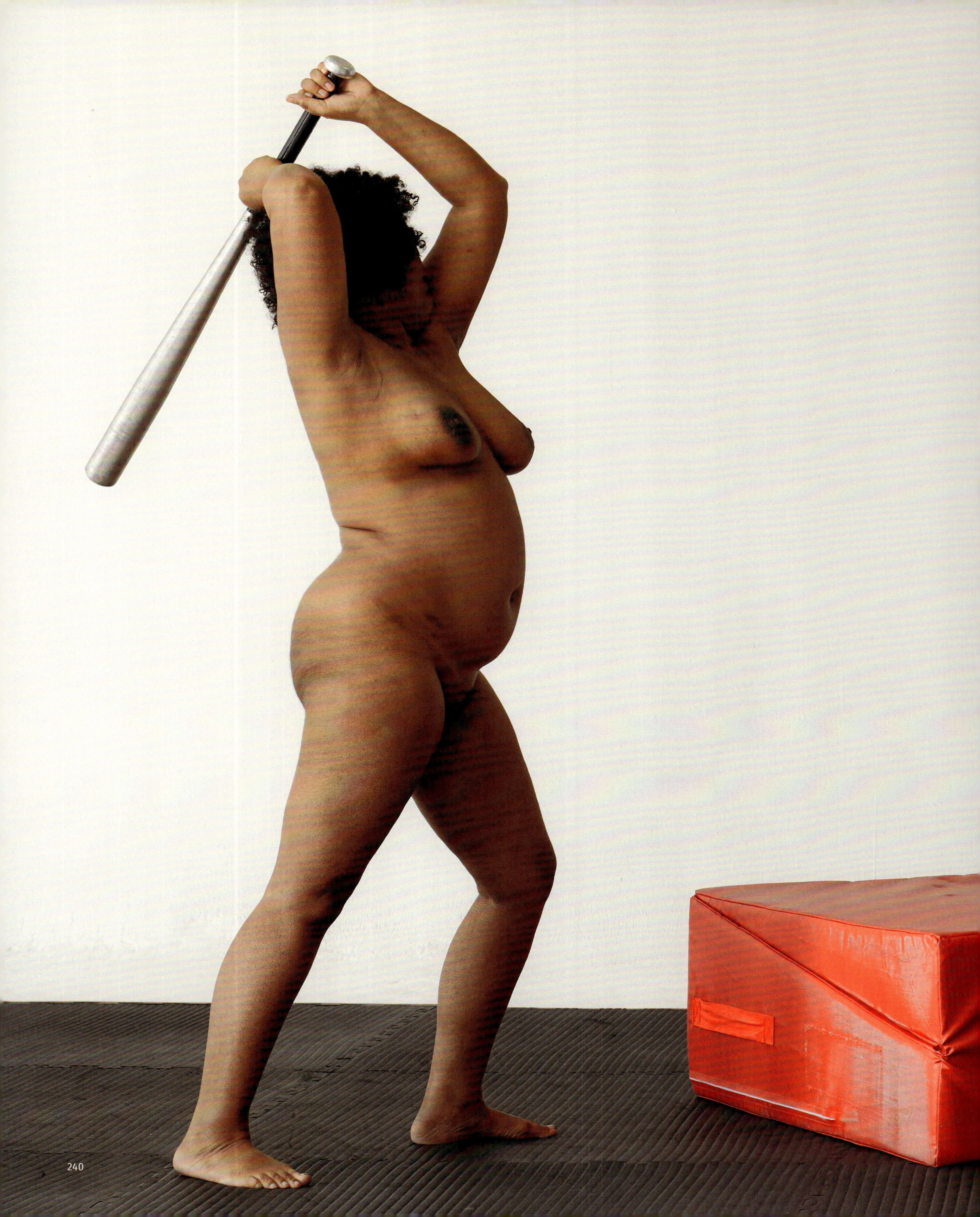

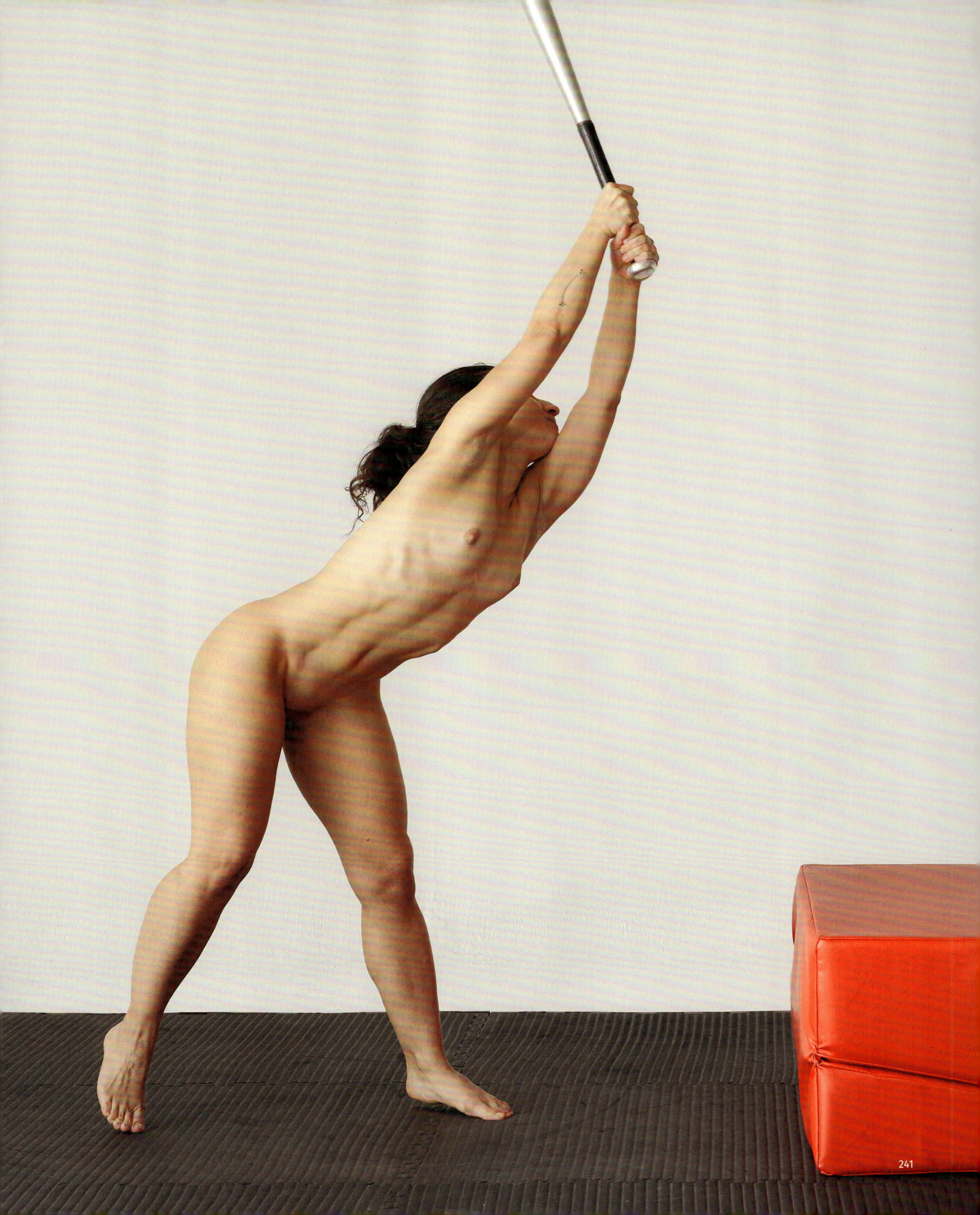

Getting up from sitting down

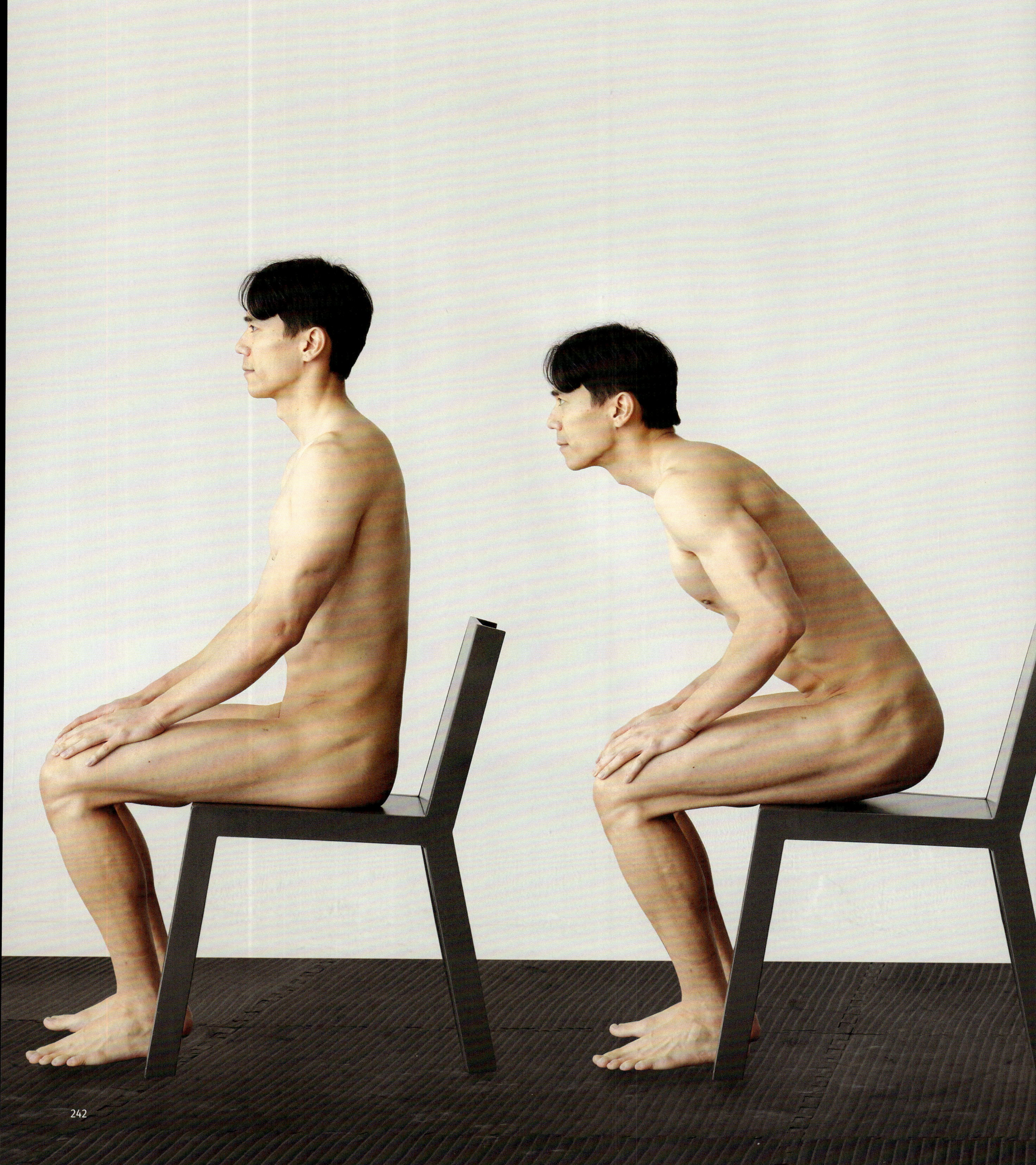

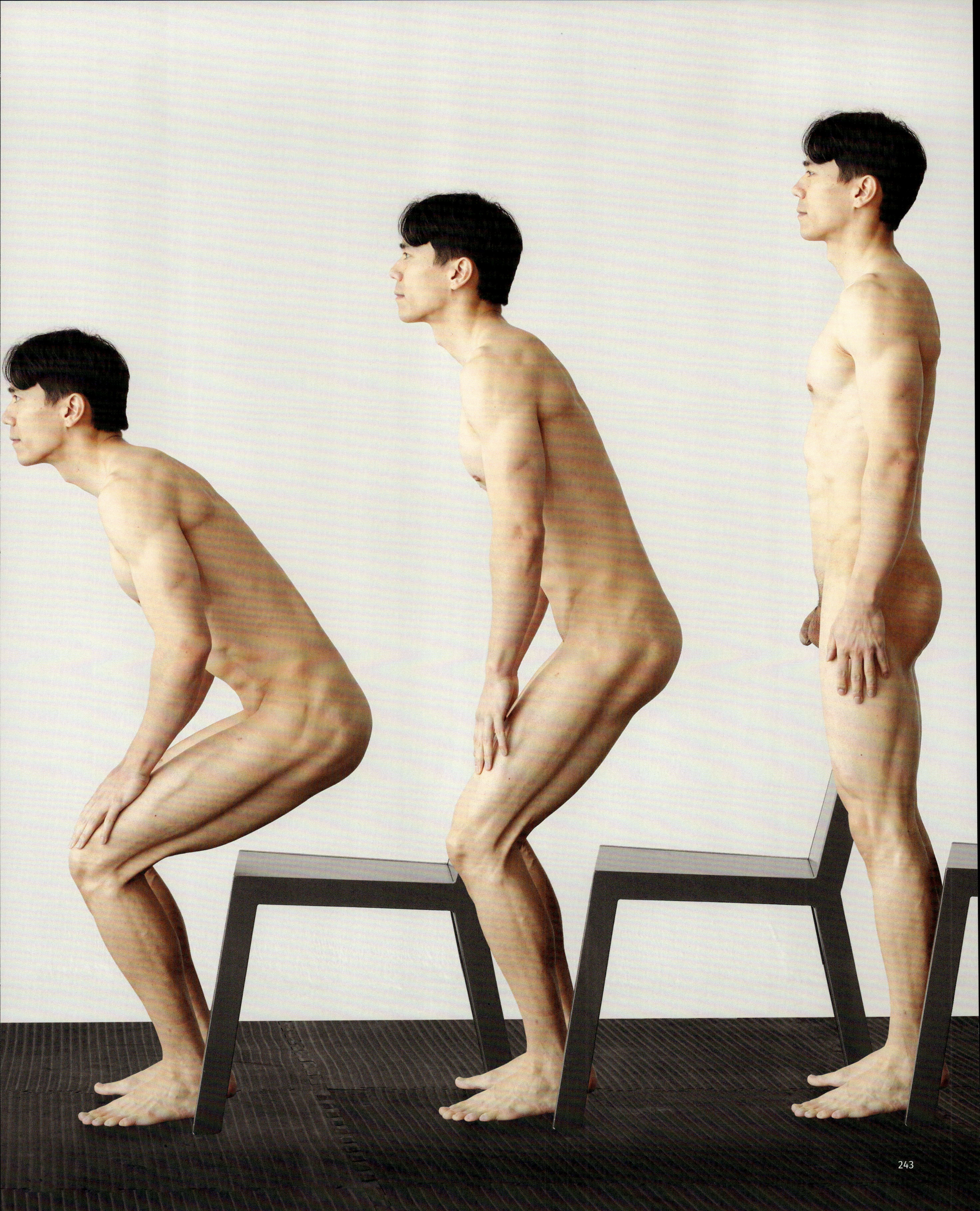

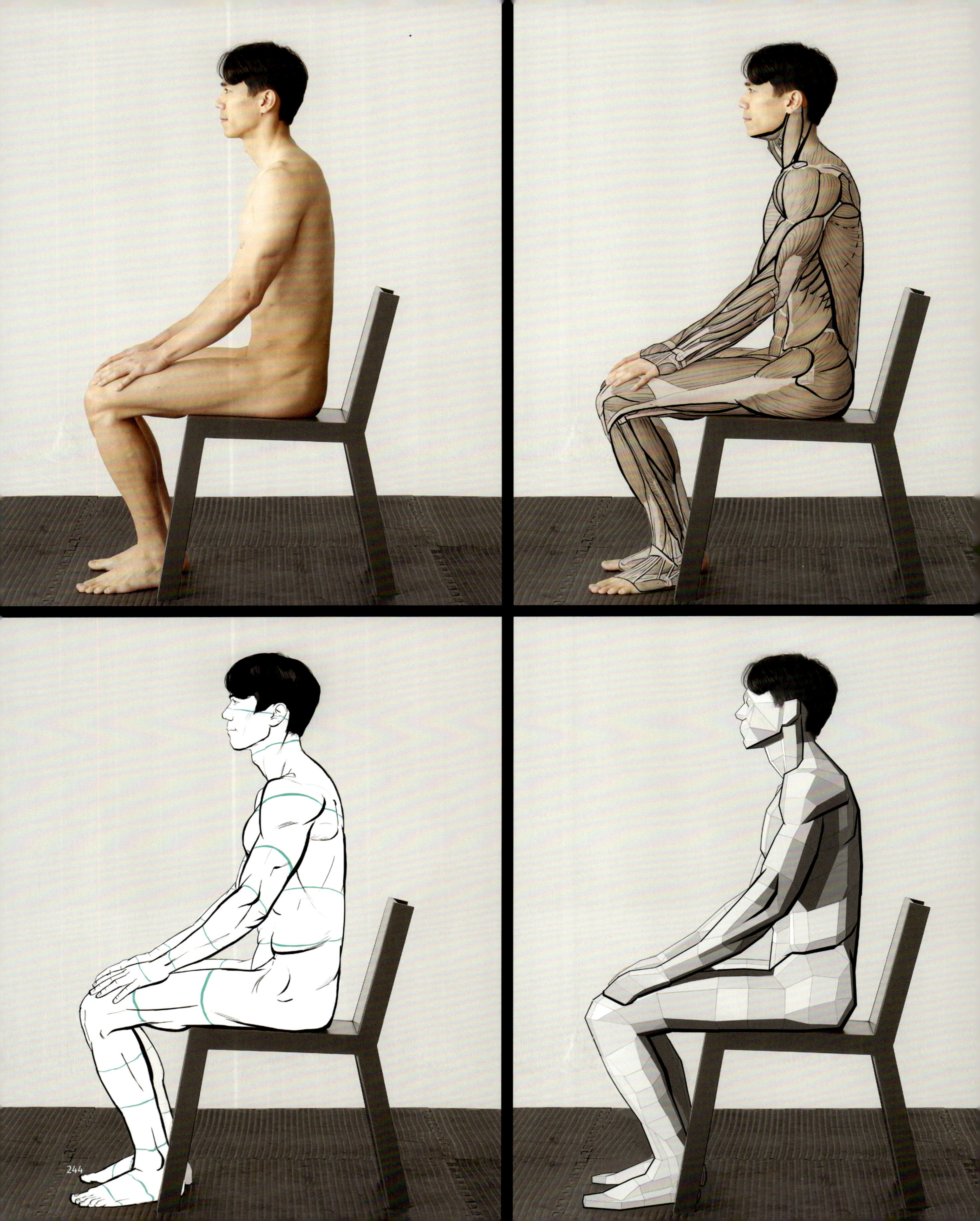

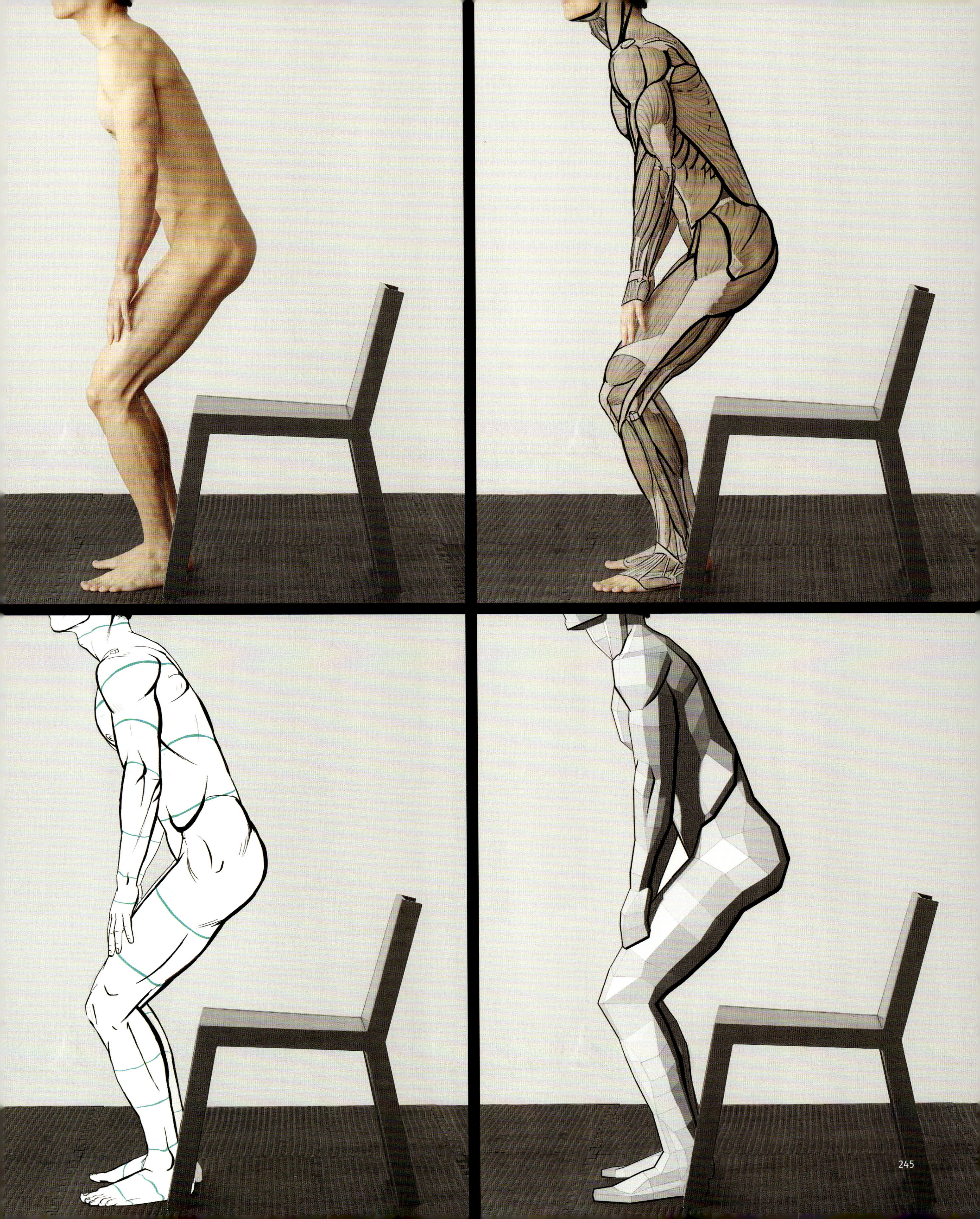

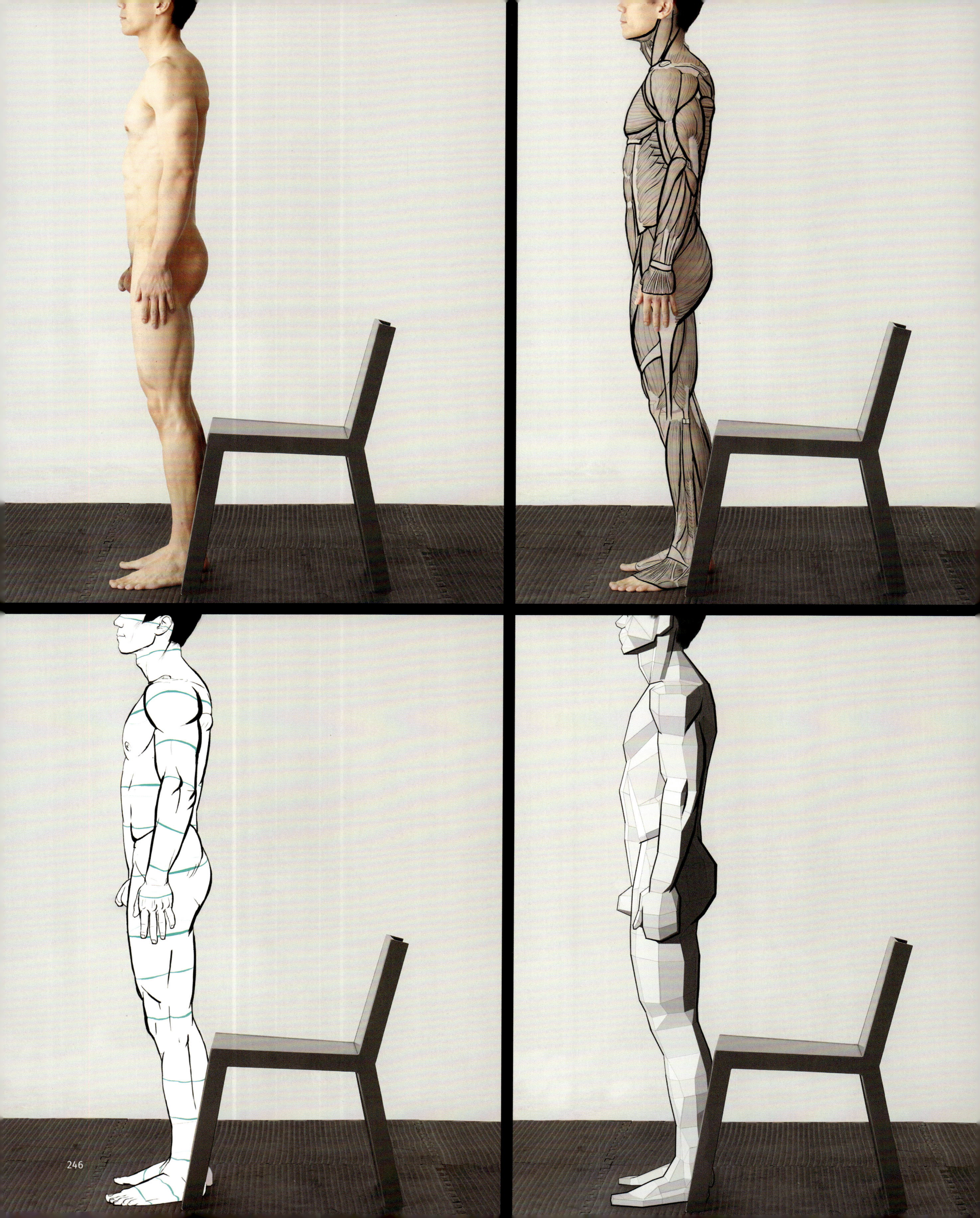

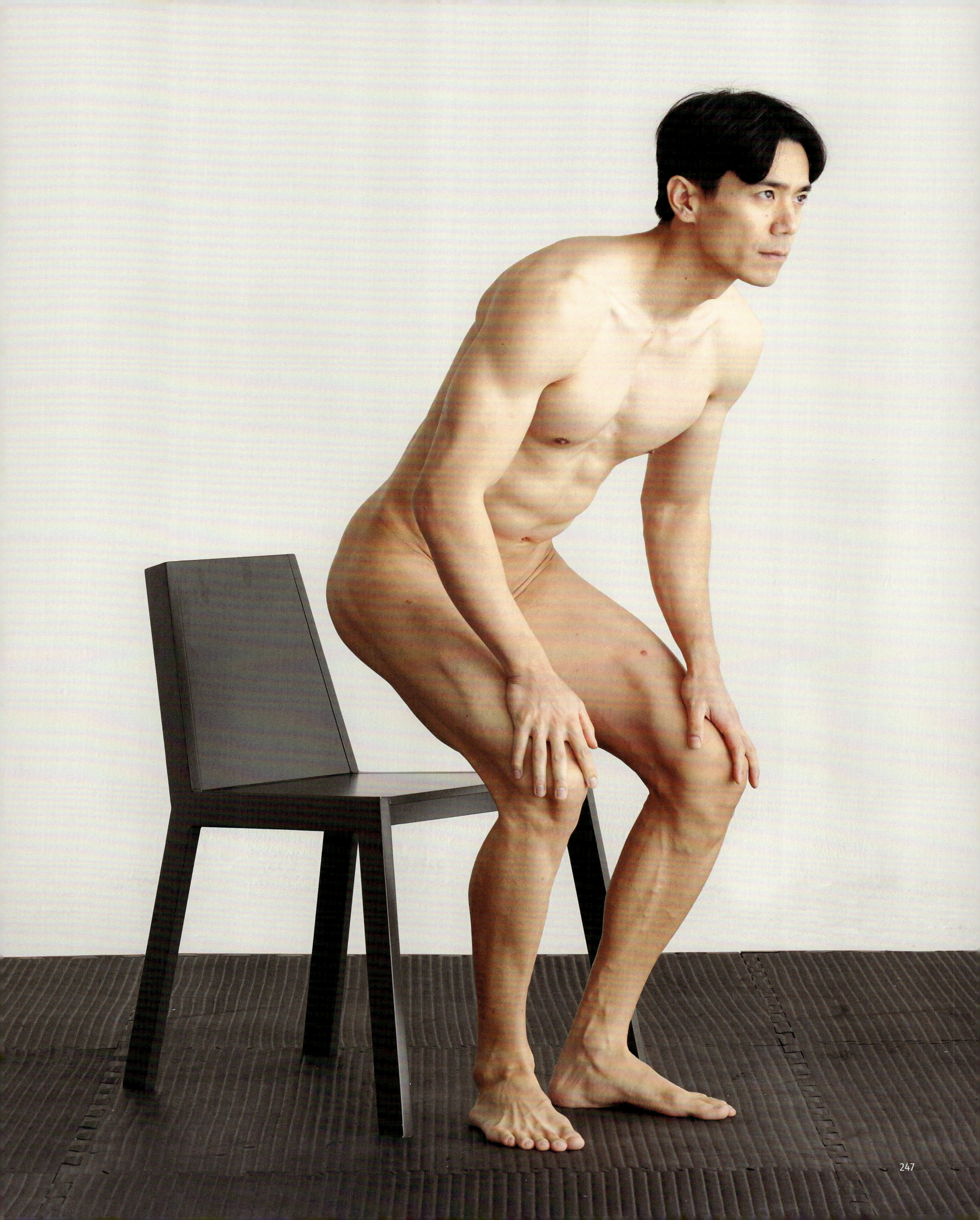

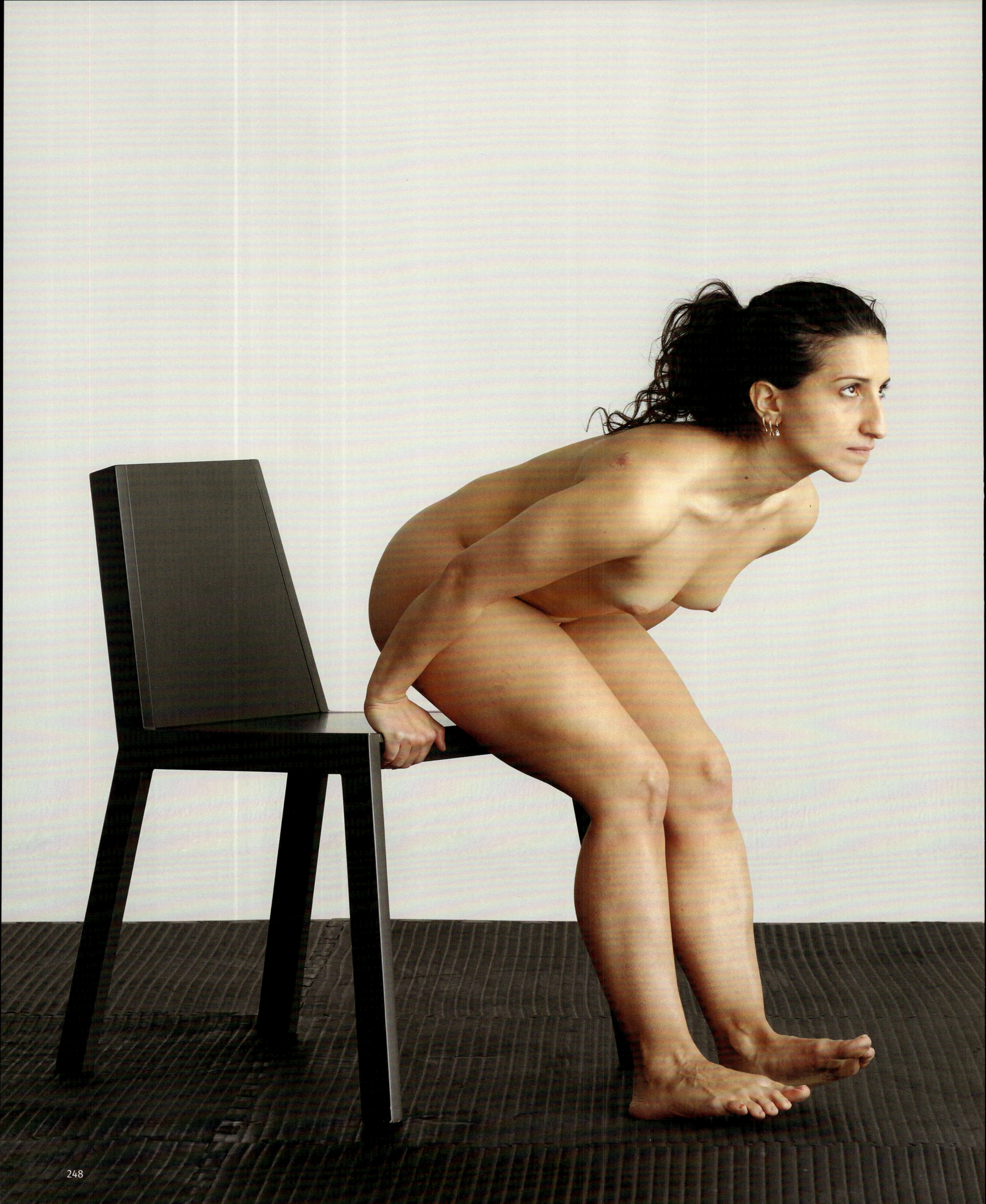

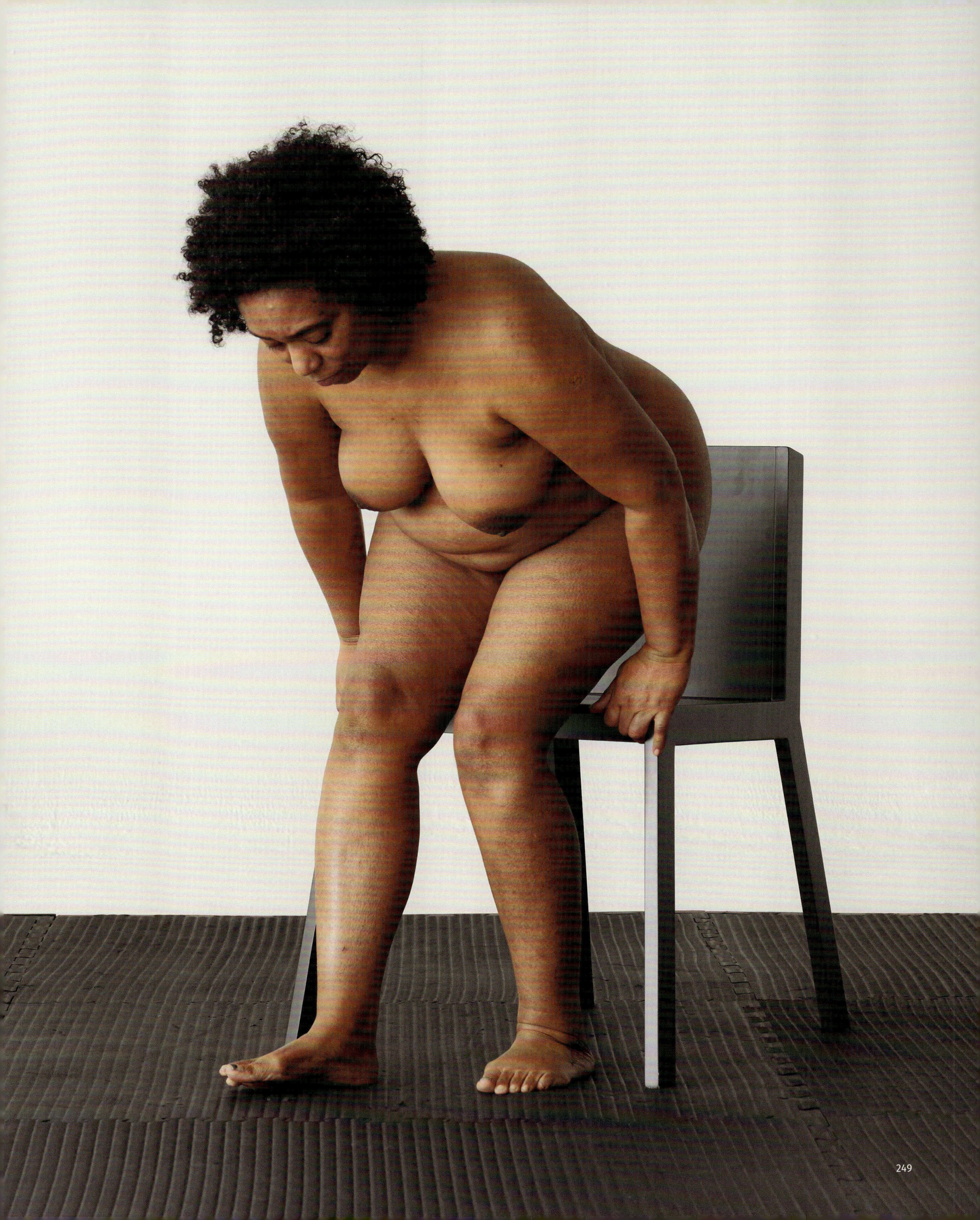

Getting up from lying down

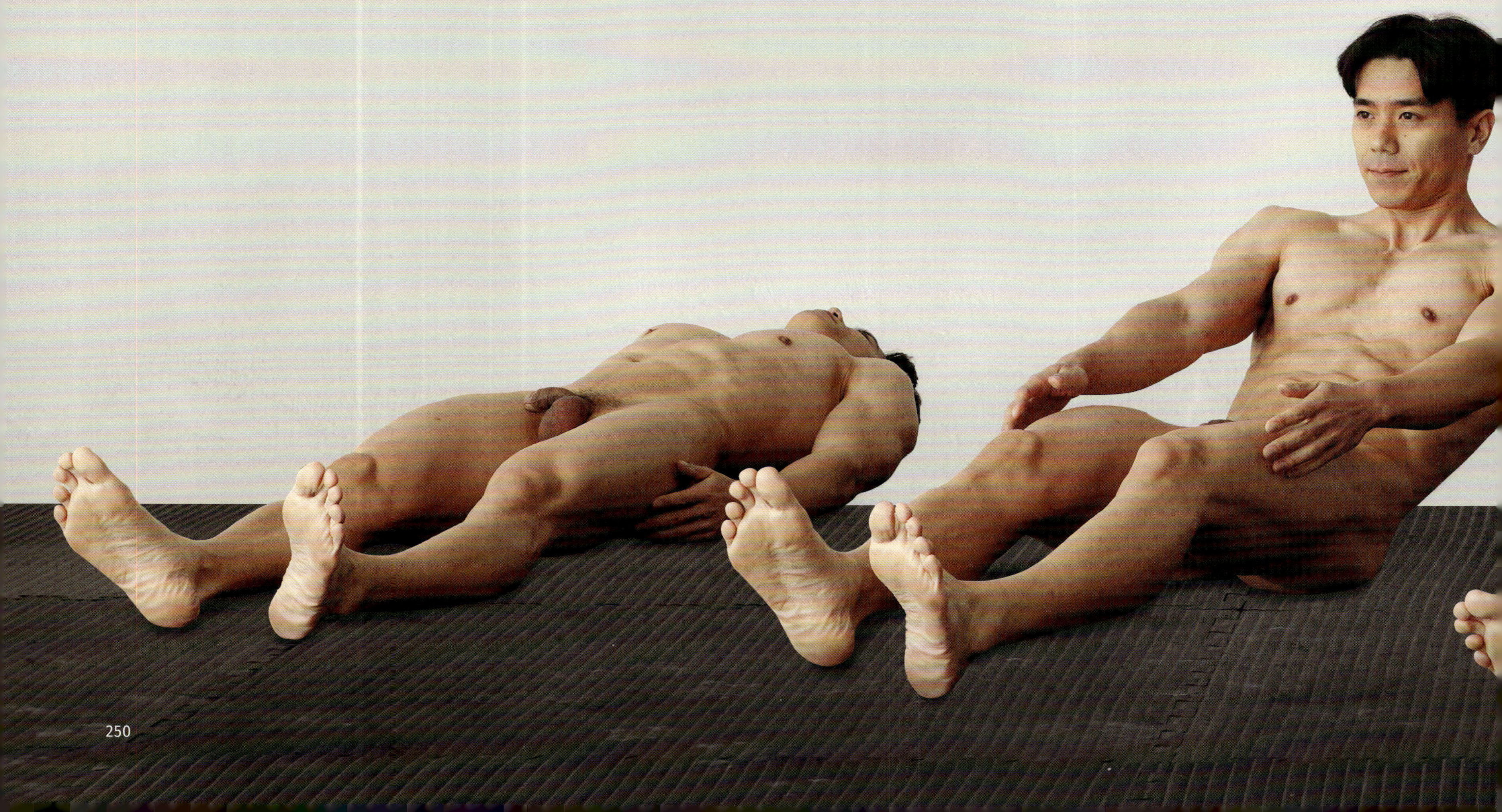

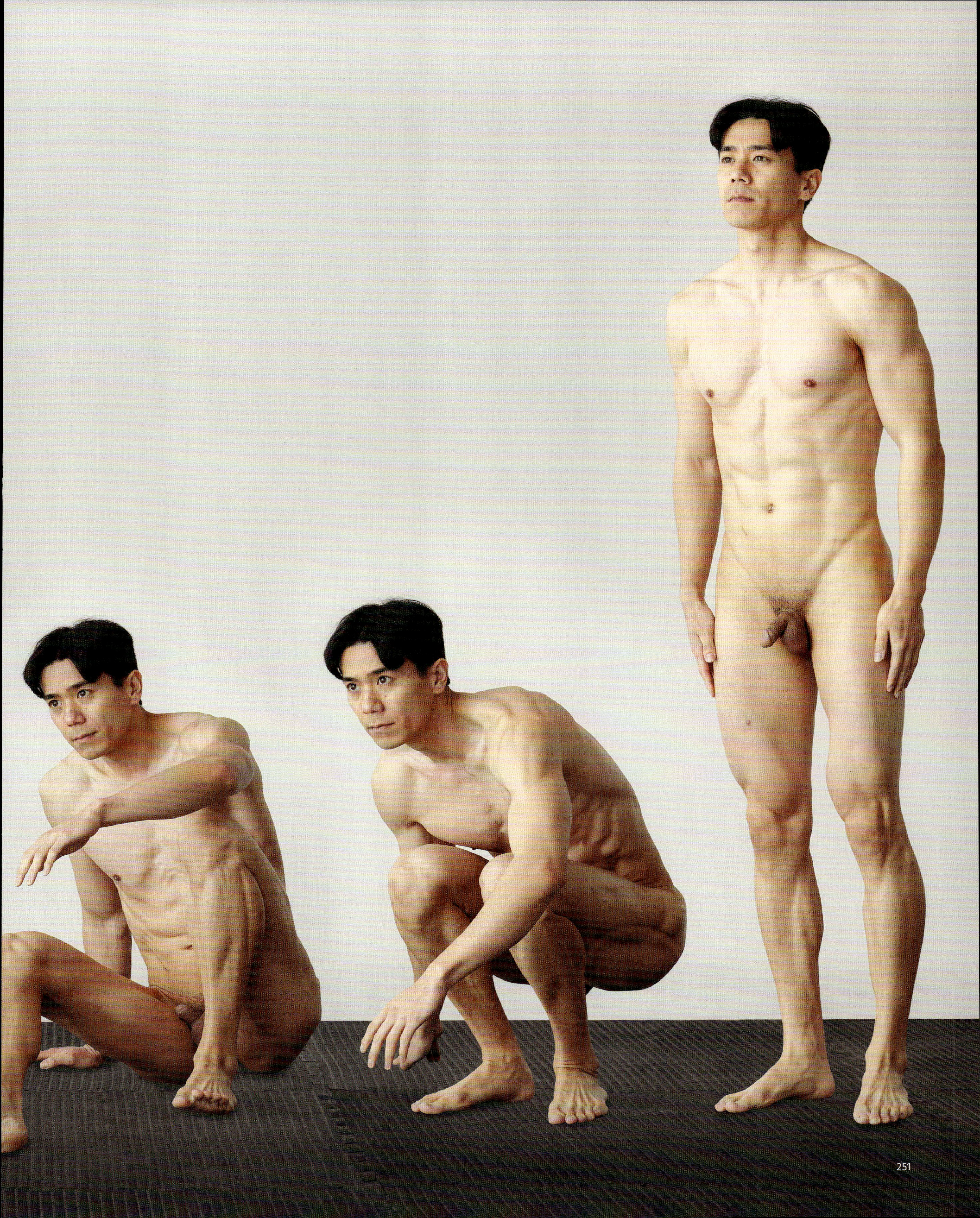

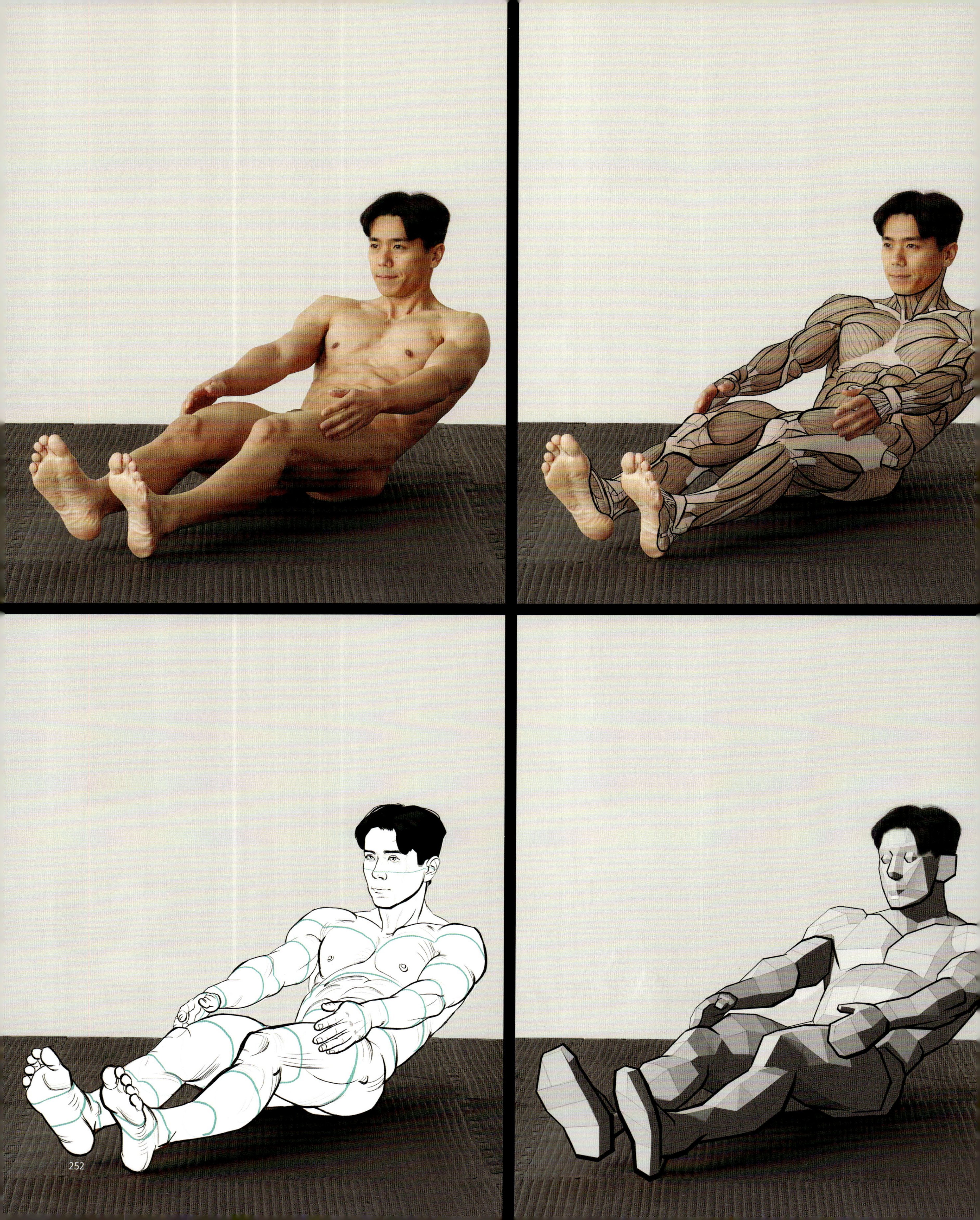

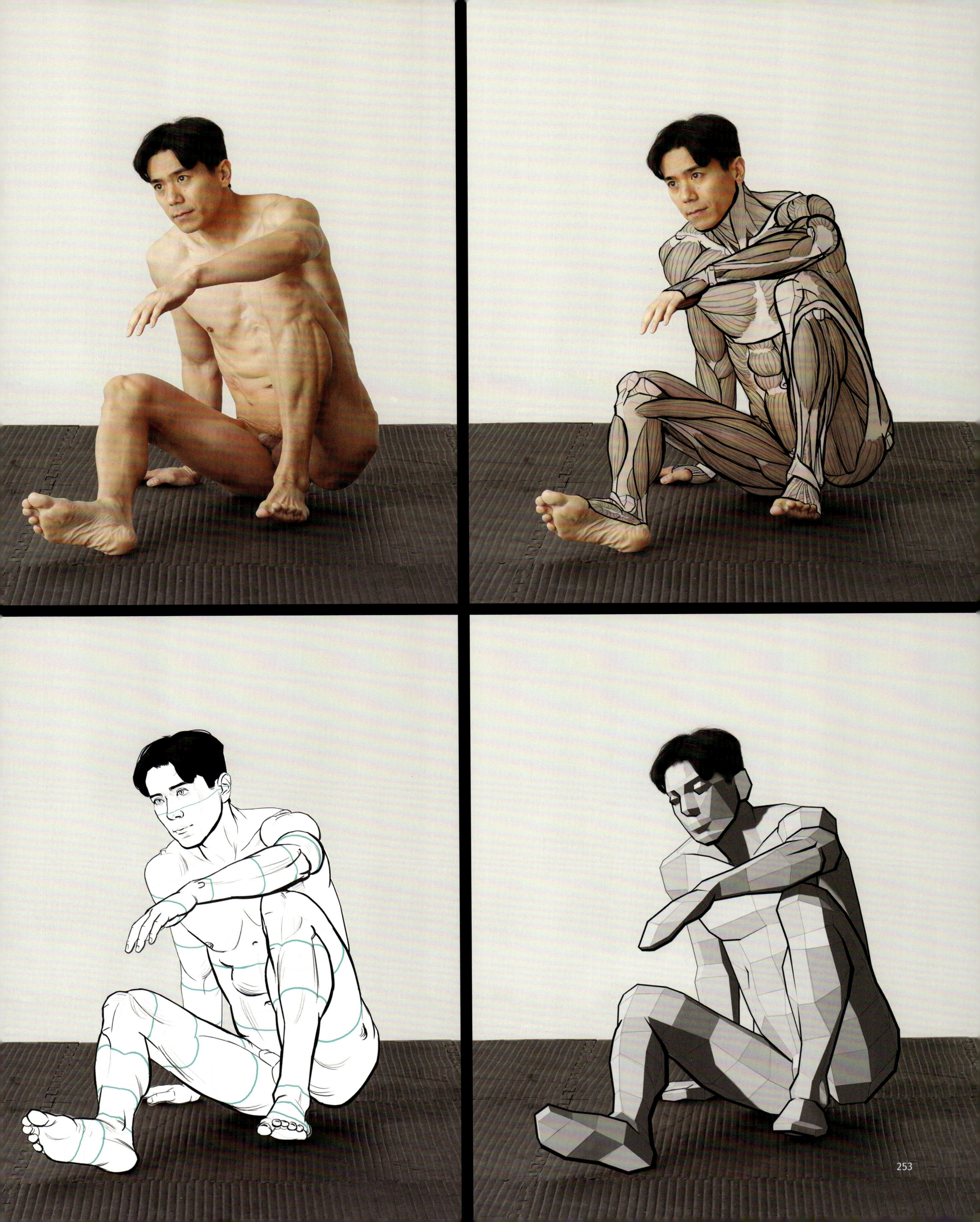

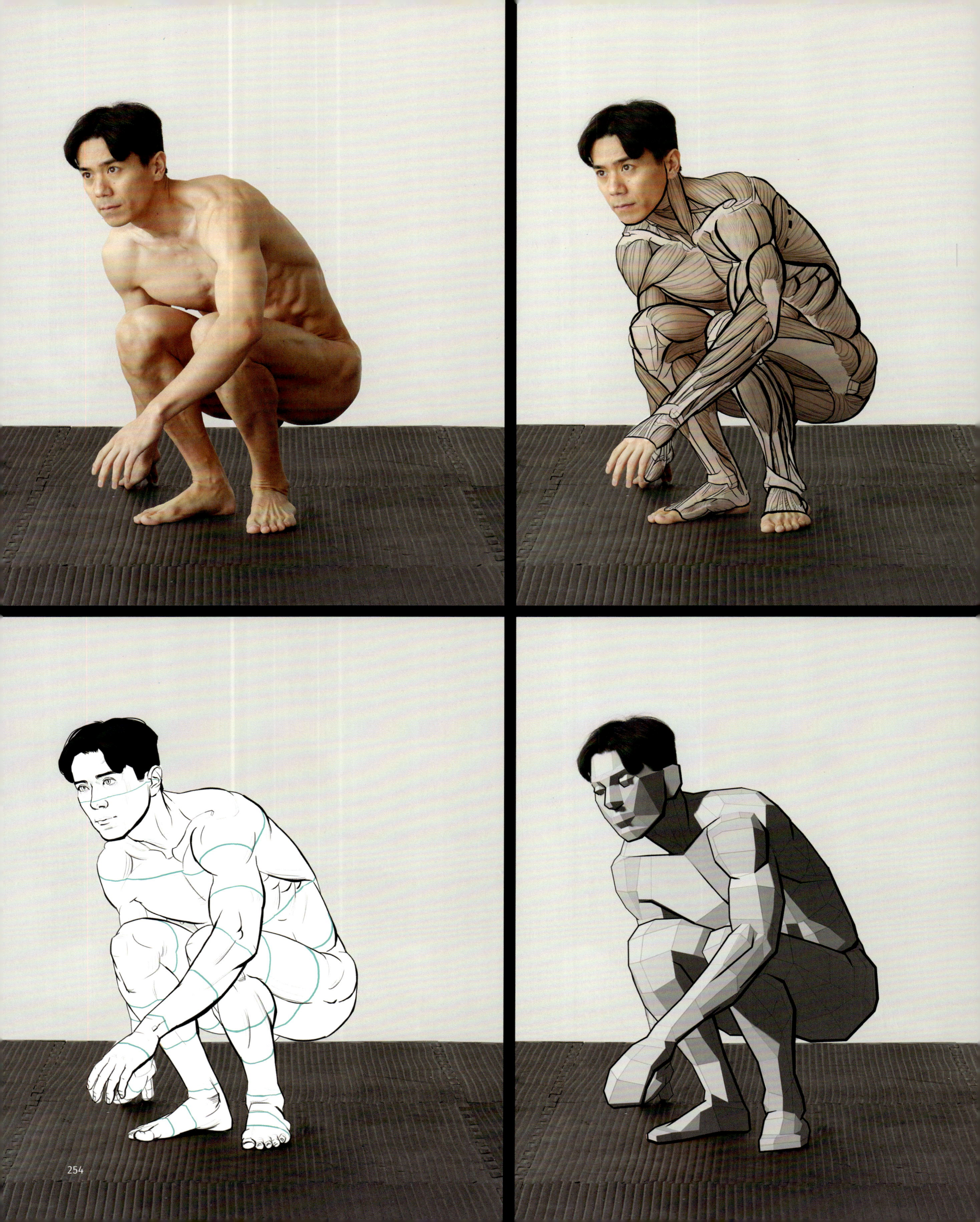

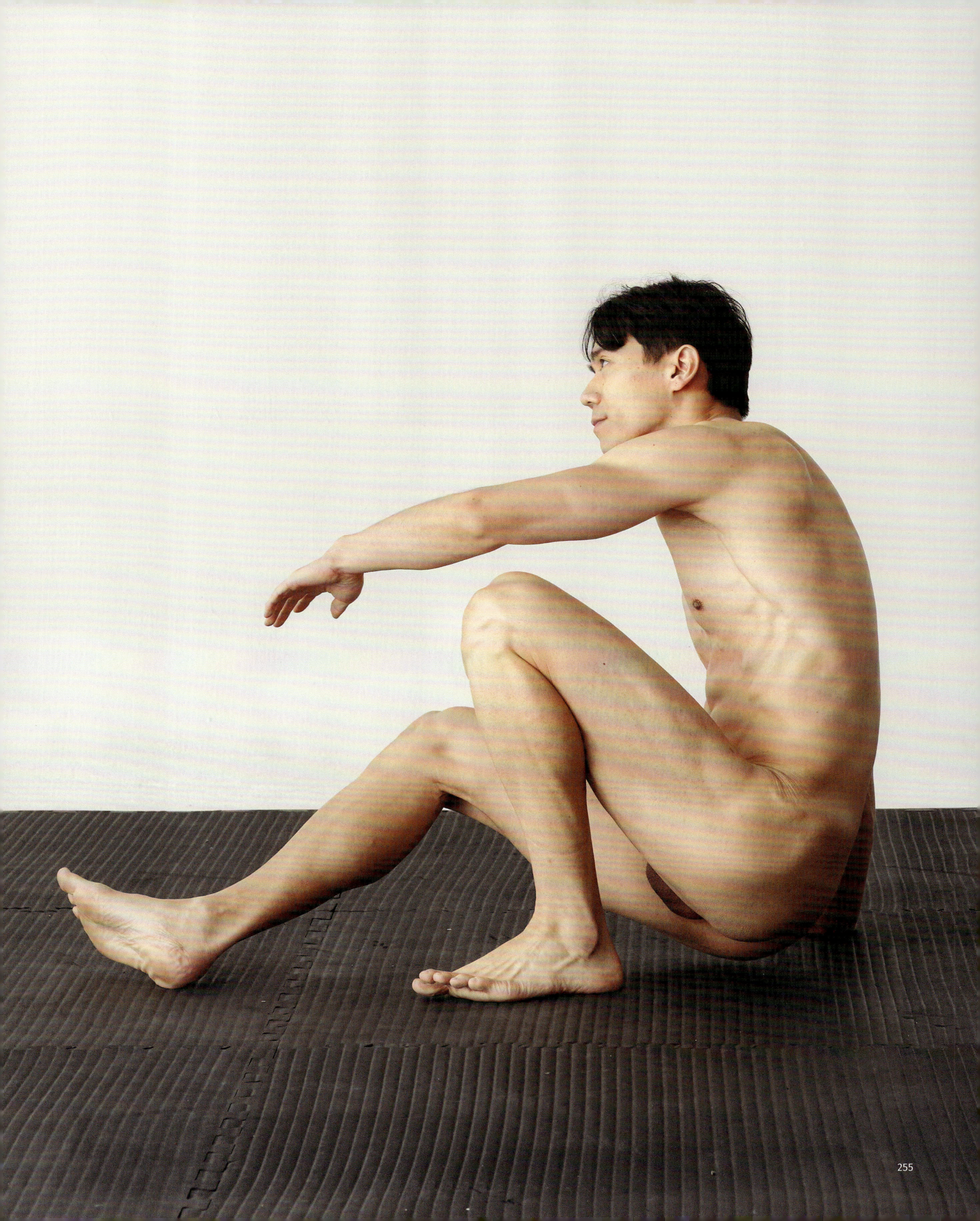

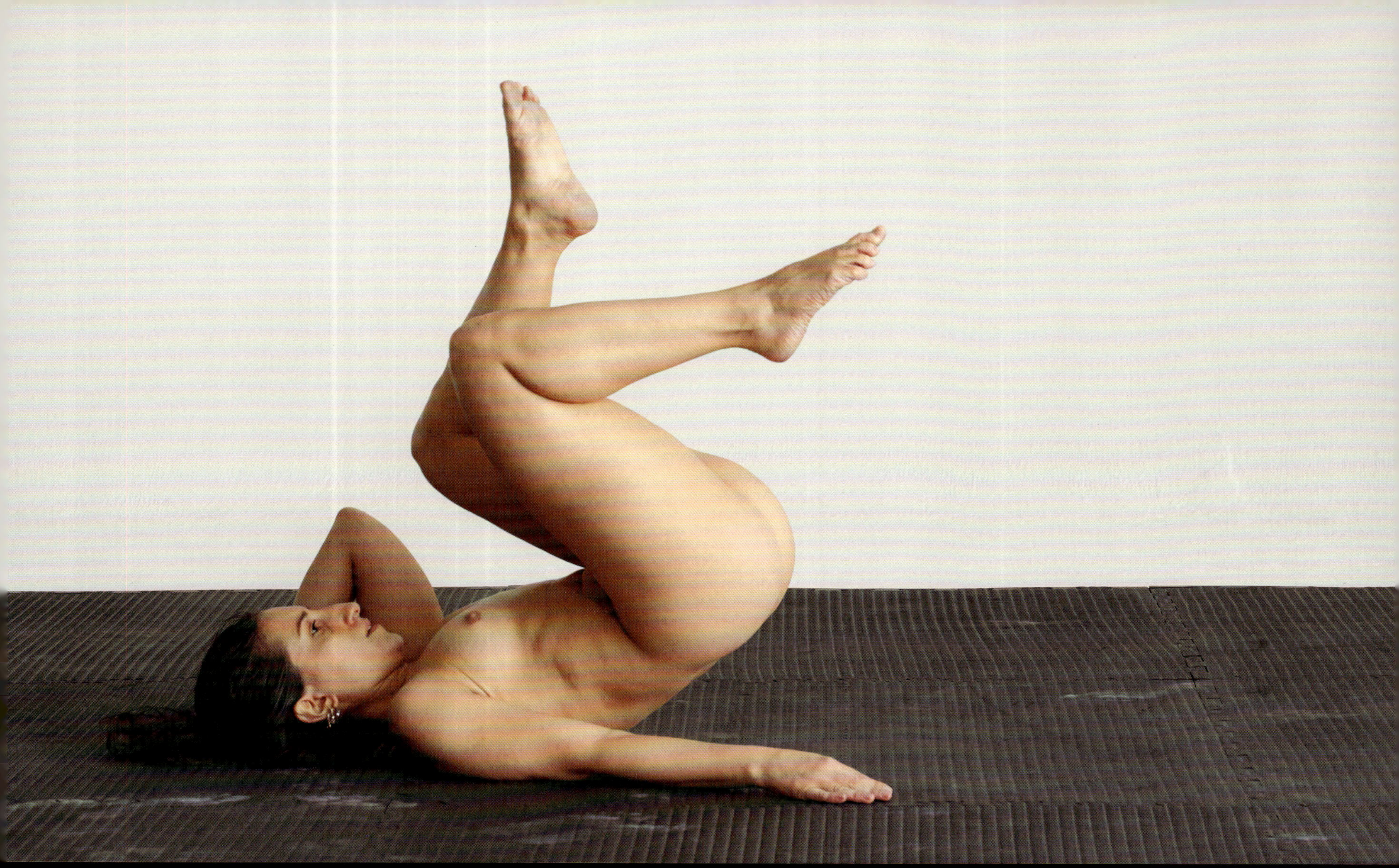

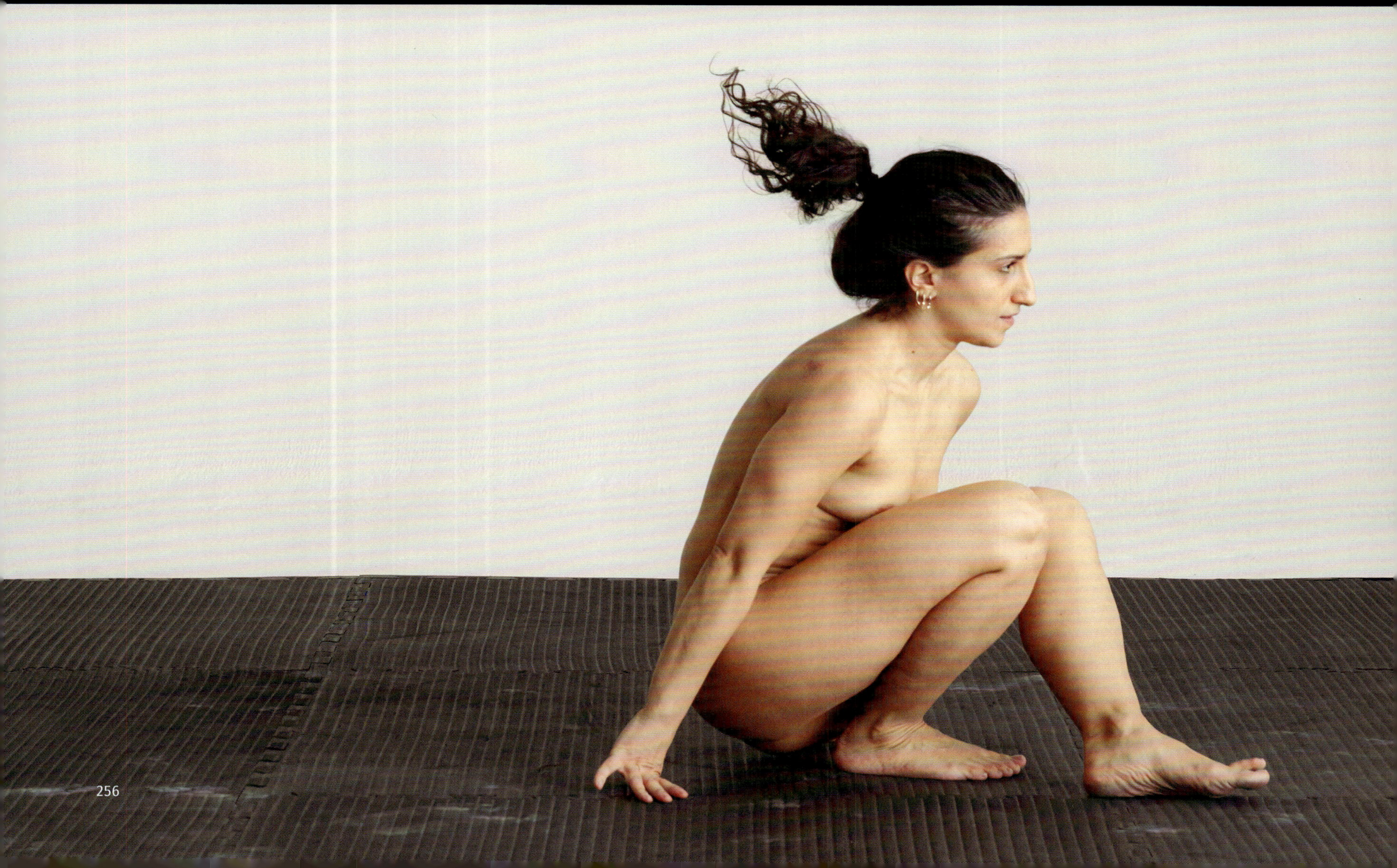

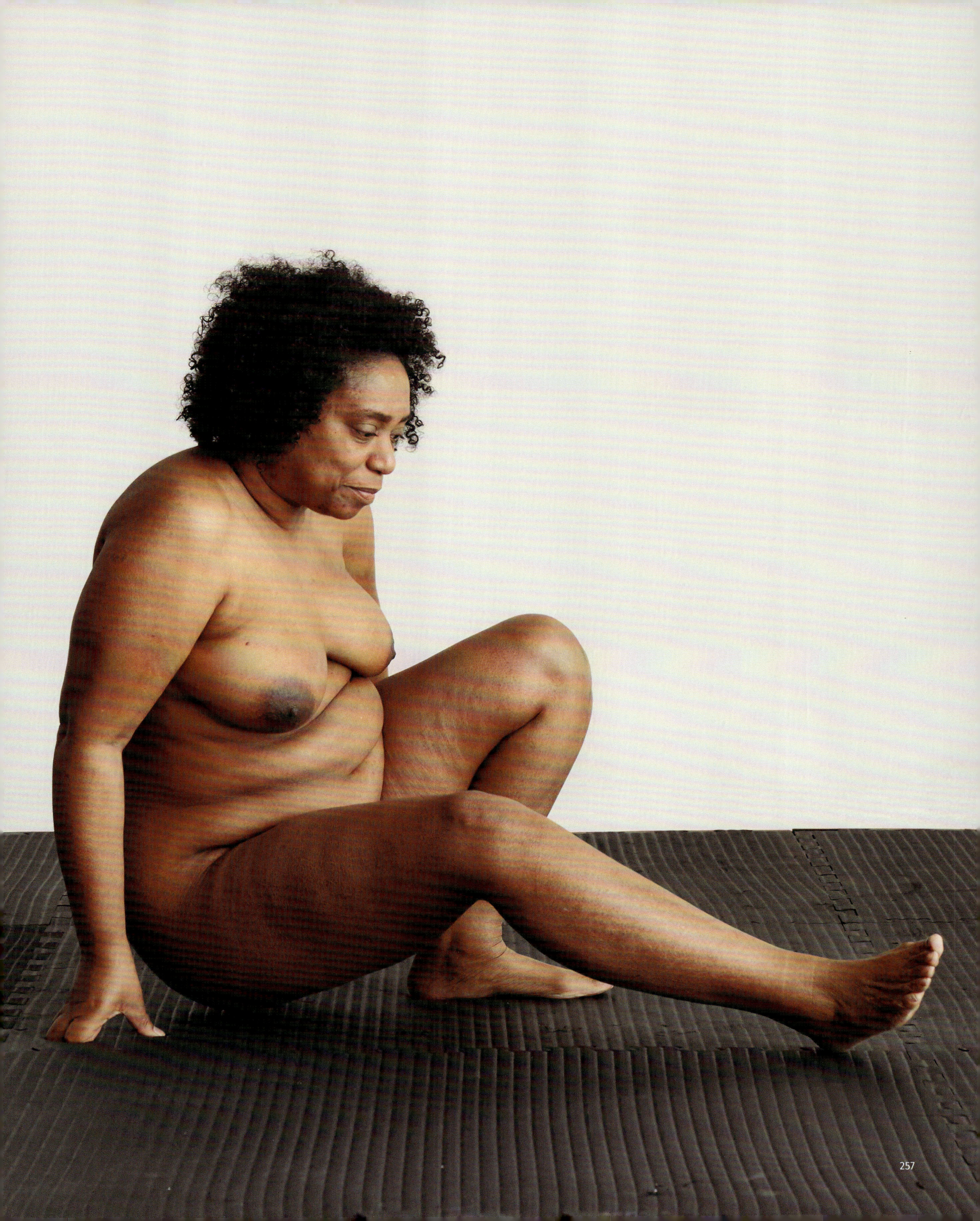

Batting a ball

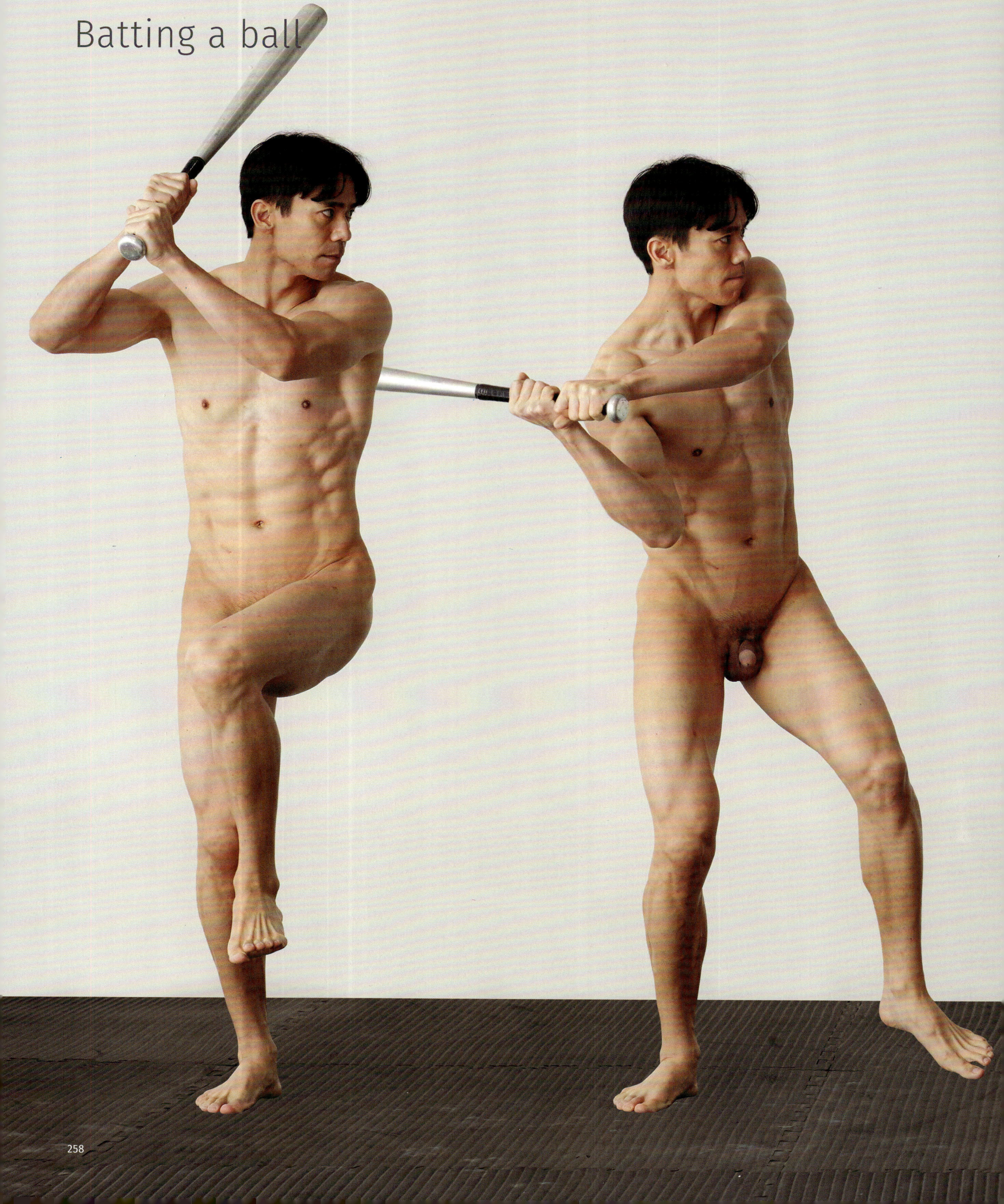

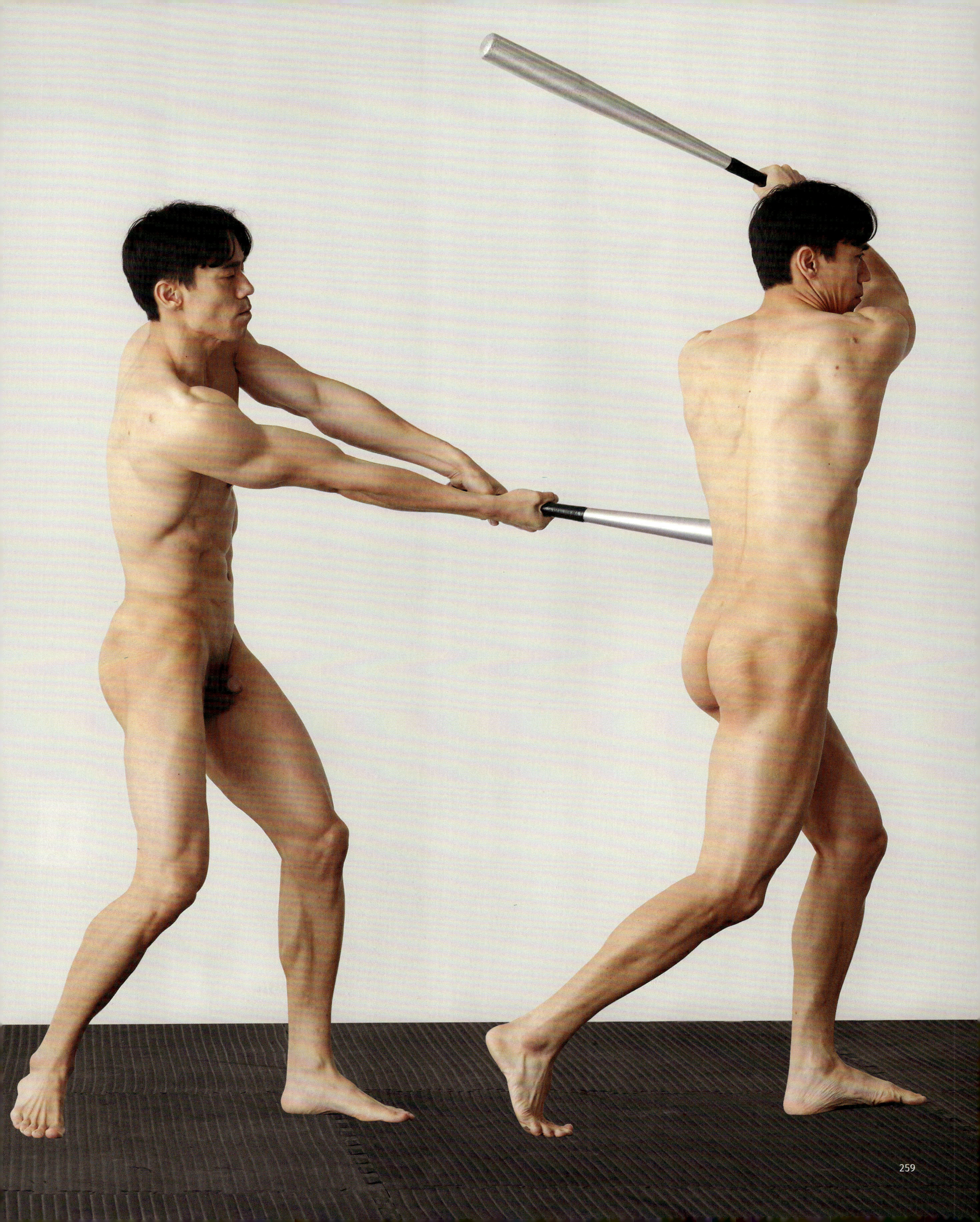

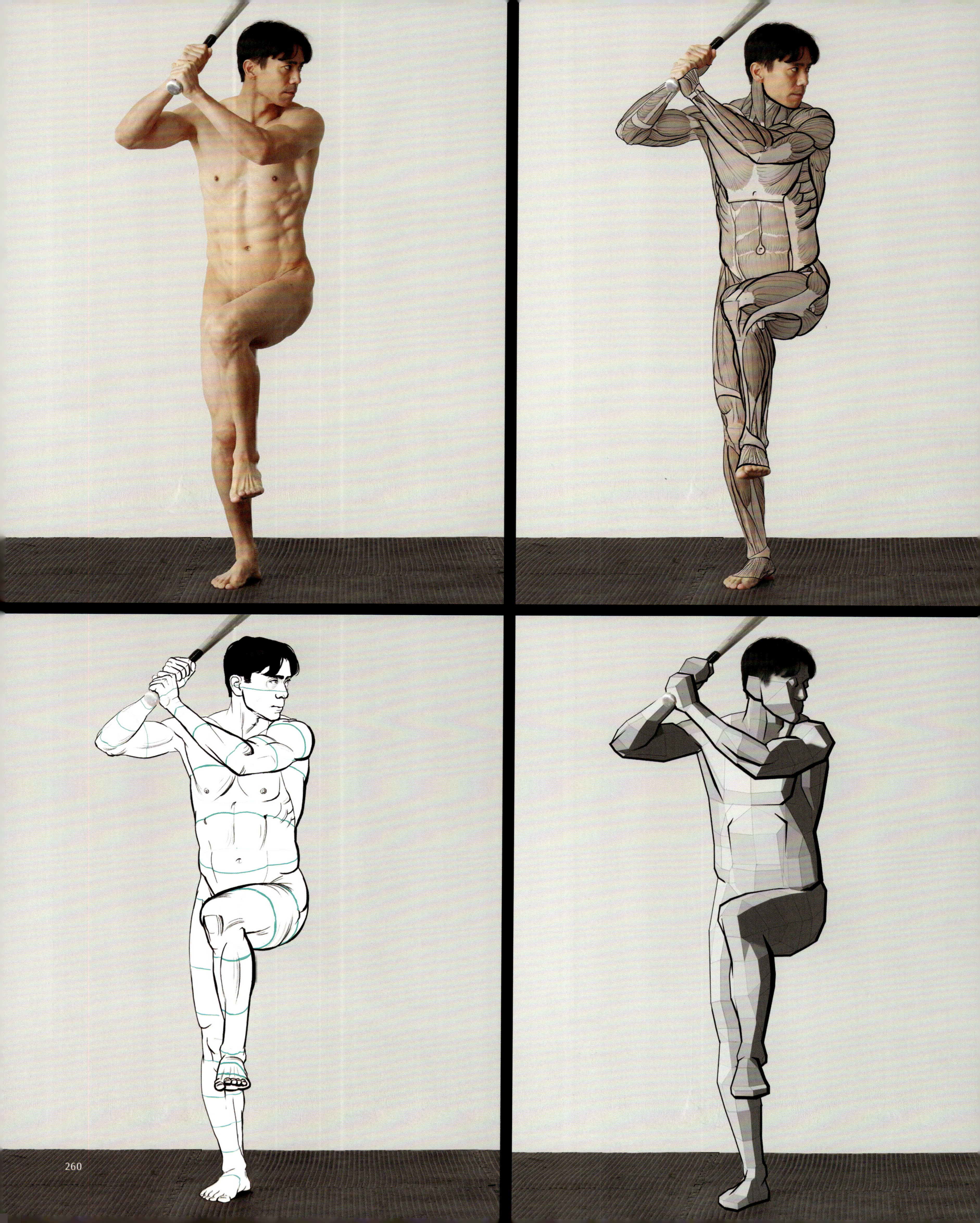

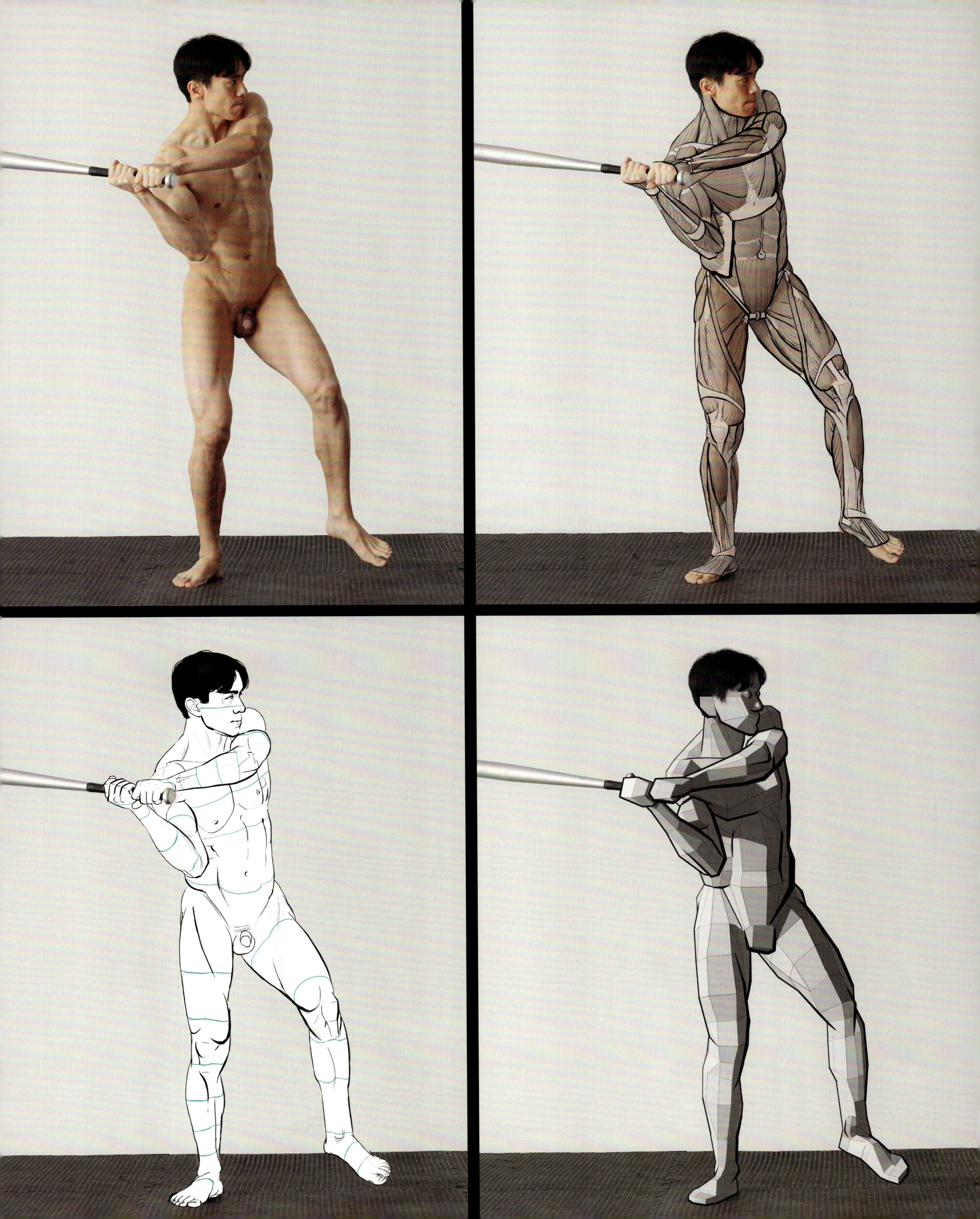

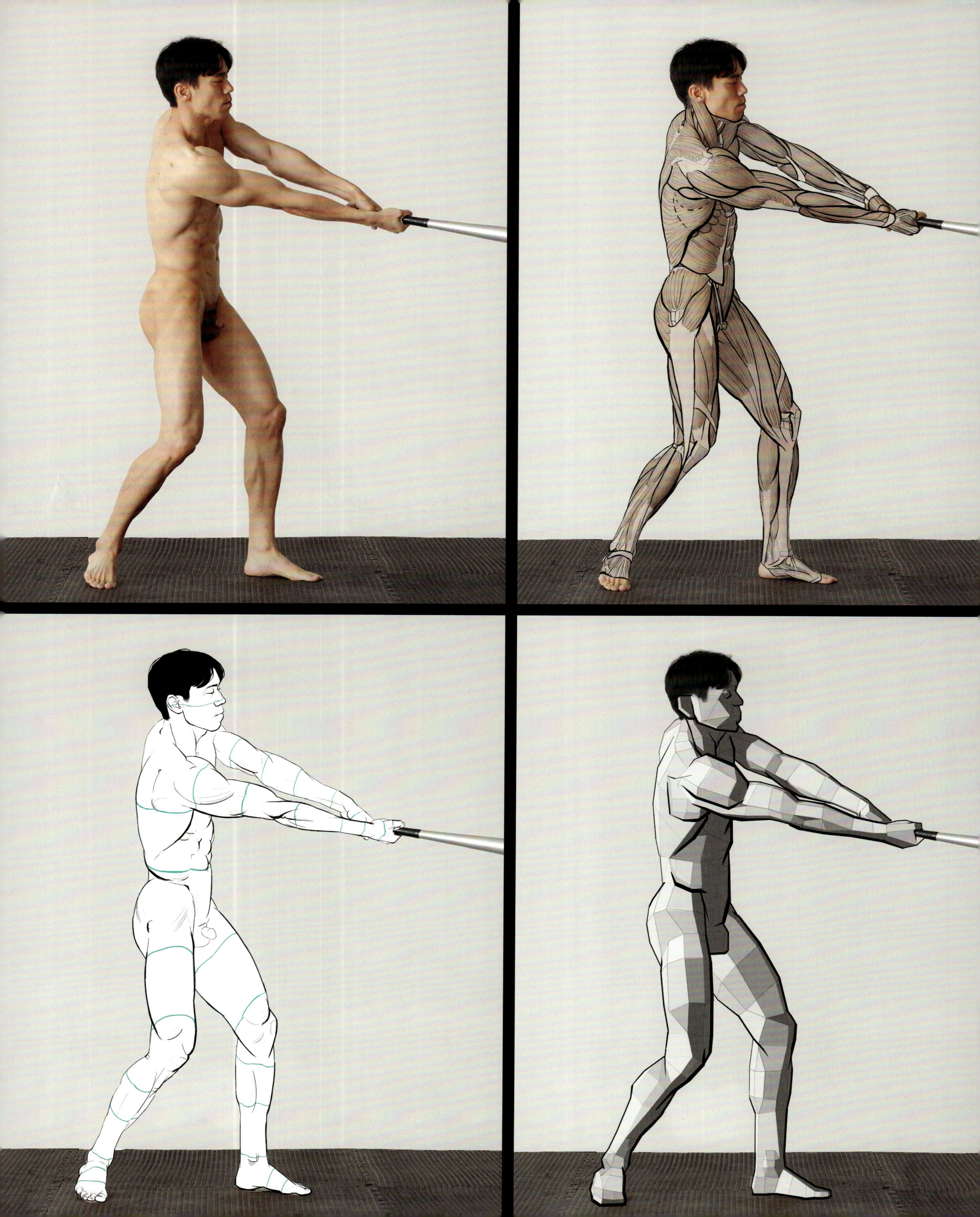

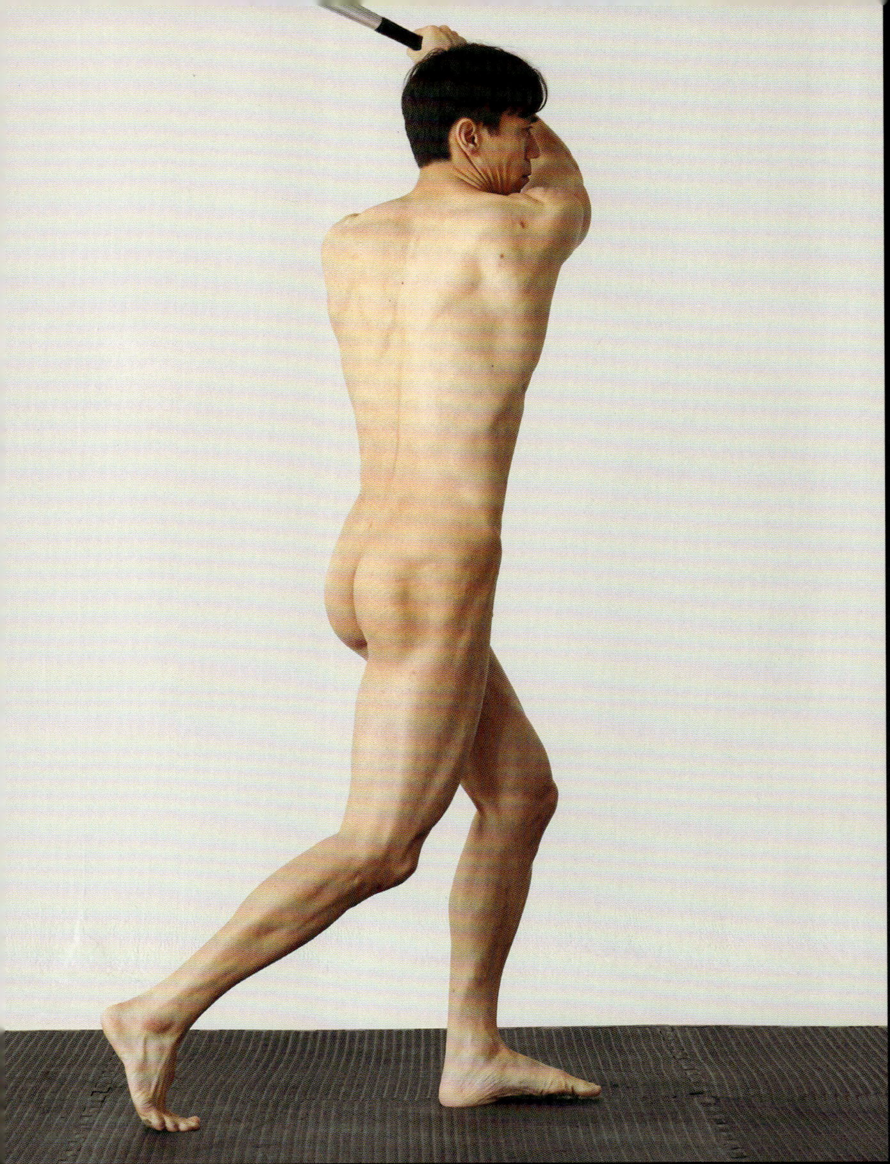
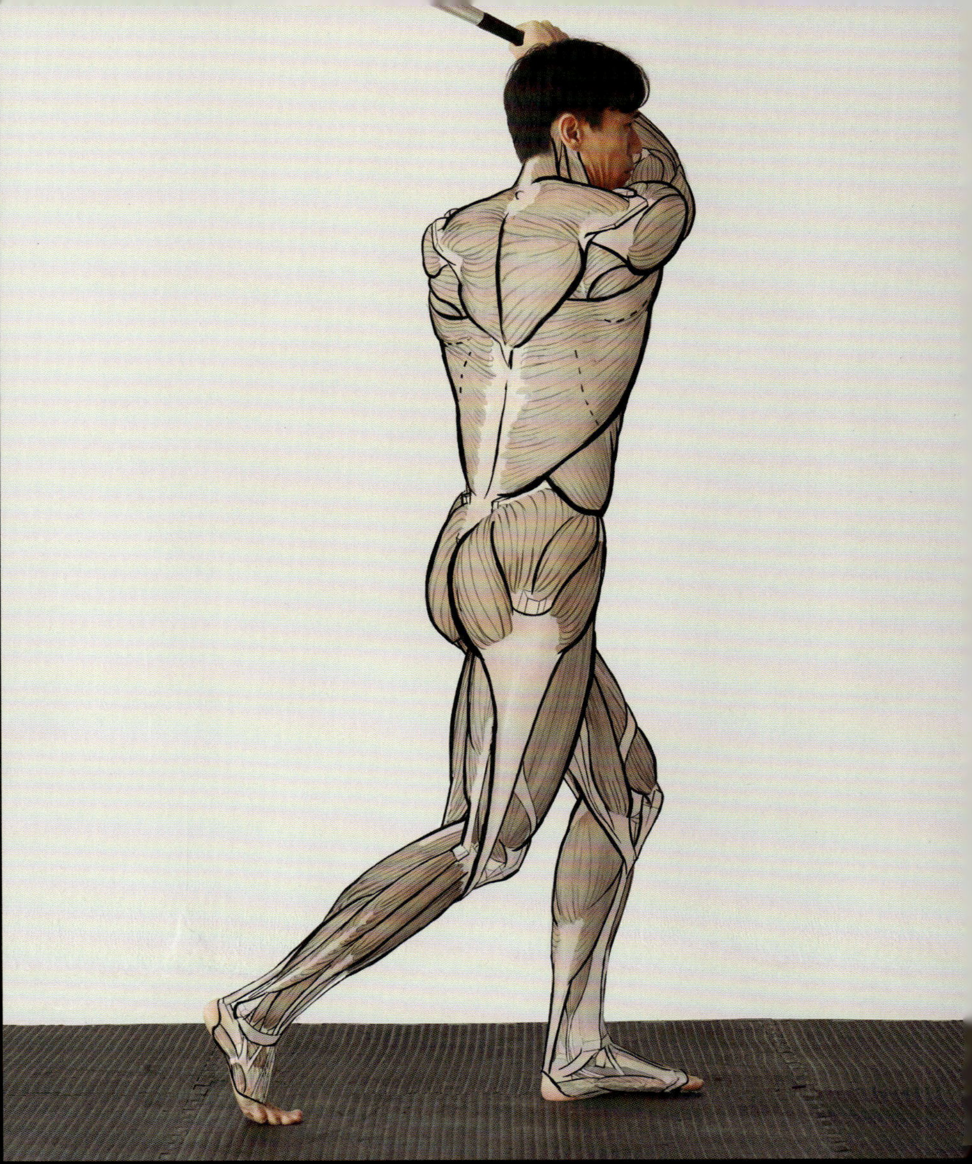
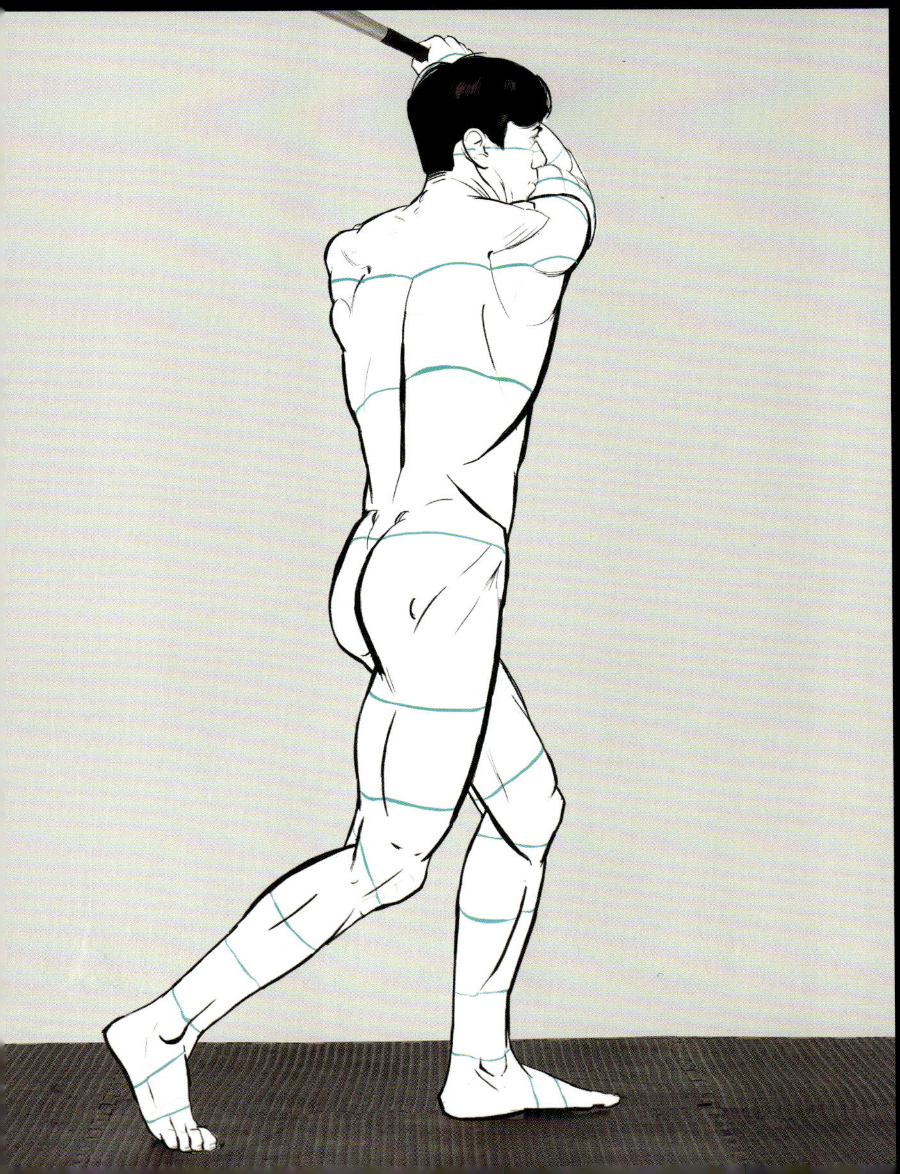
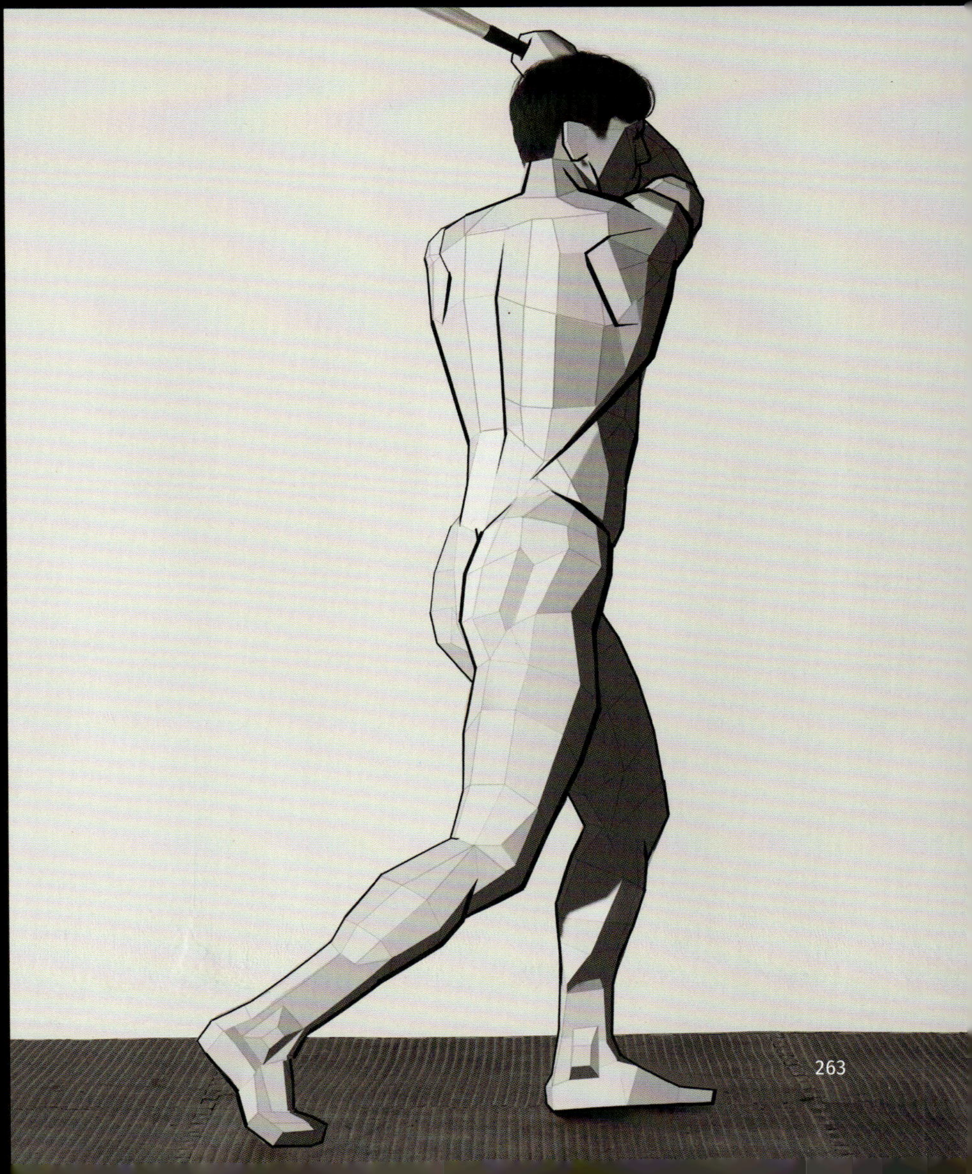

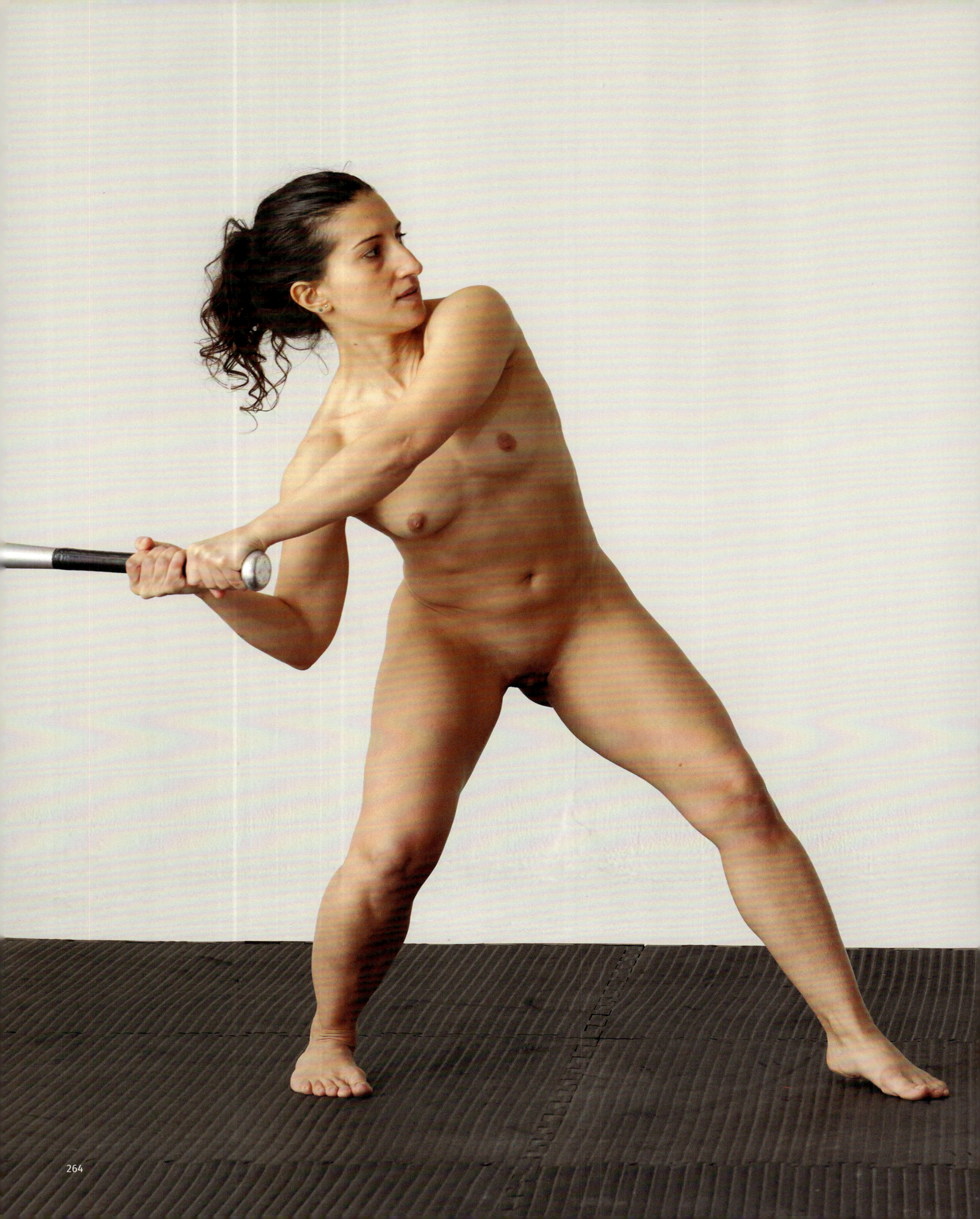

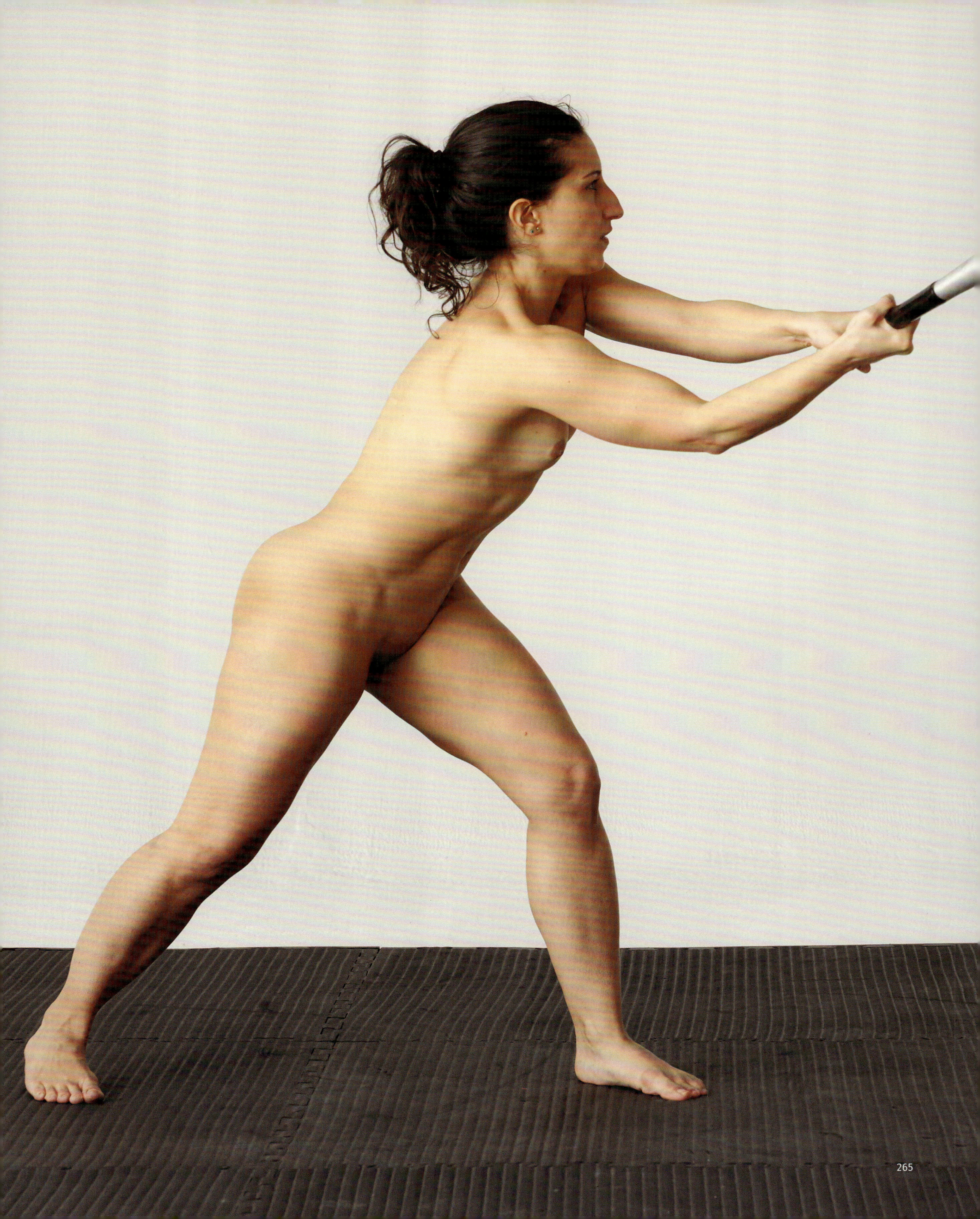

Catching a ball

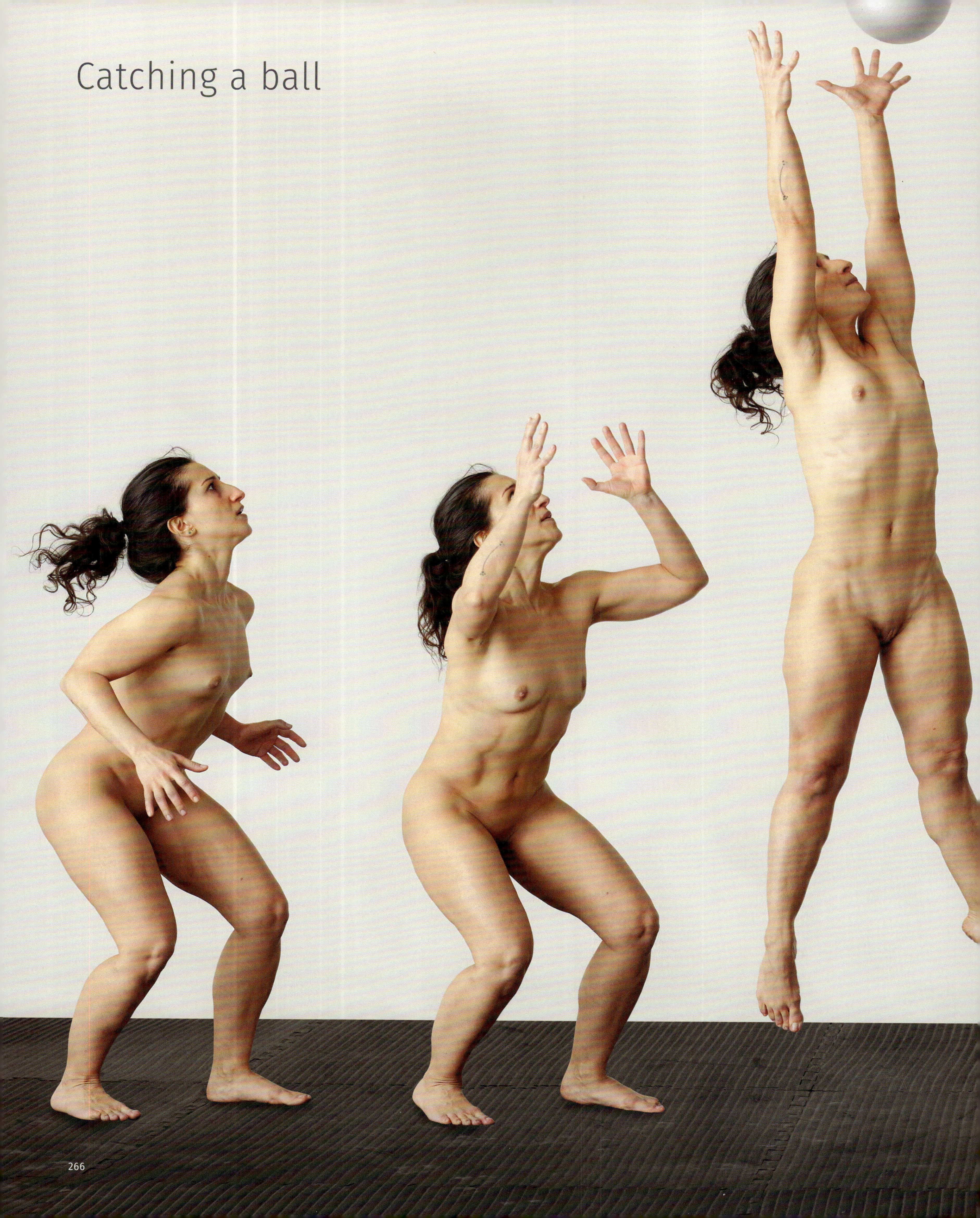

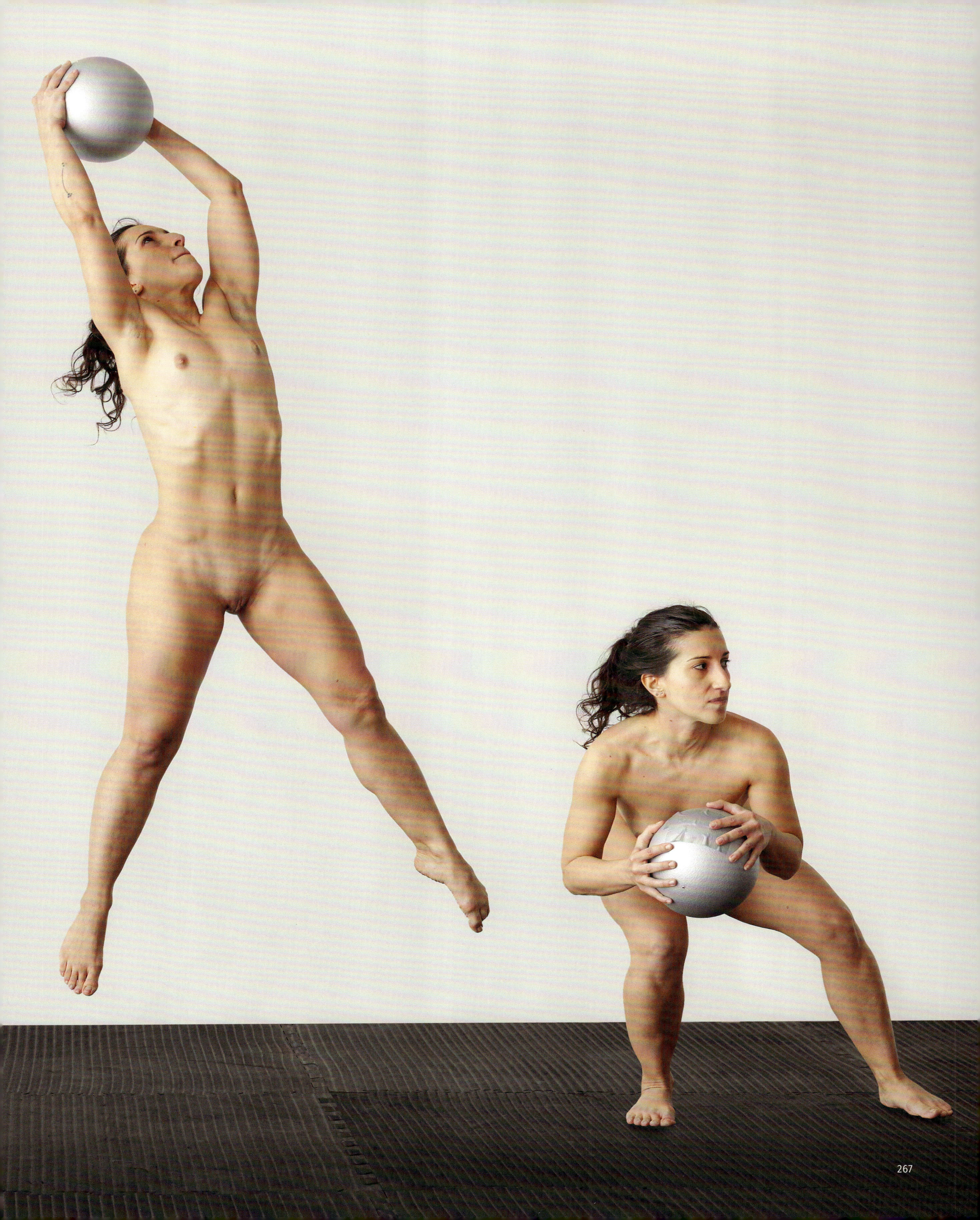

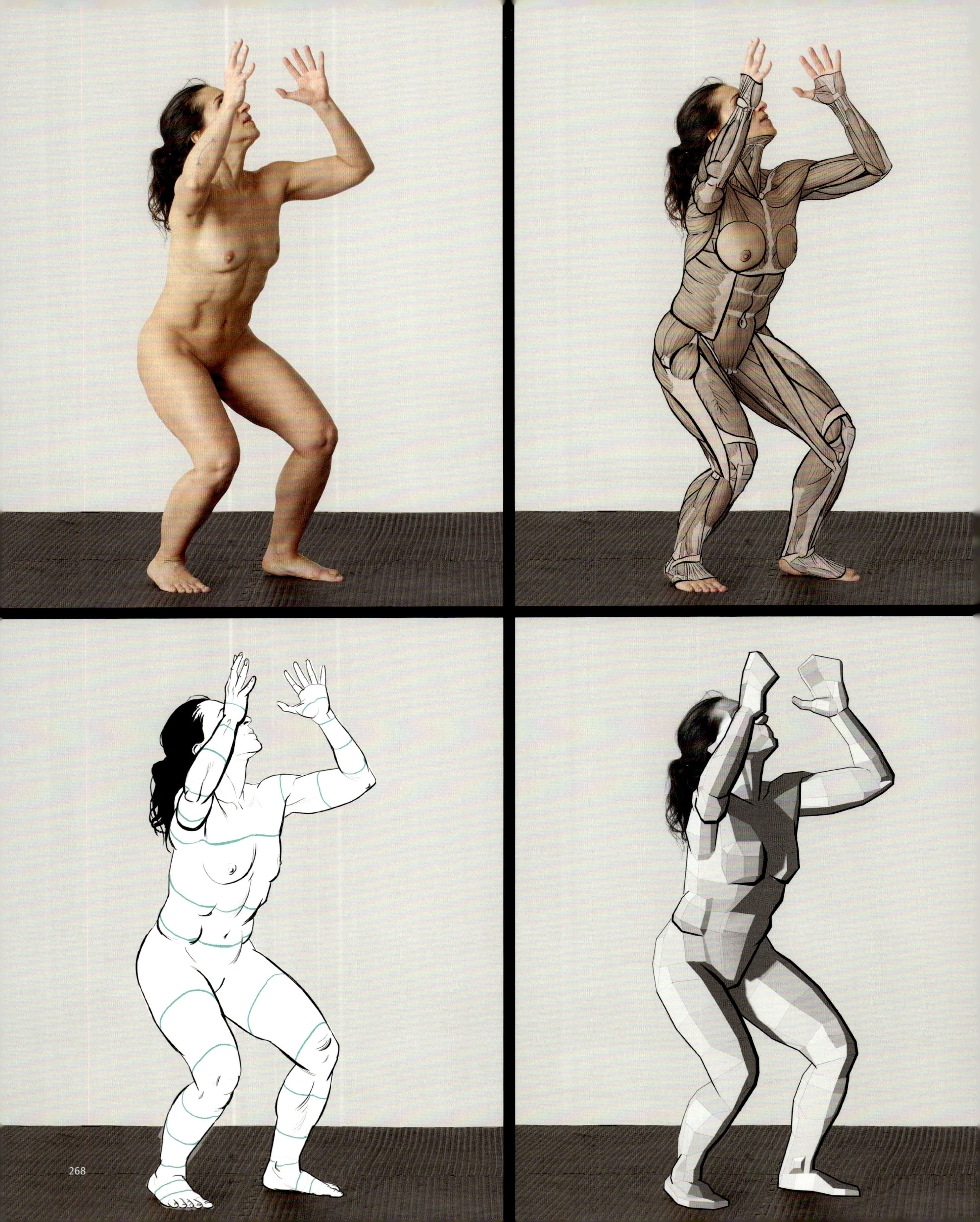

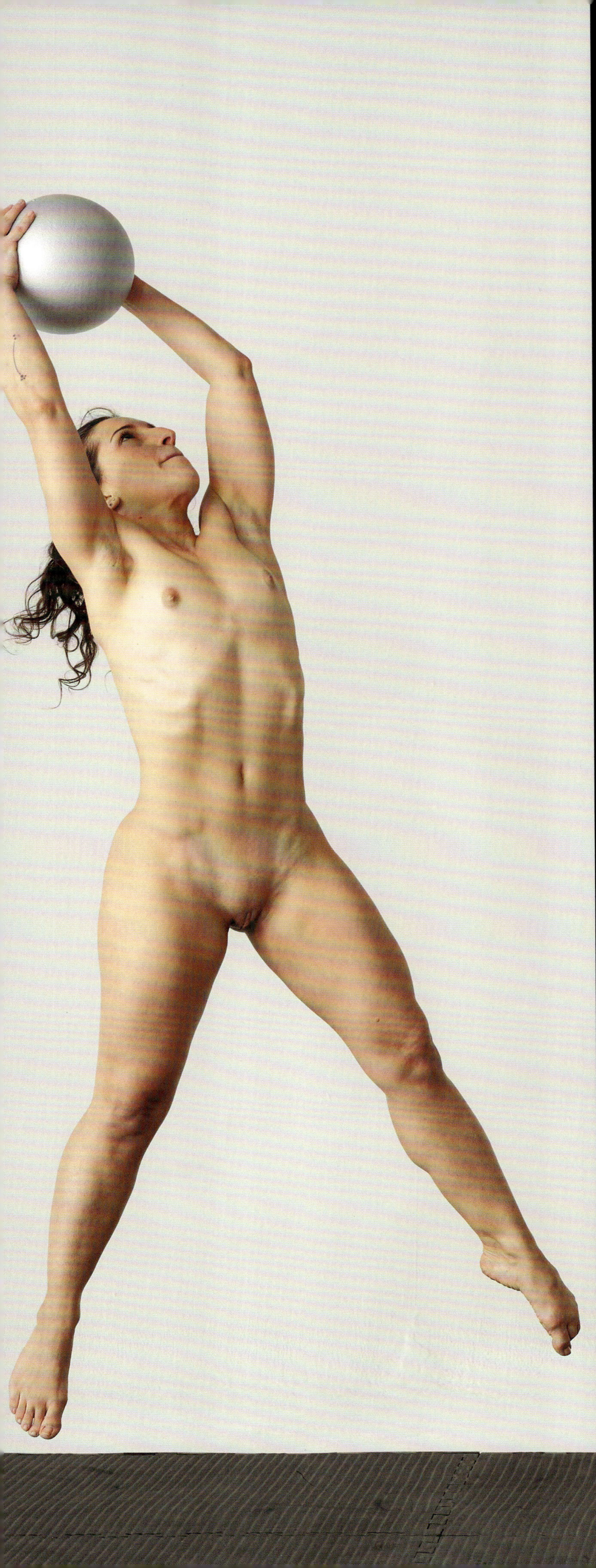

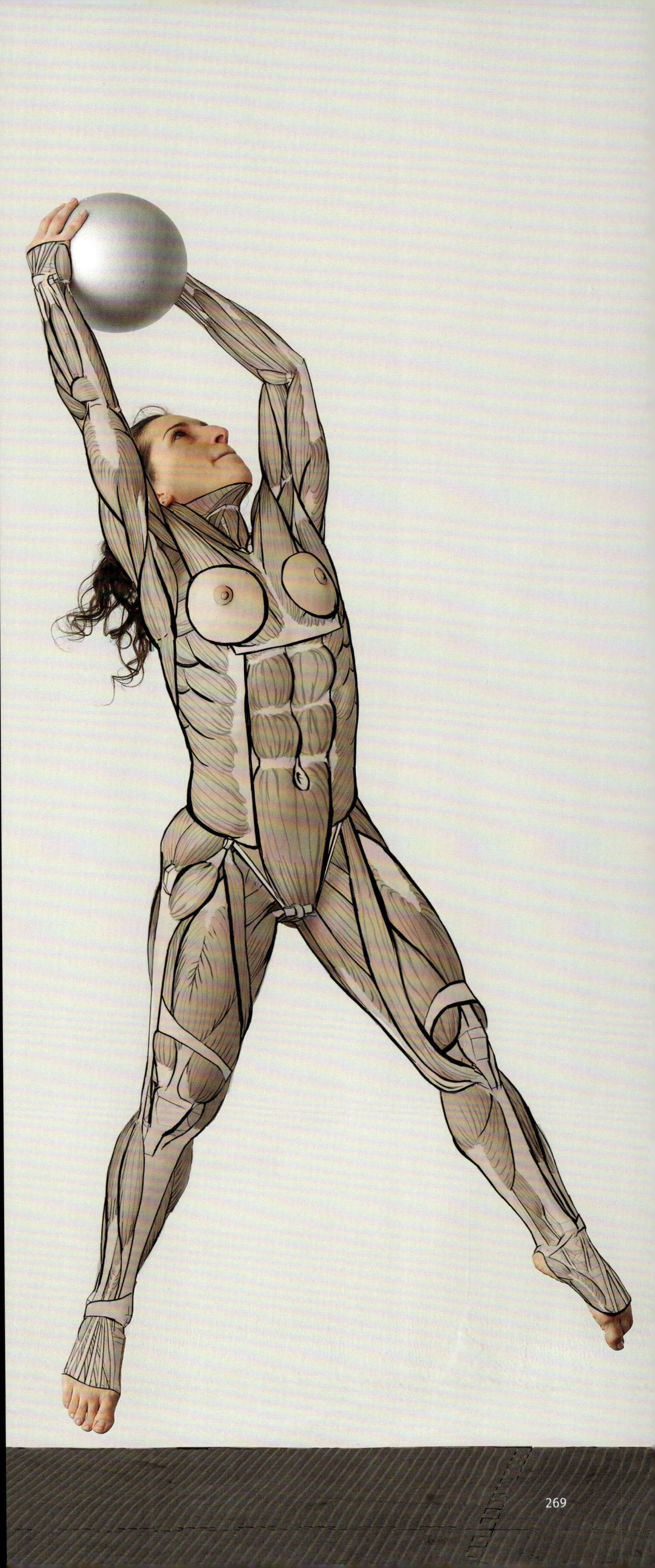

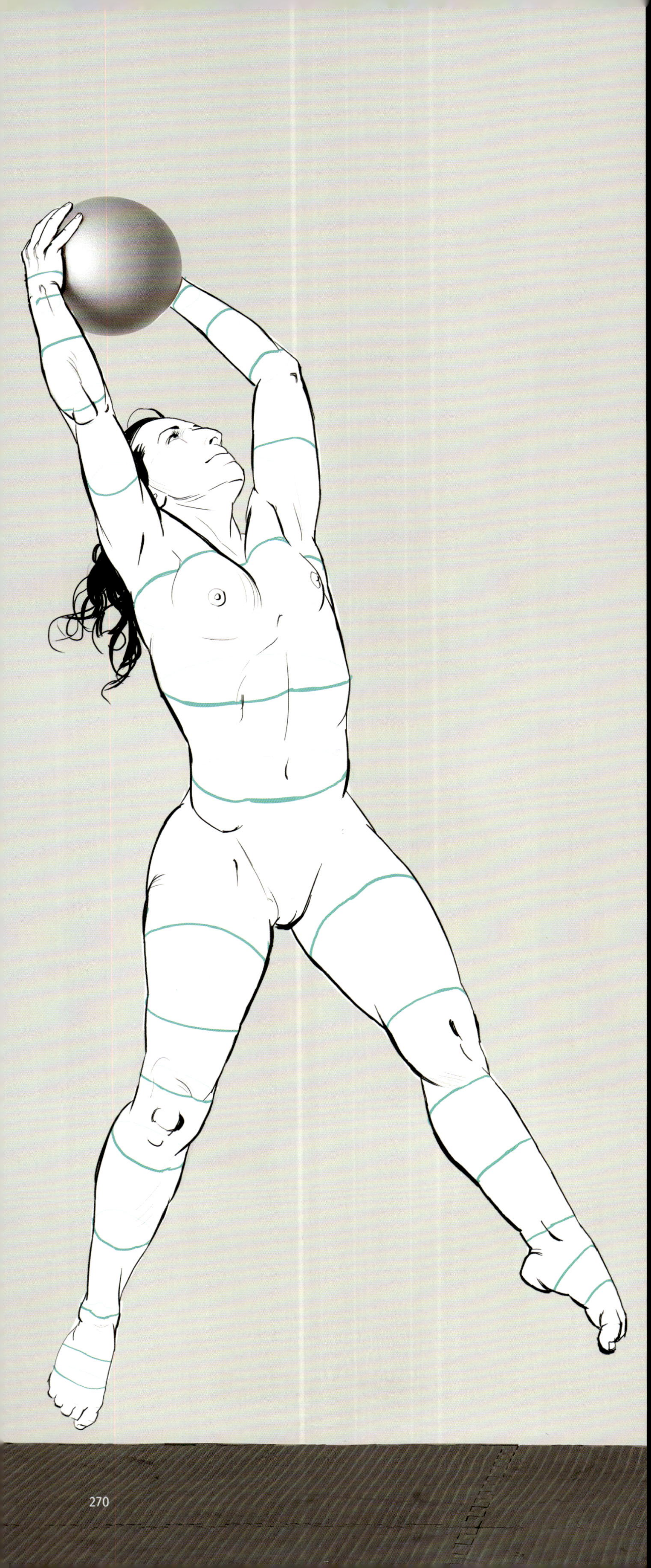

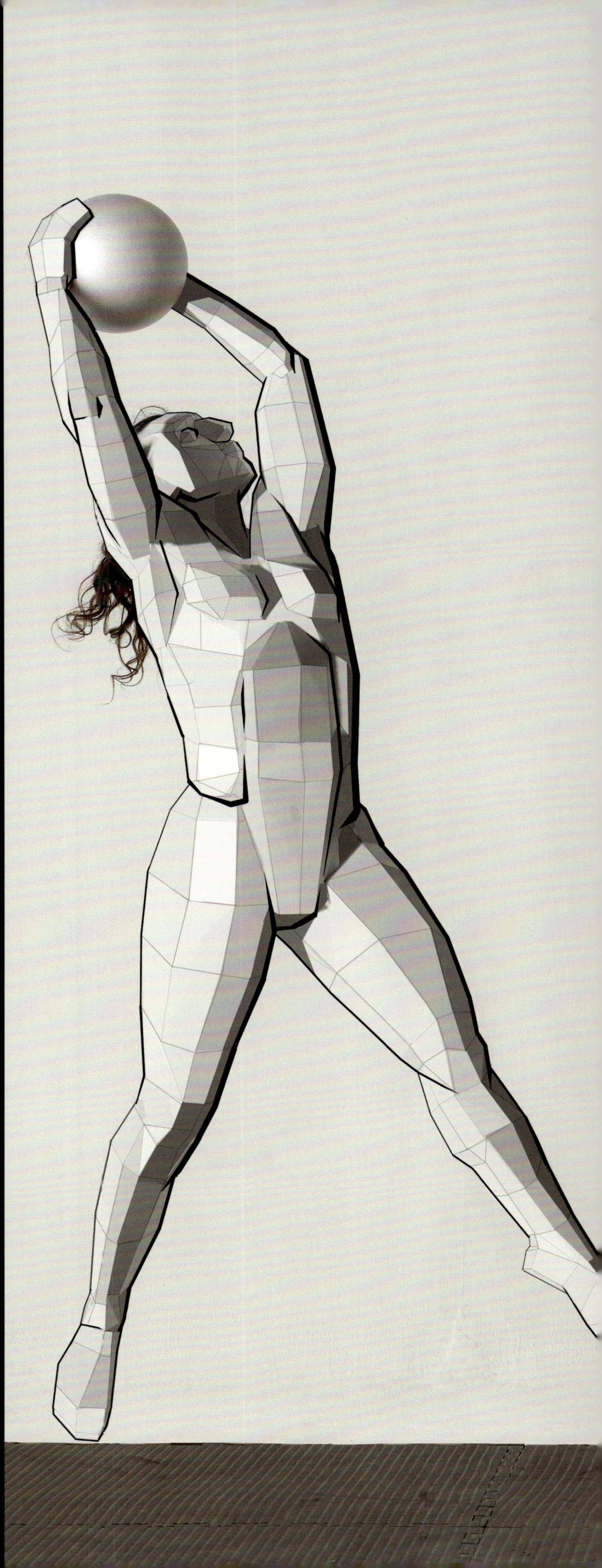

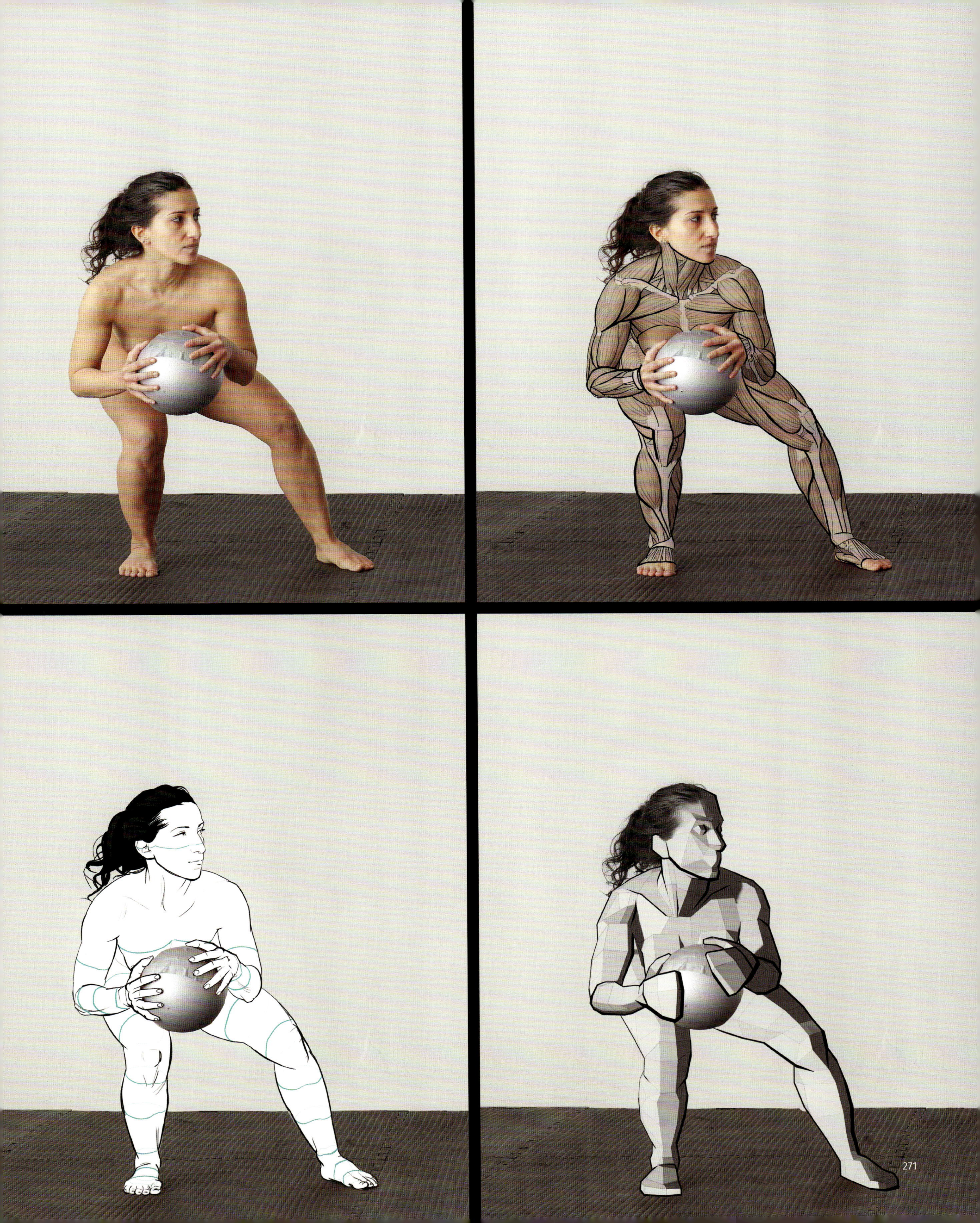

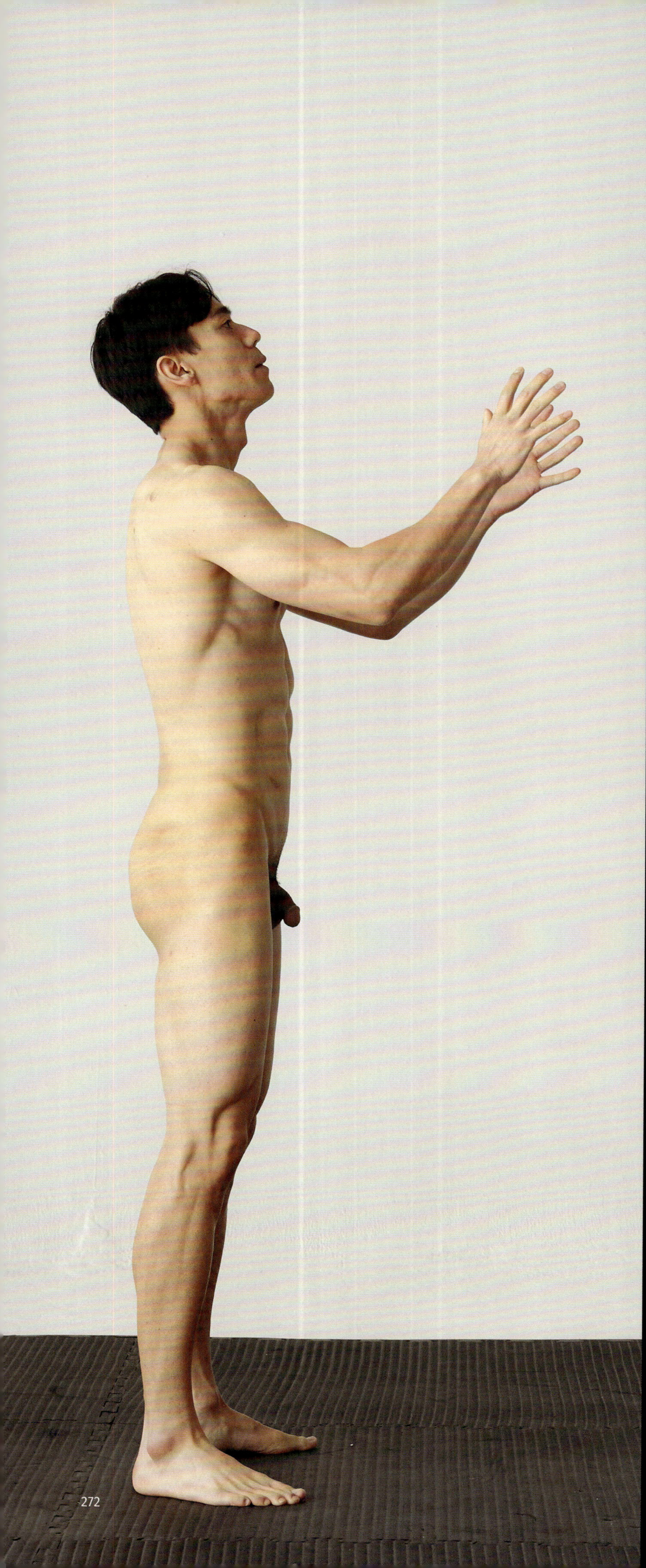

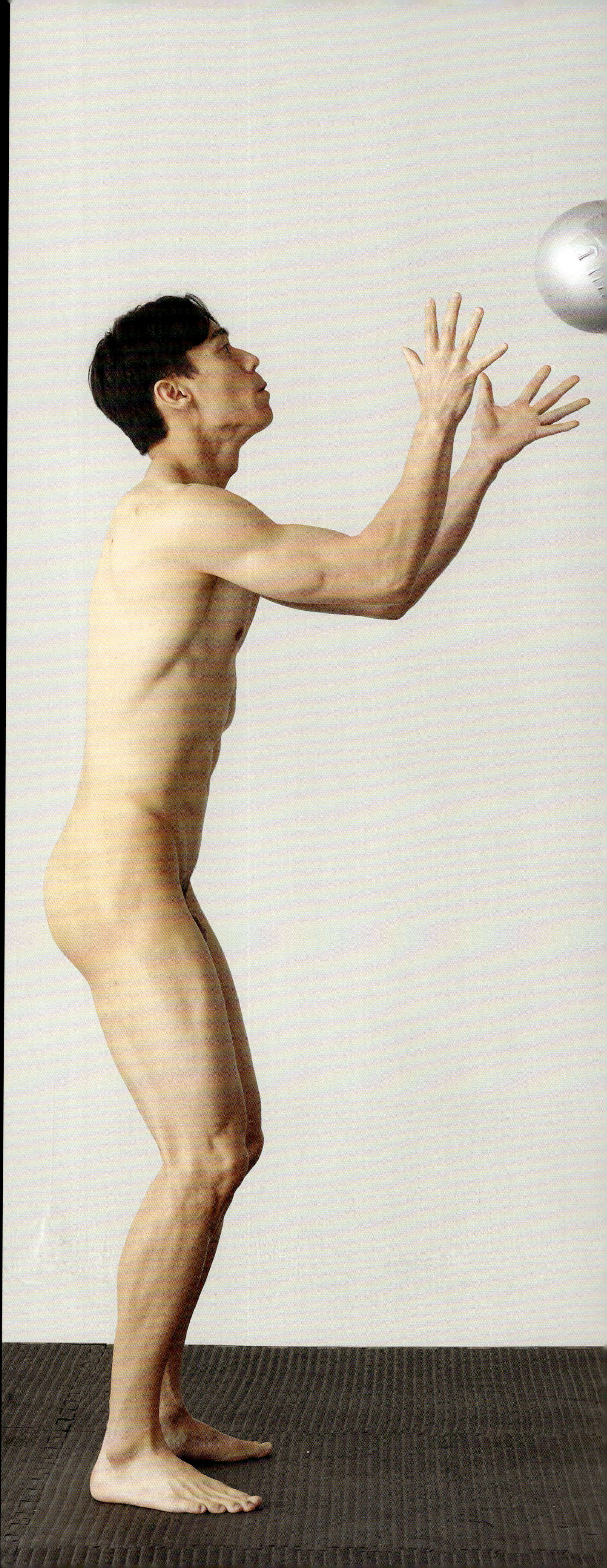

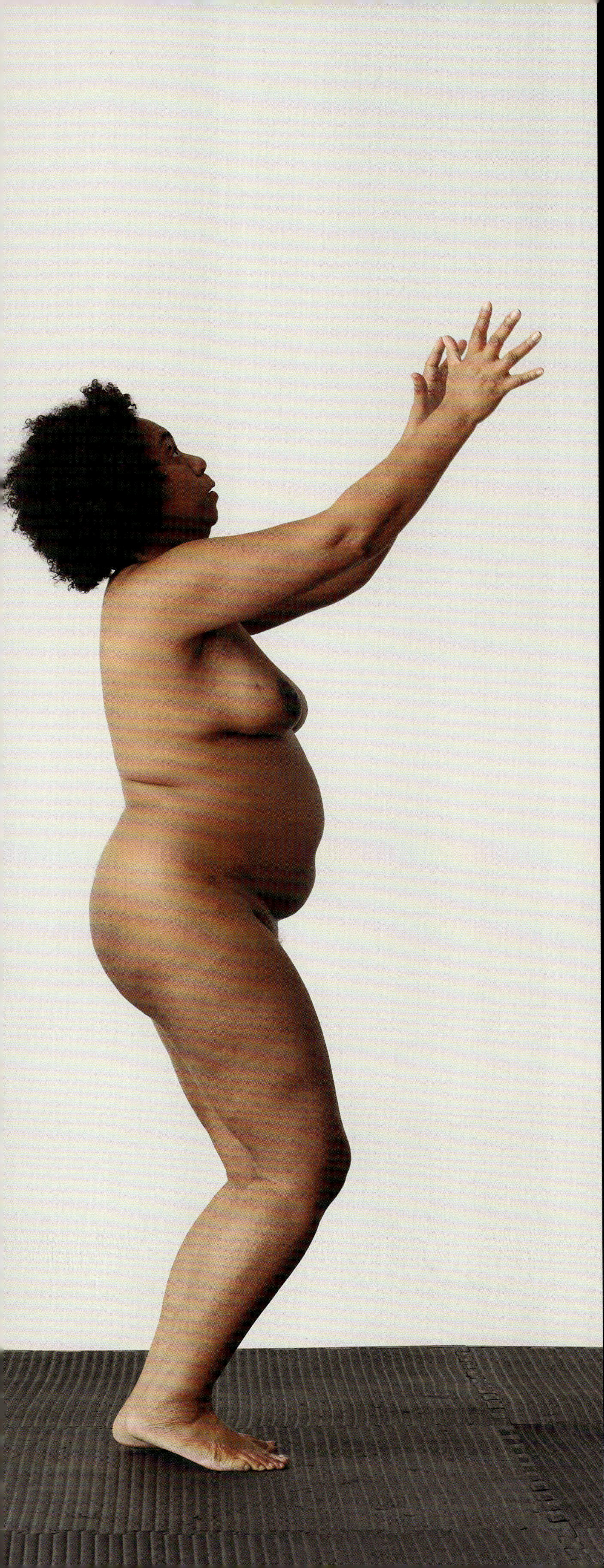

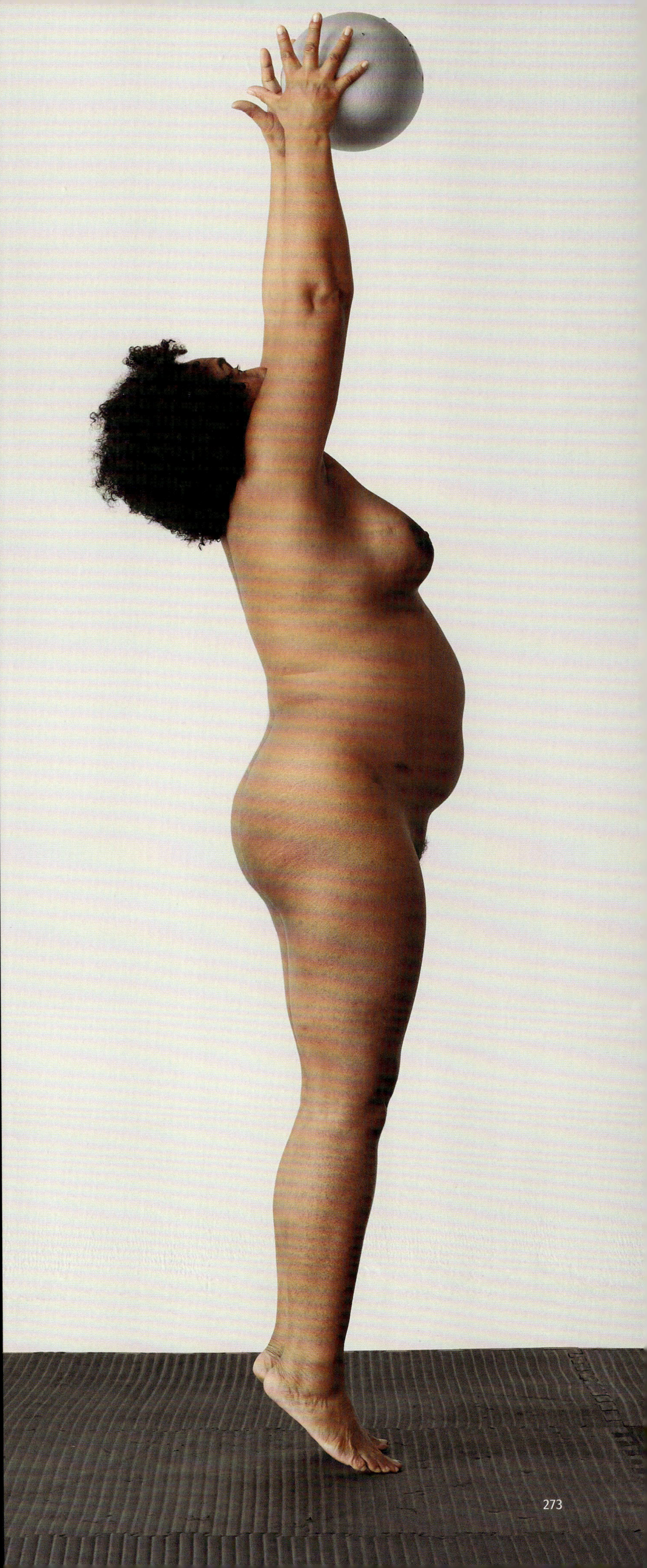

Kicking a ball

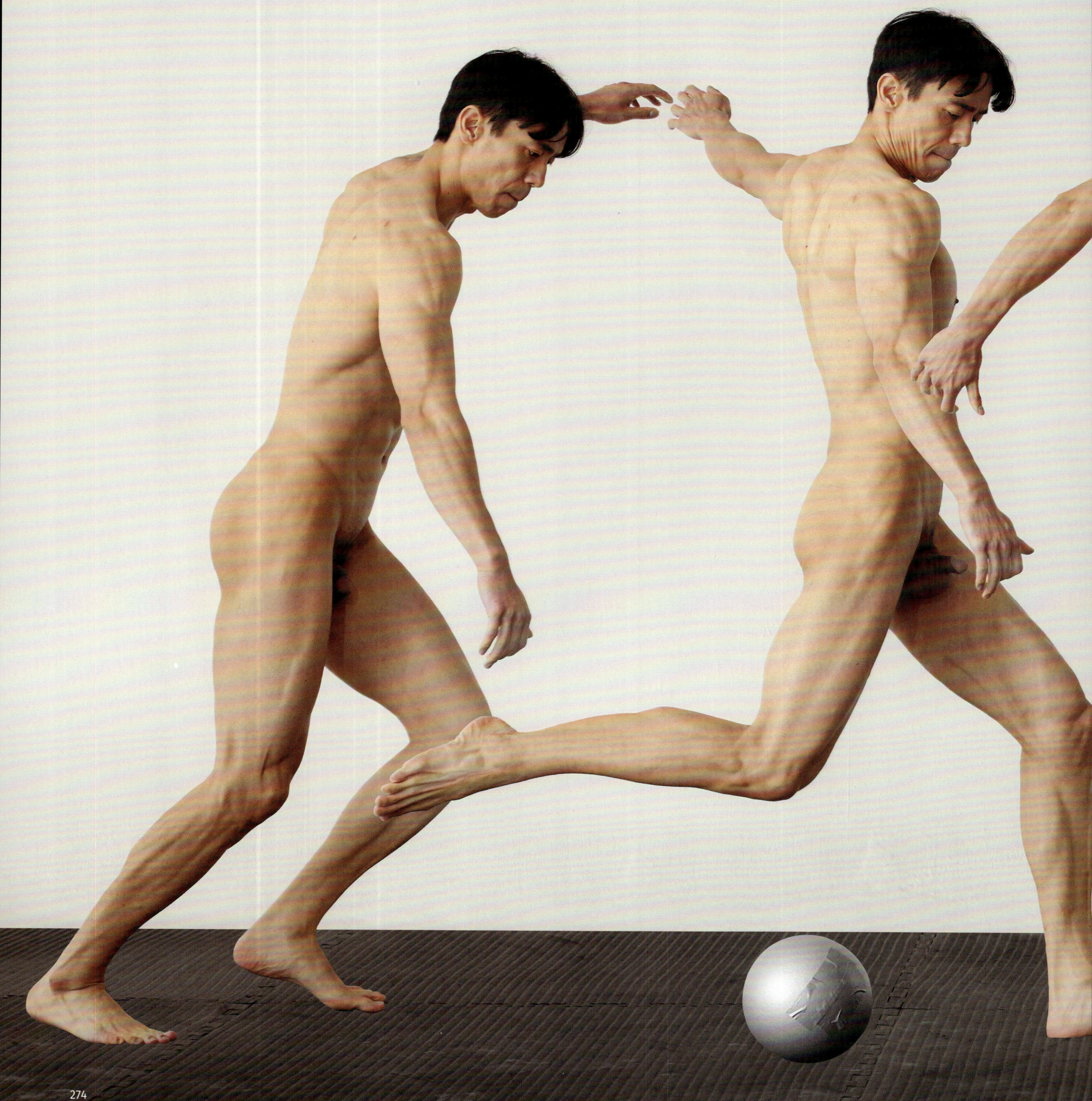

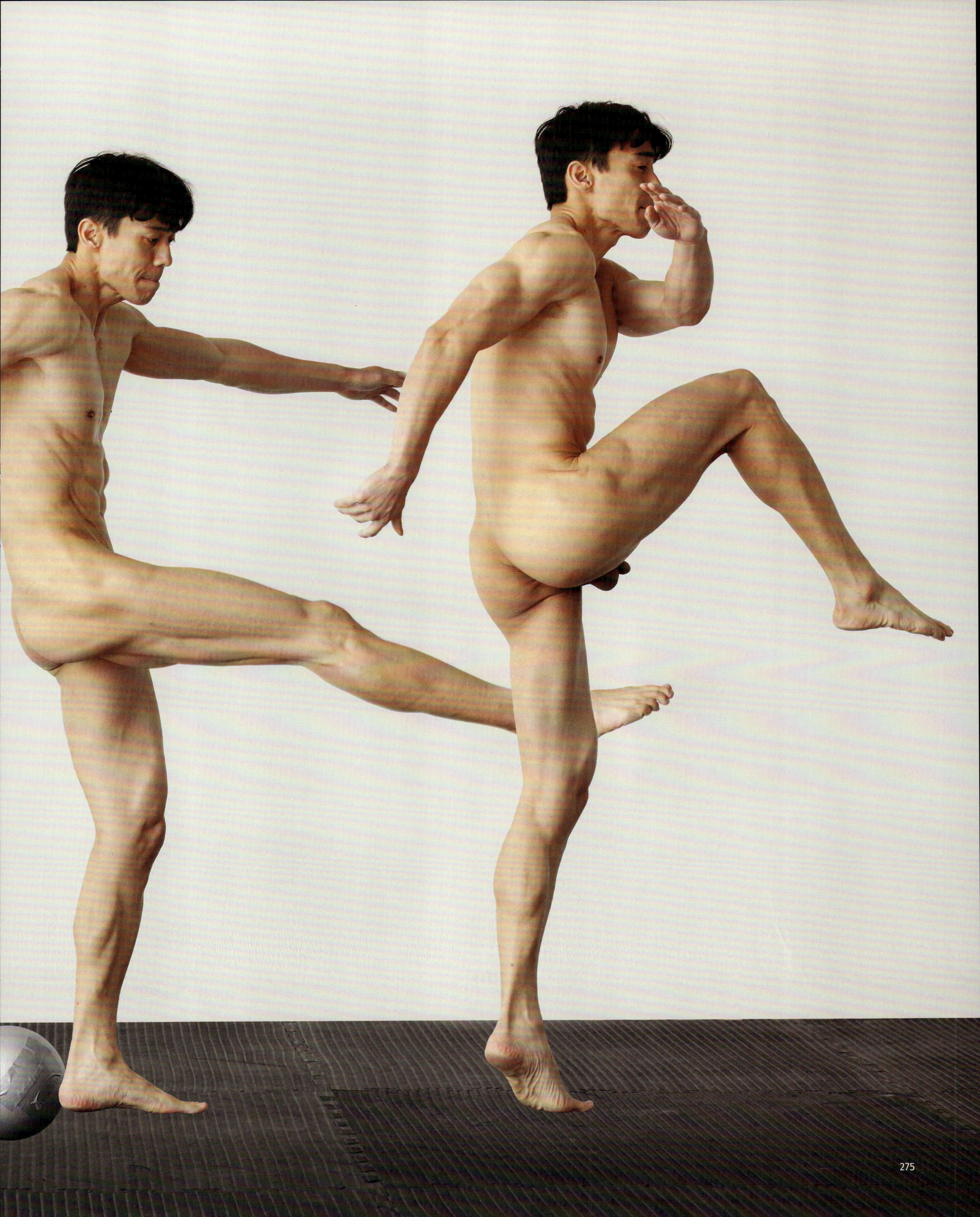

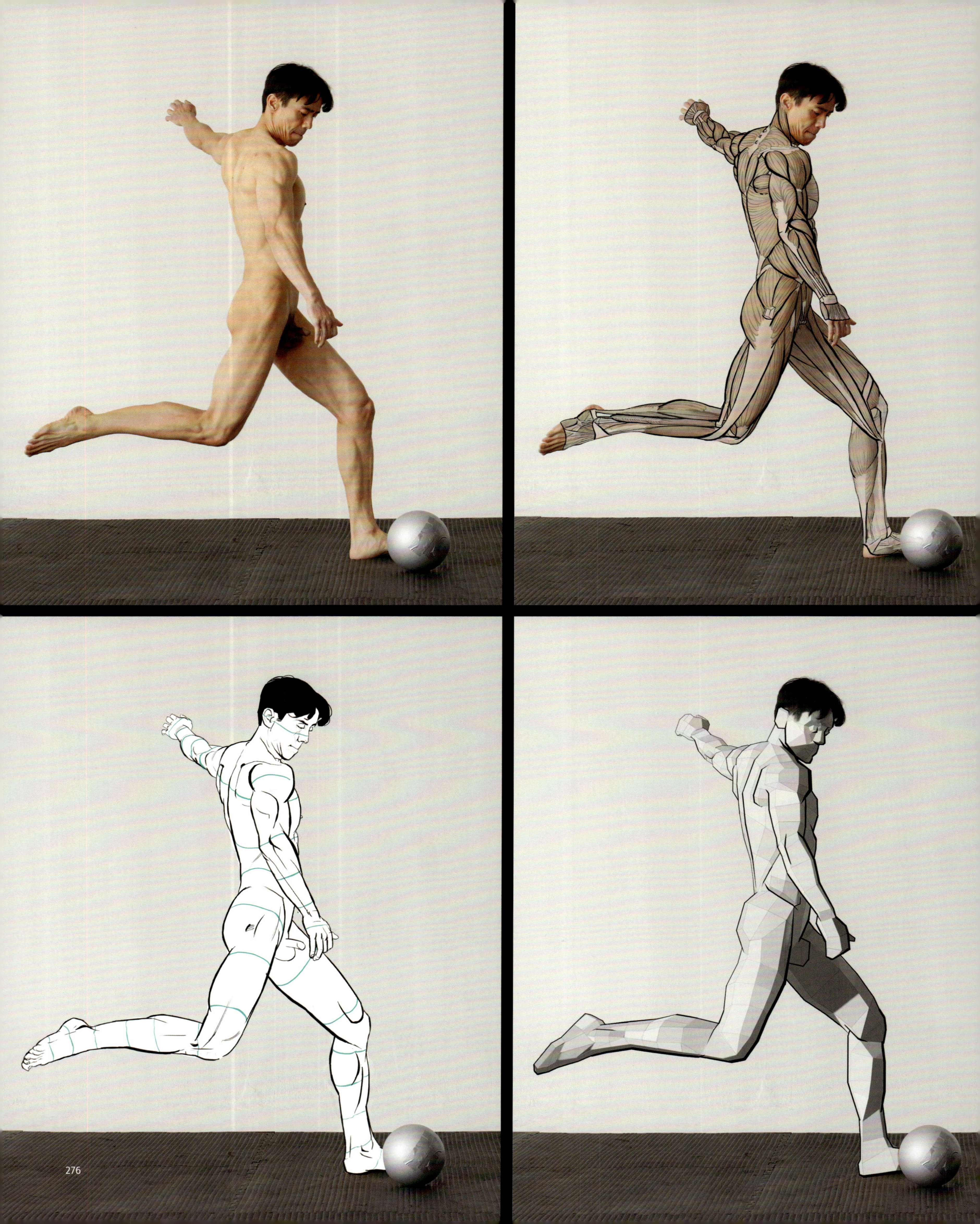

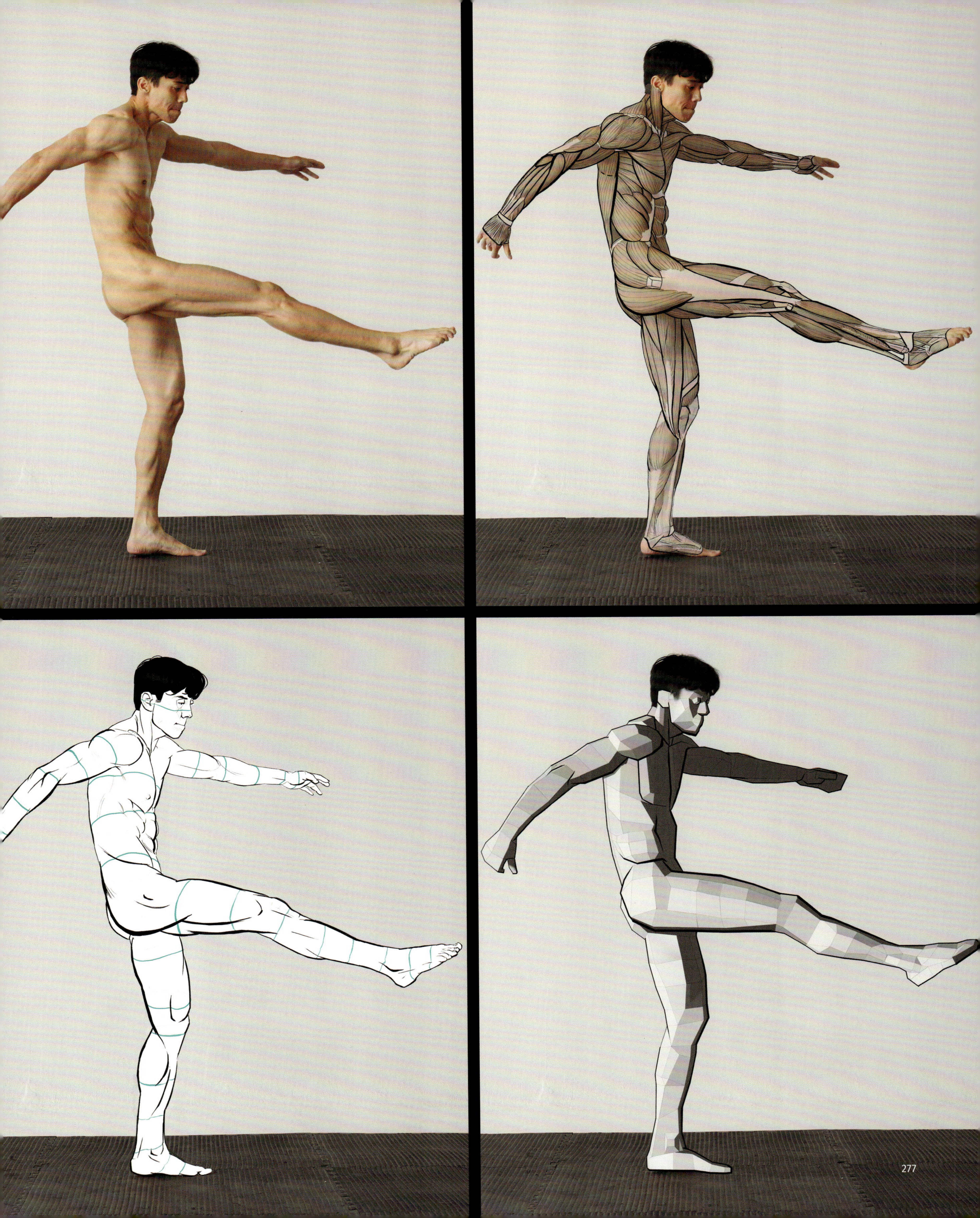

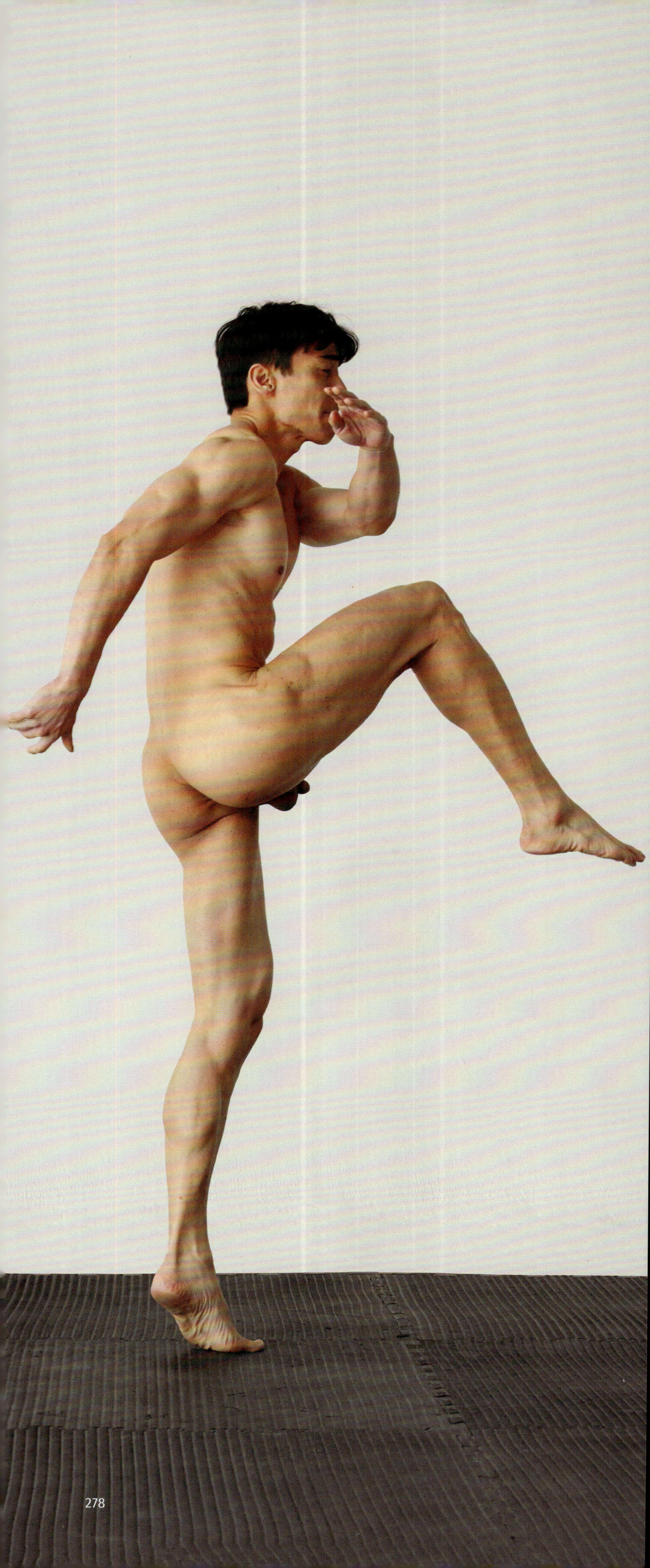

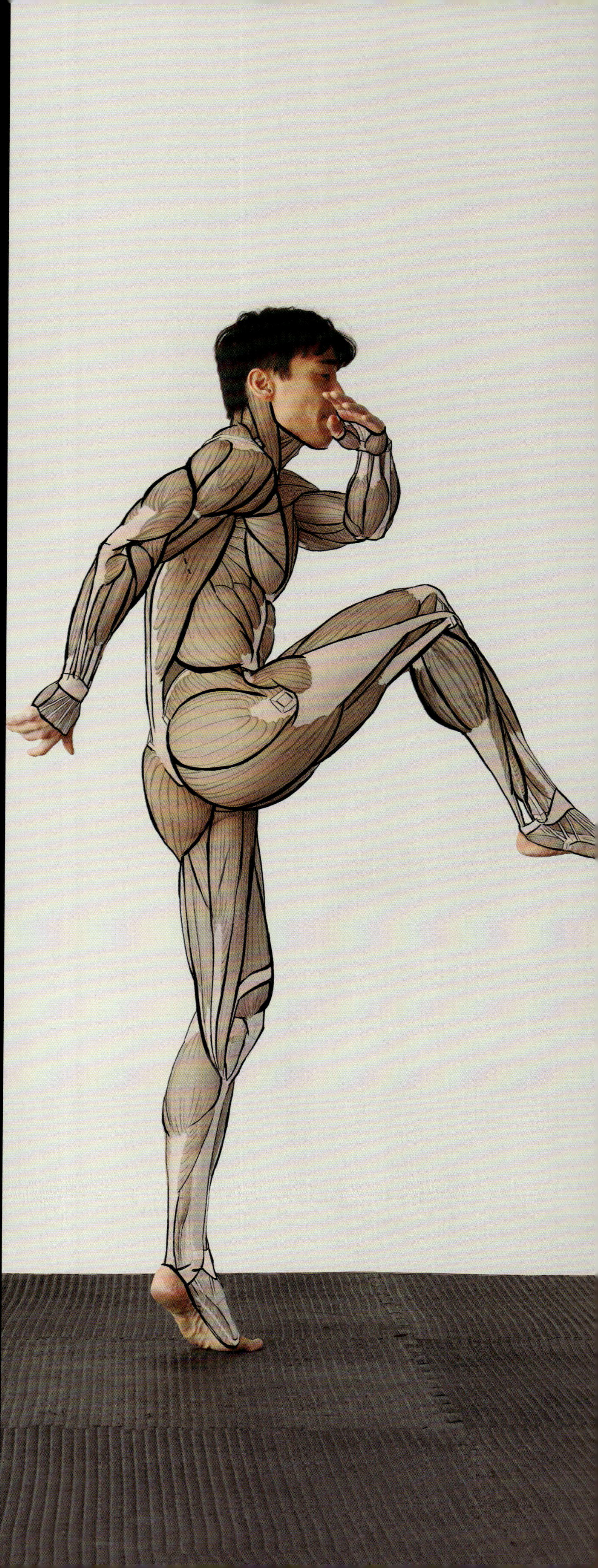

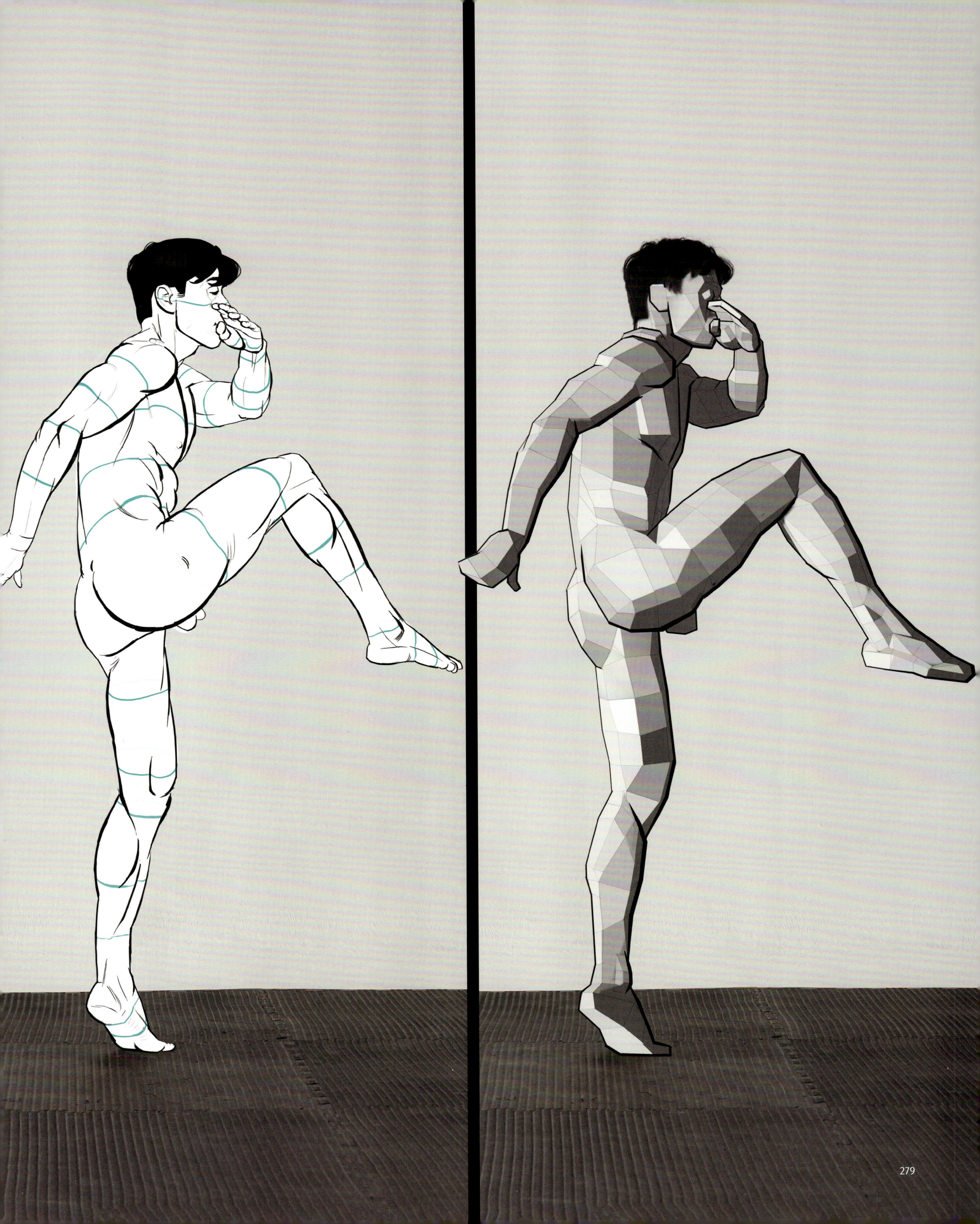

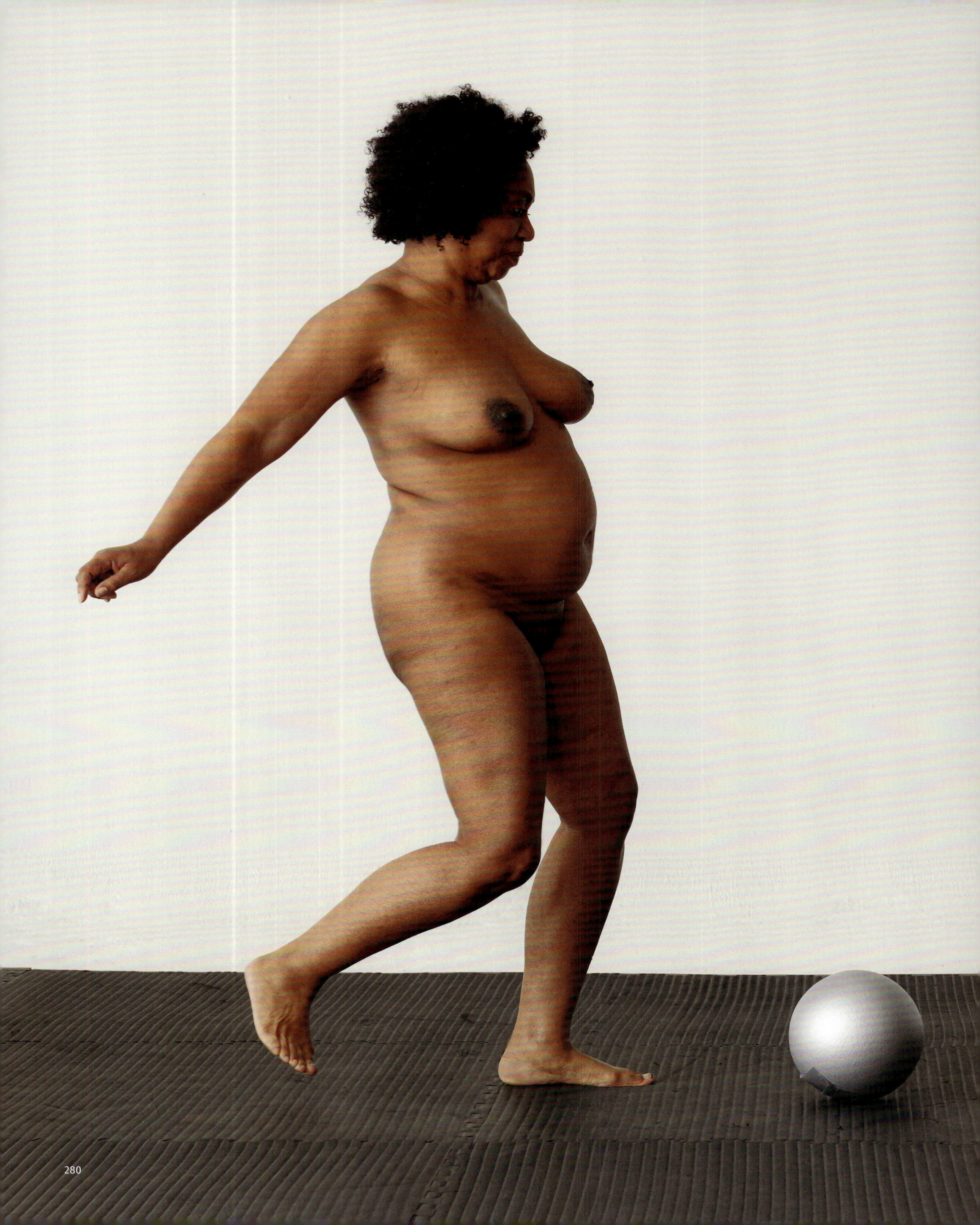

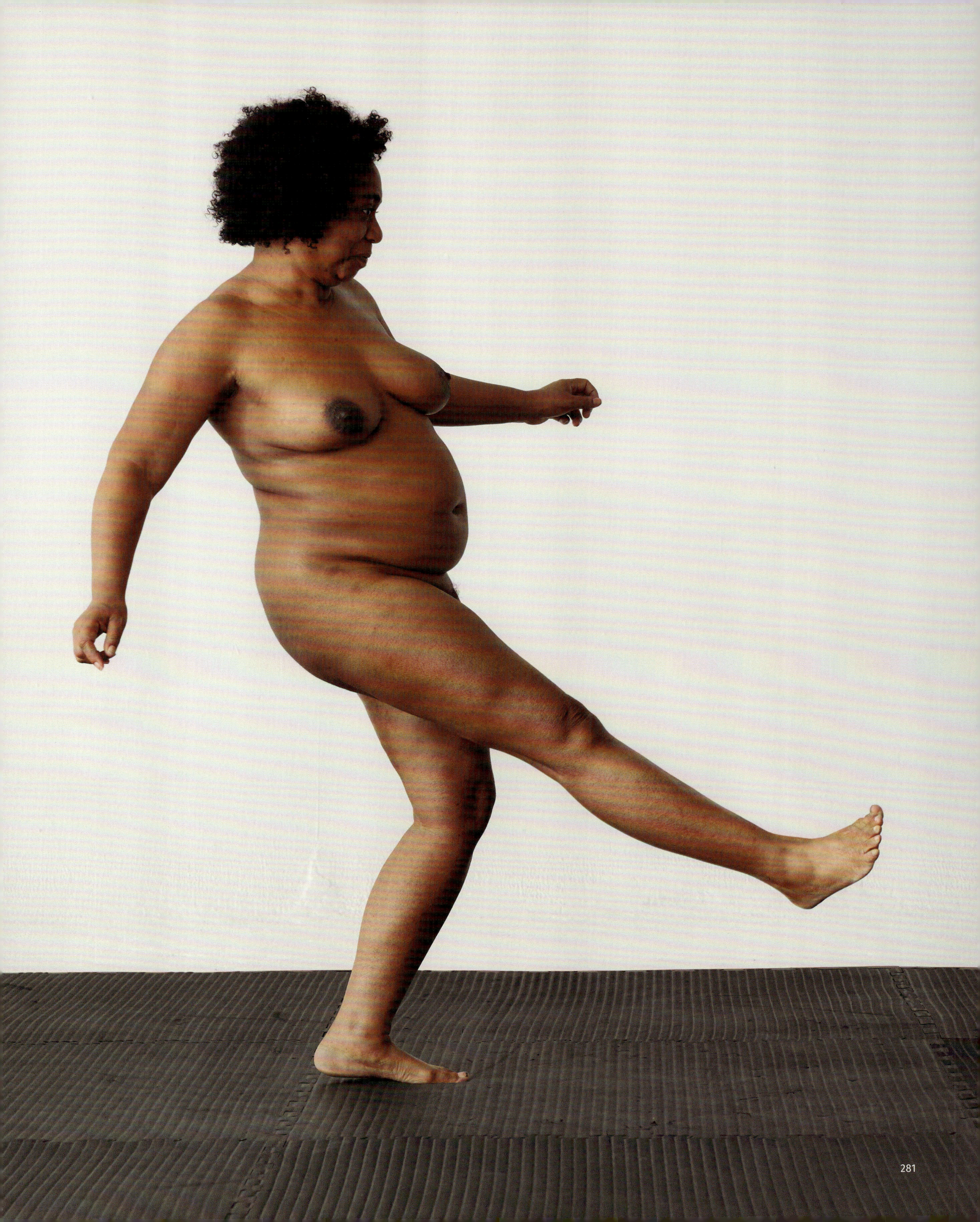

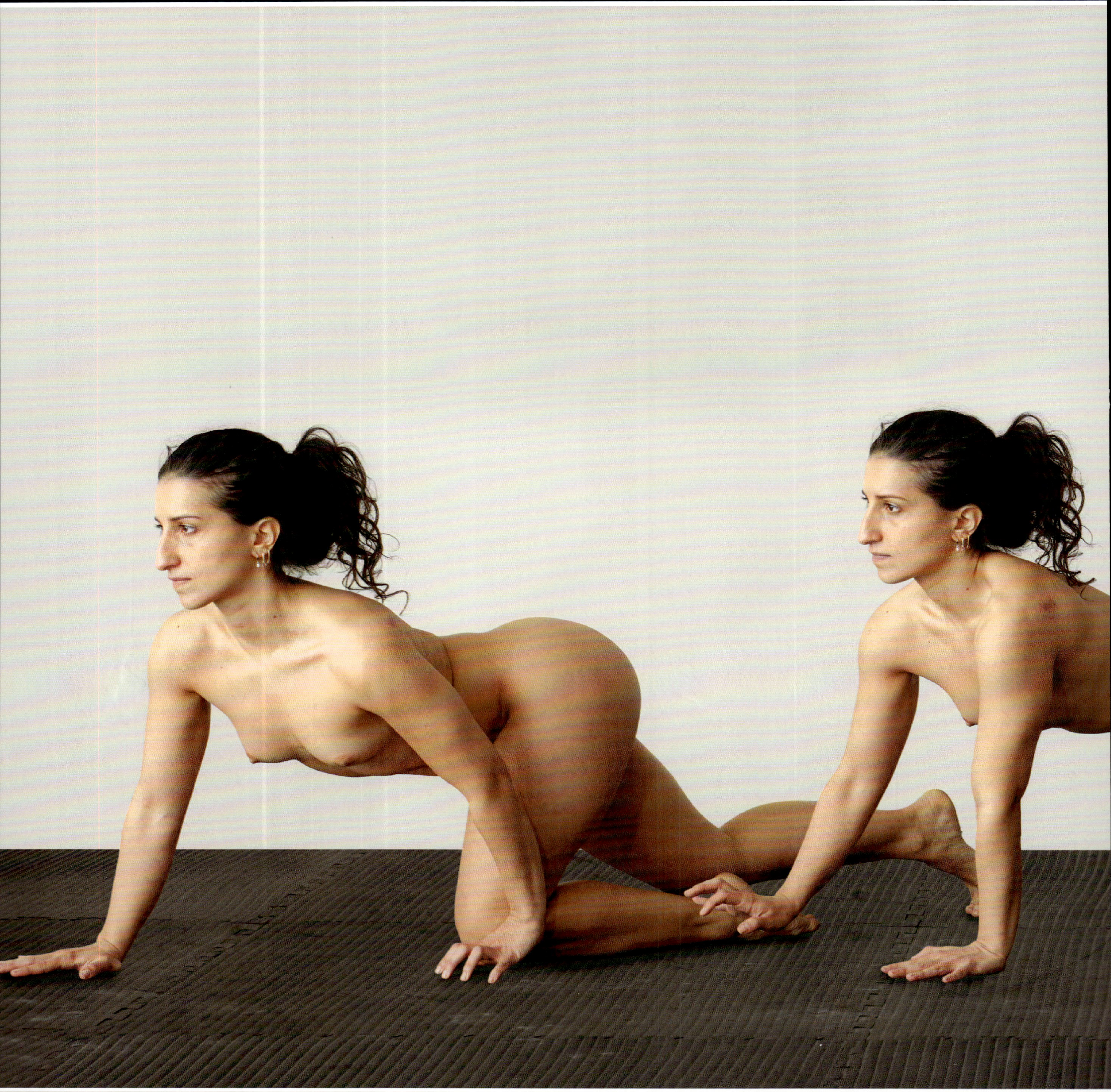

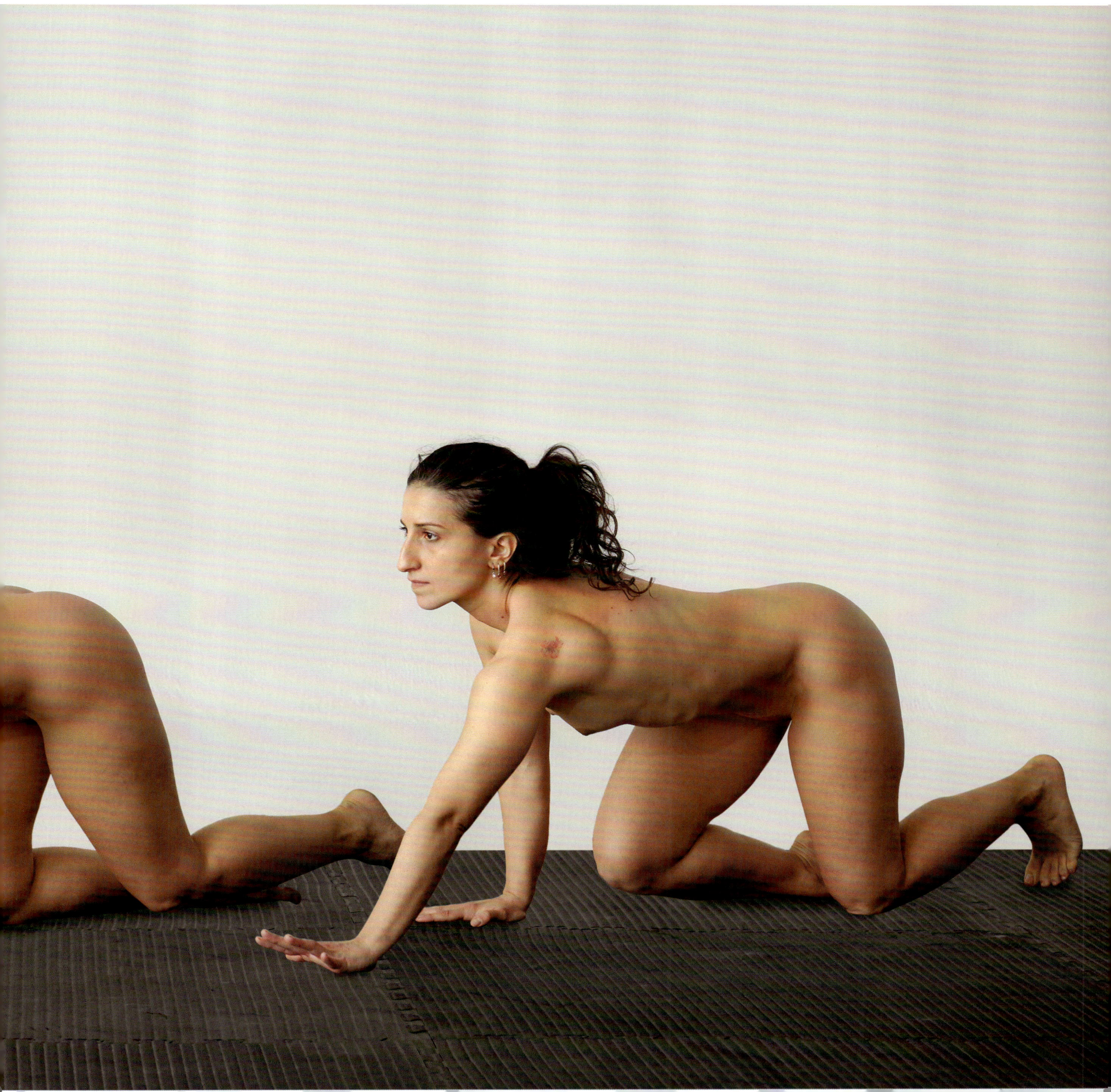

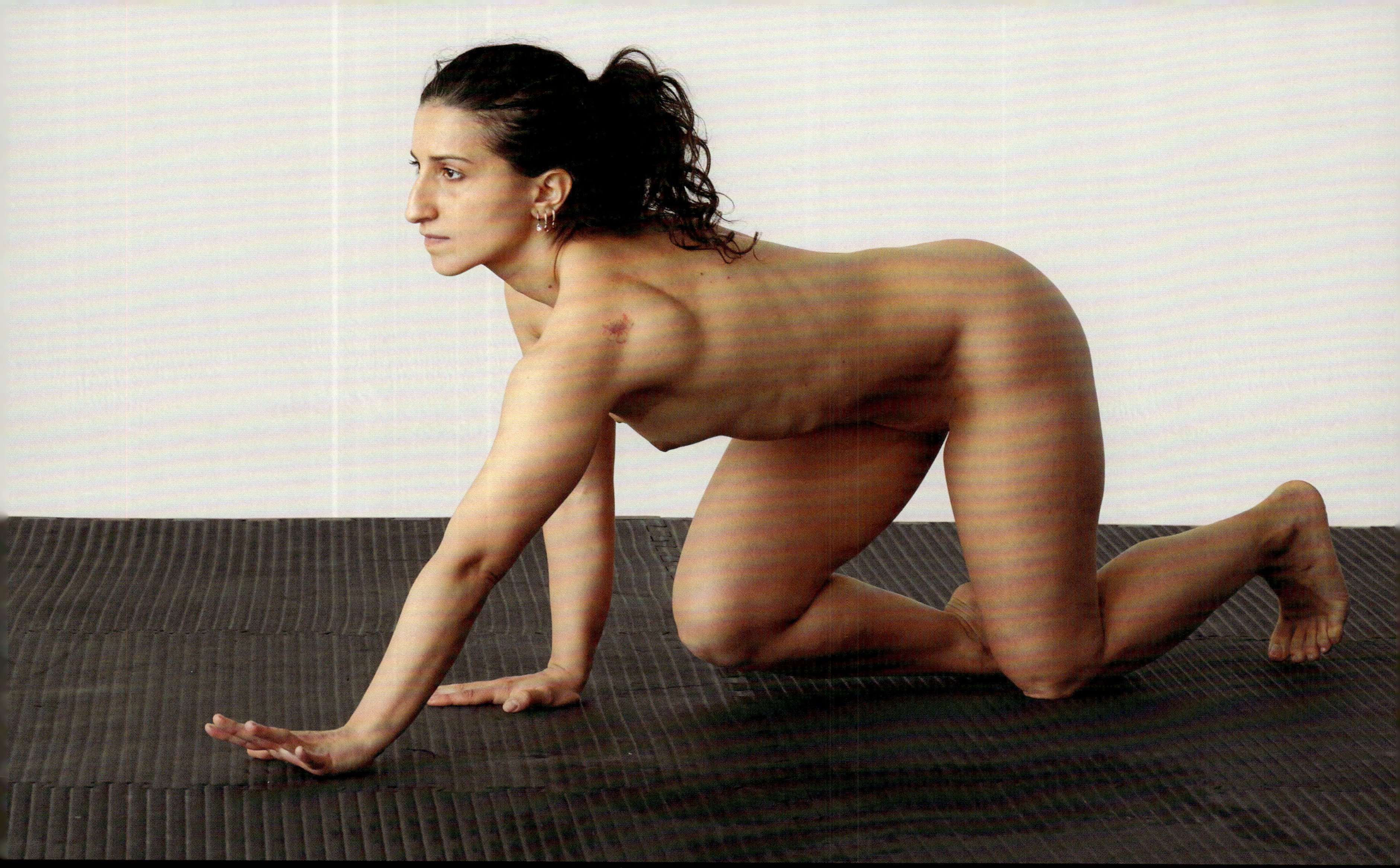

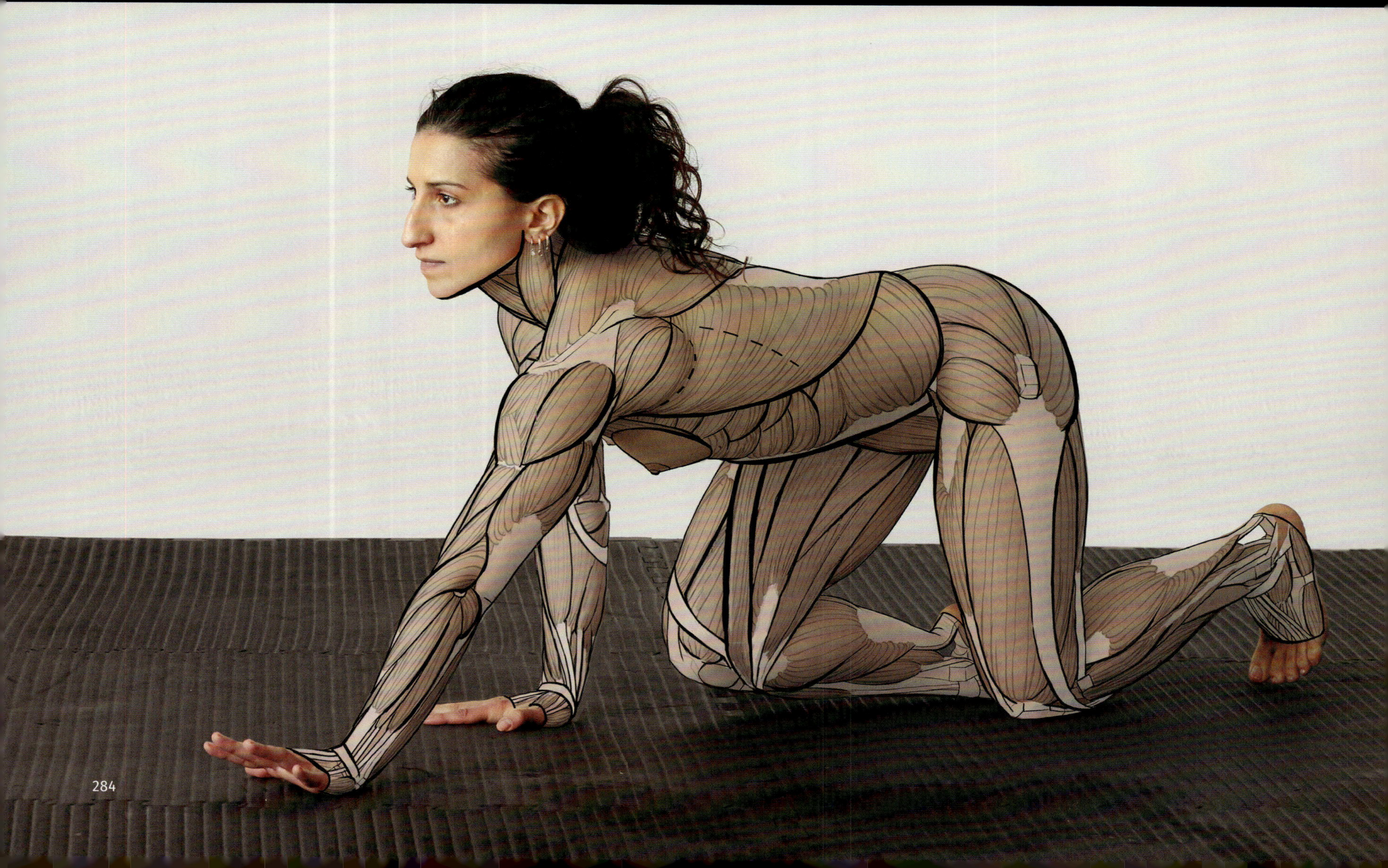

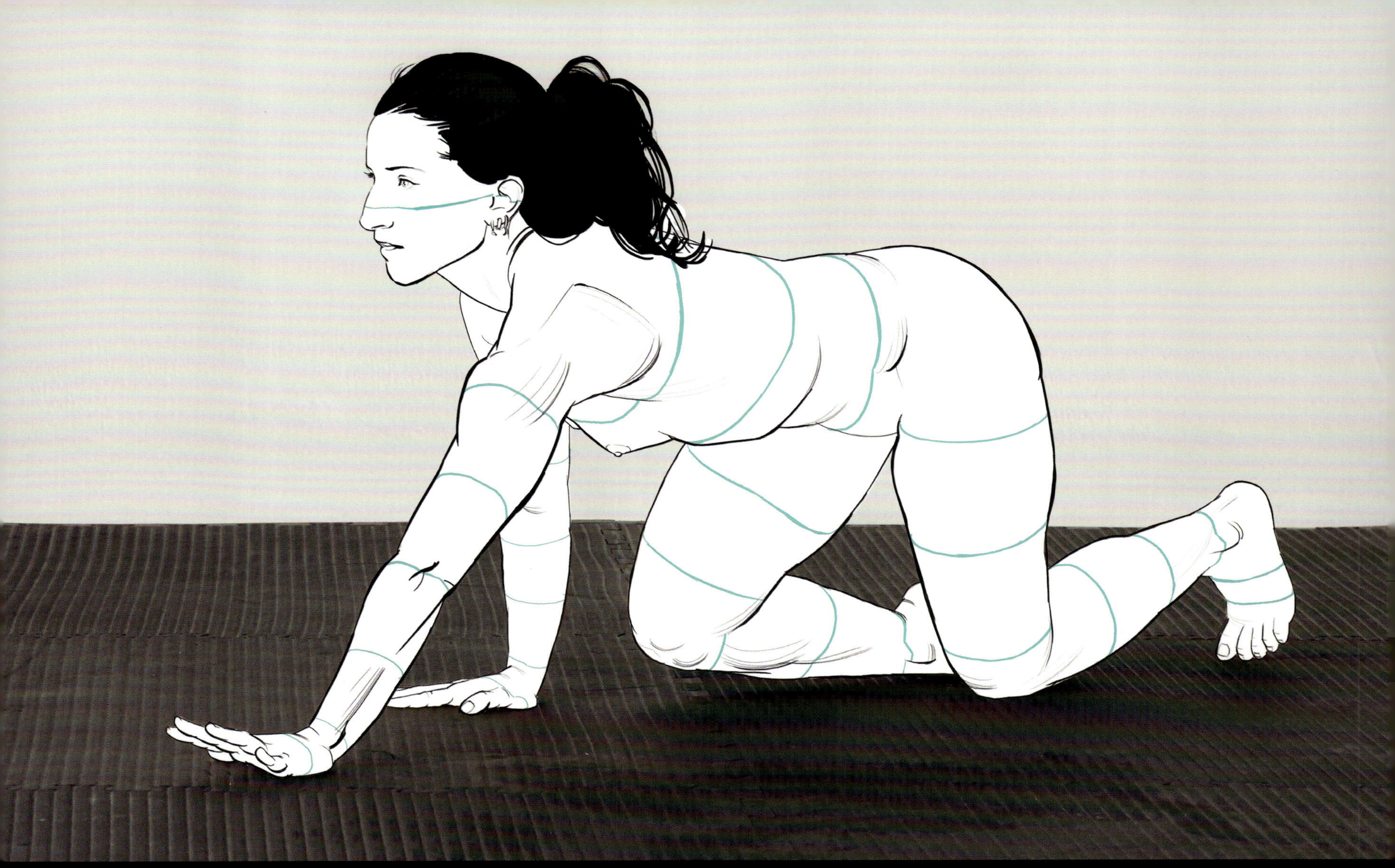

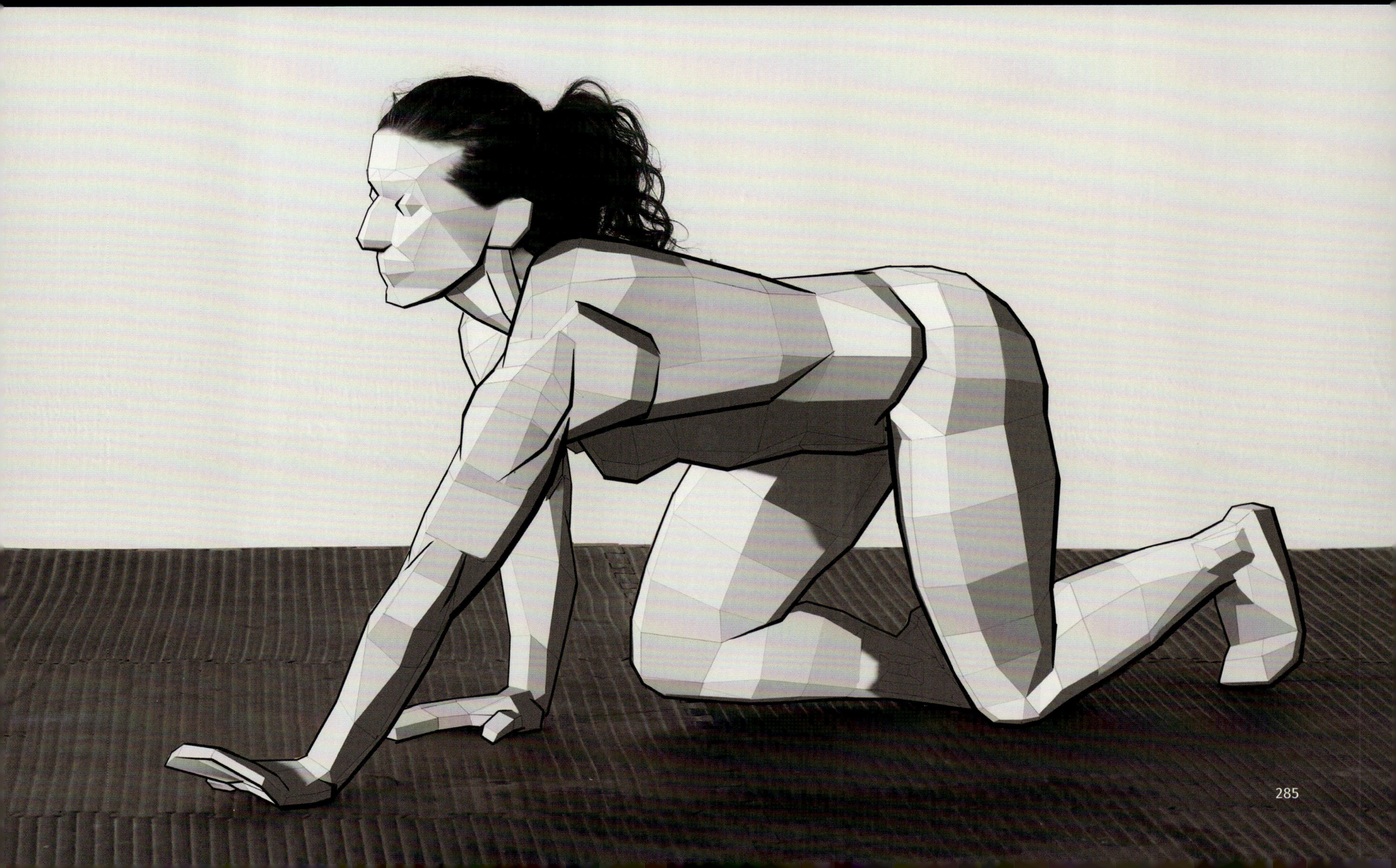

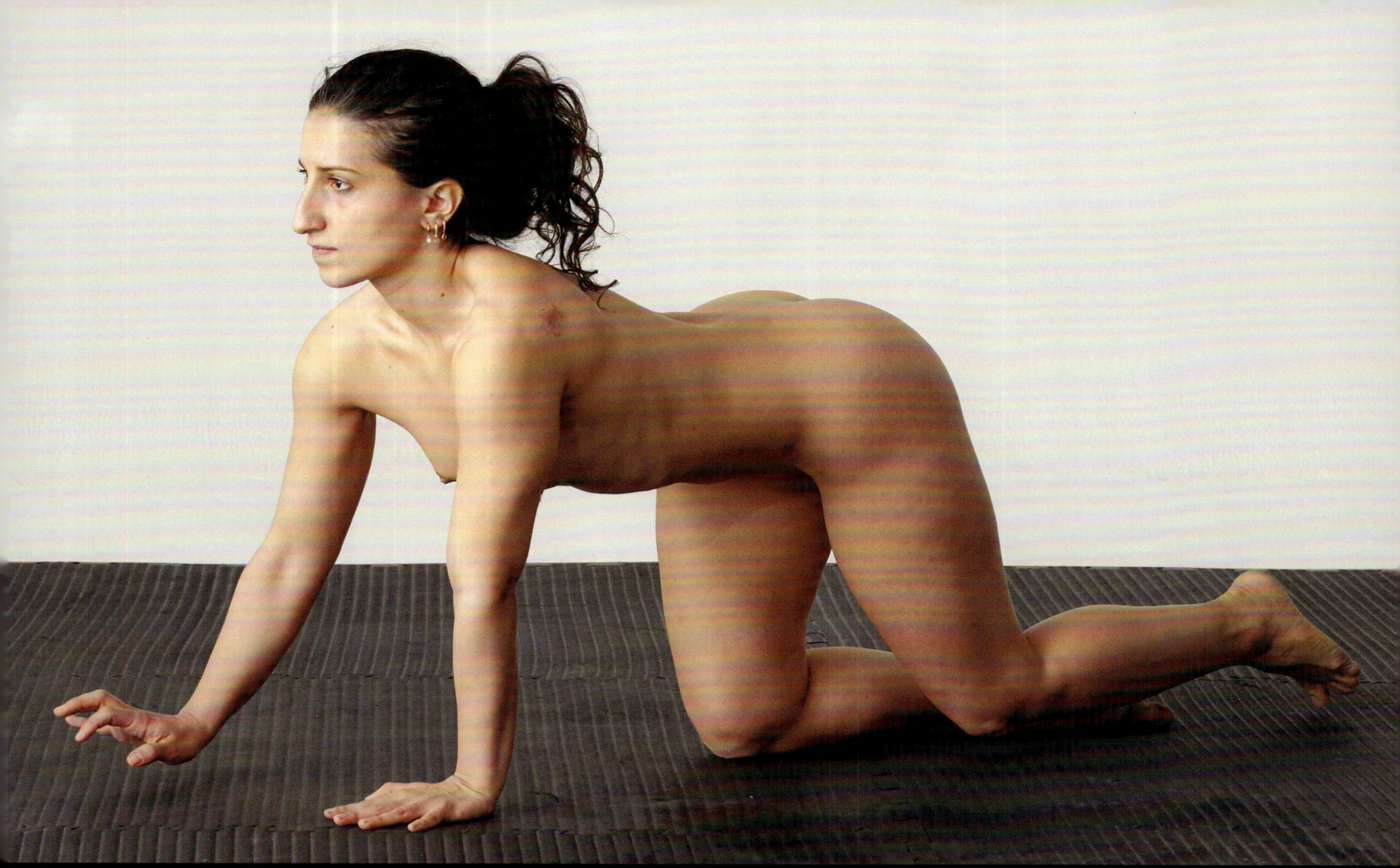

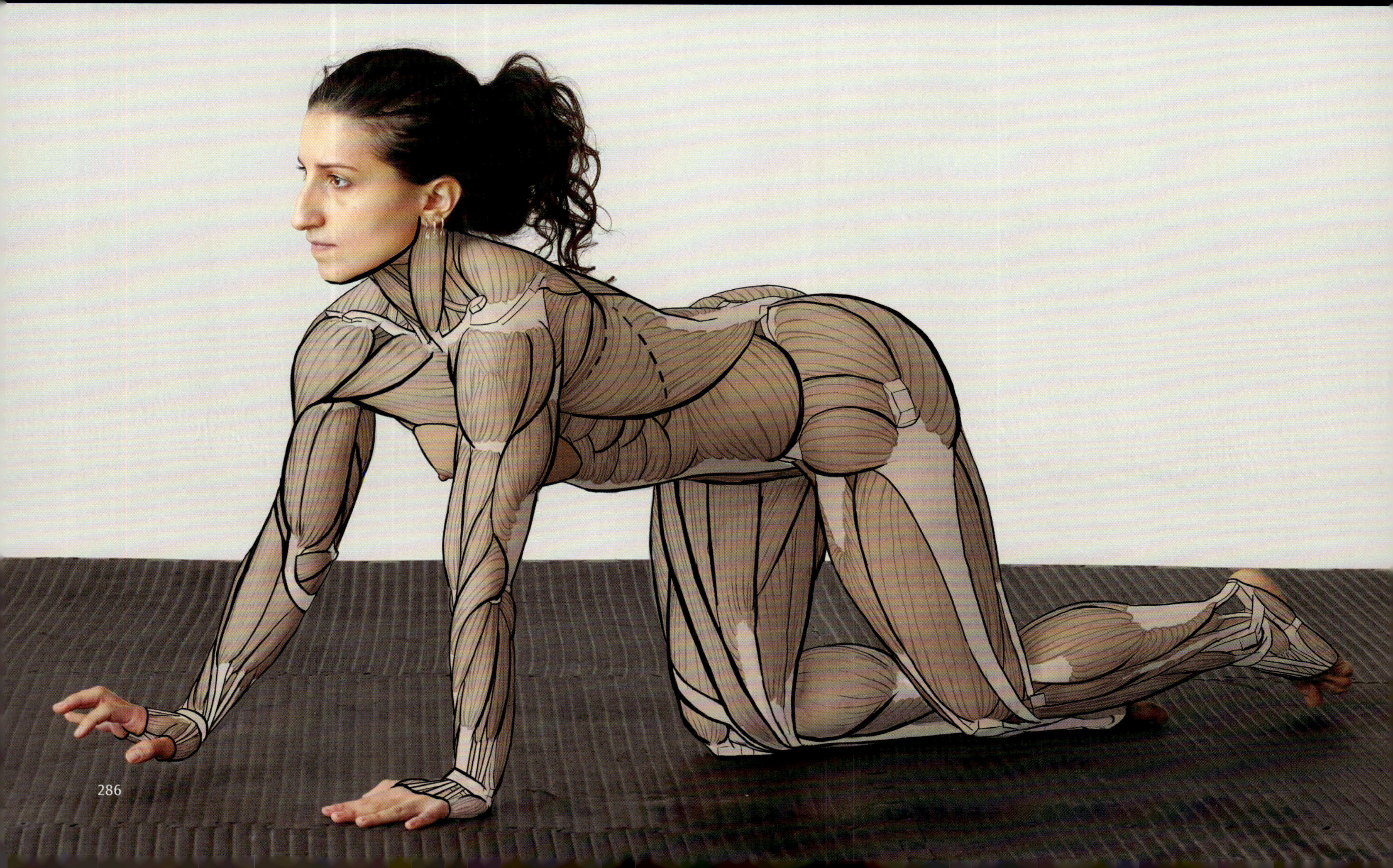

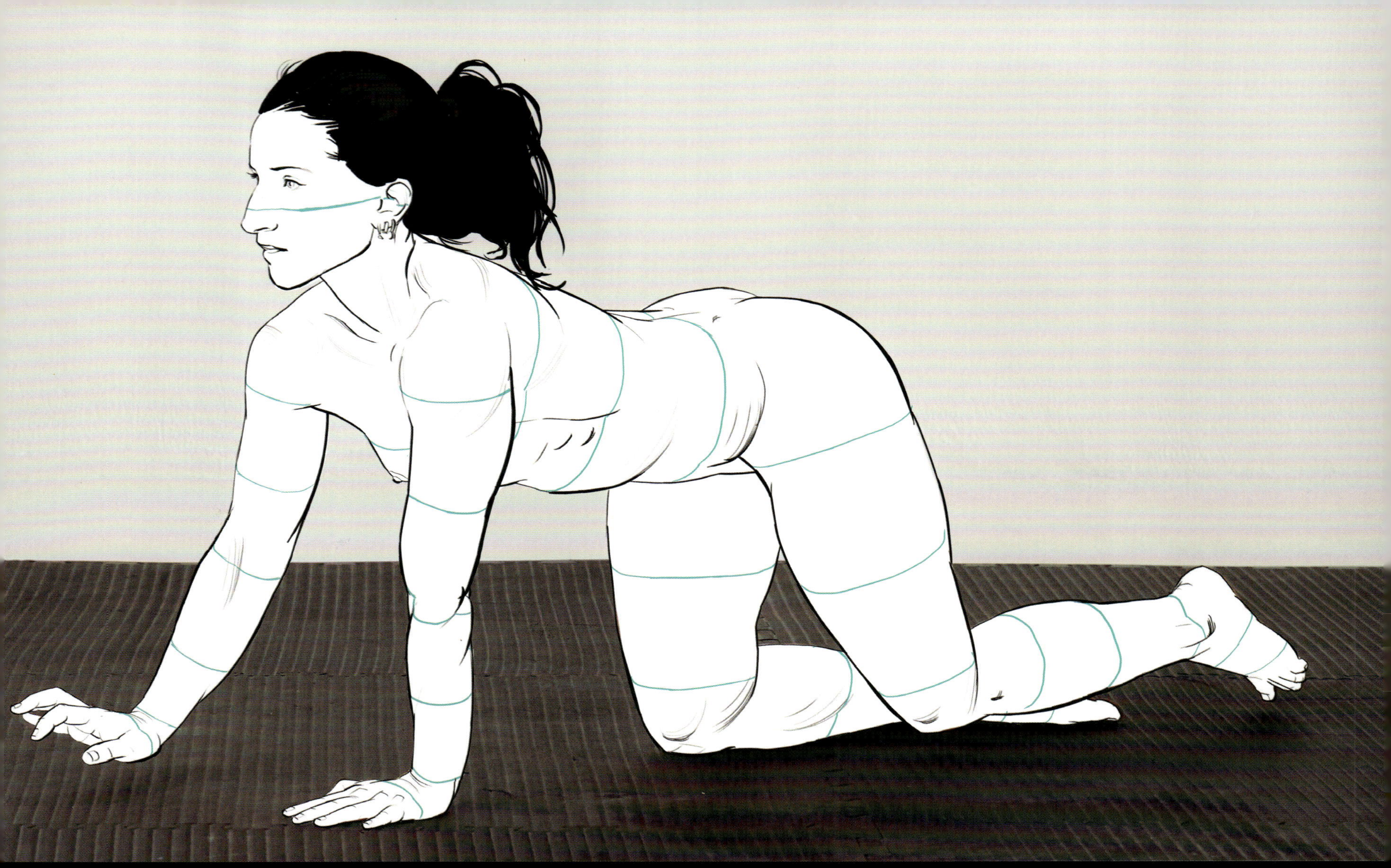

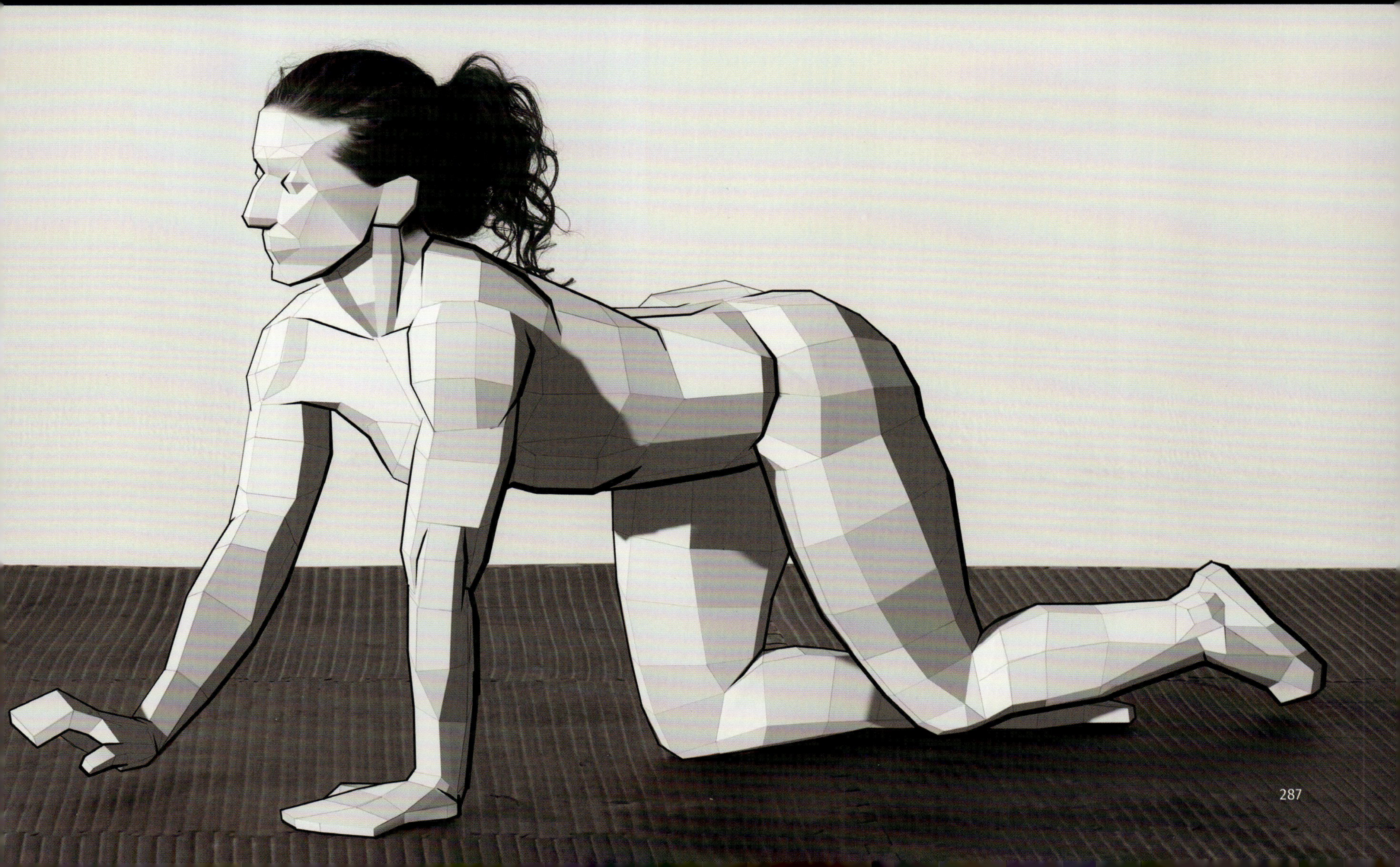

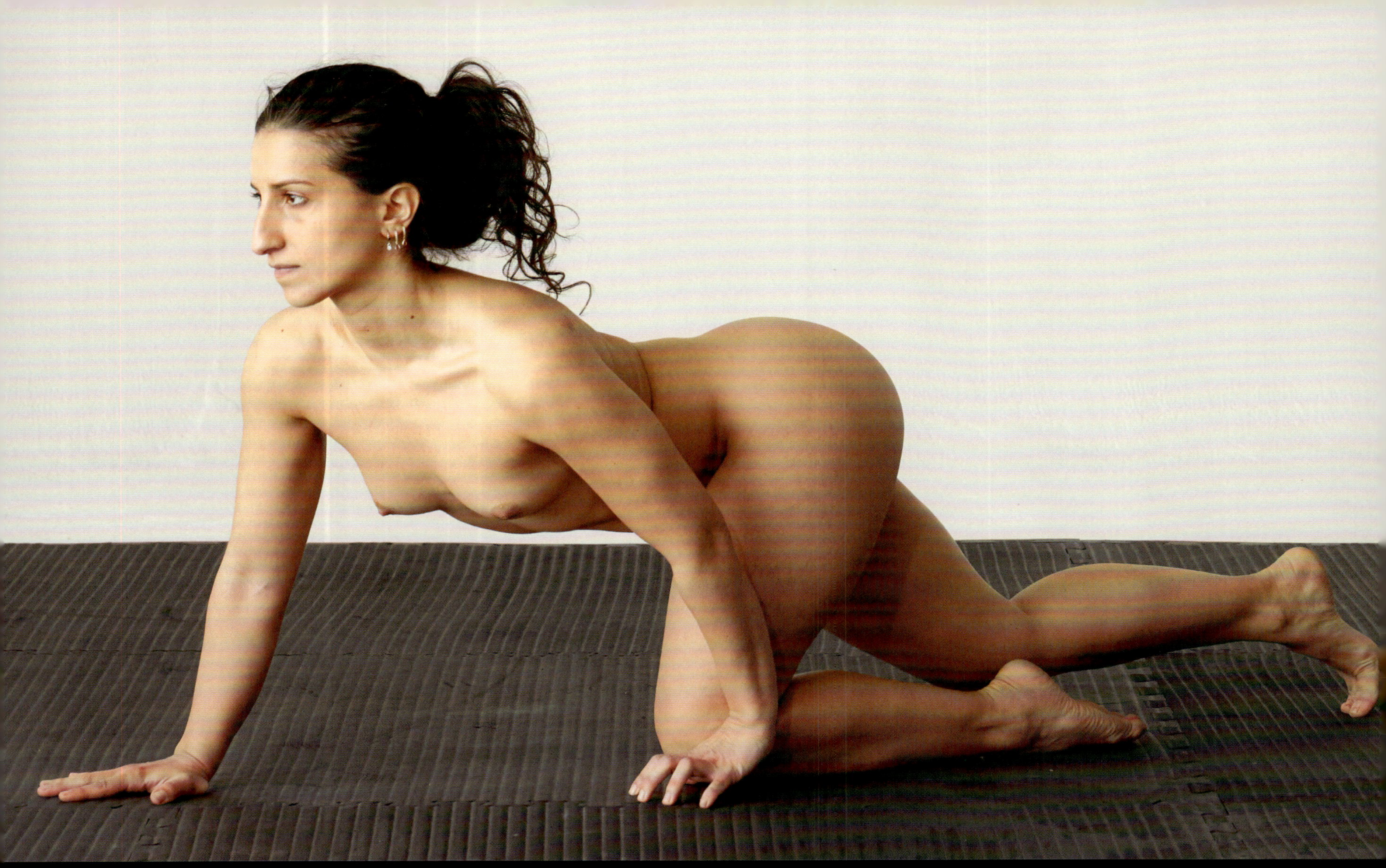

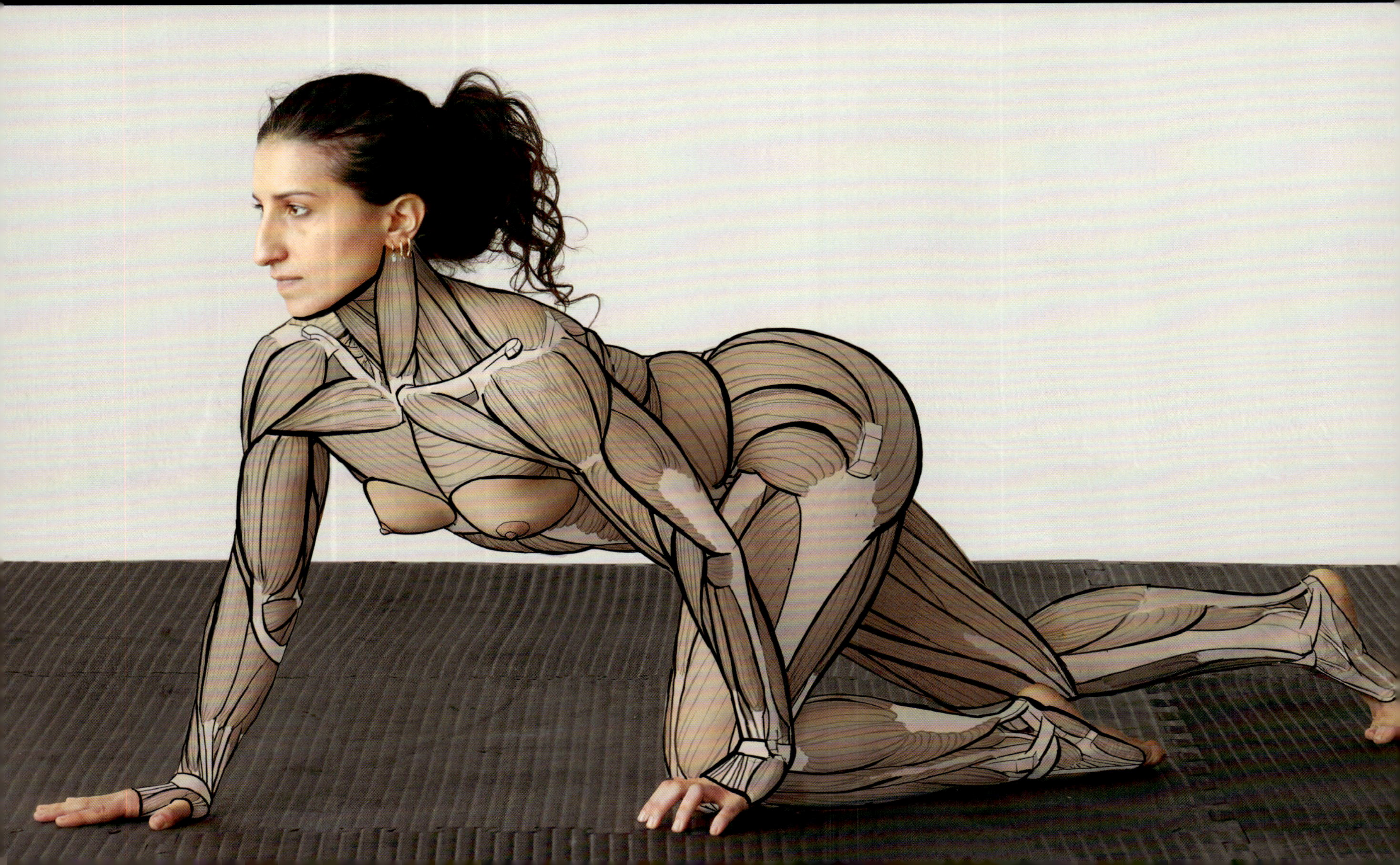

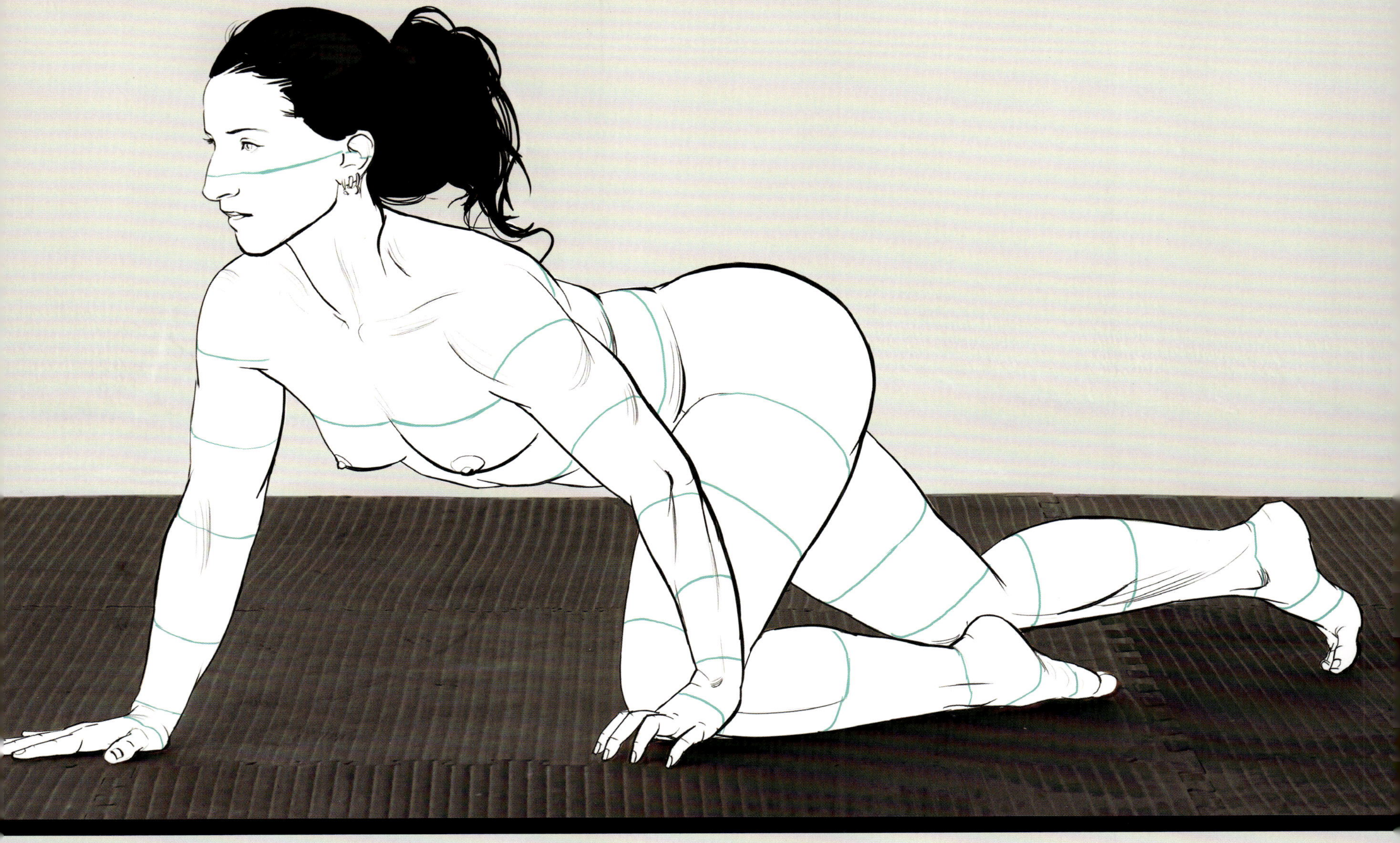

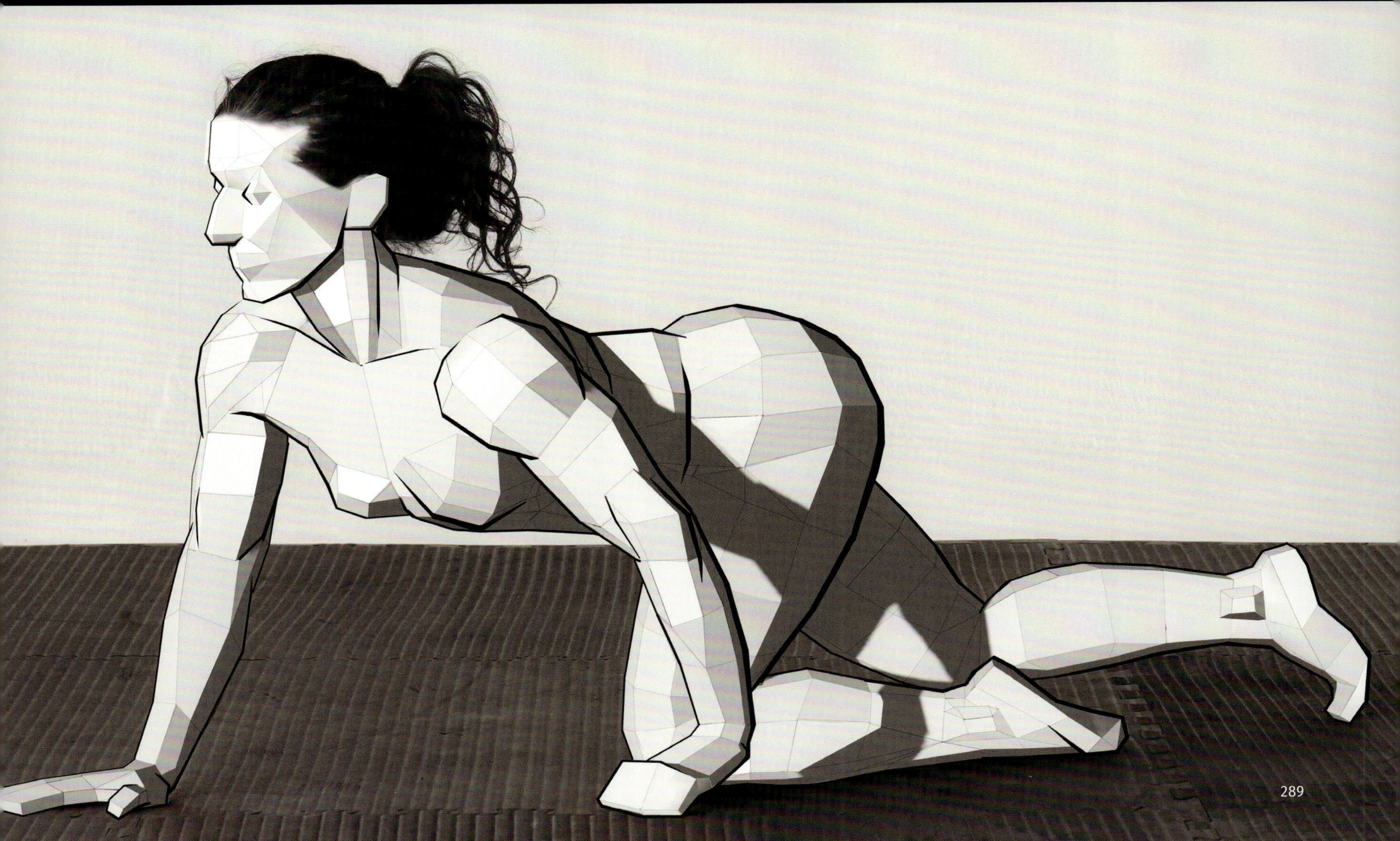

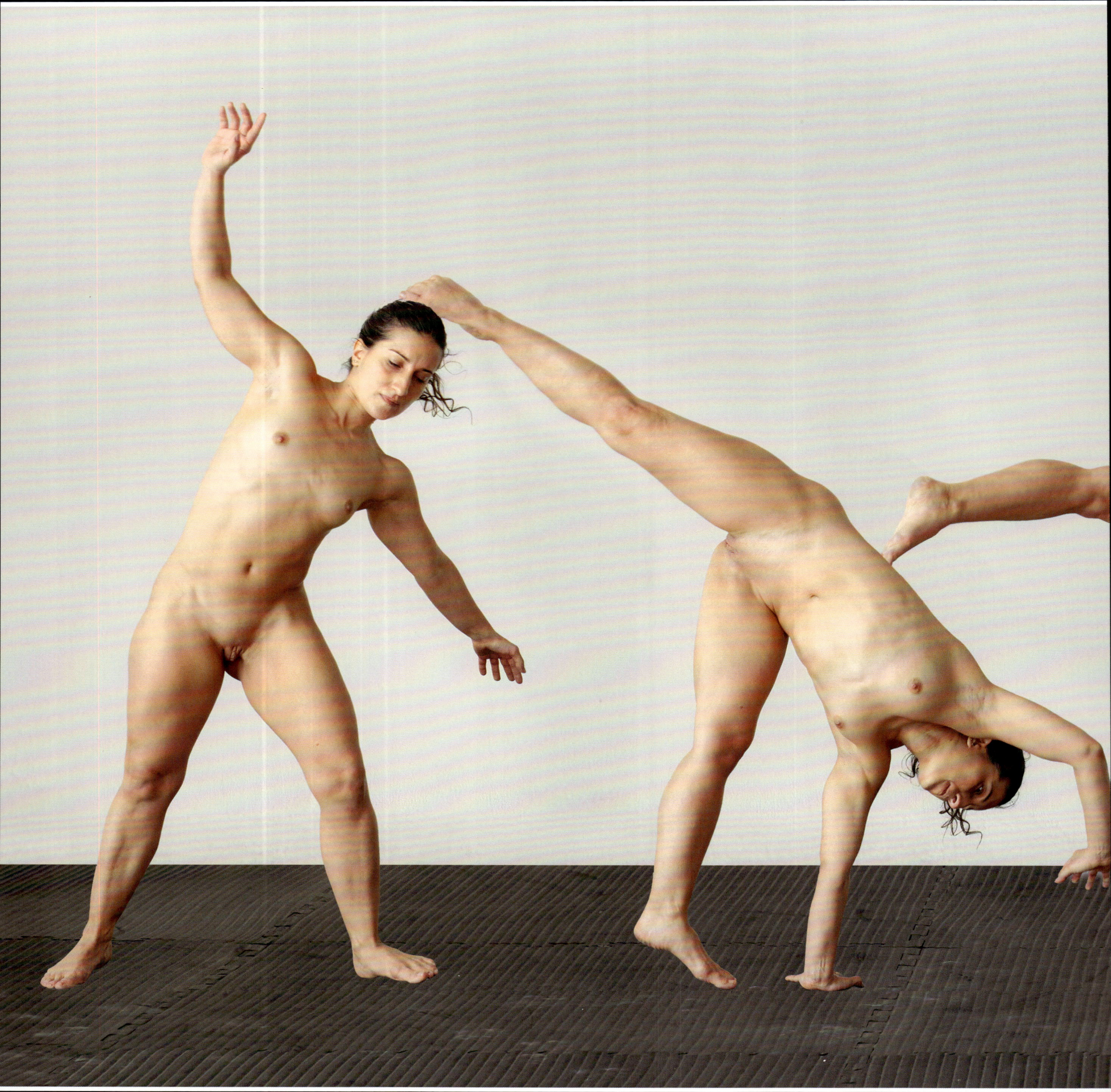

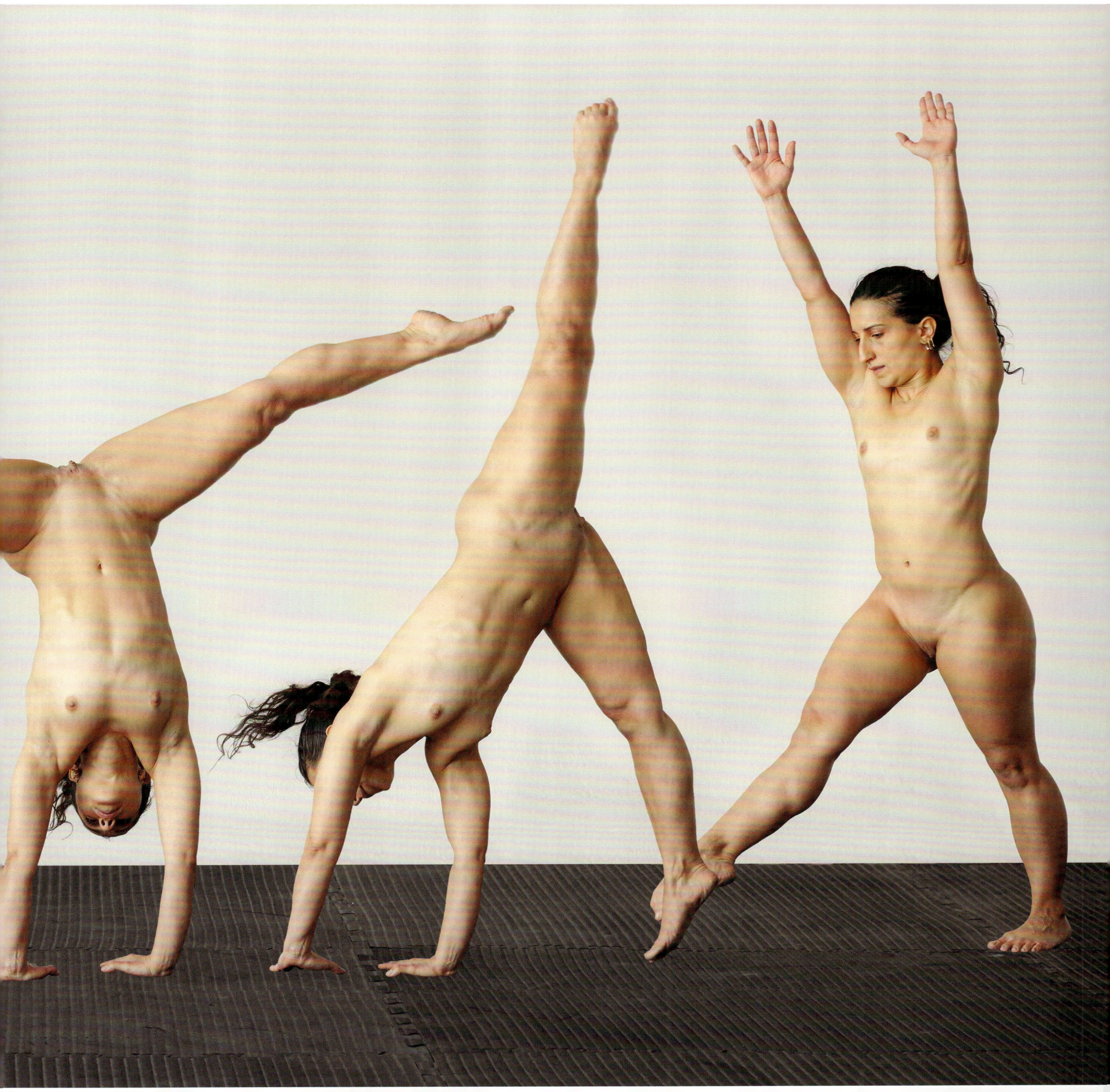

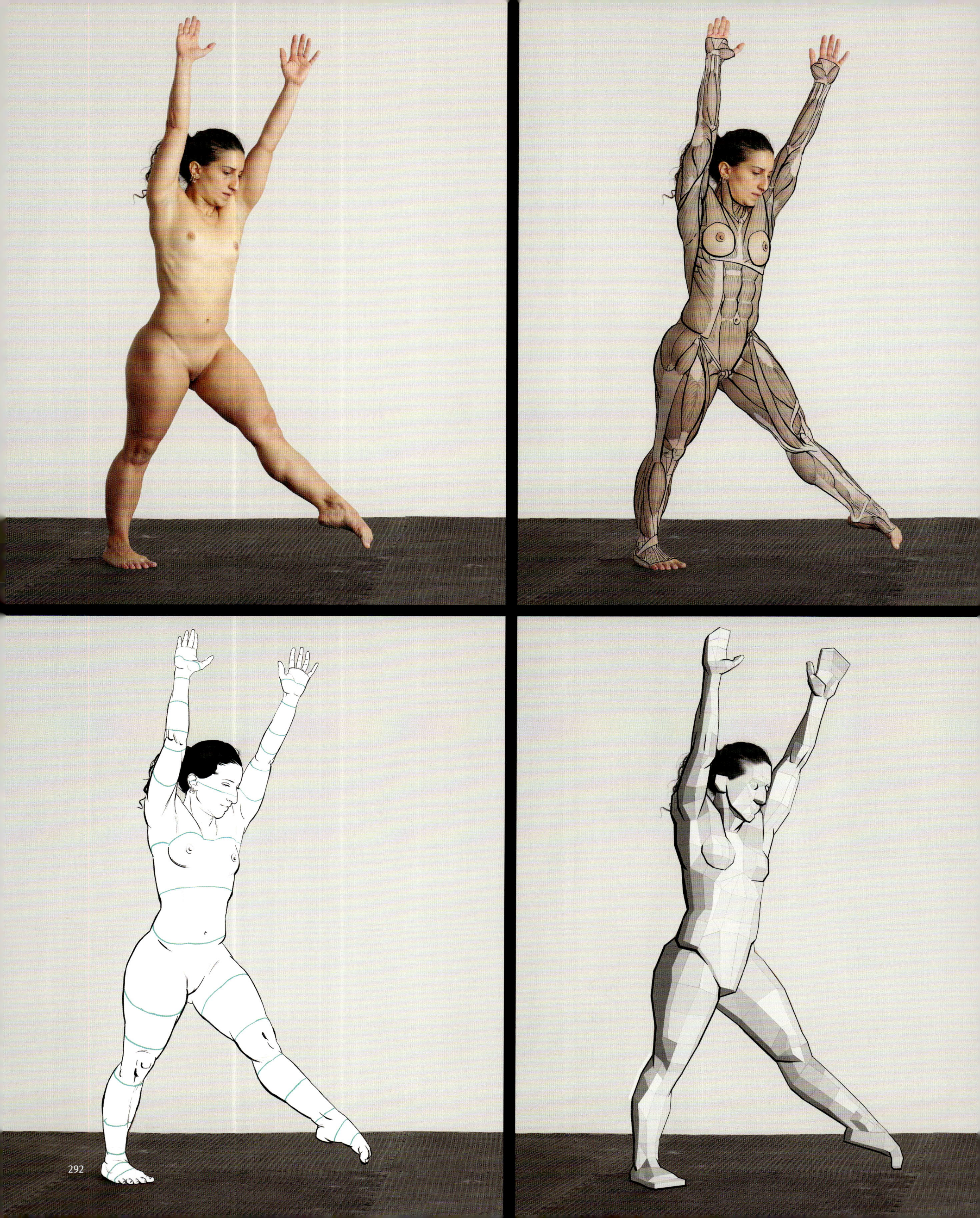

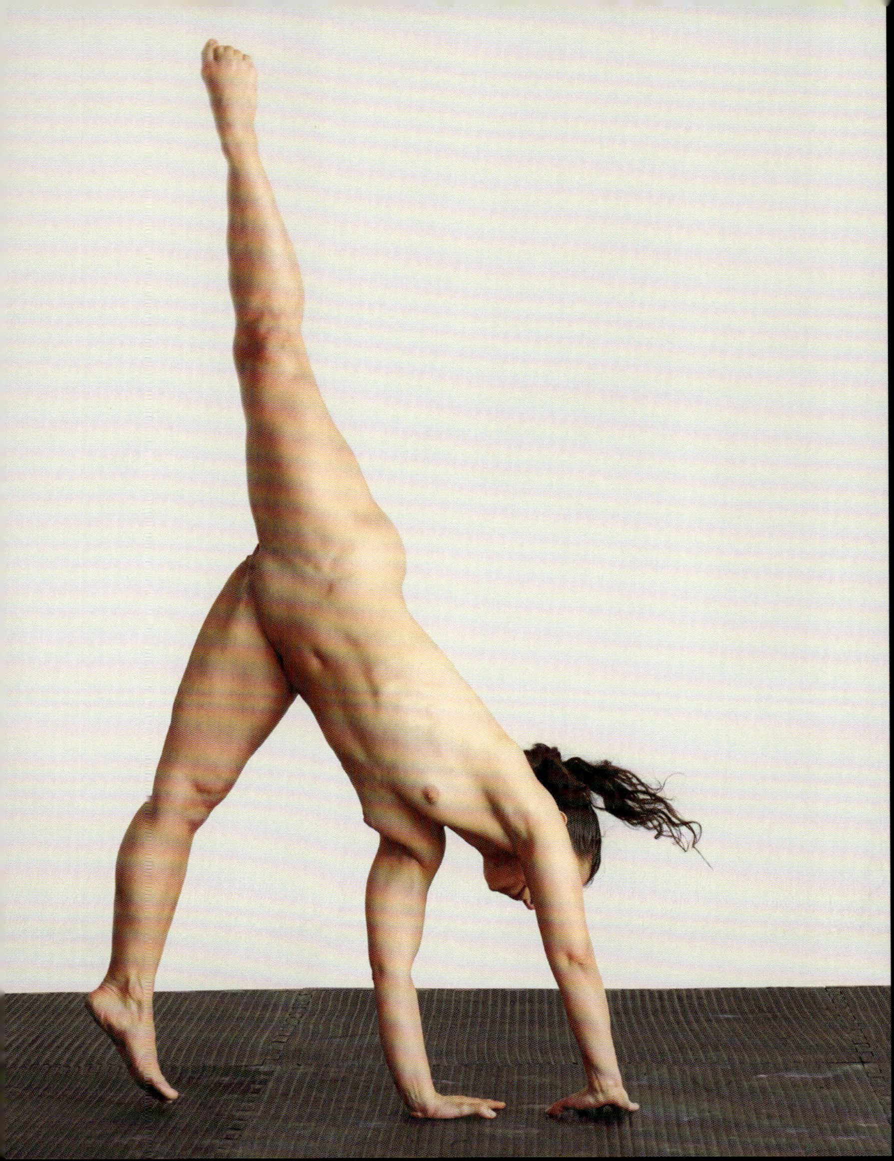
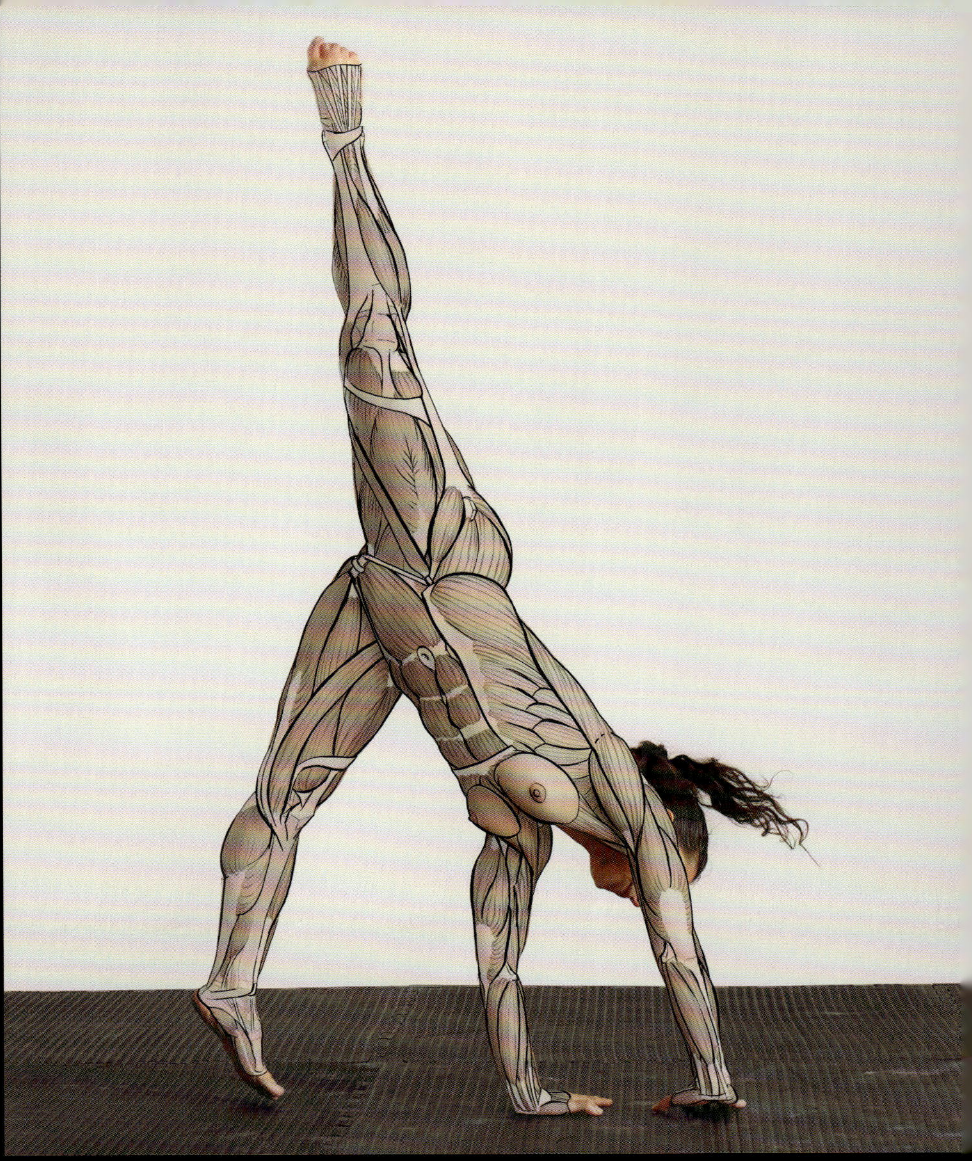
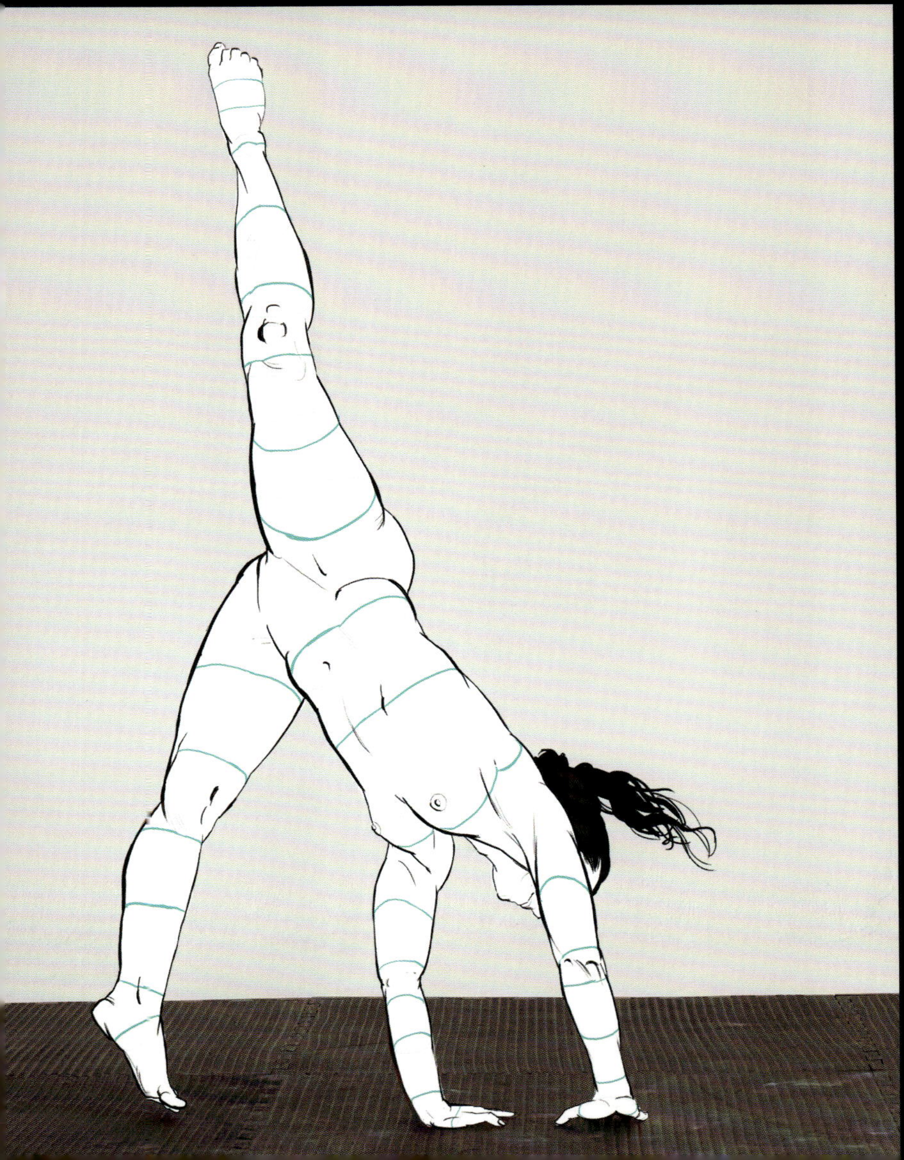
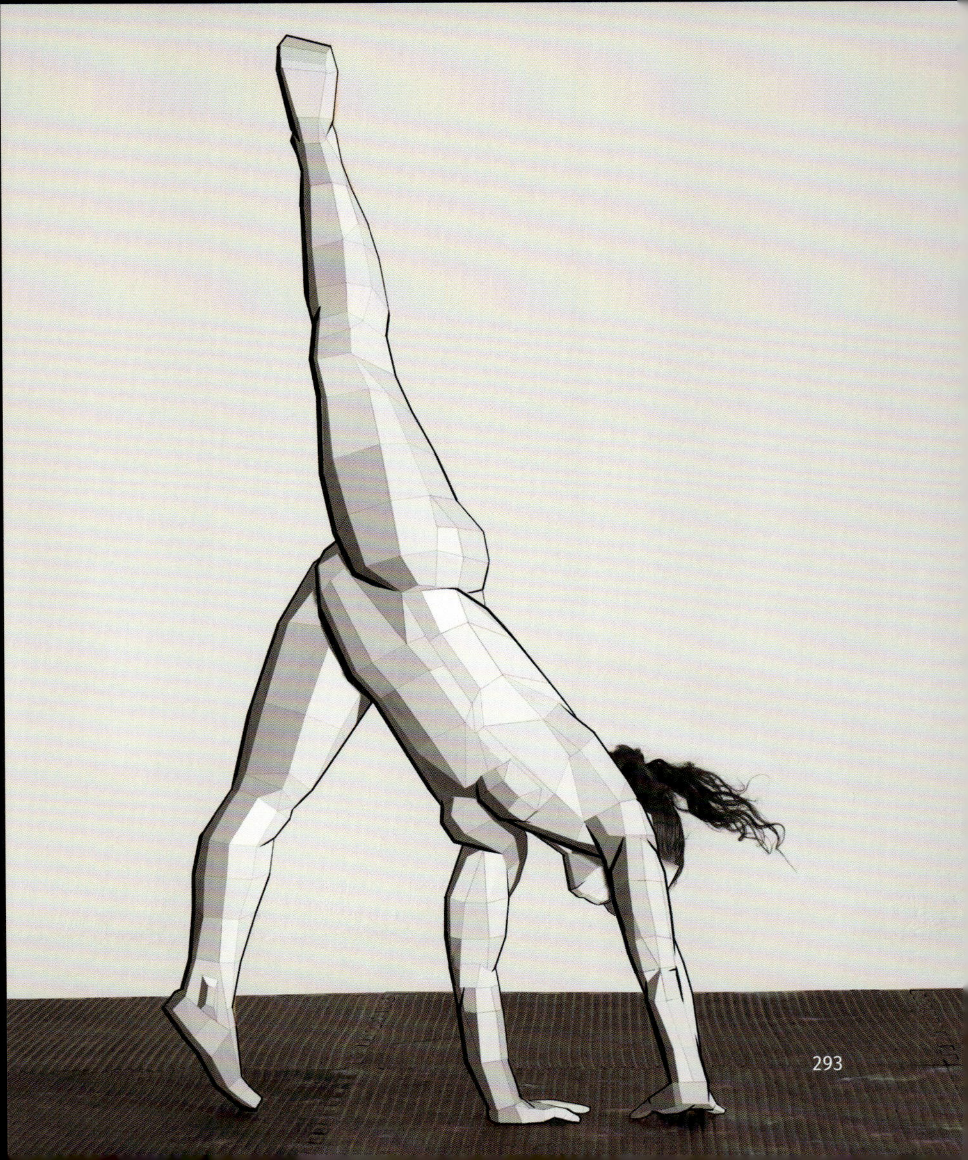

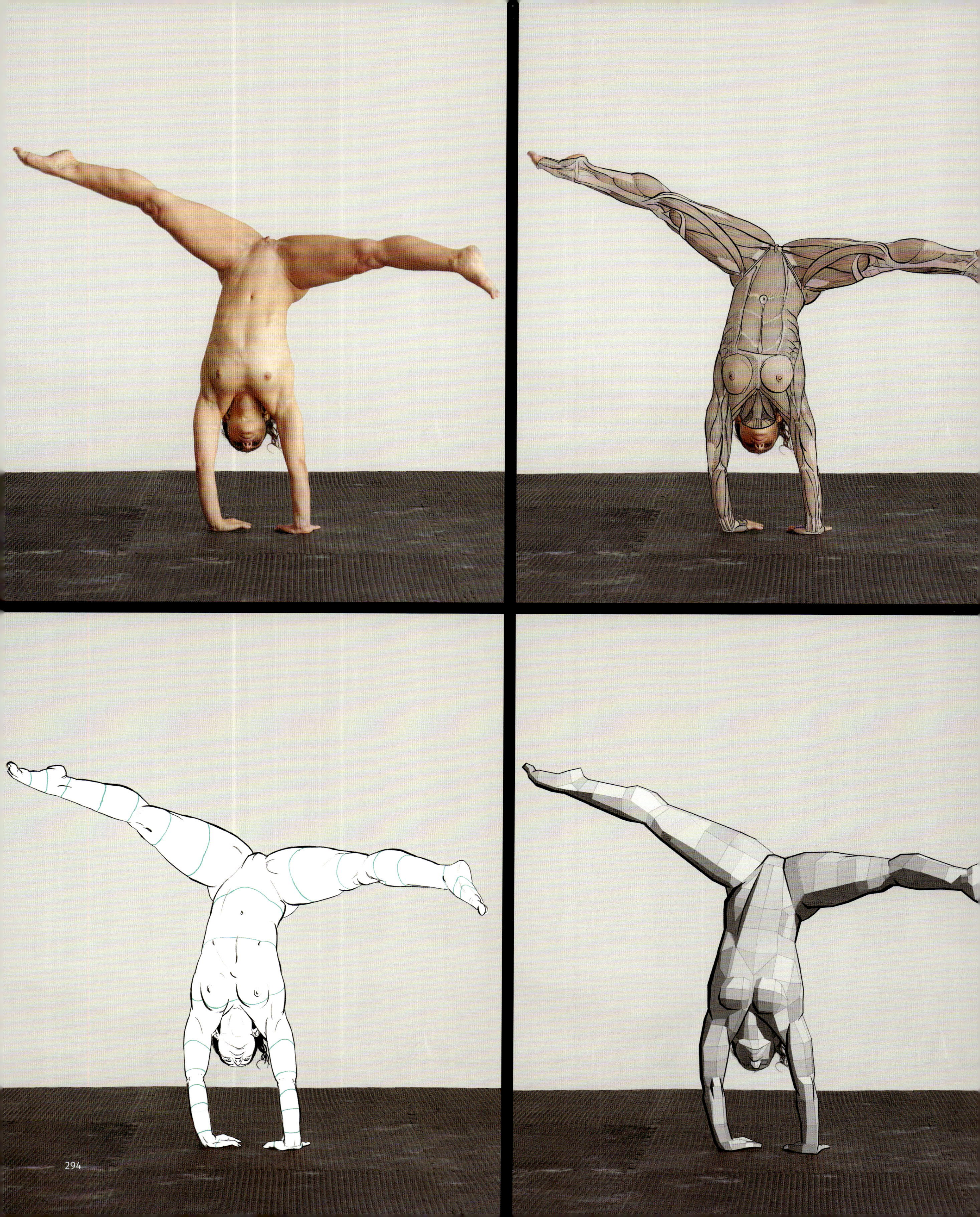

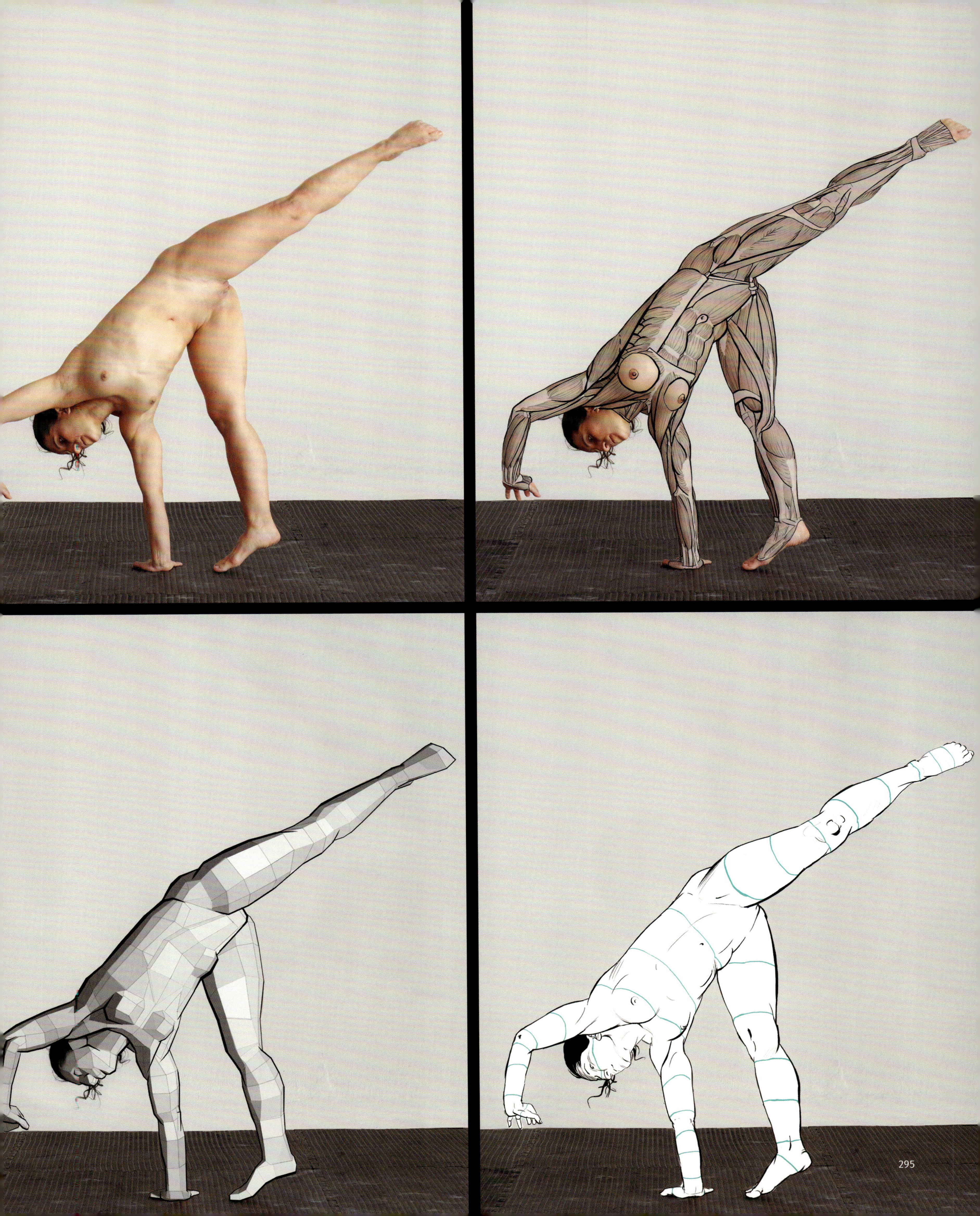

Shoulder roll/tumble

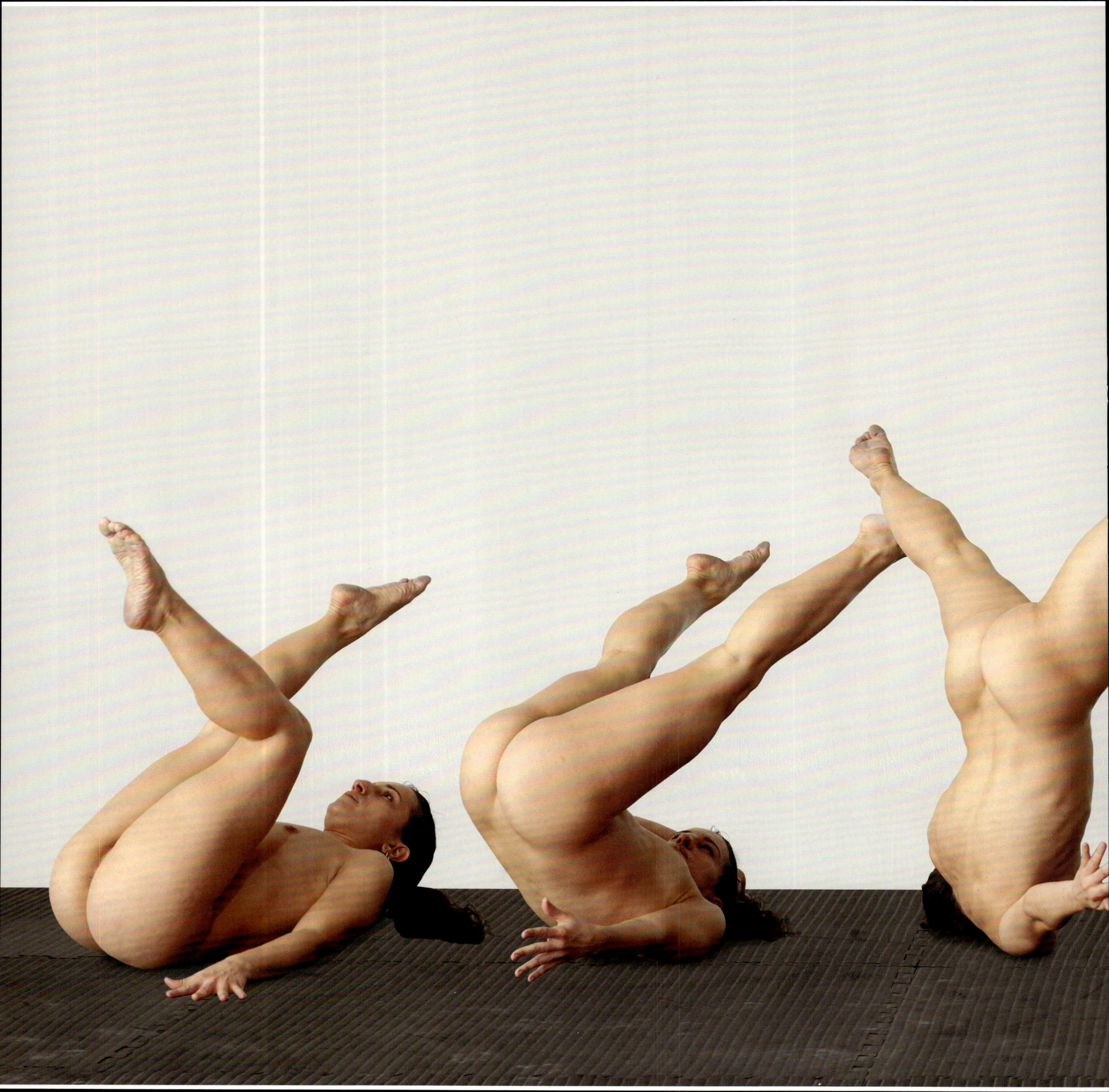

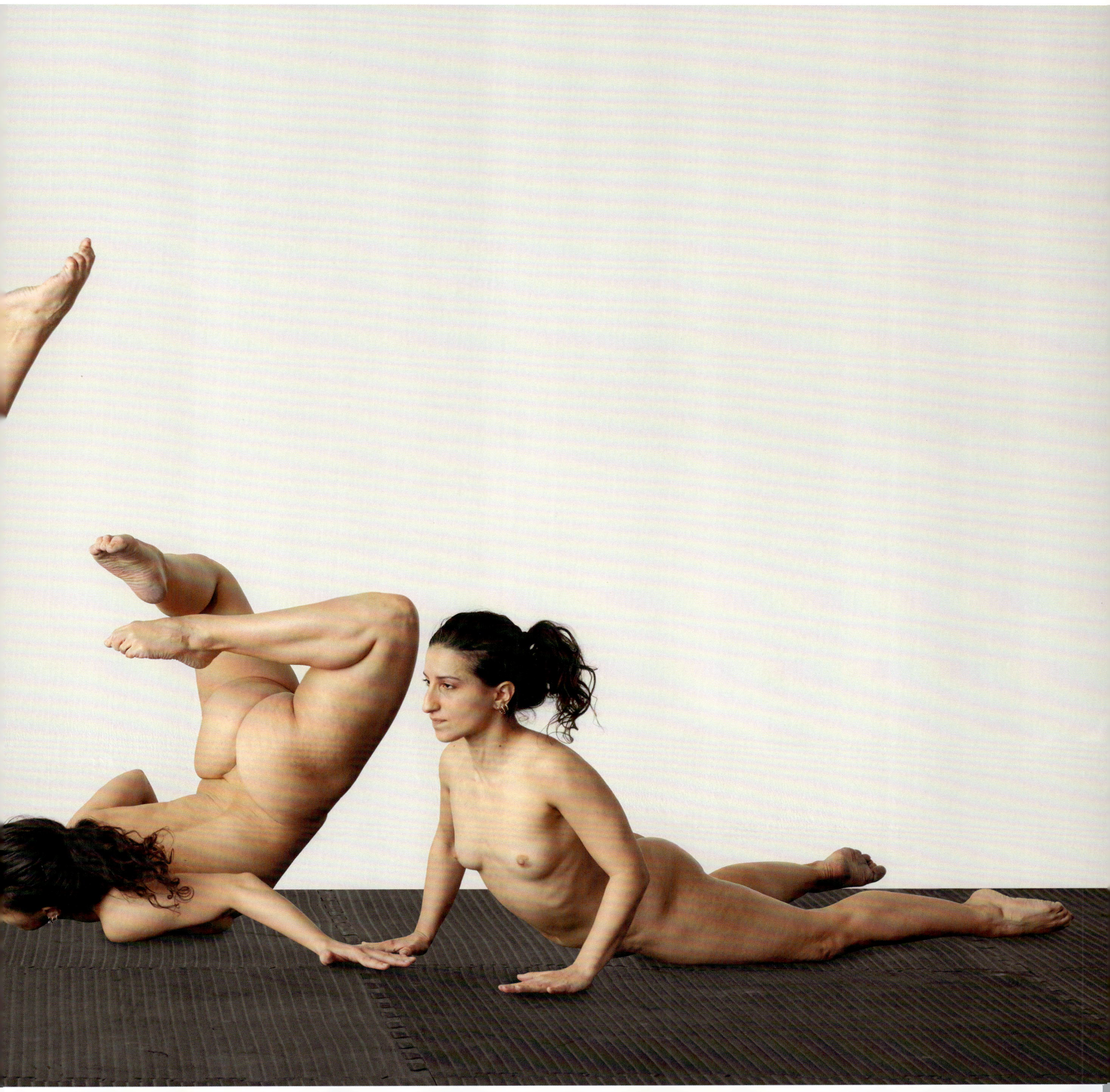

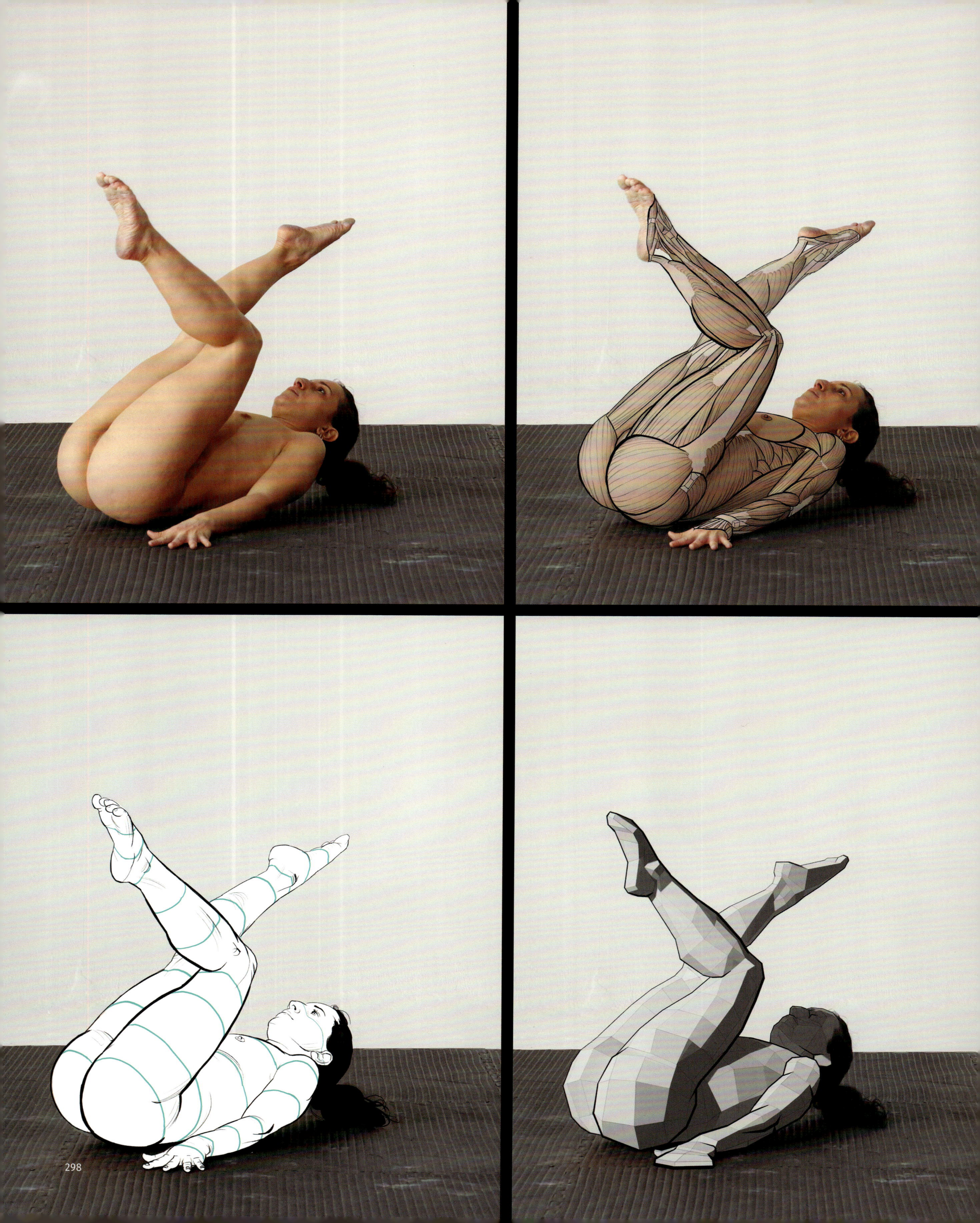

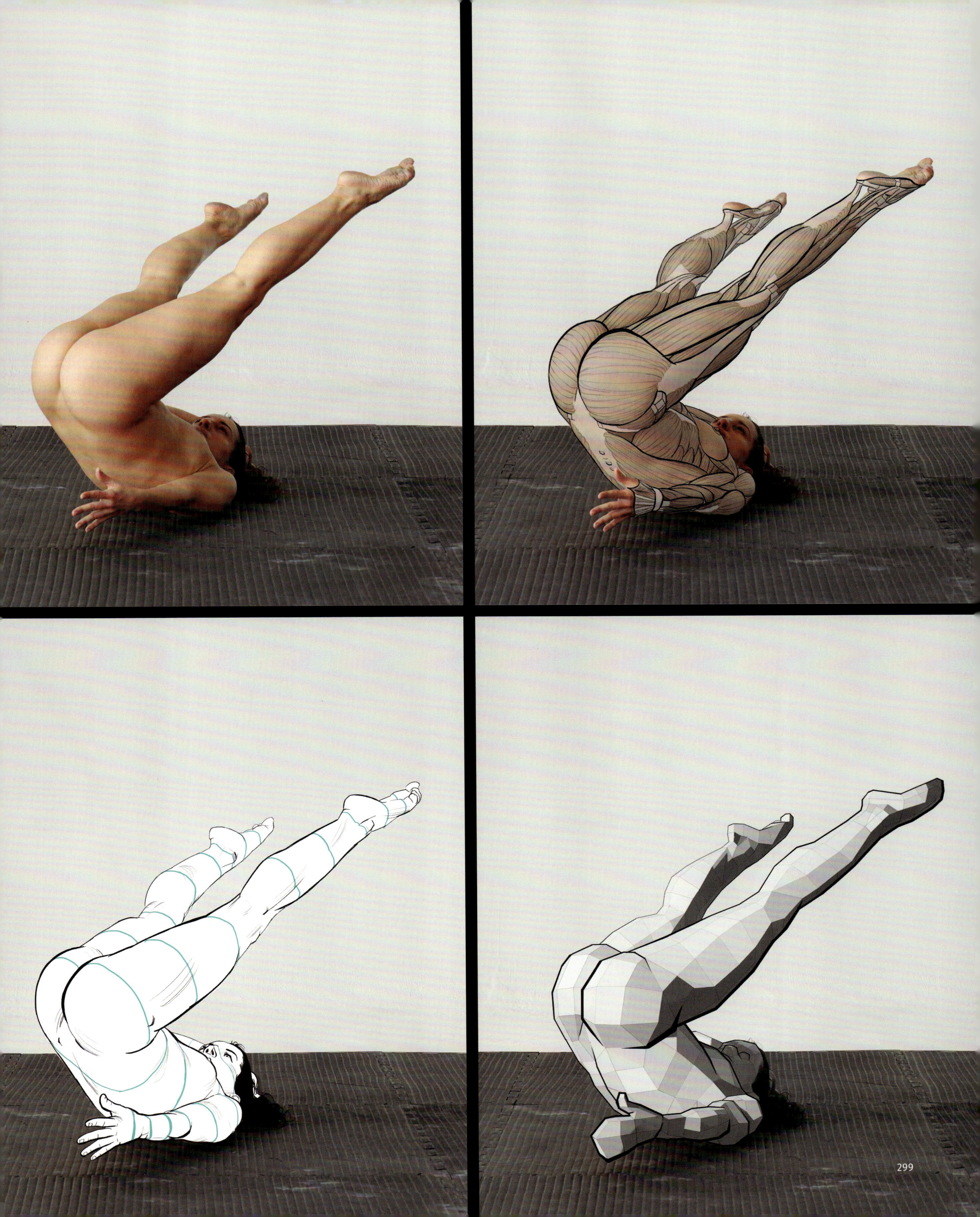

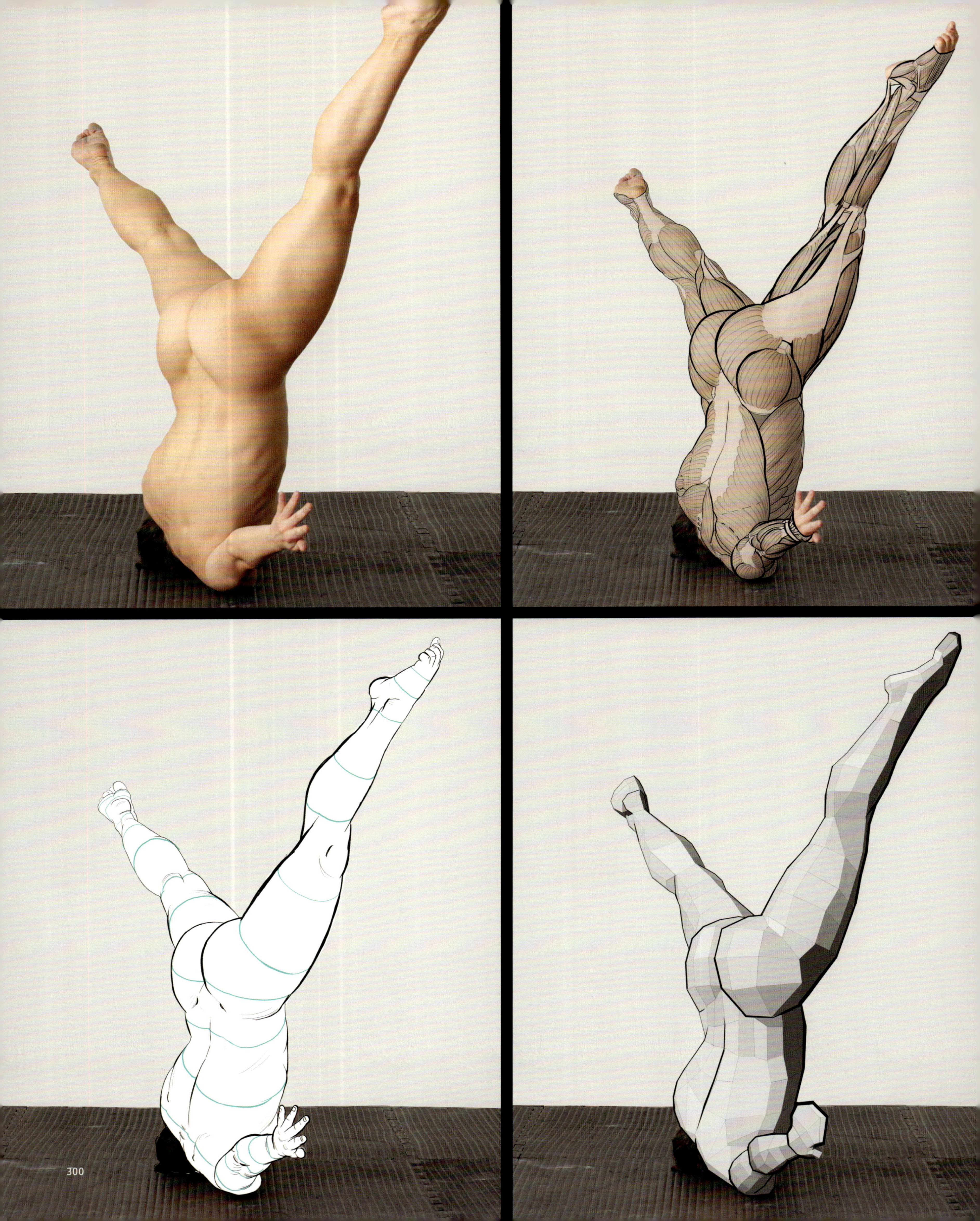

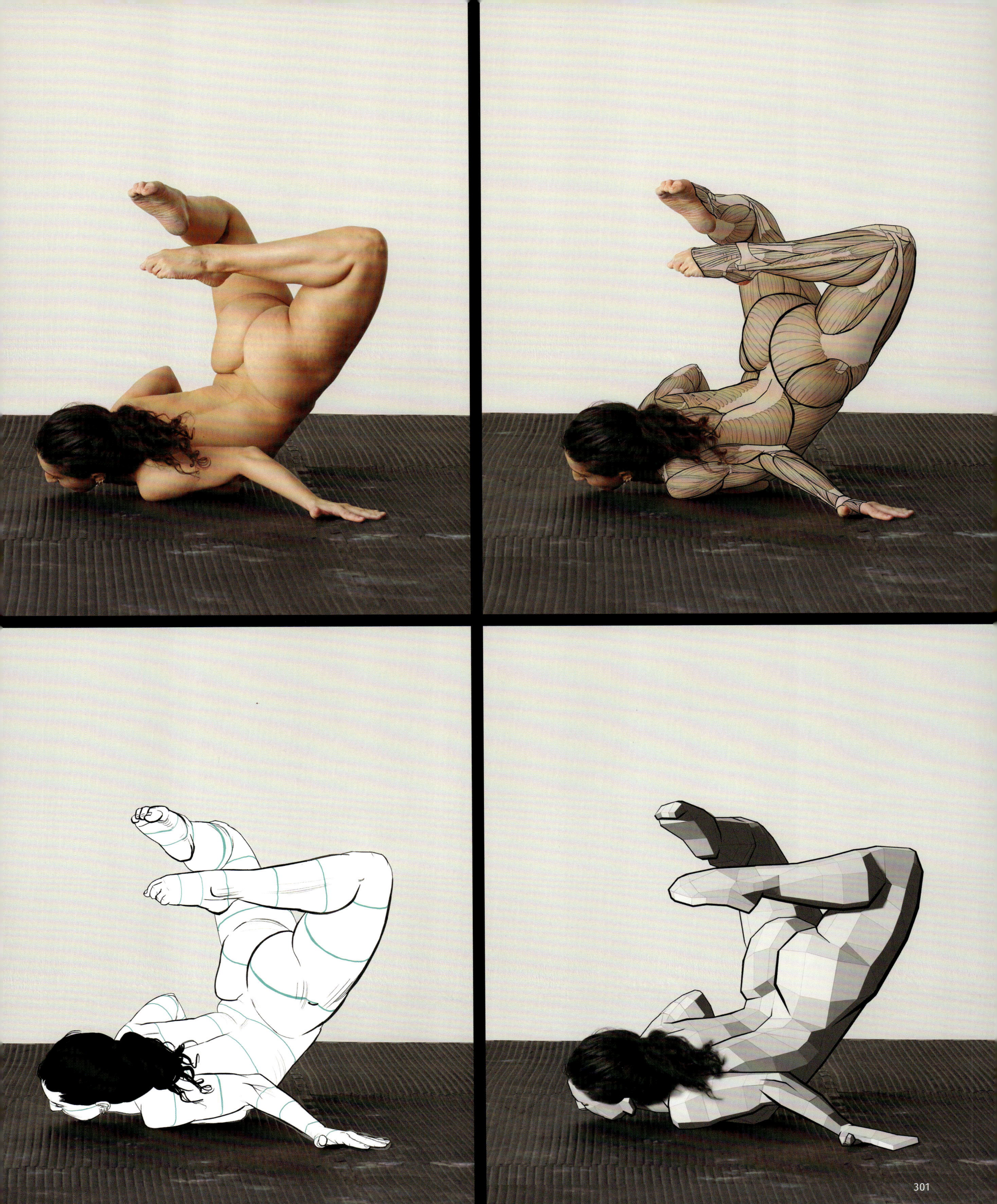

Punching

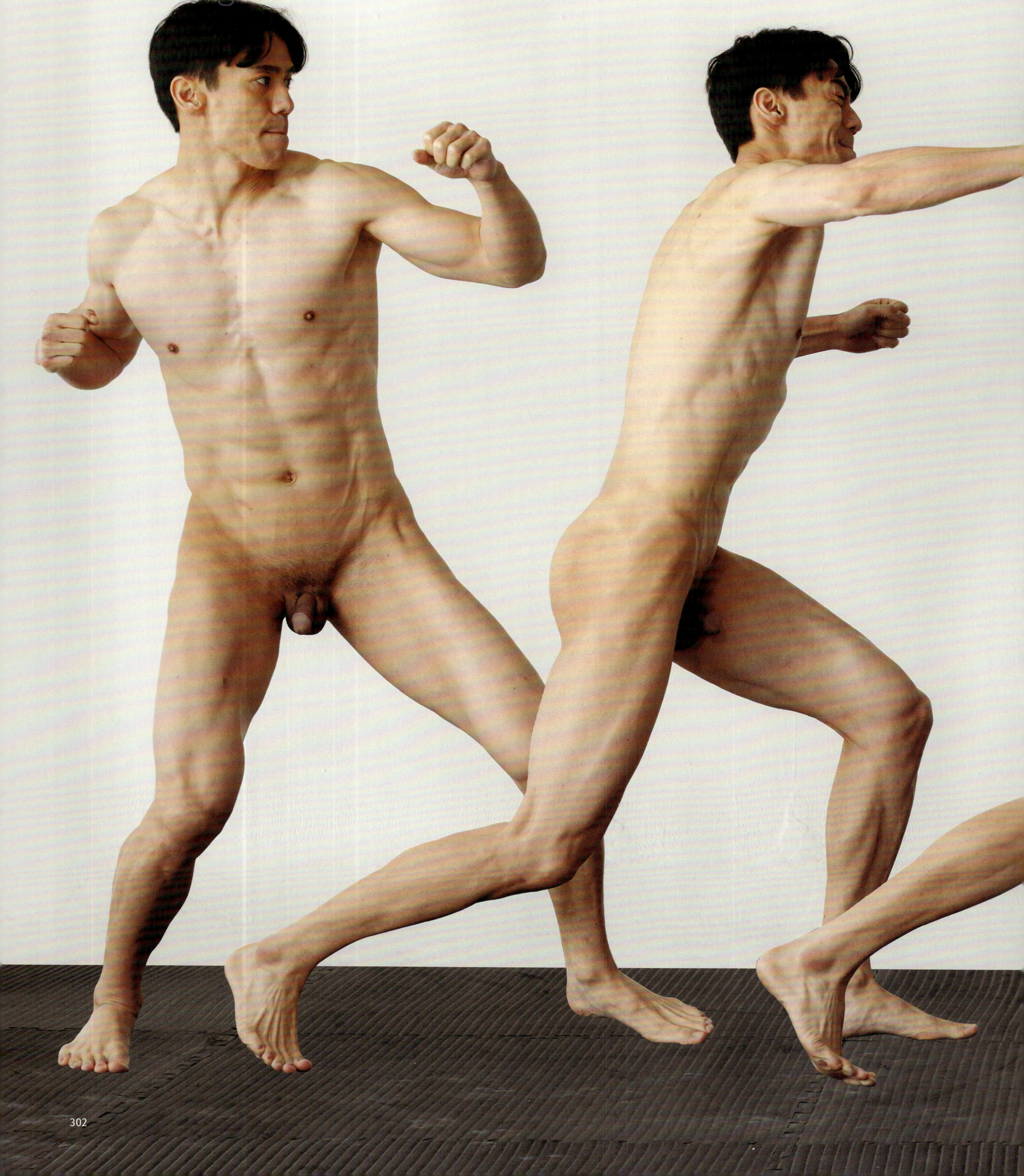

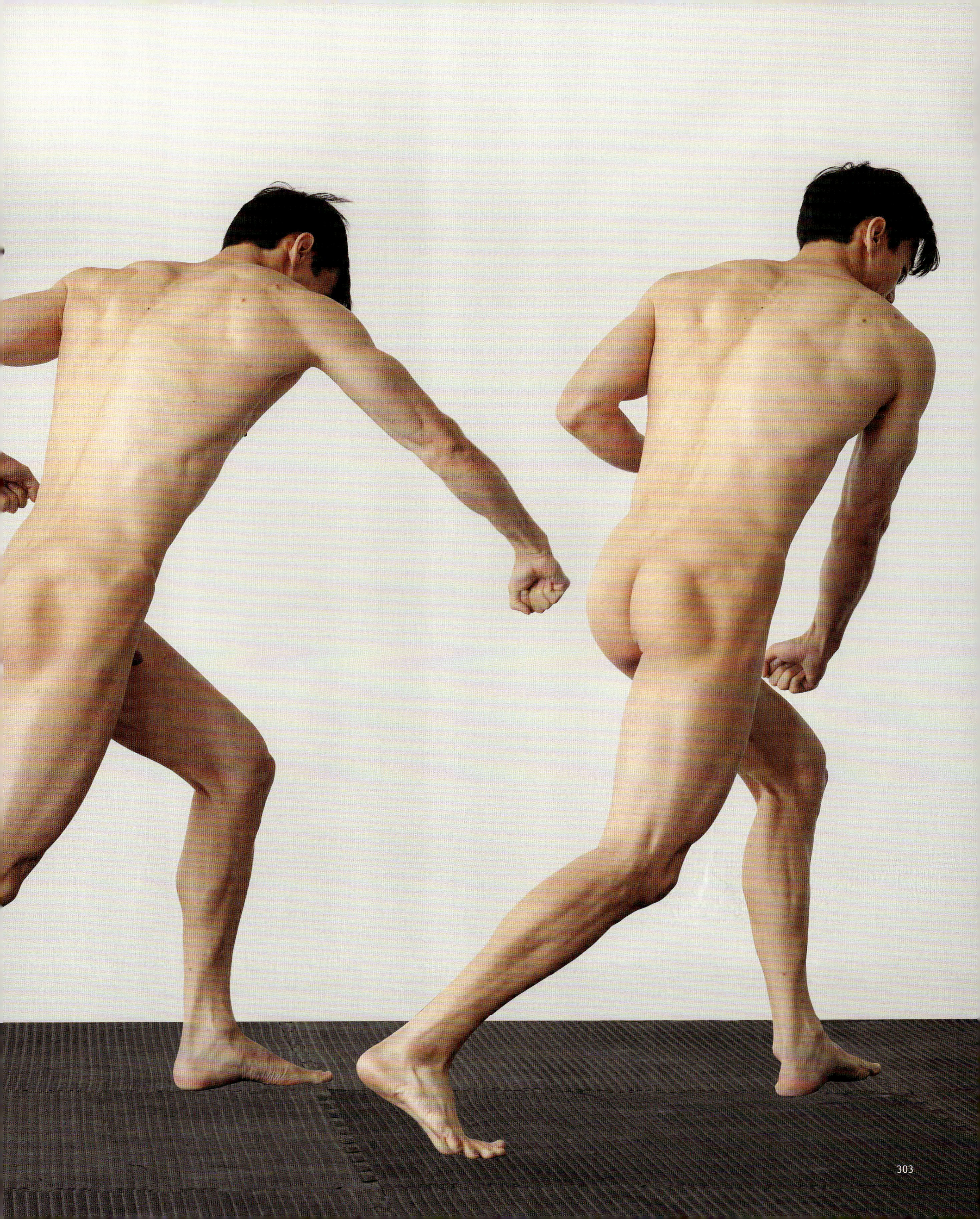

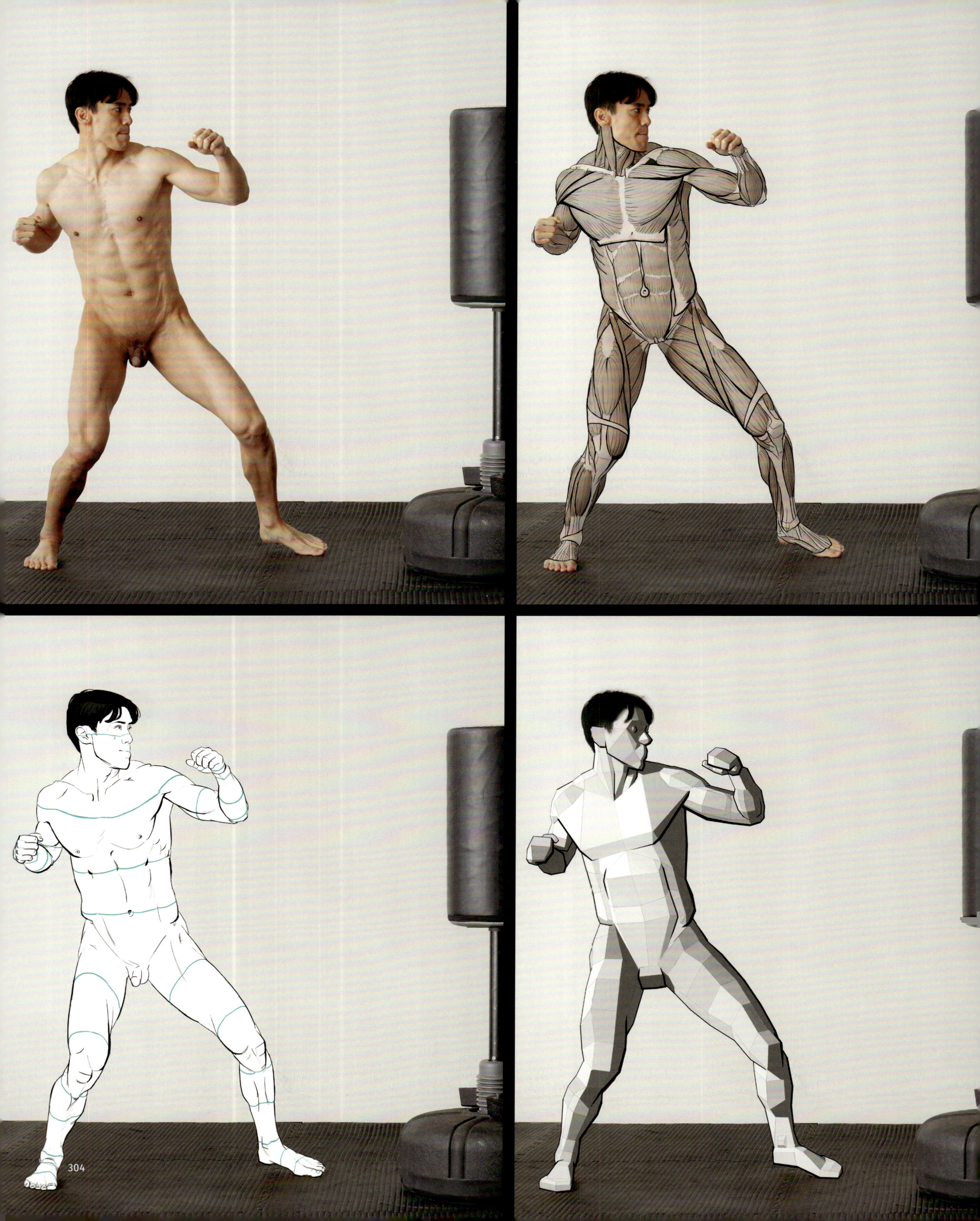

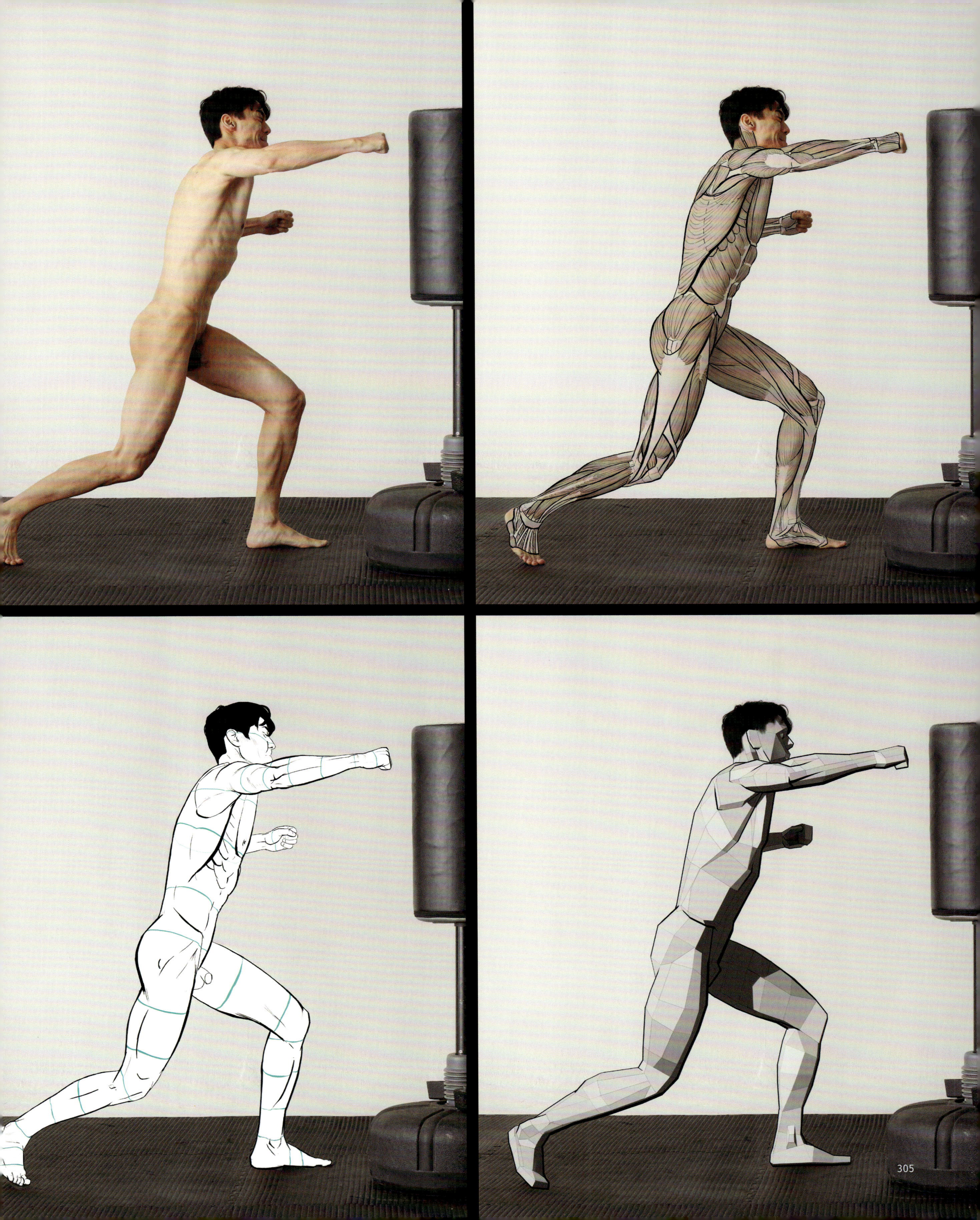

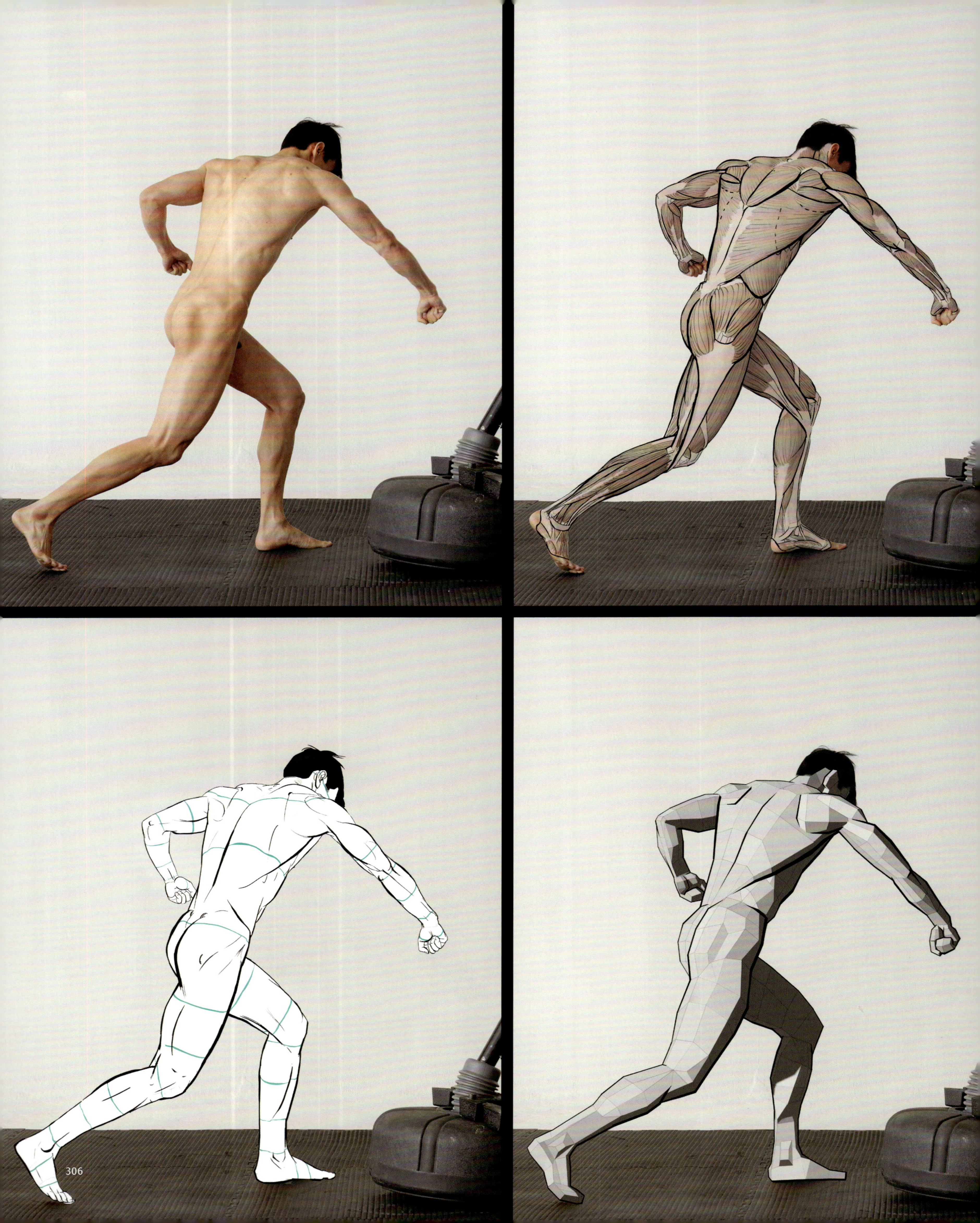

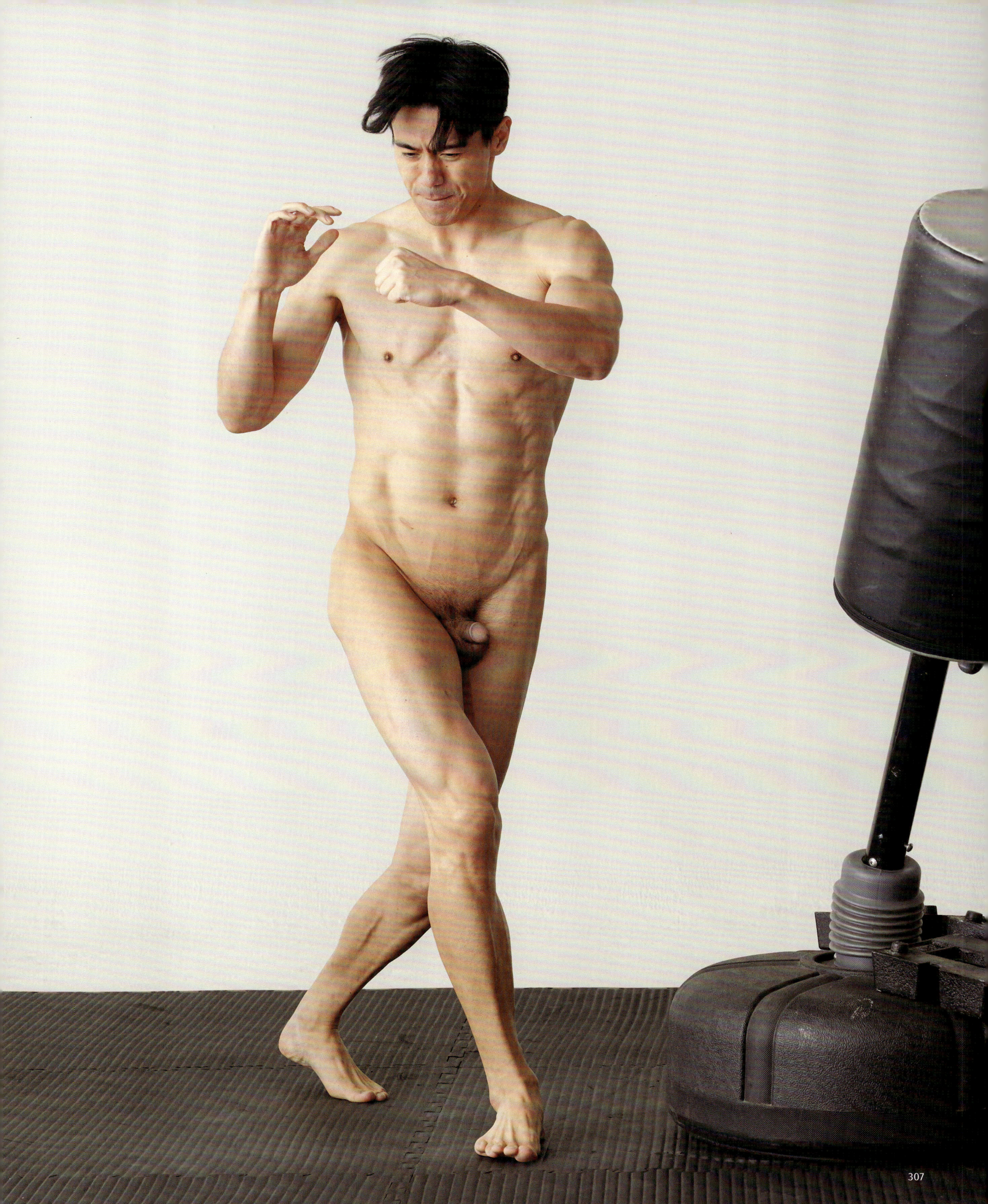

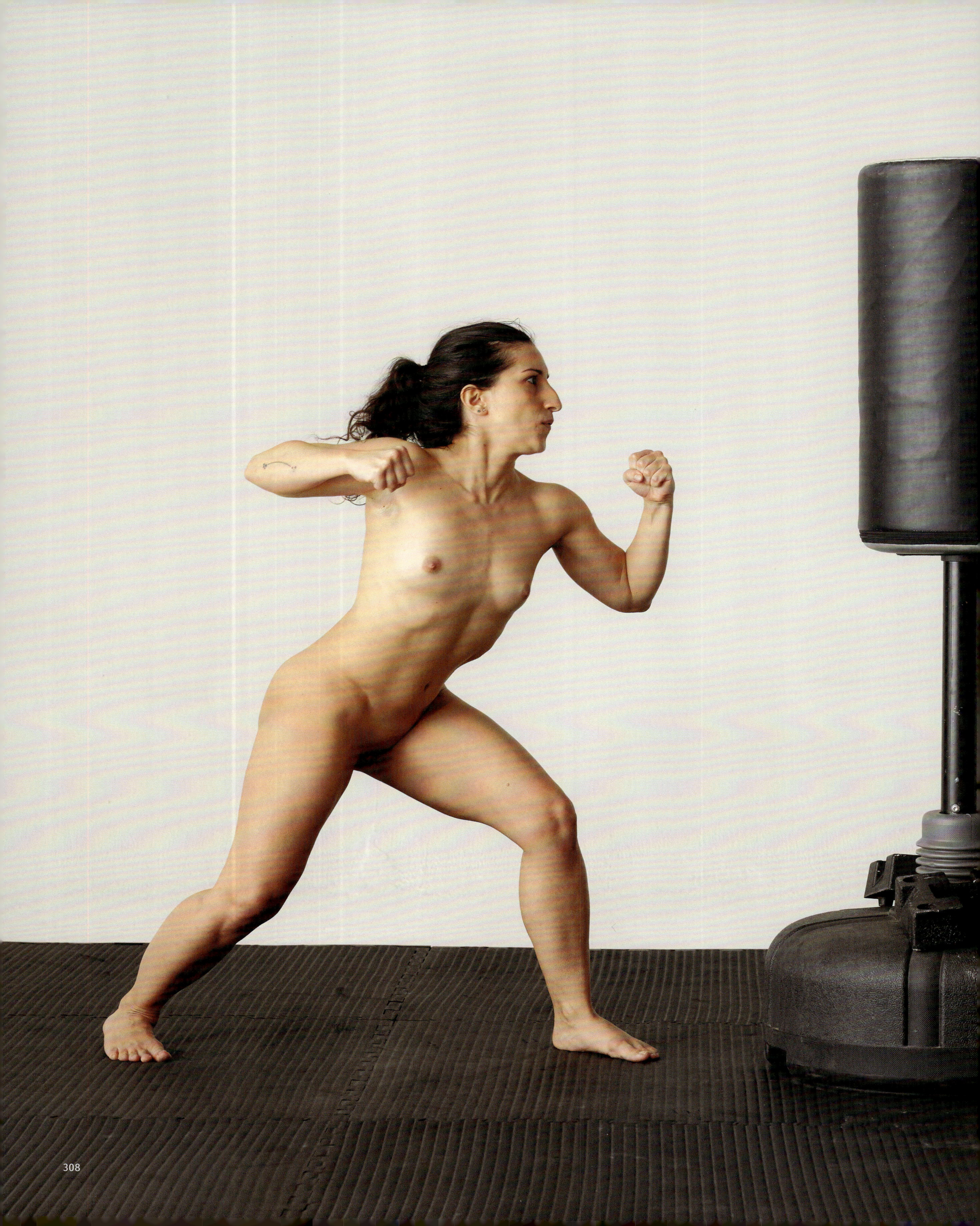

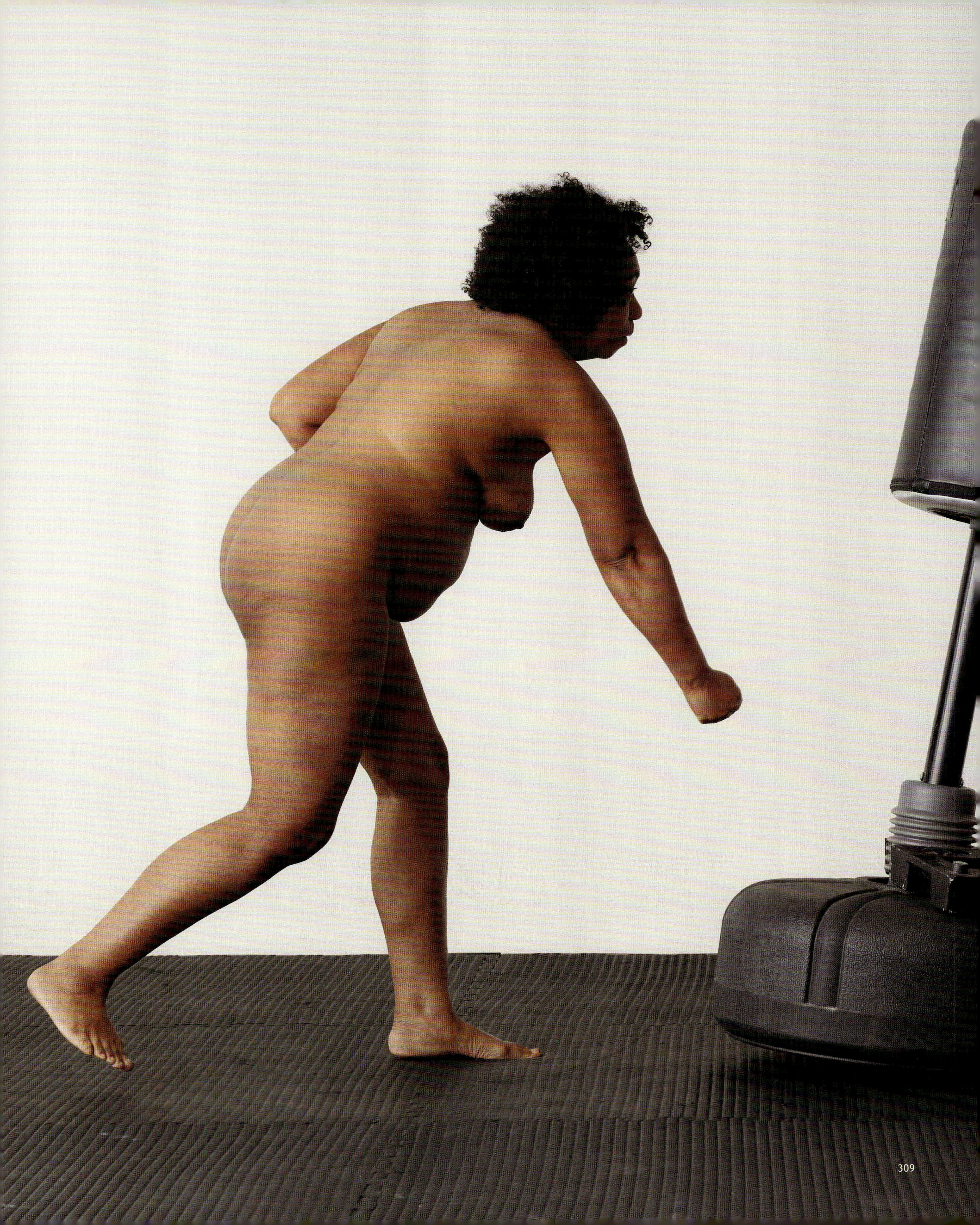

Kicking

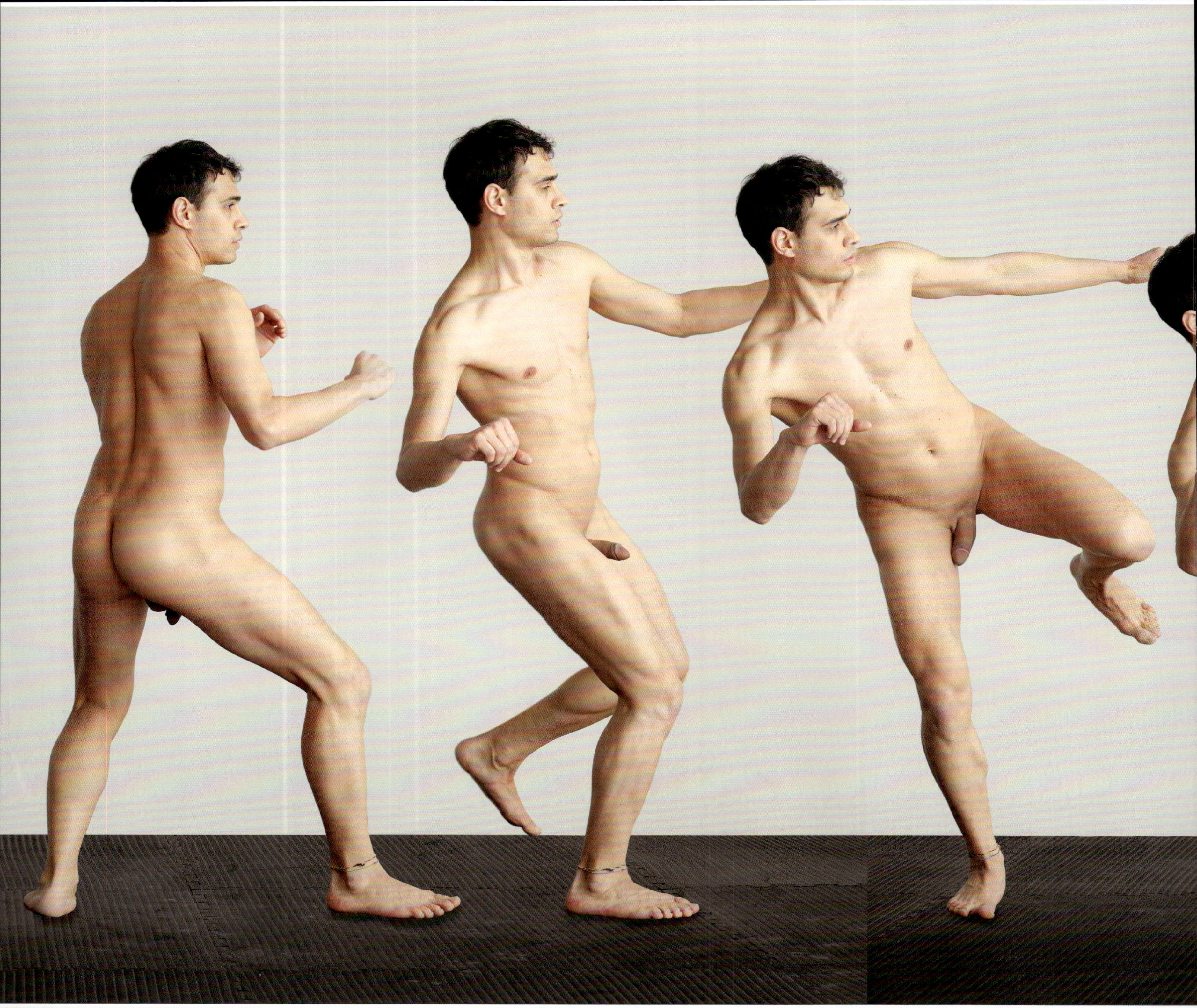

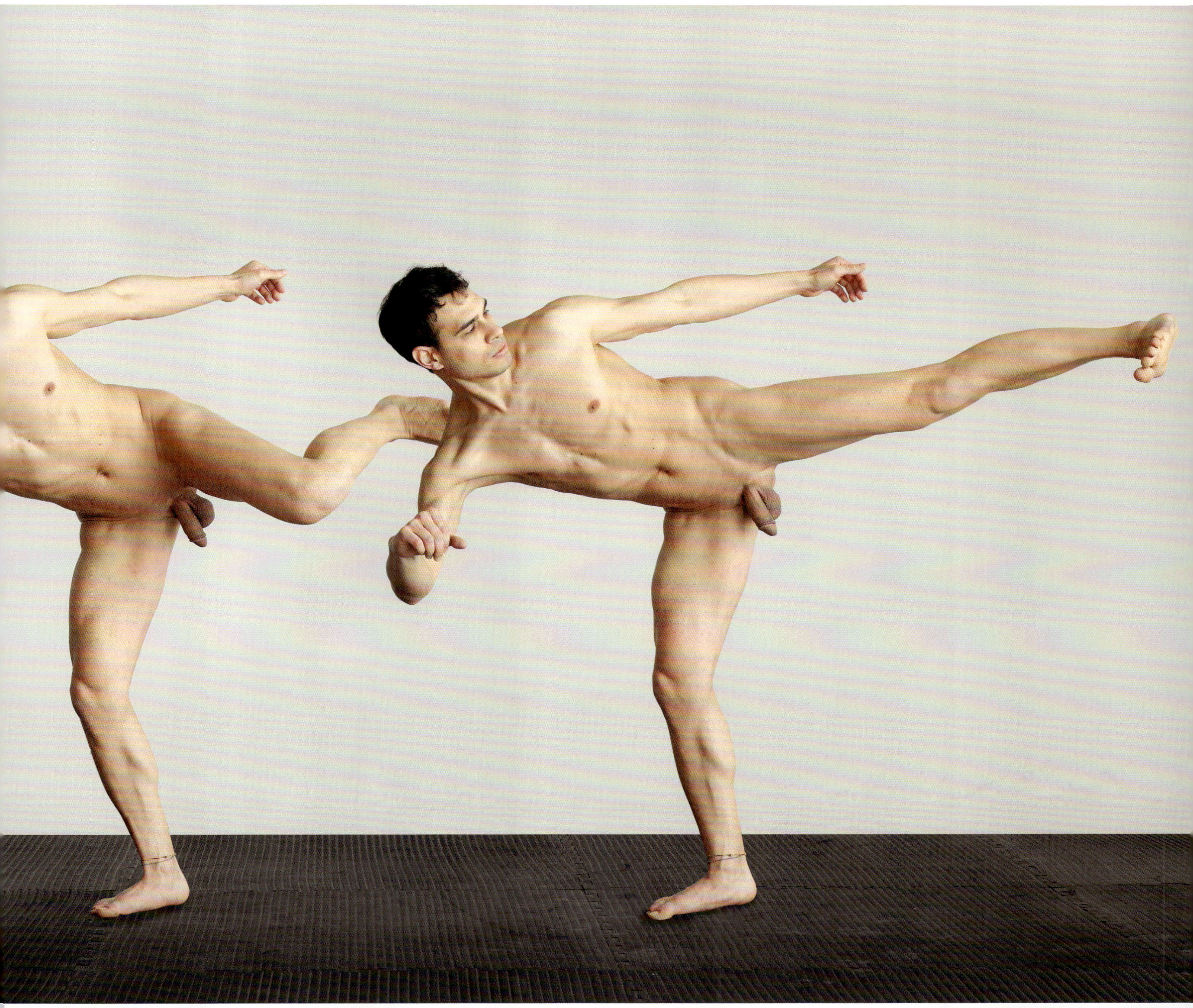

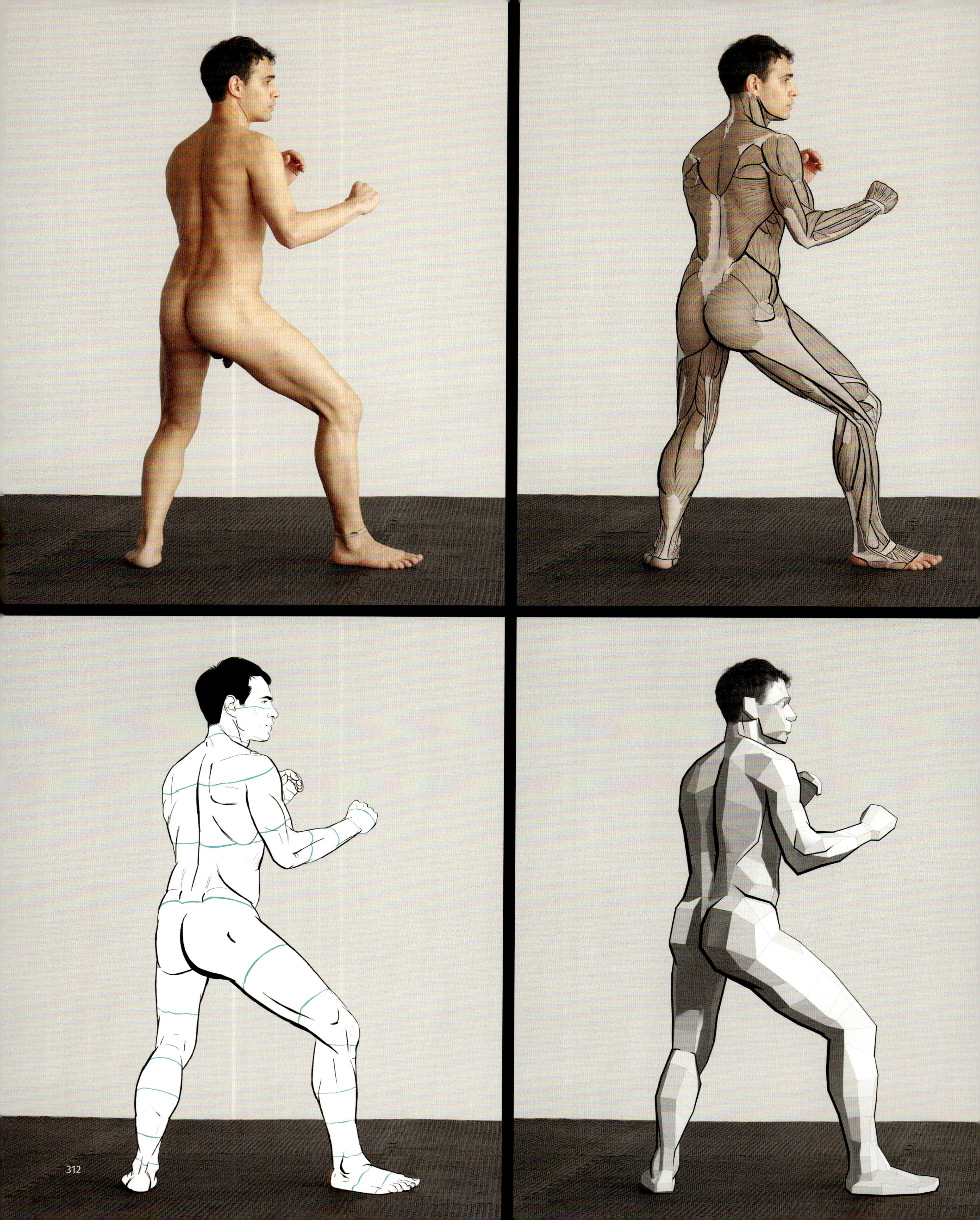

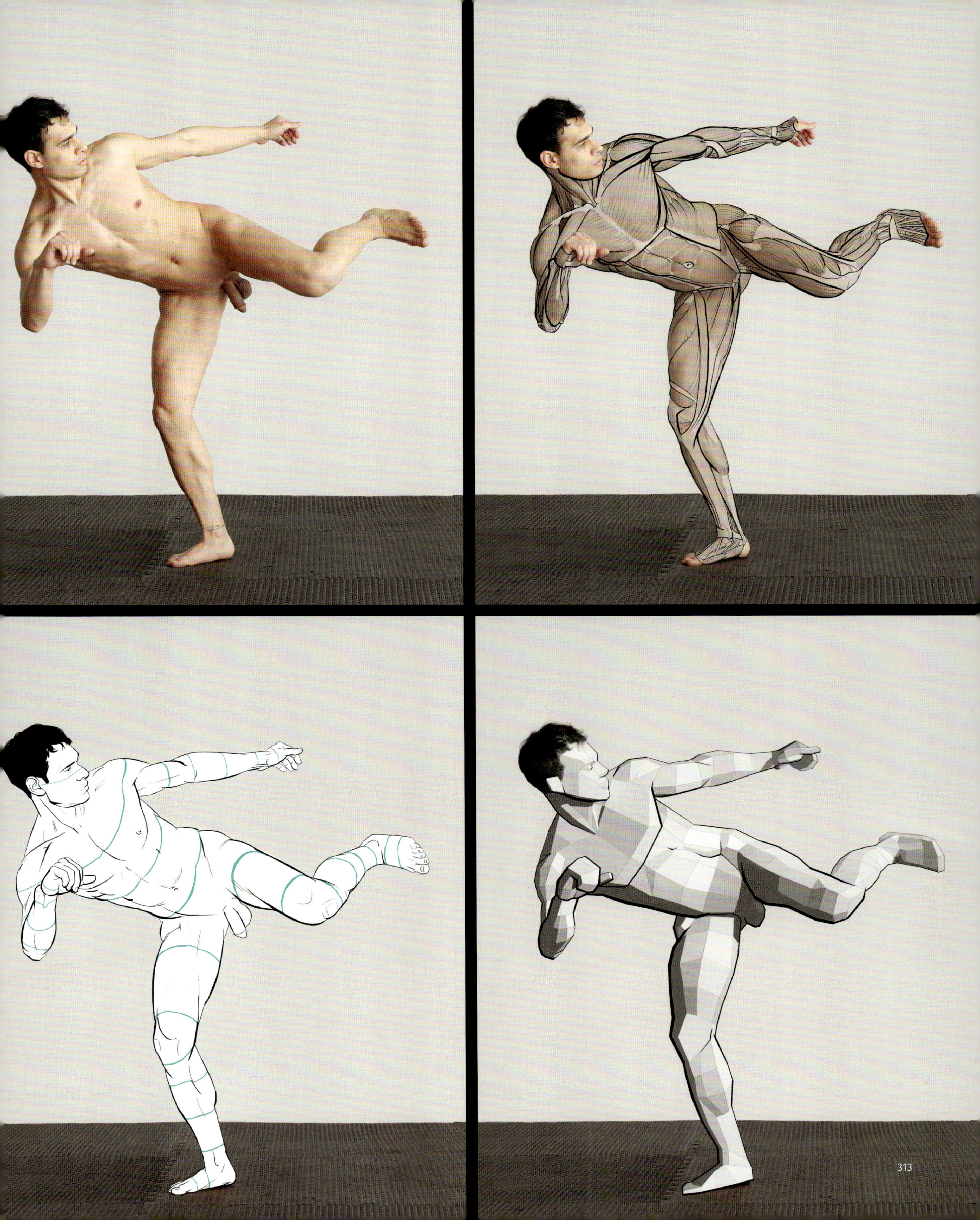

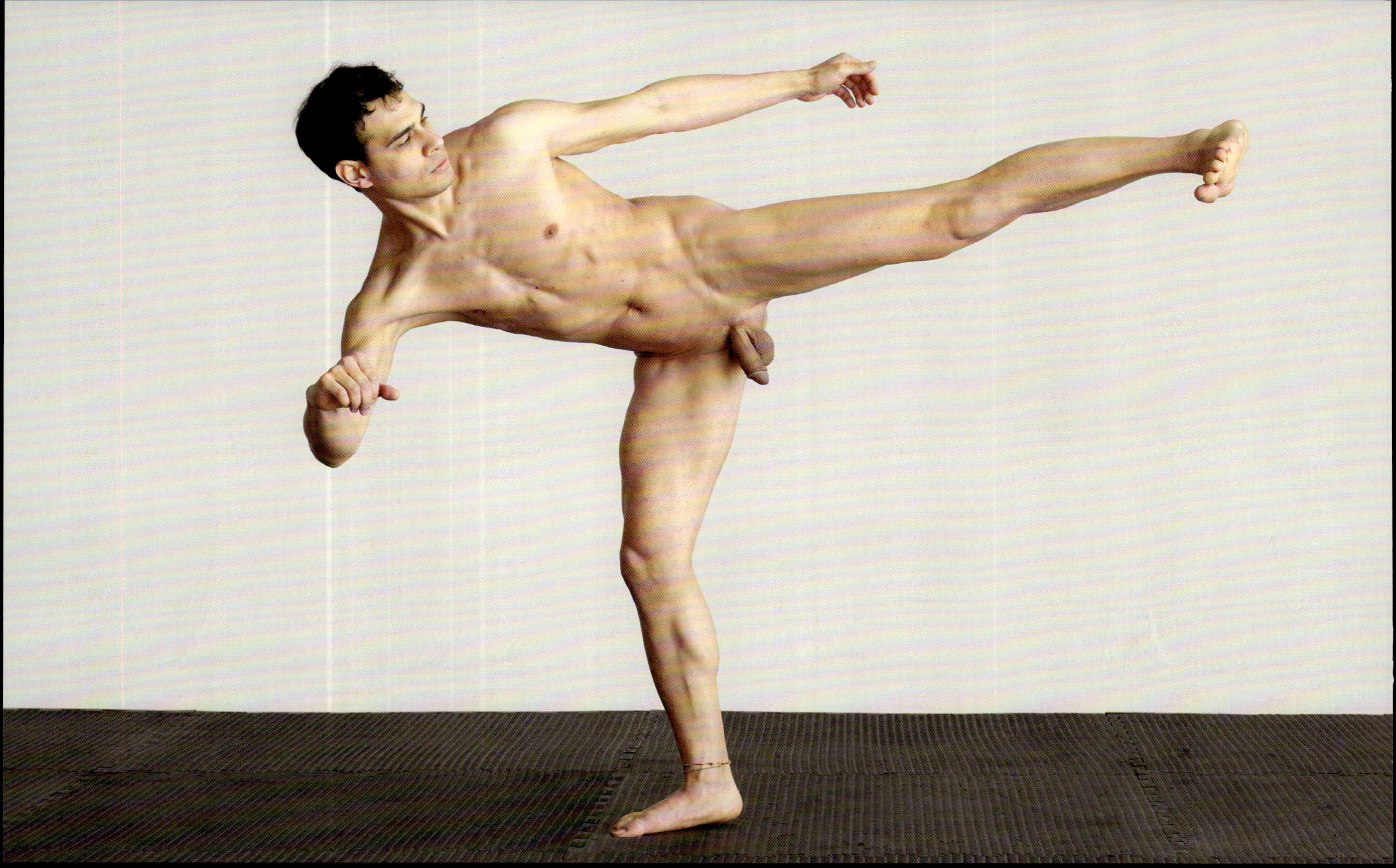

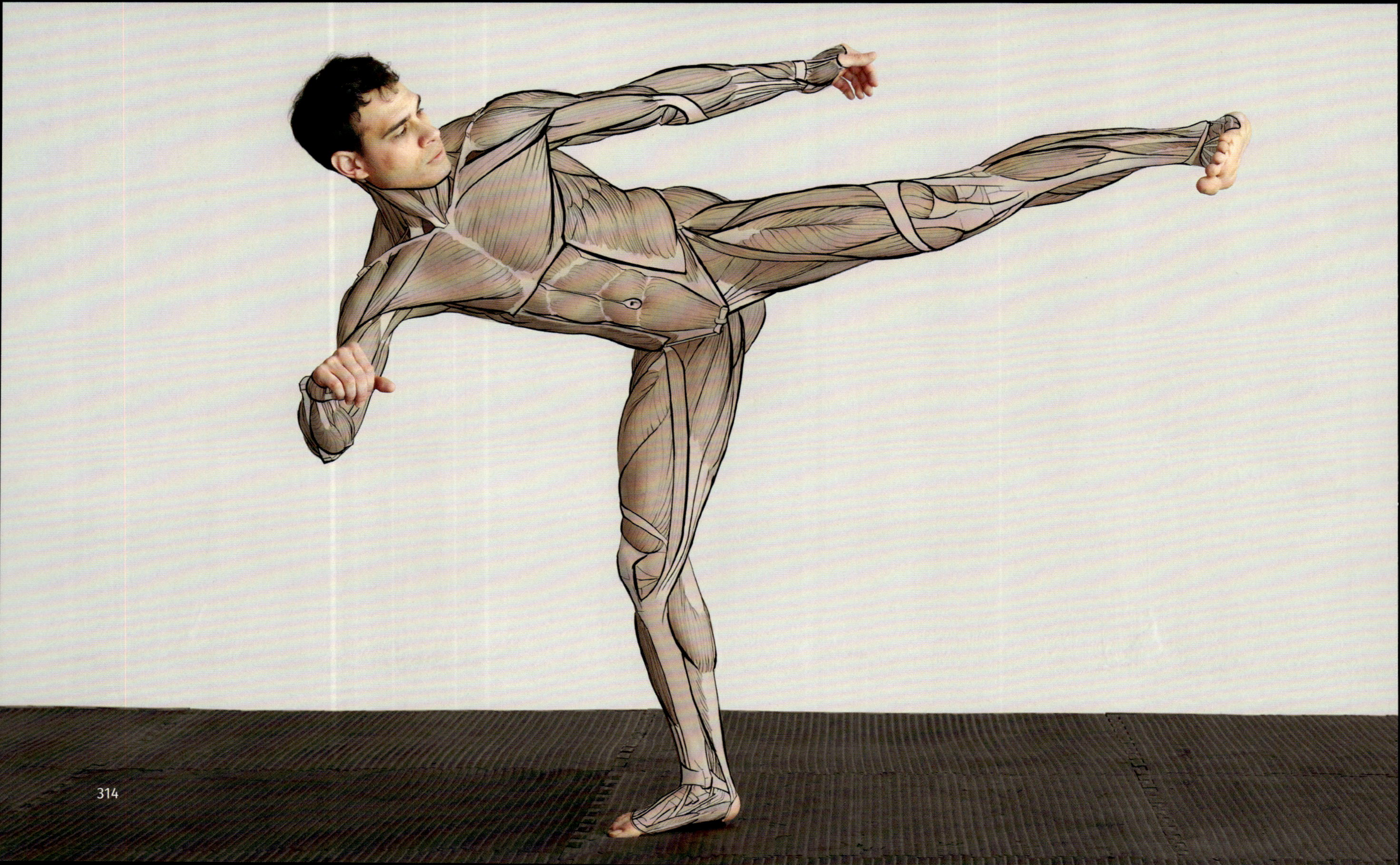

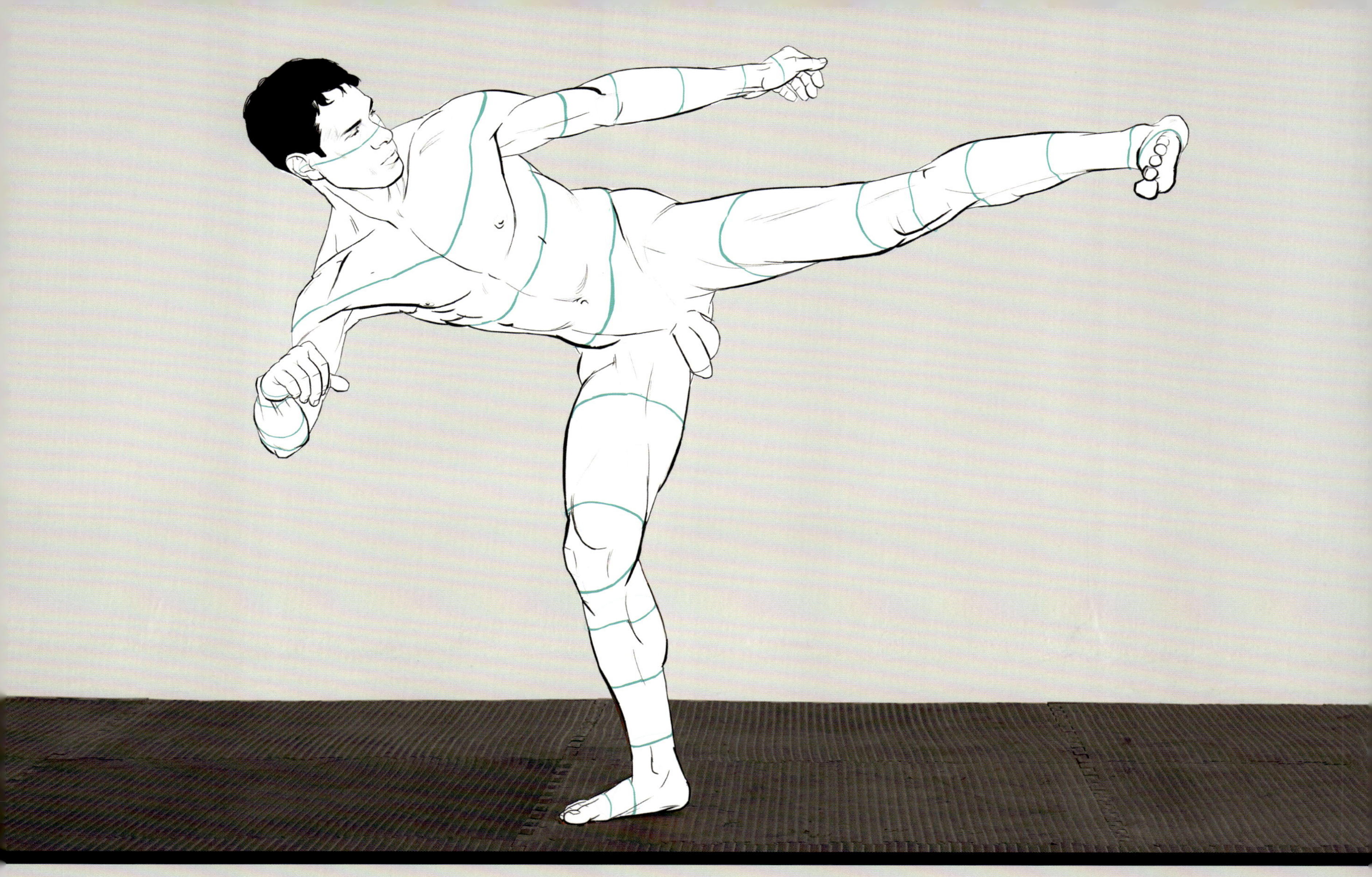

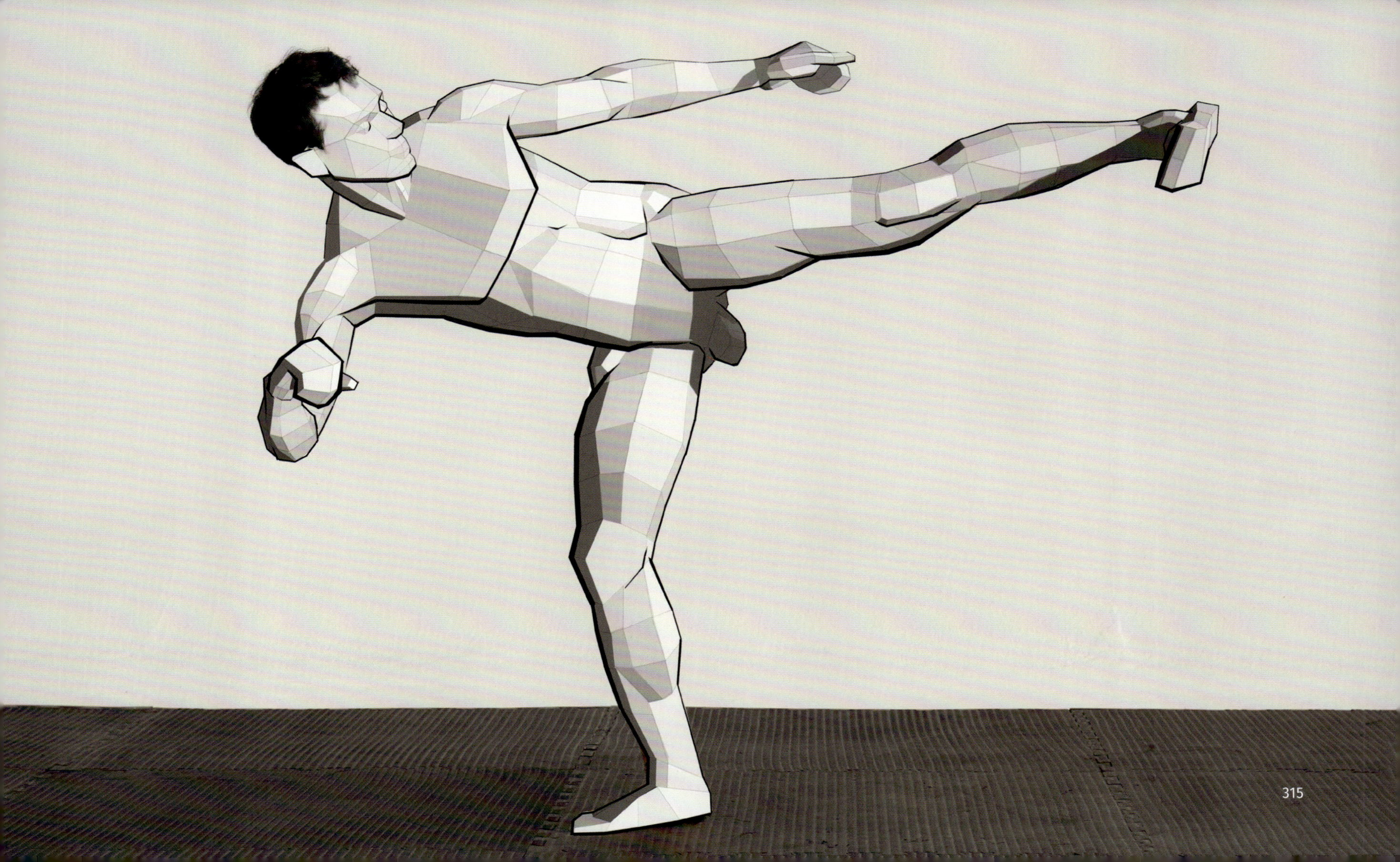

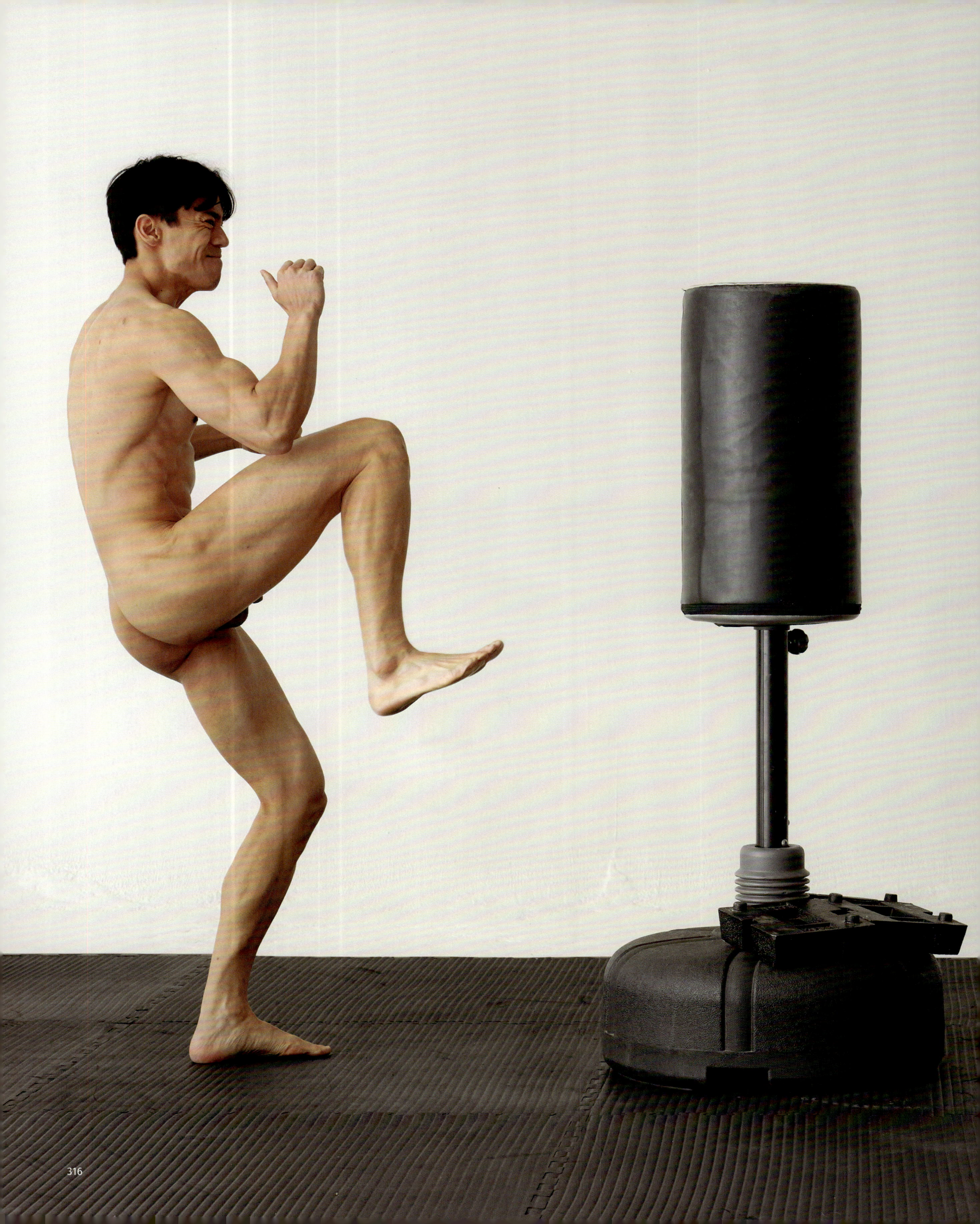

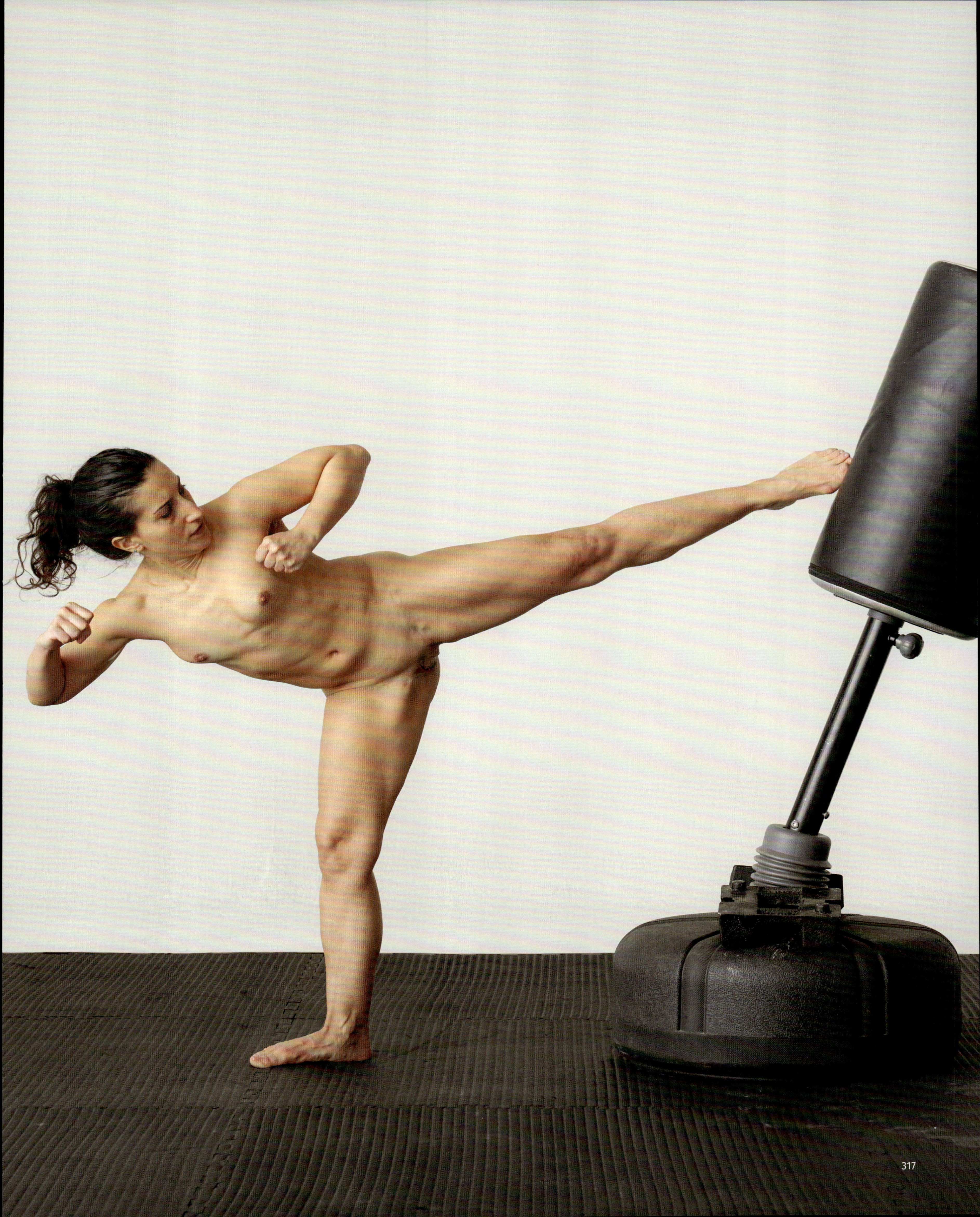

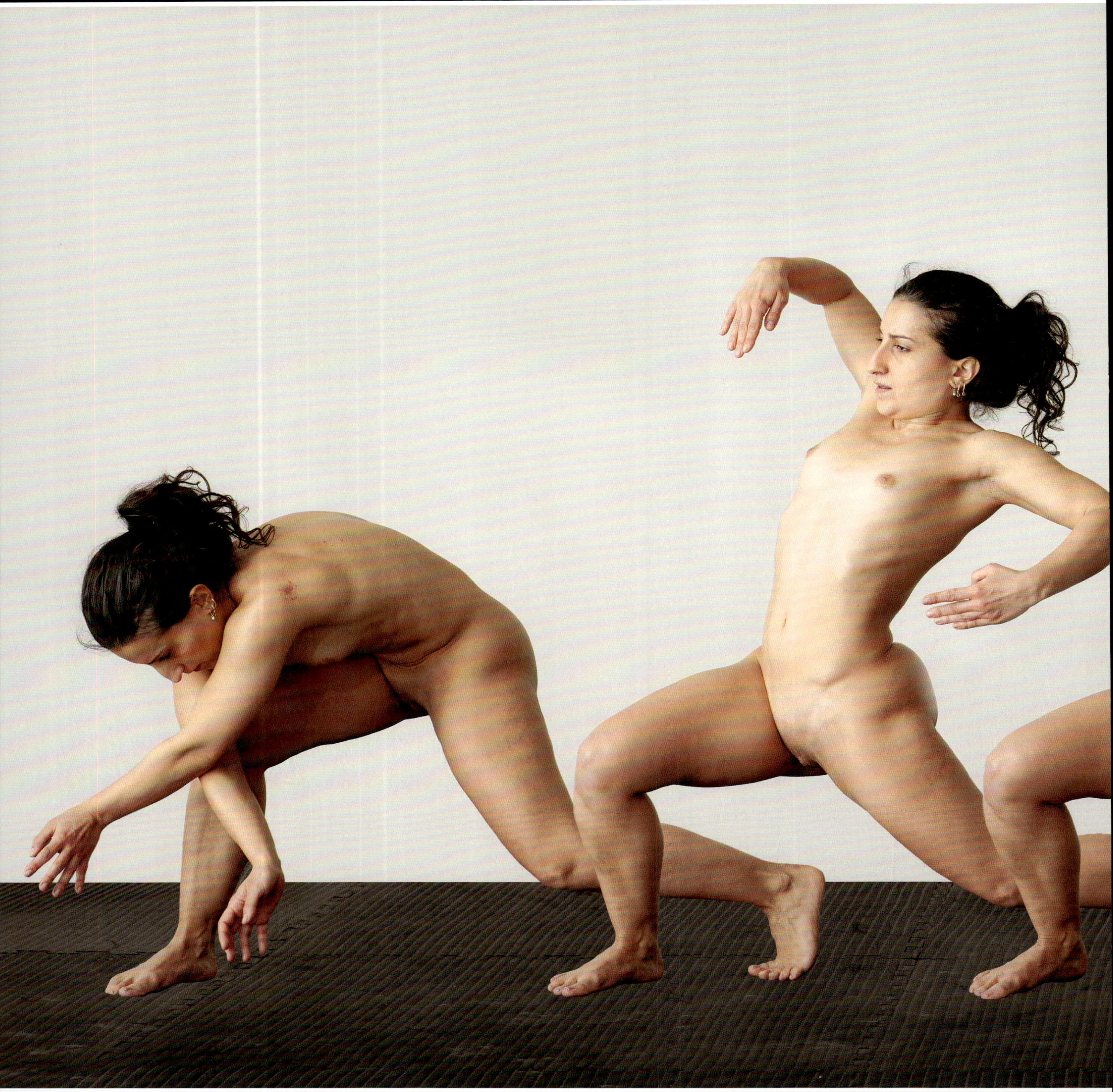

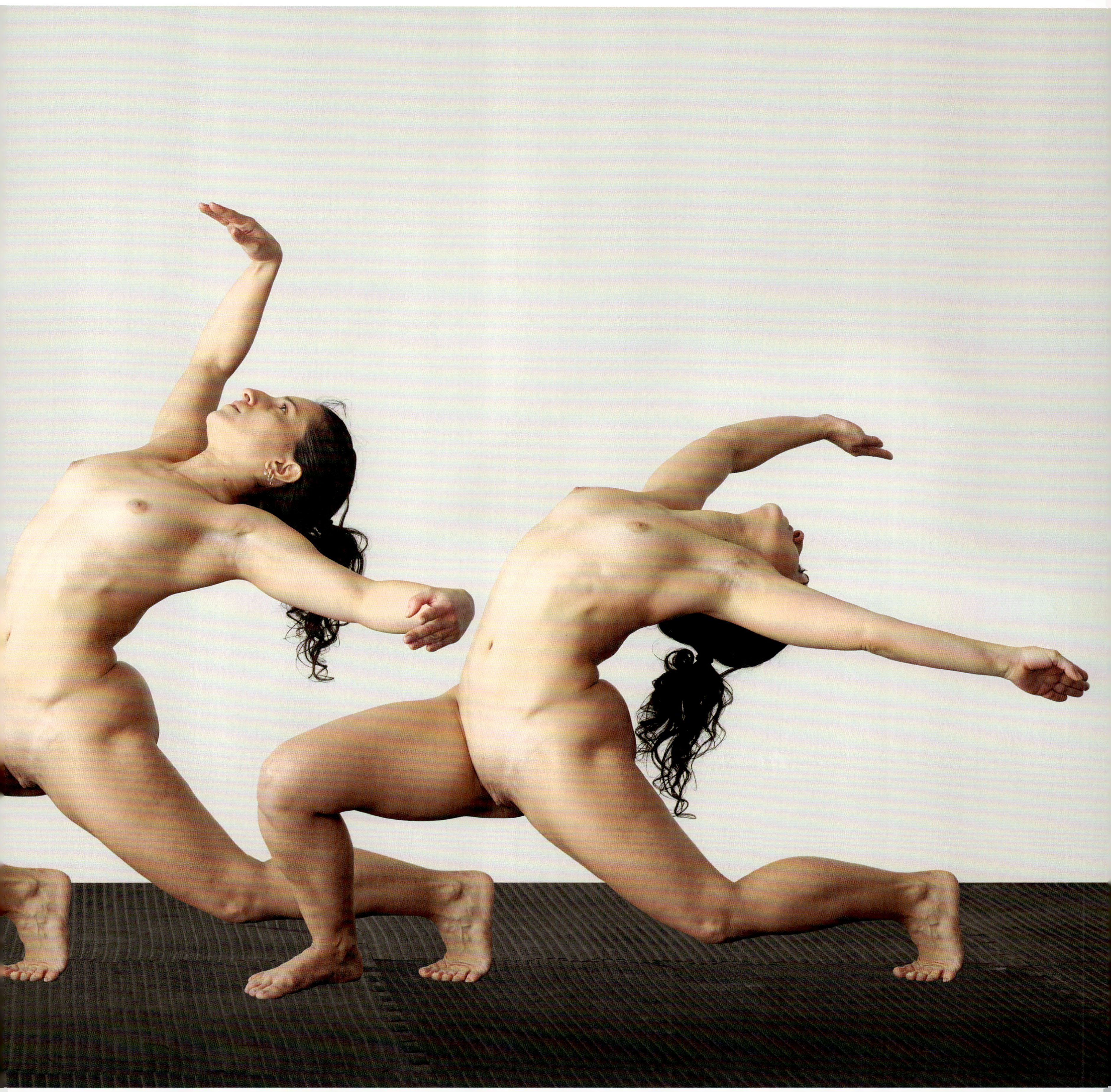

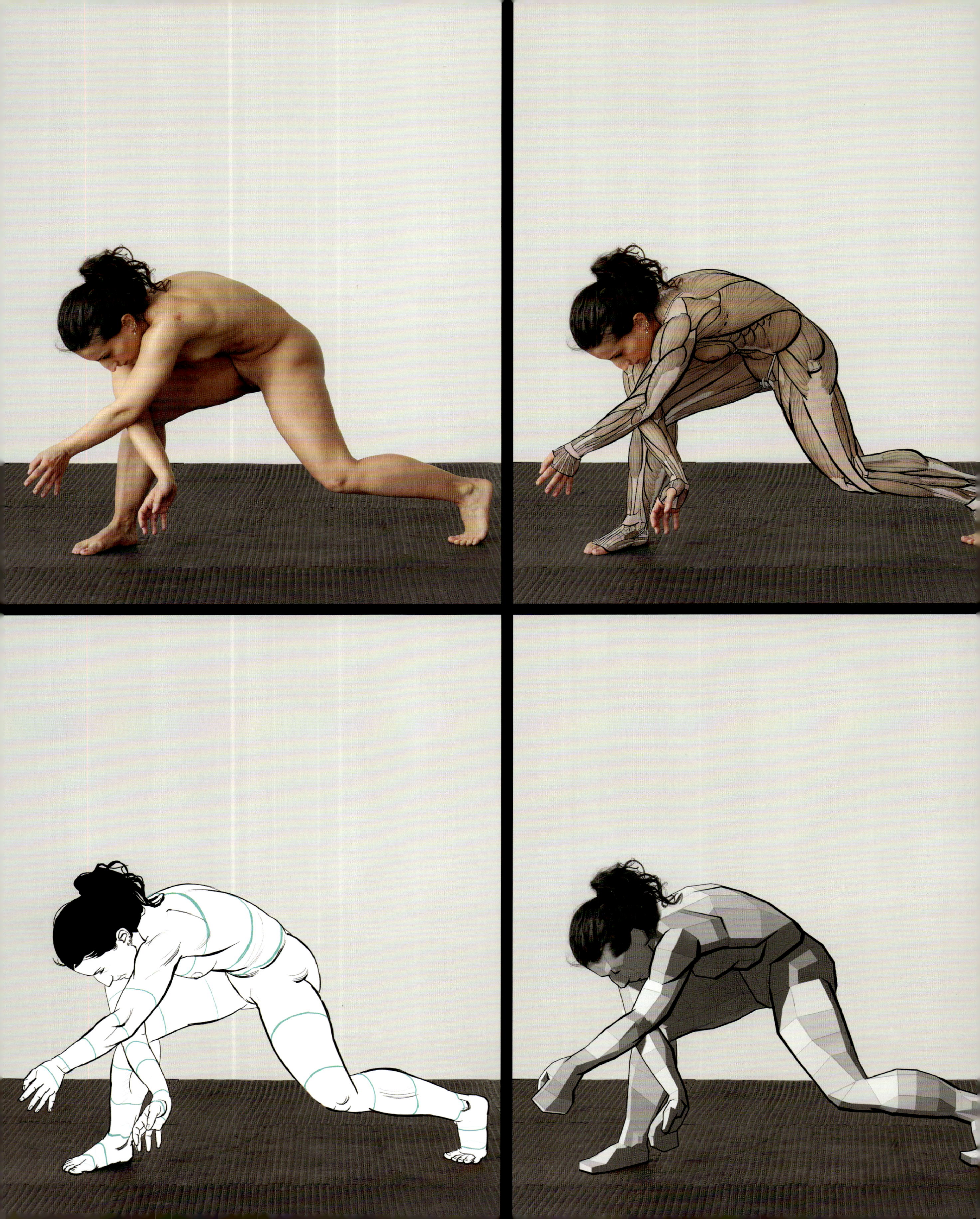

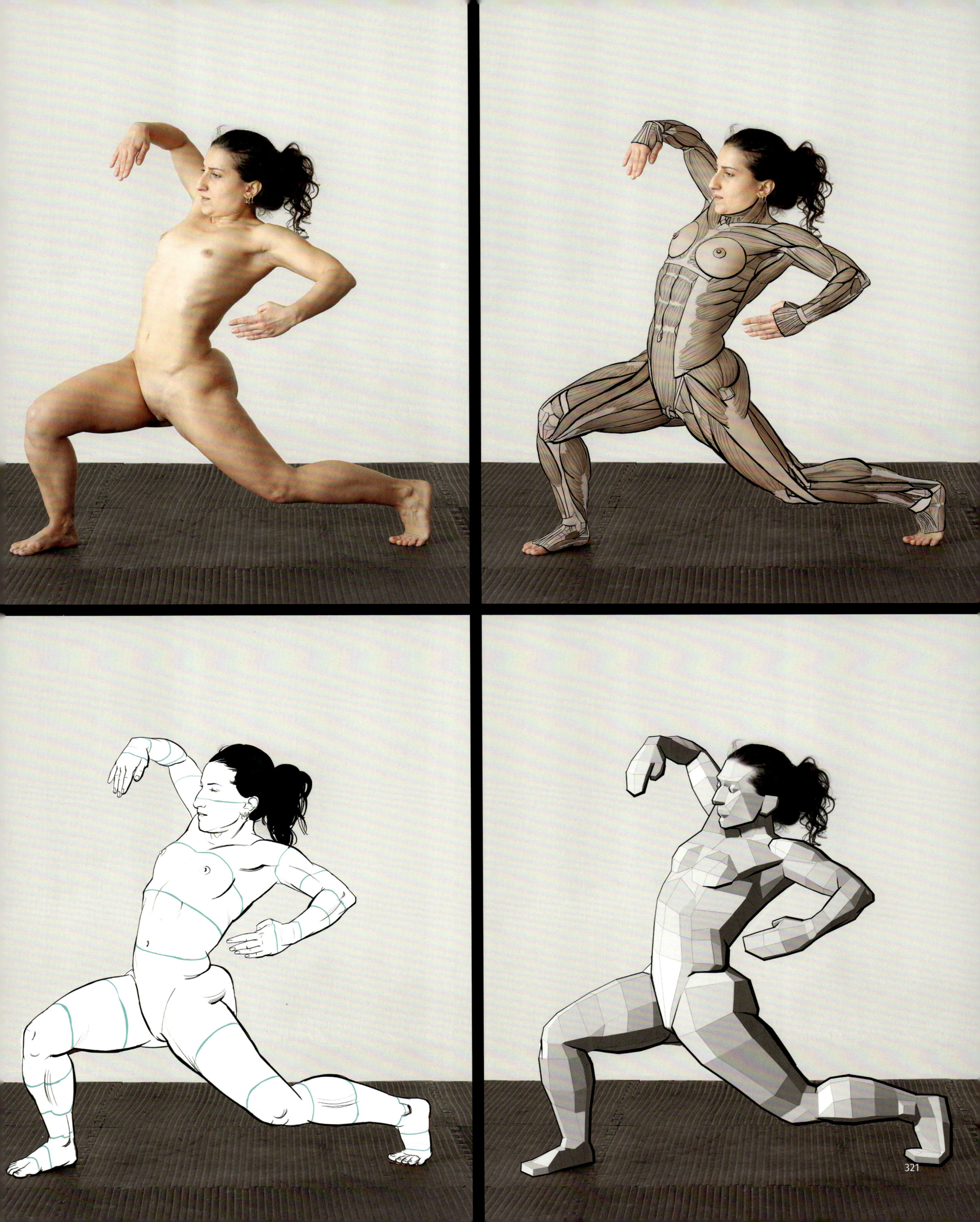

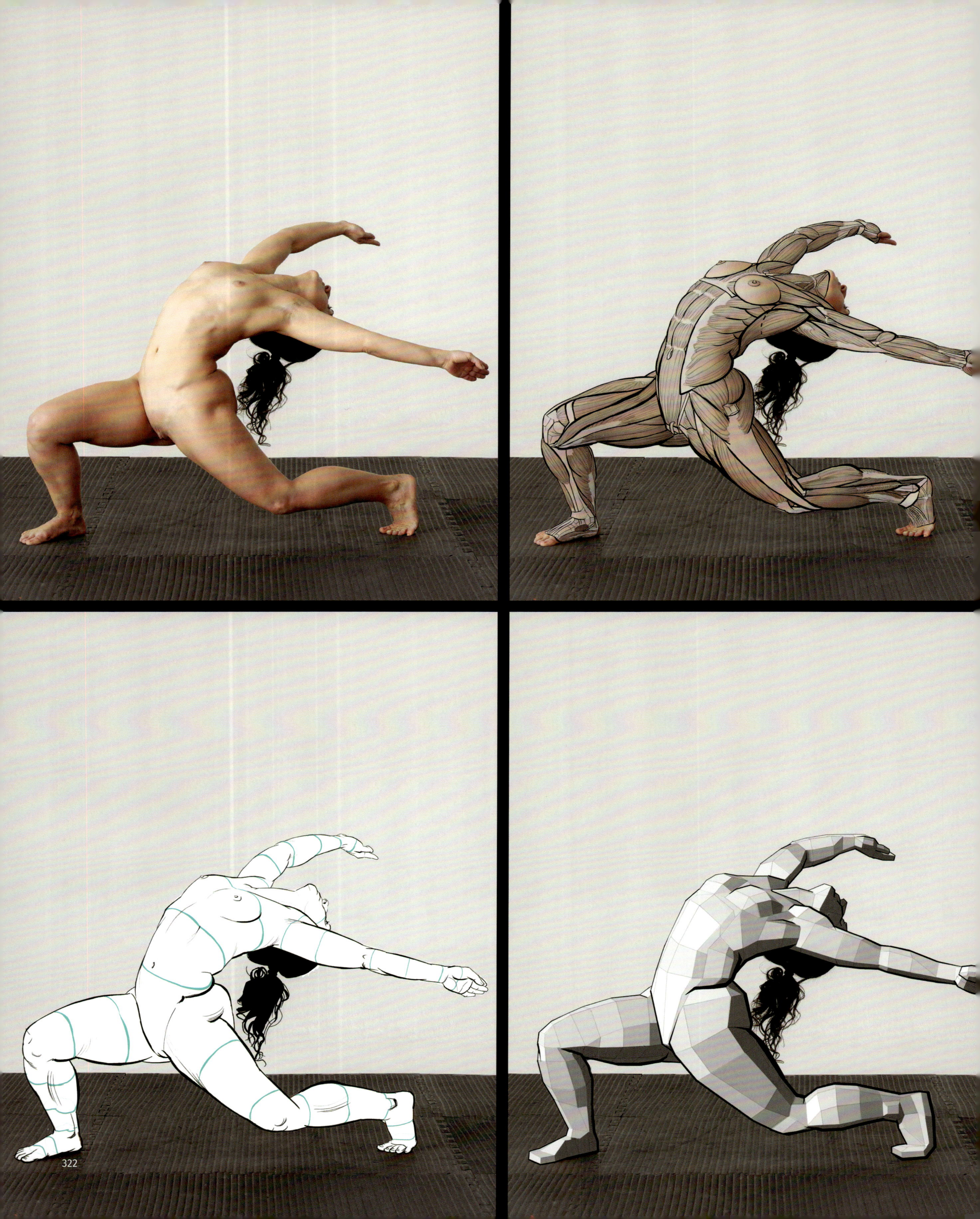

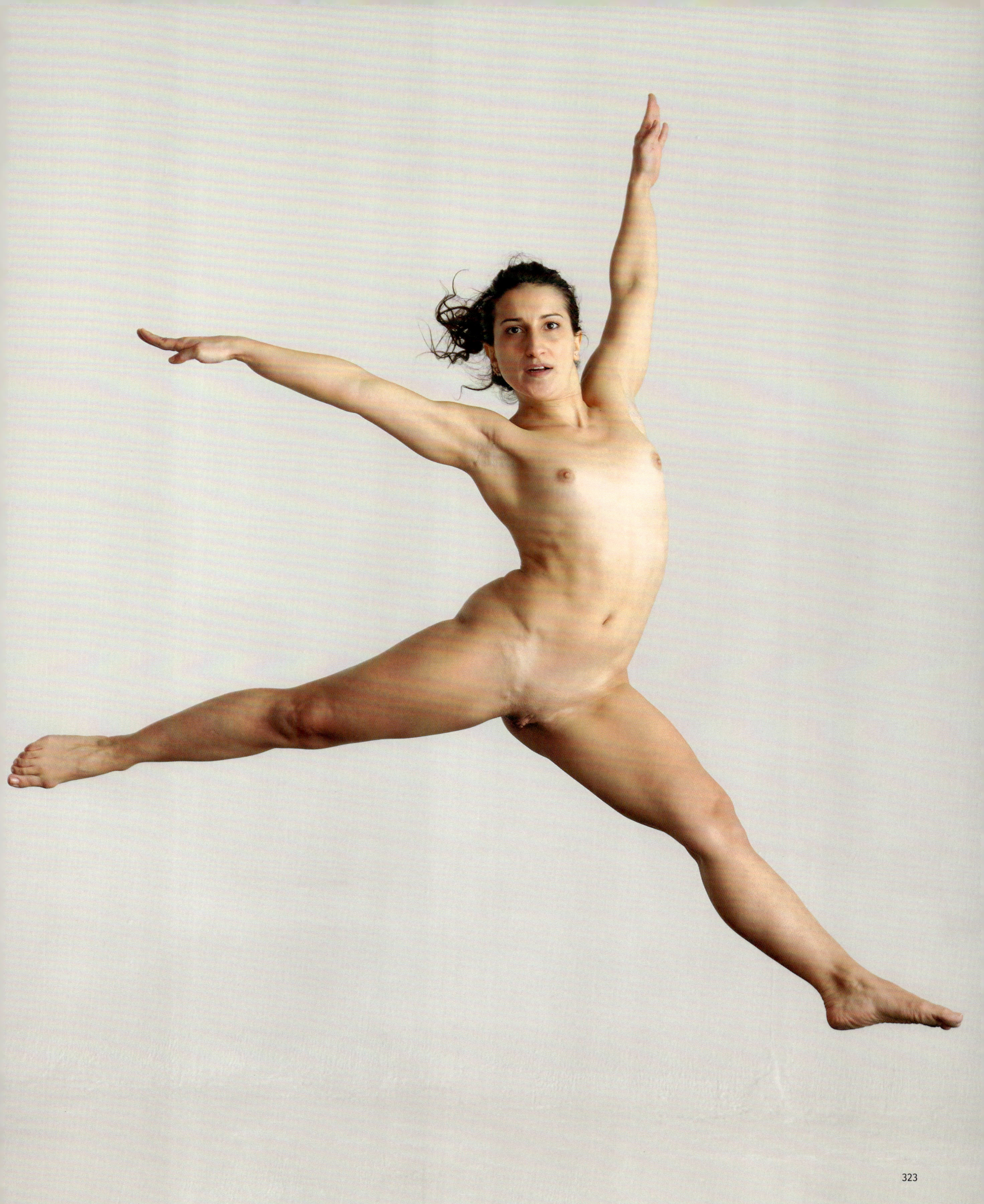

Unarmed combat

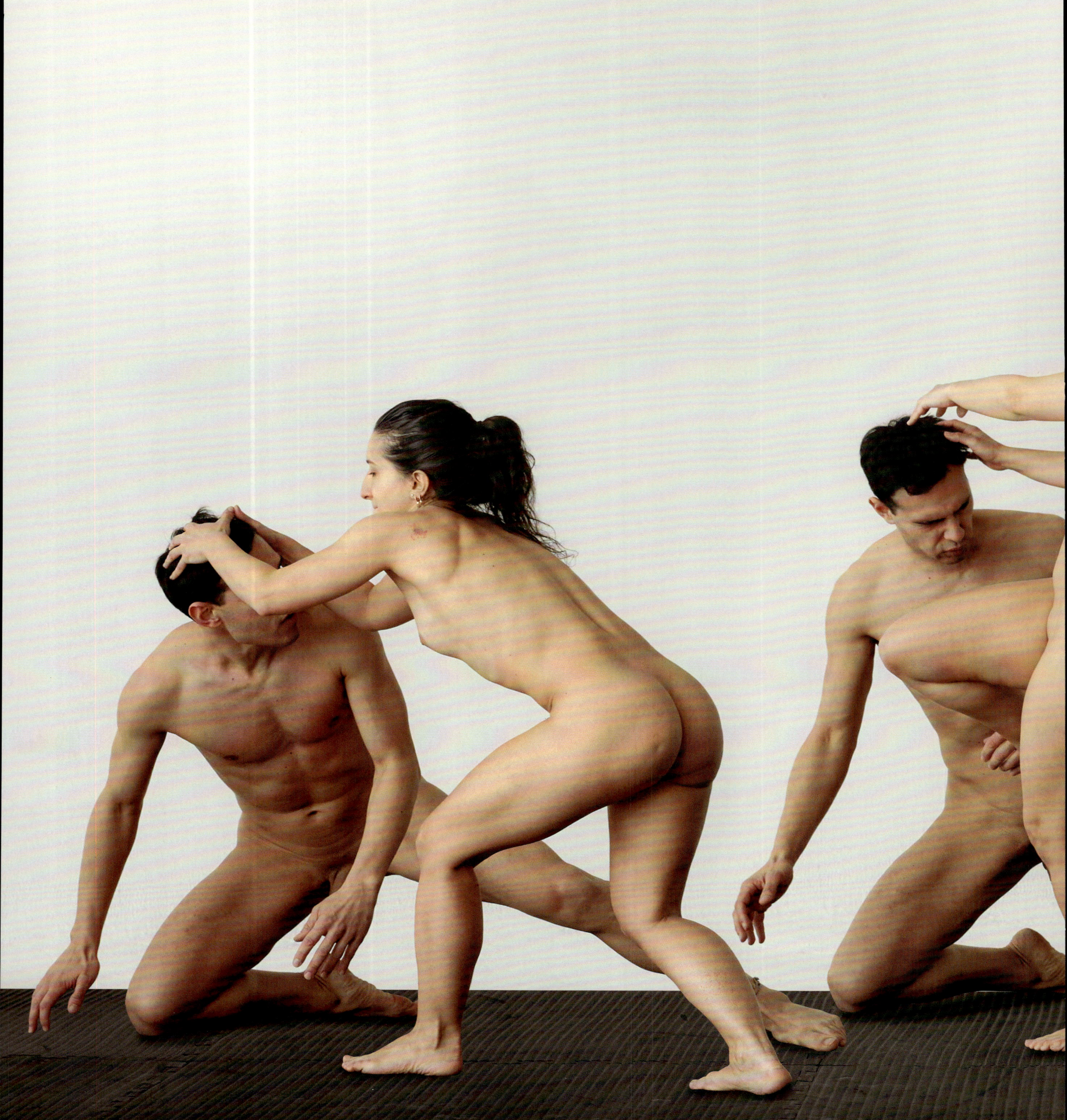

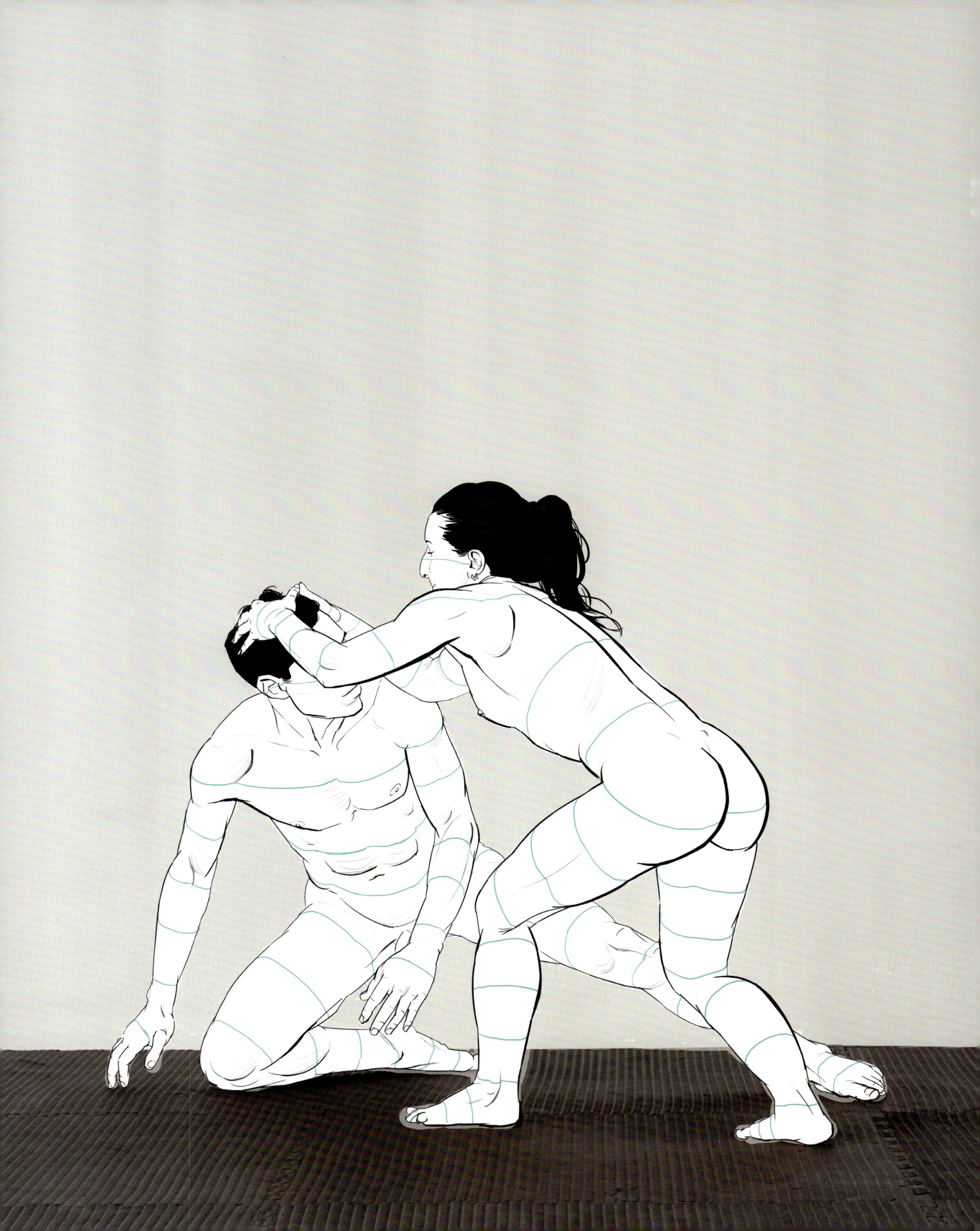

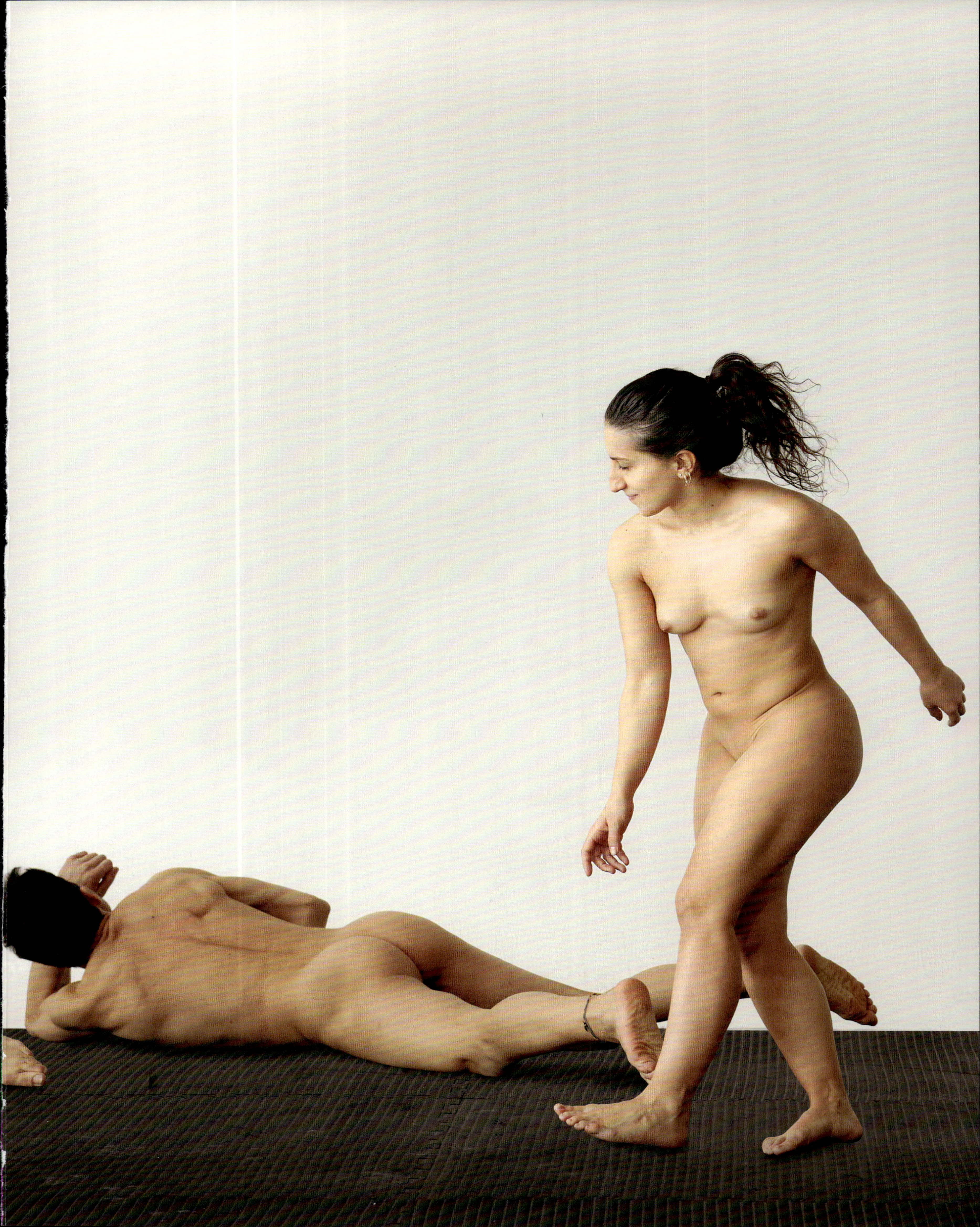

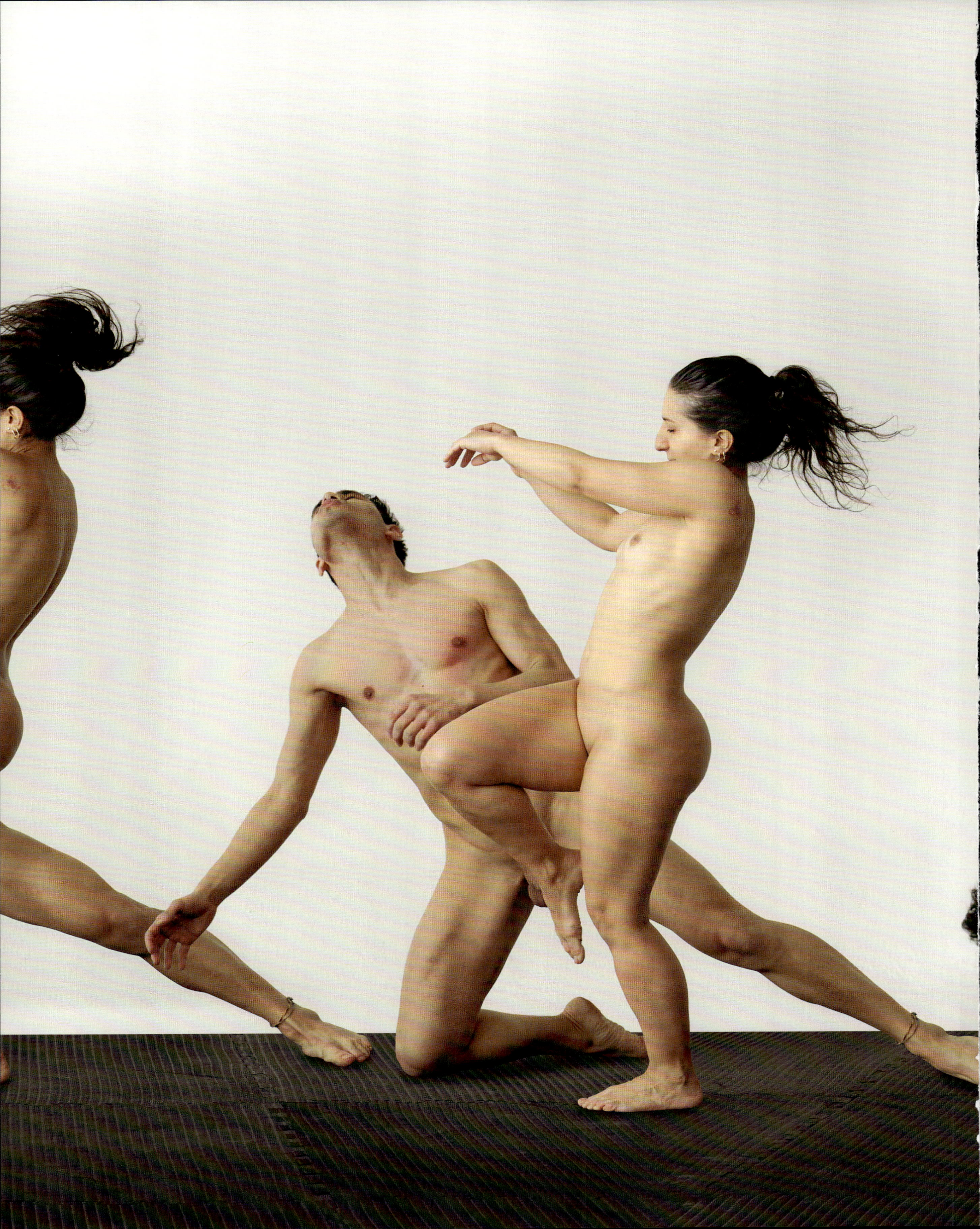

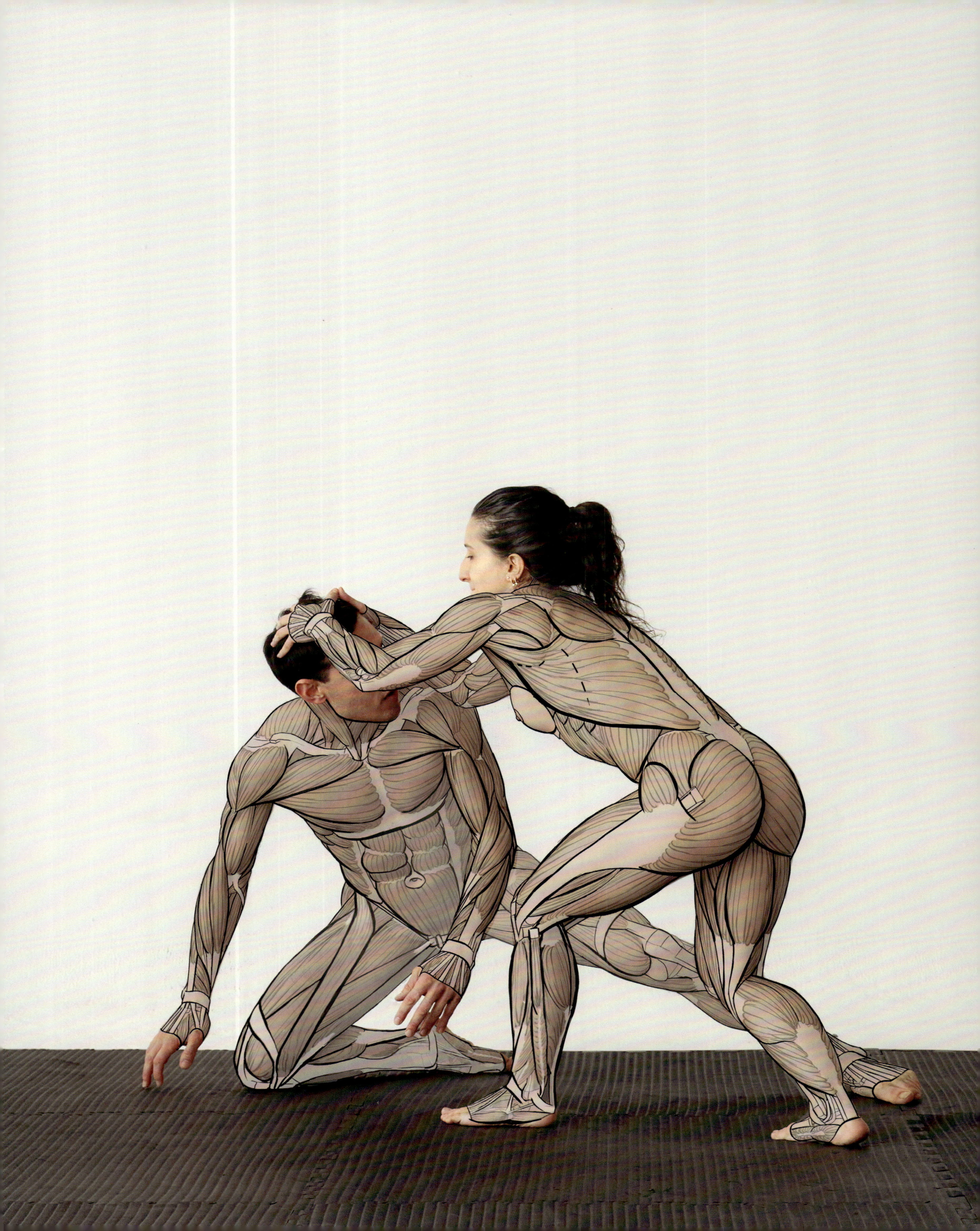

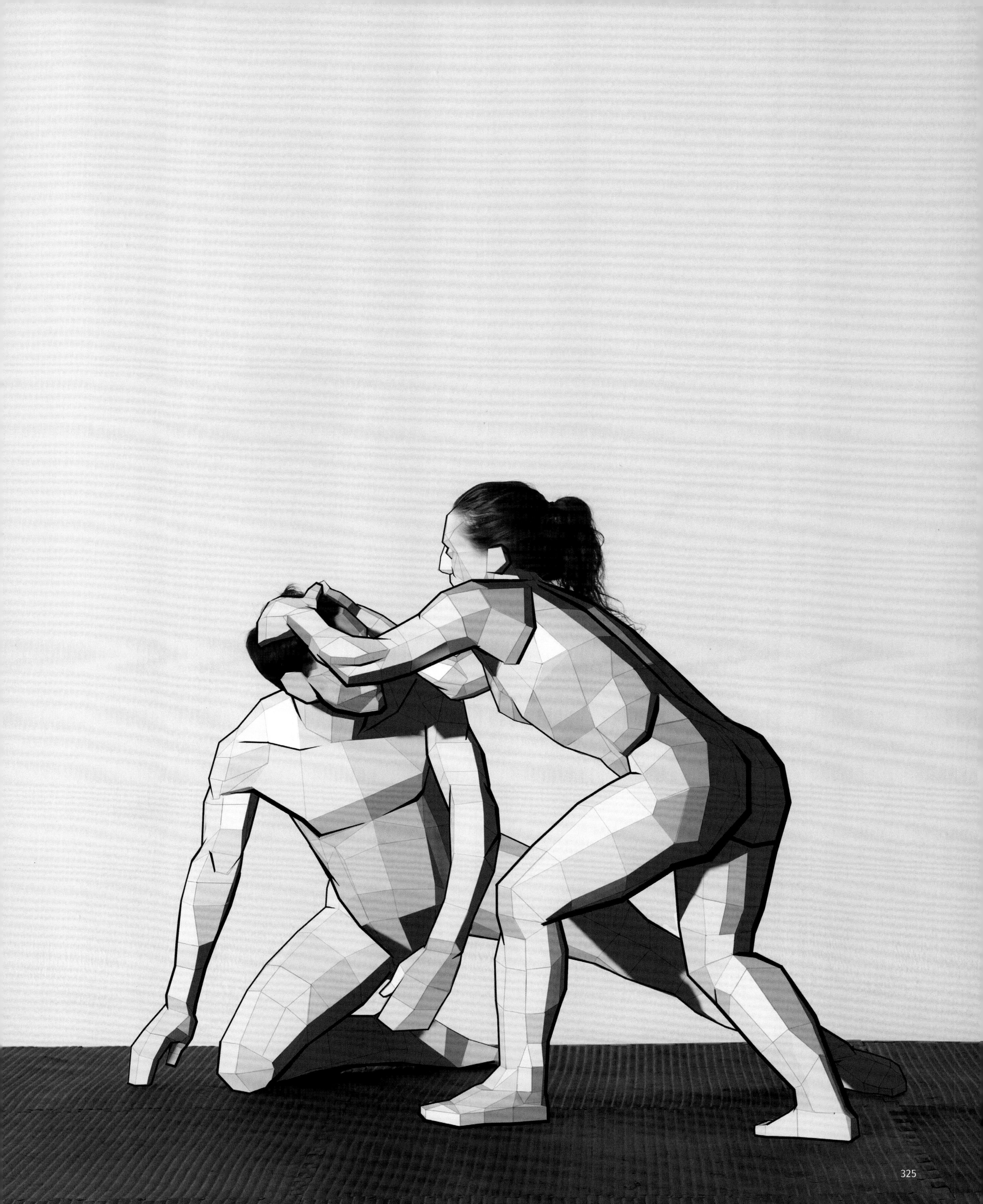

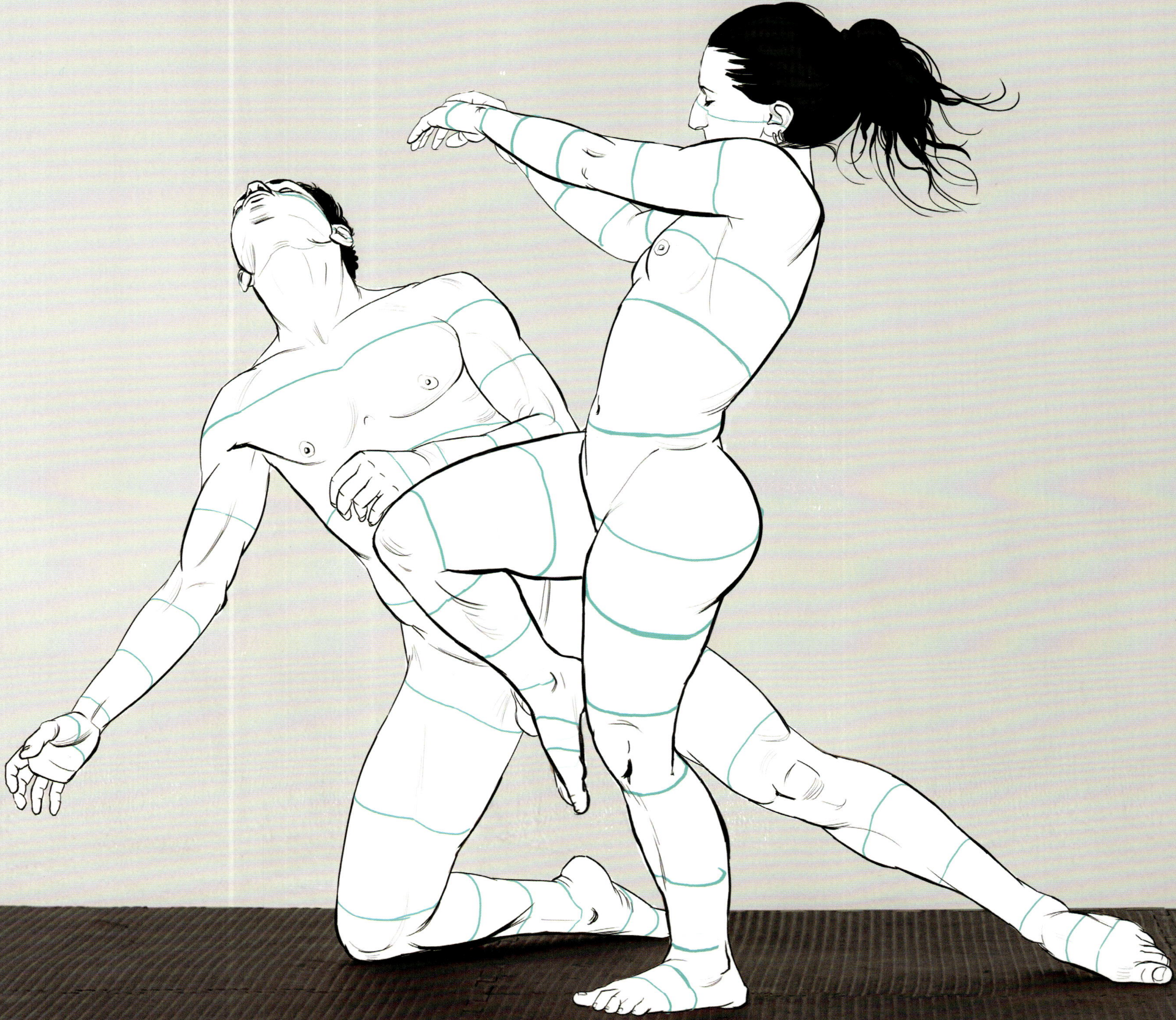

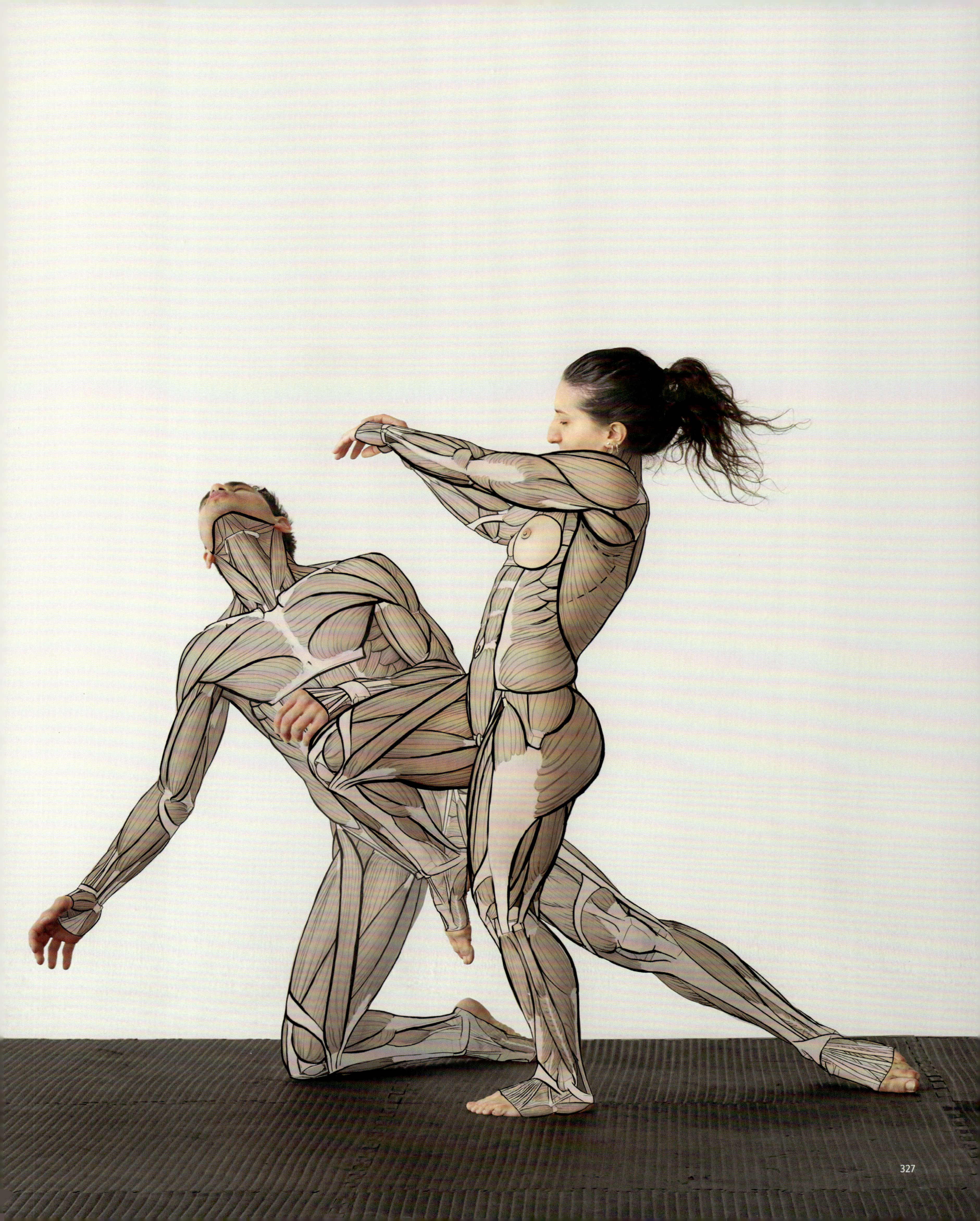

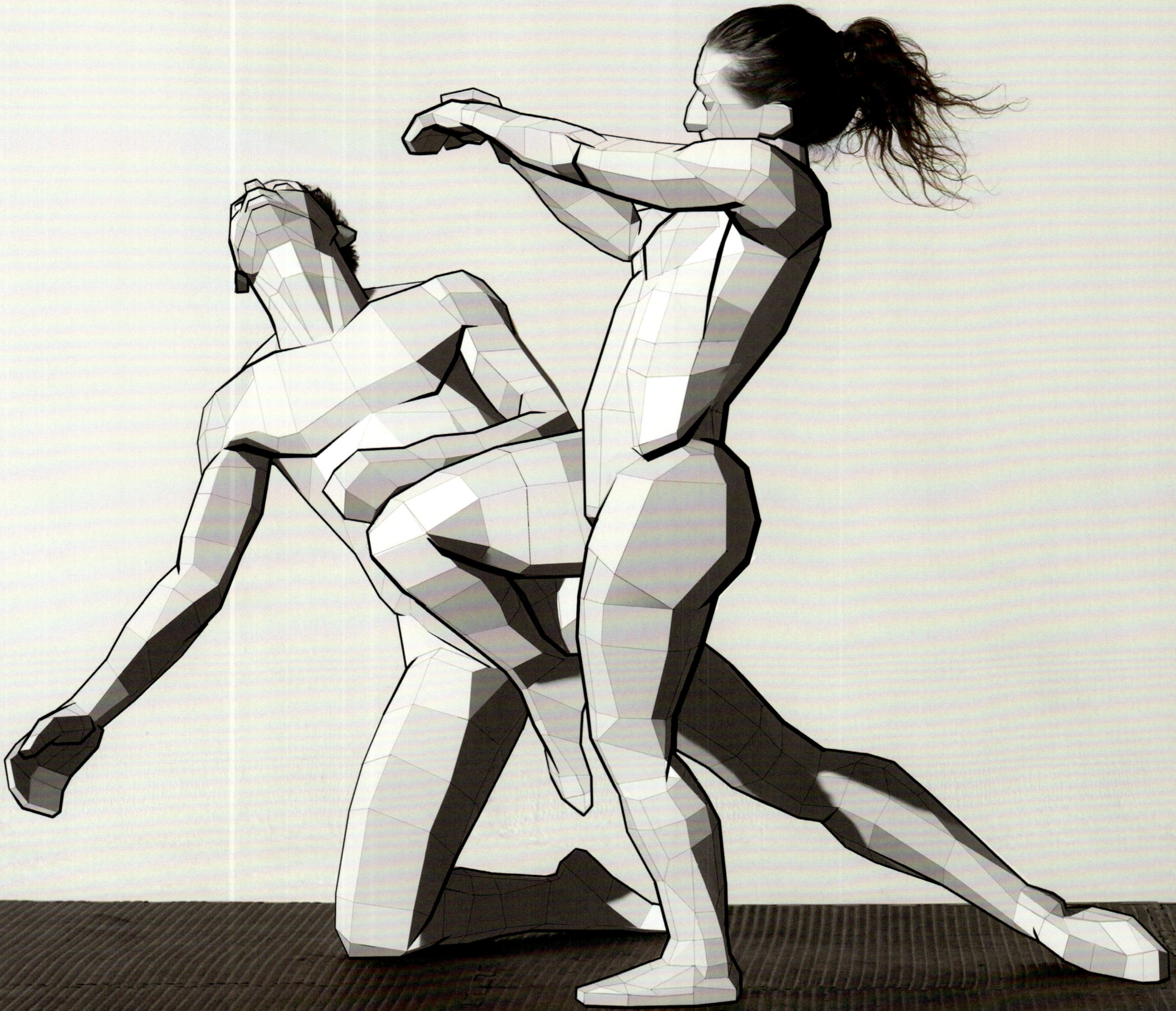

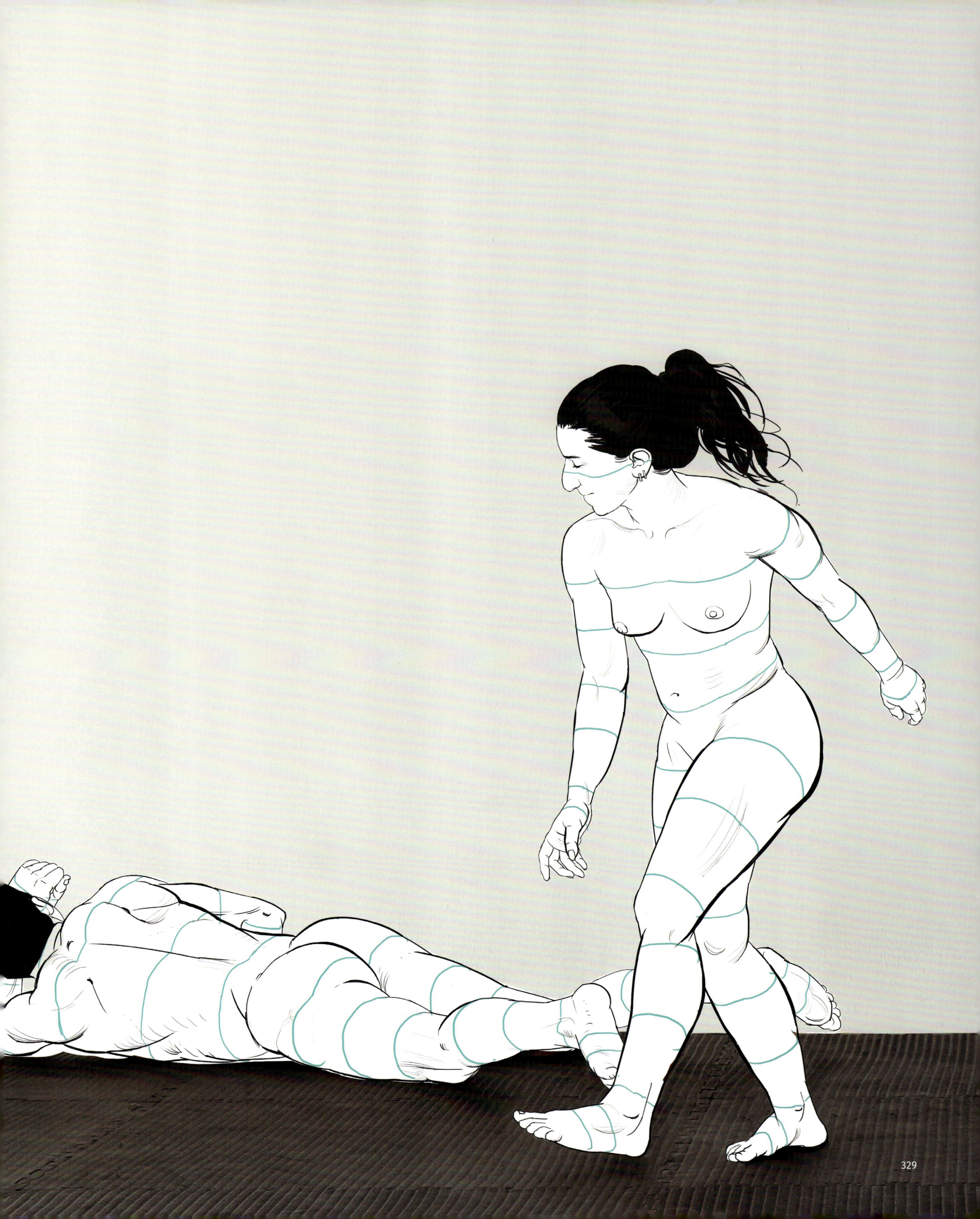

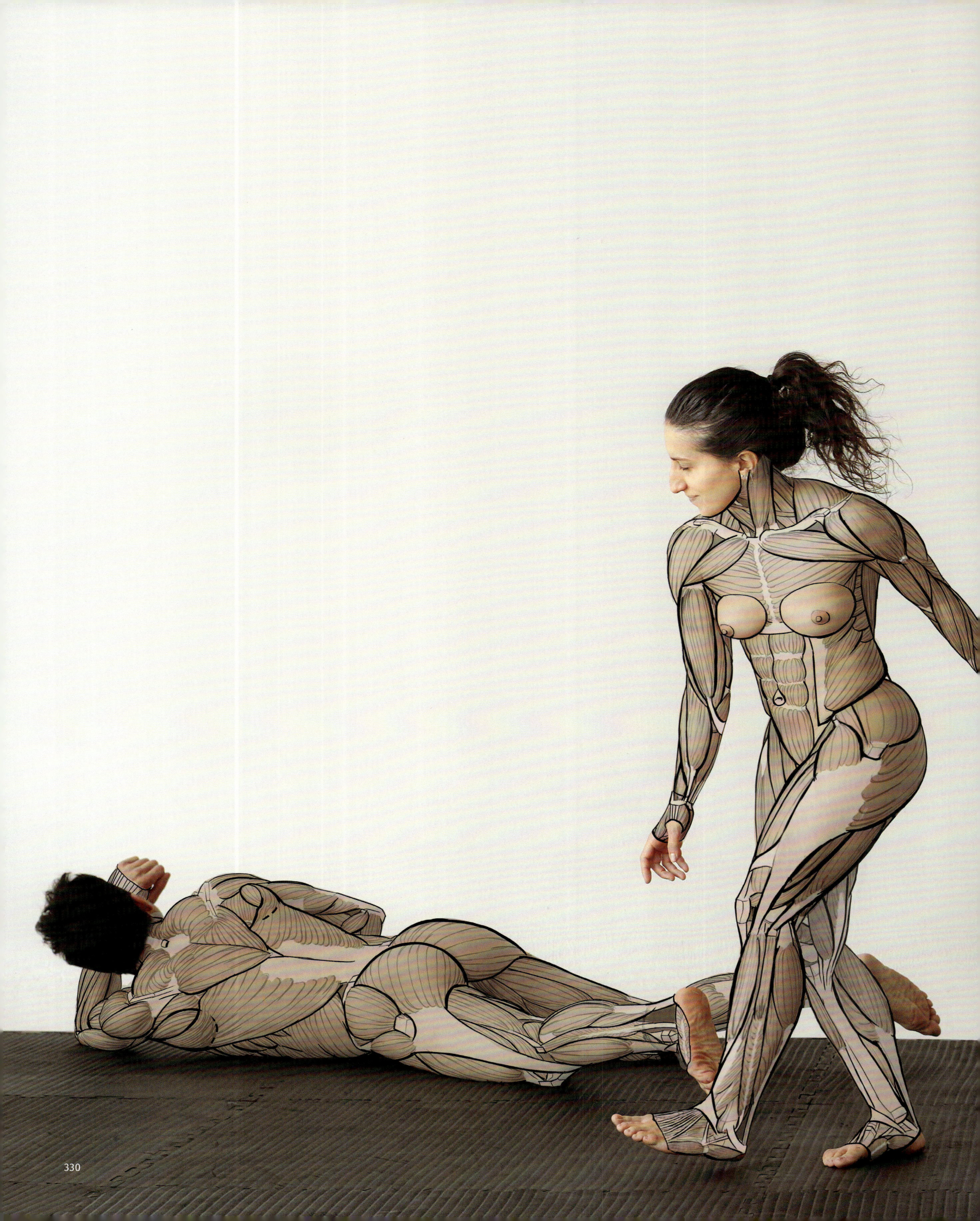

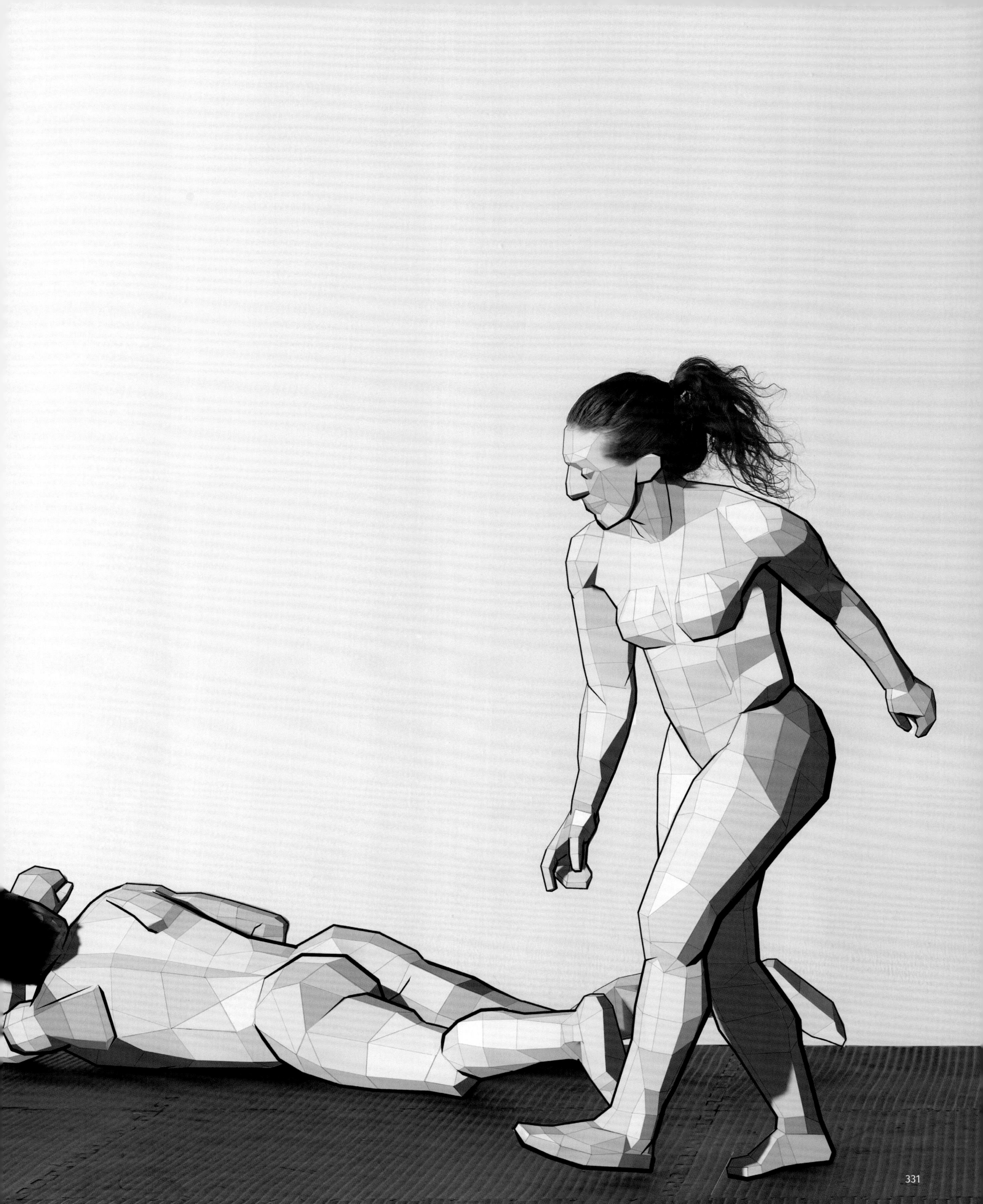

Armed combat

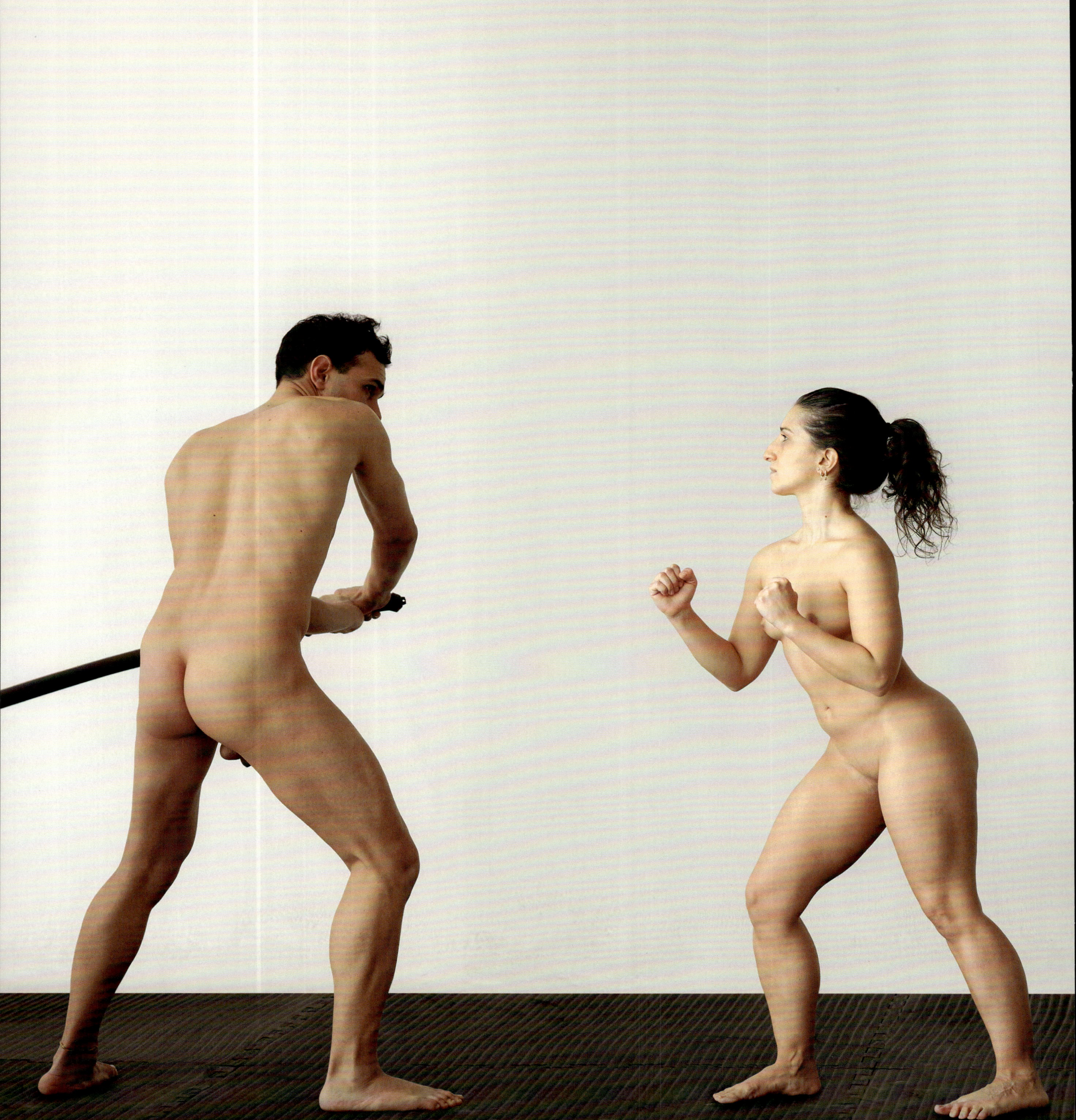

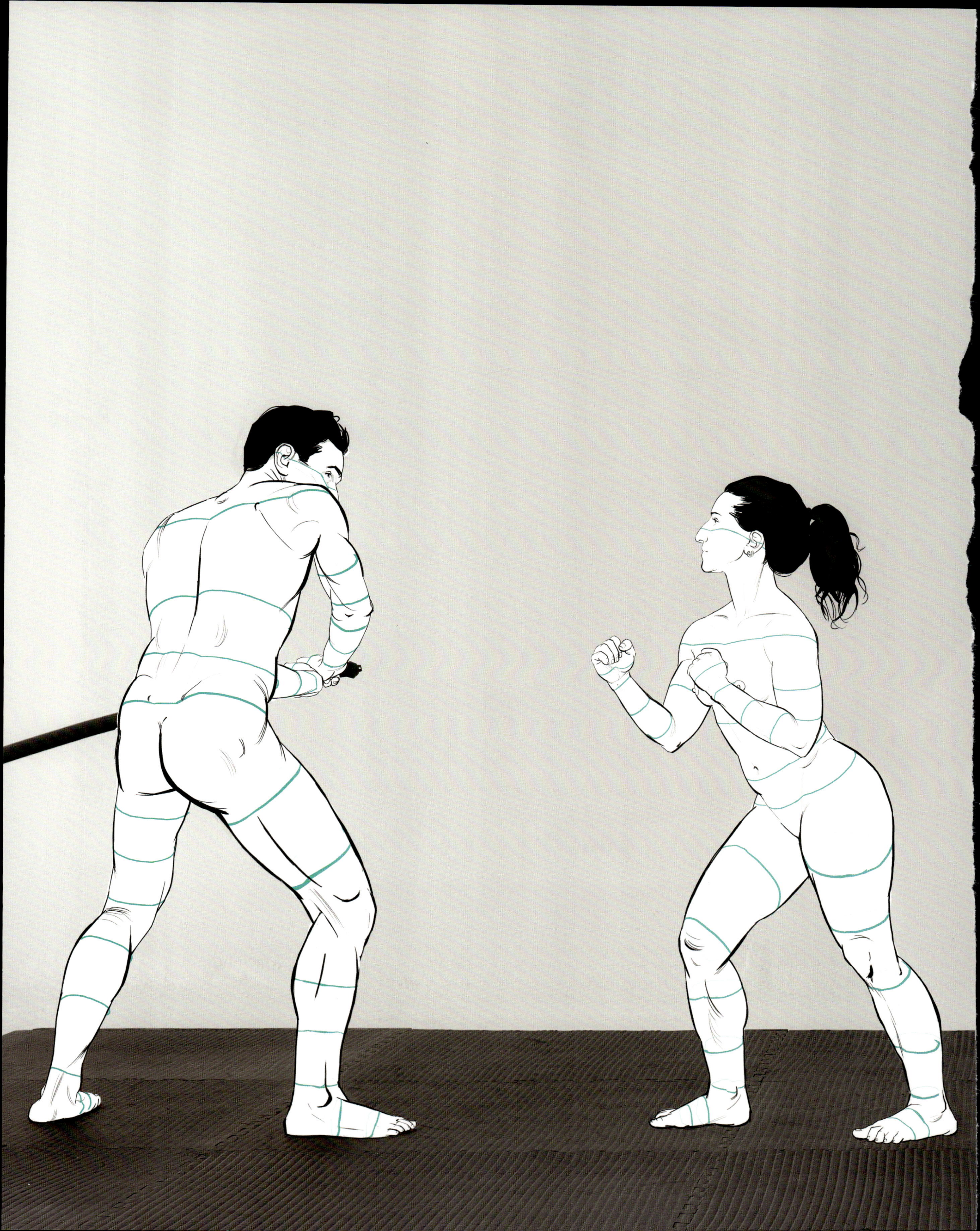

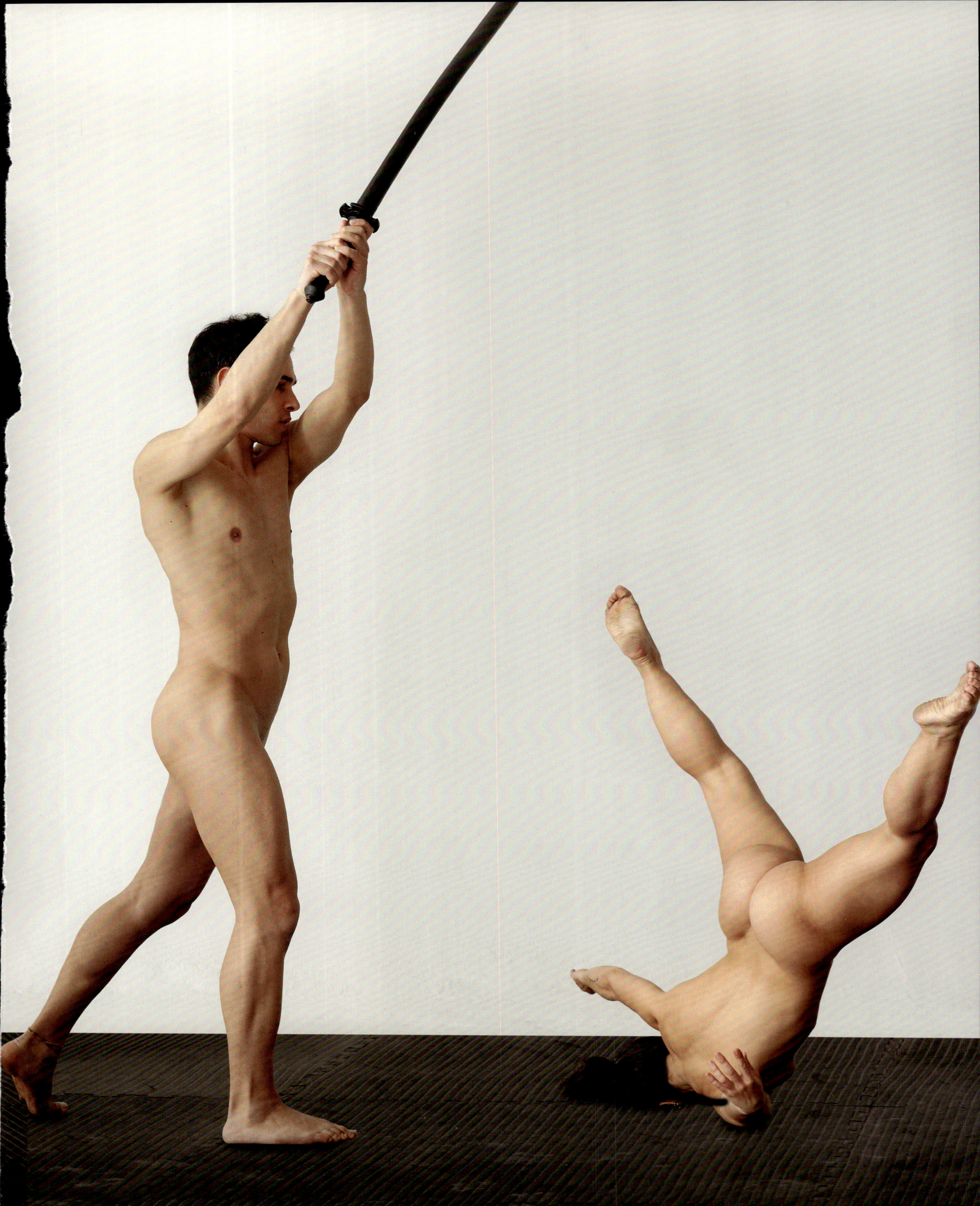

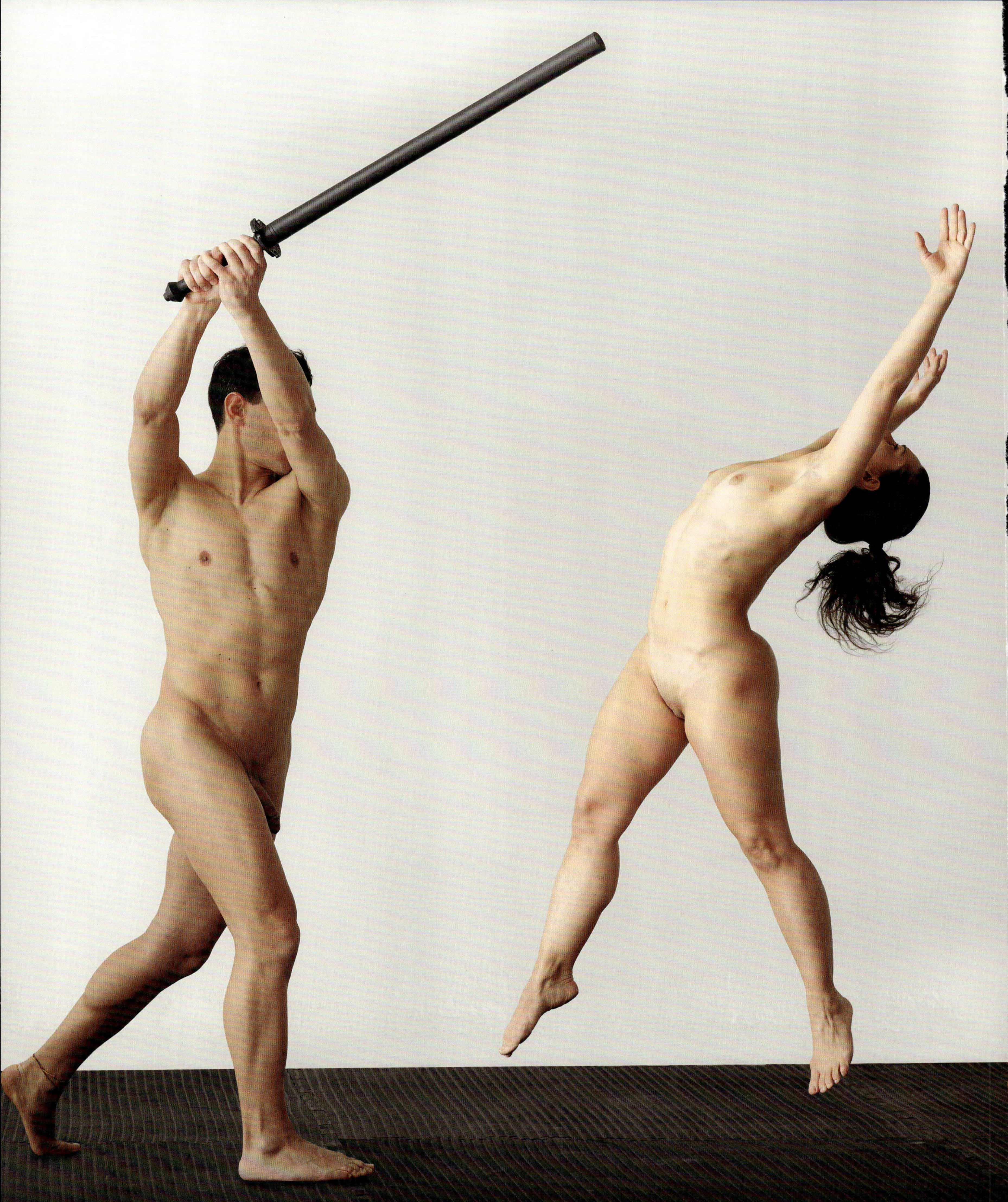

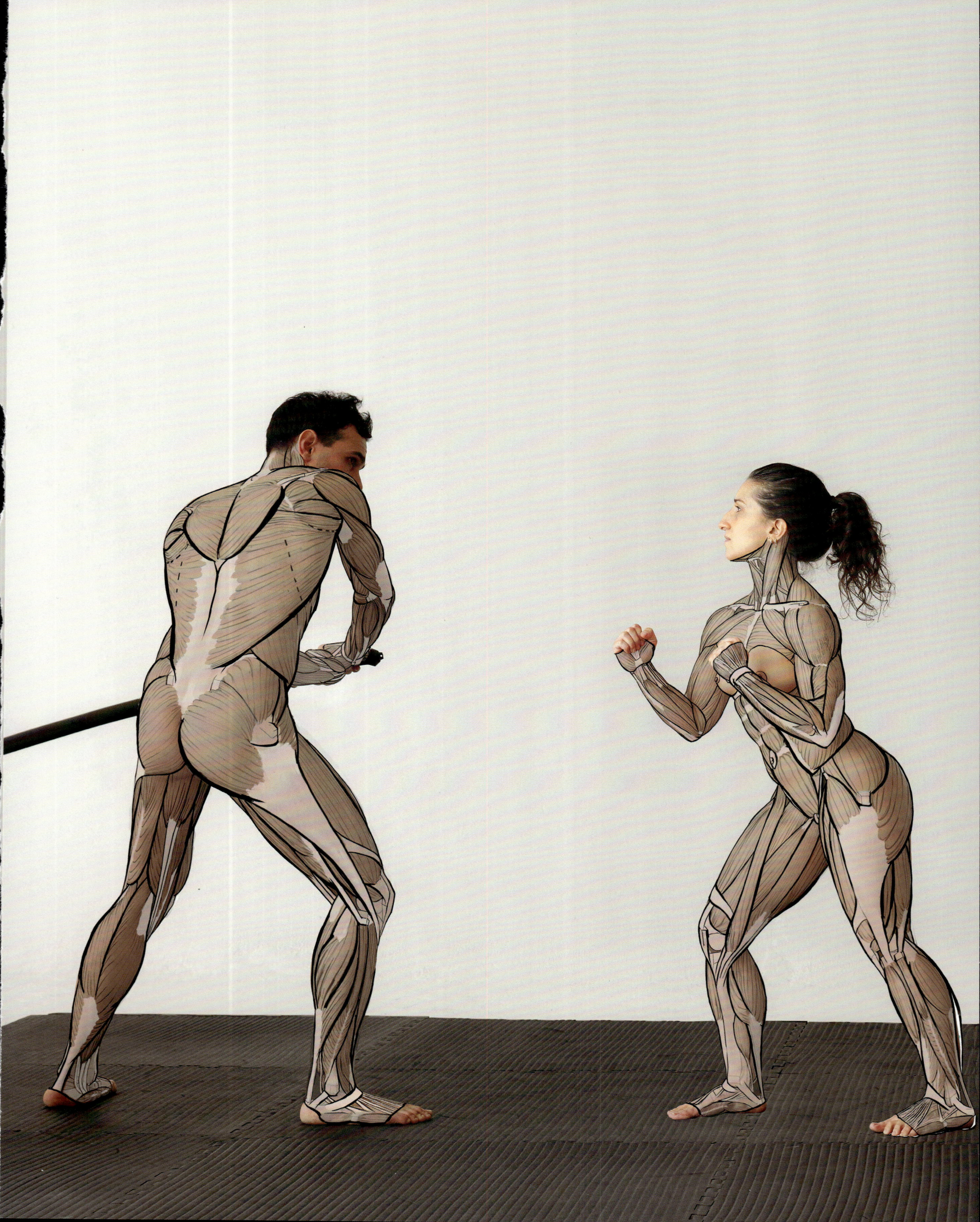

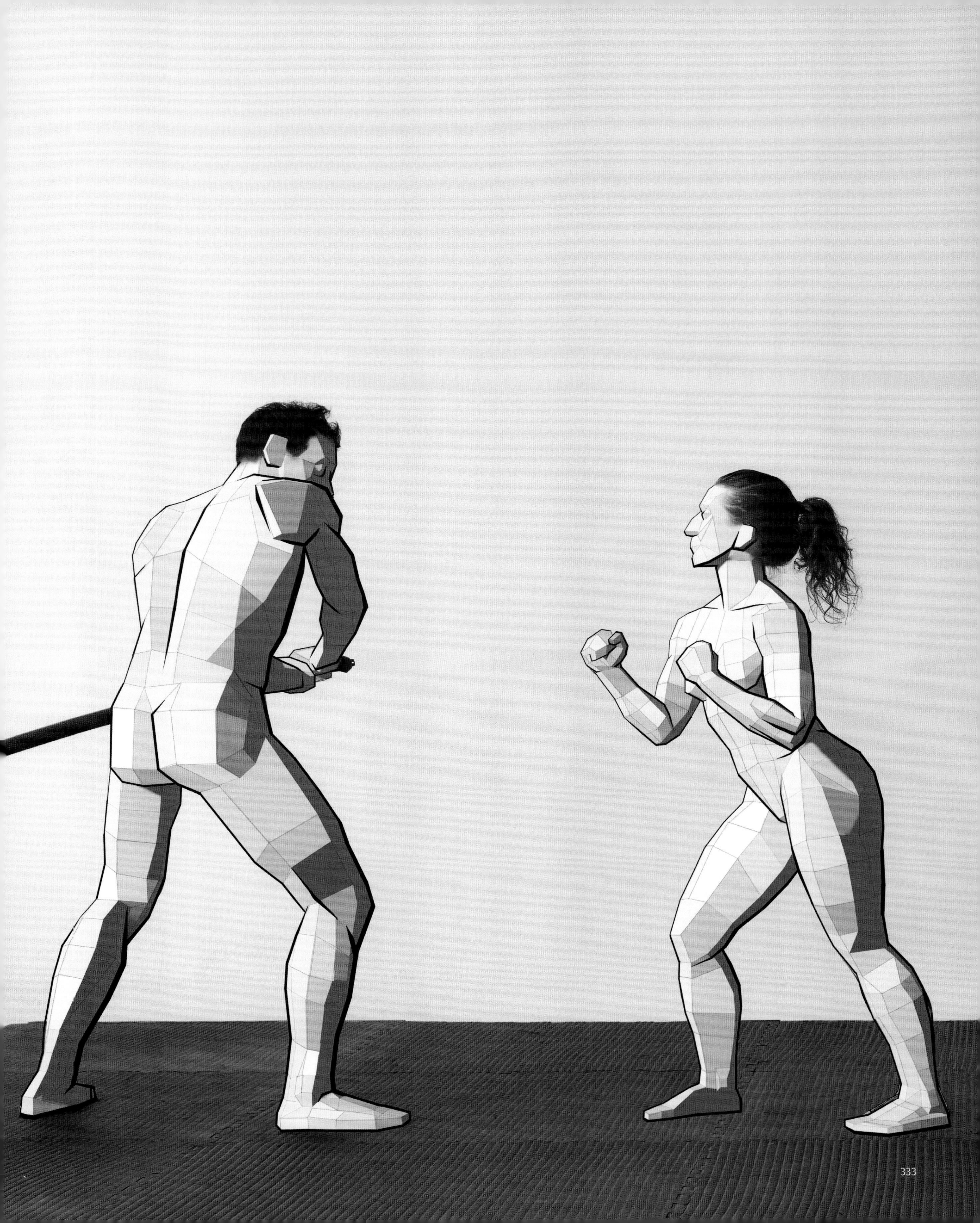

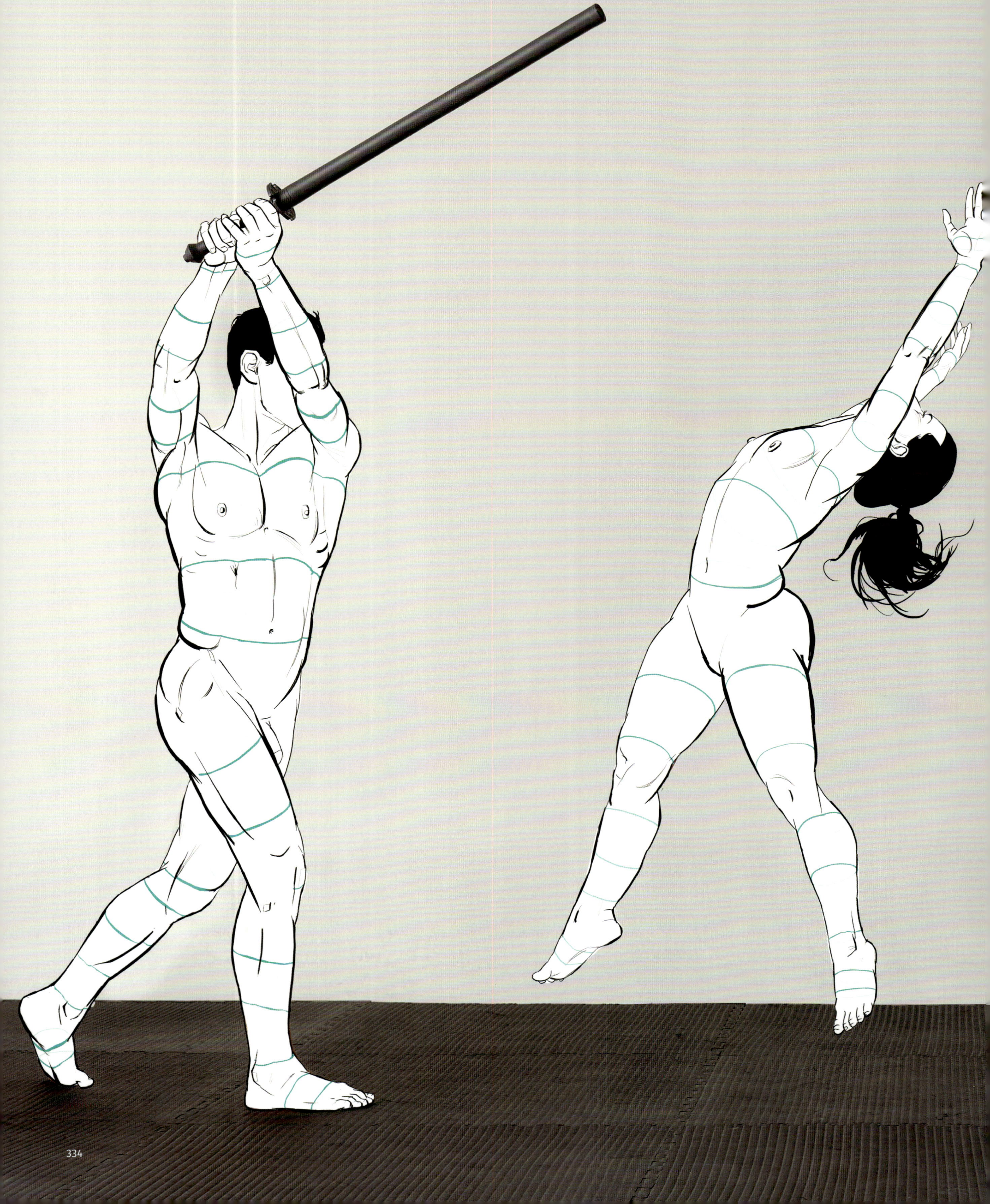

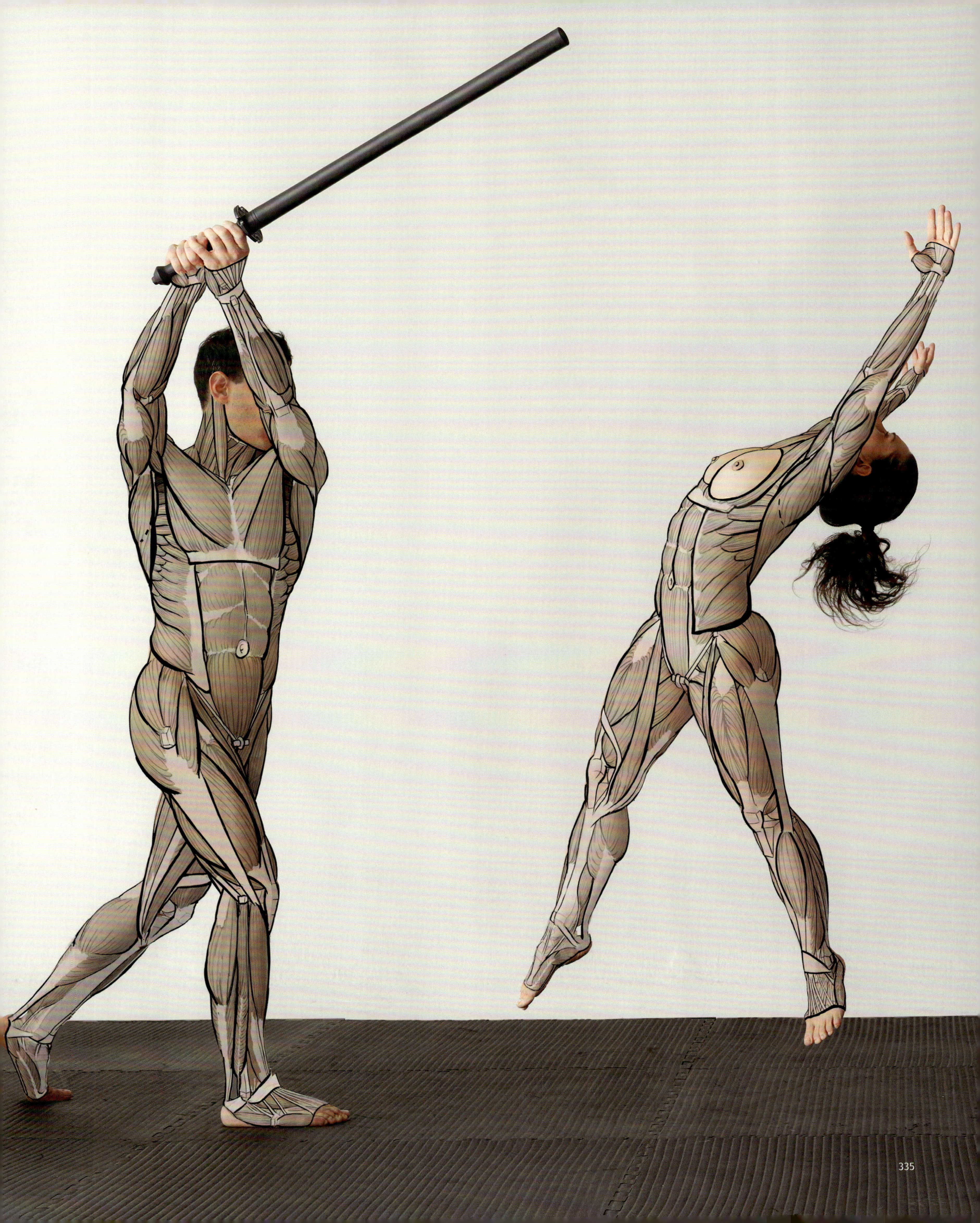

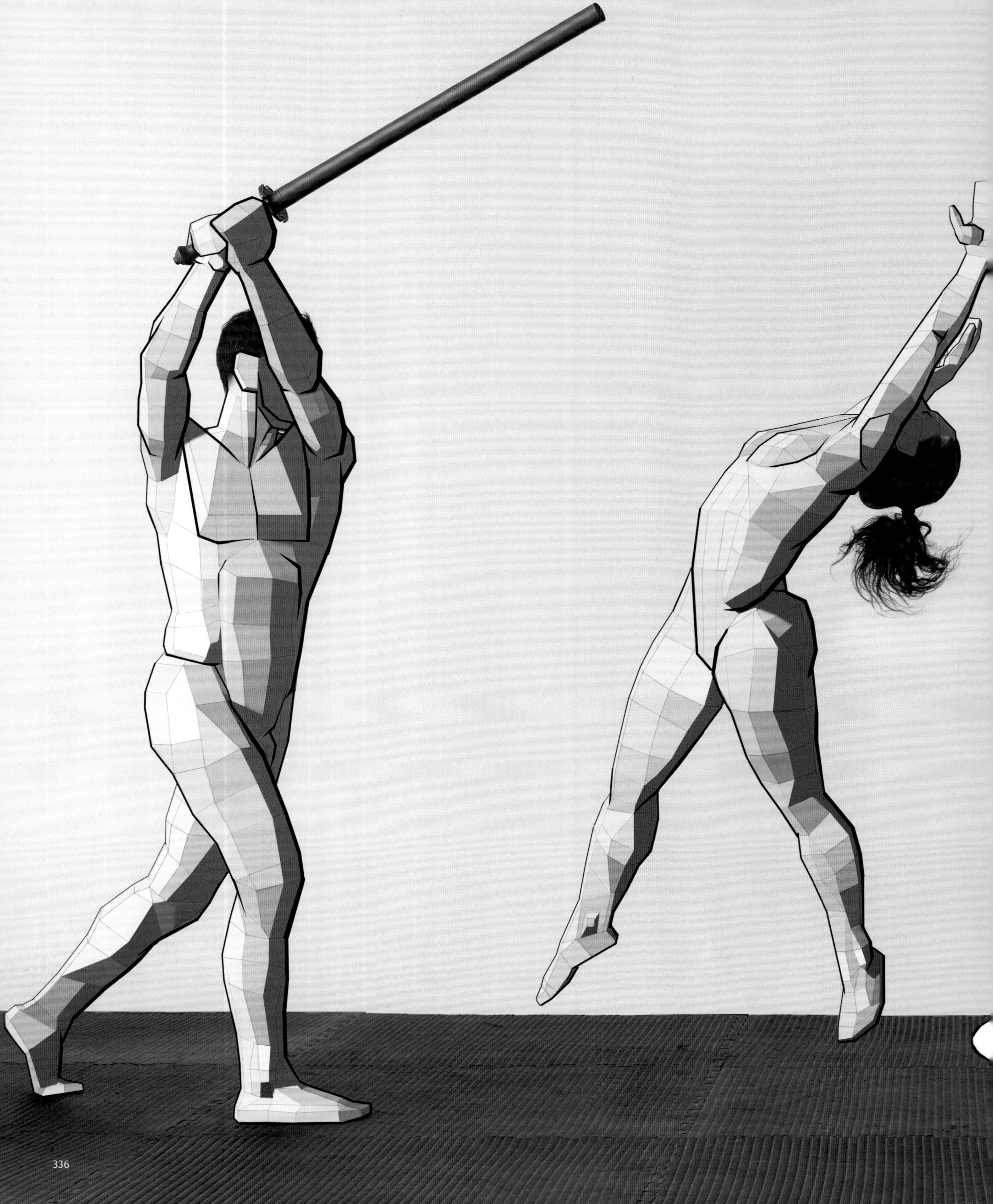

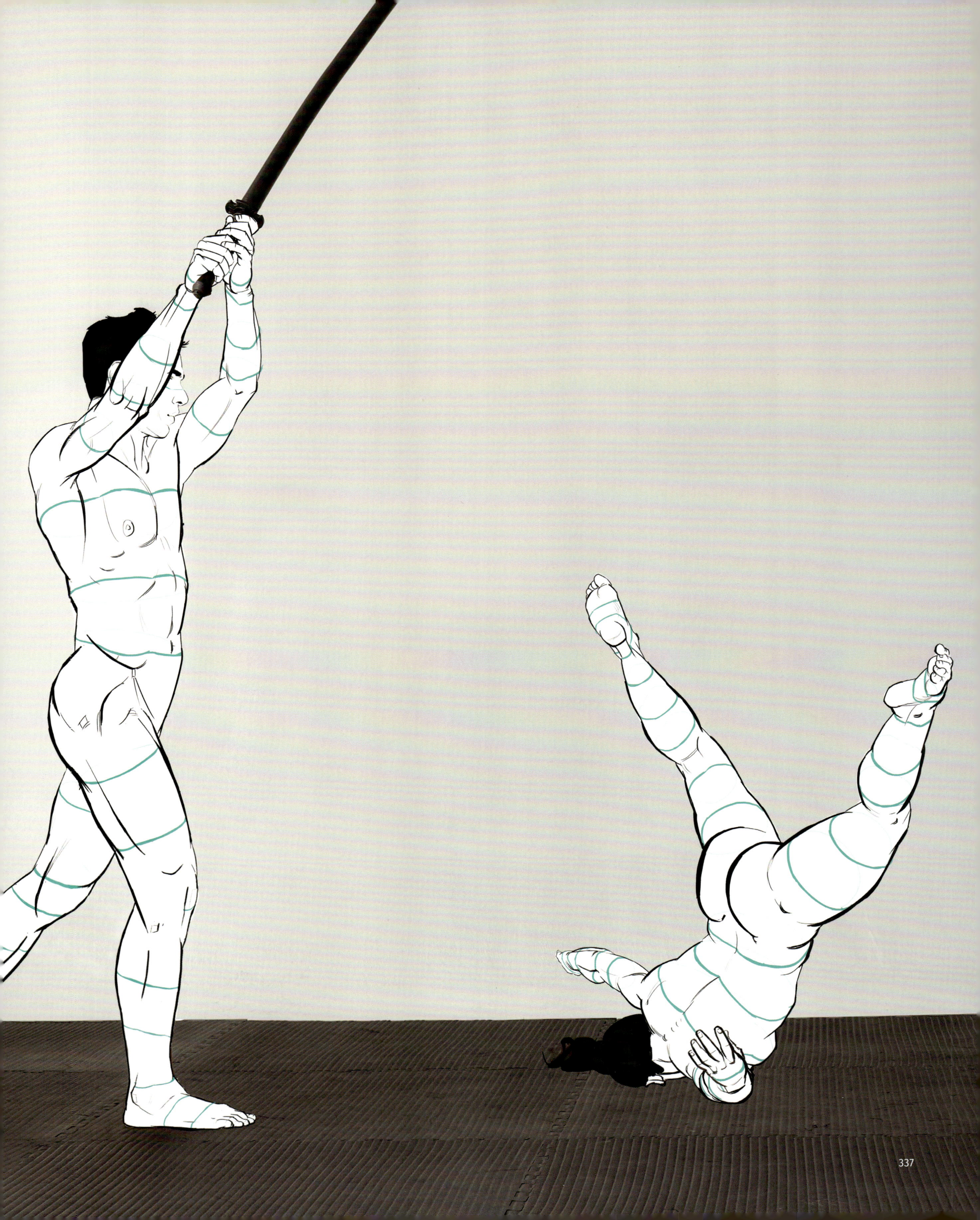

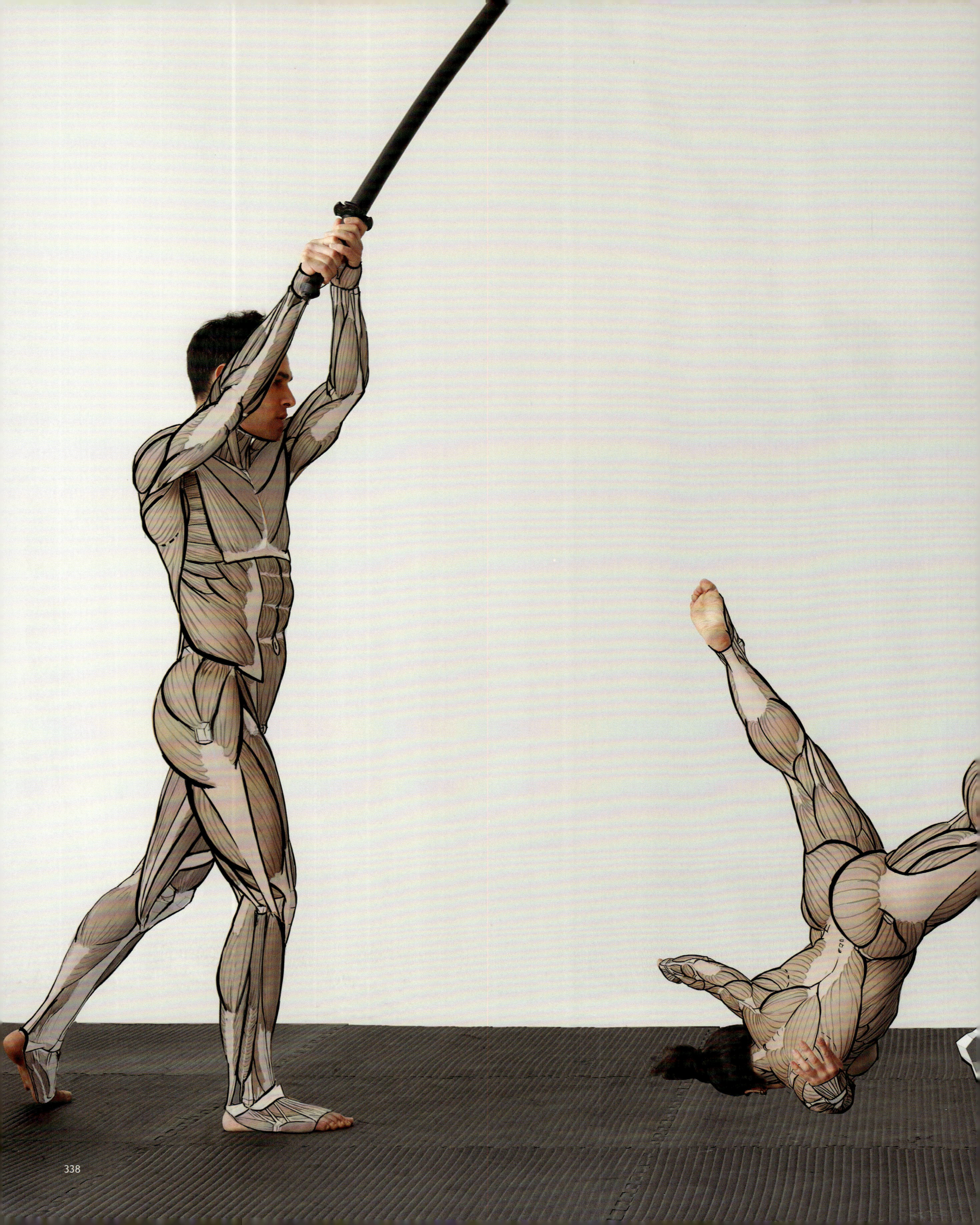

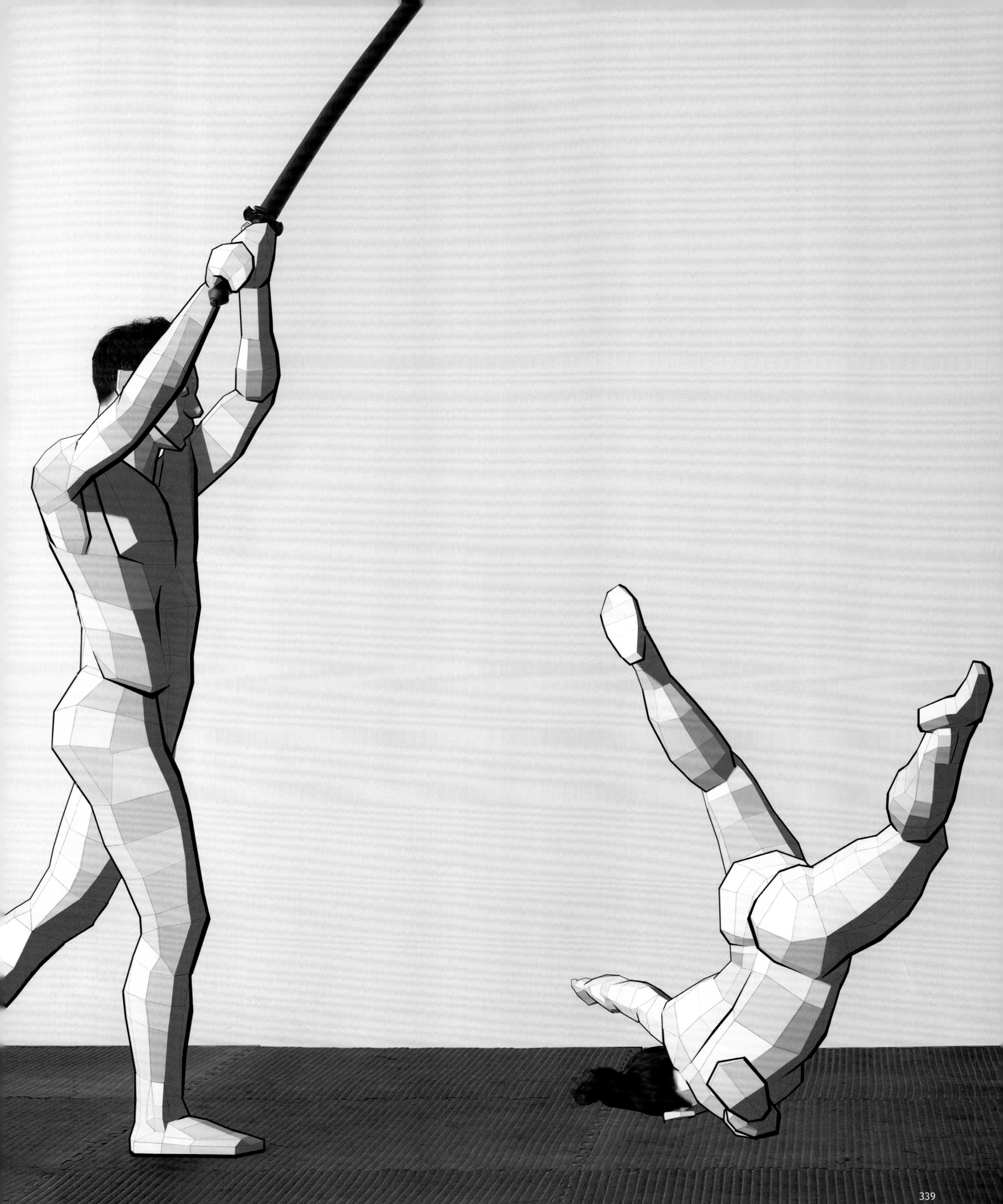

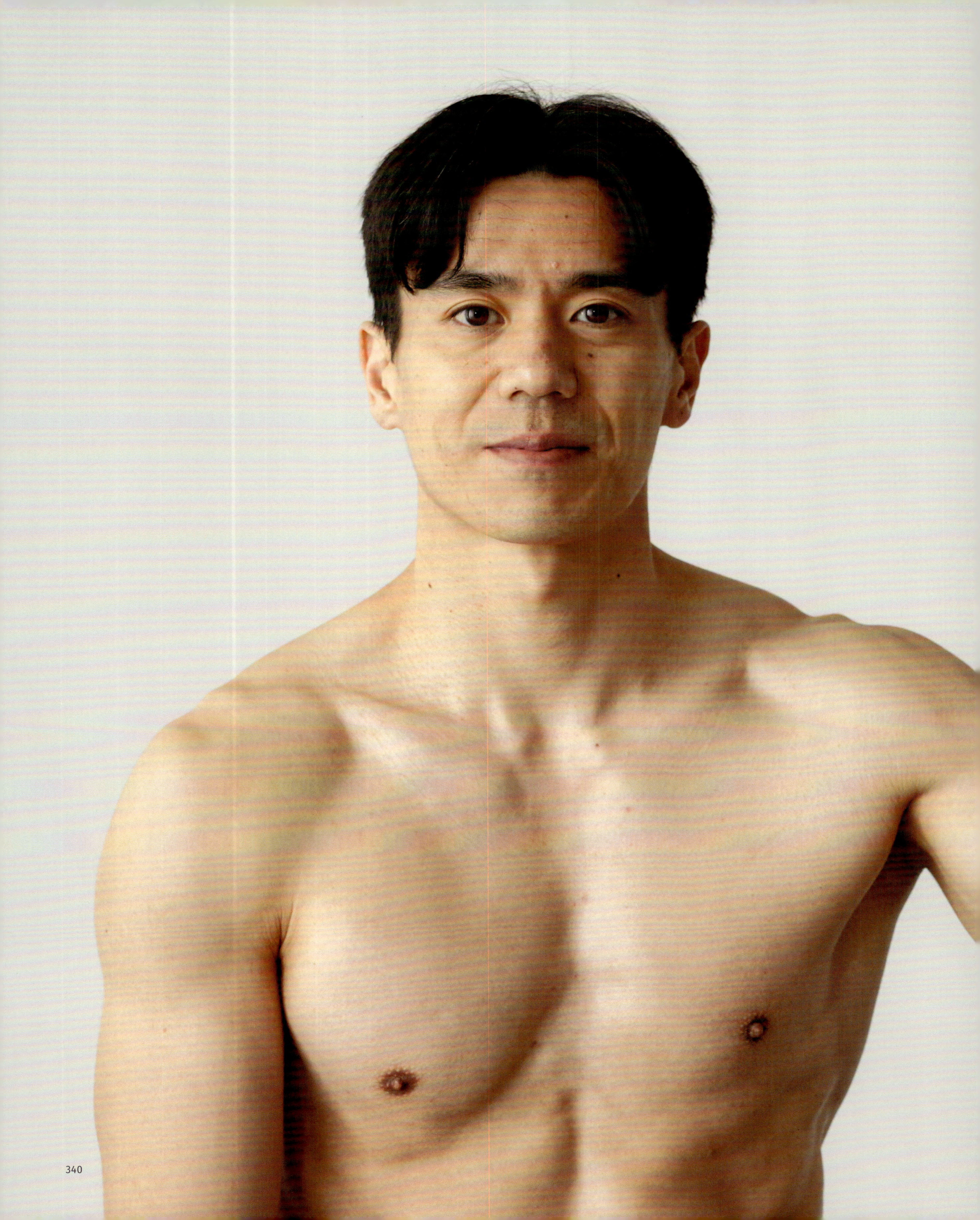

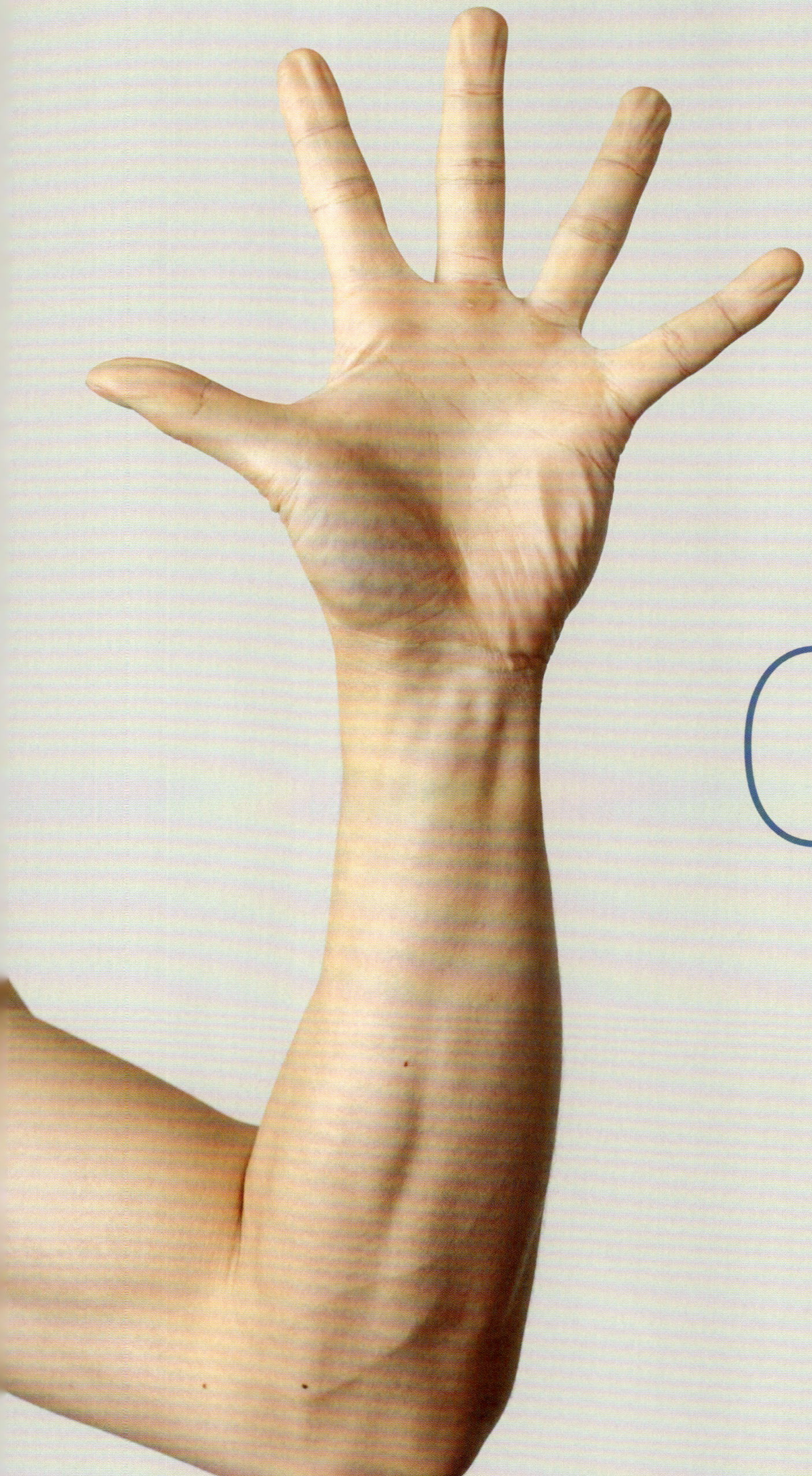

Gallery

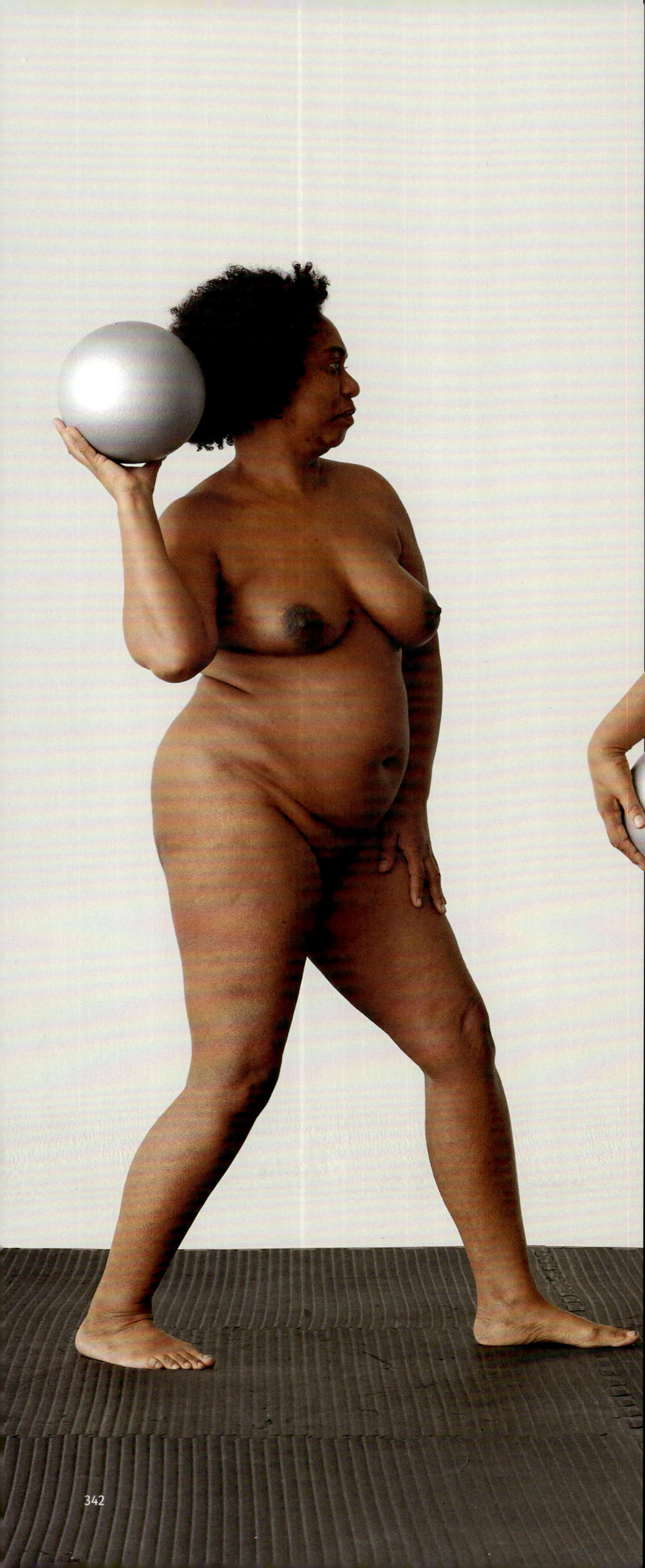

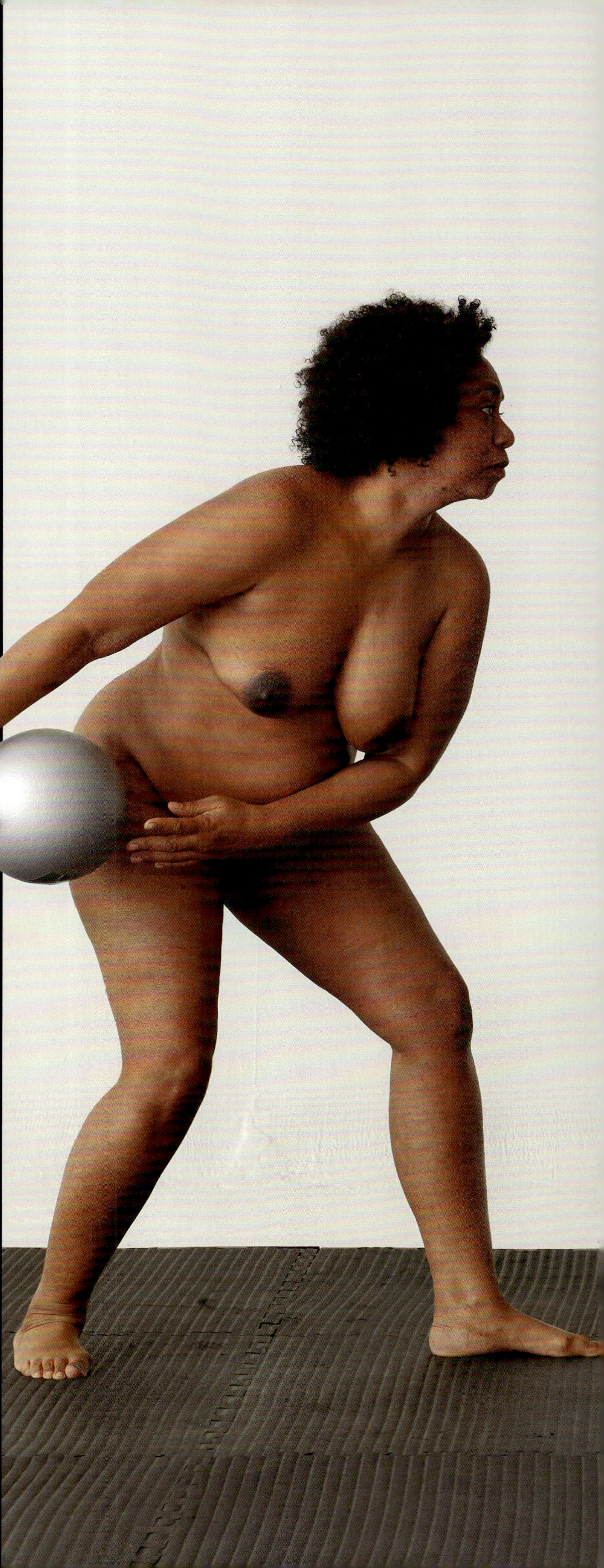

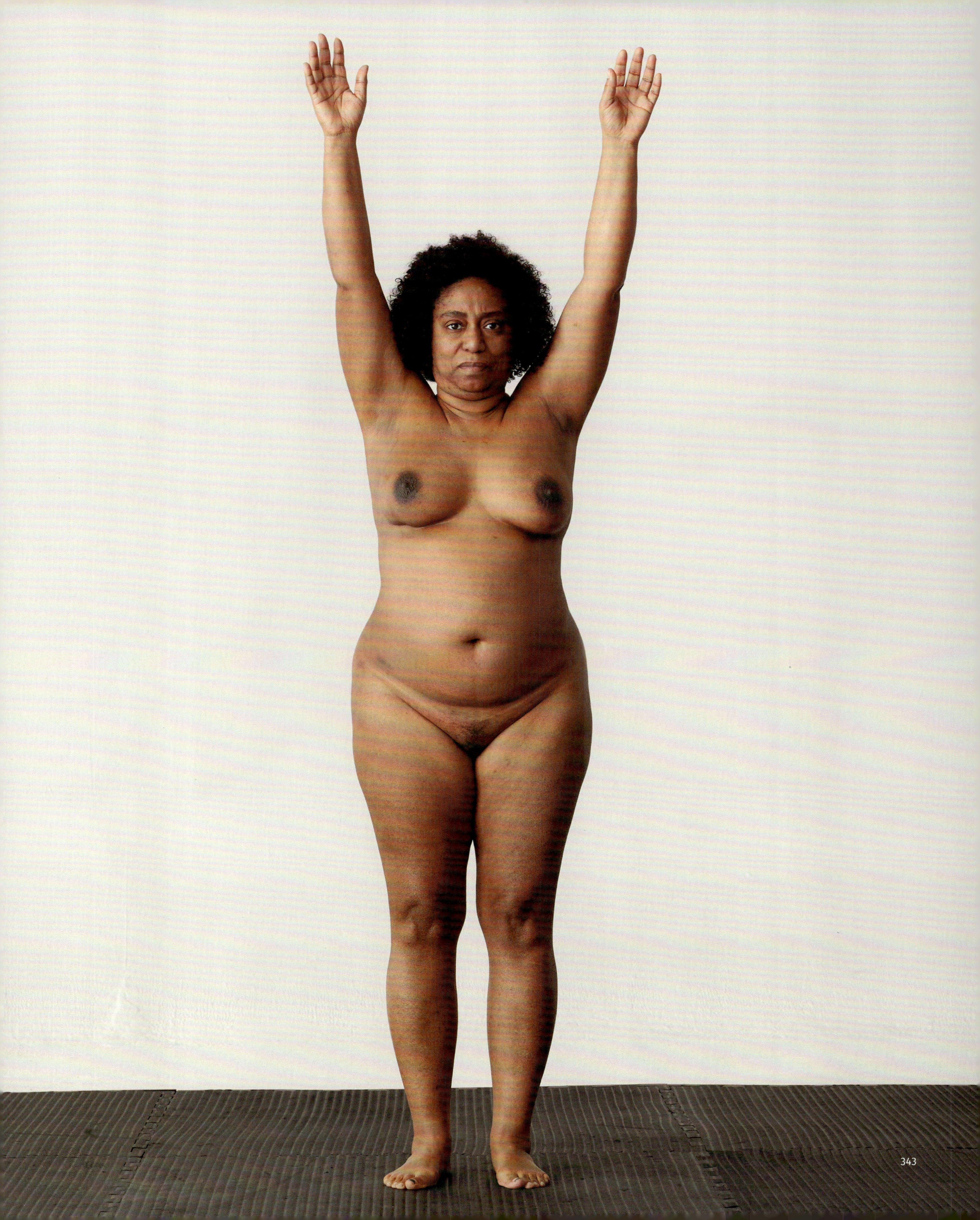

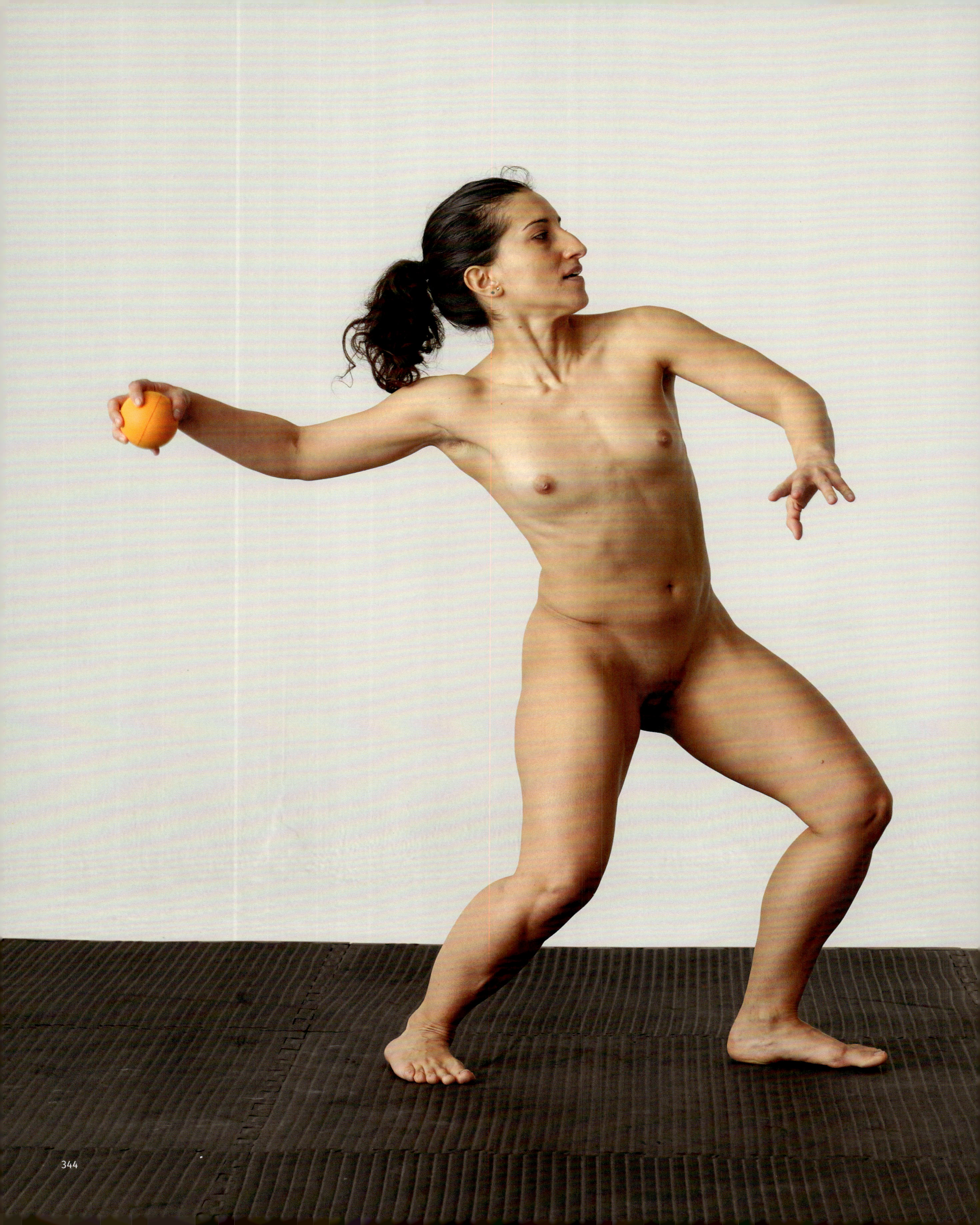

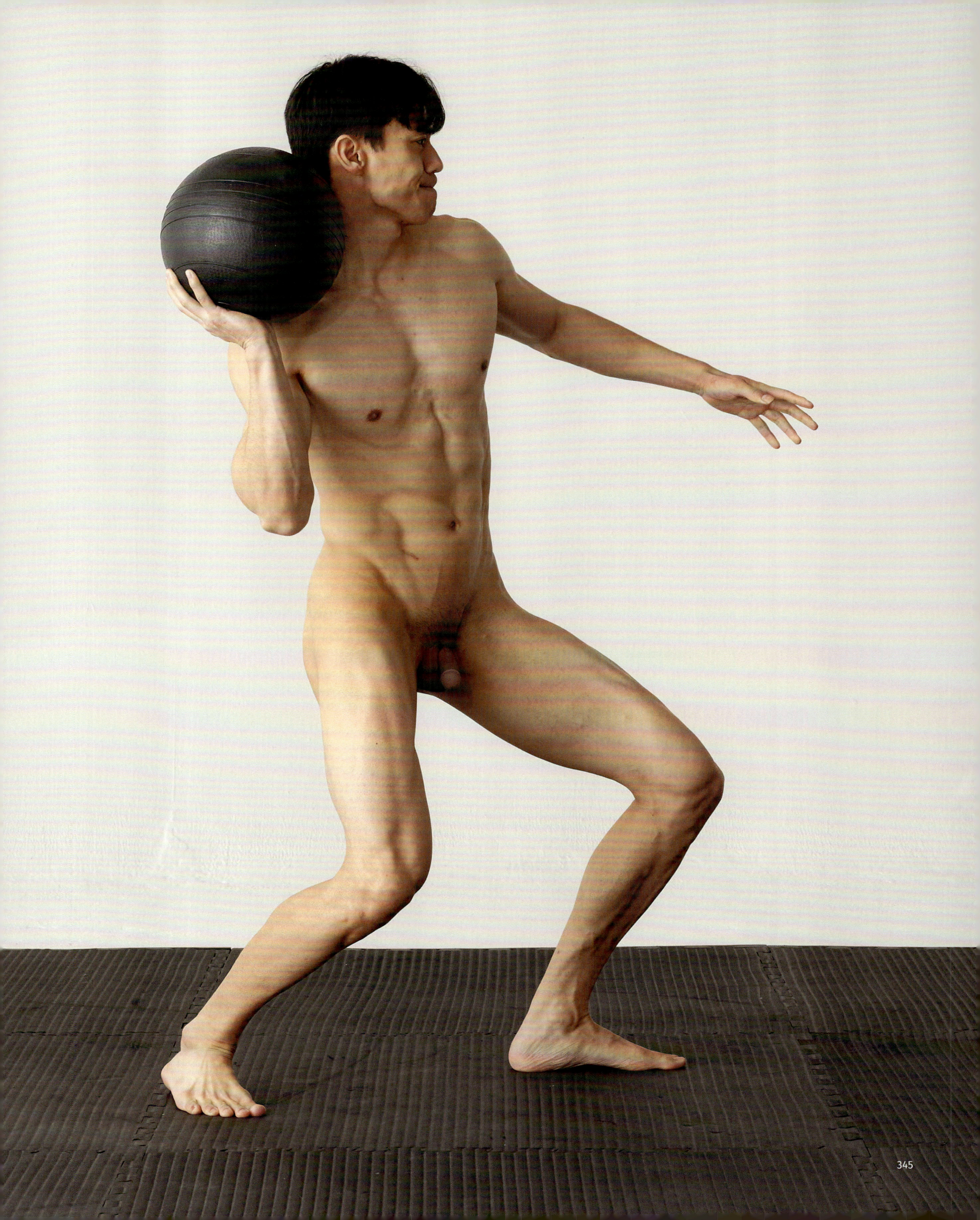

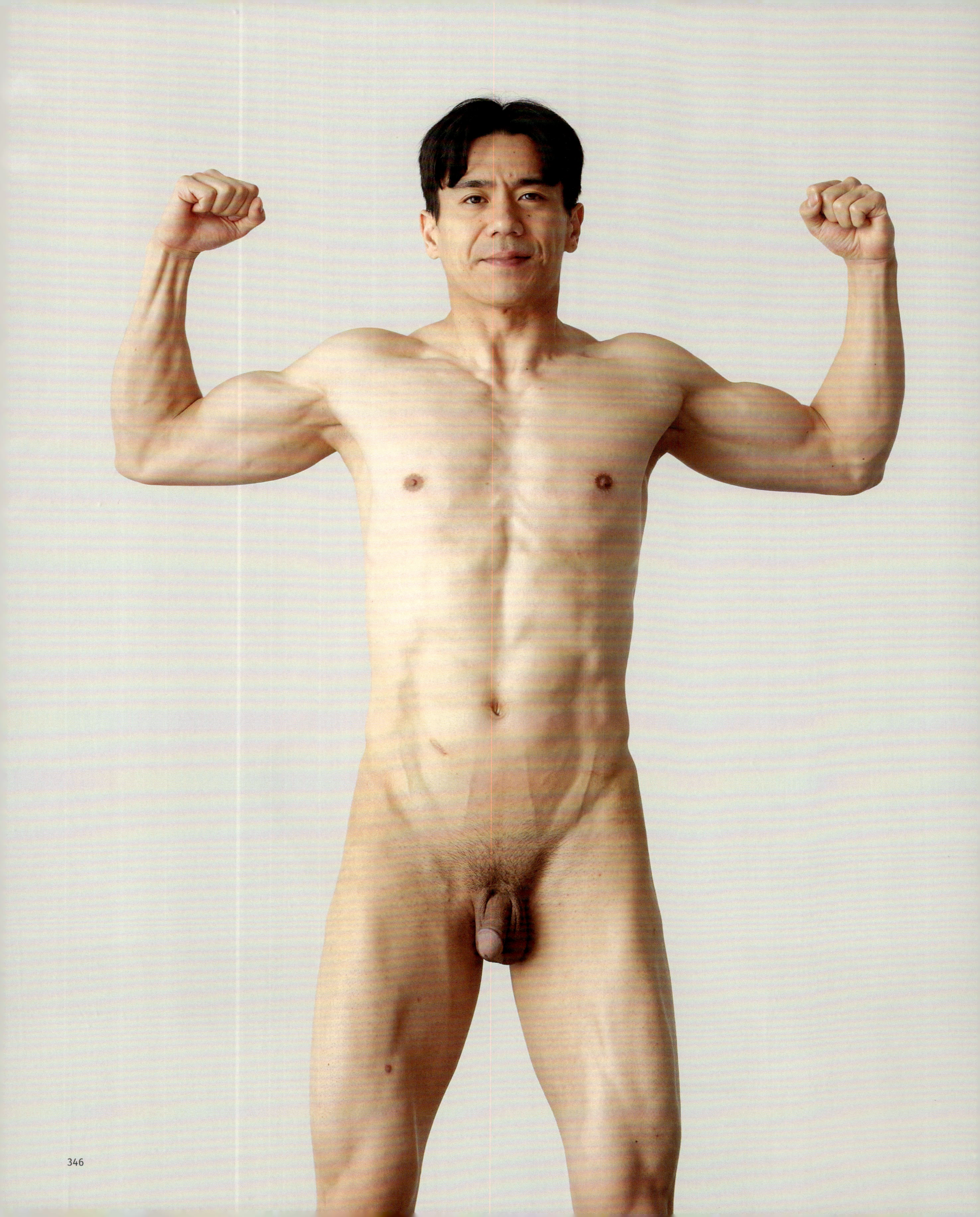

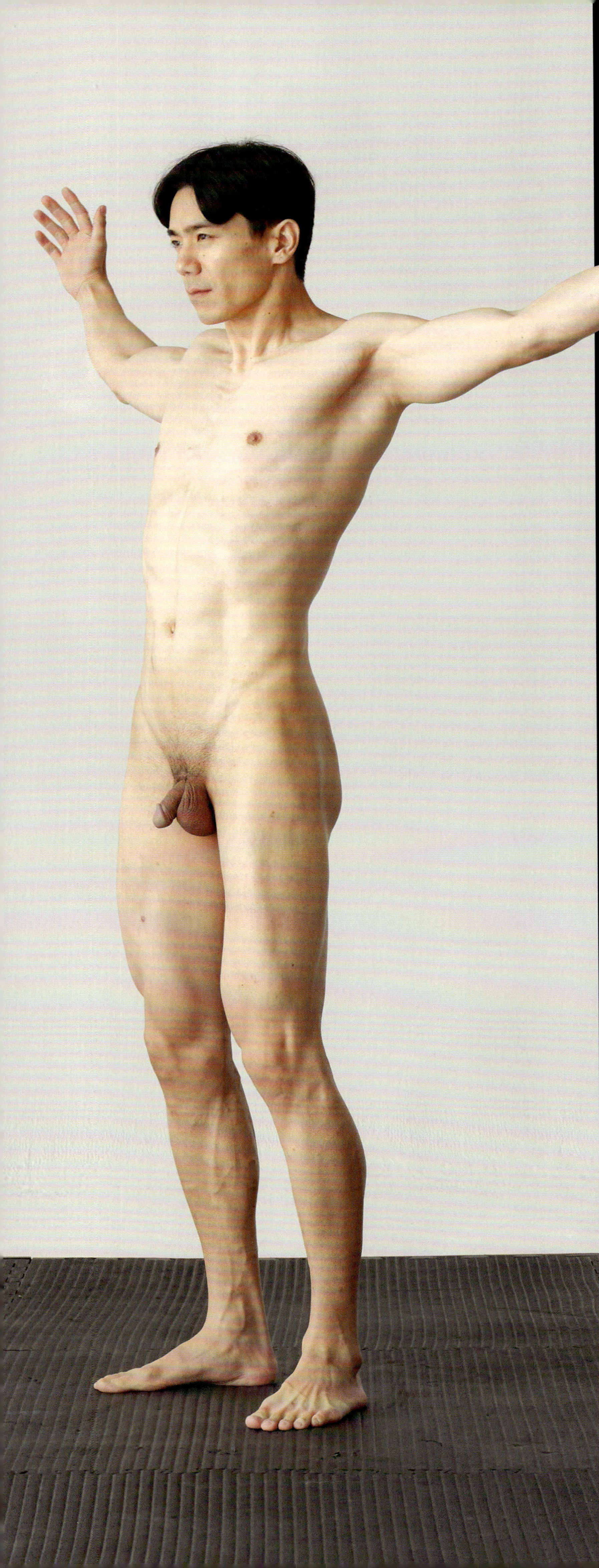
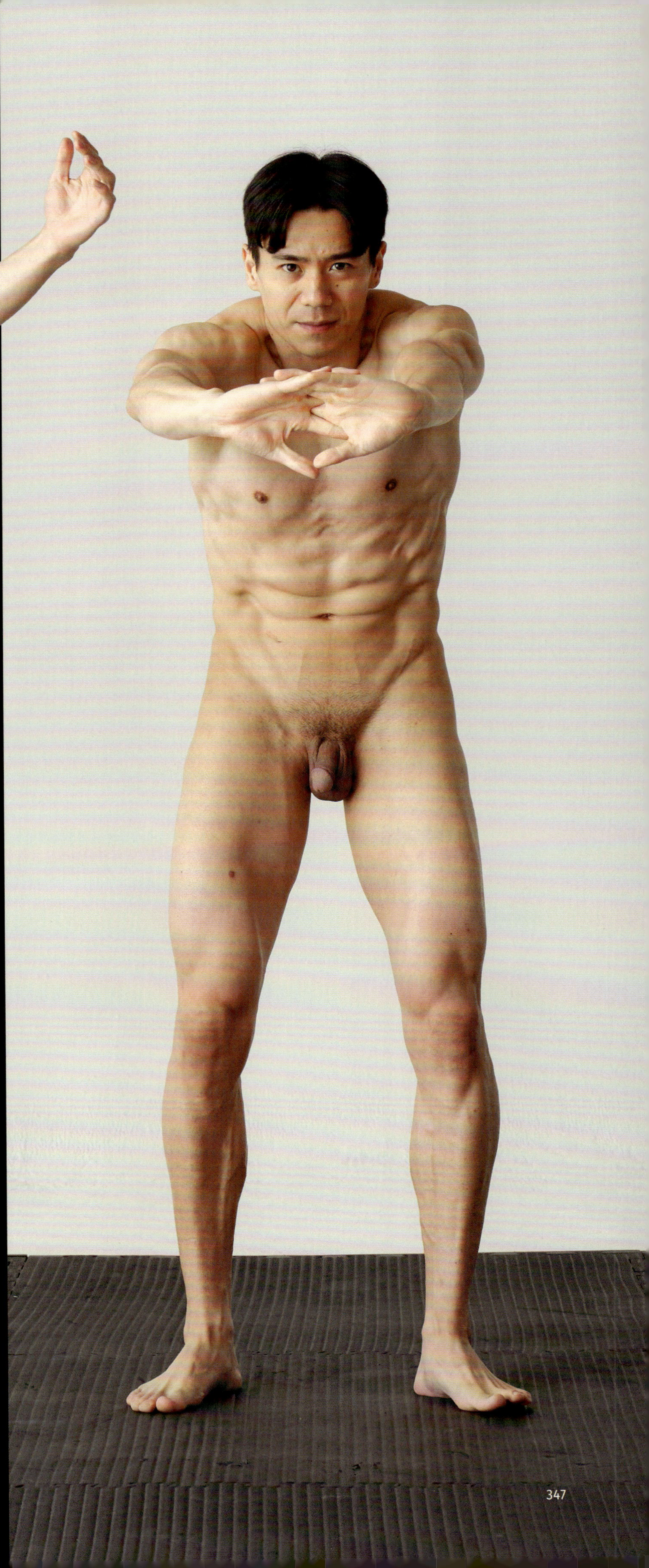

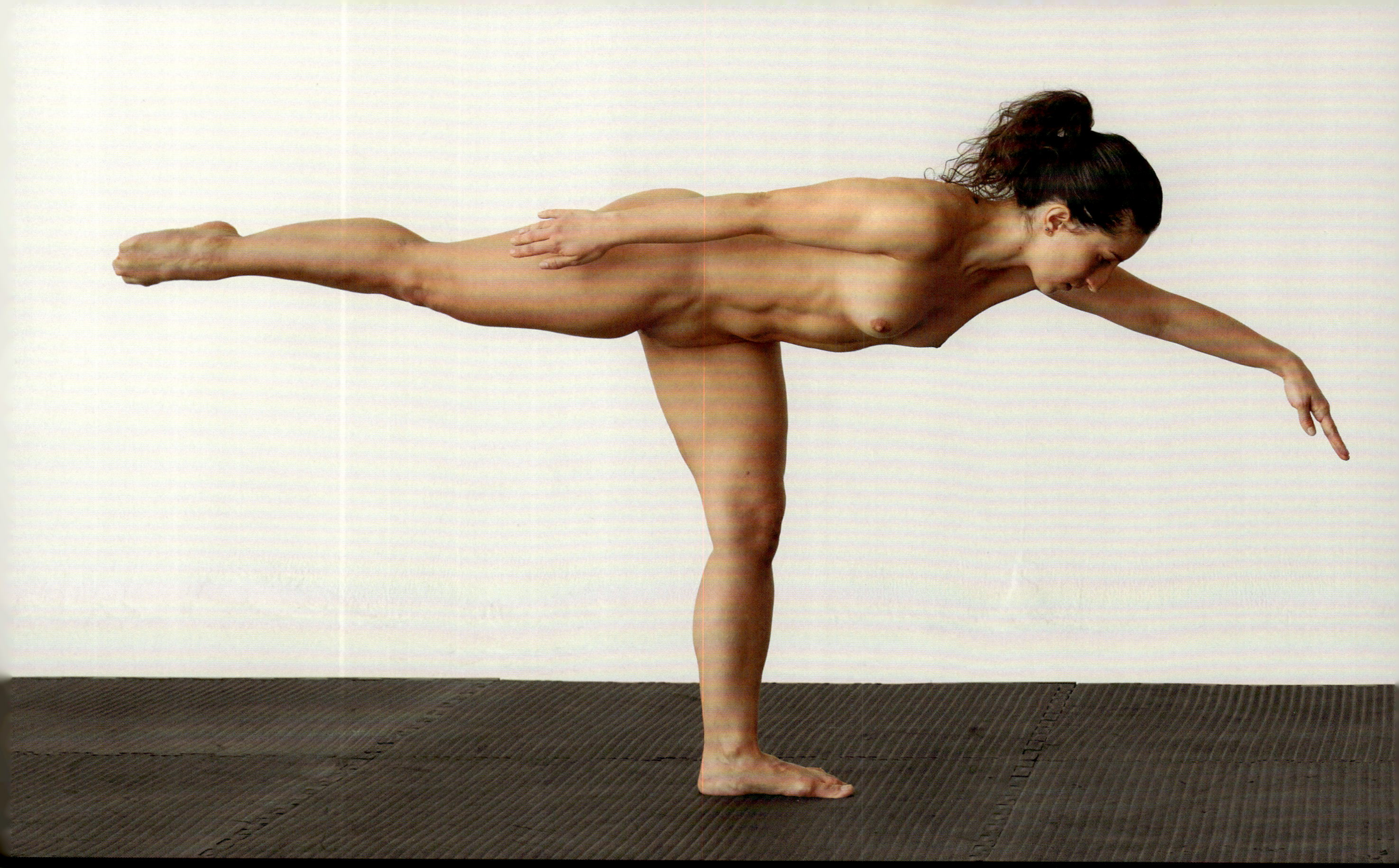

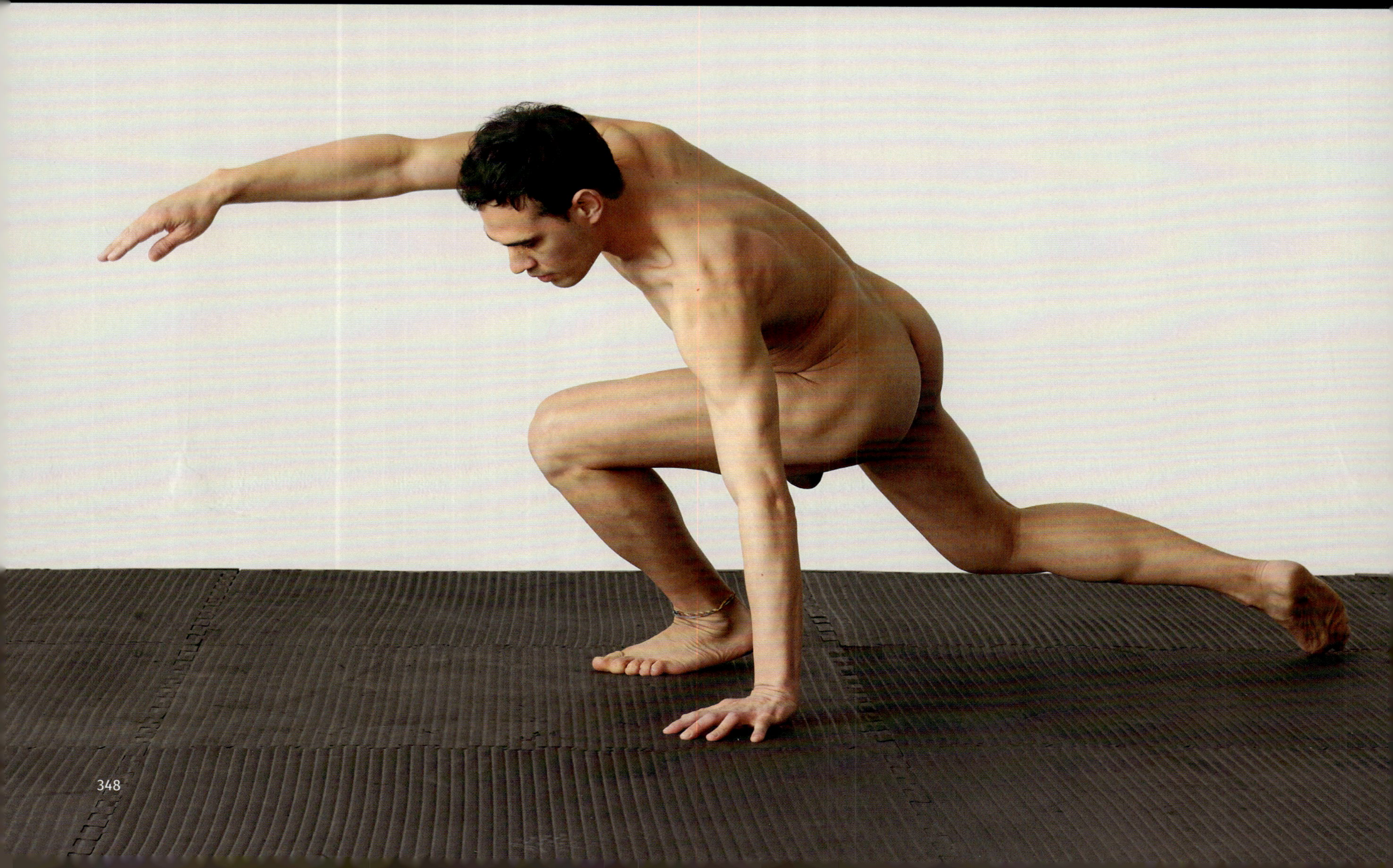

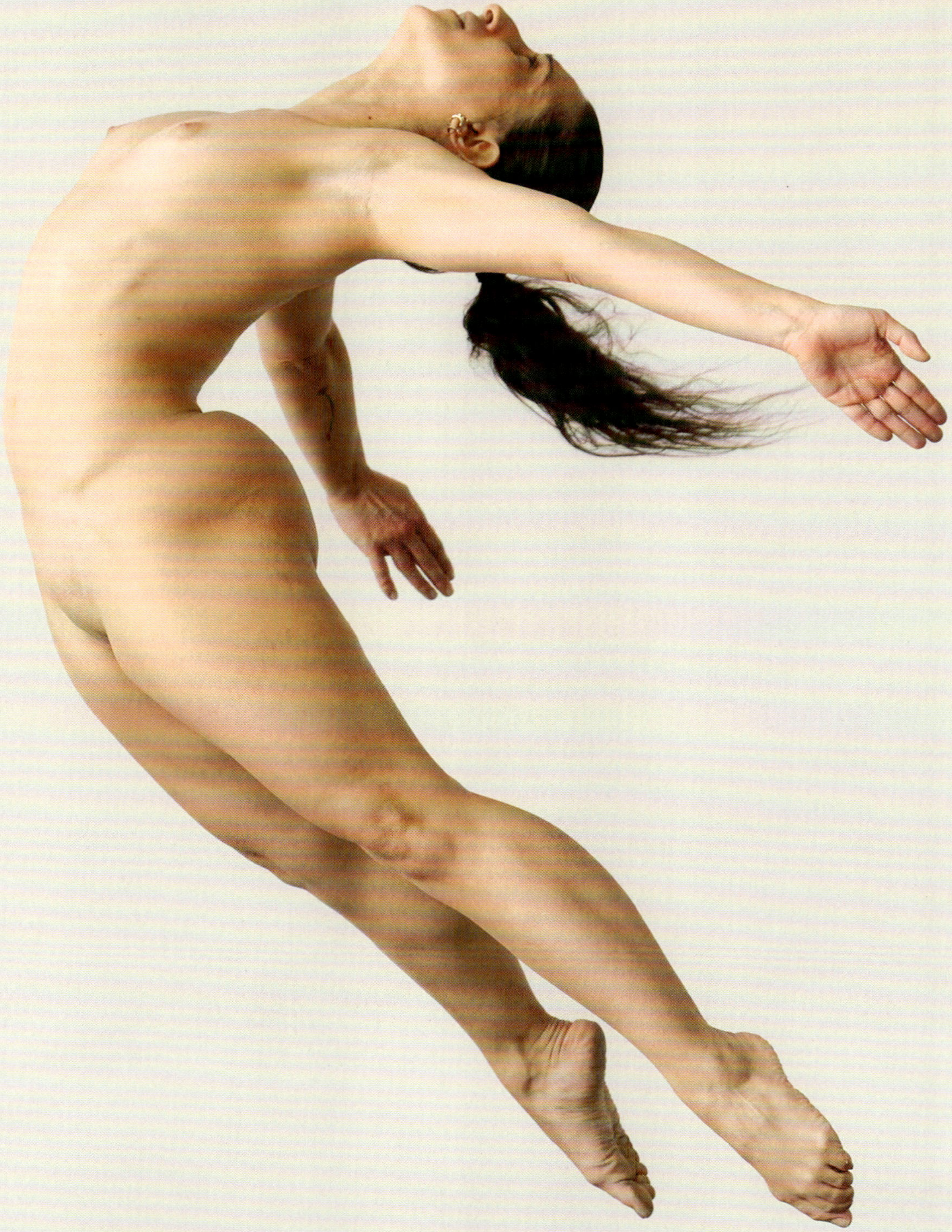

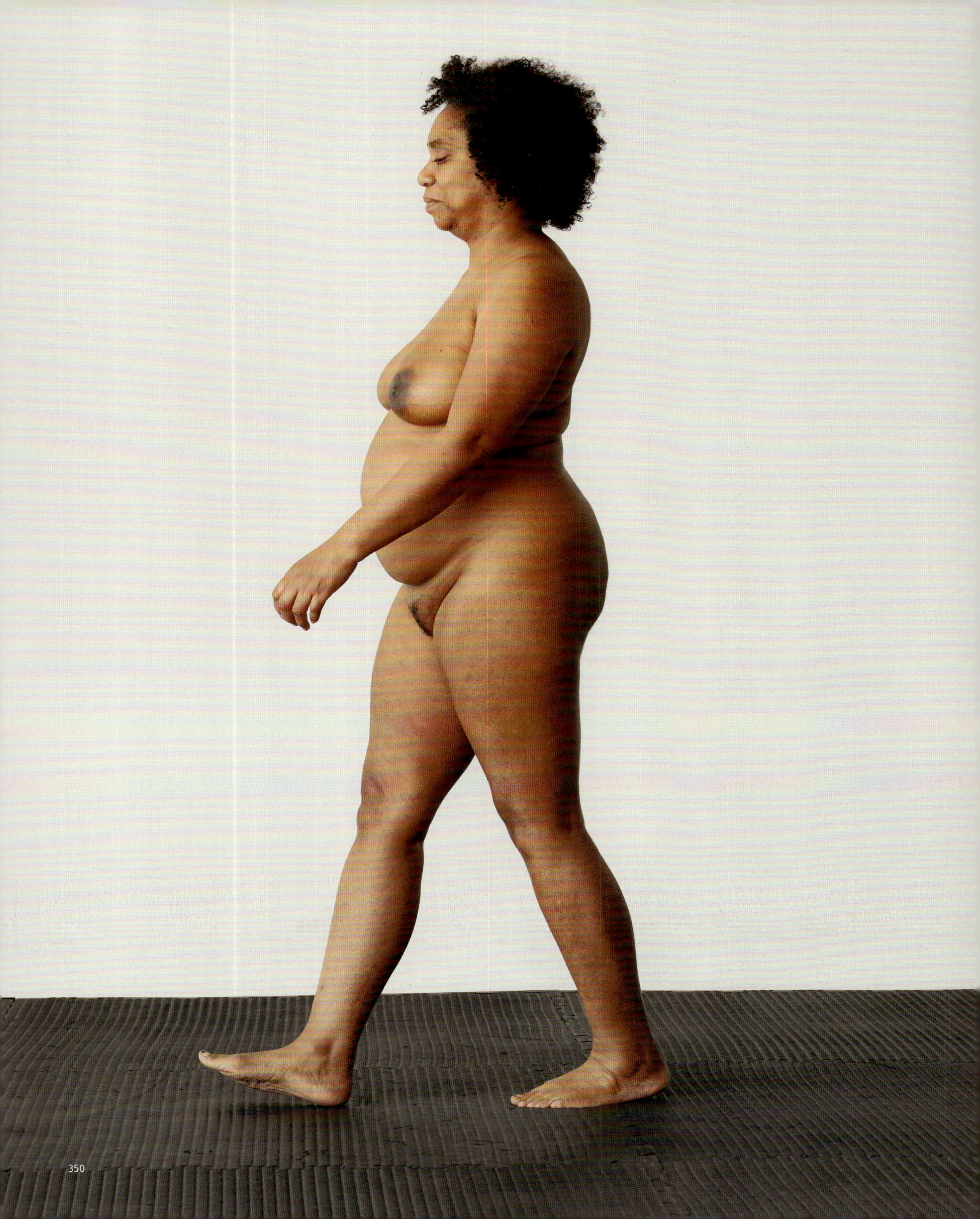

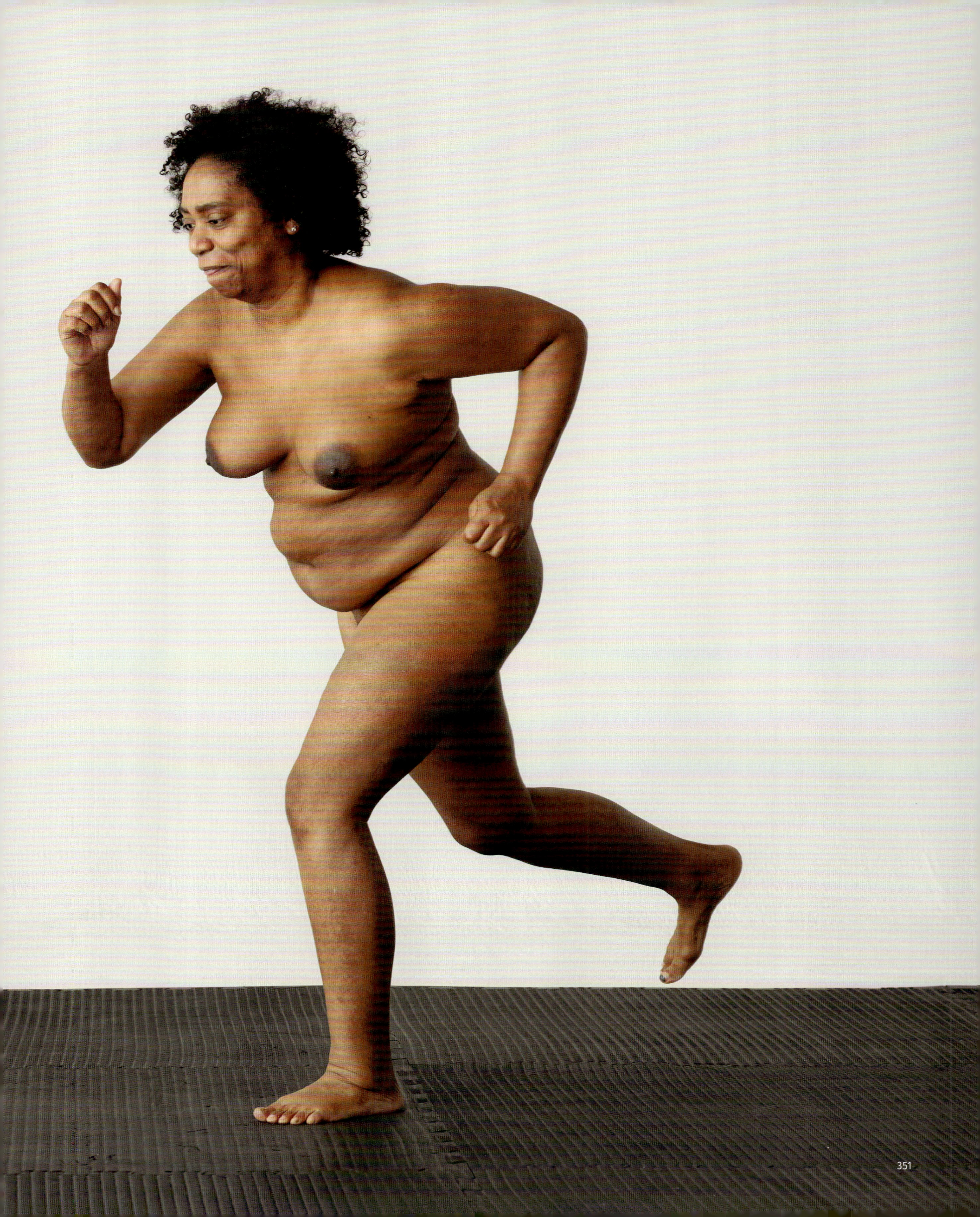

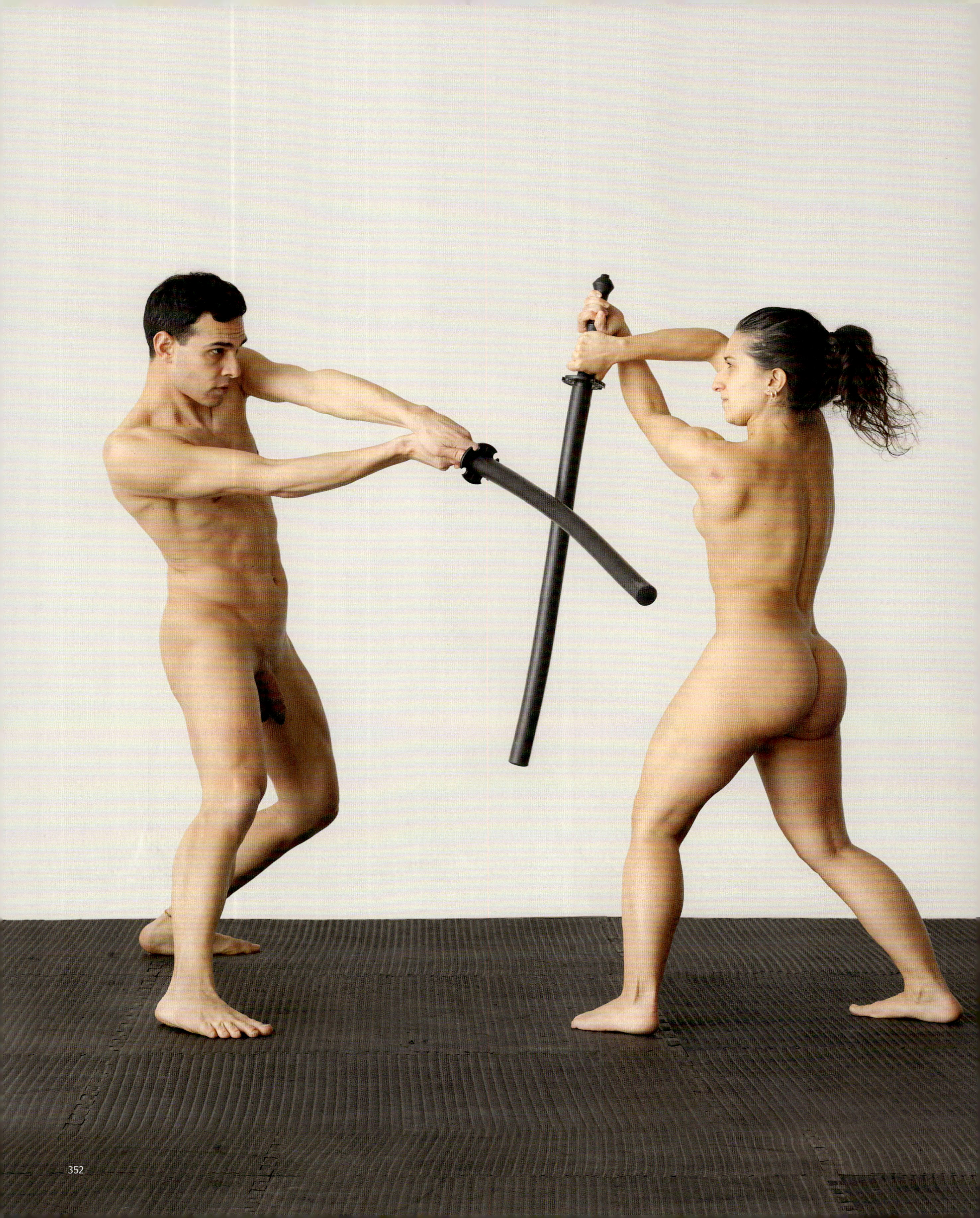

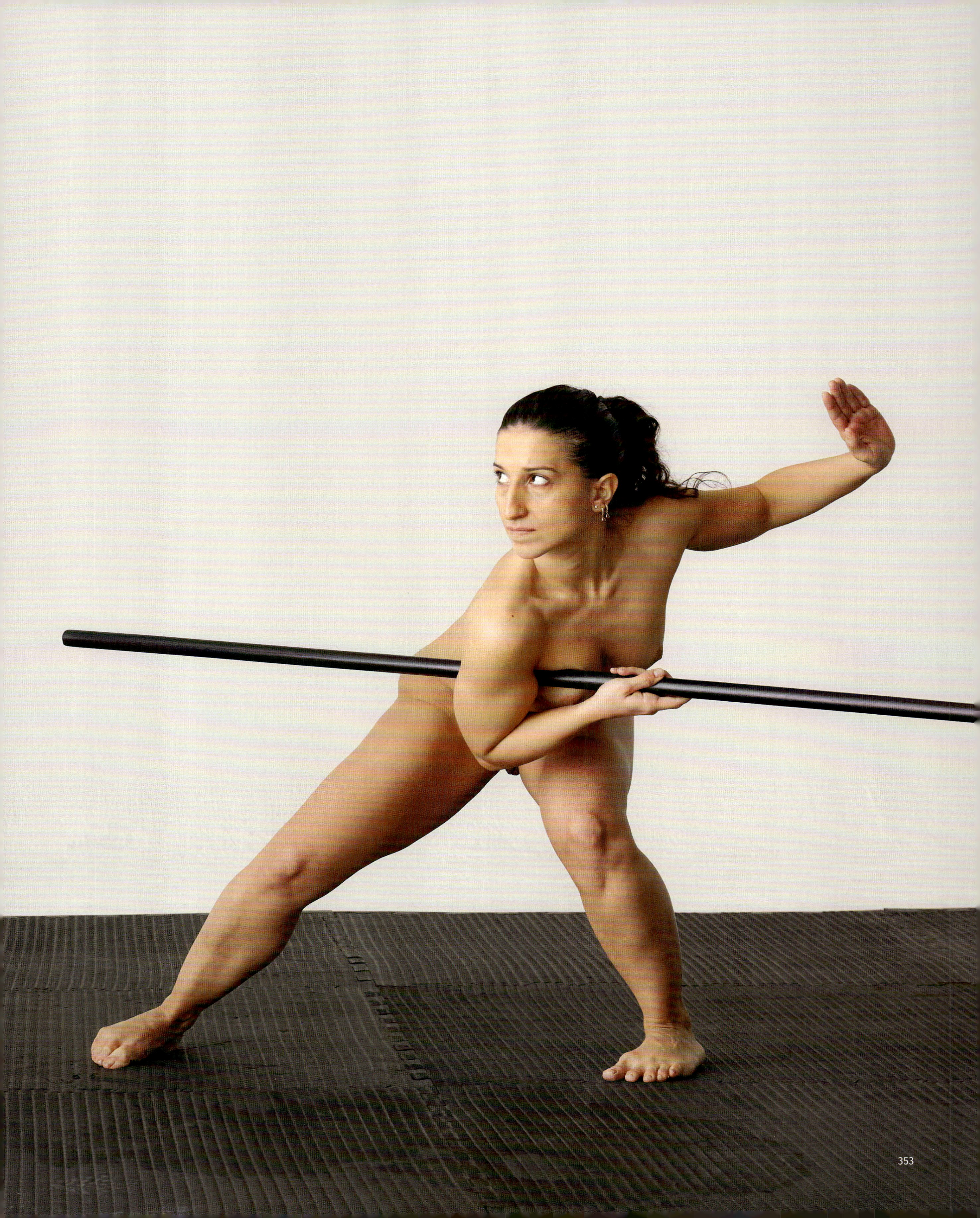

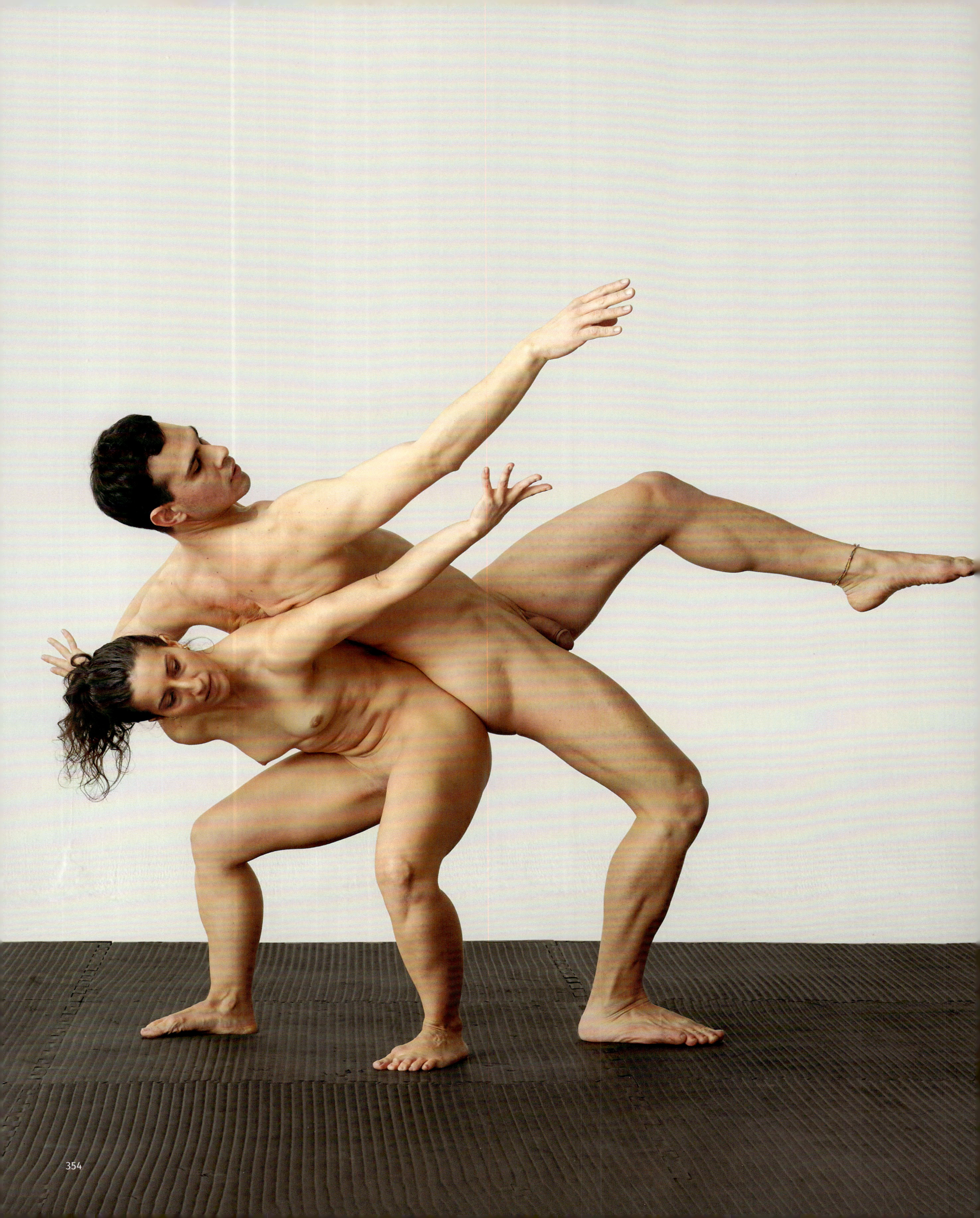

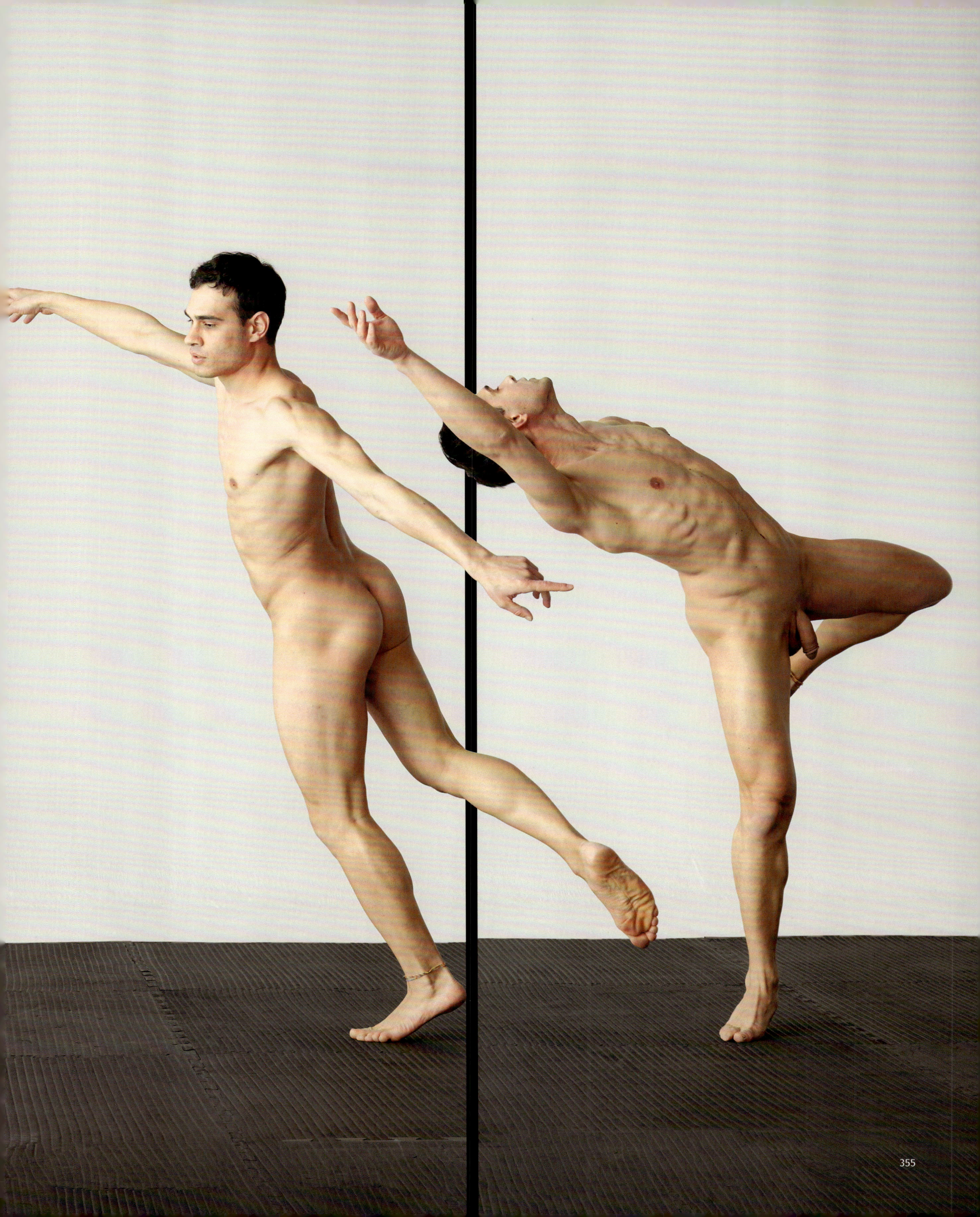

Glossary

Abduction

Moving away from the body's midline; in the case of an arm or leg, this would be swinging sideways and upwards.

Adduction

Moving towards the body's midline; in the case of an arm or leg, this would be swinging down and inwards towards the body.

Agonist

The main muscle that moves a bone in a particular direction.

Antagonist

A muscle that moves a bone in the opposite direction of the agonist.

Anterior

In the direction of or on the front side of the body.

Extension

A muscle movement that straightens a limb or appendage, increasing the angle of a joint; the opposite of flexion.

Flexion

A muscle movement that bends a limb or appendage, decreasing its angle; the opposite of extension.

Gesture

The fundamental visual flow that can give a pose or composition a feeling of movement and energy.

Lateral

Towards or on the sides of the body; a lateral motion is one that moves or turns out in a horizontal sideways direction.

Medial

Towards or closer to the midline of the body; a medial motion is one that moves or turns inward towards the centre of the body.

Midline

An imaginary guideline that runs down the vertical centre of the body.

Muscular body

The main fibrous area of a muscle, which contracts or relaxes to create movement.

Posterior

In the direction of or on the back side of the body.

Pronation

Rotation of the forearm so the palm faces downwards or towards the posterior of the body; the opposite of supination.

Protraction

Moving the scapulae forwards around the torso, hunching the back.

Retraction

Moving the scapulae backwards around the torso, pushing the chest forward.

Scapulae

The shoulder blades (plural of scapula).

Supination

Rotation of the forearm so the palm faces upwards or towards the anterior of the body; the opposite of pronation.

Tendon

The band of tough connective tissue that joins a muscle to a bone and enables it to move.

Contributors

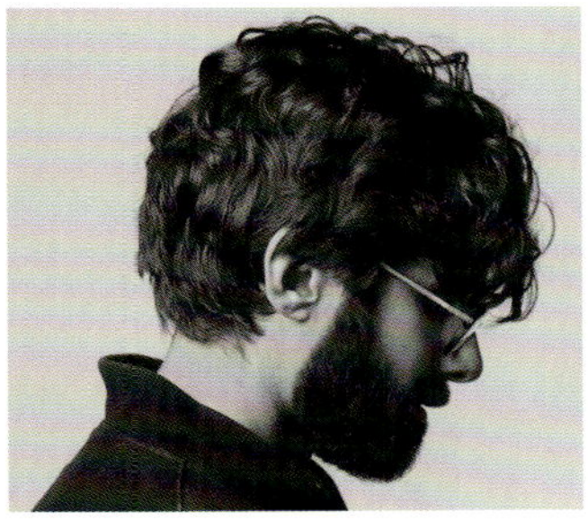

Photographer

Robin Bharaj | robinbharaj.com

Robin made his photography debut within London's underground music scene before moving into portraiture, fashion, and moving image. Recognized for his distinctive style, he is constantly working between his personal, editorial, and commercial projects.

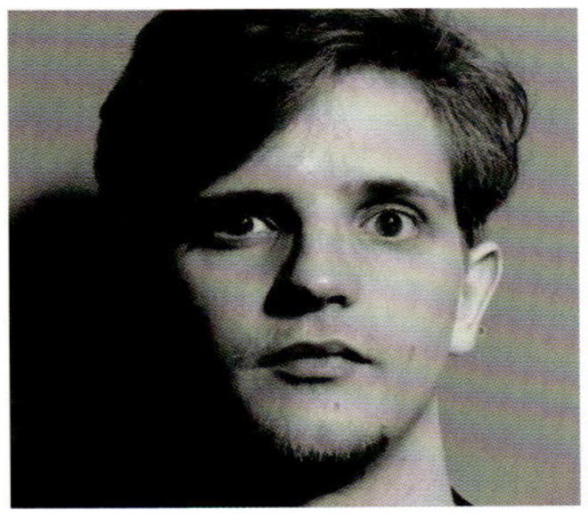

Author & illustrator

Charlie Pickard | charliepickardart.com

Charlie is a classically trained figurative artist and illustrator living and working in London. He was awarded the de Laszlo Foundation's Award for Excellence in 2020. His work is primarily exhibited in London and can be found in collections worldwide.

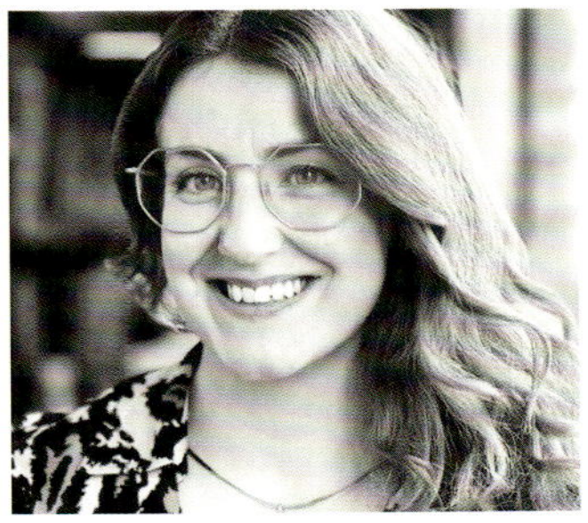

Prop stylist

Lauren Grant | laurenemmagrant.com

Lauren is a London-based prop stylist and set decorator, working on everything from feature films to stills. She has a passion for hunting out one-of-a-kind pieces and for challenging briefs.

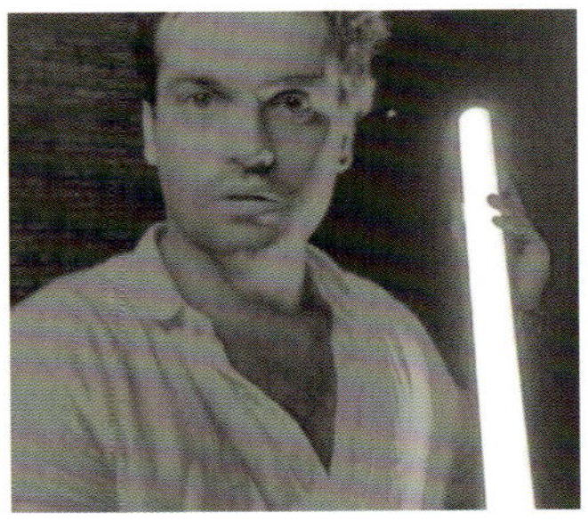

Gaffer/Lighting

Rhys Gray | rhysgray.com

Rhys is a cinematographer/DOP who has always had light at the focus of his work. With a lifelong love of the visual arts and a background in physics, he thrives on the art/science mix that is photography.

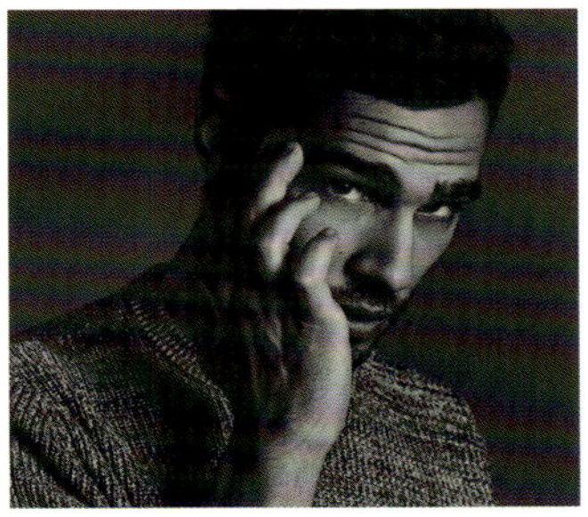

Model

Giuseppe Claudio Insalaco
instagram.com/giuseppeclaudio_themodel

Claudio is an actor, dancer, and model. He started his career when he was nineteen years old. He currently lives around London, Rome, and the rest of Europe while working as a performer and model.

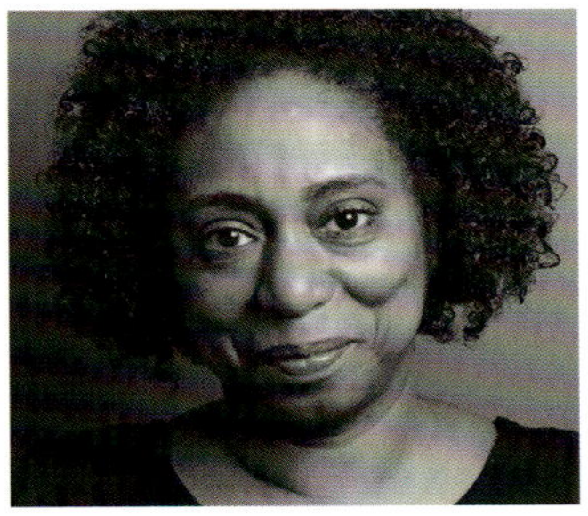

Model

Cat Smith
instagram.com/fluffykatmodelling1

Cat has posed for numerous portrait and nude sessions at art colleges, museums, and educational establishments. A Black Londoner and proud cancer survivor, she balances modelling, acting, and creative pursuits with being a part-time carer.
Register of Artists' Models no. RAM 5674

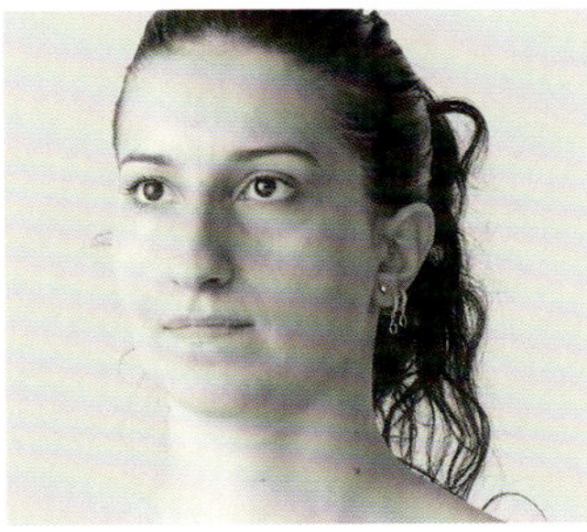

Model

Giada Palmisano
instagram.com/giada.palmisano

Giada is a dancer and choreographer with over ten years' work experience. She is trained in modern dance, contemporary dance, freestyle, improvisation, physical theatre, and more. She is also a certified pilates and yoga teacher, and has studied a range of martial arts.

Thank you to the models who helped to make this book possible, and who do not all wish to be credited by name.

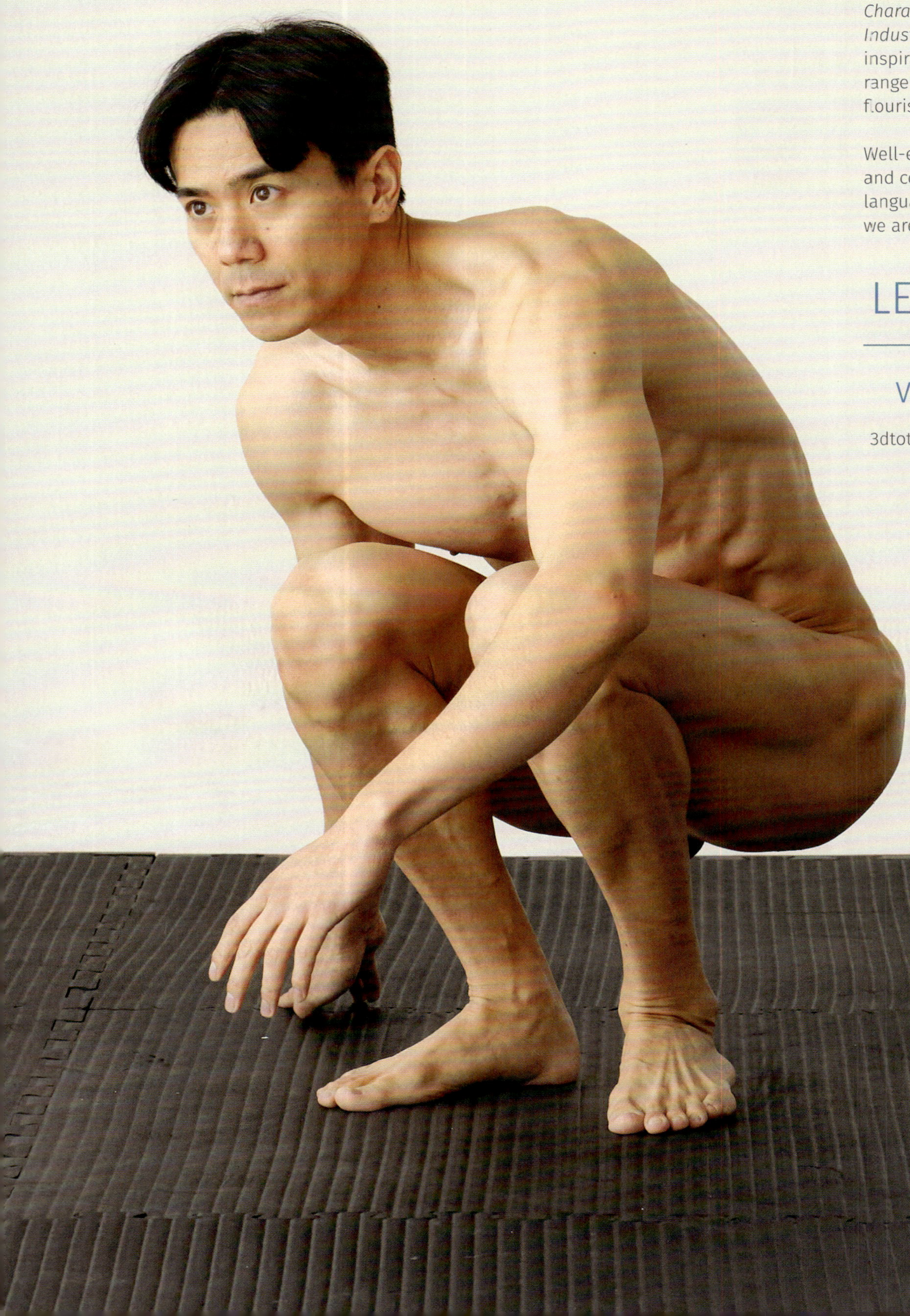

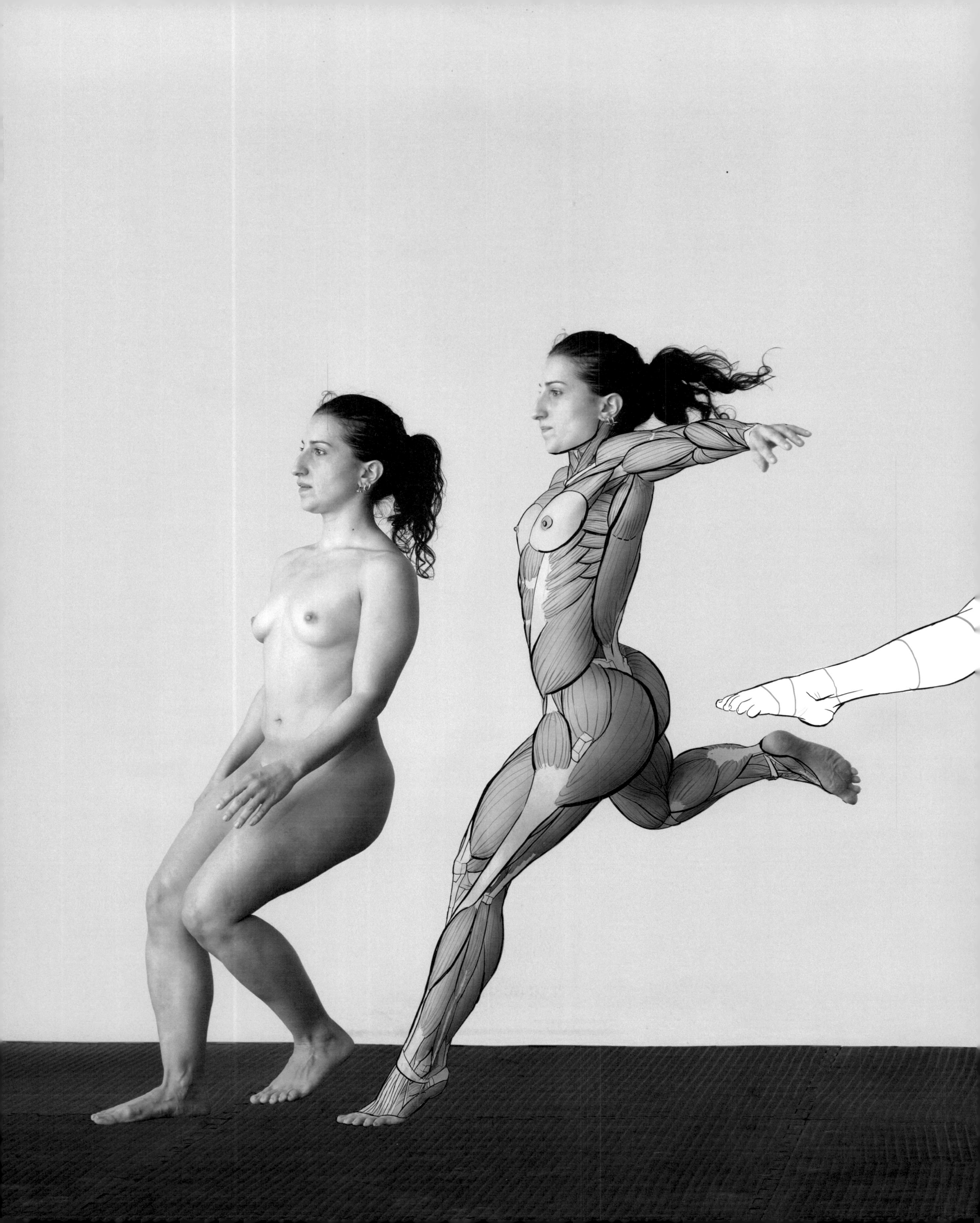